Volume 6

DEVELOPING OUR CHRISTIAN LIFE

By

Rayola Kelley and Jeannette Haley

Hidden Manna Publication

DEVELOPING OUR CHRISTIAN LIFE
Volume 6
Copyright © 2014 & 2023 by Rayola Kelley and Jeannette Haley

ISBN: 978-0-9891683-6-6

All rights reserved. No part of this publication may be reproduced or transmitted in any form or by any means without written permission of Gentle Shepherd Ministries.

Except where otherwise indicated, all Scripture quotations in this book are taken from the King James Version of the Bible.

Featuring the Following Books:

The Many Faces of Christianity
Possessing Our Souls
Experiencing the Christian Life
The Power of Our Testimonies
The Victorious Journey

You can obtain a study reference book to complement your studies of this volume at Gentle Shepherd Ministries' website at www.gentleshepherd.com.

Hidden Manna Publications
P.O. Box 3572
Oldtown, ID. 83822
www.gentleshepherd.com

Facebook:
https://www.facebook.com/HiddenMannaPublications/

Dedication

We want to dedicate this book to those
who have dared to walk where Jesus
walked in His humanity. Granted, such
stout pilgrims may not be many
in comparison to the rest of humanity.
However, know that your footprints have left
an indelible mark in the sands of time
in example and devotion. I personally want
to thank you for those precious footprints
because they truly have shown me
the way to victory and given me glimpses
of glory in regard to my eternal home.

Acknowledgment

There are many people to thank for encouraging, helping, and seeing me through the different books of this volume, such as Jo Reaves for her extensive editing of the many books that I have written, including *The Victorious Journey*.

Although there is one more volume following this one, the books in this particular volume signal an end to an extensive project that has been in the making for the past 15 years. This volume represents the last books that I wrote in regard to a series of collected information and teachings that have been written for the Gentle Shepherd Ministries Discipleship Course. It also represents years of trying to discern the possible completion of this series of volumes.

A special thanks goes to Jeannette Haley. She is the one who had to wade through each book to the bitter end, including adding her personal and important touches to *The Many Faces of Christianity*. I know, Jeannette, that it was a bitter-sweet experience for you. It was bitter because the burden was intense at times, but I also know it was sweet because the information has served as a point of edification to you and others.

I also want to acknowledge the many other people who supported us through the years. Whether it was with your friendship, prayers, financial support, and/or simply availing yourselves to the Bible studies that inspired many of these books, you have allowed me to share these insights with others. Along with your faithfulness and enthusiasm you have served as an inspiration to me. Thank you, each and every one of you, for the many ways you have been there for me.

I also want to thank those who took part in sharing their testimonies in the book, *The Power of Our Testimonies*. You were willing to expose yourselves as far as your past struggles, your present challenges, and your level of spiritual maturity. The fact that you were all willing to put the time and energy into this exercise says much about your evangelistic spirit to share Christ with others. I do appreciate each of you for sharing this very personal part of your lives for the edification of others.

Finally, I must acknowledge the one who has constantly been my source of inspiration, strength, and help through this spiritual journey for over 30 years, the Lord Jesus Christ. My hope is that these small glimpses into His character and truth contained within the pages of these books will truly edify those who are seeking to know, love, and serve Him, ultimately bringing much deserved glory to the Lord of lords and King of kings.

Contents

Volume Introduction		8
Book One: THE MANY FACES OF CHRISTIANITY		**11**
	Introduction	13
1.	The Contrast	15
2.	The Carnal Christian	21
3.	I Am A Good Person	29
4.	Associate Christian	37
5.	Religious Christian	43
6.	Sentimental Christian	52
7.	Social Christian	59
8.	Superstitious Christian	67
9.	Super Spiritual Christian	73
10.	Sanctimonious Christian	83
11.	Shortsighted Christian	90
12.	Skeptical Christian	99
13.	Sandbox Christian	108
14.	Half-Baked Christians	116
15.	Will the Real Christian Turn Aside?	124
Book Two: POSSESSING OUR SOULS		**135**
	Introduction	137
1.	What Is the Soul?	139
2.	The Soulish Man	145
3.	The Natural Man	150
4.	The Fleshly Man	156
5.	The Complacent Man	163
6.	The Earthly Man	170
7.	The War	176
8.	The Preference	184
9.	The Contrast	192
10.	Integrity of the Heart	197
11.	Opposition	203
12.	The Brutish Man	210
13.	The Desperate Man	219
14.	The Challenge	226
15.	The Promise	238

Book Three: EXPERIENCING THE CHRISTIAN LIFE 245
      Introduction 247
1. Searching For Life 249
2. Living the Life 253
3. Nominal Christianity 259
4. Preparation 265
5. Turning Aside 270
6. Encountering His Presence 276
7. The Commission 281
8. Experiencing the Mountain 286
9. Supping in the Presence of God 293
10. Waiting Before God 299
11. The Tent of Meeting 305
12. The Purpose of God's Glory 311
13. Reflecting the Glory of God 317
14. Ministration of Righteousness 322

Book Four: THE POWER OF OUR TESTIMONIES 335
      Introduction 337
1. What is a Testimony? 338
2. The Purpose of Salvation 344
3. Overcoming Hindrances 352
4. Learning of Jesus 360
5. Consecration 368
6. Detours 376
7. Experiences 386
8. Emphasis 393
9. Cultural Influence 399
10. Establishing Your Child's Testimony 406
11. Commitment 417
12. We Will Overcome 424

Book Five: THE VICTORIOUS JOURNEY 429
      Introduction 431
1. Humble Beginnings 432
2. The Purpose 440
3. The Disposition 448
4. Becoming A Sojourner 456
5. The Path 463
6. The Broad Path 470
7. The Anatomy of Defeat 480
8. Traveling the Way 488
9. The Call 495
10. Let My People Go 504
11. The Wilderness of Shur 513
12. The Wilderness of Sin 520

13.	The Valley of Rephidim	526
14.	The Wilderness of Sinai	530
15.	Judgment	539
16.	Wilderness of Zin	546
17.	Crossing the Jordan	557
18.	Rolling Off the Old	564
19.	Possessing the Land	572
20.	The Journey Continues	582

Bibliography **585**

About the Authors **587**

INTRODUCTION

Developing the Christian Life is the sixth volume in the Gentle Shepherd Ministries Advanced Discipleship Course. Volume six deals with the different aspects of the Christian walk. Few Christians consider what the Christian life is about with the intent of counting the cost to follow, know, and come into a healthy relationship with the Living God. These Christians may acknowledge that they have been endued with life from above, but they do not realize that the ways of this life have to be developed in them. They must be nurtured and brought forth for this life to become an actual possession that is valued above all other possible treasures that the world could offer.

To possess this life, the terrain of the heart and soul must be explored. Such exploration will entail mapping out the condition of the heart, exposing and uprooting the hindrances and enemies of the soul. The spiritual sojourner must also discover eternal treasures in the midst of the world's miry wells of ignorance, delusion, heresies, and anguish, as he or she tries to sidestep the dark pits of hopelessness, the lifeless caves of fear, and the cold tombs of useless activities. Granted, there are beautiful mountains to discover along the way, but there is always the reality of the harsh north winds that bring unexpected storms, causing the environment of the mountain to become foreboding and dangerous to the inexperienced. There is the beauty of springtime to enjoy, but spring reminds us that for the beauty of life to survive it must endure cold nights of testing. There are summers, but the heat purges all that has failed to find refuge in the shade of that which casts the eternal shadow of heaven. There is harvest time, but this season will prove to be short since there never seems to be enough hours in the day to complete the task put before each of us who belong to God's eternal kingdom.

Clearly the Christian life entails a walk that will cause the true spiritual strangers and pilgrims of this world to embark on an incredible journey to discover the life God has ordained for them. They must discover this life in the midst of the barren wildernesses of sin, death, and the various silent gravestones that mark the way. These various gravestones remind us of the dying out process of the various aspects of the old life and its ways. As believers, we must recognize that in order to find, establish, and develop this spiritual life we will be traveling through various terrains that will expose, challenge, and determine the character of the inner man. Such a journey entails leaving or mortifying the hindrances of the old behind to embrace the new that awaits each of us.

The new man points to the new complete, abundant, and eternal life of Christ being developed in the believer. However, for this life to be established, Christians must wade through and discern the pseudo presentations of Christianity.

The first book, *The Many Faces of Christianity,* is the only book that showcases the combined work of Jeannette and me. It considers the pseudo presentations that can be clearly observed in Christendom. Although it may not expose every false cloak or mask that people hide behind to lay claim to the title of being a "Christian", it will reveal the attitudes, false gospels, and lights that are often being promoted by these different faces.

The second book of this volume, *Possessing Our Souls* exposes the digression of the souls of those who will not be brought back to center with God in humility, repentance, obedience, and sanctification. The reader will discover the defeating route the soul of man can take as it chooses to become self-centered, giving way to the natural ways of the self-life and the world, becoming complacent towards the matters of God, and brutish towards what is honorable. This digression ultimately brings the soul to a fearful state of desperation and hopelessness in its spiritual plight.

This book is special to me as the author because it represents an exceptional part of my life as far as my own spiritual discoveries. Even though *Possessing Our Souls* shows the digression of unrepentant and unregenerate man, it also brings the contrast of the progression of the spiritual man for the reader to consider and compare. It has taken years for me to understand the plight of the soul, but through it I have discovered to some extent what it means to possess my own soul in challenging times. Do not get me wrong, I do not possess it at all times, but I do understand what it means to bring it into subjection to what is Spirit and truth to ensure righteousness.

Experiencing the Christian Life is the third book in this volume. The Christian life is a life that is actively moving forward towards the high calling that a believer has in Christ Jesus. However, the only way believers can go forward in their Christian walk is to understand that they are not living their life according to some religious code or religion; rather, they are actually living the life of Christ that is being worked in them by the Spirit of God.

In order to live the life of Christ, a believer must learn how to walk after, be led by, and walk in the presence of the Holy Spirit. This book explains how God actually manifests His presence to His people as a means to set up the proper environment in preparation for them to receive what He has for them. Such preparation entails preparing them to walk in, walk through, and walk out what He wants to entrust to them.

This book will not be easily forgotten as the reader is led from the humble beginnings of the sojourner's spiritual barrenness to experience the very heights of God's glory. It is a glorious journey that will inspire the spirit and encourage the reader's struggling or weary soul.

The fourth book in this volume is *The Power of Our Testimonies.* One might wonder what our testimony has to do with our spiritual journey. The truth is that a person's testimony develops as he or she matures in Christ. Therefore, the level of maturity, experiences, and encounters through this journey will also determine whether our testimony about Jesus is enlarged along the way. We know that our testimonies, along with the blood of the Lamb and not loving our lives unto death, are what empower us to overcome Satan.

This fourth book not only looks at what a testimony entails, but it explains how our spiritual walk affects the power and growth of our testimony. To bring home the importance and growth of our testimony in light of personal experiences, various people's testimonies have been integrated into the book to confirm the dynamics and the part that our personal witness of Jesus plays in our Christian life.

The fifth and final book in this volume, *The Victorious Journey* has proven to be a popular book with readers. It looks at what constitutes the Christian walk. Clearly, Christianity is a life that is meant to be experienced, but one cannot experience it until he or she is willing to walk it out by faith. *The Victorious Journey* illuminates the contrast between these who walk the path of righteousness and those who walk the broad path of destruction. This book enables the reader to experience the spiritual journey taken by the children of Israel from their bondage in Egypt to the Promised Land, and explains the lessons and examples that each traveler must learn and apply to finish the course set before him or her. It is a journey that will change how a person regards the struggles and failures of the children of Israel, as well as how he or she will look at his or her personal journey to discover the promised inheritance of heaven.

Book One

THE MANY FACES OF CHRISTIANITY

By
Rayola Kelley & Jeannette Haley

INTRODUCTION

Since the conception of the Church of Jesus Christ, people have tried to define Christianity. It has been reduced to belief systems, doctrines, and man-made religion. It has been redefined, counterfeited, and made into nothing more than a religious exercise that has no real power and life in it. It has been replaced with the traditions of men and mixed with the various philosophies of the world.

In a way the different presentations of Christianity are marked by religious indifference, lifeless practices, and what appears to be at times insanity. Sometimes, there is no indication of real life, authority, or power in the fruits that prevail in much of the visible Church. The struggle for many of the watchmen contending for the faith that was first delivered to the saints was and is to bring sanity and reasoning back into the equation. In such reasoning, order could once again be restored, allowing committed saints to bring a contrast between the Biblical presentation of Christianity and the pseudo presentations that are gaining popularity due to the influence of indifferent shepherds, self-serving heretics, and the philosophies and ways of the world.

Through the years you can see this struggle in the numerous books that strive to expose the nonsense and bombardment of fallacies that have rolled through Christendom. These heretical movements often gain the misdirected loyalty and zeal of the spiritually gullible, vulnerable, and immature. As you study the emphasis of each book that challenges the spiritual environment, you will see how these sources of information addressed the particular challenges and problems of that age or time in which the books were conceived.

Regardless of the ignorance or advancements of the particular time we now live in, it becomes quite obvious that the real issues and challenges do not differ with the different ages. People continue to struggle with the haunting issues of life and death. The battle for men's souls remains the same. And, such battles find their source of conflict and division at the point of truth. Like the beginning of man's relationship with God, it still takes genuine faith to receive and embrace the truths that identify and govern true Christianity.

Christianity is a way of life. Sadly, instead of people walking this life out in faith towards God and obedience to His Word, many hide behind religious masks and cloaks that they have developed. These cloaks give them the appearance of righteousness and godliness, but they lack the power of heaven. They hide sin and hypocrisy behind these disguises, while maintaining a religious presentation to the world. However, Christ came to reveal the real face of Christianity and to strip away the cloaks to expose the sin that enslaves people.

Developing Our Christian Life

    This particular book addresses the masks and cloaks people hide behind in order to reveal what the real Christian walk is all about. As the reader begins to embark into this book, he or she must be prepared to have all pretenses or false presentations of Christianity stripped away in order for him or her to come to terms with what it means to possess the real Christian life.

1

THE CONTRAST

Through the years, I have struggled with what constitutes real Christianity. When I first encountered the truth of Jesus' salvation, I was excited about my new discovery. However, my initial premise of God was based on man's religion. My excitement gave way to religious exercises of dos and don'ts. In other words, I failed to discover Christianity as a life that must be lived out in faith towards God and in obedience to His Word.

It took some major detours in my religious life to realize that I was missing the Christian life. Granted, I consoled myself with religious activities, but if I had died in such a state, I could not be guaranteed that I would not hear the terrible words of Matthew 7:23, "And then will I profess unto (you), I never knew you; depart from me, ye that work iniquity." (Parenthesis added.)

For the past 20 years the struggle has escalated for me as I have contended with others in their Christian walk. The quality of Christianity that I have encountered in the Christian realm has caused nightmares. Each encounter seemed to expose the folly of my own understanding about the Christian way. I began to question my personal standing with God. Granted, I was very aware that I was not reaching my potential, but the more I understood God, the more I became small, falling even further away from the mark.

As I witnessed the struggle of other people in their Christian lives, I became more alarmed. There were those who were striving to get it right, but they seemed to miss the mark according to the fruit of their lives.[1]

Questions begin to challenge me. I had a real experience with Jesus, and even experienced an initial change in my life. However, my detours stripped away the outward religious façade, revealing an inner disposition that possessed areas of grave darkness and inconsistent moral character.

In my quest to come to terms with the Christian life, I finally came to a place of rest. This rest was not based on my personal worth, but on the character of God. To possess the Christian life meant that I also possessed the eternal life of Christ. Christianity was not a matter of living according to some religious code; rather, it was about living according to the life of Christ in me. It was not only about living His life, but also walking it out in child-like confidence and obedience.

---

[1] Luke 13:24

As I considered the lives of those who claimed to be Christians, I witnessed conflicting messages. Some of these people declared they were Christians, but they seemed to be walking according to their own personal drumbeat.

For example, there was one individual who appeared to have power from above, but displayed a conniving character in her business dealings. How could such an individual continue on in questionable practices without conviction or paying consequences as a true child of God? Admittedly, I did not understand how this person could continue on in illegal practices and call herself a Christian minister. Even though the Bible addresses such behavior, this person possibly ignored conviction or allowed herself to become blinded by personal justification, as she disregarded Scriptural instructions. Somehow, she made such actions right in her own eyes. However, why was there not some evidence of chastisement if she was truly a Christian?[2] Did God overlook certain moral deviation in some people, while addressing it in others? This did not sound in line with His character. My conclusion to this matter was that I needed to trust that He is just in all matters whether it makes any sense to me or not.

There are also those individuals who are full of pride. Surely, you have met them. I know for me that I met one such person every time I looked in the mirror. God has been longsuffering with me in regard to my pride. Occasionally, He would give me glimpses into the wretchedness of my conceit. At such times I even felt embarrassed by the foolishness that surrounded my pride, especially when it had been operating from great heights of arrogance. Occasionally, I even questioned how anyone in his or her right mind could have tolerated me when my conceit was full blown.

God in His longsuffering did manage to bring me to places where I had to taste the shame of my pride. I realized that the depth of the abyss of its delusion and the height of its haughtiness often blinded me to its many prejudices and judgmental ways. Ultimately, it translated into self-righteousness.

Such self-righteousness has its own means of developing its personal cloak or façade to cover the hypocrisy that reigns in people's lives. For example, some people comply intellectually to give the impression that they agree about a matter, but it is nothing more than a clever means to throw others off track as to what is really going on behind their particular mask. These individuals are appearing reasonable about a matter, when in reality they see themselves as being noble for giving way to something that they may consider silly, inferior, or unreasonable to keep a surface peace. Some people will reform outward actions, but this is simply a cloak that allows these individuals to maintain the same stubborn attitude about a matter. Other people will perform by presenting a certain image or mask, while hiding an attitude of

---

[2] Hebrews 12:5-15

judgmental pride and arrogance. There are those who conform to a matter in order to throw a bone at someone to control the environment. However, this cloak hides the reality that these individuals do not intend to really change. They are simply trying to take out the element of contention in their environment so they have free rein to do as they please.

Self-righteousness also contains its own personal light. However, this light blinds the person to his or her heart condition. It will often flatter the person into thinking his or her understanding or practices are superior to the rest of the religious masses. It will ultimately create some type of elitism that will set the person up for a fall.

I have witnessed this self-righteousness in operation. It appears so clever and noble in how it judges, manipulates, and hides its obstinacy. It tries to cover up its lack of character with religious masks and platitudes. Ultimately, it will exalt itself over that which it has deemed to be inferior.

There are many counterfeit presentations of Christianity. These presentations are based on personal or religious premises that may run parallel to the truth, but miss the mark of what is pure and righteous. John the Baptist declared that an axe had been laid to the root of the lifeless religion that was in operation during his day. The writer of Hebrews tells us that everything that can be shaken will be. Only that which is established on and in the Lord, will stand during such testing. We already know that if something is not firmly rooted upon the Rock of Ages, Jesus Christ, it will fall into utter ruin.[3]

We also know that when a matter is wrong, it must be brought down to its very foundations before it can be properly established once again. Out of the destruction of the old, the new will immerge. This can truly be seen in Christianity. Christianity is about a new life coming forth to express itself in the ways of righteousness. The Bible brings this out. The Apostle Paul tells us that Jesus became sin so that we could be made in the righteousness of God. Such a life will mark us as new creations, where the old will cease, while giving way to the new that will express the very glory of Jesus.[4]

Before we can confront the counterfeit presentations of the Christian life, we have to present a proper perspective of it so people can rightfully discern a counterfeit. The glory of the new must be brought out so that believers can begin to see a contrast between the ways of the "old" man, and the ways of the "new" man. Such a contrast is what allows the believer to truly discern not only his or her own fruits, but the fruits of others as well. Clearly, a standard must be properly raised so others can begin to see how real Christianity truly affects a person.

The Apostle John describes the source of this life, "He that saith he abideth in him ought himself also so to walk, even as he walked" (1 John 2:6). The first matter about Christianity is the fact that by faith we must

---

[3] Matthew 3:10; 7:24-27; 1 Corinthians 3:11; Hebrews 12:26-29
[4] 2 Corinthians 3:18; 5:17, 21

be connected to the source of life. To abide points to the concept of dwelling, continuing, remaining, and enduring. In my Christian life, I have often sought my source of confidence in other places, rather than in the Vine of heaven, Christ Jesus. Other sources left me empty or lost.

For example, I tried to put my reliance in religious leaders, only to be disappointed. I looked to religious activities, only to be disillusioned. I even tried good deeds, only to be left with an emptiness that haunted me. I also took up moral or good causes, only to realize that in the end I came out the bad person for trying to go against the grain of what was controllable and acceptable to the world. In reality, I tried all the religious avenues to only find there was no real life in any of them.

Finally, I had to come to the harsh reality that I had left Jesus behind in all of my religious pursuits. He is the source of all life. Without His life pulsating through my inner being, all attempts, regardless of how religious, were void of substance. I was missing His vital leadership as my Lord, the inspiration of the Holy Spirit, and the awareness of being in the right place of relationship with the Father.

My challenge was that I needed to know Jesus as my only source of life and hope. In order to understand His life, I needed to become identified with Him. Such identification entailed walking even as He walked. One of the popular sayings is to avoid judging until you have walked a mile in the shoes of that person. The Apostle John stipulated that if we are going to abide in Jesus, we must walk as He walked to ensure such a relationship or connection with Him. Jesus gave the same instruction in John 15. He also stated that if we are going to follow Him as His disciples, we have to deny self and pick up our cross.[5]

As we follow Jesus as man, we can see where He denied Himself of glory and became a servant. He traveled a narrow way that required Him to submit to the will of the Father. He suffered physical pain from the whips and fists of men. He endured mental anguish as He solely walked the way of Calvary. He experienced emotional despair due to rejection, betrayal, and mocking. Finally, when He became the ultimate sin offering for each of us in His humanity, He suffered spiritual sorrow as He felt the separation from the Father.

We could try to measure each point of suffering to determine which one was greater. However, the reality is that the moment Jesus became the sin offering on our behalf was when He probably suffered the greatest sorrow. After all, it resulted in a separation from the Father, which no doubt caused the greatest point of testing and despair for Him in His humanity. If only we valued our relationship with God above all earthly matters. Sadly, very few are even aware when there is a breach in their relationship with God.

For Christians to have the discerning quality as to gauge their relationship with God, they must possess a pure heart so that they can see and hear Him. The prophet Jeremiah talked about how deceitful the

---

[5] Matthew 16:24

heart is. Solomon made reference to the fact that the issues of life come out of the heart. Jesus stated that all matters of sin come from the heart.[6]

The heart is the springboard to all matters of life, as well as the gauge that reveals the real inner state of a person. Due to sin, God must give us a new heart to ensure the right state. This state is based on the light or life of Jesus. We must walk in the light of who Jesus is to ensure the integrity of our inner state once it has been regenerated or made anew by God.[7]

The Apostle Paul talked about how to maintain the inward integrity of a righteous state. He pointed out that although our outward man is perishing, the inward man is renewed day by day. For this inner man to be renewed, believers must walk in the light of God's love to ensure that they possess the fruit of goodness, righteousness, and truth of the Spirit.[8]

In Colossians 3, we are instructed what we are to put to death, as well as what we must put off as far as our attitudes and moods. To mortify unacceptable ways and put off wrong attitudes and moods allow us to put on the new man that is renewed in knowledge. All of this must be tempered by the love of God.

As you can see, the Christian life is the path of self-denial or putting aside and neglecting personal rights to life according to the old disposition. Neglecting personal rights entails death to the ways of the flesh and following Jesus into a new life. We can talk nobly about such things, but how many of us apply such principles to our lives by walking in the light of who Jesus is and what He did for us on the cross? Such a life of awareness brings us into complete identification with Him.

Obviously, you cannot fake the Christian life. Granted, there are people who cleverly wear the masks and the cloaks, but eventually the truth will reveal their real fruits. They are void of the abiding anchor that would keep them inwardly consistent in their attitudes and actions, regardless of the tribulations that might be besetting them.

The true life found in Christianity has its very human side that reveals that the inward process to bring a person to maturity is ongoing until the flesh is put off. However, such a life possesses an inward anchor that keeps the person attached to the Rock. Such a person knows peace in the storm, the joy of confidence in uncertain times, and everlasting hope in dark times. This is what is truly discerned in the life of the Christian who truly understands the Christian walk. Like the Apostle Paul, the saint knows it is not his or her life that he or she is living, but the very life of Christ in him or her.[9]

This life is sure, abundant, and everlasting. It is not threatened by circumstances, it will not lose its substance when shaken, and it will not

---

[6] Proverbs 4:23; Jeremiah 17:9-10; Matthew 5:8; 15:10-20

[7] Ezekiel 36:26-27; John 1:4-5; 1 John 1:3-7

[8] 2 Corinthians 4:16; Ephesians 5:2-9

[9] Galatians 2:20

cease to be when all else lies in ruin. After all, it is the very eternal life of Christ that possesses resurrection power.

People who are acquainted with my studies, articles, and books might say that my presentations and concerns in this book seem redundant in light of my other writings. However, I want to point out that the Bible's message is redundant as well. It simply approaches the same subject matter, whether it is the character of God, His works, the reality of sin, the need for repentance, and so forth, from different angles and with diverse examples. However, the conclusions are the same. God is who He is. His redemption expresses the level of His love and sacrifice to save man, constantly confirming that he clearly needs to repent or he will perish in his sins.

To reiterate this point, I remember a story of how an evangelist preached on John 3:16 for a week. Finally, someone noted that he had been preaching on the same text every night, and asked when he would preach on another subject. The evangelist's reply was that as soon as everyone in the congregation finally understood what John 3:16 meant in regard to their lives, he could go on to another subject.

The reality of God's truths is that they are profound as far as the depth they can reach into man's soul to transform him, enlarging him to embrace their immeasurable power. Such power also will take him to great heights in obtaining God's heavenly perspective. These heights allow the Spirit to take such a person from glory to glory. We, as Christians, may gain glimpses into His truths that greatly impact us, but we cannot fathom their depth or height in our limited understanding.

Christianity is meant to raise the bar of excellence for believers, but sadly many have lowered Christianity into the mire of the world. As we consider the other forms of Christianity that are being presented, it will be made clear that the life of Jesus is often being perverted, adjusted, hindered, or absent altogether in the popular presentations embraced by Christendom. The masks of people who promote these different false presentations may attract you, and the cloaks may impress you, but the fruits will eventually disappoint you.

Examine yourself and see what you can discover about your Christian walk. Consider the state of your heart and the light or understanding you are walking according to. Honestly evaluate the real fruits of your life, giving the Lord permission to expose any wicked way. Then, consider if you are wearing a mask or cloak, or if you are truly putting on the very life of Christ.

2

THE CARNAL CHRISTIAN

Although this book is mainly about the false presentations of Christianity, we must also first address the different levels of spiritual immaturity in Christianity. This immaturity sends confusing signals, and often starts immature believers off on the wrong footing. If committed leaders, the Word of God, or those around them, do not properly challenge them, these young converts can become innocent victims of the different false presentations that are rolling through Christendom.

Christians experience different stages of growth during the different seasons of life. The first stage is considered the milk stage. The Apostle Peter made this statement, "As newborn babes, desire the sincere milk of the word, that ye may grow thereby, If so be ye have tasted that the Lord is gracious" (1 Peter 2:2-3). Milk is for the Christian who has just been born again. Like all newborns, they must be fed on the milk of the Word. The milk of the Word has to do with pure doctrine.

There is a lot of confusion about what constitutes doctrine. Most people believe it comes down to what they believe. This is not a correct perception. Doctrine comes down to the practices of Christianity that will clearly establish a person in godly conduct. In Jesus' Sermon on the Mount, He was presenting doctrine.[1] As you follow Jesus' presentation, you will realize that it takes a right disposition and attitude to ensure pure doctrine or pure practices in the kingdom of God. Peter pointed out that doctrine allows the new believer to taste the graciousness of the Lord. In other words, by practicing the Christian way, new Christians will become acquainted with the character of their Lord. It must be noted that without the proper spirit and attitude, doctrines or practices become tainted or perverted, reducing them to duty or works that become unclean and unacceptable before God.

New Christians need to understand how to properly conduct themselves in their new life. Granted, they begin with a lot of zeal and good intentions towards their new status as children of God. But such zeal lacks the real knowledge of God, while good intentions are heightened as they ride on the unpredictable wave of fickle sentiment and untempered enthusiasm. Eventually these individuals will come crashing down when the reality and challenges of this new life confront them head on.[2]

---

[1] Matthew 7:28-29
[2] Romans 10:2-3

Developing Our Christian Life

The pure doctrine of Christ is meant to bring much needed discipline to the Christian's conduct and order to their life. This order is to create an environment in which they can begin to properly learn about the character of God and receive spiritual matters in a right way.

The problem with Christians is that they can major in knowing doctrine, while ignoring their responsibility of practicing it in their lives. This brings us to the subject of carnal Christians. Carnal Christians are those who have had a real salvation experience, but because of their spiritual immaturity, they still can fall back in the old ways and begin to operate according to the natural man. Such individuals have not yet graduated from the milk stage to the bread and meat stage. Keep in mind the Word of God is to become the believer's food. As the believer's food, it is to bring each believer to perfection or maturity in his or her life before God. Even though Jesus serves as the essence of righteousness to each of us as believers before God, these different stages of maturity establish each of us as God's children in a proper disposition (right standing with God) and with an acceptable attitude (right doing in regard to others), thereby, grounding us in righteousness and establishing us with righteousness. Without righteousness, God cannot count our attitude, conduct, or action as being righteous, thereby allowing Him to impart His grace or favor to us.[3]

In the milk stage, Christians are learning how to conduct themselves properly so they can begin to develop a right attitude and the ability to discern between good and evil in light of God's character. They must choose to believe that what God says is truth. Pure doctrine in action will expose and address fleshly ways. Fleshly ways include a selfish attitude and worldly influences. However, the preference or tendency of Christians in their immaturity is to intellectually gather doctrine, but not really put it into practice in line with Spirit and truth.

In the bread stage, Christians are learning to partake of the divine life of Christ. To "partake" means to believe His Word, commands, and instructions. 'Believing" in this text means to assimilate the truth of a matter into our way of thinking and being. Jesus talked about learning of Him in relationship to His disposition and eating of His body and drinking His blood in regard to becoming identified to His covenant through faith.[4]

The meat stage involves knowing and doing the will of God. This stage is where a believer believes in the fullness or complete reality of Jesus in regard to His place as Lord and His work of redemption. In essence, Jesus becomes a person's all in all, always serving as his or her place of abiding, as well as his or her point of preeminence in all matters pertaining to life and godliness. At this stage a person will be able to discern between good and evil.[5]

---

[3] Matthew 4:4; 6:33; John 6:35; 1 Corinthians 3:1-2; Hebrews 5:12-14; 1 Peter 2:1-3; 2:21

[4] Matthew 11:28-29; John 6:53-58; 2 Peter 1:3-6

[5] Hebrews 5:12-14

Consider the following table as to the type of spiritual food that a Christian must partake of to reach spiritual maturity:

Food	Pure Milk	Bread from Heaven	Meat
Form in which food is revealed	Doctrine	The person of Jesus	Will of God
The way Jesus Is considered	Example	Partake of divine nature	Abide in Christ
Faith	Believe On	Believe	Believe In
Jesus as our source of righteousness	Showed what righteousness is in His humanity as the Way.	Establishes us in righteousness according to His deity as the truth about God.	Identified in righteousness by His eternal life in us.
Righteousness (Our part)	Follow what is right (Jesus) into a life of discipleship.	Apply what is right.	Do what is right
How we establish right standing in our life	Follow after righteousness.	Assimilate what is right into our lives as truth to be walked out.	Obey what we know is right.

The Apostle Paul addressed the carnality or fleshly influences that remained within the Corinthian believers. This carnal influence can be summarized in our life in this simple way: We each have been conditioned with pride and prejudices according to our worldly influences that will operate when carnality is present. Such influences manifest themselves in envying, strife, and division. This was clearly evident in the fruits of the Corinthians. Paul went on to warn these Christians that every work (practice) will be tested by fire. And, what work is not based on unfeigned faith (gold), Christ's redemption (silver), and the work of the Spirit (precious stones) will be burned up. Granted, one's soul may be saved, but there will be nothing to present to our Lord as a means to honor Him, causing grave sorrow and shame to the Christian.[6]

Even though a carnal Christian possesses a new disposition, he or she has not yet become a spiritual man. A spiritual man is in tune with the Holy Spirit. The Apostle Paul actually addressed this matter before he rebuked the Corinthians for being carnal. He reminded them that the natural man couldn't respond to the Spirit. In fact, the natural man would consider the matters of the Spirit as being foolish or silly. As believers, we cannot know the deep things of God without the Spirit bringing revelation to each of us.[7]

---

[6] 1 Corinthians 3:1-15
[7] 1 Corinthians 2:10-14

Developing Our Christian Life

The main problem with carnal Christians is that they are not firmly planted on the foundation of Jesus. They have never developed the mind of Christ. Therefore, they first must learn what it truly means to sit at His feet and learn of His disposition and attitude with the intent of putting on His mind as a means to do away with the carnality of their thinking. They must discipline their steps in order to learn how to follow His example. Such discipline will allow them to be conformed to His likeness, rather than being conformed to this present world. If new Christians fail to be properly established on the right foundation, they will find themselves being tossed back and forth by that which appeals to their carnal ways and appetites.[8] This is why it is important that those who are teaching these young believers the ways of their Lord display meekness and grace as they contend with them in their immaturity.

Another problem with carnal Christians is that they often are content to stop at the milk stage and never progress past fundamental doctrine to partake of the bread and the meat. The Apostle Paul told the Corinthians they could not bear the stronger food in their carnal state. The writer of Hebrews told the believers that they still had need for milk, rather than meat. The test that distinguishes those who are still in the milk stage is that they are unskillful in the word of righteousness. He goes on to explain that meat belongs to those who are of full age and are capable of using their senses in such a way that they are able to exercise in the ways of righteousness in discerning both good and evil. Then, he exhorted such believers that instead of trying to lay the spiritual foundation once again, they need to leave behind the milk stage and go on to perfection.[9]

When you study the concept of meat according to Scripture, you will find that it is connected to the will of God. Jesus confirmed this in John 4:34, "Jesus saith unto them, My meat is to do the will of him that sent me, and to finish his work." Jesus was spiritually nourished when He did the Father's will. He wanted to both please and glorify the Father by finishing the work set before Him. The work set before Him was the cross.

Being in the perfect will of God is the safest place to be for any Christian. When we consider His will it comes down to us believing upon His Son to receive eternal life. Belief of this nature points to a faith that responds in obedience, producing total consecration. A consecrated life means we will become a living sacrifice, allowing us to discover God's will for our lives. Granted, we must test all matters to see if they will indeed line up to His will, according to His character, His Word, and our calling. However, it is important to point out that God's will can be expressed in different ways. We can know the *general* will of God because of His Word, and we can discover His *collective* will by finding our place in His Body, but we must learn how to create a right inward

---

[8] Matthew 11:28-30; Romans 8:29; 1 Corinthians 2:14-16; 3:11; Ephesians 4:14
[9] 1 Corinthians 3:2; Hebrews 5:12-6:1

environment for us to properly discern God's *perfect* will for our lives. What we must keep in mind at all times is that God's will, will ultimately be done in the end. However, we will determine what aspect of His will, will be realized in our lives. Mediate on the following table on the next page until you understand the profound spectrum that God's will embraces.

Developing Our Christian Life

Romans 12:1-2 (Consecration)	Purpose	Test (All matters)	Forms	Types
(Prove what is the... *Good* (Beneficial) Ordained by God, results in transformation, and prepared beforehand by God.	Eternal Life *(Jn. 6:19-40)* All He does has one purpose in mind).	His Character (Test a matter in line with who He is.) This will allow you to classify according to what has been established.	General Will (Is found in His Word—requires obedience and self-denial.)	Permissive Will (He permits you to do your own thing, but consequences will follow.) (Out of order of His will for your life.)
Acceptable (Will be received by God because it is not regarded as unholy and defiled.)	Purity (Motive & Action) *(1 Thes. 4:3-6)* Has to do with disposition. Requires integrity that will determine your approach. State of holiness.	Spirit (There must be agreement with intent and reasoning.) Discern spirit (Be able to classify properly.)	Collective Will Know your position *(in kingdom)* (as His co-laborer) Your place In His (*Body* for the purpose of edification) to fulfill His purpose according to His plan. Pick up your cross.	Providential Will (Works through circumstances as a means to teach valuable lessons.) Must avoid assumptions and presumptions that you know His will. (Purpose for your life can be discovered.)
Perfect (Considered upright before God, and in doing right or being honorable by others for His glory.) ...will of God	Thankful (Attitude) *1 Thes. 5:18* Will be determined by what you expose yourself to.	Ways (To come into line with His plan/way of doing) (Righteousness) Disciplined Walk (Reflection)	Personal Will (Calling, status, And life) More about what He wants to do in you, then with you. Follow Jesus	Perfect Will (Points to one coming to maturity or reaching His-perfect order in a matter) (Stand in confidence.)

Those who are of full age are capable of properly handling the Word of God. Consider what the Apostle Paul says about this matter in 2 Timothy 2:15, "Study to show thyself approved unto God, a workman that needeth not to be ashamed, rightly dividing the word of truth." Those who are spiritually mature have studied God's Word, as well as know how to properly handle it in the right spirit.

One of the things I stress to the disciples of Jesus is that they have to give the Holy Spirit something to work with. In summation, by studying, applying, and hiding the Word in their heart, the Holy Spirit can take it and bring revelation and life to it. However, if the Word of God is not present in our lives, the Holy Spirit will not have any means by which to bring us to truth, instruct us in righteousness, and transform our minds.

Properly studying and applying the Word of God will make Christians into workmen who will not be ashamed of their work when they stand before God. In fact, as believers we are reminded that we are God's workmanship, created unto Him for the purpose of good works. God has actually ordained that we walk in these good works. We must not only ensure we bring such works to a completion, but we must remember that these good works are meant to glorify our Father who is in heaven.[10]

Mature workmen in the harvest field of humanity also realize the Christian walk is not simply about doing religious things to impress others with some type of personal knowledge or goodness. In the milk stage, new believers are basically learning how to live the Christian life. In the bread stage they are beginning to partake of the divine nature of Jesus in order to walk out the life in authority and confidence. In the meat stage, Christians are walking out this life according to the righteous and perfect will of God. Immature Christians have to learn by proving what is the good, acceptable, and perfect will of God, while the Christians being sustained by bread are learning what it means to commune and walk in step with Christ. Mature Christians will be able to simply discern what His will is based on the leading of the Spirit and the Word of God. Remember, mature saints know how to handle skillfully the Word of God. The new or immature Christian is tying to learn what it means please to God, while the Christians who live by the Bread are learning the benefits of applying the ways of God, and the mature saint will simply obey that which is right, bringing glory to the Lord.

The Apostle John also talked about three stages of spiritual maturity: children who understand their status because of the love of the Father, young people who are learning to stand because the Word of God is in them, and fathers and mothers who know God.[11] Children are learning to walk according to milk, young people who are assimilating the Bread of the Word are learning what it means to advance in their Christian maturity as soldiers of the cross, and the mature saints who partake of the meat know how to walk according to their growing relationship with God.

---

[10] Matthew 5:16; Ephesians 2:10
[11] 1 John 2:12-14

Are you a carnal Christian, or are you advancing to the stage of maturity in Christ until you are brought into God's perfect will for your life? Remember, the works you do in this life for God will be tested by fire. If you remain immature in your life before Christ, you may not have any works remaining after the fire of God has been put to them. If you are not sure, ask the Lord to reveal your level of maturity. If you are not coming to full age, you probably need to repent for failing to learn to apply and assimilate His truth with the intent of obeying His Word and discovering His perfect will for your life.

3

I AM A GOOD PERSON

One of the greatest deceptions for most people is that they think either they are good or that they are right. For those who perceive they are right, there is no need to consider any other reality. After all, if one is right about matters, it is up to others to agree, bow down, or give way to the person's conclusions. To insist on being right from this premise can become a means of control or witchcraft, where others fall victim to such control, making them feel as if they are being pushed into some type of reality that is contrary to their will. Those individuals who perceive they are right will remain unteachable as they resist coming into submission to that which is honorable and right to God.

If a person perceives that he or she is "good", there is no need to consider his or her need for salvation. Someone once stated that it is not difficult to get a man saved. What is difficult is first getting him lost so he can see his need for salvation. After all, such people perceive that they are "good" enough that they do not see that they have become lost in the darkness of sin, ignorance, and death. Such a deluded concept comes from the idea that since God is "good" surely He will see and accept a person's "goodness." However, God's perception of "good" and man's perception of it are far apart.

Such people weigh their so-called "good" against their bad. In their mind if they do enough "good" things it will outweigh what is bad and God will surely give them a pass. However, God does not weigh our good with our bad. The reason is because according to Romans 7:18, there is no "good" thing in the flesh and Isaiah 64:6 tells us our best is considered filthy rags.

It is for this reason that God weighs the type of life in us against His holy, perfect Law. Since the Law is unable to justify, it can only find us guilty when we break it. The truth is we have all broken God's Law in some way. Our selfish disposition will justify us when trespassing into forbidden areas of the Law, while our wrong attitudes will pervert its intent, and our defiant actions will transgress it.

John 3:3 and 5 tells us we must be born again to enter into the kingdom of God. Upon the new birth we receive a new heart and spirit. The new heart possesses the life of Christ and the new spirit ensures the new life is worked in, through, and out of us. Since Christ fulfilled the Law, He satisfied the judgment of death that rested upon all of us. As Romans 10:4 states, Jesus is the end of the Law for righteousness to everyone who believes.

Developing Our Christian Life

When we received Jesus, we were told in Colossian 3:3 that we became hid in Him. Since we are hidden in Him, Ephesians 2:6 reveals that we are also positionally seated in high places with Him. According to Romans 8:2, we have been placed under a more excellent Law, the Law of the Spirit of life in Christ Jesus.

When God weighs us, as believers, in the balance, the life that is weighed against His Law is the life of Jesus. Since He satisfied the Law, His life in us serves as the essence of righteousness and completes the intent of the Law. The result is we stand justified rather than condemned. Clearly, the life of Jesus must be present in a person for him or her to avoid facing the wrath of God against what His Law deems as ungodliness and unrighteousness on the part of unregenerate and rebellious man.

Through the years I have met people who perceived themselves as being "good." I am sure you have met them too. They seem nice, decent, honest, and respectful. In some cases, they are considered the "good old boy." You like to be around them because they appear positive and pleasant. They often possess a good sense of humor, and come across as friendly, with a pleasant personality and mannerisms. It is quite easy to like such a person because he or she does not come across as rude, offensive, or aggressive. Compared to other individuals these people's lives often outshine those who seem to struggle with the various issues of life. Consider the following example:

A few years ago, we met a hard-working man (we'll call him "Lyle") with a cheery disposition, out-going personality, and disarming mannerisms. His involvement in his church and community was exceptional. As a family man, he appeared to have it all together as his children were allowed to participate in every Scout, church, school, and community activity available. Lyle never missed a beat to show the world what a "good guy" he was.

Judging by outward appearance, most people would conclude that Lyle was a genuine Christian, through and through. He attended church, befriended everyone, and enjoyed the social aspects of it all. However, a closer examination of Lyle's fruits revealed that he was only deluding himself about his status as a "good guy" in God's eyes. His "good fruit" was the product of a worldly tree—not the Tree of Life which seeking souls could partake of and discover Christ. In essence, the "fruit" lacked the life of Christ. The "fruit" that Lyle produced may have served as a means of giving the appearance of a "good guy" to others, but spoke of his best and clearly fell far short of God's standard of holiness. While it may have exalted Lyle as a "good guy" in the church and community, it failed to bring glory and honor to God. His "good guy" reputation was a means of self-protection against any challenge to his immovable comfort zone. Sadly, in spite of being challenged by the truth of God's standard of holiness, the Lordship of Christ, and man's need to be broken and repent, he retreated behind a stony wall of anger.

The inspiration behind such concepts concerning man's so-called "goodness" is motivated by a worldly philosophy that one can really find some "good" in every person. For example, there are some in America who actually think God is part of the culture, along with patriotism, apple pie, and baseball. In fact, America has been presented as being a tolerant society; therefore, each of us are encouraged and instructed to find some "good" in a person as a means to give him or her a break. However, there are always those individuals in society that clearly contradict such a philosophy.

When cultural influences are allowed to define God according to the culture's particular take on life, it produces what we call the *cultural gospel*. For those who think themselves "good enough" for God, they will often adopt this gospel. In the cultural gospel, man develops his own philosophies about life according to his cultural influences and morality, and then creates and implements the idea of a god on to his philosophies to make them right in his own eyes.

In such a person's mind his or her understanding seems so wise. However, if you get this person down to the real foundation of his or her perception, you have someone who is not only quite proud of his or her so-called "goodness" but is also self-serving in regards to it. These people only do what makes them feel good about self or what makes them look good to others, bringing desired recognition or commendation. If these people have to step outside of the box of convenience or comfort, they can prove to be crude and indifferent to other people's plight.

A man we shall call "Clueless Curly" offers another example of an extrovert extraordinaire. "Clueless Curly" never met a stranger. He can talk his way around the world in one short encounter, entertaining with stories from his past that could fill volumes. However, his jovial demeanor belies the fact that when push comes to shove, he will opt to pitch in and help where he will receive the most accolades, which, unfortunately, is usually at the expense of his own family.

"Clueless Curly," like so many religious people, happily attends church and volunteers for jobs that make him the center of attention. Fueled by compliments, adoration, and his own high opinion of himself, "Clueless Curly" continues on his merry way while remaining oblivious to what is of eternal importance. He has no desire to learn of the will of God for his personal spiritual life, nor is he interested in sharing the Gospel with others. Obviously, his focus revolves around this present world and his involvement with it.

Tragically, when "Clueless Curly" is confronted with his inconsistencies, he suddenly becomes deaf, puts up an indifferent wall and shuffles off, or he jabbers his way past it. It is obvious that control is the name of the game for "Clueless Curly". He has developed his own comfortable "culture" that some would say is "located on his own little planet."

Developing Our Christian Life

The reality is that the God of heaven is not inspired by any culture nor does He exist because of the influence of culture. God stands outside of every culture, and it is up to individuals to truly seek Him outside of cultural, family, and religious influences and conditioning.

To put this in perspective, we must remember that as believers we are called to be loyal citizens of the kingdom of God. While we may have been conditioned by our worldly culture, we are called to be transformed in the mind, allowing us to be conformed to the likeness of Christ. Conformation according to the likeness of Christ points to being established as a Christian in a godly lifestyle, which involves choosing to live according to a higher, heavenly calling.[1]

As you consider those who see themselves as "good," they often prove to be *amoral* in their views. In other words, they live according to their own moral code. This code may demand the person to be honest or just, but such a person is not necessarily spiritually in tune with God. Individuals who see themselves in this light have no real inclination towards the things of God. They may not mind God being in their midst as long as He is kept within the bounds of their philosophy. However, their understanding of God is vague and perverted because it is based on personal goodness, and not according to His real character that has been revealed in the Bible. Therefore, God and some of His ways might be tacked on to moral beliefs or practices, but He will never be allowed to interfere with these people's lives outside of their personal perception of Him.

Such an attitude towards God points to the natural man being in operation. The Bible tells us that the natural man is unable to receive anything from the Spirit of God. Such a person will have no preference towards God. The Apostle Paul encountered such a man in Scripture. His name was Gallio.[2]

According to history, Gallio was considered an amiable man. When the Apostle Paul appealed to him about the matters of God, life, and eternity, he proved to be indifferent. It was obvious that he did not care about such issues. He was content in his world. However, it was said of him that he became thoroughly disillusioned in a world that eventually proved to lack the means to satisfy the inner man. It is believed that he might have committed suicide.[3]

Those who consider themselves to be "good" become indifferent to what is righteous. It is important to point out that "goodness" and "righteousness" are not the same. God is considered both good and righteous. "Good" points to that which is beneficial, while "righteousness" embraces right standing or being just in all matters.

---

[1] Romans 8:29; 12:2; Philippians 2:5; 3:14, 20
[2] Acts 18:12-17; 1 Corinthians 2:13-14
[3] Lectures on the Book of Acts; H. A. Ironside; Eighteenth Printing, August 1982; Published by Loizeaux Brothers, Inc.; pgs. 415 & 418

In light of God's goodness, we must consider whether there truly is some form of "goodness" in man that benefits others for more than a fleeting moment. If so, then one must reason that a person truly can be "good" in his own power; therefore, there would be no real need for Jesus to die on the cross. In light of this concept, one must consider why Jesus would even bother to go to such an extreme measure of sacrifice if it was not necessary. That is unless we can conclude that Jesus was just being another "good old boy" by nobly sacrificing Himself in such a way. However, such a concept is not Scriptural. "Good" in this text is contrary to God's perspective of it. The Bible is clear that only God is "good" or capable of truly benefiting people's lives.[4]

As Christians we know the truth about our spiritual plight. In the world, we may be considered "good", but in the eyes of heaven, there is absolutely nothing within us that can be considered beneficial to God or to others. Since the motive behind such worldly "goodness" is self-serving, it defiles such people's actions, and makes such deeds reprobate or useless to God.[5] The attitude behind such "goodness" is that of indifference which will rob any "action" of possible kindness or benevolence. Such acts ultimately leave a bitter taste in the mouths of the recipients who are often made to feel that they are a grave burden or are now obligated in some way to prove they are worthy of such consideration.

It is vital that we believe what the Bible tells us about humanity. We are told that there is no one righteous, no not one. In other words, there is none that stand upright before God. The Bible goes on to declare that we have all sinned, and now come short of the glory of God. The wages for our sin is that of death or spiritual separation from God.[6] Because of this premise, we are once again reminded of what Isaiah 64:6 tells us: that the man's best is as filthy rags before God.

The influence, working, and activities of sin have been passed down to each of us because of Adam.[7] Sin influences our way of thinking as it expresses itself by declaring its independence from God. After all, we think we know what we need better than our Creator does. Since we perceive that we have a right to life on our terms, the workings of sin upon our soul uses such a platform to cause us to insist on doing it our way regardless of whether it is right or wrong. The activity of sin that abounds around us encourages and condones our sin of pride in its pursuit to be exalted in all such matters, opposing God's intervention in our lives in accordance with His salvation, will, and plan.

The problem with man is that he thinks "goodness" is based on putting forth his best presentation, but true "goodness" finds its only source in God, and actually expresses itself in moral discipline and

---

[4] Matthew 19:16-17
[5] Romans 7:18; Titus 1:15-16
[6] Romans 3:10, 23; 6:23
[7] Romans 5:12-14

accountability in a person's conduct. When we consider that man now exists in a fallen disposition due to sin, we can only conclude that the best this disposition can produce in presentations and works would also fall short of the mark of excellence according to the goodness and righteousness of God.

This brings us to the inward condition of those who think they are "good enough". These people are walking according to the deception that has taken their heart captive. Their point of comparison as to their "so-called" goodness is not based on God, but on their own idea of goodness or the cultural gospel. In fact, their "goodness" serves as a false light that is actually blinding them to the real Gospel.[8] Since they feel justified based on the fact that they have not done anything really "bad," they feel secure that the just God will not reject them.

The problem with these people's point of justification is that they fail to understand that it is not just a matter of what they do, but who they presently are in their fallen disposition, and who they will become if it is not confronted. This fallen condition makes them subject to the dark dictates of sin. Such a perception may seem right, but due to the influence of sin upon the mind, it harbors the workings of death. These people's ways may seem acceptable, but because of the workings of sin upon the weak flesh, such ways lead to destruction.[9] And, the more these people give way to the activities of sin that abounds in the world, the more they become deluded about their true state before God.

Let us remember the balance where our lives will be weighed against the judgments of God's Law. Each of us have inherited a fallen state from Adam. In this state, we are not inclined towards the true God of heaven, and our tendencies are to justify such wicked and selfish ways according to the amoral, self-serving philosophies of the world. This may all seem right and acceptable to our way of thinking and being, but God in His holiness cannot accept us in such a state.[10] We are clearly separated from Him, dead in our sins, and void of real life.

Consider the following chart about sin. It gives a clear picture of how it operates in and through our lives. We see the attitude of sin, and how it works in our fallen state. We also can see what addresses the different aspects of our fallen condition, enabling us to overcome sin's influences, as well as distinguish its fruits, the forms, and types of sin. We can also clearly consider the pigpens it creates and operates within. As you study the following table, you will begin to see that the terminal disease of man's soul has defiled every aspect of our lives. It has perverted our mind, defiled our disposition, manifests itself in lifeless, poisonous fruits that are contrary to God, crosses every boundary of righteousness, and thrives in the best (pigpens) man has to offer in spite of the holiness and righteousness of God.

---

[8] Jeremiah 17:9; Matthew 6:22-23; 2 Corinthians 4:2-4
[9] Proverbs 14:12; 16:25
[10] Isaiah 55:8-9; Romans 5:12

Sin (Attitude)	Disposition (Fallen state—walking in death)	Fruits	Forms Ex. 34:7	Types	Pigpens
Independence from God's rule (I know what I have need of) Doing It my way. (I know what is right for me) Opposition against God (I will win-pride)	(Influence of sin) Inclination (What or who we serve) (Born Again)	Rebellion (Control)	Offences (Matthew 18:7) (Offend the character or pride of the person.)	Ignorance (Unaware that they have committed an offence.)	Religious (Dead men's bones)
	(Workings of sin) Tendencies (Determines what state we live in—life or death.) (Face sin, deny self-pick up the cross.)	Ignorance (Live in denial)	Transgressions (Matthew 18:15)	Commission (Idolatry)	Self (Lusts)
	(Activities of sin) Determine what we will reflect. (Godly influence) (Put on Jesus)	Delusion (Prefer own light to God's light.)	Iniquities (2 Tim. 2:19)	Omission of righteousness (Unbelief)	World (Agreement-source of dependency.)

The only way we can remedy this insidious condition of thinking ourselves to be good is to repent of our arrogance. Behind the mask of the "good old boy" is pride. God resists the sin of pride, leaving the person in his or her deluded state of ignorance and indifferent towards his or her present state of death.[11]

By repenting of this prideful state, the Holy Spirit can begin to convict such people about the sins that have taken them captive. At this point the veil can be taken off their minds and hearts, revealing their need to receive Christ as the only one who can save them from their state of death, which is leading them down the path to eternal destruction.[12]

As previously stated, upon receiving Jesus as their Lord and Savior, these people, who possessed a deceptive heart and were indifferent to

---

[11] James 4:6; 1 Peter 5:5-6
[12] 2 Corinthians 3:13-16

Developing Our Christian Life

the righteousness of God, will be born again with a new heart and spirit.[13] The new heart will be receptive to God and the new spirit will be sensitive to the Spirit of God. As they listen with their new heart to the truths of God and give way to the Spirit of God, their indifferent, selfish disposition will be transformed into a state that is truly alive unto God.

There are many who see themselves as being a "good person." They are assuming their personal "goodness" is good enough, ignoring or rejecting the redemptive work of Jesus. As a result, when they stand before the holy Judge of heaven, their personal goodness will be exposed as being filthy rags. In these rags, all confidence will fall to the wayside as they stand ashamed, rejected, and doomed.

If you have not received Jesus as the solution to your spiritual condition, it is time to do so. Assumptions or wishful thinking will not change the reality that an eternal existence is awaiting each of us, nor will it change the fact that without Jesus, people will stand in filthy rags before the One who provided the way of salvation. Such souls will have no excuse for their rags, and sadly, they will have no recourse to acquire the white linen robes of righteousness that have been allotted to those who have, through faith, received the Lord Jesus Christ.

If you feel the conviction of the Holy Spirit upon your heart to receive Jesus as Lord and Savior, but do not know where to begin, consider the following heart-felt prayer as a means to ask Him into your life.

Lord, I know that I have been prideful in trying to stand in my own goodness. I have been blinded to my wretchedness, but now I see the error of my ways and the hope of my salvation. Forgive me for my sin; come into my life and save me from my wretched state by giving me a new heart and a new spirit. By faith, I thank You for having mercy upon me and showing me grace by saving my soul from eternal separation from You. Amen.

---

[13] Ezekiel 36:26-27; John 3:3, 5

4

ASSOCIATE CHRISTIAN

Many religious people refer to themselves as being Christians, but when you consider their fruit, you have to wonder if they are simply Christians in name only. Through the years, that which was associated with Christianity has been considered in light of popular fads or movements that have rolled through the religious world. For example, when I was saved in 1976, the craze to roll through Christendom at that time was being "born again." Everyone was talking about being "born again." But, eventually the excitement over it dissipated when another fad claimed the spotlight.

However, according to the Word of God, being "born again" was never meant to be a popular fad. Jesus clearly stated that a person had to be born of Spirit and Water (the Word of God) to enter the kingdom of God.[1] It was obvious that the "born-again" experience is what ensures salvation.

Today there are many people claiming they are Christians who do not hold to even the pure doctrine of Christ, let alone possess the inner witness of salvation. These individuals hold to *antichrist beliefs* that not only present a different Jesus, but also believe in another gospel, and are being influenced by another spirit.[2] The truth is that this is acceptable in many religious arenas and is classified as being "Christian." However, the attempt to bring all religions under one so-called "covering" referred to as "Christianity," is a deceptive means of conditioning those who are part of the visible Church to embrace a lie. The lie is that there is no real distinction between the Christianity established over 20 centuries ago, and the one that is being promoted as a new move or work of God. However, the real name of this so-called "covering" is *ecumenism*, and it promotes a *false gospel of peace* that will label those who refuse to come into agreement with its abominable ways as being hateful fanatics that must be reconditioned or destroyed for the good of all.

Recently, this harsh reality was brought home to me. I was saved out of a popular cult over thirty years ago. When I was part of this cult, the leaders were adamant about claiming their distinction as the true church from the many other "false" Protestant Churches. Recently, I encountered two missionaries from this cult. To my surprise these two youthful zealots purported that they were Christians. It was obvious that

---

[1] John 3:3, 5
[2] 2 Corinthians 11:2-4; 1 John 4:1-3

Developing Our Christian Life

these two young men had been well trained to actually speak the lingo of Christianity to put forth an image, while maintaining an antichrist belief that claims a different Jesus and gospel behind their false light. Notice, they could speak the lingo because Christianity is now presented as a subculture in this world with its own terminology.

When I shared with them that I was a former member of their cult, and that at the time of my membership the cult would have never made such a claim as being "Christian," one of the young missionaries arrogantly mocked me. My thought was if they were truly Christians, why were they trying to proselytize me into their church? When I challenged them about the variation that existed between our concepts of Jesus, they kept insisting we believed in the same Jesus, even though there were obvious differences. These young men were clearly blinded to the dissimilarity between our two faiths.

In John's second epistle he gave this strong admonition,
> Whosoever transgresseth, and abideth not in the doctrine of Christ, hath not God. He that abideth in the doctrine of Christ, he hath both the Father and the Son. If there come any unto you, and bring not this doctrine, receive him not into your house, neither bid him Godspeed; For he that biddeth him Godspeed is partaker of his evil deeds (2 John 9-11).

There are those in the Christian realm who are submitting to the *liberal philosophy* of "political correctness" that calls for tolerance and understanding towards others in their error of unbelief and cultures that harbor the ways of death. This tolerance is supposed to be in the name of love and peace, but these false, worldly presentations cleverly replace any real responsibility in maintaining Scriptural truth and obeying the Word of God. They are enlarging the narrow entryway of true salvation as clearly outlined in Scripture to embrace what is being considered popular and acceptable to the religious environment. Sadly, those who are claiming to be believers are actually partaking of the evil deeds of those who hide behind a false mask of Christianity, but clearly do not have the real witness or testimony of salvation.

This brings us back to those who associate themselves to the Christian faith, but in name only. The Apostle Paul related that if Christ is not in a person, his or her confidence or so-called "faith" will prove to be useless, discrediting these people's claims or appearance of being associated with the Jesus of the Bible. However, it is not enough to be associated with Jesus; one must know the true Jesus of the Bible to lay claim to the status of being a Christian.

We not only find this association happening in beliefs that are counterfeiting Jesus, but we find it among those who are part of the Christian scene. Let me give you some examples.

Family: When people grow up in a particular religious environment, they automatically become associated to that religious preference. In such a case, it is assumed by such individuals that their elders must be correct in their understanding of such knowledge. Often in the minds of these people they logic that since they belong to the family, they will presume that their family has the right take on God, which also makes these individuals part of the church or belief system. Even if they have a disagreement down the line, there is still a loyalty that binds them to the religious affiliation.

For some religions you might be associated to them through family ties, but to be a child of God, there must be a verbal confession that clearly expresses a heart revelation. The Apostle Paul declared this in Romans 10:9-10,

> That if thou shalt confess with thy mouth the Lord Jesus, and shalt believe in thine heart that God hath raised him from the dead, thou shalt be saved. For with the heart man believeth unto righteousness; and with the mouth confession is made unto salvation.

The Bible tells us that every foundation will be shaken. Only that which is eternal will be left standing. However, people who are associated with the Christian faith through family influences will find that they are standing on a foundation made up of assumed beliefs. These beliefs do not belong to them; rather, they are assumed. In assumed beliefs, people presume they are saved, but when challenged, they cannot give a reason of the hope in them.[3]

Religious Affiliation: Being affiliated to a particular church, religious leader, or theology also becomes a point of being associated to Christianity. However, church, leaders and theology cannot save a person. The Bible is clear that we must be identified with Jesus in His death, burial, and resurrection, as well as identified in Him as our source of wisdom, righteousness, sanctification, and redemption. It is all about personal identification that takes on the very life of Jesus. Clearly, to be an associate of Jesus actually puts people outside of the gate that leads to identification to His life.

Good Deeds: Some people believe that works associate one to Christianity. Such works can include going to church, being benevolent towards others, and giving time, support, and energy to worthy causes. However, the Bible is clear that we are saved by grace, not works. Granted, we are saved unto good works, which means that works ordained by God will become a natural extension of our service and worship to God.[4]

People who think that "good works" identify them as being Christians ultimately throw bones at Jesus to keep Him "happy" and off their backs so they can maintain their personal identity and lifestyle. However, Christ will not recognize these people on Judgment Day, and their works will prove to be temporary, clearly marked for judgment.

---

[3] Hebrews 12:27; 1 Peter 3:15
[4] Ephesians 2:8-10; Titus 2:14

Developing Our Christian Life

There was a man we shall call "Ramone." Ramone was a romancer, but he also wanted to go to heaven. Therefore, he followed his wife to church, and went through all the motions of being an enthusiastic Christian during praise and worship. He dressed nice, carried his Bible to church, and even paid "tithes." He seemed to enjoy home Bible studies because he could socialize, show off, and eat desserts. It appeared that his favorite part of church life was the social aspect (especially where food and women were involved) and where he could put forth an image of being "one of the group," in spite of the fact that he really did not have a testimony, or anything of spiritual value to offer.

Ramone looked every bit the part of a committed Christian in church, but it was a different story behind the scenes. As an "associate Christian," he had no genuine interest in personal Bible study, prayer, or witnessing. On the one hand, he wanted to wear the title of "Christian," but on the other hand, he wanted what the world had to offer, including women. Thus, Ramone had one foot in the world, and one foot in the church, but neither feet were firmly planted in the kingdom of God.

The question is how can people be so close to the kingdom of God, but fail to enter in? The answer is simple; such people refuse to be converted. They like being associated with Christianity to receive the possible benefits from it, but to truly be converted to the lifestyle of a Christian would prove to be contrary to their personal agendas, pursuits, and goals. As a result, they may strive outside of the gate, but they will never enter into its narrow entrance.[5] Like the thieves who are trying to climb unnoticed into the sheepfold in John10:1, these people are trying to enter the kingdom of God unnoticed on the shirttails of others or because of personal actions. Such attempts make them thieves because they are trying to lay claim to God's kingdom that they do not have any part in.

Christ is clear that unless a person becomes converted, as well as takes on the disposition of a child, he or she will never enter the kingdom of heaven.[6] Conversion means one is going to adapt to a whole new lifestyle. This adaptation will begin with an exchange at the altar of the cross of Christ. The exchange involves giving up the right to have life according to personal agendas, pursuits, and goals to become identified to a new way of living. In exchange for the old way, one will receive the new life of Christ. His life presents a completely different lifestyle. And, to give way to this new way of living, a person must become a child in disposition to take on the very attitude and ways of Jesus.

One of the greatest examples of an associate Christian is Judas Iscariot. He followed Jesus for three years, even after some of His disciples turned back and followed Him no more. Judas had preached the Gospel, as well as witnessed the many miracles that Jesus performed; yet, in the end he betrayed Him. This man may have followed

---

[5] Matthew 7:13-14; Luke 13:24
[6] Matthew 18:2-3

the Lord of lords and King of kings, but he was never really converted to the Christian life; therefore, he never became identified with Jesus. Judas maintained his same attitude and mannerisms for he remained a thief to the end of his life.[7]

We are told that Judas repented of his actions. However, there are two different forms of repentance. There is worldly sorrow where people feel sorry about a matter due to how it personally affects them, and there is godly repentance where a person sees what sins cost others including God, thereby, ceasing from it, confessing it, and turning around to walk according to a new way. Judas felt sorry about betraying Jesus because apparently his conscience bothered him after he learned that Jesus was to be crucified. However, he did not repent in order to convert to a whole new way of life. As a result, he continued on his old path, which resulted in him hanging himself.[8]

The reason that "associate" Christians, such as Judas Iscariot, are content to maintain an outward impression of Christianity is because they have a *disconnected heart* when it comes to the things of God. Those who think they are good people take pride in their so-called "goodness", but such individuals are actually full of pride. They may have some head knowledge about the Christian life, but there is no heart revelation. The Holy Spirit is clearly absent in these people's lives; therefore, they do not have any real connection to God. They have simply tacked God or Christ on to their life, but there is no evidence of His life. After all, their self-centered agendas, pursuits, and goals, are what motivate them. If something contradicts these focal points, they will become treacherous, and betray that which exposes, opposes, or challenges them.

The main platform associate Christians effectively operate from without being tested or challenged is the *watered-down gospel*. The watered-down gospel operates from the premise of God's love and "easy believism." In the watered-down gospel, the good news is that God loves you. Granted, God loves us, but such love is presented from a worldly perspective, causing it to be improperly emphasized. This improper presentation allows the issue of sin to be downplayed, redefined, overlooked, and compromised. As a result of this presentation, God is made out as someone who will overlook sinful lifestyles because He so loves us. Since God loves us, He will receive us if we simply say a simple prayer asking Jesus to be our Savior. Once we do, we can go merrily on our way because we are now saved. Sadly, many of these people never really make the heavenly connection by realizing they must truly repent of their sin with the intent of being converted to a new way of life that will clearly identify them to their Lord and Savior, Jesus Christ.

I remember talking to a man who was struggling with his Christian life. He truly fit the criteria of being an associate Christian. He had grown up in what would be considered a Christian family. He went to church

---

[7] John 6:60-66; 12:4-6
[8] Matthew 27:3-11

Developing Our Christian Life

when he was not fishing and camping. He paid tithes, and when it was convenient, he would occasionally show religious participation. However, it was obvious that his agenda was self, his pursuit was the world, and his goal was to possess the materialistic lifestyle of an American. But such pursuits will leave one empty after offering temporary happiness.

This man came face-to-face with the reality that the quality of his life really depended on the type of relationships he had developed. He was having relationship problems due to the fact he lived for self while expecting those in his world to adjust to his whims. As a result, his relationship with his spouse was crumbling around him. He had become frustrated by his selfishness, as well as left empty by the world and feeling quite miserable and lonely in the midst of all of his stuff. In his apparent despair and frustration, I asked him if he ever really received Jesus into his heart. I will never forget what he said. "I don't know how many times I have to ask Jesus into my life before I am saved!" I instructed him that he had to get Jesus from his intellectual understanding into his heart before he could be truly saved. The man sat in total despair because he could not fathom how to make such a connection with his heart.

There is a saying that the longest distance exists between the head and heart of a person. The reason the distance is so long is because of the enormity of pride that stands between these two areas. Pride clearly stood in a lofty position in the man's soul, preventing him from truly humbling himself and giving way to the gentle impressions of the Holy Spirit that would bring him to repentance. It was clear that he was not willing for the heavenly connection to bring him to repentance. In his pride he was resisting true conversion that would require him to cease from playing at Christianity, and truly becoming a Christian in lifestyle. He simply resorted to the worldly type of sorrow that cried about the harsh reality that truth would not adjust to his reality.

There are so-called "Christians" who are playing at being Christians. As a result, they have become Christians in name only, while claiming all the glorious benefits of the Christian life. However, there is one benefit they will not be able to claim, and that is eternal life.

Are you a Christian in name only, associated to Christianity, but not identified with Jesus because you refuse to be truly converted to being a follower of Christ and a possessor of His life? Keep in mind, one day every associate Christian will stand before Him, and the Lord will not be able to acknowledge any of them as belonging to Him. There will be no evidence of His Spirit or life. There will be no point of connection or identity in which He will be able to recognize these individuals. His sad words will no doubt echo through the very corridors of eternity, "I never knew you; depart from me, ye that work iniquity" (Matthew 7:23b).

5

RELIGIOUS CHRISTIAN

A common type of "Christian" is the religious Christian. Such a person may have the appearance of being godly, as well as some type of association with the kingdom of God; but he or she can prove to be void of the realization that Christianity is not a religion but a way of living. The religious Christian may be involved with acceptable religious activities; however, Christianity is not distinguished by certain activities, but by how one stands in the midst of the world. Does the person stand distinct because of not only how he or she lives, but also displays the proper attitude of Jesus Christ towards the world, as well as approaches it according to the ways of righteousness?

Religious Christians may hide behind an appearance of godliness, but it proves to be superficial. The Apostle Paul revealed that the surface appearance of godliness simply covered the fact that such people lack the power to be godly.[1] When people lack power, they also lack authority. Authority will always identify a person to his or her source of power.

There are two reasons as to why religious people prove to be powerless in their lives. The first reason has to do with who they truly identify themselves with. It does not take long to discover people's true point of identification, for it is natural for them to talk about it or refer to it in any conversation that involves religious matters. They often refer to their point of identification because it serves as their place of confidence. Such identification can include certain religious leaders, denominations, or practices. These points not only identify them in some way, but they also serve as the source that they assume gives them the necessary authority to maintain their particular witness or testimony about their standing in the religious kingdom.

Through the years I have heard religious Christians emphasize their pastor, denomination, and practices, such as observing their concept of the Sabbath. To give credibility to their point of identification, they talk about how popular their church is, the good deeds that the church's members are doing in the community, and/or the mission work they are involved with. It all seems commendable, but the real issue is whether God has ordained such activities to ensure His glorification.

The second point of identification has to do with theology. In other words, based on this vantage point, what a person believes is what identifies him or her in the Christian world. When you talk to religious

---

[1] 2 Timothy 3:5

Developing Our Christian Life

Christians, they are thoroughly devoted to their particular belief system. They give the impression that their belief system is superior to others, giving them authority. Notice that it is a belief system. A system may point to something as being established, organized, and arranged to ensure a pattern of order, procedure, and practice, but it does not empower a person. We are told that the Gospel, not doctrine, is the power of God unto salvation.[2] As you consider these people's emphasis on their theology, you realize that they hold to the *gospel of doctrine*. In other words, their doctrine not only distinguishes and identifies them, but also serves as the good news to others. The good news is that if you agree with their doctrine, you will also be part of the religious elite who possess the "truth" about spiritual matters.

When you question religious people about their point of identity, you realize that for many they have been indoctrinated into their theology. Such theology may not be wrong, but the reality of these people's understanding is based on theories about religious matters that they have adopted in light of what has influenced them. Granted, these beliefs may be based on the Word of God, but they are void of any real dimension that allows these individuals to step out of their limited understanding to embrace greater truths. In fact, such theories may work at different times, but they cannot always be applied to every situation. The book of Job verifies this fact.

Job and his friends operated according to personal theologies. When applied to Job's situation, Job's theology became darkness to him because it could not explain why his life went into a devastating tailspin. For his friends, their theology made them cruel and indifferent to Job's plight as they improperly judged and falsely accused him according to what they believed. These men's theories about God could have applied in some situations, but in Job's case they clearly missed the mark of truth. As a result, God made this declaration to one of Job's companions, Eliphaz, "My wrath is kindled against thee, and against thy two friends; for ye have not spoken of me the thing that is right, as my servant Job hath" (Job 42:7b)

When you study what Job was right about, and what his companions were wrong about, you will realize that Job stepped outside of his theology in order to put his faith in the living God. On the other hand, his companions maintained their theology while unmercifully justifying it at Job's expense.

The more religious people are indoctrinated, the more adamant they become about their theology being the only way in which a person will be assured of their state or place in the religious world. In fact they will walk according to the limited and often prejudicial light of their particular indoctrination. At this stage, these people have clearly developed a *legalistic viewpoint*. They will automatically consider everything

---

[2] Romans 1:16

according to their religious boundaries. As their theology becomes more cemented, it begins to serve as blinders to them.

In one incident a woman was approached to consider a valuable seminar for those who were involved with her particular ministry. At first the woman seemed open to it and genuinely interested in the spiritual status of those who were volunteering to present the information. Testimonies of Christ's salvation and work were shared with her, confirming the speakers' status as children and servants of God, as well as revealing a sound Scriptural foundation.

However, the ministers encountered a snag when the leader questioned them about their "covering." Although the Bible is clear that there is only one Head of the Church, Jesus Christ, and there is only one acceptable covering over a person, that of the Holy Spirit, this woman had been thoroughly convinced and indoctrinated that Christians must have some kind of religious leader or organization as their "covering" to be considered legitimate.[3] The speakers had advisers, but did not believe in the "covering" theory. Regardless of the established validity of the speakers, in this woman's mind if people did not have such a "covering," they were out of order. Due to her theology, this woman became suspicious of the speakers and dismissed their ministry.

When theology is put as the final authority of a matter, it will nullify the authority of the Word of God. Jesus encountered this in His day with the Pharisees. Their oral traditions had become their religious conscience concerning their beliefs and conduct. Jesus said that their idolatrous exaltation of their traditions that had added terrible burdens to the commandments of God, were in reality causing people to transgress God's commandments. After all, they were not putting faith in God's Words, but in their man-made traditions; and, what is not a matter of faith is sin. Jesus also stated that they were making proselytes to their traditions, causing such followers to become two-fold more the children of hell than they were.[4]

Sadly, religious people who are in leadership positions use their legalistic view to misuse their authority. They will overstep their authority by ignoring, neglecting, or disregarding the power of God's Word. They will also abuse their authority by demanding that they serve as others' religious conscience. Ultimately, they will mishandle their influence as they reject the truth to ensure their theology and so-called "power" over the people remain intact.

Religious blinders prevent those under false or heretical coverings from seeing that they often unfairly judge the servants and truths of God because of their theology. A good example of this can be found in how some emphasize the Sabbath.

---

[3] Isaiah 30:1; Ephesians 4:15-16
[4] Matthew 15:3-9, 14; 23:13-15; Romans 14:23

Developing Our Christian Life

Sabbath points to rest, and its observance was to serve as a shadow of a great source or place of rest.[5] This great place of rest did not involve a particular day where one physically rested from the drudgery of the week. The real rest had to do with the soul finding rest in the reality of God.

The Scriptures tell us that the Person of Jesus is our real place of rest. However, the people who keep a day, rather than embrace the real place of rest for the soul, take pride in their stand and point of identification of keeping the Sabbath. Such people often prove to be very judgmental and self-righteous towards those who do not see it their way. Even though a day cannot save a person, these people give the impression that keeping this day is necessary for salvation to take place, clearly frustrating the grace of God.[6]

Theology cannot discern what is correct, it can only judge according to its philosophy. Clearly, such belief systems lack the means to bring life. Granted, these beliefs may promote certain moral lifestyles, but they cannot produce life. These theories may subtly promote beliefs as a way to understand how to please God, but there is no life in them. It is from this platform that cults are produced or developed.

Legalistic viewpoints can develop into a cult mentality in relationship to how it views religious matters. Some cults are obvious, but sadly some of the different denominations within the Christian world have slid into the category of being a cult. A cult runs parallel to true Christianity, but it fails to line up to the Spirit and truth of the Christian faith. There are three ways to test any belief to see if it falls into the category of being a cult. In fact, if a church fails any one of these three areas, you will see the presence of the cult mentality.

The first area has to do with the foundation. Christianity is established on the Person of Jesus Christ, beginning with His work of redemption, and then evolving into a revelation of who He is based on the complete counsel of the Word of God. According to the Bible, Jesus is fully man and fully God. As man, He became God's Passover Lamb, as well as our example and High Priest. As God, He serves as our Creator, Lord, Savior, Redeemer, Truth, and the essence of our life. If a belief's foundation is not made up of the real Jesus, you will have a cult that may look right, but which is founded on shifting sand that will not endure the testing and judgment to come.

The second area that cults expose concerning themselves is by claiming that they are the only true church or that they have a corner on truth. Religious people take pride in their particular belief system. This pride turns into self-righteousness, which comes across as being judgmental and elite. The reality is that the true Church of Jesus is made up of those who believe in Jesus Christ. He is the One who serves as the essence of absolute truth. Since truth is eternal, there is no way that

---

[5] Colossians 2:16-17
[6] Matthew 11:29-30; Galatians 2:21

mere man or a religious system can conquer its heights, dredge its depths, or travel its width. In our present state, we can only know in part. If we do not receive a heavenly revelation of Jesus Christ as the way to righteousness, the truth about God and redemption, and know Him as the essence of life that is eternal and possesses resurrection power, we will remain limited by our fleshly dimension as to the reality of the life of Jesus that resides within each believer.

The third area that exposes a cult is the environment it encourages. For the Christian, there must be humility before God, meekness towards others, and godly love for the brethren. Because cults possess arrogance about their beliefs, they come across as noble instead of humble. Since they see themselves as being elite, they can only come across as tolerant or sympathetic to what they consider to be ignorance and foolishness on the part of those who do not belong to their particular belief system. Although these individuals try to come across as loving and kind, there is hardness due to their legalistic view.

We cannot help but respect some religious people because they are sincerely devoted to their beliefs, but such beliefs cannot reciprocate or honor that which runs contrary to or opposes them. We can understand why these religious people cling to their theology, but there is no assurance because theology cannot save anyone. We must also, as believers, recognize that these people may commendably defend their theology, but in the end only that which is of Spirit and truth will remain standing. John the Baptist made this statement about the Jewish religious system of his time, "And now also the axe is laid unto the root of the trees; therefore, every tree which bringeth not forth good fruit is hewn down, and cast into the fire" (Matthew 3:10).

Theology cannot produce acceptable fruit. This is why the Bible refers to such belief systems as being dead-letter because in so many cases there is no life to them.[7] This means people may know of and about God, but He will never become a heart revelation to them. Without heart revelation, religious people develop a *judgmental heart* toward anyone or anything that does not line up to their controlled, limited views. Such a heart only allows them to give lip service to God.

It is important to reiterate that these beliefs may have some semblance of truth, but the Holy Spirit will be missing from such lifeless beliefs. Such beliefs represent man's intrusion into the matters of God. Man's way in the matters of religion reveals how he can only pervert that which is of God as a means to suit his own religious notions. However, the Spirit cannot honor profane ways. And, without the Spirit, there is no life or means to develop wisdom from above and receive revelation. After all, it is the Holy Spirit who is to serve as the true covering and teacher of God's people. He alone is the one who leads people into all truth about

---

[7] Romans 7:6; 2 Corinthians 3:6

Jesus and establishes and renews the inner life of those who have been born again from above.[8]

Although religious people may possess some truth, they walk in delusion about their true spiritual state. Their self-righteousness blinds them to their religious pride and the vanity of the path they are on. Since their preference is towards a lifeless belief system rather than Jesus, they have allowed their beliefs to stand as the point of their personal identification.

This brings us to another aspect of religious people. They usually have a mediator, other than Jesus, standing between them and God. Religious people are looking to their religious leader, denomination, or religious system to mediate on their behalf. Since they have faith in their particular mediator, they now can cast aside any spiritual responsibility and trust the spiritual insight of their leader, their association with their established and respected denomination, and/or the so-called "authority" of their belief system. However, the Bible is clear that there is only one true mediator between God and man, and that is the man Christ Jesus. As believers, when we behold Jesus at the throne, we do so in light of Him being our High Priest, but the Father sees Him seated at His right hand in His deity, capable of representing man to Him and properly representing Him to man.[9]

The concept of a mediator can be seen in the children of Israel who become frightened when they received a glimpse of Jehovah God's holiness and power at Mount Sinai. At that point, they asked Moses to serve as their mediator between them and God. Therefore, they did not have to meet God on a personal level. They could leave all matters in the hands of Moses.

As you follow the children of Israel, you can see that in many ways they were religious. However, they had their own ideas of service and worship. It was clear that Jehovah God could not be adjusted to the ways they were familiar with in regard to religious worship and service. By being removed from having a personal relationship with God they could maintain their old pagan ways without being exposed or challenged. In the end, they failed to learn His ways, which prevented them from entering into rest in God's promises.[10] Ultimately, the influence of paganism was revealed when they erected an idol, disobeyed God's instructions, challenged Moses' leadership, and preferred the bondage of Egypt to the glorious leadership, provision, and protection of Jehovah God. This clearly revealed that even though they gave lip service to God, their hearts were far away from Him. In essence they walked in unbelief towards God.

This is a problem with being removed from God. Granted, man could not approach God without intervention, but God provided the means in

---

[8] Isaiah 30:1; John 3:5; 16:13; 1 Peter 1:2; 1 John 2:27
[9] 1 Timothy 2:5; Hebrews 7:19-28; 8:1
[10] Exodus 20:18-21; Hebrews 3:10-19

which man could come to Him. To visibly confirm this, His presence was evident in the children of Israel's camp, His tabernacle served as a living testimony as to His desire to reside and walk among His people, and His fire of protection at night abided in their midst to guide and watch over them.

Once again, we are reminded of the rest of the story of the children of Israel. When it came to entering the Promised Land, they did not trust God enough to possess their promise. After all, they allowed Moses to have a relationship with God on their behalf. They had seen miracles and benefited from their God's care, but they still did not know Him on a personal basis. Since they did not know Him, they could not trust Him. Without total reliance towards Him, they would not obey Him. In the end, they would fail to love Him; therefore, they would not be able to fully worship Him nor could they possess His promises.

I was saved out of cult. I had a vague notion of God, but I had no idea who He was. At different times I went through the motions of doing my religious duty, but I knew something was missing. Yes, the environment was quite religious. Morals were verbally promoted and rituals practiced. It looked like a sacred place and the people acted pious, but something was missing, causing restlessness in my soul. What was missing was the life of Jesus and the presence of the Holy Spirit.

If people view God through the tainted vision of their religious leaders, denominations, beliefs systems, or practices, He will remain vague, appearing like a lifeless image that stands far away in the distance, aloof, and unapproachable. Even though these people may hear of Christ, he is simply tacked on to the religious activities and practices to give them credibility. However, the Bible is clear, we must see, believe, know, and worship the living, bodily manifestation of God who was revealed to the world, the Lord Jesus Christ, to ensure our spiritual status.

Consider the inner state of those who worship based on a dead or pagan religious system according to the following table.

Religious Pride (Zech. 4:6)	Sin (Ro. 6:20)	Unbelief (He. 3:19)	Idolatry (1 Jn. 5:20-21)
1. Will not submit to God's authority. 2. Fear 3. Independence 4. Personal Strength 5. Results in Self-delusion	1. Rebellion against God's authority (His word-Commands). 2. Will not deny self of its lusts from having life on its terms. 3. Will not give up the world's pagan values.	1. Will mock God's authority while giving lip service. 2. Determine personal belief—how one is going to believe, and how he or she is going to receive. 3. Will mock sincere faith. 4. Produces an unreceptive heart towards truth.	1. Replaces God's authority. 2. Erect own god that will give personal identity and importance. 3. Superstition (Ignorance about God.) 4. Ends up worshipping creation rather than the Creator.
Wrong Spirit	Wrong Master	Wrong Heart Condition	Reprobate Mind (Ro. 1:21-28)

As you consider this table, you can see that being a religious Christian means nothing if it serves as a cloak that hides the fact that you are being influenced by a wrong spirit, master, heart condition, and mind. The spirit that influences religious people by seducing them into accepting a counterfeit or substitute Jesus at the point of their independent and religious pride is the *antichrist spirit*. The master who inspires rebellion in such people is the god of this world, Satan.[11] Because of unbelief towards God, the hearts of these religious people become unreceptive towards truth that does not fit into their belief systems. In this state, these individuals will create their own god, causing them to become superstitious or ignorant towards the true God of heaven. In the end, they will end up worshipping the creation instead of the Creator, losing all sense of His real identity in their inner conscience.

We know that as Christians our point of authority is the Lord Jesus Christ. Our heart must be open, tender, and receptive to Him as master,

---

[11] 2 Corinthians 4:3-4; Ephesians 2:1-3

capable of seeing, hearing, and following Him into a new life, for He alone is the One who must have complete say over all aspects of our lives. His authority becomes the means in which His Spirit empowers us to stand in confidence as we obey God's Word, and carry out our responsibilities in His kingdom. Such a walk becomes a form of acceptable worship that is clearly in line with God's Spirit and truth.

Are you a religious Christian who has put your confidence in your religious influences and practices? Perhaps you know of Christ, and even have the jargon down about Jesus being your Savior, but you still see religious matters through the narrow view of your theology, religious leaders, or church affiliation. If so, you still do not personally know Jesus according to the Bible. Scripture tells us that Jesus is all in all. In other words, He must become all that we pursue, desire, and seek. He must be found in all we do, and He must become the essence of all we need to seize as far as what is true, honest, just, pure, lovely, and of good report.[12]

---

[12] Philippians 4:8-9

6

SENTIMENTAL CHRISTIAN

The next type of Christian we must identify is the sentimental Christian. To understand how these people operate, we must understand the meaning of "sentiment." According to my dictionary, "sentiment" points to an attitude, thought, and judgment that have been prompted by some type of feeling.[1]

With such people their conclusions or ideas about a matter will be colored by the emotion that is being stirred up by the environment. Whatever emotion is being stirred up in their environment will cause them to pursue after what they desire. Usually there has been some type of importance attached to the emotion because of a past experience. In such a disposition, this type of individual can indulge in how something makes him or her feel, creating an environment that is not only pleasing to his or her emotions, but compliments and reinforces his or her particular feeling about a matter.

When you consider such a state, each of us have found ourselves giving way to sentiment when something has caught the imagination of our feelings. I remember in my days of being a cult member, my first impression of Jesus was quite sentimental. It was solely based on Him being a sweet babe in the manger. Let us face it, the innocent and purity of something such as a baby can cause much sentiment in our emotional arena. I was clearly caught up with the sentiment of Jesus as a baby, but had no idea why Jesus' particular entrance in the world should cause any more excitement than the birth of another child. Granted, I had heard about Him being born of a virgin, but such information did not make any real connection that God had become flesh by entering into the world as a vulnerable baby. Therefore, ignorance continued to keep me in darkness towards my real hope and reason why God became flesh. It was to become identified with humanity as a means to redeem each of us from the dictates and consequences of sin.

Another event that causes much sentiment in the religious world is Jesus' ordeal on His way to Calvary. It is amazing how the sentiment of Jesus' suffering is actually exalted over what He actually accomplished on the cross, that of redemption. Clearly, as we consider His steps to Calvary, we cannot help but be overcome by what He had to experience. As the gamut of our emotions take hold, we experience sorrow as we follow Him to the altar of the cross, despair as we consider His silent

---

[1] Webster New Collegiate Dictionary

suffering, and our tears flow when He cried out in despair. Yet, in this emotional roller coaster, we see some light in the midst of such grave darkness when we read His words, "It is finished."

Upon His death, we are reminded how silent it must have been for those who were left behind in the wake of what seemed surreal and devastating. It would have appeared as if wrong was victorious, hope was dead, and the world was indeed utterly insane. However, after the silence, came the victory of resurrection, flooding His followers with joy when they personally encountered Him in His new body.

It is true that each of us possesses that emotional aspect that will be present when we are stirred by some point of identification that resurrects a feeling, desire, or some type of passion. At such times we are lifted up above the drudgeries of life by a wave of sentiment. It makes us feel alive, as if maybe there is some purpose for our being. As we ride this wave, we perceive this is what life is meant to be. However, like all waves it must end by bringing us back to reality when it comes crashing down in the midst of the demands and responsibilities of daily living.

This presentation sets up the stage to uncover the sentimental Christian. These people create a Jesus according to their feelings. In other words, their Jesus has been defined in such a way that consideration of Him can stir up these people's sentiment. As their emotions are stirred up to reach a certain crescendo, they began to experience an *emotional ecstasy*. Such ecstasy is important to them because it serves as the *light* they desire to live in. It gives them a sense that all is well in their world, when in fact what they are experiencing is nothing more than a personal fantasy that keeps them from facing the dreaded drudgeries and challenges of every-day living.

It is important to point out that we can only know and experience God through the spirit, but sentimental Christians operate totally from the soul area. To operate from the soul area makes one's activities fleshly. In fact, the height of this emotional wave of sentiment in religious matters often manifests itself in fleshly worship. In fleshly worship, people worship the emotionally charged sentiment they are feeling or environment they are experiencing, rather than the God of creation.

It is also vital to understand how the soul influences the sentimental Christian. The soul area is made up of the will, intellect, and emotions. It is interesting to watch how sentiment is determined or expressed through each of these avenues. For example, the will of a person will determine how something should make a person feel. Such determination will be based on personal notions or opinions that have been influenced by concepts, standards, images, or ideas. The notions and opinions of sentimental people allow them to feel very passionate about a matter. Since passion makes them feel sure about a situation, they will become set in their opinions, making them critical towards anyone who will not come into agreement with their particular take on reality. At such times,

Developing Our Christian Life

these people's passion can turn into anger and vengeance towards those who will not placate their particular reality.

Several years ago, we knew a woman whom we shall call Valerie. She is a good example of how powerful and dangerous passion can become when fueled by a steady diet of undisciplined emotion. Valerie was quick to shed a tear whenever she heard a moving song or sentimental sermon, causing those around her to believe she was a genuine believer. Her emotions were the driving force behind the high standards she maintained when it came to her home and lawn. In fact, one could say that she was a perfectionist where her environment was concerned. However, it became evident that Valerie's outward façade of perfectionism was not so much about the love of God, life, and others as it was about her.

Everything Valerie did to impress others, whether it was through her cooking and hospitality, or volunteering her help on different occasions, carried with it an undercurrent of hardness and even anger. Some began to distrust her motives for all the good things she did for them because they could sense the emotional turmoil that was taking place underneath the surface. When others failed to respond in the manner that Valerie expected, the emotional turmoil began to surface in bad attitudes, bursts of anger, and foul language, as her emotional moods swung from one end of the spectrum to the other. Nothing that others close to her could say or do at this point could stem the rising tide of explosive passion and anger.

Rather than examining herself and asking the Lord to show her her own heart so that she could repent of her pride and sin, and receive forgiveness and healing, she would justify her attitudes at the expense of those around her. In her book, her emotions were the correct standard and if others did not agree with her and her agendas on every point, then they were the ones who were not only wrong, but who deserved to be thrown to the wolves.

Obviously, such a life may produce what appears to be genuine fruit up front, but it will only prove to be shallow and empty when put to the test. This type of person is like the one described in Matthew 13:20 and 21 which says, "But he that received the seed into stony places, the same is he that heareth the word, and anon with joy receiveth it; Yet hath he not root in himself, but dureth for a while: for when tribulation ariseth because of the word, by and by he is offended."

The intellect is also greatly influence by the sentiment of these individuals. If the right feeling is not present in these people, then the intellect will harshly judge or disregard a matter. We see this in the case of the Word of God. If the Word cannot stir up the proper sentiment about something, it will be considered invalid for that time. In fact, I have watched the Word fall to the ground as it fails to penetrate the emotional perception of these people. Sentiment clearly replaces true faith towards God. These people put a great deal of faith in the reality that has been created by their feelings or attitude. Even though the sentiment of such people may quickly change, they will still maintain that their perception is trustworthy.

The reason why these people insist on this false sense about their reality is because sentiment gives them an infallible sense that they cannot possibly be wrong about a conclusion. From the platform of their sentiment their conclusion about a matter looks accurate, sounds sure, feels right, and seems unbeatable in its presentation. Therefore, how can it be wrong?

Since these people's perception of reality is based on sentiment, truth that manages to penetrate their emotional veil will always cut across their intellectual attitude. God's truth is not sentimental. It will not try to adjust its stark reality to cater to the soft, touchy, fragile sensitive palates of these people. Truth will reveal the deception that works within the unstable, changing ways of sentiment. The reality of sentiment is that it is void of any sure foundation. It is like a wave, constantly on the move. It moves according to influences, environment, and circumstances, and will always prove to be fleshly in all of its activities. But truth is founded on the immovable Rock that will never be swayed by the flesh or any pressure or manipulation.

Emotions are what reign in the sentimental Christian. They will often search for something in which they can truly be sentimental towards. Such sentiment will give this type of person purpose, direction, and something he or she can put his or her energies and passions into. Although sentiment is unstable, it has one underlying motive, and that is to ultimately feel good about self and life. Due to this underlying motive, these people promote what I call the *"feel good gospel."*

The type of good news the "feel good gospel" promotes is that the Christian faith is all about one feeling good about maintaining the self-life in their religion according to the fleshly desires and pursuits of the soul. Such an attitude sees Christianity from the basis of what it can do for the person as far as benefiting his or her personal well-being.

Sentimental Christians seek opportunities or means to do those things that will ultimately bring them necessary recognition or exaltation, allowing them to direct their sentiment towards themselves in a positive way. What they fail to realize is that behind this sentiment is a *fragile ego* that must be placated or fed by positive feedback or reactions, or it will quickly display a touchy attitude that shows that the person has been insulted and offended.

An extreme example of such a person is a woman we shall call Mona. Mona grew up watching her mother play emotional games to manipulate those around her in order to be pampered and get the attention she craved. Even though the last person on earth Mona wanted to be like was her mother, she inherited her approach to life. Mona's friendly, outgoing manner seemed to indicate that her great love for people knew no bounds. People were drawn to her because she seemed to sincerely care for them and their challenges in life. In time, however,

Developing Our Christian Life

many who took her gregarious personality at face value suddenly found themselves the target of petty and unfounded, vicious gossip.

One such victim could not understand what had happened to cause this woman who emphasized "love," to turn on her with such a vengeance until it was explained to her Mona's pattern. While Mona disarmingly appeared to be the most loving and caring person on the planet, there was always an undercurrent of scrutiny, which escalated into judgmentalism when people failed to act, talk, or respond to her "correctly." The "right response" according to Mona's selfish standards (which were based on her view of self) would always be along the emotional lines that she felt it was her right to receive.

In time, people would tire of trying to placate and feed the immature, selfish monster that motivated Mona in her pride and self-pity. Her insatiable need for emotional reinforcement caused people to feel like the life had been sucked out of them, leaving them exhausted, confused, and depressed.

As you listen to or encounter these people, you realize that the motive behind them wanting to approach and know Jesus from the premise of sentimentality is utter *selfishness*. After all, it comes down to that fact that they want to feel good about the presence of self in their religious world, as well as maintain a certain level of sentiment towards Jesus. In summation, they simply want to feel good about their selfishness reigning in their religious worlds.

Peter is a good example of how sentiment works. We see his emotions in action when he was following Jesus. In the storm, he probably was a bit impulsive about walking on water to Jesus, and sank once he took his eyes off of Him. In the light of ministry, he tried to instruct Jesus as to how He must view a matter, only to have the influence of Satan rebuked in his life because his soul was savoring the things that are of men. The night Jesus was betrayed, he zealously claimed he would die for Him, only to turn around and deny he even knew Him. In each situation, we can see where Peter's sentiment was clearly in operation, serving as his inspiration, strength, and momentum.[2]

Obviously, sentimental Christians consider Jesus and their calling according to their emotions. Since these emotions seem so real to these individuals, they gauge their spiritual condition according to how they are feeling. The result is Jesus is constantly changing to them, as He is considered through their different moods or temperaments.

At the core of these people's selfishness and sentiment is a *fickle heart*. A fickle heart is deceitful since it has not been grounded on the truth. In fact, this heart deceives the person about his or her true spiritual status. Ephesians 4:14 best describes this type of person as being susceptible to being tossed to and fro by every wind that blows through Christendom. This type of person can be moved by anything that might feed their emotional fickleness. I have even witnessed them trying to

---

[2] Matthew 14:25-31; 16:17-23; 26:26-35

conjure up some type of sentiment in their religious environment for the purpose of experiencing some emotional high.

A fickle heart is also inconstant; therefore, untrustworthy. It is unstable, causing the person to be unstable in all of his or her ways.[3] It is not steadfast because it will not put its confidence in that which is immovable.

Jesus made this very important statement to Peter about his unstable condition, "Simon, Simon, behold, Satan hath desired to have you, that he may sift you as wheat; But I have prayed for thee, that thy faith fail not. And when thou art converted, strengthen thy brethren" (Luke 22:31b-32). Peter had to be sifted by Satan in order for him to see the fallacy of his sentiment. Take away the inspiration of it, and one finds he or she does not have any real faith. After all, the person's faith is in their sentimental notion or idea of Jesus, but not in the Person of Jesus. Therefore, when you take away the momentum of such sentiment, one actually becomes a coward. Take away the false sense of strength from it, and one becomes confused, depressed, and even angry.

These people have to come down from their sentimental wave of fickleness in order to face the crux of the matter. They need to cease from being committed to maintain their sentiment about Jesus, and truly be converted to the living Christ of the Bible. This involves becoming sober in the mind.

When Peter was sober, he got it right about Jesus. However, this sobriety involves being under the inspiration of God. For example, when Jesus asked Peter in Matthew 16:16b, "But who say ye that I am?" Peter answered with these famous words: "Thou art the Christ, the Son of the living God." Jesus then stated that such a revelation was not revealed to Peter from any human influence or understanding, but it was the Father who had brought it to his understanding. He then told Peter that He would use him to build the Church that would stand, regardless of how much hell would oppose it. However, it was from the premise of imagination that the wave of Peter's sentiment once again took hold of him, causing Jesus to turn around and rebuke him.[4]

In another situation many of the disciples were offended by some of Jesus' sayings. They went back to their old life, and walked no more with Him. Jesus turned to the twelve remaining disciples and asked them if they would also go away. Peter is the one who answered Him on behalf of the others, "...Lord, to whom shall we go? Thou hast the words of eternal life. And we believe and are sure that thou art that Christ, the Son of the living God" (John 6:68-69). Clearly, there is no trace of any emotional momentum moving him in his answer. He is quite aware of the gravity of the situation. The key to his sobriety in this situation was his faith. Even though he may have not understood Jesus' saying, and the momentum of his sentiment was not there to inspire him to show a false

---

[3] James 1:8
[4] Matthew 16:16-23

Developing Our Christian Life

sense of honor, he chose to put his faith in what he did know about the person of Jesus.

Sentimental Christians need to be truly converted to the real Jesus. He is not a notion or idea that changes with unpredictable moods. He cannot be known by the fleshly dictates of the soul, worshipped with undisciplined carnally inspired emotions, or served according to selfishness. As Peter pointed out, Jesus is true, living, and eternal.

What about you? Are you a sentimental Christian? If so, take heed to Peter's example. He was sincere in his sentiment towards Jesus, but not realistic about Him. He needed to be converted from viewing Jesus through his emotions, and behold Him in His glory as the Son of the living God.

7

SOCIAL CHRISTIAN

One of the biggest challenges for the Christian in regard to the world is to make sure that they do not make Christianity a social club or activity. Sadly, local churches unwillingly serve as a social club where people of the community get together in the name of Christ to socialize for various reasons. For some, it is a matter of status to be seen and associated with certain successful denominations. It is also a good place to do business and seek a future companion of the opposite sex, but all of these agendas are worldly.

In one such case, a woman who was involved in multi-marketing saw her church as a place to promote her product. She admitted that when she did not get the desired response, she would shun the people who did not become part of her financial pursuits.

Another time, a couple of men were overheard talking about how the best place to find single, lonely women was in a church. They concluded that by going to a church, most people would assume they were part of the church and would accept or embrace them. The church association would allow them to prey on or pursue lonely, vulnerable Christian women who would ultimately serve their purpose.

Being social in the religious arena can take on other forms. It can involve becoming part of religious groups, masses, or social, moral movements as a means to promote or bring forth some kind of agenda or cause that would "supposedly" benefit society as a whole. Such activity involves improving, reforming, or rehabilitating as a means to ensure and promote proper function and well-being of the society. It can also mean supporting or being part of organizations, political movements, or stands that support some kind of agenda such a social justice or moral responsibility.

Sadly, these *social causes* become a platform and perspective for social Christians to operate from or within. In such instances, Christians get involved with issues that seem quite moral and noble in many ways. From all appearances, moral awareness and accountability, as well as good will and deeds, are being promoted as a means to change the social or moral climate of a nation. Most Christians are aware that a nation that turns against God seals its own destruction.

Through the years I have watched many Christian movements attempt to change the climate of this nation. Christians have run for office, as well as been active in supporting certain candidates. They get involve with causes that affect the healthy function of the family such as

Developing Our Christian Life

abortion and education. In some of their minds, spiritual inspirations can clearly be found in men such as Joseph and Daniel. These men were in high positions in government, and able to impact the lives of God's people. For the family of Joseph, they were saved, and for Daniel he impacted the leaders of empires through his excellent example and steadfastness as a follower of Jehovah God, along with God's people through his prayerful intercession.

Unless a person is specifically placed or called to a political position, the problem with these causes is that they depend on worldly methods and means to bring about good. These methods can end up identifying Christians to this present age, and not to the kingdom of God. They are not seen as Christians, but as social reformers who are trying to serve as a moral conscience to this nation.

Another social Christian is the Christian who goes about doing good deeds. They see their deeds as serving as a testimony as to the level of their kindness. Others admire them because they have been giving or kind in different ways. However, the reason for them displaying such kindness is so they can feel good about their particular form of Christianity. Behind the mask of good deeds, these people often live a compromising relationship with the world.

It is vital for Christians to examine whether something that is considered good keeps them from what is best or excellent when it comes to the kingdom of God. For example, those who attend church to reap social benefits are missing the main purpose of meeting with other Christians, and that is fellowship. In social Christianity there will be no place of agreement where Christians can experience the authority of heaven, the power of the Spirit, and the work of edification. Without such agreement these people will never discover their true place in the kingdom of God, thereby, failing to make an eternal impact in His kingdom.

For those Christians that are politically involved, they need to remember that God specifically placed Joseph and Daniel in their positions to bring about specific results. They were simply fulfilling the plan of God. They served as voices of reason in uncertain times. In Joseph's case, he saved his people, but Egypt eventually enslaved them. Consider Daniel, who warned and instructed people concerning the mind of God, but he still did not prevent the fall of Babylon or avoid being cast into the lion's den.

This brings us to the responsibility of Christians as far as their particular country is concerned. First, we must remember that our real citizenship is a heavenly one, not an earthly one. Granted, the Apostle Paul used his Roman citizenship, but it was in relationship to fulfilling the plan of God to further the Gospel, not changing the moral climate. He was aware that unless the inner terrain of man was changed by the born-again experience, he might be reformed outwardly, but unregenerate man would still remain lost to God's intervention.

Such a reality stuck me when I found myself caught up in a political arena that involved educational matters. I was standing for a worthy cause, but it never saved anyone. What it did manage to do was insult and enraged others, including those who were known as Christians. I had to be honest as to my real motives for standing for causes, rather than obeying the commission set down in Scripture. Did my cause somehow exalt me as being part of a notable cause that could reform a wrong in society? Was I trying to promote some type of change that in the long run would maintain the quality of my life in this present world? Was I caught up with ensuring that my motive for my activity was to ensure that I was preserving a climate that would allow me to freely worship God? In good causes we can convince ourselves that our involvement is a matter of undertaking that which is considered noble in the name of Christ, but nobility does not constitute that which is honorable before God. In fact, honor exalts the work of Christ, while nobility simply tacks Christ on in order to receive personal recognition or benefits.

As Christians, are we meant to save a nation as a means to preserve our self-serving lifestyle in this present age? We have been told what our responsibilities are towards our nation and the world by the Apostle Paul in 1 Timothy 2:1-4. Daniel best illustrated our main responsibility as Christians towards our nation as interceding for the leaders. But, for what reason do we intercede? We must stand in the gap so we may lead a quiet and peaceable life in all godliness and honesty. Such lives will serve as a powerful, living witness for our Lord. This is what is good and acceptable in His sight. The Apostle Paul ends by expounding on the heart of God in 1 Timothy 2:4, "Who will have all men to be saved, and to come unto the knowledge of the truth."

The problem with being social Christians is that these individuals will promote a *social gospel* that may encourage moral causes, reformation, and good deeds, but such a gospel cannot save a person. It may allow individuals to hide behind the idea that through such worldly methods of social deeds, activities, and interactions that Christ will somehow be exalted or honored, when in reality He is clearly missing from the equation.

In our nobility, we may use such Scriptures as 2 Chronicles 7:14 as an excuse to try to change the terrain of this nation, but this verse was written to Israel whose inheritance was the land. For Christians, we are not called to possess land, but the person of Jesus and His kingdom. The healing that God wants to bring forth is not to lands of this present age that clearly stand judged in their wretched sins and worldly ways, but to hearts and minds that need to be changed and transformed by the reality of His truth, Jesus Christ. And, without the preaching of Christ and Him crucified, man remains separated from God, far from His salvation.

Scripture commissions us as Christians to preach the Gospel of Christ and Him crucified. It is the Gospel of Jesus Christ that can bring

Developing Our Christian Life

about healing to the inward terrain of man, changing his environment around him. It also commands us to disciple people to be followers of Christ so they can be part of His eternal kingdom, as a means to make an eternal impact in their lives.[1]

Discipleship is the means in which a person becomes identified to God in Christ Jesus. As true followers of Jesus learn to follow Him in identification and obedience, they begin to discover the character of God. As God becomes more real to them, they become more Christ-like in their attitudes and ways, as well as equipped to be discerning in spiritual matters.

The power of discipleship was made clear to me in a personal way. I was presented an opportunity to disciple a young woman who maintained some worldly attitudes towards a particular moral issue for the period of a year. I simply lifted up the character and ways of God. Although the moral issue was never addressed or discussed, a year later she revealed that her mind had been completely changed about it to line up to the character of God.

In light of our commission and responsibility as Christians, Scripture clearly reminds us that God's kingdom is not of this world. It does not function like this world, it is not moved by the same methods as the world, and its perspective is far beyond this present age. Christ stated that if His kingdom was of this world, His followers would be fighting for Him according to the world. At one point He instructed His disciples to render that which belonged to Caesar back to him, and give back to God what truly belongs to Him.[2] There must be a distinction for Christians as far as their responsibility to and interaction with the matters of the present world. The main distinction is that our lives must be consecrated to our Lord as a means to carry out His work according to His Spirit and truth.

As you consider social Christians, you will realize that their causes may vary according to their social involvement with the matters of the world and their understanding of God. But, there is one thing that identifies them to this category, and that is there is a mixture that is clearly present in their Christianity. It is the *mixture* of Christian principles with the *attitude of the world*.

When you deal with the attitude of the world, you will not only encounter some type of compromise with the world, but an inconsistency in the person's life and testimony. The reason for this compromise is because these people possess a *worldly heart* where the truths of God have been choked out by the influences and activities of the world.[3] Unbeknown to these people, they have put some type of reliance or confidence in the world to make a difference. Worldly influences not only bring these people into some type of agreement with the spirit of the

---

[1] Matthew 28:18; Mark 16:15-16
[2] Matthew 22:21; John 18:36
[3] Matthew 13:22

world, but their understanding of spiritual matters is perverted by this unholy alliance, desensitizing, and confusing them as to what is pure and acceptable to God.

This mixture can clearly be seen in these people's attitude towards the truth and others. These people perceive that they are to approach the matters of the world according to the methods, attractions, and standards of the world to successfully address it. Eventually these people find themselves redefining or adjusting their philosophies, responsibilities, practices, and standards to reach out to or confront the world. As a result, worldly philosophies often replace Scriptural truths, while "noble" causes (responsibilities) end up confusing and redefining the Christian's commission. The result is compromising practices become hidden as worldly ways are justified, while worldly standards become the means in which others are harshly judged. In the end righteousness will become confused with what is considered as the decency of the world.

The Bible is clear that agreement with the world results in spiritual fornication, putting a person at odds with God. The attitude we as Christians must have towards the world is that of being a stranger in it and a pilgrim who is seeking another place outside of the corrupt entanglements and ways of the present age.[4]

Social Christians often use their causes to hide or justify the worldly influence upon their hearts, minds, and actions. I remember when I was involved in causes, I was secretly consoling myself in regard to my hidden sins. I felt that my good deeds were outweighing my worldly ways, and that God would note that I had good intentions in spite of my worldly actions. However, this is a point of self-delusion.

A man we shall call Todd offers a good example of a social Christian. Todd often attended church, but his conversation, instead of centering on Jesus, was usually about some project or charity in which he was involved. The greater the need, the more eager he was to volunteer his services. Instead of supporting the financially struggling fellowship he frequented, he poured his time and money into whatever the latest "tragedy" was. It was apparent that his causes were not necessarily God's will for him, but rather served as a means to make him feel good about himself in spite of his questionable life style.

Like many others in this particular fellowship who promised to "some day support it," Todd preferred to "be seen of men" and faded out when challenged by the Word of God concerning true servant hood to Jesus Christ. The bottom line is, Todd was apathetic towards the truth of the Word of God and true discipleship to Jesus, but found self-satisfaction in deeds that outwardly made him look good.

It is important to understand what real Christianity entails. It is not what you do that counts to God, but what you allow Him to do in and through you. It is His life and ways that must establish each of our

---

[4] James 4:4; 1 Peter 2:11

Developing Our Christian Life

attitudes toward Him, as well as our life and our relationship with the world. Therefore, all matters must be traced back to Him and His Word if they are going to identify each of us to God's eternal plan and kingdom.

Another important matter is that there are diverse differences between the spirits that govern these two kingdoms and the unseen laws that they are subject to. For example, the spirit of the world is what influences the activities of this present world. This spirit works in the children of disobedience. In other words, those who walk according to the spirit of this world will walk in the ways of iniquity or moral deviation as they submit to the dictates of the corruption of the flesh, bringing them under the law of sin and death.[5] Their inward disposition will be that of the darkness of corruption, their heart will be inclined towards the idolatrous ways of the world as they erect another god, and their tendency will be to develop their own standard of righteousness as a means to stand justified in their own eyes. The book of Proverbs best describes such a person, "There is a way which seemeth right unto a man, but the end thereof are the ways of death" (Proverbs 14:12).

As Christians, we must walk according to the Spirit of God. He is the one who will work the life of Jesus in us as He leads us from the ways of iniquity that are inspired by the world into the very paths of righteousness. From this premise that the righteous desire to exercise all that we do unto godliness for His glory will be developed. This will cause us to walk according the law of the Spirit that ensures the presence of the life of Christ Jesus in us. Our inward state will reflect Jesus' light, our heart will be inclined towards the righteous ways of God, and our tendency will be to submit to the Holy Spirit, knowing that we stand justified by faith based on the authority of our Lord, in accordance to His work as our Savior and Redeemer.

Consider the following table on the next page to see what spirit and law you have subjected yourself to according to your attitude.

---

[5] Romans 8:2; Ephesians 2:2

Law of Sin & Death	Law (Subject to)	Law of the Spirit of Life in Christ Jesus
Iniquity	Principle (Walk according to)	Godliness
Spirit of the World	Spirit (Influence)	Holy Spirit
Flesh	Master (Who/What you serve)	Christ
Corruption	Disposition (Inward State)	Life
Erect your own God.	Inclination (Heart)	Incline towards God in the ways of righteousness
Stand justified in my own eyes.	Tendency (Submission to spirit)	Stand justified by faith in Christ.

As we consider social Christians, we must acknowledge that they accept what may be pleasurable, decent, and beneficial based on the ways of the world, to that which would be considered acceptable and excellent as far as God's kingdom. For some who are in the social circles of Christianity, they prefer to socialize with the people of God, while missing the true benefit of being part of His kingdom. Others strive to save the nation or the world, while failing to realize that only man can ultimately be saved. These individuals will gladly stand for notable causes in the various arenas of the world, while failing to stand for the truth that is found in the Gospel and the ways of righteousness in the harvest field of humanity. There are also those who like to be associated to that which can be identified by the world as being good, rather than be identified to that which is clearly distinguished by that which is eternal in purpose, holy in distinction, and righteous in its ways.

As you have considered the social Christian, would you fit in this category? The Apostle Paul's solution for Christians who are part of the social aspect of the world is simple. They must repent of touching the ways or practices of the world that brought them into an unholy alliance or agreement. They must then come out and separate from this present world, cutting off all agreement with its spirit that has subjected them to the law of sin and the ways of death.[6] The promise for such separation can be found in 2 Corinthians 6:17c-18, "and I will receive you, And will

---

[6] 2 Corinthians 6:14-16

Developing Our Christian Life

be a Father unto you, and ye shall be my sons and daughters, saith the Lord Almighty."

With this incredible promise in mind, do you need to come back home to once again discover the real beauty, standing, purpose, and calling of being a child of God in His eternal kingdom?

8

SUPERSTITIOUS CHRISTIAN

The next type of Christian we must consider is the superstitious Christian. It is important to understand how superstition works. My dictionary states that superstition is a belief or practice resulting from ignorance or the fear of the unknown.[1] Ignorance often defines matters as happening by chance, or due to fear of the unknown that often operates from the premise of the supernatural. Such superstition involves the idea of things occurring according to magic.

When you combine the idea of chance and magic together, you will find an attitude that embraces a quasi-religious concept. This concept is developed by establishing certain practices that in the person's mind will cause or produce the desired affect. In other words, you can control the events that are occurring in your particular world through these practices. Such practices point to the false religion of witchcraft. In the end, people end up devising pagan practices that will produce the fruit of idolatry.

As you follow the ways of superstition, you will see how different altars mark the ways of such fallacy. When Elijah confronted the people of Israel in 1 Kings 18:20-40 about their idolatry, he asked them how long would they halt between two opinions. They needed to make a choice to follow Jehovah God or Baal. He also noted that the altar dedicated to God had become broken down through unbelief and neglect. He not only restored the neglected altar, but he erected a new one.

As you consider how the prophets of Baal tried to get their god's attention, you can see how superstition translates into pagan acts. They cried aloud and cut themselves until the blood gushed out upon them without any results. Their god stood silent, but when Elijah simply asked the Lord God to reveal Himself, He honored his prayer by accepting the sacrifice in a miraculous fashion.

Since the people who worship different gods do not know who they are worshipping, they will erect different altars with the chance of getting it right. We see where the Apostle Paul encountered such an environment in Athens. There were various gods being worshipped, causing confusion about which one was true or the most powerful.

In the midst of these various altars, stood an altar with the inscription, "TO THE UNKNOWN GOD" (Acts 17:23). The Apostle Paul used this platform to introduce the true God to these ignorant people in

---

[1] Webster's New Colligate Dictionary

Developing Our Christian Life

the midst of all of their altars. The true God is the one who made the world, the Lord of heaven and earth. He has no need for what man can offer. He is the one who gives all living the breath of life. Even though man must seek and feel after Him in his darkness of ignorance to find Him, He is not far from any person. For in Him, we each live, move, and have our being. Paul then makes this statement, "And the times of this ignorance God winked at, but now commandeth all men everywhere to repent" (Acts 17:30).

The Apostle Paul makes it quite clear that one must repent of his ignorance towards God. One of the main reasons for repenting is because such ignorance produces idolatry. Idolatry is demonically inspired.

Satan wants our worship. He does not care how he obtains it. Any worship that is not directed at God falls into the category of worshipping false gods. In idolatry man worships the creation, rather than the Creator. It is man who gives idols their identity and power over his life. Unexplainable circumstances often cause such idolatrous individuals in their ignorance to establish some type of religious practice to try to appease their idols. This is used as a means to manipulate or change what is unpleasant and frightening to them. These practices are what establish false religions.

God will not accept such ignorance as an excuse. Romans 1:20 tells us we have the witness of creation that verifies the existence of the Creator; therefore, man will be without any excuse for his superstition towards God. The reality is we can know the true God of heaven, but we must choose to put aside all of the influence of the philosophies and conclusions of the world, as well as bring down all false altars. Such idolatrous association and knowledge not only make us ignorant towards God, but it will keep us superstitious in any understanding we may have of Him.

This brings us to the matter of superstitious Christians. The first thing we must conclude about these Christians is that they really do not know the true God of heaven. Hosea 4:6 warns us that God's people are destroyed for lack of knowledge towards Him and His righteous ways. The Apostle Paul talked about those who had zeal for God, but not according to knowledge of Him. He went on to explain that since these people were ignorant as to what constituted God's righteousness, they went about establishing their own righteousness. He mentioned the fact that they had not submitted themselves to the true righteousness of God.[2] Daniel 11:32 tells us that the people who know God shall be strong and do exploits. In the Apostle John's first epistle, he makes it quite clear that we can know, we must know, and we better know our God if we are going to come to full age in our Christian life.

The question is what makes a Christian ignorant of God? The first element that will make a person ignorant of God is the wrong foundation.

---

[2] Romans 10:2-3

For the superstitious Christian, there is a certain type of foundation that will set him or her up to consider God from such a premise. The wrong foundation has to do with the improper emphasis on the supernatural. The Word has not properly established these people; rather, they have been fed an improper diet of the supernatural in their immature state. In this environment the Holy Spirit's real work of establishing the life of Jesus within the believer's life is ignored, while His power and gifts are greatly emphasized. These people find themselves getting caught up on the wave of experience as they seek supernatural acts.

When you consider God from the *supernatural view,* you will only be versed in what He can do, and not in who He is. In this view the practical ways in which God operate in earthly matters are completely ignored or overlooked. For example, Christianity is practical in its service to others. James tells us that pure religion before God is to visit the fatherless and widows in their affliction, and to keep oneself unspotted from the world.[3] Christianity is in tune with the earthly needs and matters that affect others.

However, superstitious religious people often act so spiritual that they appear to be indifferent to basic ministry. Instead of loving God and others, they are in love with how their supernatural experiences, which has exalted them above the "common" Christian, are making them elite in their mind.

Another aspect of the earthly work of God has to do with the redemption of Christ. Jesus became man so He could become identified with us in every way except in the area of sinning. Granted, He became sin, but He did not sin. Sadly, the fact that He was lifted up on the cross from the foundation of the earth is not the main message of these people. Christ may be mentioned, but the one who is constantly exalted is the Holy Spirit. Scripture is clear, the Holy Spirit did not come to be exalted; He came to glorify Jesus because He is the One who saves and becomes our point of identification to the heavenly. The main purpose of the Spirit's power is to make believers bold witnesses of Christ, while the workings of His gifts are a means to profit or edify the Church.[4] However, superstitious Christians are in pursuit of the supernatural via their idea of the Holy Spirit. The problem with this pursuit is that it serves as an open door for any spirit to come in and counterfeit the true Spirit of God.

The main spirit that comes in to counterfeit the Holy Spirit in this religious arena is a *religious spirit.* A religious spirit can easily be discerned. It makes this type of individual very religious. This is where pagan practices clearly come into the equation in these people's lives. They will try to manipulate their reality through cause and affect. In other words, they will perceive a cause as far as making themselves more religious or "holy." They set about through certain practices or disciplines

---

[3] James 1:27
[4] John 12:32; 16:13-14; Acts 1:8; 1 Corinthians 2:2; 12:7

Developing Our Christian Life

to affect God in such a way so that in due time they will possess the power to invoke or possess supernatural powers.

In one case involving a man I will refer to as religious Bart, he actually wore an apron made of burlap. He had been told that he had a calling of a prophet. His reason for wearing an apron was not only to distinguish him as a prophet much like those in the Old Testament but to give the impression he was quite humble.

The truth of the matter is that all of Bart's attempts to prove that he was a prophet failed miserably when all he had prophesied never came to fruition. The outward appearance of humility proved to be just an appearance. Bart was a novice and the only thing that all of his religious claims and activity managed to do was grow his pride rather than bring him to a state of humility. Due to his pride and inexperience, the only thing Bart came out with was a religious spirit.

This brings us to the gospel that superstitious Christians will find themselves adhering to: it is the *gospel of chance*. The good news to these people is that there is a good chance that the right combination can be found in the different religious exercises, practices, and presentations to gain God's favor. However, God's good news is that man can be saved from sin and death as a show of His favor or grace towards him. This favor is not earned or gained by any type of religious antics or works, but comes through faith.[5] Clearly, these people do not put their faith in God, but in their religious acts to gain recognition and power. They see their religious practices and pursuits to experience the supernatural as setting them apart from the "nominal" Christian life.

The heart that motivates these people is a *fearful heart*. Superstition causes these people to fear meeting God. Since they do not know God, they must guess or speculate about what will please Him. This is why they depend on those who are "more spiritual" to give them the right insight into gaining access into the supernatural. They can never be certain that they will discover the right spiritual combination to truly appease Him. However, Scripture is clear that perfect love casts out the fear of judgment, but these people do not walk according to the perfect love of God.

In the second letter to Timothy, the Apostle Paul stated that God did not give His people a spirit of fear, but one of power, love, and a sound mind. Clearly, we can walk in the power of the Holy Spirit, but these people want to possess power for themselves. And, due to the fact these people cannot connect to reality, they are not capable of operating in a sound mind.[6]

The religious darkness that can penetrate those who are pursuing the supernatural can become quite frightening. It is in this state that people can become fanatics about what they perceive about religious matters. In some cases, they can become paranoid about their particular

---

[5] Ephesians 2:8-9
[6] 2 Timothy 4:7; 1 John 4:16-18

reality. In their mind they must maintain their cause at all costs to ensure that the affect is brought forth.

Since these people's view is the supernatural, they are the ones who are prone to seek after signs and wonders. Sadly, this is the emphasis of some of the visible Church. It is important to point out God works mainly in miracles, not signs and wonders. Granted, signs will follow the true preaching of the Gospel, but these signs are a manifestation of the Spirit. The differences between miracles and signs are that miracles are an actual extraordinary intervention of God into the affairs of man to bring about a desired result. Signs are meant to mark a matter as being significant, while wonders points to the miraculous but also describes and often emphasizes the reaction of encountering the supernatural or the unusual. Such an event brings wonderment to men's souls that surely mark such a time.

In the kingdom of God, signs mark the manifestation of the Spirit as a means to edify the Church. They are meant to confirm the preaching of the Gospel, as well as one's faith towards Jesus. As you study those who benefited from the miraculous intervention of Christ, they were not seeking signs, but the mercy of God. This search had to do with seeking Jesus in order to believe Him. In their mind, He was their only true solution and they would fling themselves upon Him in unfeigned faith. As a result, their faith was confirmed while it was also counted as righteousness, and clearly marked by the miraculous, as they were made whole. In such matters, God is recognized as the One who intervened and is glorified.

To seek a sign for the sake of experiencing some type of wonderment is a fleshly pursuit. Clearly, a person in this type of pursuit is not interested in truth. As a result, Jesus said of those who sought after signs and wonders that they were part of an evil and adulterous generation.[7]

It is clear from today's environment that such a generation is thriving. From this platform, false Christ's, apostles, and prophets have arisen and gained tremendous inroads into the visible Church as a means to rob, kill, and destroy. As they hide behind lying signs and wonders, many in the Christian realm are flocking to see these people's power. Since some individuals have appeared to be healed, they believe that such wonderment must be truly of God. However, Scripture is clear that Satan can also be behind such signs and wonders. We do not test a vessel or a matter according to signs, but according to the spirit and the fruit.[8]

At the core of such practices, one will find *doctrines of demons*.[9] The problem with the supernatural in this text is that it proves to be seductive. The supernatural is a different dimension. Unless our encounters with this dimension are within the boundaries of God's Spirit and truth, we will

---

[7] Matthew 12:39
[8] Matthew 7:16-20; 24:24; 2 Thessalonians 2:9-12; 1 John 4:1
[9] 1 Timothy 4:1

be seduced by the other unseen powers that also operate in this realm, that of the kingdom of darkness. To be seduced means to be enticed into a different reality. This reality will seem so real, but it will prove to be an endless pit that sucks the person into a dark world of insanity and destruction.

Superstitious Christians will erect altars to idols they have conjured up based on their religious notions about God. These people's altars serve as a means to strive to worship unknown entities. They will devise their own religious activities as a means to be identified with the supernatural. Since the supernatural is their emphasis, they will consider the Word of God from a superior vantage point. But all such attempts will not lead them to God; rather, it will cause them to become more superstitious towards the God of heaven.

The Apostle Paul was clear that superstitious people needed to repent of their ignorant notions about God. God is not an idol erected by the vain imaginations of man or made by his hands; rather, God is the Creator that made man to worship Him from the premise of His Spirit and truth. To repent of such ignorance will mean that these individuals must cease from seeking after the spiritual elitism that is associated to the supernatural, and by faith humble themselves to seek out the true Jesus of the Bible. By seeking after the true Jesus, the authority and power will come according to God's purpose and glory.

Jesus referred to the Holy Spirit as rivers of Living Water. His invitation to the Samarian woman was to come to Him to drink of this Water. He is the well in which this Living Water flows through as a glorious river. If we want to freely partake of this Water, we must cease to complicate the matters of salvation, and simply come to Jesus with child-like faith. We must truly be born again of the Spirit who works the very life of Christ in us and by God's Word, which clearly establishes us on the foundation of the Person of Christ.[10]

Are you a superstitious Christian? God is not winking at such ignorance. He has given His Spirit and the Word to establish you in the real knowledge of Him. You need to repent of your religious arrogance, cease your vain pursuits of the unseen, and pursue to behold the Son of the living God. Replace your fearful heart with a child-like faith towards God. Choose to walk in the power of His love, with a mind that is clearly being tempered by the transforming mind of Christ towards all matters regarding His kingdom.

---

[10] John 3:5; 4:10; 7:37-39

9

SUPER SPIRITUAL CHRISTIAN

Jesus warned His disciples to beware of how they heard or perceived a matter.[1] We perceive according to our heart condition. Our heart condition will determine how we actually receive or handle a matter. If the heart is pure before God, it will receive His truths in purity. But, if a heart is blinded by personal goodness, disconnected to spiritual matters, judgmental because of self-righteousness, fickle because of sentiment, worldly due to a social attitude, or unstable because of being superstitious and fearful, then it will receive matters according to its perverted and unpredictable environments.

Solomon tells us that the issues of life originate from the heart, and as we think in the heart, so we will also become.[2] Clearly, the condition of the heart determines the attitude we are developing about God, life, and self. From the platform of the state or disposition of the heart, spirit operates, establishing our focus as to what we will be inclined towards.

Our prevailing attitude about life serves as the reflection or manifestation of the state of the heart. It will determine the tendency that will express itself in our approach towards a matter as far as our behavior or conduct. The heart condition ultimately reveals the source of our inner person that manifests itself in the fruits of our lives.

As we consider each face of Christianity, we must note it is determined not by what people believe, but by their heart environment. Each wrong heart condition harbors pride. There is either pride in who we think we are, haughtiness operating according to our personal point of association, arrogance about what we believe, self-sufficiency due to intensity of our feelings, pride in our causes, and even in our ignorance. Such pride makes us stiff-necked towards the matters of God. It will make our mind dull towards the Spirit and our will immovable towards truth. It is because of such pride that man devises the different cloaks and faces of Christianity that hide his true state of independence and rebellion towards the authority and ways of God.

This brings us to the next mask or cloak that some Christians dare to hide behind. The name in itself points to pride personified in operation. It is the mask of being a super spiritual Christian. We know that the word "super" points to something that is over and above in its quality and

---

[1] Luke 8:18
[2] Proverbs 4:23; 23:7

intensity, surpassing others in order to become superior in status or position.

The next "word" points to what these people want to be superior in: that of spirituality. "Spiritual" points to that which we breathe in as far as the supernatural. These individuals want to possess the insight that will cause them to surpass others in their understanding about matters of the unseen world.

The notion that a person could actually attain such a status is completely contrary to the Word of God. There is no recorded super spiritual follower of God in Scripture. Granted, there were humble people in which God did extraordinary feats through. These individuals were clearly set apart by God's power, but that power was entrusted to them because they were submissive towards God's leading and subject to His authority.

If we could classify one individual as being super spiritual, we would have to note that He never claimed such a status. This man came down from the heights of heaven to the very depths of the grave. He came as a servant to all. He never stepped outside of the Father's will. He was lowly in heart and meek in attitude. He came out of insignificance, was hidden in obscurity by the irrelevant, and was prepared in the midst of what was considered unimportant. He did not reside in palaces, sit on beautiful horses, nor was He honored by the world. He prayed during the night, slept during storms, and knew what it meant to be tired. In the end, He hung on a cross, where He appeared as if His mission was a total failure. We know that insignificant servant to be Jesus Christ, the Son of the Living God.

As you follow Jesus, He did not seek out the super spiritual life. He had the wisdom of heaven at His disposal, but He remained a humble servant before the Father to ensure the integrity of such wisdom. He had given up His power and authority as God to take the disposition of a servant and to be fashioned as a man, only to receive such authority and power back in His state of submission. In His example, Jesus proved that when it comes to heaven, people are empowered when they are in submission before God. It is through submission that the power of God is able to flow through His Spirit and His authority will clearly be established by His Word.

However, the super spiritual Christian is seeking to reach heights in the spiritual realm that will clearly exalt him or her above what is considered to be peons or insignificant in the Christian realm. Once again, we must take a moment to realize how such a goal may appear commendable to others, but it is contrary to the ways of God's kingdom. Greatness is not gauged by the measure of spirituality that is obtained, but by the level of humility that is reached before God which clearly expresses itself in submission, obedience, and benevolence. The best way to describe the power of humility is that the lower you humble yourself, the higher God can take you as His servant. This is not only our Lord's example, but the Bible clearly brings this out in various ways. [3]

Humility is a state that allows a person to be convicted of sin and respond in repentance that allows sins to be remitted. It gives way in total submission to the Holy Spirit, and comes into total agreement with God's evaluation about a spiritual matter. Humbled individuals never feel at the top of the game, for they realize that they must meet God at the same place of humility. The more they perceive about the character of God, the more they are aware of how far from the mark they are in their Christian life. The greater the awareness of God's holiness and their pathetic state, the lower they become in their status before God. The lower their state, the more they are able to receive by faith from the throne of God. The Apostle Paul makes reference of this very fact in Romans 12:1-3.

In Romans 12, the Apostle Paul begins to exhort us as believers to consecrate ourselves as living sacrifices. In this position of true sacrifice, we can begin to be transformed in the mind as we learn what is the good, acceptable, and perfect will of God.

In Romans 12:3, the apostle goes on to remind us that grace or favor has been given to each of us. In other words, we do not deserve His consideration, but He is showing us grace; therefore, we must not think more highly of ourselves than we ought to think. Rather, we must be sober about having a proper inward environment so that by the measure of faith we have been allotted (because of His grace) we can correctly receive from Him.

True faith is not a matter of just believing something. We can all believe that a matter is trustworthy to consider, but if there is no application of what we believe, it simply becomes an intellectual acknowledgment. In such situations there is no heart revelation that will ensure that we have an awareness that whatever we receive from God is a matter of His grace and not a matter of any worthiness or right on our part. It is from the proper understanding of grace that a state of humility can be obtained and developed.

The question is how can these "so-called' super spiritual Christians believe that they can obtain some spiritual level that will set them apart from other believers? It is quite easy. It begins from the premise of a *deluded heart* that has clearly been deceived by its own arrogance. This delusion is based on the fact that these people truly do think highly of themselves even though the Bible rebukes such arrogance.

Since these people seek a higher realm of spirituality through various spiritual exercises such as doing good works, intercession, fasting, and visualization, they actually see themselves as earning the status of being super spiritual. For example, these people have been known to fast many days. I can remember how I was impressed with a particular pastor because he had actually fasted 40 days. The reality is that he, along with

---

[3] Luke 18:9-17; Philippians 2:5-11; James 4:6-10; 1 Peter 5:5-9

Developing Our Christian Life

his family, were also quite impressed. When he was questioned as to his motive for fasting for such a long period, he had no real explanation.

In the case of Moses, we know he fasted 40 days because he was in God's presence where he received the Law. For Jesus, He fasted 40 days because He was about to embark on His mission as the Lamb of God and His ministry as the Messiah. During these 40 days, Satan tested him. He overcame the flesh with the Word, pride with neglect, and the covetousness of the eyes with rebuke against worshipping anything or anyone other than God.[4]

Clearly there must be a reason for any spiritual exercise. There was one individual who prayed and fasted for 11 days. When questioned about her reason for such a religious practice, she admitted she was seeking a greater ministry for herself. This may seem commendable, but the greatest type of ministry has already been scripturally described as becoming the least in God's kingdom or the servant to all.[5] In the end, this woman did have a spiritual experience, but there was no real evidence that she was the wiser for it. In fact, she was more arrogant because she had the experience.

These people are seeking some type of spiritual experience that will exalt them in some way. The Bible clearly tells us what we must seek after: the Lord. We are told to grow in the knowledge of Jesus. Jesus is not some spiritual experience, but a living Person who we must seek to know in order to take on His likeness and glory. We must ensure that we never become barren in the knowledge of Him or we will fail to develop the character that truly reflects Him in this dark world. Without His character being unveiled in and through our lives, we will fall short of fulfilling our commission to preach the Gospel and lead others into a greater relationship with Him. Jesus is the One who must be lifted up in our lives as the source of all hope and reality. In summation, we must seek to know Him as a means to abide in Him. This will allow the Holy Spirit to unveil Jesus in Scripture to us, making Him real, alive, and eternal. Such revelations will bring about the necessary inward environment that will develop a growing devotion that ensures greater consecration, acceptable service motivated by godly love, and genuine worship based on Spirit and truth.[6]

Spiritual growth of this nature establishes us on the true foundation of Jesus as we discover the essence of our life in Him. This life secures His wisdom (that is far above the wisdom of this world), His righteousness (that is far above the ways of man), His sanctification (that is far above the good of man's religion), and His redemption (that is far above the best of man). The Apostle Paul tells us if we are in Christ, we

---

[4] Matthew 4:1-11
[5] Matthew 20:25-27
[6] Jeremiah 29:13; Amos 5:4; John 4:23-24; Ephesians 4:13; Philippians 3:8; 2 Peter 1:3-9

are actually seated in high places with Him, firmly established above the activities of the world and the influences of the kingdom of darkness.[7]

Those who want to see themselves as super spiritual Christians are not content with being positionally placed in such an incredible position with Christ. They want to strive beyond their heavenly place in Christ to secure their own status in the unseen kingdom. They want to feel that they have somehow earned this position or scaled the necessary heights to be regarded as super spiritual in understanding or experience. Obviously, these individuals do not want to share with or accredit their spiritual status to Jesus.

Years ago, we met a certain woman whom we will name Fonda. The first thing that people in the fellowship she attended noticed about this quiet woman was her sad countenance. She wept her way through many prayer sessions, both public and private. Some in the fellowship were concerned for Fonda, and tried to help her and her children in their struggles. The more involved they became, however, the more hopeless her pathetic situation appeared to be. Dripping with self-pity, she simply could not seem to rally enough energy to help those who were up to their eyeballs helping her inside and outside her neglected home.

While people were draining themselves trying to help her both spiritually and in practical ways, Fonda always seemed to be "drowning." People began to wonder why she could never manage to keep her home and yard up after they had worked so hard to clean and organize it for her. Finally, the truth surfaced that instead of caring for her home and children, she spent all of her free time alone in intense intercession. It soon became apparent that these long sessions of "intercession" actually gave her an addictive, spiritual "high" so much so that she opted to "hide" in her room to the neglect of her home and family in order to lose herself in this "super spiritual" realm.

This sort of practice leans toward the occult, and is dangerous as it can open the door for religious spirits, seductive spirits, and the realm of the occult. Christians who tend to be like Fonda need to understand that God doesn't call His people into extreme intercession at the expense of hands-on practical, normal work that we all must be faithful to in order to ensure that our lives and environment are clean, orderly, and inviting to both others and the Lord. God cannot honor us in pigpens of our own making if we neglect that which is necessary in this world so that we can escape into a spiritual realm that is not of God. Extremes in one's spiritual life only feed a person's pride, and make him or her feel superior over others who do not share his or her super spiritual experiences.

These are the people who can become so spiritually minded they become no earthly good to those around them. Whether we like it or not, as Christians, we are still earth bound by our flesh. We must deal with the reality of the world we live in. We are not to be so unrealistic that we cannot properly function according to our daily responsibilities. Such an

---

[7] 1 Corinthians 1:30; Ephesians 2:6

unrealistic presentation presents no real attraction to Jesus Christ. After all, experience, not Jesus, is being sought after and exalted by these people. Such experience cannot save others or serve as a valid testimony of Jesus. For those who struggle with such individuals they often see these people as being foolish, ridiculous, or insane because they cannot really connect to or handle the reality around them.

This brings us to these people's foundation. Clearly, it is not the Jesus of the Bible. He has been demoted by spiritual experiences that have supposedly brought greater "*enlightenment*" to these individuals about spiritual truths that are considered to be far beyond mere man's comprehension. These insights not only cause these people to perceive themselves as more superior or elite than other Christians, but these so-called "insights" take preeminence over the Word of God, and actually blind these individuals to the real Jesus. This spiritual arrogance causes these types of individuals to see their type of Christianity as being an exception in the Kingdom of God. What they do not understand is that their arrogance is simply blinding them to the real inspiration behind their "insights." I can give you one clue—it is not the Holy Spirit that is giving them such insights or experiences, but it is often seducing spirits that are trying to bring them into a false reality through spiritual experiences.

As we consider these people's perception, we can see that their foundation is based on *spiritual experiences* that have been brought on by their own spiritual exercises. Sadly, these people operate with a spiritual mixture. The reason for this mixture is because they are approaching the matters of God's kingdom according to their perverted desire to possess the spiritual, rather than by faith to possess the excellent knowledge of Jesus. What these people fail to understand is that in their attempt to become more spiritual in their arrogance, they have simply opened the door to the many counterfeits of the kingdom of darkness. The main spirit that comes in through this particular door is nothing more than an *antichrist spirit*.

The antichrist spirit is very religious, but its main goal is to replace the real Jesus with another one. Since these people become blinded towards the Jesus of the Bible, and downplay the simplicity and profound wisdom of Scripture because of their spiritual experiences, the antichrist spirit is able to replace Jesus with a more "spiritual" Christ that is acceptable to their particular taste. As a result, these people end up with a *mystic gospel* that places the issues of Christianity on a mystical level, where nothing is real, and that all matters have a greater spiritual meaning behind it that can only be sought out and understood by the "enlightened ones." These people can be quite sentimental about their particular concept of Jesus, but He is not the Jesus of the Bible. He is a counterfeit that is being presented by the mystic gospel.

Due to the seduction of the wrong spirit in the lives of these people, they eventually develop what we call a *new age perspective*. It is from this perspective that Christ can be reduced to a Christ consciousness where there is a sense of Jesus, but He is spiritualized as a force that is prevalent and operating in the person, subtly exalting that person in the same position as the Messiah. Needless to say, it is all quite confusing for any sane thinking individual to imagine, but for those who have succumbed to this type of pursuit, they have adopted this perspective. Sadly, they do not realize that they are blindly walking down a path of delusion and destruction.

Another fruit of super spiritual Christians is the need for them to come out on top as some spiritual expert or leader in a matter. You probably know who they are. They are the ones who always hear from the Lord about all matters. They appear to have a corner on spiritual truths. They attempt to become indispensable to those they desire to influence. Of course, they see themselves as being superior and needed because of their spiritual insight. From this premise they perceive they are much more spiritual than you; therefore, you must not only listen to them about matters, but also seek them out for their instruction or counsel. In some situations, they seek to replace the Holy Spirit in people's lives.

The problem for these people is that since the foundation is wrong, the Holy Spirit is often missing from their religious insights and activities. *Religious* and *familiar spirits* are what operate in the place of the Holy Spirit in their lives. The religious spirit makes these people feel very spiritual about what they understand. A familiar spirit is one that gives them personal insight about matters that prove to be detailed and perverted. However, these people often think this insight is coming from the Holy Spirit.

As we consider the way Satan's kingdom operates from the premise of wrong foundations, perspectives, and gospels, we can actually identify four main spirits that clearly can influence the inward environment of man. We have already dealt with these spirits; nevertheless, let us now consider a simple overview of them to gain a greater insight into how they operate in people's lives in the following table on the next page.

Developing Our Christian Life

Seducing Spirits (1 Tim. 4:1)	Religious Spirits (Ep. 2:2-3)	Antichrist Spirit (1 Jn. 2:22-23; 4:1-3)	Familiar Spirits (Le. 19:31 20:26-27)
1. Throws a covering over you to begin to seduce you into a false reality. 2. As you get caught up with the reality, you will depart from the true faith. 3. At that point, you will begin to embrace doctrines of demons. You will walk in delusion towards God and truth.	1. It is a spirit of the world, only clothed in religious garb. 2. It works off of the flesh and pride. It seeks attention and experiences. It will cause confusion to those who are of the right spirit. It wants to be exalted—as being spiritually-superior-insight. 3. Creates a false environment, deceives the person. 4. Does not want to pay the price to know God. (Rebellion) Must prove all ministry. 2 Tim.4:2, 5	1. Deny the one true God of the Bible. 2. Counterfeits the true Jesus—with another Jesus— redefining foundation (God) to erect a different, false Jesus. 3. Will reject Jesus as the Messiah or as coming in the flesh. 4. Will not be able to call Jesus LORD. *(1 Cor. 12:3)* What does it mean for Jesus to be the Lord? *(Isaiah 43:11; 44:24; 45:5, 21-22)* Do you know Jesus as the LORD?	1. Spirit of witchcraft 2. Gives personal information about others; therefore, people think it is the Holy Spirit. Gives details. 3. Comes on people in the church that have open doors (sin), but they want to appear religious and righteous. Creates an environment of oppression and fantasy. The major open door is pride.

80

Super spiritual Christians who operate from the premise of developing some type of spiritual expertise or leadership must constantly seek the confirmation and recognition from others. They must have their egos fed so that they can continue to perceive themselves as being spiritually enlightened. They strive hard to accomplish such a feat. When they do not get the desired recognition, they become offended and angry. However, most of the time these individuals prove to be an irritation to those they are trying to influence. They often are void of discretion as they overstep the personal boundaries of others as a means to influence them, revealing that they are inferior in their understanding.

Miss Tina (not her real name) serves as a good example of a "super spiritual Christian," at least when others were watching. She made it her business to know everything going on in everyone else's life in her church. Whenever two or more people drew aside to talk, Miss Tina had to nose in to get the latest bit of information. That way, if someone in the congregation was having a problem, she could go after them in order to export her "wise counsel".

Miss Tina not only had a way of becoming the "expert" on nearly every subject, but she worked hard at becoming indispensable to people. Clearly, Miss Tina desperately craved special attention and praise from those in leadership as well as others with whom she became involved.

Christianity is simply a platform from which the super spiritual Christians such as Miss Tina operate from. What this type of individual fails to realize is that people who possess the goods never have to strive for recognition. When people possess spiritual abilities, they have a quiet authority that when the time comes they will simply become doers according to what they have been entrusted with. These individuals are not striving to come out on top; they are content with the life of Christ that is clearly being established in them. They do not see such tools as a means to gain some type of spiritual leverage or recognition in God's kingdom; instead, they see these tools as a matter of God's grace that allows them the means to honor and glorify Him in true, loving service.

When we consider the core of these people's problem, we can only come to one conclusion; they do not really love the truth.[8] In our ministry we encountered a minister's wife that was operating from the premise of trying to be a super spiritual Christian. She was promoting the New Age perspective to unsuspecting Christians. When we confronted her, I asked if she ever had received Jesus as her Lord and Savior. I will never forget her answer. She admitted she had accepted Jesus as her Savior, but she discovered He was "not enough."

Jesus is our all in all. He is the way and the truth to life that is complete and eternal. Apparently, the truth of His life was not exciting or spiritual enough for this poor, wretched deluded soul who was sadly known as a spiritual leader's wife. The simple truth is that Christianity is

---

[8] 2 Thessalonians 2:10-12

Developing Our Christian Life

not a spiritual experience that exalts us above the matters of life and heaven; rather, it is a life that must be lived out in this present world according to the Spirit and truth of Jesus Christ.

This brings us to the reality of God's truth. In light of Jesus' cross, it is clear that truth is not based on sentiment or excitement. It is reality that can be seen and known by all who desire to seek it, and not a spiritual phenomenon that can only be understood by a few. It has no hidden meanings that must be sought out. It is eternal, unchanging, and absolute in its stands and presentations. It has the incredible capacity of bringing people to decisions as to whether they will receive it as their personal reality about God, life, and the world, or whether they will reject it in order to pursue or maintain their own preferred reality.

Truth sets people free to see Jesus, while it cuts across the winds of fantasy, nonsense, ridiculousness, and foolishness that so often operate in each of our darkened lives. It will not placate pride or compromise with personal deception. It will strip away the cloaks and masks to reveal the real state of every person's inner man. It will call each person to a state of humility, where he or she will be required to repent of arrogance. Such repentance allows the fallacy of all personal experiences to be rendered vain, as his or her repentant soul begins to desire and pursue the simplicity of Jesus and His Word no matter what it might cost. As Solomon wisely advised, "Buy the truth, and sell it not; also wisdom, and instruction, and understanding" (Proverbs 23:23)

The reality is simple, as truly born-again Christians we will have a preference for the truth. Granted, in our initial encounter with it, it will insult our pride as we feel the sharpness of its sword exposing the wretchedness of the self-life with all of it various "isms" that desire to exalt themselves against the real knowledge of God. It will challenge our old tendencies that will justify away any possible compromise in our conduct. It will cut deep as it reveals the real attitude of our heart towards the world and its ways. However, no matter how deep it cuts or in what way it cuts, we will begin to love it, because it represents the work of Jesus upon our attitude and ways. It represents freedom as it cuts away or circumcises the old bondage of the former way to embrace the liberty of the new. We learn to love truth because it is all about discovering our Jesus in all of His glory.

Do you love the truth, or do you prefer your own spiritual reality? If you do not love the truth, take heed, God is sending a delusion that will test the hearts of those who call themselves His people.[9] This delusion will look like the real thing, but it will lack His Spirit, His life, His powerful Gospel, and His liberating truth. In the end, people who do not love His truth will be taken by this wave of deception as it seduces them to believe another gospel. This will cause them to be become subject to the ways of death as they give way to a spirit that works disobedience, bringing them under the wrath of God.

---

[9] Ibid

10

SANCTIMONIOUS CHRISTIAN

It is easy to see how each face of Christianity can digress into different presentations of the Christian life. In fact, the different faces of Christianity can intertwine with each other. However, if you strip away the pretenses of each presentation, you will be able to see the heart condition, the perception, the gospel, and the spirit behind each masquerade, which clearly identifies the spiritual state of the person.

The digression into the different deceptive stages of Christianity does have its ultimate intensity into which it will descend. Granted, delusion has no bounds, but the stages of digression have their limits. For example, the good person can graduate to become an associate Christian and even become religious about certain matters. However, such a person will stop with the religious scene. After all, he or she cannot really afford to get emotionally involved with religious matters.

Religious Christians can find themselves becoming socially involved, while the sentimental and superstitious Christians might find themselves being caught up with trying to attain the status of the super spiritual Christian. However, the limit that can be reached for these different Christians, whether religious, sentimental, superstitious, or super spiritual can be best summarized by the next Christian: the sanctimonious Christian.

Sanctimonious Christians point to those who see themselves quite pious in their religious beliefs and conduct. In fact, this piousness is translated into personal holiness. These people consider every matter through their *personal holiness*. They believe that they have not only obtained a state of holiness, but they are also a true example of holiness to others. In fact, they serve as a conscience to others as they sanction that which they consider to be holy, acceptable, or binding. If a matter is not sanctioned by them, they will consider it profane and unacceptable.

This brings us to a very important subject. What constitutes holiness? Clearly these people have their own form of holiness, but would it be considered holy to God? The Bible is clear that no man has any personal holiness. All holiness finds its origins in our holy God. Based on His divine character, He alone determines what is holy and what is profane. The Bible clearly states we, as believers, must be holy in every manner of life.[1] In other words, we must be holy according to what our God has clearly sanctioned as holiness.

---

[1] 1 Peter 1:15-16

Holiness points to being set apart from that which is contrary to the character and ways of God in order to be set in the fashion, manner, and work of God according to His purpose. In studying the Word of God, I have discovered that there are two distinct works of holiness. There is *consecration*, which involves an *act* where one is being separated from the profane for the purpose of being separated unto our holy God for His good pleasure, service, and glory. The second type of holiness is *sanctification*. Sanctification is the *work* of holiness where a person is set apart as a vessel prepared for the Master's use unto every good work.

As you consider these two manifestations of holiness, man's part is to consecrate himself from the unholy so that he can freely consecrate himself to God according to His holy character. Consecration was what the Old Testament priests did as a means to minister in the tabernacle before God. Sanctification is God's part. In fact, what God has not properly sanctified, cannot be used by Him.

All three Persons of the Godhead are involved in the work of complete sanctification. God, the Father initially sanctifies each of us as believers to establish us in a relationship as His children by placing us in Christ. Christ becomes our place of sanctification where we are positionally set apart as His people to do His work. Then the Holy Spirit does the actual work of setting us apart in our disposition, attitude, and conduct to establish us in holy living.[2]

Consecration points to separation from all unholy agreements or appearances, while sanctification involves a cleansing that will clearly set a person apart from the defiled in order to be separated unto that which has been clearly ordained as being holy. Although man can, in a sense, sanctify himself through the cleansing of his outer body, only the work of God can cleanse the inner man from the affects of sin. This is why the inward work of sanctification rests with God, and not man. He is the only One who has provided the means to truly cleanse us.

This brings us to the subject of holiness. The writer of Hebrews tells us we are to be partakers of holiness for we cannot see the Lord without it. The Apostle Paul informs us that we are to put on the new which has been created in righteousness and holiness, and that we can only be perfected in holiness in the fear of God. As we regard this subject, we will realize that we are exhorted to continue in holiness, and that we must refrain from displaying any behavior that does not exemplify it.[3]

The One who is righteous and holy has actually created us to operate in holiness. Holiness is a state that is maintained by the right attitude: that of fearing God. We are to walk according to the ways of holiness: that of righteousness, and our behavior should express the influence of holiness in our lives through godliness. The holy state allows a person to actually come into agreement with God.

---

[2] Exodus 29:43-45; 1 Chronicles 29:5; 1 Corinthians 1:30; 1 Peter 1:2
[3] 2 Corinthians 7:1; Ephesians 4:24; Hebrews 12:10, 14

To make certain of this state, ordained acts of consecration ensure that God's followers are careful as to who or what they come into agreement with. This agreement is established according to the types of environments they expose themselves to and what they touch as coming into agreement.

Sanctification produces humility that will come into submission to the work of the Spirit through regeneration or the work of bringing forth the new life of Christ. Such submission results in obedience according to the Word of God. We are told that God's Word serves as a means that cleanses us. As a person obeys the Word through the Spirit, he or she is cleansed, renewed in the inner man, and transformed in the mind.[4]

When man takes credit for any manner of holiness outside God's ordination or work of the Spirit, he does so out of arrogance. In the infancy of our ministry, Jeannette and I encountered a man who saw his idea of piousness as being holy. His true fruits were quickly exposed. His wife was in total bondage to his idea, and when he entered our home, he became assertive with us as a means to claim his supremacy over us as a man. Instead of his form of Christian piousness proving to be worthy of any consideration or respect from us, it became repulsive to our spirits. It was clear that the real fruit of his piousness was arrogance that manifested itself in rudeness and indifference on his part.

When we embarked on the subject of holiness with this man, we stated that we could not acquire such a state through our own religious attempts. This man became visibly upset as he took offence at such a concept. In his mind, he had accomplished such a state through his pious practices that were clearly legalistic and lifeless to us. According to his logic, God had to be as impressed with his piousness as he was. After all, his practices placed him at the head of the table as the leader, regardless of his lack of humility or inner character. His arrogance had clearly demanded that his wife come into total subordination to him, while she maintained a certain religious appearance as being modest and submissive. Although he could quote certain Scriptures, he revealed that he was truly ignorant of the character of God. His piousness had clearly blinded him to his wretched condition.

This brings us to the heart condition of sanctimonious Christians. Like the super spiritual Christian, they have no humility. The reason for this ungodly state is because they possess a *proud heart*. Pride can be a state, attitude, look, emotion, and/or behavior. When pride is the motivation of the heart, a person will clearly operate in every arena of pride. For example, the state of pride is a fierce independence to rule one's life. This independence produces a *militant attitude* that has the right to aggressively push its own agendas on those who are considered stupid, inferior, or foolish, expressing itself in a certain look of superiority. Such a hard attitude is quick to judge harshly any so-called "discrepancy" in others, while feeling quite noble as it tolerantly bears with those who

---

[4] Ephesians 5:26; Titus 3:5; 1 Peter 1:22-23

are considered inferior. Of course, this pretence allows the inferior or misguided individual the opportunity of seeing the light of this particular person's piousness. In fact, these so-called "pious" people cleverly try to seduce others into their particular reality, and if they fail to seduce them, they become quite combative as they attempt to intimidate with fear of punishment, control through debasing, and manipulate through confusion.

The emotion behind pride is nothing but selfishness that continually exalts itself in various ways. For example, in the minds of the prideful souls of these sanctimonious Christians, they perceive that people should feel quite privileged to be exposed to their form of piousness. Clearly, such behavior is a façade that hides these people's hypocrisy, but the façade is powerful because its light is that of the *antichrist spirit* which is active in the false religions of the world.

Even though sanctimonious Christians promote certain types of behavior, it is simply a presentation. The outward appearance of piety simply hides these people's true behavior of pride that manifests itself in haughtiness or arrogance, which proves to be rude, cruel, disrespectful, and sometimes very cunning.

This brings us to the gospel sanctimonious Christians promote according to their personal religious piousness; it is a *gospel of works*. These people believe that they are distinguished as holy by their works. These works can involve anything from certain religious practices, a particular diet, or specific attire and outward appearance. It is important to point out that such regulations cannot save anyone, and such activities are more about religious practices that bring personal recognition than deeds that speak of benevolent kindness that would actually bring honor to God. These works are all about outward presentation, rather than the honest examination of inward character and attitude. These people's point of identification is more about them presenting their own idea of holiness rather than humbly becoming identified with the One who is holy. Such emphasis may bring distinction, but not true separation. It may be commendable in certain ways, but in the end it will all prove to be reprobate to God because it has no eternal value.

Sadly, this sanctimonious, hypocritical environment of religion has become a platform in which false ministers have come into the visible Church as prophets and apostles. These individuals claim that they are bringing forth a new work of God. Because of the vulnerable state of many in the Church, these false leaders are now riding the high wave of seduction, delusion, and destruction at the expense of many innocent souls. They have clearly replaced Jesus with their own leadership in the lives of many, as well as substituted the authority of God's Word with their own form of religious deception. This is all done while often hiding behind lying signs and wonders as a means to seduce people into coming into agreement with their agendas and false doctrine. Because of the emphasis of the gospel of good works, the followers of these wolves not only embrace the need to live a certain life according to these so-called "pious leaders," but they are also giving these heretics undue reverence by becoming totally loyal to them and militant about their religious agendas.

Many years ago, we were introduced to a particular leader whom we shall call Mr. Prophet. Right up front it became strikingly evident that everyone in "his group" was in awe of him. They revered every word he spoke, and were anxious to please and obey him without question. While much of what he taught and proclaimed had the ring of truth about it, the spirit that accompanied it brought fear and dread. This discrepancy was overlooked by many who considered themselves to be spiritually inferior to this "pious, holy man." Indeed, had they been properly discipled by their former pastors and teachers, they would have known how to test his spirit and discern his fruit.

Nevertheless, sheep are sheep and as such, they can be quite easily deceived by a wolf in sheep's clothing, especially if that wolf appears to be holier than they are, and closer to God and His "mysteries" than they are.

Many people are seduced into the sanctimonious quagmire that is now invading the visible Church. The reason why is because this particular platform guarantees that everyone can become a "somebody" in this new move of God. In fact, the sanctimonious leaders feed on people's various pride to seduce them into their religious arrogance. It is not unusual that if you attend one of the meetings of these wolves, someone will prophecy over you in such a manner that you will be exalted in some way. For example, the person could proclaim that you are a prophet ready to come forth. Perhaps, you have a prophetical ministry that will influence many or a call of an apostle upon your life. It sounds wonderful to those who feel insignificant, hopeful to those who are insecure, and exciting to those who are immature in their Christian life.

The reality of this vain exaltation is that people who come into agreement with what they hear are opening the door to *religious spirits* that will give the false perception that they truly do have the "goods" to go out and fulfill their calling or ministry. However, these people have simply exposed themselves to the poisons of false doctrine, while being seduced into total delusion. They are building on an *antichrist foundation* that will ultimately taste the wrath of God. Meanwhile, the heretical mixture is producing spiritual beasts who perceive their particular reality as pious, truthful, and superior to anything that will not come into agreement with their particular perception.

A tragic example of a person, who totally sold out to the pride associated with sanctimony, is a woman we shall call Sally. Up front, Sally appeared to be exuberant and full of the joy of the Lord. She had an outgoing personality, and could keep a person's attention for hours as she vividly related the challenges and victories in her Christian life. She gave every appearance of an overcoming Christian against incredible difficulties.

Sadly, as time went on, underneath the bubbly surface Sally was making decisions that flung the door wide open for major demonic influence. She began to see herself as being more spiritual than other Christians, which led to extreme scrutiny of everything those around her said and did. To the utter dismay and shock of some of her closest friends, she suddenly took on the role of prophet, and began viciously condemning and falsely accusing them.

Sally's sanctimonious and "holier-than-thou" stance knew no bounds as she wielded her weapon of words. People who had once loved and considered her a loyal friend and close ally were left spiritually and emotionally wounded and beaten. The devastation left behind because of her sanctimonious tirades were never considered, regretted, or repented of by her.

As we consider sanctimonious Christians, we must recognize that their form of piousness is actually profane to God. Their so-called outward sacrifices of certain practices or forms of living are unacceptable to Him. The reason is obvious; they are not mixed with true faith towards the living God.[5] These people's faith is in their form of piousness, and not in the redemptive work of Jesus.

The Bible is clear, we are saved by grace through faith, and not by any works we do.[6] Grace is God's way of bestowing His favor, such as the gift of eternal life, upon undeserving man. Such favor is not something man can earn through pious acts or obtained through certain lifestyles. It is freely given to those who believe the provision God has clearly provided in His Son.

With the provision of God's Son comes the means in which man can be established in true holiness before his Creator. Once again, holiness is not obtained through personal efforts. It is established as man obeys the Word of God and submits to the work of the Spirit being done in the inner man. As he separates from the influence of the world and gives way to the Word, he will experience cleansing in his ways. As he submits to the Spirit, his mind will be cleansed. As he insists on the ways of righteousness, his conduct will be established in godliness. As he pursues a relationship with God according to His holiness, he will become more translated in the inner man. It is the light of this translation that distinguishes the Christian as a saint, who has truly been set apart in disposition, attitude, and conduct.

This brings us to the harsh reality of the false piety of the sanctimonious Christian. It is hard to tell whether these types of people have ever really tasted of the heavenly life through the born-again experience. If they have tasted of the heavenly, then they have taken a

---

[5] Hebrews 4:2
[6] Ephesians 2:8-9

very dark detour that will lead them down the path of destruction.[7] If they have never tasted of the heavenly blessings, then they are nothing more than great pretenders that are making converts to their particular vain piety that will ultimately lead them, as well as their followers to damnation.

These individuals need to come back to the simple basis of repentance and salvation. Sadly, instead of repenting for their religious arrogance, they continue to clothe it with reprobate works that lack purity of intent. Rather than admit that their misguided faith actually has perverted the Gospel and frustrated the grace of God, causing them to neglect their salvation, they continue to insist on their religious form of holiness.[8] Instead of being truly established in holiness as blood-bought saints, they hold to their own idea of holiness. Instead of reflecting the beauty of Christ in their life, they become more deluded from the reflection of the false light of religion that covers the darkness of their own souls.

The fruit of their lives is what clearly reflect their inner state. The fruits are that of pride, indifference, and a critical spirit. Pride is the opposite of godly love, indifference is a form of hatred, and a critical spirit is a manifestation of cruelty. Therefore, the major point of identification in regard to the real spiritual condition of these people is that they lack godly love. They do not really love God, nor do they have real genuine concern for people. They simply use God as a platform to promote their own form of holiness as a way to exalt themselves in idolatrous positions, in an attempt to carry out their personal agendas.

Jesus stated that His true followers would be known by the love they have for one another, not by some outward pious lifestyle or self-serving agenda.[9] As Christians, we cannot love one another in a proper way unless we first have learned how to love God in sincerity and consecrated devotion. Love of this nature will set God's saints apart as their very lives brings glory to God, while their sincere devotion serves as a form of worship in benevolent service towards others.

Are you a sanctimonious Christian who Jesus will not be able to recognize on judgment day, or are you a saint who is being established in the holiness of God? Only you can answer the question, but if you are not a saint, you must repent of your idolatrous, unholy ways and pretense. Cease to be a hypocrite clothed in your own religious garb, and truly clothe yourself in humility and become identified to the One who alone serves as your place of sanctification.

---

[7] Hebrews 6:4-6
[8] Galatians 1:6-9; 2:21; Titus 1:15-16
[9] John 13:35

11

SHORTSIGHTED CHRISTIAN

In the last chapters, we have been exposing those who have allowed their high opinions of self to blind them to their real spiritual condition of sin, religious arrogance, and self-exaltation. Obviously, self with its pride is capable of cleverly disguising itself behind many different types of masks or cloaks. However, the truth of God's Word along with the convicting power of the Holy Spirit will rip away such façades. This is why Jesus' initial call to His followers was to deny or disown the influence of self upon their lives.[1] Such denial will keep His followers from replacing the Christian life with religious façades and appearances that never allow the Spirit and the intent of God's Word to get past the surface of religious show and pretence down into their heart.

This brings us to the next group of Christians. Their challenge is not with self, but with the world. Granted, self seeks the things of the world to satisfy fleshly appetites, but the focus is still on the self-life. The self-life is driven by its insatiable selfishness. Therefore, those whose focus is based on the self-life, consider the world only in light of how it can serve their selfishness. However, when it comes to the next types of Christians that we will be profiling, they are looking to the world for satisfaction, purpose, and identity. In fact, they are putting their faith in certain aspects of the world to obtain a particular type of life. As a result, they only think of the self-life in terms of how they can experience the world through their fleshly appetites.

Scripturally, we know the world is an enemy of God.[2] In its hatred for God, it mocks His truths with its philosophies. It attempts to extinguish the life of His light with vain, fleshly attractions. It strives to counterfeit the wisdom of God with humanistic education, the righteousness of God with "good" deeds, the sanctification of God with "good" causes, the redemption of God with false promises, the love of God with "political correctness and tolerance" and the glory of God with a false presentation of beauty that simply appeals to the fleshly man.

The reality is that man is not only attracted to the glory of the world, but he prefers it. His attraction can be traced back to the fact that he is in a fallen state. In this fallen state he is not able to see through the temporary brilliance of the world to realize that it simply covers the darkness of deception, rebellion, and destruction.

---

[1] Matthew 16:24
[2] James 4:4

It is important at this time to point out that there are different types of glory that we encounter along the way. Glory represents the beauty or majesty of something by revealing or reflecting the inner character of the life it is presenting. Such glory can blind, serve as a reflection, or reveal the real source or foundation of its light or life.

For example, God's glory can blind the sinner, reflect His character in the midst of the miraculous, and serves as the source of life for the saint. However, the world's glory blinds people to its vanity, reflects a lifeless image, and ultimately reveals that the life it advocates is nothing more than the ways of death. On the other hand the vainglory of self blinds the person to the wretchedness of pride, reflects the insipid darkness of selfishness, and advocates the ways of self-delusion.

The type of glory that someone or something possesses is determined by the foundation that has been established. Such glory will be reinforced by the cornerstone that its particular reality lines up to. This reality will be revealed in the life (structure) that can be observed by others. It will be evaluated according to the substance that is produced by its works or fruits, and will ultimately reflect the type of light that will reveal the quality of the source behind the life that is being established because of it.

To understand the significance of glory, consider the following table on the next page. We have already talked about the influence of self and man's form of religion in relationship to the type of walk or life it produces in those who call themselves Christians. But, compare each of these foundations with the cornerstone that will determine people's type of reality, their particular structure that will establish their presentation, the value of their works, and the type of glory they will ultimately emit.

Developing Our Christian Life

Foundation	World	Self	Religion	Jesus (1 Co. 3:11)
Cornerstone	Philosophies	Standards	Schools of Thought	His Word and example
Structure	Temporary	Condemned	Dead	Alive/Spirit
Works (Material) (1 Cor. 3:12-15)	Conforming (Hay)	Compliance (Stubble)	Reforming (Wood)	Transformation (Precious Stone)
Light	Fading glory	Vainglory	False Glory	God's Glory

As we consider the next four types of Christians, we will begin to see how the influence of the world is affecting them. This is why Jesus' second part of the command to His disciples was to pick up the cross. The cross deals with the influence of the world upon our lives. The Apostle Paul stated it best in Galatians 6:14, "But God forbid that I should glory, save in the cross of our Lord Jesus Christ, by whom the world is crucified unto me, and I unto the world."

The influence of the world must become dead to us. The only way a person can become unresponsive in this fashion is that his or her appetites and ways of the flesh have also been crucified. The flesh is what finds itself greatly enticed by the attractions of the world. The world is designed to offer every type of pleasure that the appetites of the flesh could enjoy, even if it is only for a season. It appeals to the pride of man as it offers avenues of personal challenges, success, wealth, and power. It also has every kind of object or façade of beauty to catch the attention of the eyes in order to stir up the covetousness of the heart.[3]

This brings us to the first type of Christian who struggles with the world. These Christians are called *shortsighted Christians*. The reason for this term is because the focus of these people can be easily swayed from the Christian life to the world's attractions. Although the glory of the

---
[3] 1 John 2:15-17

world is fading, it still has the ability to catch the imagination of such people via their active selfish appetites. They see the glory of the world as something that is worthy to partake of to experience its promised pleasure. In fact, the possibility of what they would experience heightens their imagination as to the potential of what they will be experiencing once they give way to it.

A good example of this concept is found in the Garden of Eden. In the midst of this perfect, satisfying place stood a tree of life and a tree of knowledge of good and evil. God told Adam that he could partake of all the trees except the tree of knowledge of good and evil. However, Satan tempted the woman to consider the tree, not from just a knowledge standpoint where she knew it was evil, but from the point of view that she needed to experience evil so she could understand why the fruit of the tree was forbidden. In this way she could know the difference between good and evil, which would allow her to be as God in her understanding.[4]

As Christians, we know the ways of the world are evil. We may be in this world, but we are not to be part of it. We are told to come out and be separate from it in agreement, practices, and influence. However, the world has been designed to tempt us to consider the possibilities we could experience by partaking of the many forbidden fruits of its wickedness. After all, these fruits are very attractive to the flesh, and look quite harmless to the physical eye; however, they possess the poison of death in their composition.

What many people fail to realize is that evil does not initially appear to be wicked. What distinguishes evil is the reality that it leads to vanity and death. Satan simply planted the question mark in Eve's mind as to if such enticing fruit could actually lead to death. When Adam and Eve experienced the forbidden fruit, their eyes were open to the ways of evil. They possessed a contrast between knowing that something is good and evil as far as its type of fruit. However, evil has a flip side to it. On one side is the pleasure it initially produces, but on the other side are the consequences of such pleasure. The consequences are an enlarged appetite to partake of more, the emptiness of being ruled by confusion, shame, and guilt, and spiritual death that begins to work within a person's life.

There was a man that fell into the trap of the flesh and partook of its forbidden fruit. The fruit brought temporary pleasure, but the fallout vibrated throughout his family. Bitterness took root, anger took center stage, and hatred and resentment manifested itself towards him as he stood without any recourse to change the consequences of his wicked actions. He later admitted that he had walked in blessed innocence about the powerful working of evil upon the fleshly appetites. After partaking of evil, he ended up with a contrast that perverted, tormented, and defiled his way of thinking towards that which was indeed

---

[4] Genesis 2:9, 16-17; 3:1-6

considered innocent, pure, and righteous before God. The contrast he had was clear, but also tainted and seductive.

Clearly, evil temporarily gratifies the appetites of the flesh in every excitable and sensual way, while that which is considered pure would make the flesh yawn since it lacks any sensual attraction or self-gratification. However, that which is pure was never meant to attract the flesh. It was and is meant to maintain the wholesome character of that which is right and honorable before God. It is meant to attract the approval and presence of God.

As in the case of Eve and the man in the former paragraph, they both confirm that evil serves as a door that is opened when one experiences it. It is like a Pandora's Box. Once you open it, you cannot recapture the wickedness or harm that is attached to it. Now that it is open, its despairing consequences have the capacity to forever plague each of it victims in various ways. In fact, God calculated the cost of evil upon our souls. It cost Him His Son to once and for all address its consequences and devastation.

This brings us back to shortsighted Christians. We, as believers, do not need to experience the fruit of evil to know it is evil. The fact that God identifies it as being evil, and commands us to hate it in such a way that we would automatically become repulsed at it, should be enough for us for us to flee from it.[5] However, shortsighted Christians have never developed a hatred for evil because they have not totally given their hearts to God. In fact, they harbor a *half-hearted attitude* towards the things of God because they have a *divided heart*.

When people are divided in their heart between God and the world, they never really take a matter seriously, including the consequences. In their mind, all matters are left open for debate. Sadly, the test of something for these people will not be based on truth or righteousness, but on the selfishness that is freely reigning in their divided heart. A divided heart points to an *idolatrous heart*. In other words, these people's selfish whims and preferences will be exalted over a matter regardless of how honorable it might be. Therefore, if the world offers something that clearly appeals to such people's selfishness, their heart will naturally be inclined towards pursuing it.

This brings us to the gospel these people cling to as a means to justify their half-hearted attitude towards God. It is the *gospel of convenience*. In other words, these people possess a mixture. They may believe the Gospel of Jesus Christ, and will identify with it, as well as use it to verify their spiritual status; however, they also reserve the right to conveniently fit or mix the practices of the world into their Christian life when it serves their purpose. This adjustment makes it convenient for them to be a "Christian."

These people's gospel of convenience also allows them to hide behind such concepts as *"easy believism"* that states that if you have

---

[5] Psalm 97:10-12

"accepted Jesus," you are saved; therefore, you can live as you choose. Such notions also allow these individuals to justify their involvement with the world. However, any improper involvement in the world points to spiritual fornication for the Christian. Unholy spiritual mixtures of this sort will clearly defile that which is holy.

You can watch the shortsighted Christian slide into the different traps and cycles of the world. You can observe how these cycles work. When some worldly attraction manages to catch the shortsighted Christian's selfish imagination, he or she will begin to perceive that it has something of value to offer. This type of individual will start to view different aspects of his or her Christian life as being too narrow, unrealistic, unfair, or constricted to meet personal needs. In these people's logic, they conclude that since they have to live, function, and to some extent depend on the world, it could not be inappropriate to taste a bit of it here or there.

Once again, these individuals have failed to believe the Bible. Therefore, they do not realize that they are buying the same lie Eve did in the garden. The temptation of the lie was that in light of the great and pleasurable experience the forbidden fruit would bring to her, it would ultimately far outweigh the consequences she would end up paying for her deed. Jesus refuted this lie with this simple, but powerful summation, "For what is a man profited, if he shall gain the whole world, and lose his own soul? Or what shall a man give in exchange for his soul" (Matthew 16:26)?

The *harmless, pleasurable appearance* of the world is the bait that hooks many shortsighted Christians into its destructive traps. Such a hook opens a door to the wicked ways of the world that will slowly expose these Christians to its influences and attractions. As the door opens wider, it enables them to partake of more exotic worldly activities, which causes them to become increasingly desensitized to the spiritual realm. At this point, *spirits of lust* wield great influence in their lives.[6]

As these people begin to compromise with the world, they become listless and dissatisfied in their life. They find themselves trying to balance between two diverse worlds that have absolutely no agreement, revealing that they have failed to believe a well-known Scriptural principle: You cannot serve two masters. Satan, the god of this world demands loyalty and worship from those who partake of the fruits of his world. The Lord of lords and King of kings deserves our commitment, and requires that our life serve as a living sacrifice that expresses itself in true worship towards Him in every aspect of our lives.

Eventually the struggle to try to please two masters becomes too great for these individuals. As these poor souls try to determine what part of their life is bringing the most dissatisfaction, the confusion and conflict grows as their spirit begins to long for that which has substance, while their soul groans in light of the emptiness that is now clearly plaguing it.

---

[6] Ephesians 2:2

Developing Our Christian Life

This conflict is known as the war between the Spirit and the flesh.[7] Such a war is clearly visible in the lives of many Christians, especially in those of the younger generation.

Our young believers have a tough combination in place that clearly sets them up to fall into the traps of the world. They are at the age where their hormones are raging, their arrogance is hitting its peak due to ignorance, and their immaturity reeks with inexperience that lacks wisdom about the matters of life. In this state, young people are often blinded to the foolishness that still abounds in them. This selfish disposition in these young upstarts clashes with the godly call to be excellent in character while developing godly disciplines and moral accountability. In reality, they want to taste a bit of the world before they get serious about their life in God. After all, at this point, their lives consist of a lot of dos and don'ts. In their mind, they can handle tasting the world without being affected by it. However, the fruit of it is death, whether it is in small doses or large ones.

This challenge escalates for them even more so as they confront a world that not only entices their fleshly desires, but has also made the darkness of its insanity appear fun, attractive, and normal in light of the more disciplined Christian lifestyle. At this point, it appears as though the Christian life is keeping them from something that would add value, purpose, or character to their life. As they come face to face with their responsibility towards Christ, they can become angry, despondent, or rebellious.

Jim (our name for him) was intelligent, vivacious, outgoing and curious as a child. Therefore, it was sometimes difficult to ascertain what he absorbed from church attendance and Bible studies, and what he intentionally ignored. At times, it appeared that he was making progress spiritually, but then, at other times, his lack of attention and seemingly indifferent attitude were cause for concern.

When questioned about his commitment to Christ, Jim could give all the right answers, yet his prevailing attitudes and responses in his personal life, along with his attraction to the world exposed his double-mindedness. Jim also lacked fervor towards the things of God and lacked fear of displeasing Him. He also lacked a solid testimony of real repentance for sin, and a salvation experience.

As Jim entered his teen years, he vacillated between obedience to God, and dabbling in the forbidden fruit of the world. Sadly, by the time he was preparing for college, his self-centeredness, pride of life, pride of the eyes, and lust of the flesh won out. Some day Jim will hit bottom, and when he does, we can only hope and pray that he will get real with God and renounce the vanity of fleeting pleasures of this temporal world.

Sadly, what young people do not realize is that they are simply buying the lie that the world is not that bad. Part of the lie is that the ways of the world have simply been exaggerated so they will not discover how

---

[7] Galatians 5:16-18

valuable and exciting they are, thereby, choosing it over what they consider to be the "restricted Christian life." Once again, these young people do not realize that once they experience the fruit of the world they will become entrapped in its deadly tentacles, and discover what many adults have already found out. Once someone is entangled in the tentacles of the world, it becomes harder to walk away from its lies, attractions, and vanity.

This is why the Bible speaks of young people who overcame Satan with the Word. In other words, they chose to believe the truth of the Word to the attractive lies and presentations of the world. Christians are also reminded that if they give way to the Spirit, and walk in light of His leading, they will not fulfill the lust of the flesh.[8] After all, we each pursue the world as a means to fulfill the lust that is freely allowed to reign in our lives.

We have already identified the heart as being the source for these people's spiritual plight. But the other aspect that greatly affects shortsighted Christians is that they have *no real vision beyond this present world*. The Bible tells us that people who lack vision or revelation of the eternal will perish.[9] Since these types of individuals are fickle in their vision, they will fail to develop a life according to their higher calling and purpose. Sadly, because of their selfish perspective and emphasis on the world, all these people can see are the matters of the world that personally affect them; therefore, they live in the present world and are often indifferent to their need to live in light of the next world to come.

Because of the confusion that often besets these individuals, they live in a *state of limbo* as they try to figure out how to bring the two worlds together to maintain a certain worldly lifestyle while trying to preserve some religious semblance that would assure them of salvation. They do not want to let go of the false promises of the world, but they also do not want to let go of their hope of salvation. However, this speaks of their selfishness to try to have life on their terms. These people's hope is that since they do have good intentions towards God, that He will overlook their worldly reliance and emphasis and simply bless all of their worldly plans. Their emphasis clearly reveals that they do prefer the world, while trying to hold on to the best of heaven.

The Bible is clear, you cannot love the world, while simply tolerating Jesus, and be assured of the love of the Father. You can only properly serve one master at a time. If you are trying to serve two masters, you will end up loving one of them and hating the other.[10] Since this type of person is conditioned to pay homage to his or her worldly pursuits, the master he or she usually ends up loving is the world, while resenting Jesus for causing such a conflict in his or her life.

---

[8] Galatians 5:16; 1 John 2:13-14
[9] Proverbs 29:18
[10] Matthew 6:24; 1 John 2:15-16

Without sure vision, the sad reality for shortsighted Christians is that in the end they cannot really be assured of what type of existence they will experience in the next life. Vision is meant to get each of us to our next destination, and without spiritual vision to see beyond the present world, people cannot prepare for the next.

The question is, what must shortsighted Christians do to enlarge their vision? It is simple; first, they have to repent of their idolatrous selfishness. It is their self-serving selfishness that will not allow them to commit their total heart to loving, serving, and worshipping God. From this premise, they will be able to deny the self-life the right to experience whatever catches its fancy. Once the self-life is addressed, then these individuals must totally consecrate their life to God, acknowledging that it truly belongs to Him. This will require them to come to the altar of their personal cross to nail their fleshly ways to it, causing them to become dead to the world.

Once the death to the world occurs, then these people will have the wherewithal to follow Jesus into a complete, satisfying life that will truly outshine the fading glory and false promises of the world. Jesus is the only eternal focus a Christian must have to prepare for the next world. To follow Jesus means one will develop an attitude of a stranger towards the world, and the disposition of a pilgrim who is in search of a place in which he or she can experience the fullness of God.[11]

To ensure that the Christian walk is properly disciplined according to the footsteps of Jesus, we as believers must strive to keep Jesus ever before us as our constant focus. This exercise in godliness entails falling in love with Him, believing and obeying the Word, fleeing from that which is unholy, developing a true hatred for all evil, and walking in the ways of righteousness.

What is your relationship with the world? Are you a shortsighted Christian, whose emphasis is on the world while you maintain some type of wishful thinking towards spiritual matters of life and eternity? Or, are you a saint with a heavenly destination in focus as you purpose in your heart to follow Jesus? The Bible is clear; we cannot have the best of both worlds without compromising our life in Christ. If you have an unhealthy relationship with the world, remember God wants your heart so He can bestow an eternal inheritance on you. On the other hand, the world wants your soul so that Satan can boast of another person who chose to bow down to him instead of rightfully worshipping the deserving God of heaven.

---

[11] 1 Peter 2:11

12

SKEPTICAL CHRISTIAN

When people think of idolatry, they think in terms of worshipping some part of creation such as the sun, moon, or some other object that has been formed by the hands of man or the elements of the world. The prophet, Ezekiel, was brought into the inner chambers of the temple to see that instead of the priests worshipping Jehovah God, they were not only worshipping different aspects of creation, but also the imagery that had been set up in their minds.[1] In Ezekiel 14:3, the prophet unveils another place of idolatry, "Son of man, these men have set up their idols in their heart, and put the stumbling block of their iniquity before their face. Should I be inquired of at all by them?"

There is idolatry in what we consider low and high places. For Israel, the low places were hidden in secret chambers of darkness that could not be seen. The high places were out in the open, but they fit naturally into the terrain. For example, these high places represented groves where worship was taking place. When we think of the heart, it points to the concept of secret chambers that cannot be observed or seen by others. In the case of the mind, it points to idolatry in high places where it naturally fits into the terrain of our thinking process. For this reason, idolatry can prove to be deceptive, hidden by some form of darkness and isolation, or fitting into the natural terrain of man's activities.

It is due to the fact that idolatry involves the heart and mind coming into agreement with the unholy that this sin is also referred to as spiritual harlotry or fornication. The Apostle Paul reminded the Corinthians that one spirit joined them in Christ and that they should flee fornication or unholy agreement. He also exhorted them that they are the temples of the Holy Spirit, marking them with God's ownership.[2]

This brings us to the world and its part in idolatry. The world serves as a platform for all idolatry. It is important to understand that idolatry simply changes the glory of God in the mind of the person. The Apostle Paul speaks of this in 2 Corinthians 10:5 when he speaks about vain imaginations that exalt themselves against the real knowledge of God. Man's imaginations simply change the reality of God to fit his own perception. Ultimately, man who gives way to the deceitful imaginations of the carnal mind will end up denying that the God of the Bible is the

---

[1] Ezekiel 8:11-16
[2] 1 Corinthians 3:16-20

essence of all truth. However, there is no real wisdom or place of accountability outside of God's infinite character.

In man's idolatry, he also mentally strips God of His sovereignty that identifies Him as the one and only true God. As Scripture states, there are no gods beside Him or before Him. He alone is God; and He is the one who determines what is right and acceptable in all matters.[3] In the state of idolatry, man will ultimately reject God's holy character, redefining what is holy or profane according to his own standard. As a result, there is no place of sanctification in which man can experience true cleansing. In the end, the attitude of idolatry will ignore or do away with God's work of redemption through Jesus. This allows for another gospel to be devised, as well as another Jesus to be erected or tacked on to a person's perception as he or she comes under the spirit of the world. Such activities change the glory of God in man's perception as he gives way to the false light of a different glory that is undeserving of worship and service.

Clearly, if the glory of God is changed in the minds and hearts of people and given to another source, individuals will end up with an idol. Although this idol is lifeless, it is given honor in the heart. Although it is powerless, it is given authority according to the will of a person. Although a façade, it is given identity based on the intellect. Although the idol is bogus, it is exalted as a point of personal superiority according to the mind. Behind such idols are demonic influences that inspire pagan practices of worship that can take people's emotions captive, pervert loyalty that can make these individuals obsessive, and create an insane reality that sacrifices innocence, scorns truth, and mocks righteousness.

As we consider those who regard themselves as being Christians, but have some type of agreement with the world, we must realize that they are operating from the platform of idolatry. At the core of the world's idolatrous platform are humanistic and New Age philosophies, pagan practices, and idols that have been cleverly hidden in the chambers of darkness or planted in the midst of acceptable terrain established by the world.

This brings us to the three points of agreement that a Christian can have with the world. Each point of agreement ends in some type of idolatry. As we have considered shortsighted Christians, these individuals have come into agreement in some way with the sensual practices of the world. This type of agreement points to idolatry of the heart, where affections or feelings for the things of the world are being exalted and pursued, rather than seeking out the God of heaven and the life He has prepared for them.

The second point of agreement regards the wisdom of the world. God's wisdom comes from Him, and flows down from His throne towards His people, producing inward integrity or character. However, the wisdom of the world varies according to the different arenas that a

---

[3] Isaiah 45:5, 14, 18, 21-22

person must function within. For example, there are those individuals who are considered street wise because they know how to survive on the streets. There are those who are considered to possess business savvy due to their understanding of how business works. Such wisdom points to the ability to figure out a matter based on the knowledge that has been pursued or experienced, but such knowledge will prove to be lacking if it is out of its particular element. Clearly, such wisdom not only proves to be very limited in its present understanding, but it also explains why such wisdom was described by James as being earthly, sensual, and inspired by devils. It often produces envying, strife, confusion, and every evil work among those who are striving to be superior in their particular point of wisdom.[4]

Once again, we are reminded that the world serves as a platform for idolatry. Each different age of the world presented different idols for people to ignorantly pursue. In America, some of the idols that have been cleverly presented are power, money, prestige, and education.

Education for many translates as wisdom. Needless to say, to improperly emphasize and pursue worldly education involves committing idolatry in high places. It is important to point out that when we are born our minds are pretty much an empty slate. They have the ability to take in information and process it for the purpose of recognizing, discerning, and properly confronting the reality of life. The reason for this is to learn the lessons of life in light of God and eternity. However, the main motivation behind all idolatry is not to properly confront reality, but to devise means of changing and controlling it to serve the purpose of the self-life.

Those who exalt worldly education perceive it as a means to secure a particular lifestyle, to possess the means to control the direction of their world, and to acquire knowledge that will produce superiority over those who lack such understanding. In fact, such people possess the haughty look that is inspired by the arrogance of conceit. Such a look is considered an abomination to God. The Apostle Paul also associated ignorance towards the unseen mysteries of God with personal conceits. He noted that such conceit is a form of blindness. In Romans 12:16, he described the idolatry of conceit in this way, "Be of the same mind one toward another. Mind not high things, but condescend to men of low estate. Be not wise in your own conceits." Paul also stated that those who see themselves as being wise according to the present age need to realize that their thoughts are vain, and if they are going to put it into proper perspective, they need to be willing to become fools since God considers such wisdom to be foolish. In the end, God will use these people's wisdom against them.[5]

Notice how the apostle revealed the attitude, preference, and exaltation of conceit. The attitude is that it will not humble itself in any

---

[4] James 3:12-18
[5] Proverbs 6:16-17; Romans 11:25; 1 Corinthians 3:18-20

way to come into agreement because it sees itself superior in its knowledge. It might respect the knowledge of others, but it will never truly come into agreement. Its preference is towards that which is considered elevated according to the knowledge or philosophies of the world. It will never condescend to a lower estate for it has been clearly exalted in the person's mind, thereby, blinding him or her to his or her spiritual status.

This brings us to the Christian who has come into agreement with the world concerning its wisdom. Such Christians have an intellectual understanding about salvation, but clearly remain dead towards the spiritual aspect of the Christian life. Because of their idolatry in high places, they may have allowed the idea of salvation to ascend the ladder of higher criticism to receive consideration and mental acceptance, but continue to remain skeptical towards the spiritual, unseen aspect of the Christian walk. Skepticism in this arena points to a *hard heart* that operates in the darkness of unbelief towards those things that prove contrary or inferior to these people's personal conceits. This is why this particular Christian is known as the *skeptical Christian*.

It is vital that I point out that Christians can become skeptical about certain spiritual beliefs, situations, or matters. At such times, an attitude of doubt can take hold of them because understanding is eluding them. This is why Christians are instructed to have the mind of Christ.[6] Such a mind is developed through choosing to believe God when understanding is absent, submitting to His leading when nothing makes sense, and obeying His Word when all seems ridiculous. It is during such times of darkness that true faith takes root for those who allow the mind of Christ to be established in them. However, the skeptical Christian is one who resides in the state or disposition of *suspended judgment* towards the spiritual ways and matters of God.

The main problem with this Christian is that their carnal mind has never really been transformed by the renewing of the Spirit. The Apostle Paul explained how the carnally minded mind the things of the flesh, and that its fruits are that of death. Such a mind will always find itself in opposition against God. The reason for this state, when it comes to the carnal mind, is that it finds its source in the natural man. The natural man has nothing in common with the Spirit of God, and cannot respond to Him.[7] In fact, the natural man perceives the unseen world as being foolish and ridiculous, thereby, remaining ready to show suspicion, doubt, and judgment towards the spiritual realm.

A good example of such a person was the man Festus. When the Apostle Paul was brought before King Agrippa and Festus in regard to the charges brought against him by the Jewish faction, he challenged Agrippa according to his understanding about Jewish beliefs, as well as gave those present his testimony about encountering Jesus on the road

---

[6] Philippians 2:5
[7] Romans 8:4-8; 1 Corinthians 2:10-15

to Damascus. After he was finished, Festus who considered himself to be a rational person made this statement with a loud voice, "...Paul, thou are beside thyself; much learning doth make thee mad" (Acts 26:24b).

Although Festus had his own form of knowledge, he thought Paul's type of knowledge about spiritual matters regarding the one true God of heaven and His supernatural intervention on behalf of mankind through Jesus Christ, had made him insane. After all, Paul's reality did not agree or correspond with Festus' Roman mentality. Therefore, he deemed Paul unrealistic.

The world's perception of its wisdom and knowledge has clearly served as a breeding ground for many people like Festus throughout the ages. Sadly, this particular age is no different. Many of those educated and indoctrinated by the liberal colleges see themselves very rational. This rationality is tested according to what they see. They judge all matters based on what fits into their arrogant understanding and what will fall into line with their intellectual perception. Those who take great pride in what they know often bring this perception into the Christian realm. As a result, some aspects of the Christian life will be intellectually accepted while other subjects will be considered foolish.

This brings us to the Gospel. Skeptical Christians have a very confusing view of the Gospel. In one way they secretly mock its simplicity, while accepting the possibilities of it to avoid being found foolish for not believing it. To some extent they are able to accept the fact that Jesus died for them, but they cannot respect that it is a matter of simple faith that saves them. Such simplicity seems absolutely absurd to them, making the Gospel a substandard concept in their mind. The fact that the Gospel also addresses the unseen element of the spirit and soul of man, as well as eternity are also other matters that seem irrational to these people. After all, how can they believe in what they cannot see, measure, and test in some way? As a result, these people have adopted what I call the *rational gospel*.

Even though these types of Christians display a *mocking spirit* towards the simplicity of the Gospel as being foolish, they sometimes can be pricked in their conscience to consider it according to their personal reasoning. They can occasionally see that it could be quite beneficial to them. However, if some aspect about a matter cannot fit into their rational understanding, they will deem it as being foolish and discard it as nonsense. For example, Scriptural truths may be accepted or tolerated by these people, but spiritual revelation will cause either envy or mocking in them because their perception is indifferent or unresponsive to such revelations.

Kent (not real name) was one such person. Kent's skepticism hung in the atmosphere like a wet blanket, making people feel uneasy and wary of what response might be forthcoming from him. Kent had a way of silently making others aware of how intellectually "superior" he was, and how intellectually "inferior" they were. On occasion, however, Kent would volunteer spiritual insights that were very fitting and beneficial. It was obvious that if only Kent could chuck his skepticism, and relinquish his ironclad mind and will totally to God, that he had the makings of a powerful Christian leader. The potential was there, but the intellectual scrutiny that served as a sieve for any spiritual revelations or truths kept him in total bondage.

A genuine battle was taking place for Kent's soul between Satan and God, and the amazing thing is he knew it. His anger grew as he tried to maintain one foot in "Christianity" and the other in the world. Finally, he admitted to giving way to a demon because it gave him power; and, he also admitted that God had spoken to him, warning him of the consequences of his stubborn resistance to deny his intellectual conceit and skepticism and come to Him by faith. Sadly, in the end, under the cover of "intellectual" skepticism, Kent followed his skeptical heart and chose the lust of the flesh and love for the world.

What skeptical Christians fail to realize is that the truths of God are capable of standing up against the critical eye of the best skeptic, ultimately revealing the foolishness of the skepticism of the present age that abounds. As you study skepticism, it is nothing more than the product of prejudicial ignorance. Ignorance is not always a matter of lacking education; it is sometimes the result of lacking the means to connect to reality in order to gain a proper perspective. Although contrary to worldly wisdom, the heavenly perspective not only enlarges one's limited understanding to embrace eternal possibilities, but it also reveals how worldly wisdom has been perverted and manipulated by pride.

Recently, I sought out a certain group in the medical profession that dealt with one particular area of health. These professional people explained how others in the medical field had not yet recognized their particular procedure. However, they purported that the results of their procedure verified that it worked, giving them the inspiration to ignore the criticism of their colleagues, while continuing on to help others. Sadly, some of these same people became nervous and even critical to the fact that I was involved with the natural health field. Instead of admitting that they were not acquainted with that particular field, and that each diverse field has both its strengths and weakness that can prove to be beneficial in the complete scheme of things, some of these people negated it altogether. This is the reality of the wisdom of the world. Although limited, it exalts itself as judge and jury as a means to criticize and condemn such matters that do not fit in its conceptual box of understanding. However, such condemnation reveals that because it is blinded by its limitations and ignorance, worldly wisdom simply is inspired by prejudice, while touting from its superior heights of conceit that the simple truths of God that do not fit in its box are foolish and insignificant.

God confirms that the world's concepts of wisdom, strength, and worth stand completely opposite of His evaluation of such matters.[8] Worldly wisdom has no real knowledge of eternal matters. It is limited by

---

[8] 1 Corinthians 1:25-28

its own arrogant darkness, while claiming that the wisdom of God is foolish because it is contrary to the world's view of what it perceives to be rational. Yet, some of the most intelligent people from different respected professions have embraced the Gospel of Jesus Christ and the truths of the Bible throughout the different ages of the world. These individuals have been used mightily to give an intellectual account of the hope that is in them. In such debates the real problem is unveiled. It is not that the truths of God are so simple they insult the worldly intelligence of people; rather, they are so deeply profound that they prove to be far above the ability of the carnal mind to comprehend them.

Since skeptical Christians have not been transformed in their minds, they continue to consider everything according to the *philosophies of the present age* that has clearly been entrenched in their perception. These philosophies are humanistic in nature and emphasis and New Age in attitude and religious approach. When they serve as people's foundation, they regard and judge the matters of life with a critical eye that is quick to identify and vehemently criticize others' philosophy that dare to insult, intrude into, or challenge their particular perception.

The Apostle Paul put forth this warning concerning the world's influence, "Beware lest any man spoil you through philosophy and vain deceit, after the tradition of men, after the rudiments of the world, and not after Christ" (Colossians 2:8). The apostle warns that the philosophies that find their source in the foundation or rudiments of the world and are put forth through men's traditions are not only empty but they are deceitful. As a result, they will spoil or ruin a person towards the real matters of God and life.

Skeptical Christians prefer the rudiments of the world's wisdom because of how it makes them feel in their conceits. Even though God's Word addresses such a dark preference, these people continue to walk in a *spirit of unbelief* towards the spirit and life that His Word could produce in their dark, lifeless perception. Since God's truth cannot penetrate the darkness of these people's mind, they maintain a controlled indifference towards the Christian life. It is as though they stand on the outside of the Spirit and life of the Christian walk as a means to partake of that which appeals to their conceit, while deeming anything else as non-applicable, insignificant, or foolish. Such Christians may end up with knowledge about Jesus and His Gospel, but they will never possess a heart revelation of Him.

True salvation comes through faith that reaches into the heart with a revelation that a matter is true.[9] In fact, a person chooses to believe it as being so. It is the same as saying "amen" or "so be it for it is so" to something. The Bible tells us we must believe the Gospel in our heart. We must count it as true. Therefore, the truths of God are not just a matter of having an intellectual knowledge about them, but they are the actual means in which the Spirit of God establishes the spiritual life in us.

---

[9] Romans 10:9-10; 1 Corinthians 1:17-25

Developing Our Christian Life

When truths become a point of life to us, the Spirit begins to transform our minds from the carnal stage to the spiritual. From this premise the spiritual matters of God become a reality, while the wisdom of the world becomes foolishness.

Skeptical Christians are hard people to challenge. They often prove unpredictable because you never know what part of the truth they will become offended at or take issue with. They like to play on what they consider foolishness and weakness in Christianity in order to exalt themselves over what they consider to be inferior. They often use mind games to demean those around them in order to maintain a façade of superiority. This façade simply hides the fact that these people refuse to submit to the simplicity of God's truths in order to embark on a reality they cannot control or comprehend with their carnal mind. As a result of this struggle, they become miserable in their limited worlds. However, their conceits will not allow them to humble themselves to explore the profound depths of God's wisdom and truth. They find themselves struggling between the world with its vain philosophies, while wrestling to adjust or resist the wisdom of God that would expose their foolishness and strip them of their arrogance. This ongoing struggle is a form of resisting any type of submission of their mind by faith to the simple truths of God, while keeping their heart cold and lifeless towards the Spirit of God. As a result, they never enter into rest in God where they can discover Him and enjoy a relationship.

This brings us to the final aspect of the skeptical Christian. In their suspended state of judgment, they are always waiting for some type of proof about those aspects of Christianity that they would consider worth their consideration and respect. After all, what does not fit in their understanding is mocked and discarded, regardless of the emphasis the Bible may put on such matters.

As you consider how these certain Christians often approach spiritual matters from the premise of unbelief, you realize that what they do perceive according to their hard hearts is often based on presumptions about a situation. For example, if something fits their particular perception, they will presume that it is right. If it goes contrary to their perception, they will presume that it is wrong. Presumption will provoke God because it assumes He has the same attitude about a matter; or, it will put Him to a foolish test by presuming He will defend His character, truth, or way to prove a matter. The reality is that God's thoughts are higher than ours, and He does not have to prove a matter to verify what has already been established in His Word as truth. In fact, such a state of presumption allows people to justify departing from the living God.[10] The Apostle Peter put this perspective on presumption,

> The Lord knoweth how to deliver the godly out of temptations, and to reserve the unjust unto the day of judgment to be punished; But chiefly them that walk after the

---

[10] Isaiah 55:8-9; Matthew 4:7; Hebrews 3:7-19

flesh in the lust of uncleanness, and despise government. Presumptuous are they; self-willed, they are not afraid to speak evil of dignities (2 Peter 2:9-10).

People who reserve the right, according to their own will, to determine their reality about God, life, and the world, clearly will walk after the flesh according to their carnal mind. The flesh will always pervert or profane the things of God causing uncleanness in these people's perception and practices. Since these individuals despise the rule of God, they will show contempt for all authority, speaking evil of that which is worthy, honorable, and respected.

Idolatry puts people in a precarious position before God. Up front such individuals are breaking the first two commandments. They reveal that they do not really love or desire God. If they regard Him in any way, they will simply adjust, tack on, or fit Him into their particular form of idolatry.

This is why people who harbor idols in their heart or mind, must repent of their unbelief and indifference towards the God of the Bible. They must tear down the altars that are associated with such idols. These altars not only reveal the heart devotion and the attitude towards the idols, but what these individuals are pursuing in this present world as a means to worship them. They must willfully choose to not only love the Lord, but also love His truth. By loving the truth they will begin to believe it with child-like faith.

Skeptical Christians must tear down the altar that has been erected by the philosophies of the world that have clearly honored their deceitful conceits, while deeming the unseen matters of God as a place of utter foolishness. They must repent of their abominable arrogance, and humble themselves to take on the disposition of the child so they can begin to glean the very depths of God's truths. These individuals must also allow God to penetrate their hard hearts by choosing to approach the Bible to believe it as being true. They must then consider their rational gospel as irrational in light of God's wisdom and truth. This will allow them to embrace the spiritual aspect of the true Gospel of Jesus Christ and become the spiritual man or woman of God.

Consider if you are a skeptical Christian. If you are, take the necessary steps that have been presented in the previous paragraph. You need to realize that God has chosen the foolish things of the world to confound those who perceive themselves to be wise. He has used the things that are considered base and despised to reveal that those things that are valued by the world will be brought to a place of nothingness in the end.[11] Clearly, the wise of this world will be proven to be fools for they did not believe the true God of heaven, as well as failed to value that which had no real importance in light of God's kingdom.

---

[11] 1 Corinthians 1:27-28

13

SANDBOX CHRISTIAN

Christianity becomes a lifestyle that is established on the right foundation, lived out according to a cornerstone, and lined up to the head or leadership of one Person, Jesus Christ. Jesus, who is to become the believer's all in all, serves as the foundation of this life. As the foundation, we as believers will be established according to the eternal plan of God. Jesus is also our cornerstone in which the Holy Spirit will ensure that His very life will be developed in us according to His truth and example. As our head or leader, we will be led into the abundant or complete life that He has designated for each of us.[1]

This is why the Bible clearly shows Christ is in all that pertains to God and life. Every eternal work that is being done in the lives of God's people is all about Christ's life, work, and purpose being realized in them. As our foundation as believers, we will be established according to who He is. This foundation represents the source or essence of our authority in His eternal kingdom. As our cornerstone, we will know what it means to take on His disposition of humility and His attitude of meekness. The attitude of meekness will prepare us to seek, find, and submit to the will of the Father on earth, fulfilling His purpose for our lives. As our head or leader, we are assured that all matters of His life will flow to, in, and through us from the throne of God. This reminds us of the power that is always available to us as we strive to live this life out according to our high calling and commission.

If the foundation of people's lives is not Jesus, God Incarnate, then the cornerstone of their religious life will have no power to stand, and the leadership of the "Jesus" they perceive will have no authority to bring them into the complete, abundant, eternal life. As a result, these people's lives will prove to be unsound, marked by the harsh reality of judgment.

Jesus made reference to this very subject in His Sermon on the Mount in Matthew 5-7. In fact, He actually ended with it. Most Christians are aware of this text found in Matthew 7:24-27 that warns us about the type of foundation we build upon. However, it must be noted that before He established the basis of this text, Jesus described the type of life that should be present in those who identify themselves with the God of heaven. They must have a right attitude towards God, life, challenges, and others. They must be responsible to allow this life to properly express itself towards others for the glory of God. Their religion must not

---

[1] 1 Corinthians 3:11; Ephesians 2:20; 4:13-15; Colossians 3:10-11

be a matter of outward pretence, but a life that is clearly lived out by faith that is expressed in obedience to His Word. God's followers must bring the proper sacrifice to the altar, mean what they say, require inward discipline and character in their attitudes, develop the necessary sobriety to rid themselves of any moral deviation, and be prepared to be sacrificial in their benevolence. They are to love their enemy, develop effective communication (prayer) with the Father, examine their real treasure, know their real Provider, and by faith seek that which pertains to God's kingdom and righteousness. They are not to judge from a prideful, prejudicial premise, and they must ask for God to have His way, seek His truth, and by faith be willing to knock on every door to discover the full life God has ordained according to His perfect will. These followers are to realize that the way of this life is narrow, and few will find it because most prefer to walk according to their own perception. In the end, the fruit of people's lives will reveal their true source. As a result, Jesus warned that those who choose another way will delude themselves enough to believe that their works identify them to Him, when in reality, He will not even recognize them because they were not doing the will of the Father.

After Jesus' presentation of the attitude and life of a believer, He explained how this life was established. It is established by hearing His sayings with the intent of obeying them. Sadly, many people hear Jesus' sayings with the intent of adding them to their religious knowledge, rather than assimilate them into their lives. Such people lack faith, because faith comes by hearing, and hearing by the Word of God.[2] In summation, true faith approaches the Word of God with the intent of believing it as truth, applying it to one's way of living, and daily walking it out in obedience. This is how Jesus' disciples will follow Him into the satisfying life that is marked by eternity and power.

James reiterates the truth about obedience to God's Word in his epistle. He exhorts Christians to be doers of the Word and not just hearers who end up deceiving themselves about their Christian status. He relates the hearers of the Word only as individuals who look into the mirror to see what manner of person they are. After seeing their reflection, they walk away from the mirror, but immediately forget who they are. Clearly, such people have never truly been established on the foundation, developed according to the cornerstone, and lined up to the head. James concluded that a person, who not only hears what the Word says, but also becomes a doer of it will be blessed indeed.[3]

Jesus stated that people, who do His sayings, would build their spiritual lives on the Rock. We know this rock to be Jesus. He is the immovable Rock of ages that cannot be moved from who He is by different circumstantial storms.[4] His foundation is clearly rooted in

---

[2] Matthew 7:24; Romans 10:17
[3] James 1:22-25
[4] Matthew 7:24-25; 1 Corinthians 10:3-4

eternity, ensuring us that He will never move or be removed from His truth, work, or plan. He is sure, stable, and trustworthy.

Jesus goes on to warn those who do not hear these sayings in a proper way because they fail to do them, are likened to foolish men who build their houses on the sand. When the storms of life come rushing in with their various winds of judgment to shake the foundation of these people's religious lives, they will end up having a great fall. Keep in mind every foundation will eventually be shaken by such storms to expose the spiritual condition of people.[5]

As we have considered these different faces of Christianity, it is clear to see that many of the people that wear these façades are not founded on the right foundation, have failed to develop their life according to the cornerstone, and/or have never grown up into the leadership of Jesus. As a result, they must wear different masks or cloaks to cover up the inconsistencies in their Christian life.

This brings us to the next type of Christian, the *sandbox Christian*. If there is one type of Christian that emulates the foundation that has been clearly established on nothing more than sand it is the sandbox Christian. In fact, these people not only pride themselves on how well they are establishing their life on sand, but they have established such a clever presentation of their type of Christianity that many are not able to even see the sand beneath their life.

The reason that many fail to see the sand underneath this type of person's foundation is because, as observers, they are caught up by the *sandcastles* these individuals have brilliantly constructed. These sandcastles represent these people's many good and noteworthy deeds. The problem is that the observers are not aware or properly discerning what they are really regarding. These castles can look so real, as well as appear strong, but they are made of the same type of sand the castles are sitting upon. These presentations are merely miniature replicas or imitations of what could be considered the Christian life, but they are not real.

The sandbox Christian plays at Christianity by building and establishing their personal idea of this life. Their ideas are often based on what is popular in the religious world. However, their presentation is nothing but a glorified sandcastle that will eventually be brought down by the storms of adversity that periodically roll through life. Once the castles are brought down, then the winds of judgment will scatter the sand in every direction, wiping out any memory that the castle really existed.

This brings us to the topic of judgment. Judgment is a form of separation. There will be a time when the tares will be separated from the wheat, the goats from the sheep, and the profane from the holy. Each form of separation shows us that the counterfeit will be separated from that which is real. In such judgment there is no way a person will be able to hide his or her true foundation, cornerstone, and source of

---

[5] Matthew 7:26-27; Hebrews 12:27

leadership. All works that are not marked by the will of God will be stripped away and burned up by the fires of judgment.[6]

There was a young man that once mocked some Christians by saying that they would be rejoicing in heaven over his existence in hell because it would prove they were right. Talk about the voice of foolishness and disrespect. The truth of the matter is that all tears of sorrow that have been experienced by Christians in this present world will be wiped away, while the memory of the wicked will be remembered no more.[7] God's people will not be in heaven mourning for those who did not make it; rather, they will be rejoicing in the glorious revelation that they are going to bathed in the unhindered presence and glory of their precious Lord forever.

However, I can tell you that those tormented in the bowels of hell will be quite aware of their past life. The rich man in hell recognized Abraham, and the beggar, Lazarus, who he had ignored when he was dying at his gate. This tormented soul also was fully cognizant that he had five brothers who were going to end up in the same place if they did not change their ways. The issue of our eternal existence all comes down to whether our names are found in the book of life, which identifies us to the redemption of Jesus. The other prospect has to do with people's names being blotted out of the book because of their refusal to believe in the Jesus of the Bible, while choosing to walk the broad way of personal theology in light of worldly preferences.[8]

We know that the shortsighted Christian is focused on tasting the world to fulfill self-serving appetites. Skeptical Christians are considering Christianity through their worldly philosophies as a means of covering all their intellectual bases, but the sandbox Christian sees the world as their treasure chest. This brings us to the type of religious sandbox that these people are playing in. The box is nothing more than the world. These people love the world, and simply see Christianity as their personal platform in which they can give an impression of personal righteousness while disguising their worldly involvement and practices.

For example, these people can be greedy, which expresses itself in stinginess and hoarding. However, they hide such idolatry behind an appearance that such covetous practices are for the sake of good causes. The harsh reality is that if a matter fails to serve their purpose or bring them proper recognition regardless of its righteous status, they will disregard, mock, or demean it in some way to alleviate themselves from any moral obligation.

These individuals can also prove to be very shrewd in their affairs, but tout that such cleverness is for the purpose of being good stewards. They often situate their activities in such a way as to present themselves as being benevolent and sacrificial. However, if you peek behind the veil,

---

[6] Matthew 7:21; 13:24-30; 25:31-46; 1 Corinthians 3:13-15; 1 John 2:17
[7] Psalm 109:5-15; Revelation 20:11-15; 21:4
[8] Psalms 69:28; Luke 16:19-31; Revelation 3:5

you will see that every activity ultimately benefits them in some way. In fact, if the activities did not benefit them in some way, they would not even consider them for a moment. In essence, these people use Christianity to serve their worldly purposes, agendas, and causes. As a result, there is no purity in anything they do, which makes them untrustworthy.

A number of years a go we met a married couple that we shall call Sam and Smiley. Sam was a hard working, shrewd businessman who was financially successful in his investments and his line of work. He was a well-known, upstanding respected member of his community, and was involved in different charitable organizations and causes. It was assumed that Sam was a bona fide Christian because of his associations, activities, church attendance, and his commitment to talk to people with personal problems.

Smiley gave the impression of a bright, happy, friendly, caring, "chipper" person. Both Sam and Smiley were associated with a particular ministry that served needy people in very poor third world countries. Since Smiley's passion in life was to travel to every country in the world, this ministry gave this couple opportunities to go abroad. They also spent several weeks out of every year traveling the globe for personal pleasure. Undoubtedly, many people were under the impression that it was all for the purpose of "ministry."

While people may have been caught up with Sam and Smiley's "sand castle" storybook life, the truth is, neither one had a solid testimony of Jesus Christ, whom He is, nor what He had done for them in their life. Instead, their brand of religion was a hodgepodge of beliefs that mainly consisted of always being "positive" (at the expense of reality and truth) and being politically correct.

Clearly, Christianity is not a way of life to sandbox Christians. They will use it as a means to attract people to or gain credibility about their particular presentation. The fact that these people use Christianity becomes quite obvious, as they are quick to divorce themselves from it when worldly preferences or philosophies would serve them best in a situation. Therefore, as you regard these individuals in their religious presentation, you become aware that certain aspects of Christianity may be shaped or adjusted in some way to fit into their worldly agendas, but in the end it will be sacrificed to ensure that the ways of the world are ultimately honored.

The reason for these people's attitude is quite evident; the world allows them to be exalted to a place of importance and example, while in Christianity, Jesus alone is to be exalted and honored. Jesus put it best, "And I, if I be lifted up from the earth, will draw all men unto me" (John 12:32). Jesus must be lifted up because He is the only one who can save man from His plight. He does not share this position with any one man or woman. As man, He became the Lamb that paid the price for our sins, and as God, He became our only hope for life, and our only way to obtain it. Regardless of what sandbox Christians may have that is attractive and noteworthy, it cannot save people from spiritual death, give life, or offer hope. As the Apostle Paul summarized, no flesh will glory in our Lord's presence.[9]

This brings us to the point of attraction that these people possess. They possess a certain sense of self. In their minds, this sense of self translates into self-worth. The idea of being worthy becomes their point of faith or confidence. According to their perception, they are worthy of everything they pursue or desire. After all, they have established a sense of their worth through their abilities, deeds, or diplomacy. For example, they have proven their worth through abilities, earned their worth through deeds or works, and/or have secured their worth through diplomacy. Therefore, they have gained the right to partake of the treasure chest of the world with all due honors and recognition.

The harsh reality of sandbox Christians is that their greatest ability is that they know how to effectively play the games of the world. The greatest game is you scratch my back and I will scratch yours. These people must have their prideful, overrated perception of themselves constantly fed so they can continue in the self-delusion they have erected about themselves. They have devised deceptive ways to manipulate people to adjust to their reality. In this deception, they secretly pride themselves in knowing how to play on the pride of people to gain personal status in these individual's eyes, all the while seeing these people as foolish and inferior.

They also know how to play with the emotions and needs of people to gain their dependency. Clearly, these people exalt themselves at the expense of others. What these individuals fail to realize is that other people are playing them as well. These games represent a false way that must be hated by those who call themselves Christians.[10] Such games have nothing to do with integrity, truth, compassion, genuine concern for souls, or the ways of righteousness. They are simply the means for these people to maintain or gain control of their sick, fragile, perverted realities.

Another sandbox Christian is a person we shall call Raymond. Raymond found himself in a situation where it was to his advantage to tack Christianity and Christ on to his life. After some exposure to a run-of-the-mill church, Raymond felt satisfied that he was assured of heaven in the end, but as far as selling out to Christ in the here and now, he only went so far. The reason for this was that he felt he deserved the best the world had to offer, and he had a lot of living to do. In other words, he did not mind being a Christian as long as it did not interfere with his worldly pursuits. After all, the things in this world that were on his agenda to do and acquire were not wrong in and of themselves. The problem was, Raymond's heart was more caught up with the vanity of this life than in pursuing a life in Christ, and eternal rewards.

---

[9] 1 Corinthians 1:29
[10] Psalms 119:128

Developing Our Christian Life

    This brings us back to the original lie of Satan back in the Garden of Eden. Since Satan is the god of this world, the lie he sold in the garden can be found in every fabric of the world. Needless to say, each of these different worldly Christians have bought part of the lie. Shortsighted Christians believe they can taste some evil of the world without reaping the consequences of death. Skeptical Christians believe that worldly wisdom will mean that their eyes will surely be opened to embrace important knowledge that will exalt them in a greater standing. In the case of sandbox Christians, they believe that in their particular standing they shall be like God, capable of serving as an example to others and able to determine what is real and acceptable.

    Sandbox Christians judge everything according to their personal perception about matters. Since they see themselves as being important, clever, superior, and in control of their realities, they feel that they have the privileged status to judge others. This judgment is based on how something makes them feel. For example, if a person fails to approach a matter that lines up to their personal approval, sandbox Christians will judge the person, while touting that the transgressor needs to adopt their particular way (game) as an example.

    Needless to say, sandbox Christians judge people based on their own high opinions of self. Their judgments reveal that they are not in touch with reality. They may think they know a matter, when in reality they have absolutely no clue. When they expose their way of thinking, they prove they are out in left field, playing their own individual game that proves to be separate from the rest of the world. Ultimately, they end up looking like fools to those they are falsely judging.

    This brings us to their idolatry. Since the world is their treasure chest, they have idols in the heart that they greatly value and pursue, such as money, prestige, and worldly success.[11] Given that their heart is with the world, they harbor an *unstable heart* that has no sure foundation. It lacks real dedication as it can change its attitudes, adjust presentations, or comply with the winds of worldly popularity.

    Due to their high opinion of their worth, these sandbox Christians have idols established in the high places of their mind. These people often pursue the respect and recognition of the world as they strive to establish reputations that will bring them honor from the world. They often desire people to speak well of them as a means to verify their self-worth. As a result, much of their actions are simply a matter of show. However, the Bible is clear; the fear of pleasing others is a trap. Hence enters the warning of woe, "beware when all men speak well of you," because in the end such recognition will be your only reward.[12]

    This brings us to the gospel these people proclaim. Sandbox Christians hold to a *self-serving gospel.* Keep in mind, these people are all about appearances, but if something does not serve their purpose,

---

[11] Matthew 6:21
[12] Proverbs 29:25; Matthew 6:2, 5, 16-18; Luke 6:26

they will discard it as rubbish and pursue other avenues. Therefore, these people will present a gospel that somehow will exalt them in their religious activities. For example, their gospel can embellish such things as works or love. But, as you consider the fruits, depth, or source of their particular, biased gospel, it does nothing more than exalt them as the example for others to regard. These people are simply stamping Christianity onto their activities and claims in order to delude themselves and others to their real spiritual status of standing on shifting sand that one day will cause their façade to cave in around them.

The harsh reality about sandbox Christians is that you will not find any truth in their activities, nor will you find any real lasting fruit. They have simply tacked Christ on to their activities or claims to verify their selfish, worldly pursuits. Therefore, these people remind me of the tree that Jesus cursed. The fig tree was green and looked healthy, but it lacked fruit. Even though it was not in season to bear its summer fruit, according to Herbert Lockyer in his book, *All the Parables of the Bible*, the tree had failed to produce its first initial fruits that came even before the leaves to benefit the Lord when He walked past it; therefore, He cursed it.[13] Like the fig tree, these people look productive, but they have no real fruit that identifies them to the kingdom of God. Since they desire the world, they will never come to a season in their life in which they will truly benefit God's kingdom or bring glory to Jesus; that is, until they truly repent of their insidious masquerade.

Perhaps you somewhat relate to some aspect of the sandbox Christian. You need to give the Lord permission to shake your sandy foundation of self-worth as a means to expose and convict you, providing the means for you to repent of your self-serving, idolatrous pursuits of the world. You need to mourn your pretense of being a Christian while pursuing the ways of the world. You need to choose to love the God of the Bible, rather than your personal reality. By embracing the truth and choosing to love God, you will experience true liberty from the wretchedness of your false reality, and avoid hearing Jesus' question, "And why call ye me, Lord, Lord, and do not the things which I say" (Luke 6:46)"?

---

[13] Mark 11:12-14; Luke 13:6-9

14

HALF-BAKED CHRISTIANS

When I consider the status of Christians who play around the fringes of the Christian life, while giving the appearance of being religious and pious, they remind me of half-baked Christians. This is where people have been exposed to enough religion that they have somewhat been tempered by it in their practices, but they remain fleshly in their view about the matters of God and life as they pursue the different elements of the world that have gained their attention. Since they expose one aspect of themselves to religion, you have people who appear pious, but when you taste the fruit of their lives, they will prove to be doughy, inconsistent, and undone.

I was first introduced to the concept of half-baked Christians when I was studying the tribe of Ephraim. Ephraim was the younger of the two sons of Joseph. Since Reuben had lost his status as the first-born son due to committing fornication with one of his father's concubines, it was passed on to the oldest son in Jacob's union with Rachel, Joseph. Although the custom was to pass the birthright to the older son of Joseph, it was prophesied that the seed of the younger brother, Ephraim, would be greater than the older brother, Manasseh.[14]

It is interesting to follow the course that the descendants of these two brothers walked. When you consider that the tribe of Manasseh became divided when one group laid claim to the Promised Land, and the rest of them would end up on the other side of the Jordan River, you realize why it became weak in its own way. You cannot divide something without compromising its strength.[15]

Out of Ephraim would come the first king of the northern kingdom of Israel, Jeroboam, exalting it to the forefront as a tribe who would influence and lead Israel.[16] We can see where God used Jeroboam to contend with Solomon and his son about the oppressive taxes they were putting on the people of Israel. The fact that he had been used as an instrument of God revealed that Jeroboam had been exposed to Jehovah God, but when his commitment towards the one true God of heaven was being challenged, we see another side of him that revealed that he was half-baked and would remain quite undone before the Lord.

---

[14] Genesis 48:17-20; 49:3-4, 22-26;
[15] Numbers 32:31-40; Joshua 1:12-17
[16] 1 Kings 11:26-40; 12:2-24

As king, Jeroboam became concerned that if he did not provide some religious life for the people under his auspice that he would lose some of his subjects to the house of David, the southern kingdom of Israel. The result of this king's insecure, fearful conclusion is that he started the northern kingdom of Israel into a downward spiral into idolatry that ended with its demise as a nation 200 years before the kingdom of Judah fell to Babylon.[17]

The question is how does an individual begin with God but end in blatant idolatry? If you follow the descendants of Ephraim, you can begin to see how religion may temper some aspects of a person's life, but is unable to bring him or her to any real spiritual growth or completion. This digression will also reveal why man's religion is never enough. The Christian life is meant to completely transform or revolutionize an individual from within.

In Hosea 5 we see the Lord lamenting the spiritual fornication that the people of Ephraim (also known as Israel in Scripture) had been committing. The people did not know the Lord God. In their idolatrous ways they had become prideful, had dealt treacherously with the Lord, and did not see that they were about ready to fall into utter destruction because of their iniquity. Even though they would seek the Lord, they would not be able to find Him. In the end, they would be left desolate, broken in judgment, and sick from their rotting ways. The prophet Hosea would describe Ephraim as a cake that was not turned, or what I would call half-baked.[18]

What kind of heart would a half-baked state produce in a person? According to Hosea, Ephraim was willing to hire lovers for her protection and was like a silly dove that flitted from one idol to another, but was found to be *heartless* towards the matters of God. The people of Ephraim had erected many altars to their idols. Such altars would be counted as sin by God, eventually left broken down, desolate, silent, unused, and useless.[19] Clearly, there was no spiritual maturity to be found in Ephraim. The people were untamed, unpredictable, and juvenile concerning what was important to their spiritual well-being.

Even though the people of Ephraim proved to be silly on one side, on the other side was fierceness that revealed just how unpredictable they were in their loyalty and life. Like their ensign, the bull, they were ready to push all opposition back when push came to shove. We see this in the case of wartime efforts. The men of Ephraim were ready to go to battle and occasionally became insulted when they were not called to be part of the wartime effort. Yet, we are told that they failed to drive out the Canaanites from their inheritance.[20]

---

[17] 1 Kings 12:26-33
[18] Hosea 7:8
[19] Hosea 7:11; 8:9, 10:1-2
[20] Judges 1:29; 3:26-30; 7:24-25; 8:1-2

Developing Our Christian Life

In today's Christendom, it is not unusual to encounter those who are ice cold towards anything that challenges their way of thinking. When you consider what is behind such people, you realize that they have constantly exposed themselves to unholy mixtures of partial truths that have been undermined with lies. Various false, heretical preachers and teachers have flooded the airwaves of so-called "Christian" radio and TV stations for the past four decades with these lies. These dammed, foolish, heretical infidels send forth their mixture of so-called "Scriptural truths" and "revelations" that have been cleverly laced with poisonous heresies to promote their own personal kingdoms. The more these deluded followers expose themselves to the unholy damnable, deadly mixture of these false ministers, the colder and more unreasonable they become towards truths that would otherwise challenge them.

Randy (not his real name) had a genuine testimony of salvation from sin through Jesus Christ. His life changed 180 degrees, and he sought for ways to serve the Lord through his many talents and abilities. Unfortunately, Randy was not properly discipled in the truths of God's Word. Thus, like so many others, he found his niche in Christendom by tuning in to the many false teachers and heretics on "Christian" TV. In addition, the churches he sought out and attended helped to lay the same false foundation.

Because Randy lacked the bedrock of biblical truth by which to discern and test the spirit behind what he exposed himself to, he was thoroughly indoctrinated in the "positive confession" or "faith in faith" mind-science dogma. Therefore, on those occasions when he fellowshipped with Christians who had a biblical perspective about matters, he would become confused and unable to fully comprehend what people were saying because it didn't fit into his mental frame of reference.

One Christian leader warned him more than once to turn off TBN and get into the Word. He stubbornly ignored this advice and continued to embrace unbiblical teachings. As time went on, his attitude noticeably began to change towards those who maintained the truths of Scripture, and it became almost impossible to communicate with him from a sound biblical standpoint.

Where the people of Ephraim were concerned, there was a real absence of personal integrity or character. They appeared to decide their own moral code as they maintained a fierce attitude about their independence. They could prove to be brave on the one hand, but due to a heretical, worldly mixture they could easily be rendered complacent and unreasonable on the other hand. In a sense, they held to what I would consider an *impractical gospel* that served their fierce independence and worldly view of life.

When we consider the impractical gospel, we realize it is comprised of rigid rules and standards that are put on others, while covering up a personal state of paganism. These rules and standards prove to be heartless as they judge and condemn those who are considered inferior because they do not live up to these people's ridiculous and unpredictable religious notions or ideas.

I have encountered the same scenario in half-baked Christians. There are those Christians who may have a religious side to them, in that they can prove to be quite noble about religious beliefs and causes, but flip them over and you will discover a side that is fierce in maintaining their independence as they insist on life according to their terms and whims. If challenged, such individuals can prove to be heartless as they charge against being brought into line with that which is righteous and godly. On one side these individuals may appear to be tempered by religion, but turn them over and you will soon discover someone who will not be tamed by any part of the Christian life. They prefer their worldly perversion as they flit from one fleshly desire or idol to another. They will never concede to true righteousness, but they will succumb to the fleshly ways, while becoming complacent and content to be half-baked in their commitment and devotion to God.

Even though they may erect an altar to God in their heart, they are like the people of Israel during the days of the prophet of Elijah; they will neglect the altar to God as they sacrifice on the many other altars erected to their fleshly idols. They may try to console themselves that they have some remembrance of their God in their midst, but the reality is that the altar of God is unused because it is not preferred.[21]

We knew a man we will call Jake who was a prime example of such a Christian. He could talk the talk profusely, and charm the spots off a leopard, but in his personal, private life, he lacked the necessary discipline to walk the walk. Jake could become very emotional about Jesus, and he could give a good defense of the written Word. However, when it came to totally selling out and giving up his right to himself, Jake balked. Suddenly he would throw up a wall of confusion, which was often reinforced by intense anger.

In Jake's cycle he wanted attention, as well as affirmation that he was "okay" and on his way to heaven; yet, he often found himself in a pit of deep depression and self-loathing because of besetting sin. When confronted with the fact that he loved his sin more than he loved God, he would confess it and feel remorse about it, but there never was any real repentance or genuine change in his life.

Half-baked Christians refuse to consecrate their lives totally to God. They may seek God, but they will resent His intrusion or suggestion that they must concede all of their life to him. They do not mind benefitting from being associated in some way with Him, but they will not give up their godless mixture that allows them to maintain their fierce attitude, heartless ways, and impractical gospel with it rigid rules and standards that they quickly apply to others to justify personal iniquity.

This unholy mixture simply reveals that at the core of these people is nothing more than paganism. Granted, they are idolatrous, but their ways

---

[21] 1 Kings 18:30

Developing Our Christian Life

are pagan. They are fierce, but it is because they are fleshly. They are ready to battle, but it is because they are contrary and desire self-glory and recognition. They may seem rigid in their religion, but such rules distract from their moral inconsistencies. They may be honest about their struggles, but it is a way to throw people off to the reality that they have no real intention of giving up their pagan or idolatrous preferences. They may even cry about their failures, but such tears are not towards the offences they have committed, but because they do not really want to lose that which has become dear to their way of living and being.

The truth of the matter is that it is easy to become a half-baked Christian. I know in my own personal life I have been such a Christian. It comes down to what we expose ourselves to. Most of us are content to expose ourselves to religion while refusing to expose ourselves to the penetrating, purging light of God. We do not want to be undone by God so that we can become completed in His Spirit in accordance to our high calling.

In such a pagan state, we have enough religion to put on a show, while making us delusional in regard to ourselves and unmercifully dangerous to those who unsuspectingly cross our path or challenge us in some way. In such a state, we can go off half-cocked with religious fervor in our causes, while arrogantly maintaining our rigid standard and being partially aware and ignorant of what is really going on. We can be quite content in presenting an impractical or foolish perception of our particular take on the Christian life, while missing the Spirit of God. It is the Spirit of God that brings discipline, wisdom, compassion, and real inspiration to our lives.

Sadly, in such a pagan state it is easy to remain content with our religious experiences, involvements, or causes, while failing to go all the way in our devotion to God. It is unproblematic to settle for a pious appearance while failing to possess any real fruit. It is convenient to hold onto our fleshly view of life while touting religious knowledge that can sound so wise to those who do not know us. It is so easy to maintain an outward façade while lacking inward character.

However, when people partake of our life, they will know differently. They will taste of a doughy substance that is repulsive in texture, undone in content, and unacceptable in quality. In the end, we will be regarded as silly, foolish, and untrustworthy.

When people partake of your life, what do they taste? Are you done on one side, but not on the other side? Are you just surface in your life and devotion with God or do you possess real substance?

***

We have considered different presentations of Christianity. As you can see, each presentation has it own attitude, light, gospel, heart condition, prevailing spirit, and spiritual state. Sadly, each presentation falls short of what real Christianity is meant to be. In each presentation, Jesus is subtly replaced with man, false lights, religious activities, the counterfeits of the world, and with an unacceptable state that is devoid of real faith and falls short of true holiness.

It is important to point out that all wrong spirits come under the auspice of the spirit of the world. There can also be more than one wrong spirit tormenting, driving, or oppressing those who open the doors of sin (rebellion and compromise), self, and the world.

Since we have considered these different presentations of Christianity by the variations of cloaks and masks that are apparent in the visible Church, thereby, exposing their attitudes to what is influencing them or how they perceive themselves, let us now summarize them in the following tables created by the religious environments and the world. Consider if you fit into any of these false categories. If you find you do, make sure you get it right with the Lord before you journey any further in your spiritual life, for as the Apostle Paul declared in 2 Corinthians 6:2 that today is the day of salvation or deliverance.

The following table on the next two pages reveals the religious perceptions of each type of Christian that has been outlined in this book.

Developing Our Christian Life

Presentation	Attitude	Light (View)	Gospel	Heart (Spirit)	State
Good Person	Do not need to be saved. (Good enough)	Personal Goodness (Amoral)	Cultural Gospel	Deceptive (Self-righteous)	Pride
Associate	I am okay due to my association.	Culturally Acceptable. Liberal Philosophy	Watered Down Gospel	Disconnected (Spirit of the Age)	Never really converted
Religious	Personal beliefs or points of identification	Mediator of some type. (Legalistic Elite)	Gospel of Personal Doctrine	Judgmental (Religious)	Cult Mentality
Sentimental	Adjustable Jesus according to feelings	Emotional Ecstasy (Selfishness)	Feel Good Gospel	Fickle (Perverted)	Unregenerate/ Fleshly
Social	Mixture of Christian principles and worldly attitude.	Social reform, causes, or promotion. (World's methods)	Social Gospel (Ensure worldly lifestyle)	Worldly (Spirit of the World)	Spiritual Fornication
Superstitious	Ignorance about God.	Wrong Foundation (Supernatural)	Gospel of Chance	Fearful/Uncertain (Antichrist)	Idolatrous
Super Spiritual	New Age	Spiritual Enlightenment	Mystic Gospel	Deluded (Seductive)	Spiritual Arrogance
Sanctimonious	Militant Attitude	Piousness (Rituals)	Gospel Of Works	Proud (Critical)	False Authority

Presentation	Attitude	Light (View)	Gospel	Heart (Spirit)	State
Short-sighted	Half-hearted	Easy Believism	Gospel of Convenience	Divided (Lust)	Spiritual Limbo
Skeptical	Worldly Philosophies	Presumption (Foolish)	Rational Gospel	Hard (Unbelief/ Mocking)	Suspended Judgment
Sandbox	They are Worthy	Christianity is a Platform	Self-serving Gospel	Unstable (Hypocritical)	Exalted State of Mind
Half-Baked	Fierce	Fleshly about God/life.	Impractical Gospel	Heartless (Untamed)	Paganism

15

WILL THE REAL CHRISTIAN TURN ASIDE?

I have discovered that one of the hardest realities that most Christians miss is the fact that they are not to live their life according to some religious creed or exercise; rather, they are actually living the life of Christ. The Apostle Paul clearly brought this fact out when he stated in Galatians 2:20 that because he (his old life) was crucified with Christ, even though he was living, he was living according to the life of Christ in him. He was in fact living this life in the flesh or in his earthly body or tabernacle by faith according to the character, life, and example of the Son of God.

The reason most Christians become dissatisfied with the Christian life is because they are basically living their own life, while adjusting their notions or concepts about Christ into their particular lifestyle. In other words, their Christian life has become man-centered and not Christ-centered. Without Christ as the center, one cannot live the Christian life.

Life outside of Christ in this present world will prove to be nominal at best. In such a life, there is nothing that really stands out in such an existence unless it is traumatic, overwhelming, or beyond mere comprehension. Instead of realizing that by assimilating Christ into the way we think and who we become by constantly challenging our nominal existence in this world with the eternal treasures of heaven, our sense of His life becomes lost or misplaced in the drudgery and foolishness of it all. When it comes to the life of Christ that we are called to live in our bodies, there is nothing nominal about it. It is the most challenging and rewarding life we could experience.

If we are really living the life of Christ, there must be a constant stirring of our inner, spiritual man to not lose a sense of possessing a discerning edge of His truth in this world. We must insist on steadfastness to maintain the integrity of the life of Christ, as well as stir up the necessary devotion or passion to make the right decisions in the midst of the various temptations that this current world will present.

In Exodus 3, we see a lone man by the name of Moses swallowed in the midst of drudgery in the wilderness. In the center of this drudgery, God intruded into his reality. Moses turned aside to consider the great thing that was taking place. Like Moses, we Christians need to turn aside to get our spiritual bearings. Perhaps we need to go back to the cross to remember our small beginnings. Maybe, we need to go back to the simplicity of the Gospel to regain our child-like trust. The Bible clearly reveals some places in which we can get a sense of our spiritual condition.

First, we must confront the problems before we can present the solutions. We have identified many of the problems in this book, but it is vital that we bring the immerging picture from each Christian masquerade together.

The first main problem has to do with Christians' attitude towards the world. As ministers of the Gospel, we constantly must challenge ourselves beyond what is considered nominal and acceptable Christianity according to the times we live in. We must honestly consider if our understanding and practices of Christianity truly represent the Christian life. After all, in our three decades of ministry together, Jeannette and I have witnessed the different so-called "phases", "movements", "fads", and "beliefs" that have rolled through Christendom in America. We have been aware of how many in the Church appear to be conditioned according to the influence of the world. In some cases, the influence of the worldly systems has greatly come into the visible Church to the point that there appears to be no distinction. In some ways, the Christianity of today has been rendered into just another subculture in America that needs to become tolerant towards other cultures to become competitive. This competitiveness will supposedly give the "Church" the opportunity to show Christianity's so-called "love". On the other hand, it is clear that the world has never been rooted out of numerous individuals that claim some type of Christian heritage.

There are a couple of reasons for this condition. One, is people have not been properly discipled. The second reason is because there is no distinction or real challenge coming from the majority of the pulpits, calling for separation from the world. Therefore, those who sit in the pews have never really been discipled to love God, nor have they learned what it truly means to follow Jesus in obedience. This has caused these people to interpret Christianity according to the world, and to adjust their understanding of it to the world's philosophies, ways, and practices. Again, from this premise there is no real distinction.

Although the influence of the world has always been the major challenge for all of God's people, it has also been made clear that in order to properly love, serve, and follow God, His people must separate from the influence of the world, and stand distinct in disposition, attitude, and conduct as a peculiar or special people.[1] Such distinction would prove that God's people belonged to Him, and not the present age.

God's people were also to reflect His light in the midst of the world's grave darkness. They were commissioned to represent the ways of God by being holy, obedient, and upright in all matters according to their high calling.

---

[1] Deuteronomy 14:2: 1 Peter 2:9

Each age has presented different challenges to God's people, but at the core of each challenge, temptation, or point of defeat is the world's influence upon their hearts and minds. When the children of Israel came into the Promised Land, God told them to rid themselves of the temptations that would present themselves in the idolatrous and pagan practices of the people of the land. If they failed to root out such influences, these people and their pagan ways would eventually become terrible snares to them and bring judgment upon them.[2]

We know that the children of Israel did not root out idolatry and pagan practices. Although they took these pagan people captive to use as slaves, their idolatrous and pagan ways eventually took the people of Israel captive. In the end, they ended up with an unholy mixture that eventually brought them down as a kingdom, and caused them to be dispersed throughout the world as a form of judgment.

The Church has been called to separate itself from that which harbors a wrong spirit.[3] Sadly, once again there is no real distinction to be found in some of the presentations and activities of what is referred to as the Church. In such a state of mixture God is often being redefined, Jesus is rendered into a vague, controllable concept, while a different gospel is developed, the Word is used to justify deviant beliefs and practices, and personal reality of piousness exalts the individual to a place of arrogance. Such a place allows people to be god of their particular reality, making them judge and jury towards all that would dare to contradict or challenge their so-called "truth".

As Christians, what must we do when such insanity rules in the religious world? Should we simply become part of the scene to keep the peace and maintain an appearance that is acceptable to others? Or, do we flee in order to seek out the place or person where we can begin to truly hear the voice of our Shepherd speaking to us? Either way, we are going to incur some type of wrath, either from those with whom we refuse to play their particular game, or from God who never changes, adjusts, or bows down to such an absurd environment.

The harsh reality about Jesus is that the world hated Him. He said of Himself that He would prove to be an offense to many.[4] He enraged the religious leaders, insulted some of His disciples to such an extent that they ceased to follow Him, and frightened others because of the changes that became apparent due to the power of His presence in their midst. Jesus understood that what offended people the most was His truth.

Jesus' uncompromising truth exposed the deviant cloaks of the religious people, and cut across the various realities of those who followed Him to expose their prejudices, limited understanding, and unbelief. He exposed the false piety of those at His hometown and the utter darkness of the world. As a result, He was worshipped by some,

---

[2] Joshua 23:12-13
[3] 2 Corinthians 6:14-18
[4] John 6:60-66; 17:14-18

hated by others, and tasted the cruel indifference of those who did not think it was important to even consider Him.

As the world is winding down to the climatic event of Jesus' second coming, this insanity is clearly abounding in our present age. My suggestion is quite simple, we need to turn aside from all of our activities regardless of how religious and good they may seem, and truly examine whether we are in the true faith that was first delivered to the saints. We must start at our altar, the cross of Christ, and choose to remember we have been purged from our sins, for some have forgotten their small beginning and have become barren in their knowledge of Jesus. It is such remembrance that will establish a right environment, allowing for God's presence to make itself known.[5] But, once again, we must do this by faith.

This brings us to another major problem that plagues God's people, that of unbelief. Wherever the world has made inroads into the lives of God's people, the snare of unbelief will be in operation. Jesus asked if He would find real faith when He returned. Once again, we are reminded of how the Apostle Paul talked about the true faith in 2 Corinthians 13:5, "Examine yourselves, whether you are in the faith; prove yourselves. Know ye not yourselves how Jesus Christ is in you, except ye be reprobates."

As believers, we are told that our faith must be towards God, not this world or personal abilities and accomplishments. Such faith is not about changing reality, but about being able to walk through the challenging times of life while maintaining total reliance on God. It is about clinging to the Rock while all else is caving in, trusting His character when the waves of uncertainty are about to destroy all we know to be true. It is about standing on His promises when our confidence in the Rock is being threatened by uncontrollable circumstances that are about to consume us in hopeless despair. Since unfeigned faith is the only way we can truly please God, it is what assures us that He will be in the midst of our lives.[6]

Once again, we must remind ourselves that genuine faith means we will approach God's Word to believe it as truth with the intention of obeying it. The Apostle Paul summarized this by stating that faith comes by hearing, and hearing by the Word of God.[7] Clearly, what we believe must be based on the Word of God. However, many people do not approach the Word to believe it, but to judge it as they justify, adjust, or fit it into their personal religious concepts. Since the Word contains the revelation of God, these same people fail to discover who He is, and because they have no real revelation of God, His presence will be missing as they devise a different Jesus.

---

[5] 2 Peter 1:3-9
[6] Luke 18:8; Hebrews 11:6
[7] Romans 10:17

True faith leads us into our life with Jesus. The Apostle Paul put it best when he asked if the believer really understood that his or her life was hidden in Christ. He is the bread that we as believers must daily partake of by faith and assimilate through obedience. He is also the well that contains the rivers of Living Water that we must freely drink from if we are going to experience the abundant and eternal qualities of His life. Once again, we must remind ourselves that it is not our life we are living, but His life. It takes child-like faith in God to give way to His Spirit as He works this life in us. It is His Spirit who leads us by faith into this glorious life that is free, rich, and glorious.[8] Such a life serves as the living, eternal presence of God in us.

As we have considered the different faces of Christianity, we must note that because of unbelief towards God and His Word, many religious people have faulty foundations. People who possess such a wrong foundation have failed to believe the Word of God at some point. Such unbelief opens for another problem to take center stage, that of coming under another spirit. Depending on these people's emphasis, the spirit of the world that is working disobedience in their life can influence them. If religion is a major emphasis, these people can come under a religious spirit, causing them to mishandle the Word of truth, as they adjust everything to their religious perception. Still, some have come under an antichrist spirit that will clearly establish them on a different foundation that will delude them. Sadly, each person who is walking in the dark arena of this age has been marked to taste consequences or God's wrath.[9]

Each person who has a wrong foundation and spirit will reflect a different light or life. For the religious, they will reflect the false, harsh light of self-righteousness. In the case of those who are pursuing the ways of self, they will reflect the vainglory of pride, and when it comes to the world, these people will reflect the fading glory of that which is surface, temporary, foolish, and doomed.

As Christians, we must examine whether we are truly walking according to the light or life of Jesus in us. Such a light will expose all sin and illuminate our Christian walk according to the spiritual insight or understanding that has been unveiled to us by His Spirit. However, the intensity of this light will vary according to the level of Jesus' life that is in us.

The diversity of lights reminds me of the seven churches in Revelation 2-3. Jesus threatened to remove some of these church's candlesticks because they were not reflecting the essence of His life. The Church of Ephesus was reflecting commendable works, but lacked Jesus' true likeness because these people were not compelled by a love for Him and because of Him. The reflection of Jesus in the Church of Smyrna was being refined in persecution. This church was told to be

---

[8] John 6:35; 7:37-39; Romans 8:14-17; Galatians 2:20; Colossians 3:3
[9] Romans 1:18; Ephesians 2:2; 2 John 7-11

faithful unto death. The Churches of Pergamum and Thyatira had commendable qualities, but they both had unholy mixtures. One allowed heretical doctrine into its midst, while the other one came into union with spiritual harlotry or idolatry. Therefore, their lights were being perverted and defiled. Sardis' light could not be seen for the life was gone, while the Philadelphia Church had little strength, but kept His Word and had not denied His name. As a result, a door was opened through which its members could enter. The final church was Laodicea, the church that perceived itself as being rich, but was considered wretched because of its lukewarm spiritual state. It is at the end of the challenge to each church that Jesus reminded His people that the presence of His life and fellowship was what will ensure that their particular candlesticks would remain in place as a burning light to those who were lost and seeking, "Behold, I stand at the door, and knock; if any man hear my voice, and open the door, I will come in to him, and will sup with him, and he with me" (Revelation 3:20).

The different foundations and lights of Christians are also fueled by the gospel they adhere to. This brings us to another problem as well as one of the aspects of our lives we need to examine, and that has to do with the Gospel. As we have seen, different gospels can embrace denominations, works, or such emphasis as love. Some people think the good news is being part of a religious group. Others believe that their works will gain them recognition, and then there are those who think if they display a sentimental, wimpy love that people will be attracted to it causing them to accept some type of religious perception or affiliation. Once again, we are saved by God's grace, which is received by faith. To add something to the redemption of Christ such as church affiliation or works is to pervert the true Gospel, stripping it of its power to save.[10]

The Bible is clear that our works do not save us; rather, we are saved unto good works. Good works naturally accompany salvation, but do not necessarily serve as a proof of it. As Jesus stated, "Let your light so shine before men, that they may see your good words, and glorify your Father, who is in heaven" (Matthew 5:16). Remember, such light also represents the presence of our Lord's life and glory in our midst.

Genuine faith walks hand in hand with God's love. Love motivates the type of life we are to live by faith, but faith ultimately embraces the life we are called to live according to godly love, and begins to walk it out in obedience. Jesus stated that if we love Him, we will obey Him. This shows us that God's love is not one sided as it has been presented by many in Christendom. The lopsided and unrealistic presentation of over-emphasizing the love of God often serves as a sick substitute for failure to preach the Gospel and invest Christ in the lives of people through proper discipleship. However, improper spiritual emphasis will frustrate His grace, preventing salvation from truly taking place in a person's life.[11]

---

[10] Galatians 1:6-9
[11] John 14:15; Galatians 2:21; 5:6

Developing Our Christian Life

As Christians, we know God's love serves as a genuine solution to the many issues confronting the Church, but few understand what it is and how it truly operates. The love that many are clinging too or hiding behind in the religious arena is not godly love, but worldly sentiment. This is evident when people are quick to sacrifice truth to maintain some type of façade of agreement or peace in the name of love. Keep in mind, love does not rejoice in iniquity but in the truth, for truth is able to set the captive free.

People who cling to their foolish idea of love, instead of to the Rock of Jesus, are not interested in the love of God, but in the idea of love. Such ideas are always self-serving and unrealistic; therefore, the ideas are quick to resent truth that would challenge the fickleness and hypocrisy of such emotional nonsense. This prideful, self-serving love will always prove to be very touchy, and can become quickly offended when people do not bow down to it. It is clearly contrary to the love of God as described in 1 Corinthians 13.

Such individuals also use the idea of love to bring people into agreement with their perverted reality, causing bondage to those who embrace their false presentations. This worldly love is used to promote "ecumenicalism" and "political correctness." However, such love has no regard for the eternal destiny of souls. It avoids confronting sin, becomes offended by truth, and mocks true righteousness.

Back in April of 1991, a pastor's wife wanted to share about God's love with the congregation of their local body. She asked Jeannette about her understanding concerning our Creator's incredible love. Consider Jeannette's following insightful description of it. Although the pastor's wife disregarded it altogether, and chose to ride the sentimental wave of the world's perverted presentation of love to stir up the emotions of those present, she did receive an insightful contrast and challenge to her personal perception of the world's fickle, fleshly love.

> "Until we realize how depraved we really are, we will never even remotely begin to comprehend how <u>great</u> the love of God is. The higher we elevate self (humanity) the narrower the distance becomes between the sinner and the Savior, thus minimizing our understanding of the unfathomable love of God.
>
> "But, once a sinner glimpses the glory, majesty, and holiness of God Almighty, then he will cry "Woe is me; for I am a man of unclean lips." Truly, he who has been forgiven much loves much!
>
> "To represent man as being anything other than what the Bible describes him of being is to cheat the sinner of the joy of true repentance and forgiveness, and puts the preacher in danger of wrongly dividing the Word of God. It diminishes the truth of the great unchanging love of God.
>
> "We should never be guilty of minimizing the extent of the fallen state of man for fear of failing to maximize the unchanging love of God. Christ, rather than humanity, must be exalted. By elevating

humanity and de-elevating God, the sinner is put into the position of choosing who his savior...self (because he's "not so bad"), or God (whose nature has been badly misrepresented).

"We must always preach TRUTH—it always edifies because it sets us <u>free</u>. Flattery fails to set people free, but rather fosters corruption.

"Thus we see that the unchanging love of God is understood in greater measure when we also understand the lengths to which He had to reach to lift us up!"

The main problem with the Christian life is that most believers forget it is all about relationship with God. Clearly, religion points to practice, but not necessarily relationship with God. Causes and works point to deeds, but can prove to be indifferent to any real relationship. Sentiment speaks of feelings, but does not serve as a basis for the steadfast commitment that must be present in a relationship. Spiritual experiences speak of an encounter with the unseen world, but relationship with God speaks of actually experiencing His reality in a personal way that will transform a person. Piety points to some form of personal holiness, but it does not necessarily identify a person to a personal relationship with the holy God of heaven.

When relationship with God is missing, there is only one response that will change the direction that a person is walking in, and that is repentance. Repentance will bring straying Christians back to the place of forgiveness for failing to properly love, honor, and serve God. It will end with reconciling them back into a relationship with God, thereby ensuring spiritual restoration of their status as His children, their spiritual inheritance that is waiting for them, and their place in Christ. True repentance is always taking responsibility for one's true spiritual condition by the renunciation of sin for either breaching the Law of God or omitting righteous responsibilities that have been clearly established by His covenant. It is a complete turn about from walking in the ways of sin and death, and walking in a complete opposite direction towards the true light of the world.

Scripture points out that the one way leads to hell, but the other way leads back to God, to His presence, and the life He has prepared for each us as His children. When we make such a change, we have one goal in mind and that is to respond by faith in obedience to what has been clearly established by God in His Word. Such repentance will result in a changed inner life that will clearly produce the love of God. God's love will compel us to pursue His righteous ways, love His unchangeable truths, and receive the fullness of His everlasting life.

As long as God's presence is missing in matters, Christianity will miss the mark of fulfilling it highest potential to reflect His glory. If the Christian life recedes into the nominal ways of the world, it will lack the boldness of the Spirit and the passion of Christ's life to inspire the person to experience the fullness of God. If Christianity simply serves as an outward cloak, there will be no spirit or life to it. If it is simply tacked on, it ultimately becomes a reproach to all that is pure, righteous, and holy.

This is why those who call themselves Christians must step aside to examine if they are truly in the faith, possess His love, and walk according to His life. If they find they are lacking in their consecrated life in Christ, then they must come to the place of true repentance in a spirit of contrition and brokenness. From this premise they must choose the way of self-denial, total death to the world, and complete abandonment to Christ to truly strive to live a life that clearly reflects Christ.

Obviously, what we Christians reflect, stand for, and truly confess, not only with our mouths, but also by our lives that serve as visible living epistles to others, will determine what Jesus will say to us on judgment day. The question that I continue to ask myself as a means to test my relationship with Him is would He acknowledge me as a faithful servant and identify me as a friend, or will He declare He never knew me. As a faithful servant, I will be able to rejoice in the assurance of being in His presence forever, and as His friend, I can joyfully live in expectation of beholding His glory in immeasurable ways for ages to come. But, if my life on earth causes me to become a person that He does not recognize on judgment day, all I will have to look forward to is to live in a Christless eternity in utter despair and spiritual ruin. For this reason, I must soberly examine whether I am in the true faith that was first delivered to the saints. And, with the same sober intensity, I adjure you to honestly examine whether you are in the faith.

Let us now sincerely consider the possibility of losing our substandard idea of the Christian life that can be easily adopted in this present age. Consider for a moment what would it profit you if your so-called "goodness" is considered filthy rags to God, your real association is not with God but with death, your religion is lifeless, your good works considered reprobate, your causes lack no real eternal significance, your spiritual experiences are fleshly or demonically inspired, and your piousness is nothing more than an unacceptable wedding garment that will end up identifying you as one who will be cast into outer darkness?[12]

Perhaps in this examination, it is revealed that your self-life perceives that it can maintain its rights, while giving an appearance of godliness. However, such a concept is self-delusional because the self-life is void of any godliness or means to please God. Therefore, are you willing to lose your right as a child of God to maintain your personal rights to the self-life? Granted, the world placates all religious notions about God, but it does so in order to hide its hatred and unbelief for Him. You can buy the worldly delusion about the matters of God, but are you willing to ultimately lose your soul?

There is a cost to possess the Christian life. To the self-life, the cost will appear noble but not convenient and acceptable. After all, it will cost self its right to reign. The world will mock and reject such a notion

---

[12] Matthew 22:11-14

because it will cost all identification and agreement with the world. However, we must honestly count the necessary cost to acquire this heavenly life or suffer the loss of our souls, our place in God's kingdom, and an eternal inheritance.

With this in mind, what price are you willing to pay? Perhaps you must consider what you are unwilling to pay in order to consider what you must choose to pay in the end. Will you pay the cost of your existence in this present world or your soul in the next world? Will you give way to the preference of death and hell because is it easy on the self-life and attractive to the flesh? Or, will you choose God's everlasting life by deciding to disown self and crucify the flesh as a means to put to death the influence of the world on your life, while giving way to the Spirit and Word of God to follow Jesus? There are only two choices: the Lord or Satan, two different prices: life or death, two diverse ways: obedience or sin, two types of realities: truth or delusion, and two dissimilar destinations: heaven or hell. Now you must honestly choose what you ultimately want to possess in lieu of counting the necessary cost.

What way will you choose? Your choice will determine what type of Christianity you are reflecting to the world. Does it truly identify you to the life of Christ that is being lived according to unfeigned faith in Him, or does it reflect the selfishness of self or the ignorance and resentment of the world towards the matters of God? The truth is, you are either denying Christ by your present life, or you are denying any association or relationship with the world. Heed Jesus' words,

> Whosoever, therefore, shall confess me before men, him will I confess also before my Father, who is in heaven. But whosoever shall deny me before men, him will I also deny before my Father, who is in heaven. Think not that I am come to send peace on earth; I came not to send peace, but a sword (Matthew 10:32-34).

Book Two

POSSESSING OUR SOULS

By
Rayola Kelley

INTRODUCTION

As I watch the time we live in spiral out of control, my question is, as believers, what must we do to be prepared for the world around us as it drastically changes? The insanity that presently exists is even now appearing to give way to total fear, as people's hearts grow colder and more indifferent to the virtues that bring value to life.

From all appearances, we are in the end days. Whether it is the end days as far as watching the demise of the American way of life, or whether it is the end days as mentioned in the Bible when Satan's one-world government, economic, and religious system take center stage, we are most assuredly witnessing many frightening realities occurring around us. We must be honest about the signs in order to properly discern the days in which we live. We also must be prepared to face such days.

When I consider God's instructions concerning the end days, one of the things that stands out is that believers are told to watch. In other words, we must be alert and vigilant as to what is happening around us. This is important if we are not to be caught off guard by events that could swallow us in hopelessness, causing us to deny the true faith once delivered to the saints.

This is why the Scripture tells us to stand and withstand. We must stand on truth by faith towards God, withstand with truth according to faith in God, and stand because of truth that is clinging to the eternal Rock because of faith firmly established on God. It is with such steadfastness directed towards our Lord that we are going to maintain the integrity of the faith that has been entrusted to us. "Standing" does not point to advancement, but to maintaining the territories of our spiritual lives that have been established in our relationship with God through Jesus Christ. It also means we will be ready to stand when our present life, or the world around us, caves in.

We are also to pray. But what are we to pray for? Are we to pray in regard to being spared from such times? The reality is that the sun shines on both the wicked and the righteous, just as the rain falls on both. Clearly, blessings from above are afforded to both groups of people, as well as the consequences of sin that plagues the world. We all have to face the harsh realities of life. No one person has been made an exception to the sorrow, losses, and tragedies that confront people during their journey through their particular age.

The Bible does instruct us to pray that we are counted worthy to avoid tasting the bitterness of the tribulation that will be upon the earth in the last days. But, what does it mean to possess such an environment that God would spare us in such a way? We know that because Noah found grace in God's eyes that he was instructed to prepare an ark of safety and deliverance, allowing him and his family to be spared from tasting God's judgment over the whole earth. Clearly, the Bible tells us what to pray about in such times. However, my prayer is simple if I am to be offered up in uncertain times, "Lord, like the apostle Paul, I want to be able to say that I have fought a good fight, finished the course, and kept the faith."

Since the Bible has instructed believers to be watchful, ready, and in prayer, can we assume that this points to the proper environment in which confidence in God can ensure deliverance in, through, or from such times? No doubt these three actions to maintain our life in God point to personal preparation. However, there is also another important Scripture that gives insight into the type of environment that must exist for believers to stand in tumultuous times. It is found in Luke 21:19, "In your patience possess ye your souls."

The instruction in Luke 21:19 sounds wise, but what does it mean to possess our souls in patience? Such an instruction reveals that it is not optional for us to seize our souls. Clearly, it is vital that our souls are properly maintained to ensure the right inward environment in these uncertain times. This book is going to answer such a question in regard to possessing our souls with the hope of instructing, encouraging, and edifying God's people in this day.

Are you ready to come to terms with what it means to possess your soul?

1

WHAT IS THE SOUL?

What does it mean to possess our soul? Notice we have the responsibility to possess our own soul. But, before we can honestly possess our own soul, we must understand what constitutes the soul. The Apostle Paul stated that we are made up of body, soul, and spirit. The Bible instructs us to love God with all of our heart, soul, mind, and strength.[1] These different compartments, elements, or arenas point to the inner working of the unseen man.

It is important to distinguish these different arenas of the inner man in order to bring a proper perspective to the soul. The two most valuable resources that enable one to understand these different elements, besides the Word of God, are *Strong's Exhaustive Concordance of the Bible* and *Vine's Expository Dictionary of Biblical Words.*[2]

When we think of heart, we think of our physical heart. However, the heart of man determines what will motivate and influence a person. It represents the inner being that we often relate to as being the source or substance that brings an inner knowing to us about the matters of life.[3] It also will determine what will ultimately rule man. In a sense, the heart serves as the connection between the spirit and soul. The condition of the heart will establish the condition or state of man's spirit. Man's spirit will establish the inclinations of the heart. Clearly the heart serves as the bridge that connects the motivation of the spirit to that which will inspire the soul.

Granted, this information may seem somewhat confusing to some people. The words "spirit" and "soul" are interchanged at times in Scripture, but I believe that the soul may house the spirit. Regardless of their location to one another, there must be a connection between the spirit and soul because they have separate functions that clearly influence each other. We can call such a connection a door, avenue, or some type of entryway. The heart or inner being of who a man is and who he is inclined to become serves as the entryway between these two unseen compartments.

This brings us to the spirit. Spirit can be related to the very breath or air that we take in. The type of breath or air that we take in will determine how we live life. For example, Adam was a living soul. This meant God put His very breath or spirit in him as a means to relate and interact with

---

[1] Mark 12:29-31; 1 Thessalonians 5:23
[2] In Strong's Concordance see the (NT) # 1271, 4151 & 5590
[3] Proverbs 4:23

Him on a spiritual level, making him a spiritual man. When Adam rebelled against God, God's breath or Spirit departed, leaving Adam an earthly man, bound by the air, elements, and laws of earth. He became soulish in the sense that the air or breath he now relied on was from the earth; therefore, he could only interact with the earthly environment around him from a fleshly premise.

Since the spirit is unseen, it actually serves as the vital principle as to the type of life we will live, as well as develop in these earthly tabernacles or bodies. It represents what we would refer to as the higher state of man. The reason for this is because only the unseen and spiritual can affect the spirit of man. This aspect of man is what distinguishes him from the rest of creation since God formed this very spiritual element in man in order to bestow upon him the life principle of His Spirit. It is from the life principle of His Spirit that the very power of God's life will flow through the inner being of a person, identifying him or her as a spiritual man who belongs to that which is heavenly.

It is the activities within the spirit that will determine the type of character that is being established in man. Character points to the moral qualities of a person. Such qualities will determine the very disposition or inner state. The disposition of man points to what a man will be naturally inclined towards. Keep in mind that the inward character determines a person's particular bent towards the matters of life.

There are only two ways people can be bent. They can be bent towards the things of the self-life and the world, or they can be inclined towards the heavenly matters of God. When people are bent towards bowing down to self according to the world, they will be inclined to walk in the ways of the world. If they are directed heavenwards towards God, they will be upright in character as they pursue after, are guided by, and learn how to walk in the Spirit of God.

Such people's vision is beyond this present world, always focusing on that which is unseen by the physical eyes. They are walking according to an inner voice, a heavenly drumbeat of all that is contrary to the world. This spiritual walk causes those of the world to become uncomfortable. Contrast of this nature can cause persecution to come upon those who refuse to be bent towards the self-serving ways of the present age they live in.

As we consider the heart, we must now come to terms with the mind. One would think that there is not much difference between the heart and the mind. According to Jesus, the heart is the springboard to the issues of life. Clearly, the heart influences the mind, but the mind is what connects the heart to the worldly activities surrounding a person. It will often reinforce the heart in its deceptive ways, adjusting the matters confronting a person according to his or her own point of view.

The mind serves as a seat of reflective consciousness. In other words, it determines how we perceive the world around us. Perception will determine how we judge and approach matters that we see or witness. Our approach will be based on our moral reflection of the issue, which is often referred to as our worldview. Therefore, the mind is motivated by what we value or regard in light of the type of moral character that is being established in our inner man or heart. The mind will reflect how we understand an issue. This is why Jesus instructs His disciples to beware of how they perceive or hear a matter. They may perceive it according to their own darkness or personal take on life.[4]

The reflection of the mind will find its source in our sentiment or attitude. Again, this may seem confusing, but we must remember what motivates our logic. It will be influenced by our values. Values will be determined by our agendas and priorities, which will find their support based according to our heart condition.[5]

The Spirit of God must renew the mind before it can function properly. In other words, before one can think in an upright manner, the mind must be changed or transformed by the Spirit.[6] As the mind is transformed, it will be able to perceive, receive, and properly respond to the things of God.

It is in the mind that we choose to remember, regard, or consider something in light of what is influencing our way of thinking or perceiving. There are two types of minds mentioned in Scripture: the carnal mind and the spiritual mind. The type of mind we must possess is a mind that can be influenced by the Spirit of God. A mind that will consider a matter in light of the spiritual is a mind that will have the interest of heaven as a focus and priority. It is a mind that constantly chooses the ways of God to meditate on. It wants to be enlarged in its understanding in order to embrace the revelation of the eternal. After all, spiritual truths must be revealed by the Spirit of God and received in the heart as truth before the mind can be enlarged to receive it as a revelation.[7]

Heavenly inspired revelations that are walked out in obedience become a reality in the conscious mind. This allows the person to discern the spirit or intent of a situation in order to come to a proper judgment. This is what Jesus meant when He instructed His followers to judge with righteous judgment in John 7:24. As Christians, we cannot properly judge unless we start from the right premise.

It is in the mind that we can come into agreement. The Bible talks about being likeminded.[8] This is where two minds meet together as one in spirit and truth. If the Holy Spirit motivates the spirit of a person, such agreement will be confirmed by truth. It is in such spiritual agreement that those who are likeminded can reason together.

The prophet Isaiah tells us that God desires to reason with us about our sin.[9] Once the person agrees with God's evaluation about a matter,

---

[4] Matthew 6:23; Luke 8:18
[5] Matthew 15:16-20
[6] Romans 12:2; Ephesians 4:23-24
[7] Romans 8:5-7; 1 Corinthians 2:9-13
[8] Romans 15:5-6; Philippians 2:2
[9] Isaiah 1:18

such reasoning can bring agreement between man and God. This is especially true in the area of personal sin where one needs to confess it in order to seek forgiveness and deliverance as a means to come into agreement with God.

As we consider how each area is reflected in a person, we can see where the spirit and heart are reflected through the person's very countenance. For the mind, it is reflected through our notions, opinions, judgments, and ideas. If we prove to be stiff-necked instead of humble about our conclusions, we will be reflecting the carnal mind. Such a mind will fail to have the inclination or interest in being sober minded about the issues of God. Without such serious inclination, this type of mind will fail to make the connection to the spiritual realm. Such a mind will fail to be roused in remembrance to where all loyalty and true devotion must reside in order to ensure discipline and integrity in the thought life. In fact, the thought life must be brought into subjection to Jesus Christ.[10]

This brings us to the issue of the soul. The spirit of man is considered a higher estate because it is what connects him to the spiritual dimension. However, the soul, especially in its unregenerate state, is considered the lower element of man's estate. The soul is made up of the will, intellect, and emotions, and will connect him to his outward environment.

The will decides who or what will reign in a matter. It will influence a person's behavior towards a situation, as well as decide what will be received or rejected. It sits at the door of the heart as to the type of reality a person will actually embrace. This is important to understand. God is the only One who can will a matter into being. However, when the right spirit is not influencing our will, it will strive to control reality. The best our unregenerate will can do as far as influencing our reality is to lead us into total delusion. Once again, we must be reminded of the purpose of our will. It is to decide who or what will serve as master or lord. It will determine the focus and emphasis of our affections, devotion, and commitment towards something.

The intellect of the soul is what will influence the state of our mind. It connects us to our ability to rationalize with the type of reality that we encounter. It will take what it knows and begin to logic out, or reason, about how a matter must be perceived. From this premise, it will develop its own code of truth. The problem with the intellect is that it often rationalizes away the very reality of the true God, and erects a god of its own liking.

Finally, we have those fickle emotions. Emotions were meant to sense the unseen aspect of an environment. Under the control of the Spirit of God they can discern the spirit behind a person or environment. However, if the emotions are not properly disciplined, they will interpret reality according to how a matter is affecting the person. It is important to understand if the emotions are undisciplined, there will be no sound

---

[10] 2 Corinthians 10:3-5

boundaries in which they can interpret what is happening around them. As a result, they will be affected by anything that has the means to arouse them. However, they will judge as a means to define reality according to how something makes them feel. It is within the emotional arena that man will justify or compromise wrong conclusions, attitudes, and actions.

This is when the intellect comes into play. Regardless of how wrong a person may be about a matter, emotions will perceive that his or her particular take on reality must be right because of how it is affecting him or her. These emotions will therefore call on the intellect to rationalize its conclusions. Needless to say, the mind will agree with the evaluation of the emotions. In such situations, the heart will become more delusional in its attitudes about God and life.

As we consider the makeup of the soul, we can begin to see how it serves as the seat to one's personality. It is from this seat that self is defined by that which influences the will, affects the perception, stirs the emotions, and rules the appetites. It is from this seat that man will perceive a matter, reflect his true intentions, contend with his feelings, channel his desires, and control his emotions. In this seat, he will decide who he is, and who he desires to become in order to discover his personal identity.

One of the main problems with the soul is that it can be sentimental towards spiritual matters, but remain incapable of responding to the Spirit of God due to the powerful influence of the world. Obviously, the soul serves as the means by which man interacts with his outward environment, which will influence the state of his inward environment. On the other hand, the spirit of man will determine what environment man will be so inclined to interact with.

If man has not been born again from above of Spirit and water (the Word of God), he may prove to have some sentiment towards God, but will be void of interacting with God on a spiritual level. Instead of the spirit being able to connect to the soul, the soul will be inclined towards, and subject to the world. As a result, it is only able to interact with the world. As the world gains influence upon the soul, the person is brought under the spirit of the world. This spirit entangles a person's soul as it enlarges the appetites that are attached to his or her affections, enslaves the will, perverts the intellect, and entices the emotions

The spirit of man is reflected through the countenance of a person and the mind is manifested through the conclusions. However, the soul is reflected through a person's attitudes. In fact, attitude reflects who or what is truly ruling the inner man.

To possess our souls as Christians, we must bring the heart into submission to our Lord, the will into subjection to His Word, the thoughts into captivity (for the mind to be transformed), and the emotions into line with the leading of the Spirit of God. By bringing the inner man into total agreement with God, the outer man will begin to reflect His very glory.

The soul was meant to interact with God on the spiritual level. It was meant to sense His presence, reason with Him about the matters of eternity, walk according to His truth, commune with Him in Spirit, and experience the fullness of His life. However, the entrance of sin broke that interaction. Clearly, man has lost control of his soul. It now dictates to him according to the fashion of this present world. Due to the spiritual breakdown, man is unable to operate on a spiritual level. As a result, man must now take possession of his own soul. He must do so with the patience of a saint.

Let us now consider the plight of man's soul. It will become clearer as to how these different arenas can affect man in his present state. As we come to terms with what has happened to the soul, we will understand what it means to truly possess it in the days in which we live.

Meanwhile, consider what these different arenas that make up the inner man are reflecting about your inner character. Does your reflection identify you to this world or to our Lord and Savior, Jesus Christ?

2

THE SOULISH MAN

What happened to man that caused him to fall from his original spiritual state? To answer that question, we must consider Adam. Adam was created in an innocent state. In fact, Adam was distinguished from the rest of creation by his ability to interact with God on a spiritual level. In his innocent state he was free from guilt brought on by sin for he was not as yet personally acquainted with evil. He stood blameless before God, and possessed simplicity towards the matters of life. Such simplicity made him open to the spiritual realm, able to interact with God on an intellectual and emotional level as he walked in the garden with Him in blessed fellowship.

God had placed Adam in a perfect environment. It was said in Scripture that God beheld all that He had made and He considered it good, delightful, or pleasurable. In light of God's approval of His work, it is obvious that the essence and joy of Adam's existence in the garden truly depended on his fellowship with his Creator.

However, there was something that proved to be terribly amiss in the garden. We can debate about the fall of man in paradise, but the harsh reality is that man began to toy with another existence outside of the blessed reign of God and the life of communion he shared with Him.

Job gives us an insight into the separation that was beginning to happen between God and Adam, even before Adam blatantly disobeyed God. "If I covered my transgressions as Adam, by hiding mine iniquity in my bosom" (Job 31:33). The first thing we must acknowledge about Adam is that he was hiding some iniquity or moral deviation in his heart. But, what type of moral deviation was Adam hiding? Was it a desire to be independent from God's reign? In other words, did Adam want to call the shots in order to be served and worshiped, as well as determine his own reality? We can only speculate, but Adam's blatant rebellion by transgressing the command God set before him concerning the tree of knowledge of good and evil spoke of the decision to have independence outside of the reign of God.

How could Adam choose a lesser existence than a blessed, intimate relationship with God? Hence, enters the will. Remember, it is in the will that a person decides who will reign in his or her life. In the will area, Adam had freedom to toy with what he most likely perceived in his mind to be optional or possible.

When Adam experienced evil by partaking of the tree of knowledge of good and evil, he fell from his innocent state. He now stood guilty before the holy God for he had sinned. What Adam failed to realize in his

Developing Our Christian Life

inward moral deviation of toying with unacceptable possibilities is that it would ultimately lead him into rebellion that would move him out from under the authority of God and put him into a lower state of being. In this lesser state, he would be unable to interact with God on a spiritual level. Since God is unable to accept such a lesser state, a gap or division was created in the area between the spirit of man and his soul. Man could not enter into the spiritual realm in communion with God until the gap was addressed. We know that gap was addressed by Jesus' death of the cross. The cross lifted Jesus up in such a way that He became the bridge that actually could close the gap in the spiritual realm between man and God.

What state did Adam fall into? To answer this question, we must first examine the state that Adam experienced. It was intended that man would experience God in an intimate communion as his Lord, Master, and Creator. In such an environment man's heart would be openly devoted to God, while his will came into subjection to God's will. God would therefore influence the mind of man, as he intellectually sought wisdom from above. Such wisdom would enable man to properly discern and worship God through his emotions. We know that when Adam sinned, he fell into a state that ceased to have any type of agreement or fellowship with God. From that point, a veil came over the heart of man, blinding his mind to the real light of heaven and the glorious Gospel. However, when people turn to the Lord in repentance, the veil shall be taken away.[1]

The state that Adam fell into is what we would refer to as a soulish state. In this soulish state, man would be inclined towards, as well as develop and constantly give way to, a selfish disposition. This is where self sits on the throne. In fact, everything done, considered, or pursued would be in line with self, for self, and because of self. Needless to say, there is no Spirit or life in this state; therefore, man became incapable of interacting with God in a spiritual arena. In fact, all Adam was aware of in his fallen condition was his shame that had clearly separated him from God. He responded to his state by trying to hide from God. Clearly, his guilt had taken center stage, creating a clear division or gap between the holy God and sinful man.

Man, in his disobedience, had become independent of the Spirit and life of God. Instead of being a living soul, he became a fleshly soul that lived unto the wicked ways of self. Since the soul was not being properly disciplined and challenged by the right spirit within man, man's will, intellect, and emotions became the means that would define him rather than his Creator. Since self was now on the throne, the heart would become self-serving, idolatrous, and deceptive as it declared that it would ascend to heaven to ultimately rule.[2] All matters involving life would be required to bow down to the self-life that would now be fully

---

[1] 2 Corinthians 3:14-16; 4:3-4
[2] Isaiah 14:13

pursued without any interference or opposition. The prophet Jeremiah described such a heart, "The heart is deceitful above all things, and desperately wicked; who can know it" (Jeremiah 17:9)?

Who can know the heart? We know that such a heart will deceive man as to his true spiritual condition. However, Jeremiah goes on to say that the Lord will search the heart. He will test the reins or conscience of what motivates and inspires it. In fact, He will turn man over to his self-serving ways to reveal the fruits of his practices.[3]

In man's selfish deposition, he will try to get reality to bow down to his self-life. In his attempt to accomplish such a feat, reality would become perverted. Such perversion would serve as darkness upon the dictates of his mind. As a result, man would not be able to perceive anything outside the dictates of his selfish pursuits. As long as the selfish pursuits made him feel good about self or brought forth a false peace, he would perceive such darkness as being light or truth.[4]

Sadly, it is the selfish disposition, or state of man, that has been passed down to everyone born of Adam. In this state, sin now dictates to man, while spiritual death or separation from God, is the consequence.[5] In the darkness of this sinful disposition, man has become lost as self consumes him into a world that is empty, lifeless, and doomed by the death that now resides in and upon him in all he does.

The Apostle Paul described this state in Romans 3. He stated that no one can be considered righteous in this dark state. Because the darkness is so great, man no longer understands what truth is, and has no real inclination to seek after the God of heaven to possess His truth.[6]

Because of this hopeless state of the soul, as well as man's inability to save his wretched soul from the claims of death upon it, God had to redeem him from the reign of sin and its consequence of death. The Bible talks about how the Lord converts and delivers the soul from its hopeless state. He also must heal and restore the soul as He lifts it above the pit of its present destruction.[7]

The question is how can a person's soul become living after being dead in this sinful, selfish state? Jesus gives us insight into this in John 3:3 and 5, a person must be born again from above. This means he or she will be born of the Spirit of God according to the water or Word of God, restoring him back to the original state of being a living soul.

Jesus provided the means through His death on the cross by which man can now be restored to his original position as a living soul, once again capable of interacting with his Creator on a spiritual level. By receiving the life of Christ in the spirit, the veil will be taken away from the heart and mind, as the wall of resistance that has been erected in the

---

[3] Jeremiah 17:10; Matthew 7:16, 20
[4] Matthew 6:23
[5] Romans 5:12
[6] Romans 3:10-11
[7] Psalm 6:4; 19:7; 23:3; 34:22

Developing Our Christian Life

will area is broken down through humility and repentance, resulting in reconciliation. God will then give the person a new spirit along with a new state or heart. The spirit of man will once again be inclined towards God, and his heart will be made alive unto God for His purpose. Instead of remaining soulish, man can once again become spiritual as he is restored in a relationship with God through the ministry of reconciliation. Reconciliation is what brings peace of mind and rest to man's tormented soul.[8]

By being born again, man's vantage point changes from the soul area to the spiritual heights of God. It is by positionally being seated in high places in Christ that the spirit of man can soar on the wind of the Holy Spirit, the soul of man can be lifted up in praise and worship to embrace the eternal, and the mind of man can be transformed to consider and discover the nuggets of heavenly blessings.[9]

It is from this vantage point, that man will once again discover the paradise Adam lost when his fellowship with his Creator was broken by his disobedience. The present paradise is not found in a perfect environment, but it is found in a relationship with the Living God. To know Him as Lord, Master, Provider, Protector, Father, and yes even, Friend, makes the revelation of heaven a reality to our spirits.

Clearly, to enter God's unseen kingdom, one must be born again. There are people who tack on the concept of Jesus' salvation, but there is no indication that they truly have been born again. The person who never progresses past the soulish dictates of self must question if he or she has truly been born of the Spirit of God in accordance with believing His Word about sin, repentance, forgiveness, and reconciliation.

Today is the day of salvation from the despairing selfish state created by independence from God. This independence has caused separation from God. As man, Jesus cried out in utter despair when He experienced the darkness of such separation.[10] Heed His cry. Granted, the selfish man may not recognize the spiritual separation that leaves an empty vacuum, but the Word clearly states that it is present in the lives of those who do not have the Spirit and life of God in them.

If you are not sure if you have experienced this new birth, cry out to God in humility, seek His mercy, knowing that He does want to show you favor by giving you the life of His Son. If you are not sure how to ask God to save you from your wretched condition, consider the following prayer:

Lord Jesus,

I have been told I am separated from You by sin, but by believing that You died on my behalf, I can be forgiven of my sins, spiritually reconciled back to You as my Creator, God, and Lord, and restored back

---

[8] Ezekiel 36:26-27; Matthew 11:29; John 14:27; 2 Corinthians 3:14-16; 5:18-19; Ephesians 2:13-18

[9] Ephesians 2:6

[10] Matthew 27:45-46; 2 Corinthians 6:2

into a relationship with the Father. Therefore, by faith I make this humble request. Show Your mercy towards me by forgiving me of my sin and bestowing Your grace on me by coming into my life as my Lord and Savior, saving me from the entanglements of sin and death upon my wretched soul.

By faith I thank You for saving me today from a miserable state of vanity, despair, and eternal damnation. Amen.

3

THE NATURAL MAN

When Adam fell into a soulish state, man's premise about the matters of life started from the influence, workings, and activities of the soul. The question is how would the soul operate based on its fallen status? After all, when man falls or departs from God, he will cease to start from the true center of Spirit and truth. From such a deviant point man will begin to operate in a state that will be off base in his reality, identity, purpose, and destination.

Before the fall, Adam's availability to the spiritual realm would have caused him to initially have inclination towards a relationship with his Creator. His natural tendencies would be to desire to walk with his Creator in order to establish his identity in creation and fulfill his purpose. But, when he fell from his innocent state into a soulish state, his inclinations and tendencies changed. Instead of a graduating from an innocent state into a spiritual man, he became a natural man.

"Natural" in this text points to the base aspect of man's disposition where he becomes bestial or sensual in his desires and pursuits.[1] At this point there is not much difference between man and the savage beast that must prey upon others to feed its appetites that are influenced by survival instincts and the need for dominion in its territory.

The Apostle Paul talked about the natural man in 1 Corinthians 2:14. He stated that the natural man could not receive the things of the Spirit. The reason for being unreceptive to the unseen is because the natural man in his base state thinks that the unseen matters of heaven are foolish. No doubt the natural man perceives that the preaching of the simple Gospel as being idiotic as well. This is why he is perishing in his foolishness.[2] Such an attitude points to a foolish heart.

The Apostle Paul also dealt with the foolish heart in Romans 1:21-23. He said of those who had a foolish heart that they refuse to glorify the true God of heaven. One of the reasons for this refusal is because the natural man puts tremendous confidence in his personal strength, which replaces the power of the Spirit of God in his life. Personal strength is not just based on physical strength, but on possessing the abilities of surviving the different challenges of life. These natural abilities or strengths give the natural man the sense of being shrewd, clever, and

---

[1] Strong's Exhaustive Concordance of the Bible, #5591
[2] 1 Corinthians 1:18

crafty as a means to control reality, circumstances, and people. In fact, the natural man thinks quite highly of himself.[3]

As the natural man exalts his strength over that which is considered weak and inferior, this debased man will perceive his abilities as outshining those around him. In fact, he thinks that that he is so shrewd that no one will see his deception; that he is so clever people will not see the foolishness behind his logic; and that he is so crafty that no one will catch on that it is all a game of control and manipulation. Such arrogance points to the pride of life that believes it will ultimately prove its worth and strength in a matter and come out on top.[4]

Another aspect of the natural man is that he is unthankful. In his arrogance, he believes he deserves to be honored by all. After all, he is quite wise in his thinking and ability. Such a perception can make the natural man touchy; therefore, he is quick to be rude when insulted, mean spirited when angered, and vindictive when not placated. As a result, Scripture refers to him as a fool. The reason for the natural man's foolishness is because he is vain in his thinking. There is no truth to his conclusions, no reality to his understanding, and no real wisdom behind his knowledge.[5] King David best explained the reason for the natural man's true foolishness in Psalm 53:1, "The fool hath said in his heart, There is no God. Corrupt are they, and have done abominable iniquity; there is none that doeth good."

The natural man lives as if there is no true God. Granted, the natural man has some conscience about the need to worship something, but there is no real inclination towards the true God of heaven. In his mind he is quite independent and self-sufficient; therefore, he has no need for God.[6] After all, his strength or abilities are what he honors. He greatly admires them, and has faith in them because he walks according to his own understanding. Obviously, he worships what God has created, and not the Creator. How foolish the natural man proves to be in his endless pursuit of that which is idolatrous, vain, and destructive.

This brings us to the darkness permeating the soul of the natural man. Remember, Adam hid from God. He was aware of his shame, but he still refused to humble himself, confess his sin, and ask for mercy from his loving Creator.[7] He refused to turn from his moral deviation in repentance so he could be restored to a place of worship and communion with God. He simply hid from his Maker, ignoring or denying the fact that God already knew about the wretchedness of his condition.

The wretched condition brings us to another aspect of the natural man. His natural tendency is to hide from God behind the cloaks of darkness. Adam put on fig leaves to hide his shame. This flimsy attempt

---

[3] Romans 12:3
[4] Isaiah 14:13; 1 John 2:16
[5] Romans 1:21-22
[6] 2 Corinthians 3:5
[7] Genesis 3:8-11; Proverbs 28:13

could not hide the humiliation brought on by sin. God took the life of an innocent animal to clothe Adam and Eve. The death of this animal may have served as a means to cover them, but it would not take away the shame and separation brought on by sin.[8] It would take Jesus' death on the cross as the Lamb of God to take away the devastating fruits of sin.

Sadly, man continues to hide from God with flimsy coverings. Due to the independence, arrogance, and vanity of the natural man, he refuses to receive the remedy that God has provided. In utter vanity, the natural man continues to try to cover up the reality of his spiritual state. Jesus said in John 15:22 that His truth would strip away the cloak of the natural man that hides the influences, workings, and activities of sin. In fact, people would hate Him for exposing their inner darkness.

The question is why does the natural man refuse to repent of his foolishness? Jesus answered this question in John 3:19-20. The natural man refuses to repent because he loves his darkness due to his self-serving preferences. In other words, he prefers life according to his personal preferences.

Preferences are made up of agendas and priorities. Such preferences serve as a darkness that will cover the evil deeds that are produced by this self-serving reality. The Apostle Paul describes the way and deeds of the natural man. He states that he has gone out of the way that God has provided for him. As a result, he has become unprofitable in all he does; proving that he does not have the ability to do what is good or beneficial.[9]

The natural man clearly likes to have life on his terms. In darkness he can justify his wicked attitudes and evil deeds. He can portray a false way to maintain his desired reality without his deviant character being exposed. He can appear wise in his conceits, while hiding the foolishness of his thinking. He can deceive himself about being right concerning questionable practices, regardless of how they may be affecting others.

Cain is a good example of the natural man. Adam hid from God, but Cain departed from Him, and became a wanderer. Cain's plight started because he wanted to impress God with his accomplishments, rather than honor or obey Him. Cain, with his brother, Abel, offered sacrifices to God. Cain's offering was from the ground and Abel from the best of his flock.[10] The Lord had respect for Abel because it was a shadow (or type) of the sacrifice that He would offer on the cross.

Cain became angry because God would not show respect for his sacrifice. The Lord confronted Cain about his jealous attitude, and warned him of the sin of hatred that was waiting at the door. But, the natural man in Cain had become fierce in its independence. Obviously, the natural man would not accept the reality of God's truth. It would not

---

[8] Genesis 3:7-8, 21
[9] Romans 3:12
[10] Genesis 4:3-5

bow in humility at God's warning. It would come out on top no matter what the cost. Sadly, it cost Abel his very life.[11]

When God confronted Cain about his wicked deed of killing Abel, Cain tried to play ignorant. He had tried to hide his sin by burying Abel, but God knew what had happened. Instead of confessing his sin and crying out for mercy, Cain stood his ground. God was given no other choice but to pronounce judgment on him. He would become a wanderer or fugitive in this world.[12]

It is said of Cain that he mourned his punishment but not his actions. He felt sorry for himself, but not repentant about murdering his brother. Clearly, the natural man refuses to take responsibility and agree with God about the matters of sin, death, and judgment. Cain would be a marked man who would die in his hopeless state, but meanwhile he would be a fugitive from God who would leave the presence of his Maker and wander far from his ordained purpose.[13]

Cain also built the first city.[14] Again this points to the natural man's refusal to be ruled by God. Man would establish his own government outside of the rule of his righteous Creator. After all, man is self-sufficient and has no need for God. He is clever, gifted, and capable enough to successfully rule his own life and control his destiny. Of course, such a perception has constantly proven to be bogus throughout the history of mankind.

It is obvious that the natural man is unable to truly repent. He may show worldly sorrow, but it is only when he starts paying the consequences for his evil deeds. He will cleverly try to comply without giving up his independence; he will outwardly conform without coming to repentance; he will religiously perform to hide his deviant ways, and he will occasionally reform in some of his ways without giving way to the rule of God. It is all outward show because the natural man has no intention of giving way to God. He is not inclined to do so, and deems much of the religious exercise of faith, devotion, and obedience to God as being weak and foolish.

Another good example of the natural man in operation is Esau. As you study the life of Esau, you can see that he had no inclination towards spiritual matters. He actually sold his birthright to Jacob.[15] The birthright pointed more to maintaining and bringing forth the spiritual legacy of the covenant God made with Abraham. However, Esau's only interest was receiving the blessing that was attached to the physical inheritance. Hebrews 12:16-17 calls Esau a fornicator or profane person who sold his birthright for one morsel of meat. Because of his disregard for his birthright, he was rejected from inheriting the blessing as well. Even

---

[11] Genesis 4:8; 1 John 3:12
[12] Genesis 4:9-16
[13] Genesis 4:16
[14] Ibid
[15] Genesis 25:27-34

though he sought the blessing with tears, he found no place of repentance.

It is important to point out that without the conviction of the Holy Spirit, man cannot truly come to a place of repentance. The natural man can only feel sorry for his situation, but since he has no real inclination towards the conviction or work of the Holy Spirit, he cannot respond in the spirit of true repentance, which requires humility towards God and brokenness over sin.

Esau was bitterly upset over losing the blessing, but he could not truly come to a place of repentance in order to secure it. He was not being convicted; therefore, he failed to see where his attitude about the birthright was sinful and unacceptable towards God, causing him to be found unworthy to receive the blessing that was also a big part of ensuring the birthright. His mind was clearly darkened by his pursuit for that which was seen and temporary.

The grave deception of the natural man is that he perceives that he can figure his way around any obstacle. Since he thinks the things of God are foolish, he often despises and rejects anything attached to the unseen. In his mind he has no time for what he considers to be folly. He perceives if he plays the game well enough that in the end he will get his way. However, Esau tasted the bitter reality of his folly when he forever lost his blessing.

As we can see, the natural man will not allow anyone to be his lord or master. Since he is cleverly independent, he will not be managed. Since he wants to go with the sentiments of his own way, he will not be disciplined. Because he wants to determine his own reality, he will not yield to any other way that does not bow down or recognize what he considers to be superiority on his part. Since he wants to be in control of his world, he will not be ruled. Therefore, that which motivates him is unmanageable. That which inspires him proves to be undisciplined. That which stirs him up is unyielding, and that which serves as his point of strength is unruly. Ultimately, he refuses to humble himself so he truly can come to a place of repentance. After all, to the natural man humility implies losing control, becoming weak, and vulnerable. He will have no part in what he perceives to be a feeble state.

Proverbs 25:28 describes the condition of the natural man in this way, "He that hath no rule over his own spirit is like a city that is broken down, and without walls." Due to the absence of the Spirit of God, the natural man is like a broken-down city because death reigns. Since the natural man is not under control to that which is worthy or greater, there will be no self-control. Without discipline, there will be no real place of accountability where one can truly test or discern the fruits of his or her way. Clearly, the natural man will find that he is a city without walls because his strength will ultimately be defeated by his own foolishness.

Without the proper protection of God's Spirit, ways, truth, and life, the natural man will not only suffer defeat, but total ruin. After all, the Bible tells us we do not fight against flesh and blood, but against that which is unseen and holds power in this present world.[16] Such reality proves to be the greatest point of foolishness for the natural man. He is unprotected because God is not his fortress or high tower. He does not believe in what he cannot see. He walks according to his own foolish wit and glories in his limited abilities. Such delusional foolishness clearly makes him a sitting duck when it comes to withstanding the real unseen battle.

The natural man will be defeated in his foolishness. He has no future. His natural strength will be taken from him, and his abilities will become traps that will bring him down into utter shame and hopelessness. He will eventually realize that all his rational arrogance simply sets him up to prove him to be an utter fool in light of eternity. And, all of his justifications for his folly and compromise with darkness had simply deluded him to the damnation that is awaiting him.

We know that for the soulish man he must be born again, but the natural man must clearly be denied of any right to rule or have life on his terms. Jesus put it best when He told His disciples that they must deny or disown self if they were going to be His followers. It is not enough for the soul to be connected to the spiritual realm by being born again; the natural man must be completely transformed much like a caterpillar experience when it goes through metamorphoses in the cocoon.[17] Transformation of this nature cannot begin until a person comes under the leadership of God and walks in obedience to His righteous ways.

Such leadership points to a person being managed by the Spirit, disciplined by the Word of God, yielded to the life of God, and ruled by the Lordship of Jesus. A person must seek the strength of God, knowing that even God in His power does everything through His Spirit.[18] Such a person must live the life ordained by God, not according to that which is based on his or her personal sentiment and abilities. Ultimately, the vainglory of the natural man will give way to the majesty of Jesus, as the person realizes the blessed glory that awaits him or her beyond this present world.

The question is, are you giving way to the foolishness of your natural man? Granted, such foolishness will blind you to the seriousness of your independent ways, but eventually you will prove to be a fool, deluded by your own folly.

---

[16] Ephesians 6:12
[17] Matthew 16:24; Romans 12:1-2
[18] Zechariah 4:6

4

THE FLESHLY MAN

It is important to understand how man truly digresses into utter hopelessness and spiritual ruin. Because of Adam, man became soulish. In such a state, he regressed into a natural man that simply became subject to his own soulish preferences. Such preferences are self-serving, not Christ centered or Spirit inspired. As man gives way to natural preferences of the self-life, he becomes fleshly in his ways. Since man's ways often identify him to the type of person he is becoming, such unregenerate ways will classify him as being a fleshly man.

The Bible speaks much about the flesh. However, there are two meanings to the word "flesh." The first meaning points to the skin of our physical body or what is often referred to as our tabernacles. The flesh is simply our covering. It is within these fleshly bodies or tabernacles that our soul and spirit reside. The soul uses the body to interact with the world around it and pursue the life it is seeking. For the spirit, the body becomes the means to reflect the light or glory it is walking according to. In fact, the body will ultimately reflect the type of light or glory that is motivating and inspiring the inner man.

It is important to understand what happened to man's tabernacle when he sinned. God intended for man to live forever in a state of blessed communion with Him. As a result, man had been created to be an eternal being. I once heard that those who study the makeup of the human body admitted that they do not understand why a person dies. It is able to repair itself if given the right means to do so. As we come to a greater understanding of the body, we cannot help but readily agree with the Bible by admitting that the body is wonderfully made.[1]

Therefore, why does the body die? As believers, we should be able to answer this question. The outer man is perishing because of sin. When Adam sinned, the corruption of death came upon all men. As a result, our bodies are now corruptible, and from the premise of spirit and soul man has been separated from God, pointing to a spiritual death. Physical death begins to work within the members of our body when we are born. Granted, our body has certain defenses that may combat death for a season, but eventually physical death will win out when it comes to our physical tabernacles.

The Bible describes our flesh in vivid terms. The Apostle Peter stated that all flesh is like grass and the glory of man like the flower of grass. The grass will wither and the beauty of the flower will fall away. He

---

[1] Psalm 139:14

referred to his body as a tabernacle, and stated that in a short time he would be putting off his tabernacle.[2]

If any one aspect of our makeup gives us a clear picture of how fragile, and limited, we are in our present state, it is our flesh. The natural man may glory in what it perceives to be its strength, but as the flesh digresses in its ability to function, man's strength will also fade. The end is made obvious by every obituary and funeral we take note of or participate in. We are reminded of our mortality and that in light of eternity our present life in these bodies is nothing more than a vapor.[3]

The flesh clearly reminds us of how weak we are in our present state, for in the end it will succumb to physical death. Once this type of death comes upon our flesh, our spirit and soul will cease to know and experience life according to our earthly tabernacles. Physical death will simply serve as a door in which our spirit and soul will exit the body to encounter a different existence. Whether we encounter the environment of hell where there is no real life, or the blessed glory of heaven will be determined by what we do in these earthly tabernacles.[4]

The Apostle Paul also reminded us that our bodies are the temples of the Holy Spirit. He warned us that if we destroy this temple with sinful practices and unholy agreements, God would destroy us. Our bodies should be used to glorify our Lord.[4] After all, the activities of our bodies will become some type of expression of the life we are living and pursuing.

As we consider the weakness of the flesh, we must remind ourselves that the body of man has only one good purpose, and that is to be offered up in consecrated service to the Lord.[5] In our bodies we serve as the mouth, hands, and feet of Jesus. We are vessels that pour His life into others. In fact, the only victory the flesh can lay claim to came through the door of death. Jesus took on flesh in order to become the Lamb of God. The Apostle Peter makes this statement, "For Christ also hath once suffered for sins, the just for the unjust, that he might bring us to God, being put to death in the flesh but quickened by the Spirit" (1 Peter 3:18).

This brings us to the second meaning of the word "flesh." It has to do with the appetites that are associated with the bodily functions. Such functions are also related to our needs, desires, passions, and obsessions. In many cases this causes much confusion for Christians. The body has certain needs that must be maintained for us to live in this world, but since death works in these tabernacles, bodily needs can take tremendous time, energy, and resources. Depending on what type of emphasis we put on an activity, the body often operates according to

---

[2] 1 Peter 1:24; 2 Peter 1:14
[3] James 4:14
[4] Matthew 26:41; Luke 16:19-26; 2 Corinthians 5:8-10
[4] 1 Corinthians 3:16-17; 6:15-20
[5] Romans 12:1-2

desires and passions that are being stirred up to pursue a matter. However, many of these desires and passions prove to be ungodly; therefore, they are void of any real substance. As a result, a person can become enslaved to obsessions that leave him or her spiritually empty and hopelessly being consumed by an unseen bondage. Ultimately, many people find themselves serving their fleshly ways, rather than properly confronting the driving force behind them, that being fleshly appetites.

The flesh can become a powerful, insatiable god we constantly bow down to. The Apostle Paul talked about the lusts and desires of the flesh and mind. He said of them that because of their nature or disposition along with their influence and ability to enslave, they would make people into children of wrath. The flesh is also quick to declare that in the end it will find the necessary avenue to sit in a place of dominance, importance, and significance in our lives regardless of how weak and fragile it is.[6]

The natural man operates with a foolish heart, but when you add the fleshly ways to such a heart, you end up with a proud heart. Pride can serve as a premise we start from in our fallen condition, a state we reside within, an attitude that will become apparent in our look, a trait that will manifest itself in our fleshly body, and a way of doing something. It is motivated by selfishness and inspired by foolishness. It walks in delusion to it arrogance as it disguises itself behind a veil of fake humility. The flesh serves as its platform to explore, as well as experience and partake of the world according to the natural man's preferences. After all, the natural man has a right to survive according to his terms. This is why pride sets a person up to explore in his or her flesh what God has already marked with a "No Trespassing" sign. For this reason, God resists pride at any level.[7]

Although the flesh is weak in many ways, in the mind of the natural man it can easily be controlled. However, the flesh possesses a door that once a person opens it, he or she will find him or herself spiraling downward into a hopeless abyss of ruin and death. James explains how this door works. It begins with temptation that will catch the attention of the natural man. As the natural man foolishly toys with the temptation mentally, he is drawn away by the possibilities of how it is going to feed his ego or make his flesh feel. After all, the natural man perceives that he has a right to experience what he considers the "good things of life". Once he has given way to the justification and enticement of the temptation, he will sin against God by submitting to the temptation.[8]

Sin always leads to the ways of death. The door that is opened by way of temptation is referred to as lusts. The Apostle John referred to this door as the lust of the flesh. The Apostle Paul referred to such lust

---

[6] Isaiah 14:13; Ephesians 2:3
[7] Psalm 138:6: Proverbs 6:16-17; 11:2; 15:25; 16:18; 18:12; 21:4; Jeremiah 49:15-16; 1 Timothy 6:4-6; James 4:6
[8] 1 Corinthians 10:12-13; James 1:13-15

as youthful lusts that one must flee, instructing people to follow righteousness, faith, charity, and peace. If these lustful appetites and desires are not kept in their proper place, they will cause such an individual to become a castaway, even in his or her Christian life.[9]

To put the ways of the flesh in perspective, keep in mind the flesh can only produce fleshly ways. When we live according to the corruptible flesh, our ways will also prove to be corrupt. The man who puts his trust on the weak arm of the flesh will have to depart from God as Cain did and stand cursed. The Apostle Paul made it quite clear that there is no good thing in the flesh. In other words, any matter that finds its origins in fleshly appetites will not be beneficial to our spiritual well-being. It will prove to be corrupt, full of decay as it disfigures our reality and puts us on the path of spiritual ruin and death. The apostle also described how the flesh in its wretched state conducts itself through its members. The throat proves to be a sepulcher (lifeless), the tongue deceitful (no truth), the lips poisonous (deadly), the mouth full of cursing and bitterness (hateful), and the feet swift to shed blood (murderous). It is clear that destruction and misery are in its many perverted, godless ways.[10]

The Apostle Paul dealt with the fleshly man in great detail. The flesh is what is warring against the Spirit. It insists on its pagan, idolatrous ways. The apostle stated that we either are walking according to the Spirit or according to the flesh. Therefore, if the natural man is calling the shots, a person will be walking according to his flesh, making him or her a fleshly man. Such a walk points to a carnal mind in operation.

The carnal mind is the product of a perverted perception. Remember, the natural man has a darkened mind due to a selfish perception of his right to secure life on his terms. Once the natural man begins to pursue his preferences according to the flesh, his mind becomes carnal as it begins to mind the things of the flesh. We know the carnal mind represents death because it is enmity against God and is not subject to the Law of God.[11]

This fleshly man is subject to the dictates of sin. He is sold under sin's wages of death, causing the person to yield his or her personal members of the body as a servant to all that is unclean and morally deviant. The Apostle Paul also stated that if we walk according to the flesh, we will come under the law of sin and death. After all, if one sows in the flesh, he or she shall reap corruption. Obviously, in such a state, the flesh stands condemned in all of its ways.[12]

A good example of the fleshly man is Ishmael. Most Christians should know the story of how Sarai (Sarah) was barren. She took matters into her own hands, and according to the customs of the land gave Abram (Abraham) her maid, Hagar. Hagar conceived and began to

---

[9] 1 Corinthians 9:26-27; 2 Timothy 2:22; 1 John 2:16
[10] Jeremiah 17:5-7; Romans 3:13-16; 7:18; Galatians 6:8
[11] Romans 8:5-7; Galatians 5:17
[12] Romans 6:19, 23; 8:1-2; Galatians 6:7-8

Developing Our Christian Life

despise Sarai. Sarai would not tolerate such disrespect from her servant; therefore, she chastised her. Hagar fled from Sarai. In the wilderness, the Lord instructed the bondwoman to return to her mistress, for she would bear a son whose seed would multiply. She was to call him Ishmael for God had heard her cries.[13]

Hagar went back to Sarah. We know that eventually Isaac was born to Sarah due to the miraculous intervention of God. The Apostle Paul explained how Ishmael, the son of the bondwoman was born after the flesh, but Isaac was born of the freewoman according to the promise of God.[14]

When you study the life of Ishmael, you will see the contrast between the flesh, and that which was the product of God's promises. The first contrast is that the fleshly attempts of man will only bring one into bondage. Ishmael was described as a wild man, implying that he would run wild. This is true for the flesh. It can run wild according to its lusts.[15]

Ishmael was a warring man who had no concept as to the ways of peace for his hand was against every man, and every man's hand was against him. There is no real peace in the flesh. It continually wars against the Spirit.[16]

Like his mother who had showed contempt toward Sarah in her barren state, Ishmael became mocking towards Isaac, the one who represented the promise of God. As a result, he along with his mother were cast out. That which represents the flesh of man will have no part with that which has been brought forth by the promises of God.[17] The Apostle John makes this incredible statement about the children of God who are joint heirs with Jesus due to His redemption, "But as many as received him, to them gave he power to become the sons of God, even to them that believe on his name; Who were born, not of blood, nor of the will of the flesh, nor of the will of man, but of God" (John 1:12-13)

Clearly, there is no life or promises of God to be found or obtained in the flesh. It is dying, and it walks according to the ways of death. Jesus stated that the Spirit is what gives life, but man will profit nothing from his fleshly attempts. The Apostle Paul tells us that we cannot please God in our flesh, and if we live after the flesh, we shall die.[18]

This brings us to the ways of the flesh. The Apostle Paul summarized the ways of the flesh in Galatians 5:19-21. Each way shows how the flesh clearly transgresses the Law. In other words, it commits the sins of commission, where it clearly breaks the Law or covenant of God as it gives way to iniquity or moral deviation. The apostle is clear

---

[13] Genesis 16:1-11
[14] Galatians 4:22-23
[15] Genesis 16:12
[16] Genesis 16:12; Galatians 5:17
[17] Genesis 21:9-12
[18] John 6:63; Romans 8:8, 13

that those who practice the ways of the flesh will not inherit the kingdom of God.

As you consider the ways of the flesh, you can see how they take captive every aspect of our lives if we willingly give way to our fleshly appetites. For example, adultery will improperly enslave our affections in a lustful way. Fornication brings us into agreement with unholy alliances, which are inspired by our vain imaginations. Unclean practices expose us to wrong influences. Lasciviousness or debauchery feeds the lusts of the flesh according to its corrupt and immoral preferences. Idolatry stirs up the emotions to pay homage to idols, while witchcraft seeks ways to control reality and others as it insists on its own way. Hatred causes anger, unforgiveness, or indifference to come to the forefront of our emotions. Variance means we are operating from a disposition of pride, causing us to be contrary and argumentative. Emulation is just a clever way of trying to be on equal footing with others in order to excel above them, creating an environment of superiority. Wrath requires a person to bring judgment on those who have wronged him or her, while strife results in opposition and division as one demands his or her own way. Seditions points to division caused by dissension; and heresies come from disunion created because there is a lack of agreement in spirit and truth. Reveling simply means that one is letting loose in his or her actions and pursuits.

It is important to note that in 1 Corinthians 3, the Apostle Paul referred to the Corinthians as carnal or fleshly Christians. What constitutes a carnal Christian? The main reason that Christians remain carnal is because they have not denied the natural man his right to exist by repenting of and rejecting their worldly attitude towards life. Even though a Christian may be born again, and has subdued many of his or her fleshly ways, he or she can secretly maintain the right to life on his or her terms. Such people will decide when to deny themselves, as they boast or flatter themselves that they are not subject to their former lusts. Although this may be true in part, such people still are responding in fleshly ways. In fact, the Corinthians were experiencing divisions because of their carnal ways. The Apostle Paul rebuked them because they were still at the milk stage of knowing about spiritual matters, but unable to bear meat. We are told that the meat stage implies one is being brought to perfection as far as establishing righteousness in their ways.[19]

What must we do with the ways of the fleshly man? The Apostle Paul instructs us to mortify the deeds and members of the flesh. For the natural man, we must deny or disown self, but when it comes to the flesh it requires death. As Christians, we must pick up our cross and die daily to the fleshly man with his lustful, pagan, sensual, unclean, and idolatrous desires and ways. As we crucify the fleshly ways, we become

---

[19] 1 Corinthians 3:1-3; Hebrews 5:12-14

Developing Our Christian Life

crucified to the world.[20] We actually close down the platform of the natural man that serves as the avenue in which we can become entangled with the attractions of the world. The Apostle Paul makes mention of this in Galatians 6:14, "But God forbid that I should glory save in the cross of our Lord Jesus Christ, by whom the world is crucified unto me, and I unto the world."

The natural man must give way to the Spirit through humility, but the fleshly man must exchange the old ways with the new by putting on the life of the Lord Jesus Christ and walking according to the Spirit of God. This is the only way a Christian can be assured of not fulfilling the lust of the flesh.[21]

How about you? How much of the fleshly man reigns in your life. If he is not losing his right to reign through death, you will prove to be a carnal Christian that is still partaking of milk, rather than coming to full age in your spiritual life. Ask the Lord to reveal your level of spiritual maturity.

---

[20] Luke 9:23-24; 14:26-27; Romans 8:13; 1 Corinthians 15:31; Colossians 3:5
[21] Romans 13:14; Galatians 5:16

5

THE COMPLACENT MAN

The soulish man is selfish and independent of God's reign. The natural man is self-sufficient, as well as obstinate when it comes to God's authority. The fleshly man is lustful, as well as rebellious towards the ways of God, but the next man, the complacent man gives an appearance of outward compliance to the ways of righteousness, but remains unresponsive towards the Spirit of God.

It is vital to see the progression of the unregenerate man. From the deceptive heart, a person will develop a foolish heart that will not be reasoned with concerning the matters of God. As the heart gives way to foolishness, it becomes rebellious. The fleshly ways of the proud, rebellious heart will cause a person to become unmoved towards God. After all, without truth there is no real standard of accountability. Man can adjust his reality to what serves his preferences. Without truth to guide man, he will lack the true wisdom from above. He will become flippant and disrespectful as he strives to control reality. In his foolishness he will seek his desired reality according to the attractions and appetites of the flesh.

Each time he gives way to deception, he will justify any compromise with the world. As he comes into agreement with the world, he will prefer the ways of the world. As he gives way to the world, he will come under the influence of the spirit of the world. At this point the man has now become a man of the world. The world has become the source of his identity and the point of his purpose. After all, the world serves as a source of incredible attraction to the soulish man, feeds the ego of the natural man, and offers all the temporary favors of hell for the fleshly man to pursue after and freely partake of.

We know according to the Bible that the world is at odds with God. There is no agreement, causing the world to resent the obvious contrast between the profane and the holy. As a result, Jesus stated that since the world hated Him, it would also hate His followers. There is no greater example of the intensity of such hate as that which is found in religion.[1]

Man's religion appears righteous, but it has it own agendas. Jesus challenged the attitude behind man's religion at different times. The problem with the soulish man is that he will put on a religious image that will give an appearance of godliness, but ultimately denies the power of it. The natural man can sound quite religious in his logical presentation, but there it no life behind his self-serving conclusions. Eventually, his

---

[1] John 17:14; James 4:4

Developing Our Christian Life

religious philosophies are traced back to the world, exposing the influence of an antichrist spirit. The fleshly man puts on a religious cloak to cover his fleshly activities, but truth will eventually expose the activities of sin.[2]

This brings us to the next stage of the fallen man, that of the complacent man. This man has an indifferent heart towards God. Such a heart may consider God, but it will fail to really tune in and care about what God might really think of a situation. In its sensual state it may desire to please God at different times, but it is too lazy to carry it out. In its arrogance it may devise great notions about God, but is too apathetic to see a matter through. Such a heart may possess sound ideas, but is obtuse in its ability to truly relate to its environment so that it can successfully see a matter come to fruition.

The complacent man is caught up with the world. He strives to have both the seen and unseen worlds without having to make a clear-cut decision about which master he is going to serve. This man wants to experience certain aspects of the world, while outwardly trying to silence any personal religious conscience as a means to keep God at bay. In a way, this man is simply an associate of the kingdom of God through religious activities. But such activities simply serve as a means to pacify this man's conscience, while he avoids truly becoming identified as a real citizen of the kingdom of heaven. This type of man simply impresses himself with religious knowledge, appearance, or activities. However, this particular man cleverly remains in the valley of indecision when it comes to deciding which master he will truly serve. After all, he has no intention of truly coming out and being separate from the world or being identified as a hypocrite in religious circles.

As the complacent man gives way to the world, he becomes more desensitized to God. He will come to a point where he will not be able to discern the profane from the holy. He will think his form of religious devotion or activity is acceptable to God. However, God will have quite a different opinion of it. The Apostle Paul describes the state of this man. Even though the complacent man appears at peace with the matters of life, there is no peace because there has been no reconciliation made between him and God. The other aspect of the complacent man is that although he may appear wise, he has no real fear of God, which means he is void of true wisdom.[3]

A good example of the state of the complacent man can be found in Revelation 3:14-19. These Scriptures are in regard to the Church of Laodicea. It is amazing to consider how Jesus is introduced to this church. It would be beneficial to note how Jesus is introduced in relationship to the churches in Revelations 2-3. The introduction gives us insight into a particular church's weakness or point of hope and encouragement.

---

[2] John 15:22; Colossians 2:8; 2 Timothy 3:5; 1 John 4:2
[3] Psalm 111:10; Romans 3:17-18

To the Church of Laodicea, Jesus is introduced as the faithful and true witness, the beginning of the creation of God. It is clear from this perspective that when complacency is in operation, the fruit of it will be deception that will justify unfaithfulness. Faithfulness points to being faithful to see a matter through or to endure to the end in personal commitments or agreements. Those who are complacent will fail in both arenas. They will lack the personal initiative and character to see a matter completed that might prove inconvenient or unpleasant to the fleshly ways, and foolish to the mind.

Jesus said of the Church of Laodicea that He knew their works. Most people think of those who are complacent towards a matter as being lazy. This is not true; complacency simply means a person is unresponsive towards matters that do not personally stir them up. Complacency is very fleshly; therefore, it can be easily stirred up emotionally to matters that will serve its particular purpose. However, if a matter does not stir up the sentiment, desire, or emotional zeal, it will not respond.

We know the soulish man does not mind God in his midst, but he will not be inclined towards His rule. The natural man will tolerate God, but is incapable of receiving anything from the Spirit for he deems such matters as being foolish. The fleshly man wars against the Spirit for there is no agreement between them. For the complacent man, he may be busy in regard to the matters of God, but will prove to be unresponsive to the true call for consecration and obedience.

We see that the Church of Laodicea did works, but their works revealed that they were neither hot nor cold towards God. Jesus' response towards what I would consider "half-baked" works was to spew them out of his mouth.

As we consider each form of judgment pronounced upon each stage of the unregenerate man of this present world, it proves to be quite sobering. The soulish man was completely separated from God to partake of a cursed life outside of what his Creator truly desired for him. The natural man would eventually be turned over to a reprobate mind. The fleshly man would not inherit the kingdom of God. For the complacent man, once his works are spewed out in repulsiveness, his true state of wretchedness will be revealed as he stands in utter misery, spiritually bankrupt, blinded by delusion, and naked before the Lord.[4]

Obviously, the complacent man will end up being deluded by his own form of righteousness. Consider the Church of Laodicea in Revelation 3:17, "Because thou sayest, I am rich, and increased with goods, and have need of nothing, and knowest not that thou art wretched, and miserable, and poor, and blind, and naked." These people equated what they considered to be blessings of God according to worldly evaluations. The Word of God is clear that those who believe or teach that true godliness is measured or associated with the physical blessings of the

---

[4] Genesis 3:14, 22-24; Romans 1:28; Revelation 3:15-17

world are perverse, and to withdraw from them. It is the rich who often fall into temptation and the snares of destruction; for the love of money is the root of all evil. However, the things of the world will ultimately pass away, but those who do the will of God will live forever.[5]

It is interesting to observe how the complacent man responds to truth. The soulish man hides from truth, the natural man becomes offended by truth, and the fleshly man rages against truth, but the complacent man will respond in one or two ways. He can easily be frightened by it, choosing to ignore, deny, or downplay it in some mocking, degrading way. Otherwise, such fear can also turn into anger towards God, because this man is not willing to do what is right. He prefers his comfortable world of darkness and indifference towards what is true and acceptable to God. He resents the fact that God would strip him of his religious cloak to expose his indifference towards Him. After all, indifference comes from a lack of love or a type of hatred that causes many to grow cold in their attitude and response towards God. The truth is the complacent man prefers his pigpen to that which is holy and honorable before God.

The other way the complacent man will respond to truth is with fake nobility. In other words, he will quickly agree with a matter, and even say "amen" or "so be it" in regard to the situation. As a result, this man seems quite agreeable to any wrong or consequences that might be a result of his complacency. However, such fake nobility is nothing but an outward façade of pride that is being noble about excusing itself from being humble and repentant. A good example of this fake nobility of the complacent man can be found Eli.

Eli was the priest of Israel. The problem is he had two sons who were serving in the priesthood, but they were worthless men. They not only offered to God sacrifices that were unacceptable, but they were morally corrupt. It was said of their sin that it was very great before the Lord.[6]

It was Eli's responsibility as the High Priest to rebuke his sons, and remove them from the priesthood to ensure its integrity before God. We are told that Eli rebuked his sons, but he did not remove them from the priesthood. Since God already marked them for judgment, they did not hearken to their father's rebuke and warning.[7]

Eli may have appeared honorable in rebuking his sons, but he did not do what was honorable before God. Clearly, he was not zealous towards truth, righteousness, and purity. He did not insist that the standard set forth for priests was strictly observed.

This brings us to the harsh reality behind a complacent man. He is very self-serving. God sent one of his servants to rebuke Eli. In his rebuke he exposed what was happening behind the priestly garbs. Eli

---

[5] 1 Timothy 6:3-12; 1 John 2:17
[6] 1 Samuel 2:12-17
[7] 1 Samuel 2:22-25

was also enjoying the part of the offering that was to be dedicated to the Lord. He was partaking of his sons' abhorrence they showed to the offerings to the Lord, thereby trampling also upon the sacrifice. God made it very clear through His messenger that Eli's sons would die, and He would raise up a faithful priest who would do right in this holy position. God confirmed it through Samuel that what was pronounced upon Eli and his sons through this messenger would come to past.[8] Consider the arrogance behind Eli's fake nobility according to his answer in 1 Samuel 3:18b, "It is the LORD; let him do what seemeth to him good."

There was no indication of repentance on the part of Eli. God was not calling him to agree with His judgment; He was calling him to repent for abhorring the offering that belonged to Him. However, Eli would rather be noble in his complacency than repentant for his sinful participation.

Judgment did come upon Eli's household. The uncircumcised Philistines killed his sons, while the Ark of the Covenant was taken captive by them, and placed in their pagan temple. The Ark of the Covenant represented the presence of Jehovah God in the midst of His people. But God will not reside in the midst of an unholy priesthood and a wicked people. Eli and his sons had brought a terrible reproach upon Israel because of their disregard for their positions.

When Eli heard of the fate of the ark, he fell backwards in his chair, breaking his neck. Apparently, God's offerings had made him very fat. And, when he fell backwards, his age and weight also were a factor in his demise. In his complacency he proved to be a foolish man in his lukewarm ways. As a result, he died a foolish death. There was no honor to be found in his life or death. The legacy left by him was one of disgrace and ruin.[9]

How do we address the complacent man in our fallen state? Jesus gave the people of the Laodicean Church this instruction,
> I counsel thee to buy of me gold tried in the fire, that thou mayest be rich; and white raiment, that thou mayest be clothed, and that the shame of thy nakedness do not appear; and anoint thine eyes with eyeslave, that thou mayest see (Revelation 3:18).

We know that our faith must be refined in the fires. As believers, we must be tested, proven, and found true in our life before God to gain eternal riches that will last forever.[10]

White raiment points to righteousness. We must be clothed in humility by Christ's righteousness to ensure we are able to stand without shame before our Lord. We must be healed of our spiritual blindness caused by delusion in order to see the truth about our Lord. We must

---

[8] 1 Samuel 2:27-36; 3:16-18
[9] 1 Samuel 4
[10] 1 Peter 1:6-9

come into agreement with God's evaluation about a matter before we can be healed.

It is the Lord's heart to chasten those whom He loves so that they will be zealous in repentance, and to ensure they will partake of His holiness. He so desires to have a relationship with us as His people that He stands at the door of our unreceptive hearts and knocks on them to gain entrance. His hope is we will respond and interact with Him at the table of communion.[11]

We know that the soulish man must be born again, the natural man must be transformed, and the fleshly man crucified. However, the complacent man must be revived. The Apostle Paul talked about the awakening or quickening of our spirits towards God and the need to cease from sinning in our unresponsive state. After all, the complacent man is dead or asleep towards God. In Romans 13:11, Paul states that it is high time to wake out of sleep, for salvation is nearer than before. In 1 Corinthians 15:34 we are told to awake to righteousness. Ephesians 5:14-15 gives us these instructions, "Wherefore, he saith, Awake thou that sleepest, and arise from the dead, and Christ shall give thee light. See, then, that ye walk circumspectly, not as fools but as wise."

There is a reason that we must awake from any dead, complacent state, and that is to follow Jesus.[12] Jesus is the one who will lead us to the life He has designated for us. But we must daily stir ourselves up to defeat the complacent man who simply floats with the different tides of the world on the self-serving waves of what represents personal comfort and convenience.

We must stir ourselves up to love God with all of our heart, mind, soul, and strength. Stirring ourselves up to love God in such a manner requires a daily choice of the will to do so. Love is opposite of self-serving complacency; therefore, we must choose to love God if we are going to know our Savior and submit to His Lordship in our lives.

Consider the following table on the next page in regard to the different states that the unregenerate man digresses into.

---

[11] Hebrews 12:5-15; Revelation 3:19-20
[12] Matthew 16:24

Condition	Soulish	Natural	Fleshly	Complacent
Heart	Deceptive	Foolish	Proud/ Rebellious	Indifferent
Mind	Independent	Darkened	Corrupt/ Carnal	Desensitized
State	Fallen	Obstinate	Sensual	Lukewarm
Ways	Selfish	Self-sufficient	Idolatrous	Self-serving
Attitude Towards the World	Attractive to what it can offer.	Feeds ego	Feeds appetites	Allows for Self-justification
Attitude towards God	Hides behind religious image (Tolerant of God)	(Departs from God) Can sound religious	Offended by truth and wars with the Spirit (Religious garb)	Unresponsive (Fake Nobility) (Will come in own filthy garb)
Restoration	Born Again	Transformed	Crucifixion and Exchange	Zealous in repentance (Revived)

What about you? Are you giving way to the complacent man because you will not sell out in order to follow Jesus? If you are not following Jesus, He cannot lead you into the paths of righteousness to discover the life He is calling you to.

6

THE EARTHLY MAN

We have been considering how the soulish man digresses in his fallen state. He has fallen away from the source of real life, God. Due to his fallen condition, he can no longer walk with his Creator in a relationship because there is no agreement. As Amos 3:3 asks, how can two walk together unless there is agreement?

Without a relationship with God, man has developed his own means to have some type of religion on his terms. In his religion he is able to erect a god that will bow down to his particular notions. This god will accept personal exaltation, as well as fleshly, profane sacrifices. The idol will also accept a mere covering to a heart revelation. According to these people's particular form of worship, God will surely overlook their unrighteousness because He will see how good they are trying to be in this fallen state. After all, God will not mind the fact that self is reigning, and that it will not share or concede its throne with Him.

In explaining how self reigns in his small booklet, "31 Kings or Victory over Self," A. B. Simpson relates the god of self to the 31 kings whom the children of Israel had to overcome to possess the Promised Land. This is true for us. We must overcome the reign and influence of our own self-life to possess the life of Christ.[1]

Mr. Simpson pointed out that these kings belonged to Arba, the father of Anak. The name Arba means "the strength of Baal," pointing to the natural man who depends on the strength of self to rule. Anak points to being "long-necked" or "stiff-necked" in his ways. A neck that will not bow is one that will insist on ruling from the heights of personal pride according to its own will.

Let us consider the ways in which self reigns in our life. We already mentioned the self-will. In the self-will of our fallen man, we will never really yield to God. In a sense, we will give God permission as to what part He will have in our lives, but we will always seek the next type of reign, that of self-glorying.

This "selfism" seeks the recognition and praise from others. It will not submit to that which is truly worthy to ensure the reign of the One who deserves to sit in such a place of honor. In fact, self-confidence will exalt its personal wisdom, strength, and righteousness, stripping God of His rightful place in our lives. Since I am now exalted in my wisdom, I will become self-conscious about my abilities and ways. I will cater to my

---

[1] Joshua 12:7-24

emotions, placate my religious notions, justify my fleshly ways, and become quite enamored with how wonderful or self-important I am becoming.

If I am criticized, I will either resort to self-depreciation that will impress others in regard to my fake humility, or I will vindicate self through personal justification. Of course, I cannot let anyone see how sensitive I am due to the reign of my self-life, for the person will see how fragile my ego really is. I must be sure that I cleverly adjust all matters around how I see things in regard to my self-life to hide not only my sensitivity to self, but my perverted introspection that allows me to appear wise and noble. At all times, I must cleverly hide the fact that I really love self, revealing that I am unable to love others, unless they are willing to adjust to the particular regard I have for self.[2]

In my fallen state, I cannot let anyone know my affections are self-centered, my motives come from my own self-absorption that I have concerning my selfish ways, my desires are self-serving, my choices are selfish, and my pleasures are always done for my sake. I hold on to personal possessions to gain the world, while fearing I will lose them, as well as greatly obsessing about how I can preserve them.

As a result, my greatest sorrow is over what I might lose, not what I fail to gain in light of eternity. My sacrifices are profane because they cost me nothing, and I deny myself of nothing that will impact my life on a personal basis. The virtue and morality I possess is not a matter of being honorable before God, it is about looking a certain way to others. My self-righteousness is an outer cloak that hides my arrogance, and the personal so-called "sanctification" that is taking place in my life is sanctimonious. It is all a façade to hide the fact that I do not possess true charity that is sacrificial, nor do I truly offer gifts that are pleasing to God. My so-called "good works" are based on what is convenient, and my prayers are about getting my will done. My hopes are nothing but personal wishful thinking that will hopefully end with my expectation being realized, and not the expectation of heaven.

This is the essence of the self-life. This digression of man brings him back to his original state—that of being an earth-bound man whose identity, purpose, and hope are associated to that which is doomed and will ultimately be purged by fire.[3] In the beginning man possessed the very breath and life of God, but when he sinned, he resorted back to being an outer body or shell created from the dust. Granted, he housed a soul, but it was now undisciplined and no longer inclined towards the spiritually unseen influence of the heavenly.

As a result of the separation between God and man, the terrible digression of man's inner state entered into a free fall into utter spiritual darkness. He was driven out of the place of communion with God into a world of struggle, toil, loss, and sorrow. There, instead of living a life of

---

[2] Mark 12:31
[3] 2 Peter 3:10-12

blessed harmony with God, he would have to strive to survive the world he once had dominion over, as the earthly elements would give way to the workings, destruction, and judgment of sin upon the world around him. Since man was driven out of paradise in his fallen state, he became a wanderer like Cain. Instead of looking beyond this world towards a city built by God, he built his own city where he would govern himself in a natural state, thus removing himself further from the true source of his origin and purpose.

As man digressed further away from God, like Esau, he would end up pursing the blessings of the present world, rather than desire a spiritual inheritance that would identify him to the next. As a result, he would never be able to find the place of true repentance to be restored back into a relationship with God.

As man's pursuits become worldlier, like Ishmael, he will begin to mock the actual promises of God. Ishmael represented the fleshly aspect of the soulish, natural man. He may have desired the promises of God, but as a fleshly man he could never become spiritually identified to them. The flesh always represents the earthly man's best intentions and interventions. However, God's promises represent God's miraculous intervention. Since the flesh cannot have any part in God's promises, it will try to counterfeit or mock them.

As man ventures further away from God, he becomes complacent towards the matters of God. For the soulish man, he may tolerate God, but he will never allow Him to reign. The natural man will always depart from God so that in his self-life he can reign without any competition. Granted, he might become self-sufficient in his religion like those who build the tower of Babel or the self-righteous Pharisee in Luke 18:9-14, but he will never stand justified before God. As the fleshly man, he might clothe himself with religious garb while he offers fleshly sacrifices and worship as he justifies away the darkness of his own soul. But like those in Noah's day, the fleshly man will be stripped of all religious façades, revealing that he still stands condemned and doomed in his fallen, unchanged disposition. The complacent man may even stir up his flesh to become religious, but such attempts will prove to be self-serving and temporary. He may accept the wedding invitation, but he will come in his own filthy garb, resulting in him being cast into outer darkness. This is why many are called, but few are chosen.[4]

This is the harsh reality of the self-life. It will simply digress to the point that man will simply be identified to the earth from which he came. At best he might wear a religious cloak, but the truth about his identity is that he is of this earth. He will mirror it in a darkened, temporary state. His natural preference will be for the world, making him worldly like Balaam who preferred the wages of unrighteousness. Such people who walk according to the earthly man will live in error, choosing the vanity of a worldly inheritance to the eternal promises of God. They will ultimately

---

[4] Genesis 6:3-8; 11:1-9; Matthew 22:1-14

live in complete opposition against God. These individuals represent wells without water and clouds that are carried about by the storms of judgment.[5]

As we consider the earthly man, we can identify a man who has come under the spirit of the world and harbors a heart of unbelief. Since there is a gulf of separation between God and man, the spiritual aspect of man's inner being is vacant. Left with an emptiness, he strives in futility to satisfy the appetites of his self-life. Even though often tormented in his soul, he remains deluded, proud, disobedient, and indifferent to God. As a result, in his earthly identification he walks in unbelief towards God's character and Word.

The earthly man who has walked according to the whims of the self-life will cease to exist, leaving the spirit and soul to reap the consequences of a vain, useless life on earth. Sadly, man wants to make an impact in this world. He wants to leave a memorial, a legacy marking the significance of his life. In some cases, history serves as such a memorial, but it can be perverted, temporary, and uncertain. The reality is many people have passed through the corridors of history that remain unknown or appear insignificant in the scheme of things.

The truth is man will barely leave a significant mark even in history. He may leave stuff and records behind, but in a couple of generations he will be reduced to just a name on a tombstone. Perhaps, there will be a face put to his name via a picture, but as an earthly man in his corrupt state, he will return to the earth that will embrace his outer shell with a dead, cold silence.

The truth is Jesus must mark our life if it is going to make an impact. We have been given a physical life, but we have also been entrusted with a spiritual life. The life we must be living must be the life of Jesus. Otherwise, we will become identified to the earth as our flesh falls into utter decay and ruin, without any future hope for our soul and spirit. A. B. Simpson put it best in his small booklet about the 31 kings of the self-life when he stated, "Our very life must be held not as a selfish possession but as a sacred trust."

The earthly man must give way to a spiritual man. This requires each of us as believers to take on the likeness of Jesus. We must be born with His life from above. We must neglect the natural preferences to gain His life. We must crucify the fleshly ways to ensure that His life is established in us. We must stir ourselves out of indifference in a spirit of revival if we are going to walk His life out in obedience. Clearly, it is Jesus' life in us that will make us a spiritual man. The Spirit of God in us will identify us as belonging to that which is eternal, but it will be the life of the Son of God we will be living out by faith. In the end, the spiritual man will be raised up with a new, glorified body. However, there must be an

---

[5] 2 Peter 2:15-18

exchange made at the cross of Christ. The old selfish disposition must be exchanged for the very life of Jesus.[6]

The soulish man represents the state man fell into, but the spiritual man represents the heavenly state man can be raised to. The natural man represents what man is, but the spiritual man reveals what man can become according to His Creator. The fleshly man reveals the best man can obtain from his base status, but the spiritual man reveals the best God can accomplish from heavenly heights. The complacent man represents man in his best presentation concerning religious matters, but the spiritual man will represent the majesty of heaven as he reflects the very glory of Jesus to a lost world.[7]

The Apostle Paul talked about this great transition for Christians from being an earthly man into the spiritual man. He tells us that what has been sown in corruption and dishonor, our earthly tabernacles, will be raised by power in incorruption and glory. He declared that the natural body would one day be raised up a spiritual body. Although the first man, Adam was made a living soul, the second man, Jesus was made a quickening or life-giving spirit. The first man, Adam, was initially able to interact with God on a spiritual level, but as believers in Jesus, we have been raised up to commune in heavenly places with our Lord.[8]

The apostle goes on to explain that the first man was from earth, but the second one, Jesus, was from heaven. Those who remain earthbound by the old disposition will be considered earthly, but those who become heavenly in their lives and identification will be considered heavenly. We have all been born with the image of the earthly (Adam), but as believers, we should bear the image of the heavenly, Jesus. After all, flesh and blood cannot inherit the kingdom of God; neither can corruption inherit incorruption.[9]

Consider the following choices on the next page to see what category you fall within as to your point of identification.

---

[6] Romans 6:5; Galatians 2:20; Ephesians 4:23-24; Colossians 3:10
[7] 2 Corinthians 3:18; Ephesians 2:6
[8] 1 Corinthians 15:42-49
[9] 1 Corinthians 15:46-50

Type of Man	Earthly Man	Spiritual Man
Identification	Earth bound	Heaven bound
State	Fallen into a doomed state of death.	Will be raised up in a new state.
Status	What man is in his fallen state: (perverted).	What man can become in his new state.
Works	Best man can do: (defiled).	The best God can accomplish in and through man.
Body	Corrupt and used in dishonorable ways.	Will be raised up in power in an incorruptible state of glory.
Soul	Once a living soul that gave way to death.	Possesses a life-giving Spirit.
Potential	Used to interact with God.	Will experience communion in heavenly places.

Clearly, the earthly man must be put off to put on the heavenly. This entails the soulish man giving way to a heavenly identification. The natural man must cease to be in order to become spiritual. The fleshly man must be put to death to become a Spirit-led man. The complacent man must become revived to experience the heavenly heights of communion. The soulish man must learn of Jesus' disposition, the natural man must let the mind of Christ reign, the fleshly man must die to put on the new man, and the complacent man must follow after Jesus into a new life.

It is clear that we must put off the old disposition to take on the life of Jesus. The question is what man are you reflecting, the earthly man who is yet unregenerate or the heavenly man? Are you becoming fleshlier in your ways or are you becoming spiritual in your attitude and conduct? It is vital as believers we bear the heavenly image of Christ to stand distinct in this dark world of sin, unbelief, and rebellion.

7
THE WAR

We must learn how to possess our souls in patience if we are going to finish our journey through this dark world. It is interesting to note that we can only truly possess our souls through patience. "Patience" in this text is a matter of expectation, knowing that something that is enduring or possesses a far greater eternal significance will be brought forth. It is clearly not a matter of personal strength, but one of inward character that enables us to have the fortitude to endure the trials we encounter to the end. Such strength is developed by us being constant in our devotion to the Lord, and upright in our walk before Him regardless of what we may suffer. It is truly learning to abide in Jesus even when our world appears to be caving in.[1]

The Apostle Paul described the place in which patience is developed and brought forth.[2] He reminds us that we stand in the place of justification before God. This place came by way of faith. Faith serves as an access into God's grace or favor. It is God's grace that allows us to stand and rejoice in the hope or expectation awaiting us in light of His glory.

It is in this place of justification that we can glory in tribulations, knowing that they are what will work patience or that inward character in us. Patience leads to experiences that establish greater hope or expectation in us because we have witnessed the faithfulness of God in each tribulation. As a result, we have grown in the love of God that is now shed abroad in our hearts by the Holy Spirit. It is for this reason that we have been instructed to possess our souls with this inner character or strength that will ultimately cling to the reality of God.

This brings us to the importance of possessing patience in regard to those matters that clearly affect our souls. We have considered how the soulish man digresses in his fallen state of sin and death. Now we must understand the war that is raging. At the center of this war is man's soul.

Man's soul is the prized territory that the unseen forces are targeting. Who will possess the will, intellect, and emotions of man? This is why we are told to possess our own souls in patience, thereby, choosing in what way our will, will be disciplined, our intellect will be influenced, and our emotions will be directed. If we do not possess our souls for the sake of

---

[1] Strong's Concordance, (NT) *#527 &, 5281*
[2] Romans 5:1-5

realizing Christ in our lives, we will become subject to tyranny, sorrow, and destruction in this dark world.

There are three main battlefronts in regard to our souls that we must prove victorious in to be assured of possessing our inner man. Jesus confronted these three avenues when He was tempted in the wilderness. The Apostle John speaks of these three avenues in his first epistle, identifying them to the world. However, it is important to understand how this unseen battle rages *over* our soul, *in* our soul, and *for* our soul.[3]

The first battle can be seen in Job's life. Job was considered a righteous servant, but he found himself in the middle of a battle he did not understand. He did not understand that his soul had become a battleground between God and Satan. In a sense, they were fighting *over* his soul. The test was simple, take everything away from Job except his life, and he will end up cursing God. Would Job in the end prove that his soul truly belonged to God, or would it become Satan's sick possession?

The temptation that was raging in Job's life seemed senseless to the natural man, insane to the fleshly man, and ridiculous to the complacent man. As a result, his best friends even falsely accused him. Job could not see the reason for the battle, but in the midst of it he made a decision to trust God, not curse Him.[4] God knew Job would pass the test, even in the midst of grave darkness. He knew that he would choose to trust His immutable character, rather than his personal understanding or theology of Him. Such understanding or theology was proving to be clearly limited, as well as incapable of answering the tough questions surrounding his trials.

The battle in regard to Job was *over* his faith. This battle is also clearly established in Scripture. The soulish man puts his faith in his right to be independent of depending on God. The natural man puts his faith in his own strength or abilities. The fleshly man puts his faith in his ways, and the complacent man tacks his faith on to his present reality to produce a false assurance. Hence, enters the battle in regard to the faith that was first delivered to the saints.[5]

The battle over our faith is intense. At the core of this battle over the soul of the unregenerate man stands his insidious pride to always prove his ability to reign in his own life. Jesus was tempted in the area of the pride of life when Satan tempted Him to prove He was the Son of God. Jesus was the Son of God and Satan knew it; therefore, it was not necessary to prove what was already established as being true and obvious. He rebuked Satan by reminding him that no one should put the Lord to such a foolish test. After all, pride is the open door that allows the flesh to claim it rights to partake of the glory of the world according to its selfish dictates.

---

[3] Matthew 4:1-11; 1 John 2:15-17
[4] Job 1:1, 5-12; 13:15; 19:25-27; 23:10
[5] Jude 3

Scripture is clear; we must not be weak in faith, causing us to walk in the sin of unbelief. Rather, we must allow it to serve as our shield. In fact, we must stand steadfast in faith, as well as continue in it. It must be without hypocrisy, mixed with all we do in regard to our life in Christ, and must serve as the substance of all that we hope for in God so we can overcome the world and inherit the promises. It is able to sanctify us, as well as serves as one of the virtues that will follow us into eternity. Ultimately, our true faith towards God will become precious as pure gold when it is tested and tried in the fiery ovens of trials and temptations.[6]

The next battle takes place *in* the soul. The first battle is over the matter of dependency or trust. But, the second battle has to do with our preferences. We have already discussed our preferences, but they will determine who or what we end up serving. Service also will determine how we walk out a matter. The preference of the unregenerate man comes down to the works of darkness. These works hide the fact that his deeds are indeed evil.[7]

Scripture describes the battle that takes place in the soul of man. The Apostle Paul is the one who gives the most concise description of it in Galatians 5:17, "For the flesh lusteth against the Spirit, and the Spirit against the flesh; and these are contrary the one to the other, so that ye cannot do the things that he would."

Most people understand that a battle is raging in their soul. They know it is a battle between good and evil, but they do not understand that it comes down to who or what will have authority in their lives. In other words, will they serve their flesh or the Lord Jesus Christ? The Spirit of God is trying to lead each of us into a life of humble and obedient servitude to our Lord. However, the flesh wants people to serve its whims.

In our initial state as believers this battle can prove to be intense. After all, before our born-again experience, we constantly gave way to the preference of the flesh. We have been bent towards trying to satisfy its various appetites. As a result, the war in the soul as to who or what will gain our loving devotion and service will take center stage until we learn what it means to actually give way to the gentle leading of the Spirit, rather than giving way to the demands of the flesh.

I have seen this battle in many Christians' souls. Needless to say, they are miserable as long as this battle rages, but they have not quite made peace with the fact that their fleshly ways must be crucified. Oftentimes these poor tormented souls focus on the battle, rather than the victory.

Overcoming the flesh is a matter of submission to the Lord and His righteous ways. However, the natural man presents a logical argument

---

[6] Acts 26:18; Romans 14:23; 1 Corinthians 13:13; Ephesians 6:16; Colossians 1:23; 2:4-6; 2 Timothy 1:5: 2:22-26; Hebrews 4:2, 12; 6:12; 11:1; 1 Peter 1:6-8

[7] John 3:19-20

as to what one will miss if he or she allows the fleshly man to be put to death. Therefore, the natural man is trying to bring the fleshly man into a place of prominence and peace through a false justification. Such peace simply translates into complacency because there is no real peace, just a state of delusion that has silenced the conscience about a matter. Of course, to make peace with the fleshly ways will cause the Holy Spirit to withdraw His presence, as well as silence the impression that He is trying to make upon the conscience about the person's need to repent and come into submission to the ways of God.

In such a state of delusion the battle may be over, but the war has been lost for the poor, wretched soul. Sadly, I have seen where the war has been lost for some individuals. Such souls have digressed into the state of the complacent man, thinking that all is well with their souls. However, the Spirit has withdrawn, leaving the soul in delusion about its true spiritual status. Jesus has left such a person behind as well, even though such an individual believes that He has been "cemented in place" according to his or her own personal preferences.

Coming into submission to the Holy Spirit allows us to walk after Him in the ways of life, be led by Him in the paths of truth and righteousness, and to walk in Him by faith in Jesus and obedience to the Word of God. Scripture states that those who walk after the Spirit will not know condemnation; those who are led by the Spirit are no longer under the Law; and those who walk in the Spirit will not fulfill the lust of the flesh. In fact, by submitting to the Spirit, we are brought under the law of the Spirit of life in Christ Jesus.[8]

It is our life and walk in the Spirit of God that allows us to know our authority as God's children as we truly discover "what is that good, acceptable, and perfect will of God." We will know freedom as we explore the depths of His ways and experience the heights of His purpose for our lives. However, before we can become humble, devoted servants to our Lord, we must cease to allow our flesh to war against the conviction and work of the Holy Spirit. We must deny the soulish man his selfish rights, neglect the natural man's justification to sin and compromise with the world, and crucify the fleshly man in order to follow Jesus into righteousness, faith, charity, and peace. To follow Jesus, we must choose to walk after, be led by, and live in the presence and power of the Holy Spirit.

When Satan tested Jesus to silence the lusts of His flesh by using His authority and power to turn the stones into bread, He spoke a simple sentence, "It is written, Man shall not live by bread alone, but by every word that proceedeth out of the mouth of God" (Matthew 4:4). Jesus made it quite clear that He would not bow down to the dictates of His flesh. He would live according to the authority of the Word of God for it was meat to His soul. In John 4:34, Jesus told His disciples that His food was to do the will of the One who sent Him.

---

[8] Romans 8:1-2; Galatians 5:16-18

Developing Our Christian Life

It is important at this point to understand that the Word of God does have a flavor to it. In fact, it will even give us insight into where we are spiritually as well. Examine how the Word is tasting to you to see where you might be in your spiritual walk and what state you must come to, to ensure that the powerful intent of God's Word has its way.

Taste	Heart	Condition	Response to Ensure Intent.
Bitter *(Rev. 10:9-10)*	Should lead to contrite heart	Humble, repentant state	Seek new vision.
Salty *(Mt. 5:13)* *(Truth)*	Been set free	Has been enslaved	Liberty to find life.
Sweet *(Ps.34:8)* *(Goodness)*	Tender before the Lord.	Agreement or Oneness	Communion or Fellowship
Lean *(Ps. 106:14-15)* *(Dissatisfy)*	Seeking	Spiritual Wilderness	Cause us to rise up to seek Him.
Dry *(He. 3:10)* *(No life in it)*	Divided (Idolatrous)	Spirit is missing	Repent of unbelief
Boring *(Does not feed the flesh)*	Half-hearted (Fickle)	Not consecrated *(Mt. 16:25-26)*	Abandons all to God.

The Word of God is meant to bring each believer to perfection in his or her life before God. It is also meant to bring a challenging reality to the unsaved that hopefully will bring conviction to their souls. As you consider how God's Word might taste to a person, we can begin to see how it will expose a person's inward condition. For example, it will prove to be bitter to the soulish man, dry to the natural man, boring to the fleshly man, and the complacent man either discovers leanness in his spirit or he tastes the salt in way of judgment. On the other hand, the Word will prove to be both bitter and sweet at different times with a clear touch of saltiness to the spiritual man.

This brings us to the final war that takes place *for* the soul. We know the war *over* the soul has to do with dependency and the war *in* the soul has to do with who or what we will serve. But, in this final war *for* our souls, it comes down to who or what will influence us. Influence points to the spirit that is in operation. Spirit determines what will motivate, drive, or lead us in our walk. It will also determine what we will expose ourselves to, as well as what we pursue after and worship.

The Apostle Paul talked about the aspect of this particular battle in Ephesians 6:10-17. We are told that we are in a battle with an unseen kingdom. In order to fight this battle, we must learn to stand, so we can withstand, thereby, establishing the resolve to stand when all has been done to resist and overcome these enemies.

As Christians, we are told that we have been given an armor to stand against the unseen forces that are positioned in this world, as well as in high places that greatly affect the welfare of our soul. We must put on the whole armor if we are going to possess our souls. Such possession means we will be protecting ourselves from the unseen enemy taking captive the different aspects of the selfishness firmly motivating the soulish man. We have to stand with the confidence of truth, ensuring that the deception of the natural man does not take hold in our perspective. We must put on the breastplate of righteousness to avoid the wicked ways of the fleshly man. We must shod our feet with the preparation of the Gospel of peace to leave the complacent man behind with all of his false pretenses. We must then take up the shield of faith to quench all the fiery darts of the enemy that could rob us of our resolve, kill our devotion, and destroy the work of the Spirit in our lives. We must take the helmet of salvation to remind us of our true hope that is in Christ, and pick up the sword of the Spirit to nullify any claims the enemy may have upon our lives with the powerful truth of God. According to the Apostle John, we overcome Satan when the Word of God abides in us.[9]

Satan is a clever unseen enemy. He knows how he can use our pride to set us up, our flesh to pursue idolatrous ways, and our eyes to covet ways that would cause us to fall down and ultimately worship him as the god of this present world. He understands that the soul presents the different avenues in which he can take captive the soulish man. Once the soulish man has been taken captive, then the enemy is able to blind the natural man to the penetrating light of the Gospel, enslaving the fleshly aspect of man in the affairs of this world. As the fleshly man becomes entangled, the complacent man takes center stage in an environment where his desires and lusts can be stirred up at anytime by the attractions of the world. Sadly, Satan's kingdom is not met with much of a challenge when it comes to taking captive souls of men due to the fact that in their fallen state they are already bent in their souls towards the ways of his kingdom.[10]

Jesus understood that Satan was after His worship. This prince of darkness wanted to influence Him according to the ways of darkness. However, Jesus only subjected Himself to one influence: that of the Father. He was led by the Spirit, and only exposed Himself to the ways of righteousness. As a result, He never deviated from His calling as the Messiah, His mission as the Lamb of God, and His ministry as a humble Servant. This is why when Jesus was tempted by Satan to worship him in exchange for the kingdoms of the world, Jesus rebuked him in this manner, "Get thee hence, Satan; for it is written, Thou shalt worship the Lord, thy God, and him only shalt thou serve" (Matthew 4:10b).

---

[9] 1 John 2:14
[10] 2 Corinthians 4:3-6; 2 Timothy 2:3-4, 19-26

Developing Our Christian Life

Satan is after our worship. He does not care whether he uses man's pride, fleshly appetites and needs, or worldly desires to gain access into his life. This enemy of God and man's spiritual well-being knows that each avenue of the soul serves as a possible means for him to bring man into his camp of slavery and destruction.

One of the greatest examples of this spiritual war in Scripture can be found in the case of Amalek.[11] Amalek clearly represented the ways of the flesh. The Amalekites were the first enemy that the children of Israel had to confront in the wilderness. They had been delivered out of Egypt (the world), but as the Amalekites remind us, God's people still had the battle with the flesh before them.

They met this enemy in Rephidim. Moses stood at the top of the hill with the rod of God in his hand. As long as the rod remained outstretched, Joshua and the inexperienced children of Israel would prevail, but when Moses' arm became too heavy to hold it up and he begin to let it down, Amalek would begin to prevail. Eventually, a stone was put under Moses, while Aaron and Hur held up his hands. As a result, the children of Israel discomfited Amalek.

Let us consider the example we have in regard to the fleshly man being brought to naught in our lives. It will be the first major battle we fight in our Christian life. We may come out of the world, but it must lose its influence, via the defeat of the flesh in our lives. In order for us to prevail we must stand on the authority of our foundation, Jesus, and we must hold up our rod, the Word of God as our source of victory until we overcome.

The Lord instructed Moses to write in a book this memorial, "That He would utterly put out the remembrance of Amalek from under heaven." During King Saul's day the Lord commanded him to carry out this memorial. However, Saul failed to carry out God's command when he spared the life of the king of the Amalekites, Agag, along with the spoils of war. Saul did not think one man or insignificant animals that could be used as sacrifices would be important. However, Agag represented the pride or authority of Amalek, and the animals represented a bribe that would surely pervert the ways of righteousness.

Samuel's response towards this wicked king shows us that such pride had to be cut off, and the flesh hacked in pieces to ensure that Amalek would never again rise to power. In spite of Saul's outward show of remorse regarding his disobedience, his complacency towards God's instruction was a sign of rejecting the authority of it. As a result, the Lord rejected Saul from being king.[12]

There is much instruction about how we as God's people must confront the flesh. If we fail to carry out these instructions, it will simply show we are rejecting the truth and authority of His Word. In the end, God could very well reject us in our fleshly state.

---

[11] Exodus 17:8-16
[12] 1 Samuel 15:1-33; 1 Corinthians 15:50

The war that takes place in the flesh is ongoing in our lives, but one day it will be utterly put down by the Lord, to never rise again. As stated, flesh and blood will not inherit the kingdom of God. This is why we must cease to be a fleshly man, and become a spiritual man that is identified to the heavenly man, Christ Jesus.

We need to take heed the examples in Scripture. We need to believe what God reveals and instructs us about the war in regard to our souls. This is clearly brought out in Ezekiel 14. Jerusalem was about to be completely destroyed. Who could be saved from such destruction? The prophet Ezekiel answers such a question in Ezekiel 14:14, "Though these three men, Noah, Daniel, and Job, were in it, they should deliver only their own souls by their righteousness, saith the Lord."

The question is why these three men? Each man represented the war that is raging over, in, and for souls. Noah was in the midst of great wickedness, but in spite of it he walked with God, finding favor and deliverance out of the judgment that came upon the whole world. Daniel was in the midst of great paganism that could have easily taken his soul captive through fleshly attractions, but because of his excellent spirit he was delivered through its various temptations. Job was righteous before God; as a result, his faith enabled him to stand when Satan tried to destroy the light of his testimony in the world.

Scripture clearly instructs us to overcome the flesh, the world, and Satan. However, it requires us to learn how to walk with God in an excellent spirit so that we can be assured of standing upright in faith. The question is, are you overcoming in the different battles that rage in regard to your soul? If you are not, you most likely are also failing to possess your soul in patience.

8
THE PREFERENCE

We have been following the destructive digression of the fallen man. It has taken me years to realize the significance behind the words found in Isaiah 55:8-9, "For my thoughts are not your thoughts, neither are your ways my ways, saith the LORD. For as the heavens are higher than the earth, so are my ways higher than your ways, and my thoughts than your thoughts." As I have dealt with people, one of their greatest obstacles comes down to them believing that their particular way must be right, simply because everything within their inner being, their mind, and emotions agrees with it. They have approached if from every direction to come into some type of understanding that fits in every way. They have figured it out, tested it according to how it made them feel, and considered all the possible affects it would have on them. In the end, they come to the same conclusion; therefore, how could they be wrong?

Since these people have proved their conclusion to be sure and valid in their own mind, they automatically believe others should see the "truth" behind their reality. In these people's minds they believe that any real intelligent person would see how right they are in their thought processes; therefore, come into agreement about a matter.

However, there is one that is usually not in agreement about our conclusions as to the way something should be. The one who opposes our conclusions has a far greater perspective. His vantage point is a heavenly one. In other words, He sees the whole picture, from the beginning to the end. He knows about it in light of the past, the present, and the future. He knows the spirit, purpose, and end result of it. He knows, and He is forever trying to get man to realize that no matter what he thinks he knows, he still only knows in part.[1]

The One who often opposes our thought process and often considers our ways to be perverted is our Creator, the God of the universe. Scripture is clear that we can only know the real matters of God by His Spirit. It is the Spirit who unveils the matters of heaven to our spirit. He is the one who serves as our true teacher and leads us into all truth about Jesus. If a teaching does not come from Him, there will be no life to the Word of God. It will be just words, concepts, philosophies, and lifeless doctrine that enslaves a person, rather than inspires, enables,

---

[1] 1 Corinthians 13:9

and empowers him or her to walk out its truths and principles in child-like confidence and obedience.[2]

Individuals have come to me with a big question mark on their face after I have challenged them about approaching the Bible for the purpose of gaining religious knowledge about God. The correct reason to approach the Bible is to seek to know God. In other words, if the knowledge about God never gets into our spirit, we will never really know Him. These individuals ask me how they can get such knowledge into their spirit. This is an easy question, but not an easy answer. The reason that God's truths often do not become life is that most people are looking for some type of religious formula that they can put into practice that would cement them in truth and righteousness. However, there is no real formula as far as allowing the Spirit to take what we know and connect the dots in order to unveil God to our hearts, thereby, bringing life to our understanding.

I explain to people that our initial error is simply that we seek to understand God, rather than seek to be brought to an understanding of who He is according to the revelation of the Spirit. When we approach the Word to understand God, it is often for the purpose of controlling our understanding as to who He will become in our lives. Such an approach lacks faith. We see this lack of faith in each stage of the fallen man.

For the soulish man, the concept of God is allowed, but not the reality of God that would shake his personal kingdom. After all, God deserves the right to be God in each of our lives, but the soulish man must keep Him at bay so he can maintain his independence from Him.

For the natural man, God is tacked on as an option, but will never become the solution. For the fleshly man, God simply becomes a platform that allows one to believe that all experiences attached to religion are from God. In the case of the complacent man, God is put into a nice little "box" that allows the religious side of the fleshly man to be comfortable in his religious world. And, if anyone or anything challenges that "box" the complacent man can become belligerent. It is at this point he will try to take back his idea of God by not only fitting Him back into the "box", but he will actually cement his idea of Him in it to avoid any future conflict. Needless to say, God is not in the complacent man's "box."

Scripturally, we know that the Bible was written to bring contrast to our lives through examples.[3] Therefore, it is vital that examples regarding the earth-bound man and the spiritual man be presented to enable us to examine them in light of our personal walk. When I think about two people whose lives serve as such a contrast, Saul and David come to mind.

---

[2] Proverbs 21:2, 8; John 6:63: 16:13; 1 Corinthians 2:10-13; 2 Corinthians 3:6; 1 John 2:27

[3] 1 Corinthians 10:11

Developing Our Christian Life

    These two men stand at opposite poles of one another. Since their lives were intertwined, we can begin to see the distinct contrast between their character and ways. In fact, the earthly man will become jealous and resentful of the spiritual man. If you have any knowledge of these two men, you will automatically know which one serves as the image of the earthly man and who will ultimately develop the image of the spiritual man.

    It is vital that we set up the environment in which these two men's lives crossed paths. The environment in which these two men met started with the children of Israel wanting to be like the rest of the nations around them. In other words, instead of God being their only Lord and true King, they wanted a man to rule over them as king. This demand for a king greatly distressed Samuel, their judge. However, the Lord instructed Samuel to hearken to their demand. He also told him that they were not rejecting him as their judge; rather they were rejecting their Creator's reign in their lives.[4]

    We see Samuel warning the people about the consequences of mere man reigning over them. He would require their sons, daughters, labor, the fruits of their fields, and the best of their flocks. As seen from history, earthly or worldly kings will usually put their subjects in bondage. After all, they will do everything in light of that which will serve their own preferences and lust. Samuel made this statement to the children of Israel, "And ye shall cry out in that day because of your king whom ye shall have chosen; and the LORD will not hear you in that day" (1 Samuel 8:18).

    Scripture tells us that the people refused to obey the voice of Samuel. They had already made up their mind. They wanted to be like the pagan nations around them. In essence, they were saying they would rather have an earthly king than a heavenly king. Once again, it comes down to preference. At least they could see an earthly king, but this king would not have a heavenly vantage point; and his power would depend on one or two sources: heaven or the people who set him up as king.[5]

    God told Samuel to make the people of Israel a king. This is interesting statement. In other words, any mere man can be made a king, but there is only one who is truly king of all. How do you make a person a king? We must follow Samuel's steps to understand how easy it is to make someone a king.

    It is important to note that Saul's history as king begins with Israel's rebellion. As we will see, King Saul serves as a clear example of how the flesh works from the premise of rebellion. After all, rebellion can only produce rebellion. As we study Saul's example, we will see the fallen man's limited vision, independent ways, rebellious heart, perverted perception, and ultimate destruction. Although, Saul had the potential to be king, his fleshly decisions resulted in him wasting his life as he gave

---

[4] 1 Samuel 8:5-7
[5] 1 Samuel 8:19-21

way to fleshly compromise, and an existence that was riddled with judgment.

As we study the rebellious foundation being established by the children of Israel, we can see that all rebellion towards God is marked by a change in leadership. In other words, they wanted to dethrone God. The reasons for dethroning God bring us back to the presence of idolatry. However, anytime a person dethrones God, he or she must expect judgment.

God permitted the children of Israel to dethrone Him. However, God's permissive will simply means He is permitting a person's rebellion. But there will be consequences that will follow.

God was permitting the children of Israel to have their king. What kind of man would fit these people's concept of a king? Remember they wanted a king like the pagan nations around them. Their concept of a king would be based on the fleshly realm influenced by idolatry and paganism.

The answer to this question can be found in the description of Saul in 1 Samuel 9:2, "And he had a son, whose name was Saul, a choice young man, and goodly (handsome); and there was not among the children of Israel a goodlier (more handsome) person than he; from his shoulders and upward he was higher (taller) than any of the people." (Parenthesis added.) Saul fit their perception of a king because he looked like the idea they had about a king. However, did Saul have the inward character to be king? It did not matter to the children of Israel. He had the image of the earthly man that was appealing to the eyes according the attractions of the world. After all, anyone at this point could be king that had the right appearance.

Saul must have presented a striking impressive image of a man. However, the flesh's preference is contrary to God's choice. Granted, God was permitting the children of Israel to have their king, but they would discover that their choice for king was greatly lacking in discernment. Their choice was based on outward vanity and not inward character.

In tough times outward vanity will not be able to address the ethical and spiritual issues of a matter. It will not have any real discretion in matters that require diplomacy and wise decisions. It will lack true leadership ability. However, to the shortsighted people of Israel, it did not matter whether Saul had any type of spiritual life in God that would ensure morality and wisdom in leadership. He was the people's choice for king because of his outward appearance. One of the greatest kings of Israel, Solomon summarized the dilemma of a people whose leaders prove to be foolish, "When the righteous are in authority, the people rejoice: but when the wicked beareth rule the people mourn" (Proverbs 29:2).

To me the biggest point of insight into Saul's character can be found in 1 Samuel 10:9: "And it was so that, when he had turned his back to go from Samuel, God gave him another heart; and all those signs came to

Developing Our Christian Life

pass that day." Character always comes back to the heart condition. God actually had to give Saul another heart in order to be ruler. Does this mean that Saul did not have the heart to be a leader of Israel?

Let us consider the events surrounding Samuel anointing Saul as king. We know that God was giving the people of Israel what they wanted, but sometimes this means judgment, not blessings. Samuel reminded the people that they had rejected their God, who had saved them out of adversities and tribulations. He later told them that their wickedness was great in the sight of the Lord in asking for a king.[6]

When Samuel went to anoint Saul, he was hiding in stuff or baggage.[7] Remember, the soulish man will hide from the light and calling placed before him by God. Of course, God knew where he was. Saul had to be fetched. When he was presented to the people, he stood taller than anyone else. They now had their king, but what would they do about it? They simply went back to their old way of life. However, matters had changed, and things would never be the same. Consequences would follow their unrighteous request. They had proven to be rebellious towards God's leadership.

Consider what Samuel said in 1 Samuel 12:13, "Now, therefore, behold the king whom ye have chosen, and whom ye have desired! And, behold, the LORD hath set a king over you." Clearly, Saul was their choice of king, but based on his inward character what kind of leadership would he bring to them?

As you follow Saul's life, you will realize that at the beginning there was a mixture. In other words, Saul did not have any real faith in God; therefore, he would end up in fearful, compromising, and defeating situations.[8] Before we follow Saul's digression as a king, we must first recognize some interesting aspects about his life. Keep in mind that he is the example of where the flesh will lead a person in his or her ways.

Saul had some real encounters with God as a confirmation to him being king. He had a prophecy spoken over him, as well as the fact that the Spirit came down on him and he prophesied among the prophets. God had also given him a new heart.[9] You would think with these types of experiences that Saul would prove to be a godly man. However, in my own encounters with fleshly people who had some type of supernatural experience, it often proves the opposite. Such people may be sentimental about such experiences, but they are void of real faith.

In a sense, it is as though the supernatural experiences simply reveal such people's real heart as far as God. These people really lack inward integrity. Without inward integrity, a changed heart will become darkened by old ways, instead of transformed by a new way of living.

---

[6] 1 Samuel 10:19; 12:17
[7] 1 Samuel 10:22
[8] Hebrews 4:2
[9] 1 Samuel 10:1-13

The new way of living is clearly motivated and disciplined as a person seeks out and learns how to serve the Lord with all of his or her heart.

Therefore, such spiritual experiences often serve as some form of judgment against these individuals who fail by faith to direct their changed heart in a right way. Faith is never established by spiritual experiences; rather, such experiences will confirm faith according to the Word of God. This is why faith comes at the point of hearing, and not from the premise of experiences. It is based on believing an actual record that has been confirmed in some way.[10]

What we will discover is that Saul did not really believe God, therefore, proving to be void of inward character towards spiritual matters. In light of Saul's example, as Christians, we must remember the warning found in Matthew 7:21-23. According to these Scriptures, many will come to Jesus calling Him, "Lord," and reminding Him of their many accomplishments that they did in His name. However, His answer should bring sobriety to us, "And then will I profess unto them, I never knew you; depart from me, ye that work iniquity." Even though these individuals were doing works in the name of Jesus, they were not doing the will of the Father.

Let us now consider Saul's digression. Initially, God touched the hearts of some men who became followers of Saul. In His first battle with the Ammonites, the Spirit of God came upon Saul, and he and his army were victorious in slewing the Ammonites. It was upon this victory that the people at Gilgal confirmed Saul's kingship.

In the next situation, Saul became fearful as he and his army were hedged in by the Philistines. The people hid themselves in caves as they waited for Samuel to bring the required offerings. However, Samuel did not come at the appointed time; therefore, in his natural state, Saul took matters into his own hands by trying to fulfill the responsibilities of the priest. This was unacceptable to God. As a result, the possibility for his descendants to remain sitting on the throne of Israel would never come to fruition. This ended any notion of a royal dynasty coming out of his family.[11]

In another incident Saul became impulsive. Impulsiveness proves to be a response of the flesh. There was a stalemate between the Philistines and the Hebrews. Clearly, Saul was not an effective leader to spur his army on to victory. However, his son Jonathan was a man of faith. He proved victorious over the enemy, inspiring the rest of the army on to victory. However, in his impulsiveness, Saul cursed anyone who would eat any food until the enemy was put down. Jonathan did not know about his father's rash, unrealistic command. He ate a bit of honey, and because of his father's rash curse, his simple action almost cost him his life.[12]

---

[10] Romans 10:17
[11] 1 Samuel 13:8-14
[12] 1 Samuel 14:6-24, 42-45

Developing Our Christian Life

One of the major incidents of Saul's career as king involved the Amalekites. We already dealt with this issue in a previous chapter. Saul was commanded to kill all of the Amalekites, but he spared the life of the king and the lives of the flock. He was trying to act noble about sparing the flock. However, in his fleshly, complacent state, he had been indifferent about carrying out God's command. Samuel put Saul's rebellion in perspective,

> Hath the LORD as great delight in burnt offerings and sacrifices, as in obeying the voice of the LORD? Behold, to obey is better than sacrifice, and to hearken than the fat of rams. For rebellion is as the sin of witchcraft, and stubbornness is as iniquity and idolatry. Because thou has rejected the word of the LORD, he hath also rejected thee from being king (1 Samuel 15:22-23).

Saul sought pardon in the midst of the kingdom being ripped from him, Samuel mourned, and the Lord repented that he had made Saul king over Israel.[13] The real issue with Saul is the same for every individual who gives way to the fallen man. He or she refuses to let the rightful Lord and King, Jesus, reign in his or her life.

Who we serve is a choice of the will. Who we follow is a choice of the heart. Who we honor is a choice of the mind. All three arenas must come together to ensure that one truly loves or serves his or her particular lord from the heart. The fallen man will choose his natural preference of worldly rule, but the spiritual man will choose the One who is truly Lord and King to rule from his heart. The contrast between these two types of men is that the flesh will always bring bondage, while the spiritual pursuit will ensure liberty for those who follow the ways of the second Adam, Jesus.

Twenty centuries ago, some of the Jewish people had a choice between their real king Jesus, and the worldly leadership of Caesar. Listen to their choice, "But they cried out, Away with him, away with him, crucify him! Pilate saith unto them, Shall I crucify your King? The chief priests answered, we have no king but Caesar" (John 19:15). The natural response of the fallen man is to crucify the spiritual man.

The same error is being done today as it was during Saul and Jesus' day. People would rather have the earthly reigning over their lives than the spiritual. After all, fleshly ways appeal to the ego of the natural man, as it feeds the appetites of the fleshly man, and justifies the complacent man in his indifference. Such individuals resent the contrast between the fleshly and the spiritual. They want to put out the light and voice of the spiritual so they can maintain an outward façade of nobility and religion.

Clearly, the first stage of possessing our souls comes down to who we allow to reign in our lives. It is easy for Christians to fail to learn the lessons of Israel and choose the wrong king. Jesus did not come in the way that the people of Israel were looking for Him. He did not bring a

---

[13] 1 Samuel 15:24-35

physical sword to set them externally free from Rome's reign of bondage. Rather, He brought a spiritual sword of truth that would expose hearts with the intent of setting them internally free from the deceptive work of sin. However, each man in the fallen state will clamor to reign in his own way, but each one must be addressed and properly dealt with to ensure the reign of Jesus. Jesus' reign is what will bring needed discipline and character to our inner man.

Therefore, who or what are you allowing to reign in your life? Is it the old man reigning from behind a form of godliness, hiding behind the worldly leadership of Caesar, or is it the Lord Jesus Christ? We each need to answer this important question to ensure that we possess our souls in patience.

9
THE CONTRAST

King Saul had it all. He was preferred by the people, sought out by the Lord, and anointed by Samuel. He was given the promise that if he obeyed, his family would retain the crown. At times the Spirit of God would come upon him in different situations. Saul had it all, but because of his independent, foolish, prideful, indifferent heart towards God, he ended up losing it, not only for himself, but also for his family. How can someone who has it all end up in utter desolation? It comes down to one main culprit. The flesh was allowed to reign in Saul's life.

There are clearly pinnacles in King Saul's life, but they are surrounded by the intervention of God working on his behalf. However, the godly life is not lived out from the premise of the pinnacles of our lives where fragile egos can be exploited by others, but in the valleys of testing and humiliation. This is how character is established in the inner man.

For Saul, there is no real record that he sought God about the matters that confronted him. He often ended up going in his own power, which exposed his limitations and foolishness as man. As you study his life, the people who were involved with him that had faith towards God were the ones who proved to be victorious over enemies.

We need to meditate upon Saul's life to understand what happens when we, in our fallen state, insist on giving way to the flesh. This should also remind us of another Saul who went around persecuting the new Church in the name of God. How foolish he proved to be in his fleshly pursuit. However, he encountered Jesus on the road to Damascus. The life of this Saul was turned upside down by his encounter. He ceased to be a Saul (desired by those around him), and became a Paul (small or little) before God. This allowed God to do great things in, through, and with him.[1]

We all start out like Saul, but we must learn what it means to come to a state of smallness or humility before our Lord. We need a new disposition, a right attitude, and the power of the Spirit in our lives to walk in these valleys of testing and humiliation by faith, and come out victorious.

Obviously, we must change our foundation if a new life is to be produced. If we start from rebellion, we will end in rebellion if there is no

---

[1] Acts 9:1-31

true repentance. We must ensure a right premise to be guaranteed of a right ending. Although God gave Saul the tools to end in a right light, this foolish man gave way to his natural preferences rather than chose to trust God. Probably one of the greatest consequences for Saul's fleshly ways was that he lost his spiritual edge when the Spirit of the Lord departed from him altogether, leaving open a door for an evil spirit to trouble him.[2]

The reality of the earth-bound man is that a wrong spirit motivates him. Either his natural spirit is causing him to toy with sin, as well as the temporary things of the world, or, the spirit of the world, Satan is enticing him to oppose God, rather than submit to the Holy Spirit. He is either being pushed by some form of pride or he is deluding himself by some religious spirit that inspires him to accept a substitute for God, His truth, and salvation.

This is the sad epitaph of the earthly man. It is one of defeat and utter spiritual desolation. As Christians, we must mark this sad epitaph because God has also given us all things that pertain unto life and godliness.[2] There will be no excuse on judgment day as to the path we prefer or choose to walk.

As a result of Saul giving way to natural preferences rather than choosing the reign of God, his life spun out of control as he spiraled downward into a hopeless, dark abyss of vanity. He had indeed walked in the ways of the first man, thereby, reflecting his failure to reach his ultimate potential as the second man. In Saul we see the reflection of the first Adam, that of rebellion and treachery towards God.[3]

Hence enters the contrast between the earthly and the spiritual man. The earthly man will always war against the spiritual man. The reason for such a battle is because the spiritual man will always bring contrast. Contrast will expose the real motive and character of the fleshly man. We actually witness this very struggle between the religious leaders of Jesus' day. Jesus constantly exposed the self-serving religious spirit that motivated them. The religious spirit was of the world. The Apostle Paul best described how such a spirit will express itself in 2 Timothy 3:5, "Having a form of godliness, but denying the power thereof: from such turn away."

Since Jesus was exposing the heart condition of these men, they became fearful, jealous, angry, and hateful towards Him. Clearly, the first Adam was warring against the second Adam, because the light of the world was exposing the darkness of the fallen man.[3]

This brings us to the men who brought contrast to the ways of Saul. The first man was his son, Jonathan. Jonathan was a man of faith. While Saul found himself at a stalemate due to confusion and fear in one of his

---

[2] 1 Samuel 16:14
[2] 2 Peter 1:3
[3] Hosea 6:7
[3] John 1:4-5

battles with the Philistines, Jonathan went into battle in the power of his God. As a result, he not only experienced victory, but he inspired others on to victory. It is interesting to note that eventually division occurred between these two men. The Bible warns us of such division in families. We know that division in households signals a fall within such homes. The conflict between this father and son that brought this difference to the forefront involved the second man who definitely brought contrast to Saul, and that was David.[4]

It is interesting to study the conflict that arose between Saul and David. As we will see, David was not in competition with Saul. After all what would the spiritual man desire or seek after in regard to the first man? The second man is satisfied and content in his life and pursuits. He may not be rich as far as the world, nor hold any real place of importance in his particular age, but such a man will be at ease in his life because he will be in a place of godly service. However, the problem the second man poses for the first man is the light he walks according to. The light will not only expose the inner darkness of the first man, but it will expose the weak character of his fleshly influences and ways.[5]

King Saul had proven to be soulish in his disposition. He started out strong, but it was according to God's mercy and grace. His reliance on the personal strength of his natural man revealed his moral inconsistencies early in his reign. Although he displayed worldly sorrow for his disobedience, he never repented of or changed his self-serving old ways. As a result, his fleshly ways were given free reign since they were never really addressed or put down.

In his first act of disobedience, Saul revealed that he not only lacked true faith in waiting on God, but he did not respect God's order in spiritual matters when he intruded into the priest's office. It was at this time that the Lord took the kingdom of Israel away from him and his family and began to seek after a man after His own heart.[6]

His improper intrusion into the matters of God rendered Saul powerless before his enemies. After all, if you do not overcome the inner enemies of the soul, how can you expect to overcome your other enemies that operate in any other arena?

God had given Saul a new heart to reign over Israel, but it did not prove to be a heart inclined toward Him. Saul failed to recognize his strength was not in his ability to be king, but in having his reliance on God. His authority did not come from being in a leadership position, but by being obedient to God. This is brought out in the case of Jesus in His humanity. Hebrews 5:8-9 states, "Though he were a Son, yet learned he obedience by the things which he suffered; and being made perfect, he became the author of eternal salvation unto all them that obey him."

---

[4] 1 Samuel 14:3-23; 20:18-34; Matthew 10:34-37; 12:25
[5] Ephesians 5:1-17; 1 Timothy 6:6-12; James 2:5
[6] 1 Samuel 13:14

Saul's second act of disobedience was in relationship to God's instruction. God's instructions are His commands. Saul's actions in regard to the Amalekites made it quite clear that he had rejected God's Word to him. "Reject" in this text points to abhorring, casting away, despising, disdaining, or loathing something.[7] The flesh will always reject the things of God because they are contrary to its ways. In fact, the flesh sees the ways of God as being unrealistic or foolish. It perceives that God will tolerate some compromise as long as He benefits from it. However, God does not need to receive any benefits. He desires our obedience to sacrifices that cover up disobedience. Saul clearly cast away God's instruction. Granted, he justified his rebellion, but he discarded God's command. Since he rejected God's instruction, God rejected him as king.[8]

It is from this premise that Samuel was sent to Bethlehem to anoint God's choice for a king. At this time the prophet was concerned about King Saul. He knew that he was untrustworthy. As an earth-bound man, Saul didn't care about God's plan for His people. He was blinded by the loss of his own dynasty because of his rebellion. Therefore, Samuel was discretely sent to a man named Jesse to anoint one of his sons as king. He had eight sons.[9]

The oldest son of Jesse, Eliab, passed before Samuel. His outward stature gave him an appearance of a king. However, God set the record straight. Man's appearance has nothing to do with whether he is qualified to be king. Granted, that which is of this world judges according to such appearance, but God judges according to the heart. The first type of judgment is based on shallow standards, but the second one ensures righteous judgment. Jesus even made reference to this in John 7:24, "Judge not according to the appearance, but judge righteous judgment."

Seven of Jesse's sons passed before Samuel, but God chose none of them as king. The prophet asked Jesse if he had another son. He admitted that his youngest son was tending their sheep. We all know that the youngest son was David, the one Samuel anointed as the next king of Israel.[10]

Who was this unknown shepherd boy? We could conclude that he was not regarded as significant because he was left with the sheep. However, this is not true. This young man had to be proven responsible as a shepherd to be entrusted with the sheep. Jesse had no doubt that his youngest son could take care of the sheep on his own.

We already know that David had a heart for God. Regardless of his age or stature, his heart was right before God. We get an insight into David's heart in 1 Kings 9:4a, "And if thou wilt walk before me, as David, thy father, walked, in integrity of heart, and in uprightness." We see that

---

[7] Strong's Concordance, #3988
[8] 1 Samuel 15:12-29
[9] 1 Samuel 16:1-3
[10] 1 Samuel 16:5-13

David had a heart that possessed integrity. It was from this premise that David would walk out the life that was set before him in an upright, honorable manner.

It was obvious that David could be entrusted. This brings us to how the path of David finally crossed the path of King Saul. The Spirit of the Lord had departed from Saul. As a result, an evil spirit was tormenting him. To soothe his tormented soul a skillful player of the harp was sought out. David was not only a responsible young man, but also a talented one. He could play the harp in such a way that even Saul's tormented soul could be refreshed.

Let's just summarize the type of young man David was. He was responsible, upright, talented, and anointed. David had not only been anointed to be king, but there also had to be an anointing on his music in order to refresh the tormented soul of Saul. Such an anointing can only be established in a relationship with God. Did David have such a relationship with God?

The most famous incident concerning David reveals that he did have a secret life in God. To have such a life, David had to have faith. Genuine faith is what establishes people in the strength of the Lord. Out of such strength come boldness, authority, and victory. The incident that reveals each of these virtues in David's character clearly can be seen in his encounter with the giant, Goliath.

I wonder how many sermons have been preached on this particular text. How many times have people heard this story and found comfort and hope? I am sure David had no idea when he was with the sheep that centuries later his very life would be recorded in the most prized book, *The Holy Bible*.

Let us now consider the incident of David and the giant. Saul once again found himself at a stalemate with his enemies. Not only was he being rendered powerless, but also some giant who was blatant about defying both the army of Israel and the God they claimed to serve was clearly mocking the ineptness of the army. Who had the courage to become a possible sacrifice on the battlefield on behalf of the rest of the army of Israel to secure victory?

The very size of Goliath intimidated the soldiers of Israel. Here again is the example of appearance being exalted over character. Do you presently have some Goliath in front of you, intimidating you from moving forward in your spiritual life? In light of the next chapter, consider what it will mean to have victory over such a giant.

10

INTEGRITY OF THE HEART

We have been considering the examples of Saul and David. Their outward behavior reflects the heart condition of their inner man. We already know that God had to give Saul a new heart because he was not prepared to fulfill his calling as a king. However, this changed heart did not incline Saul towards the Lord. He kept walking according to the ways of his selfish disposition. Granted, he had religious experiences but none of them changed his inner man. Such a change comes from making a right choice in a matter once the heart has been changed. Saul continued to follow the ways of the soulish man.

In Saul's first point of rebellion God started to look for a man with a heart for Him. We know, according to the heart condition that there are four ways in which man responds to God's truths. There is a hard heart that will not be able to receive truth in any form. It will reject or ignore it altogether. There is stony, selfish heart that will initially respond with fleshly excitement towards the idea of truth, but will become angry or resentful when it experiences any type of inconvenience because of it. Then, there is a worldly heart that will lose sight of truth, and becomes desensitized towards the profane ways of the world as it comes into agreement with the spirit of the world. Finally, you have an open heart towards the truth that can be convicted by it in regard to sin, challenged by it in light of righteousness, and brought to a place of separation by the judgment it is able to bring to one's life.[1]

Obviously, Saul possessed a stony, selfish heart towards God. In his second rebellion, God rejected Saul, because he rejected his Word. Here again, Saul showed no real inclination to obey God. He gave an outward appearance of obedience while adjusting the lines of righteousness to his own conclusions about a matter. According to Saul's actions, God would surely accept a matter as long as there was sacrifice, and surely He could be reasoned with in regards to His ways. In such logic, man will perceive himself as showing more tolerance for such matters than God.

It never ceases to amaze me how people somehow reason that their tolerance towards sin is considered a matter of love for the person, when in fact it is simply an indifference that serves their particular philosophies. Such perception actually deems God as being unreasonable and cruel for insisting on repentance, cleansing, separation, and obedience. However, God cannot accept anything contrary to His holiness. Out of

---

[1] Matthew 13:1-23; John 16:7-13

love, He has provided the means in Christ in which people could be deemed righteous before Him. But they still have a responsibility to repent of the profane, and turn towards that which will impress and influence them in the ways of righteousness in order to be holy in their disposition and lifestyles.[2]

In my need to understand the difference between Saul and David, I had to go back to the heart of David. We are told that David had a heart after God. The question is how did this young man develop such a heart? In the case of Saul, he had no such heart, and the heart that was given to him did not seem to change his attitude towards God.

In 1 Kings 9:4, we are told that David walked in the integrity of the heart before the Lord. Solomon tells us that out of the heart comes the issues of life. He also stated that as a man thinks in his heart, that is who he becomes.[2] Clearly, a person determines who he or she becomes by how he or she processes a matter according to the moral and spiritual temperature of his or her heart condition.

We are told that David walked according to the integrity that was present in his heart. Such a quality points to inward character. Integrity in this text means complete, pious, gentle, and dear combined with perfect, plain, undefiled, and upright.[3] David was complete in his life before God because his heart was single towards Him. He was pious in his devotion, gentle in spirit, and dear to God because he was righteous in his ways, pure in his motives, and upright in his conduct.

It is obvious that such a heart is developed in a person. In other words, David had to develop this inward condition. We only get glimpses into David's life before he was flung to the forefront. We know that he experienced some challenges as a shepherd. He had to fight off the predators and did so in the confidence of his Lord. Therefore, the first aspect of his integrity is that he had tremendous faith in God. He trusted God to preserve him and fight for him.[4] We know that Saul lacked such faith.

The next aspect of David's integrity is that it was wrought through travailing. Saul may have hidden from his calling because he lacked the necessary character to be king. Inward character is developed when one goes against the selfish tendencies of the soulish man, the preferences of the natural man, the strong appetites of the fleshly man, and learns to reject the indifference of the complacent man. Saul's life as king revealed that he had not developed such character. He had the opportunity to oppose the ways of the earthly man through the power of the Spirit, but he failed to do so.

David's character was clearly developed in obscurity. When compared to others, there was nothing that stood out about this young

---

[2] 1 Peter 1:13-25
[2] Proverbs 4:23; 23:7
[3] Strong's Concordance, #8537
[4] 1 Samuel 17:37

man as far as his outward appearance. From Samuel's perspective David's older brother, Eliab, had a more attractive appearance. However, God considers the condition of the heart. We know from reading Eliab's reaction towards David that he thought his brother to be prideful and wicked. Obviously, by David's reaction to his brother's false accusation, it was not the first time he had innocently brought displeasure to him without a cause.[5] Eliab represented the earth-bound man, who no doubt was jealous of the spiritual man that his younger brother was becoming. Eliab's reaction was a prelude to the attitude that Saul would develop towards David.

Saul had been presented with much without really travailing for it. The glimpses we see of his life were that he did not have to contend with the challenges that young David confronted. As a result, David developed his life in God in the secret places, away from the popularity and limelight of others. He was a servant at heart who was learning to become a soldier in the arena of life. After all, he knew God was on his side. Even though his brother Eliab falsely accused him of wanting to see the battle, the truth was David was prepared to fight the battle.

David was also tender and open before God. It takes discipline to remain tender towards the matters of life when you are being prepared in the darkness of obscurity. We see this gentleness coming out of David towards Saul when he ministered to him in music.[6] Saul was a tormented soul, but David was pure; therefore, his music had the ability to subdue even the evil spirit that would torment Saul at different times.

We can also see that David understood how to stand against his enemies. This was a big issue with Saul. He never really knew how to stand because it takes faith to stand in the power of God. It was others who usually inspired the troops on to victory. Clearly, Saul was often rendered ineffective in battles.

The Lord was about to bring David to the forefront. However, this position would bring on even more tribulation for this young shepherd. He had already been secretly anointed as king. However, he was not ready to take this position. God would first take him through a process to refine and ensure the integrity that had already been established in the young man. This would be the way God would maintain David's heart towards Him. It would not be an easy process as the fallen man would vehemently oppose him in every way, but David would choose to walk according to the integrity of his heart. He would not betray his inward condition, but maintain it in patience. Each right decision would reinforce his integrity; his righteous ways would distinguish his upright character; and his godly devotion would cause his life to bring contrast to those who were reflecting the fallen man in their disposition.

---

[5] 1 Samuel 17:28-29
[6] 1 Samuel 16:14-23

David brought his brothers food on the frontlines of a battle that had been rendered a stalemate by one man named Goliath.[7] Goliath was a giant in stature, but he was about to meet another giant. However, this young man's inward character is what made him a giant. David knew what it meant to stand in God, letting Him be his fortress and high tower in his battles.

This young shepherd boy heard the claims of the giant. He had taunted the soldiers of Israel to send out one man to fight him. If this soldier lost, the Hebrews would become the Philistines' servants, but if the giant lost, the Philistines would become their servants. Needless to say, his size frightened the Hebrew soldiers.

David considered this uncircumcised Philistine who enjoyed defying the armies of the living God. This young man had confidence that the Lord would deliver him out of the hand of the brutish giant. David volunteered to take on Goliath. Most of us know the story. But it is important to point out how David defeated the giant.

The first point to note is that David did not confront this enemy in his own power. Saul tried to discourage David. He noted that the Philistine was a man of war, and David a mere youth. David did not listen to the bad report. It was obvious that he was a youth and this man a seasoned soldier, but the victory does not rest with the natural man who has obtained experience and strength along the way. This young man knew what it meant to go in the power of the Lord. This showed his incredible faith towards God.[8]

Saul offered his armor, but it was not made for David. David understood he could not go in the armor of another. God had personally trained him with other tools of the trade. For David his main weapon would be a simple slingshot and a stone. The fleshly ways of humanity complicate victory. It is thought that numbers and show of strength are what will secure victory. For God, victory is a simple matter. It does not require a show of strength on God's part for it is already wrought in the spiritual arena according to His plan and Spirit. By faith David would make the victory a reality in the earthly arena.

Most people noted that David took five stones, but only needed one to bring down the giant. It has been speculated that David took other stones in case he had to face Goliath's brothers. Regardless, of his reasoning, the number "five" reminds us that all of God's intervention on our behalf is a matter of his grace or favor.

Can you imagine how the giant looked compared to David? It must have been quite a sight. I am sure no one was betting on David to win. However, the giant was not facing a young boy. He was coming up against God Almighty. Although unseen, David understood that he stood in the strength and power of the living God of Israel. He even stated as much to the mocking Goliath. "Thou comest to me with a sword, and with

---

[7] 1 Samuel 17:17-24
[8] 1 Samuel 17:32-47

a spear, and with a shield; but I come to thee in the name of the LORD of hosts, the God of the armies of Israel, whom thou hast defied" (1 Samuel 17:45b). David goes on to say that the Lord would deliver this giant into his hand, as well as the host of the Philistines; and the people would know that the battle belonged to the One who saves, Jehovah God.

It is interesting to note that David ran to meet the enemy. In Christ, we can run to meet any obstacle. We do not have to cower before it or be paralyzed in fear by it. We can have the confidence of meeting each challenge, knowing that the real victory will always rest with our Lord.

David prevailed over the Philistine with a simple sling and stone. God knows how to bring all giants down regardless of size and number. He is our fortress and high tower. We stand against all enemies while resting in Him, as we stand above the battles in complete victory. However, we must remember that such victory comes by way of integrity. Integrity comes by way of travailing in simple faith before God concerning the matters of life.

This young victor, David, stood on top of the dead Philistine. We need to remember with God's help He will bring all of our enemies under our feet. It tells us in Romans 16:20, "And the God of peace shall bruise Satan under your feet shortly. The grace of our Lord Jesus Christ be with you. Amen."

He also took Goliath's sword from its sheath, and finished off the giant. The sword represents the Word of God. We must take the Word of Truth from its sacred, silent places and properly use it to silence our enemy's mocking ways. David then cut off the head of the giant. Cutting off the head reminds us that the reign of the natural man must be silenced, and the ways of the fleshly man must be put to death in order to stir the complacent man out of a state of indifference towards the matters of God.

David's victory inspired the other soldiers to stir themselves out of the stalemate they had been experiencing, and prevail over the defeated enemy. Remember, once Goliath was defeated, the fate of the rest of the Philistines in the battlefield was sealed as well.

God had clearly brought David to the forefront. He was a shepherd boy who had been prepared in obscurity to become a leader. He learned how to stand in the power of God against bears and lions in order to withstand the giants of the land. He had subdued the evil spirit of Saul, as well as silenced the defiant cries of the uncircumcised.

David was graduating from being a musician in the court of Saul to becoming a soldier in his army. He had clearly gained Saul's attention. Even though Saul knew him one way, he was now seeing him in a different light. Who was this young man?

David was brought to Saul with the giant's head in his hand. Saul asked him whose son he was. David's answer will ring down through the corridors of time, "I am the son of thy servant Jesse, the Bethlehemite" (1 Samuel 17:58b). David's answer was a humble answer. He was saying I am the son of your simple servant named Jesse, from Bethlehem.

Developing Our Christian Life

However, this simple genealogy would be expounded upon in many ways. The prophet, Isaiah would prophesy that out of the stem of Jesse, a Branch would come forth and the Spirit of the Lord would rest upon Him. The prophet Jeremiah tells us that out of David would come a righteous Branch and a King who shall reign, prosper, and execute judgment and justice. Zechariah stated that this Branch shall build the temple of the LORD, and He will bear the glory as He shall sit upon and rule from His throne. He will also be a priest upon this throne.[9] The descendants of David would not only mark a royal line, but it would be the lineage that the Promised, Blessed Messiah would come from.

Surely, as David declared his source of identity, he could have not known the impact his life would have on future generations. He was simply a young man who walked according to the integrity of his heart in light of his great confidence in his God. No doubt this seemed normal, acceptable, and honorable to David. It did not seem extraordinary or unusual to him. However, his integrity served as a breeding ground in which God would do the extraordinary. As Creator, He could see this young man's potential, and David's integrity would allow the Lord to use him as a means to bring salvation to future generations. Ordained as king, God would establish an everlasting kingdom, king, and throne through this young shepherd boy.

Generations have been inspired by the story of a young shepherd boy who brought down a giant. Many struggling individuals throughout the centuries have found encouragement in believing and knowing that in God all Goliaths stand defeated by His power.

David clearly shows us we can victoriously possess our souls in simple faith. We can know that if we develop integrity in our heart towards God, we can be assured that the impact of our life will be no small matter to God. It will have a ripple affect that will impact eternity.

The question is simple. Based on your inward heart condition, is God able to make such an impact in, through, and with your life?

---

[9] Isaiah 11:1-2; Jeremiah 23:5; Zechariah 6:12-13

11

OPPOSITION!

God was ready to bring His choice for king to the forefront. Before this time, David was being prepared for his calling. It is true God calls us, but few are chosen because they are not willing to go through the preparation.[1] Such people want the greatness without experiencing the smallness that every true servant of God must truly come to an understanding of when it comes to his or her strength, abilities, and purpose. God's servants must recognize that they have nothing to really offer God. As they become small in their ways before God, they are able to discover the glory and power of His ways. For this reason, the prophet Zechariah reminds us of an important perspective in regard to establishing a matter such as the foundation of the temple, "For who hath despised the day of small things? For they shall rejoice, and shall see the plummet in the hand of Zerubbabel with those seven; they are the eyes of the LORD, which run to and fro through the whole earth" (Zechariah 4:10).

David had been made small in order for God to be magnified in his life. He recognized that victory belonged to God. Without His intervention there would be no real power to stand against the lion, bear, or giant. We know that David displayed great faith in God. He clearly stood in his faith, withstood by faith, and when all was done he continued to stand because of faith.

David had discovered God in obscurity, but now he would be graduating to a different level. He would have to learn to walk in light of God in order to withstand the opposition that lay before him. Although the opposition would express itself in the physical realm, it would start in the unseen realm.

King Saul was thankful that David proved to be victorious over the giant. In his humble attitude towards Saul, he did not pose any threat to the king. In fact, David's boldness and valor identified him as a courageous soldier who would prove to be an asset to Saul's army.

In due time, David even proved himself worthy of Saul's trust. He was set over the men of war. It was said of David that he behaved himself in a discrete or wise manner in all that he did. The consistency that was obvious in his character made him acceptable in the sight of the people, including Saul's servants.[2]

---

[1] Matthew 20:16
[2] 1 Samuel 18:5

Keep in mind, eventually the earthly man will oppose the spiritual man. We can clearly see this even with the religious people and Jesus. At first, all seemed well between these two parties. After all, David was serving Saul, and Jesus properly maintained the ways and teachings of God before the religious people. However, the spiritual man will eventually threaten to upset the façade of the earthly man. For example, Saul lacked the character and means to be an honorable king and maintain his kingdom; and the religious people lacked the spirit and truth to properly represent the matters of God. Saul as well as the religious people of Jesus' day wore masks and cloaks to cover their rebellious ways. Such masks and cloaks will always be stripped away by the example and truth that is characterized in the life of the spiritual man. Jesus confirmed this when He stated that He had taken away the cloak that had covered the sin of people.[3]

King Saul was about to come face-to-face with the character and authority of the spiritual man. The people that stirred up the complacent man in Saul to see the contrast were the women. After each victory, the women came out in the streets, singing and dancing. On one occasion they spoke these words to one another as they rejoiced, "Saul hath slain his thousands, and David his ten thousands" (1 Samuel 18:7b).

The natural man will not be outdone in his selfishness. If the complacent man is stirred up to recognize that one is indeed being considered or honored above the strength of the natural man, it will give way to the jealousy of the fleshly man. Needless to say, out of such jealousy comes anger. Saul was displeased that David was being honored above him. It was said of Saul that he was very wroth or angry about the comparison. He began to watch David with envy.[4] Clearly, the selfish disposition was fully in operation in Saul.

When challenged, the selfish disposition immediately becomes treacherous. Granted, it can hide such treachery, but eventually it will manifest itself. For Saul, the darkness of his disposition manifested itself in a couple of incidents when he tried to kill David with a javelin. Of course, David escaped both times. This caused Saul to become even more afraid of David because it was obvious that the Lord was with him.[5]

What does the spiritual man do when the fleshly man tries to destroy him? Since David was honorable, he could do nothing more than behave himself wisely before Saul in all matters. As a result, the Lord was with him.[6] Wisdom is an obvious virtue of the spiritual man. Jesus never stepped outside of the heavenly wisdom He possessed. As a result, He never fell into the treacherous traps of His enemies.

David's discretion was not only obvious to Saul but to others as well. Saul became increasingly afraid of David, while the people began to love

---

[3] John 15:22
[4] 1 Samuel 18:8-9
[5] 1 Samuel 18:10-12
[6] 1 Samuel 18:14-16

him because of how he handled himself before them. Obviously, David was not a tyrant, disrespectable, or arrogant. He must have maintained the same attitude of humility at all times no matter who he was around.

Since Saul could not openly come against David, he began to formulate a plan that would put David in harm's way as a means to cleverly destroy him. To put someone in harms way you must bait the trap. Saul would use his daughter Merab to bait David to valiantly and sacrificially prove himself against the Philistines. When Saul offered the hand of his daughter to David in return for the lives of the Philistines, David humbly questioned whether he was worthy to be the son-in-law of the king.

Scripture tells us that Saul gave the hand of Merab to another. The soulish man will maintain his independent reign at all costs. This reign means that since the natural man is treacherous, he will resort to flattery, while the fleshly man will attempt to entice one into a trap, and the complacent man remains indifferent and deceptive about honoring any promises and commitments. Although such treachery can discourage the spiritual man, he will not betray the integrity of his life before God and lower himself to any type of wretchedness.

Saul's plan to destroy David in a deceitful way was clearly thwarted by God. Saul's daughter, Michal, informed her father that she loved David. As a result, it pleased Saul to give his daughter to the trustworthy soldier. However, it must be noted that Saul agreed to this union because he saw his daughter as becoming a snare to David, not because it was the honorable thing to do.[7]

As a man of the flesh, Saul schemed to establish his reality in regard to his spiritual plight. God had already stripped the kingdom of Israel from his family along with his crown. No matter how Saul plotted to secure both, his plans were already doomed to fail. However, the unregenerate man in him would never concede to such a reality. After all, the soulish man would not give way to that which is worthy or greater if it required him to sacrifice his independence. The natural man would resent any aspect concerning the spiritual that cannot be controlled, while the fleshly man would become jealous and fearful of that which will not bow down to its perception, and the complacent man would always be stirred up to anger against that which challenges complacency in its comfort zones. Underneath the fleshly man resides the pride that continues to believe that it will succeed and survive, even when it comes to God.

David was once again enticed to prove his valor by avenging the king's enemies, the Philistines, in order to win the hand of Michal. To David it was not a challenge that he would back away from. In fact, it pleased him to prove that he could be worthy to be placed in such an undeserved position as the son-in-law of the king.

---

[7] 1 Samuel 18:20-21

Developing Our Christian Life

Clearly, David maintained his humble stance before his Creator and king. God once again honored David in his humility. The courageous soldier brought the foreskins of 200 Philistines to Saul. It was clear to Saul that the Lord was with David. As a result, the king became more frightened of David as he conceded to give him his daughter in marriage. However, it is said that Saul became David's enemy continually. Every aspect of Saul's soul escalated in its opposition against the spiritual man, while the spiritual man even behaved himself more wisely than all the other servants of the king. This caused the spiritual man to be much more esteemed by others.

The separation between David and Saul finally came to an abrupt head. The king could no longer tolerate the presence of David. The soldier's presence not only tormented him, but it reminded him of his present state in relationship to God, and his future in light of judgment.

Saul not only tried to personally smite David, but he sent messengers to David's house to watch him with the intent of slaying him. However, Michal warned David of Saul's scheme, helping him down through a widow, where he fled and escaped.[8]

When we think of such windows, we are reminded of the small window of opportunity we are often given by God to escape the divisive plans of God's enemies. The temptation is to ignore such warning and not accept the small, but simple way out of such dire situations. For the spies in the wilderness, they were let down by a cord through the window of a harlot in Jericho. The Apostle Paul was let down the side of the wall in a basket so he could escape the fanaticism of religious Jews bent on killing him.[9]

Such windows remind us of our gate, door, and veil. We know that Jesus serves as the only gate that leads us into eternal life. He is the only door that will truly identify us to His leadership. Such honorable leadership will lead us into the ways of righteousness. He is the only veil that will open the way for us to come into sweet communion with the Father, producing and ensuring godly attitudes and ways in our lives. As we consider these three entryways, we must realize that God's way of deliverance, righteousness, and grace comes through faith and godliness.[10] If we fail to respond to a matter by faith, we will fail to discover the righteous path that will lead us away from the snare of destruction.

Although there was an attempt on the part of Jonathan to bring reconciliation between the earth-bound man (Saul) and the spiritual man (David), it was short lived. There is no point of true agreement once the fleshly man gives way to the deviant spirit of this present world. In fact,

---

[8] 1 Samuel 19:11-12
[9] Joshua 2:15; Acts 9:23-25
[10] Psalm 23:3; Matthew 7:13-14; John 10:9; 1 Corinthians 10:13; Hebrews 10:19-21

such a man becomes more adamant to rid himself of the torment that plagues his wretched soul.[11]

This separation clearly marked the beginning of David's process in being brought forth as king. Leadership can prove to be a lonely walk. Those who follow cannot know the struggles or sacrifice that will challenge a godly leader. Although David was a man of faith, he would learn how to walk by faith in light of his enemies. He would learn to seek God in the midst of darkness and obey in light of the unknown.

Instead of the palace being David's rightful home as an ordained king, the desert and caves would serve as his residence. Rather, than holding a place of honor, he would be branded as a fugitive. Instead of being over a well-trained army, he would end up leading a rag-tag army that represented those who were disillusioned or disgruntled by their present leadership. David would surely have to learn to walk according to the Spirit if he was going to maintain the integrity of his hidden life in God.

David's plight should remind us of Jesus' plight. Although He was the King of kings, He stated that the foxes had holes and the birds their nests, but He had nowhere to lay His head. He was God in the flesh, but He became a servant in disposition so He could serve the Father as a means to fulfill the Father's plan of redemption. Instead of having learned, important scholars under His leadership, He took under His arm the unlearned and insignificant. He would be acknowledged as King while riding a lowly colt, only to be offered up as the Lamb of God a few days later on a brutal cross.[12]

As you follow the spiritual man, you will realize that God always provides others who not only confirm a matter, but who will go before the spiritual man. For Jesus, it was John the Baptist. He was the voice in the wilderness preparing the Jews for the Messiah. John the Baptist was considered great for he was willing to give way to the plan of God. In the end he was sacrificed.

For David, it was Jonathan, the son of Saul. Jonathan was in line to be king. However, he was not interested in the matters of the world, but in the plans of God. This potential heir to the throne knew that David was to be the next king. The man of the world would not concede to such a position, but Jonathan was not of this world, he was a spiritual man, and he would confirm that David was to be king.

It was said of Jonathan and David's relationship that their souls were knitted together. "Knitted" pointed to the agreement these men had in the spirit. Such agreement manifested itself in godly love. Out of this love a covenant was established between these two men in regard to their commitment to each other. It was at this time that Jonathan stripped

---

[11] 1 Samuel 19:4-7
[12] Matthew 21:1-9; Luke 9:58; Acts 4:13; Philippians 2:7

himself of the robe, sword, bow, and the belt he wore and gave them to David. Jonathan was clearly giving way to God, by giving way to David.[13]

It was Jonathan that tried to bring reconciliation between Saul and David. After all, he loved both, but he had a covenant with David. His soul was in total agreement with David, and he understood that David was God's choice for king. As a spiritual man, he did not reject his Creator's plan; rather, he rejoiced in it as he watched out for David's welfare, knowing that he would taste the wrath of his father.[14]

Jonathan also went to David in the wilderness when he was on the run to strengthen his hand in God. He told David that his father would never find him, and that he indeed would be king over Israel. In a way, Jonathan knew that David's exaltation not only sealed the doom of his father, but of him as well. Yet, he was resolved that the will of God had to come forth for the sake of His people.[15]

Jonathan and David made and reaffirmed a covenant three times. Covenant is perpetual or ongoing. It is an agreement that is to be passed down from generation to generation.[16] It is interesting to note what covenant was made between them. We are given insight into this covenant in 1 Samuel 20:15-17. Jonathan had agreed to warn and protect David with his very life, but David was to show kindness to his household forever.

David did honor his part of the covenant when he took Jonathan's lame son, Mephibosheth, in as his own. Mephibosheth sat at David's table. In a way, Jonathan's son pointed to each of us. Before Jesus established the new covenant of redemption with his blood, we were separated from God, unable to spiritually walk before Him in life and righteousness. However, our King and Lord secured His kingdom and crown with His very death on the cross. Upon receiving Jesus, we become adopted children of His kingdom, allowing us to sit at His royal table.[17]

As we consider the spiritual man, we have to acknowledge that due to his unfeigned faith he is ready to decrease; and because of the obedience that comes out of righteousness, he is quick to give way to the will and work of God on behalf of His people. This man may prepare or confirm the way, but will always concede that he is not the Way. The spiritual man will always be ready to be offered up to ensure that God's choice of king and kingdom are brought forth for the benefit of others and for His glory.

The end of the earthly man is death and decay, but the end of the spiritual man, is a new life and a glorious existence. As a result, the

---

[13] 1 Samuel 18:1-4
[14] 1 Samuel 20:5-13, 28-33
[15] 1 Samuel 23:16-18
[16] If you would like to know more about covenants, see the author's book entitled: *The Place of Covenant* in the Volume 1 of the foundational series.
[17] 2 Samuel 9; John 1:12; Romans 8:14-17; Revelation 1:6

spiritual man is always looking beyond this present world to a future, unseen world. His vision is clearly set, his focus unwavering, and his hope sure as he allows all that is around him to decrease in importance so he can embrace that which is truly eternal.

What about you? Is the old man in you still trying to gain preeminence over the spiritual? Or, is the spiritual man that is present in you giving way to the eternal? Only you can honestly answer these questions.

12
THE BRUTISH MAN

As human beings, we need to realize that we are always giving way to something. We are either giving way to the ways of the soulish, unregenerate man, or we are giving way to that which is new, eternal, and glorious. The key to possessing our souls is that we discipline ourselves in the ways of righteousness to ensure we are giving way to that which is eternal. If we do not, we will find ourselves giving way to the digression of the soulish man that will lead to separation from God, rebellion against His authority, controlling, insatiable appetites, indifference to the Spirit, and spiritual death.

We have been following Saul's digression because he refused to possess his inner being in patience according to the ways of righteousness. He simply gave way to that which was selfish, rebellious, fleshly, and indifferent to the spiritual arena. Eventually, the Lord departed from him, leaving him in a despairing condition of torment and hopelessness.

In Saul's state, all he could hope for was to hold on to that which God had already taken away from him in judgment. However, that meant getting rid of his competition. This caused the war between the fallen man and the spiritual man to come to the forefront. Saul no longer could hide his jealousy towards David. The soulish man was now becoming obsessed with the soldier. The natural man would not concede to any matter regardless of whether it was right or not. The fleshly man was greatly frightened by the prospect of losing what he possessed in the world, and the complacent was charged up to rid the world of the reflection and life of the spiritual man.

We see Saul pursuing David with His army. He was ready to do anything that needed to be done to destroy David. When the soul becomes possessed by its own insecurities and jealousy, it will digress into the brutish man. This is when man resorts to his base appetites. At this point he becomes obsessed in his pursuits according to that which is befitting to his fleshly desires, insecurities, and whims. Ultimately, the unregenerate man will become a complete slave to his sensual desires. In such a state he will appear foolish and insane as if he knows little and lacks any real intelligence or sensibility in which he can be reasoned with.

The brutish man clearly comes out in Saul's case regarding the priest's involvement with King David. It is important to know that when a person has digressed into becoming the brutish man, he or she is wary of anyone and everybody. Treachery takes center stage in the form of vengeance. At this stage, the beast within the inner man will rage against that which has offended the individual. Therefore, the offence of jealousy that started with the soulish man produces suspicion in the natural man, fear in the fleshly man, and anger in the complacent man. Such anger eventually turns into the vengeance that is clearly motivated by that which has become brutish. This is clearly the depraved reality of the next stage of the fallen man—that of becoming the brutish man. Since the brutish man is clearly untrustworthy, he automatically transfers that suspicion to others. Regardless of whether something is true or not, any minor discrepancy will immediately be considered treason.

The priest had unknowingly helped David when he was fleeing from Saul.[1] This priest had no idea that the king now considered this brave soldier as his personal enemy. No doubt if the priest had known, he would have never helped David. However, in his ignorance he gave David bread to nourish him in his journey.

Saul would have never discovered the innocent action of the priest, except that out of treachery comes treason of the worse type. When Saul was mourning about those who would conspire to help his enemy, including his son Jonathan, a man by the name of Doeg, an Edomite, related the incident of the priest helping David. If there was an example of a brutish man it was Doeg.

Doeg's name means "fearful."[2] The main aspect about the brutish man is that he is fearful. Since he is untrustworthy, he cannot trust anyone. Since deep calls to deep, he attracts those who are like him. He is always watching out for self as he suspiciously considers everyone and everything around him. Such fear will turn into anger and paranoia. In these people's insane worlds, they lose the ability to be reasoned with. In many cases the wrong spirit they are under keeps them separated from any real reality or point of reason that could change their direction of destruction.

A brutish person will either become pigheaded, bullheaded, mule-headed, or hardheaded in confrontation. In his pigheaded way, nothing can penetrate his insane reasoning. When he is bullheaded, he is too busy charging against what has offended him, running over anyone who might be trying to bring a reasonable perspective to a matter. In his mule-headed state he will cause a fuss with his insane suspicions and accusations, making him untouchable and unwilling to be challenged by any other reality. Ultimately, the brutish man will be found to be hardheaded. He will insist on his reality no matter how unjust it might prove to be to those who are innocent.

Doeg was set over the servants of Saul. He was a descendant of Esau. Therefore, he had no respect for the matters of God, which included the sacred position of the priesthood. He saw the opportunity to

---

[1] 1 Samuel 21:1-9
[2] Smith's Bible Dictionary, Thomas Nelson Publishers

Developing Our Christian Life

gain Saul's trust by sacrificing someone who not only held an honorable position, but who also had no intent of treason against Saul. He told Saul about how he witnessed the priest helping David, and he was the one who later executed Saul's order of judgment upon the priest and his family.[3]

In Saul's brutish state, he refused to listen to the priest's side, and ordered the priest with all of his descendants killed by the sword without a proper cause. The priest and his family came out of the lineage of Eli. Although God had pronounced upon Eli and his descendants that they would cease from performing before Him as priests in His house, one can only hear the "woe" pronounced upon those who take a matter into their own hands. It was because of Saul's wrath that Doeg executed judgment against the priest and his family.[4]

This was so in the case of Judas Iscariot. Jesus made this statement in Mark 14:21 about Judas' betrayal of Him, "The Son of man, indeed, goeth, as it is written of him; but woe to that man by whom the Son of man is betrayed! Good were it for that man if he had never been born." It takes brutish men to carry out such wicked judgments. The truth is that if the heart of these men were not primed to disregard honorable boundaries, they would never find themselves in such dishonorable roles.

David brought forth the truth about improperly taking matters into your own hands. He was ordained to be the King of Israel because of the dishonorable actions of Saul. Out of jealousy and fear Saul had relentlessly pursued David into the desert. On two occasions David could have taken matters into his own hands and executed judgment on Saul. However, David understood that God had anointed Saul as king. Granted, David could not come into agreement with Saul or follow him, but it was not up to him to take vengeance on Saul in order to be made king. God had His own way of executing judgment on Saul, as well as the timing in which it would be done.

David's disciplined actions towards Saul proved he was righteous. In one instance, David restrained his servants from killing the king, but cut off the skirt of his robe. He even felt sorrow over his actions. David followed Saul out of the cave, addressing him as his lord, the king. He paid homage to Saul, proving that he had no evil intention of causing him any harm. Since he had not sinned against the king, David asked Saul why he was hunting him. David then asked the Lord to judge between them. In the end, Saul had to admit that David was more righteous than he was, and that he was trying to reward David's honorable ways before him with evil. He even admitted that David would one day be king.[5]

In spite of Saul's admission, his base ways continued to pursue and oppress David as a means to keep him from reaching the throne. In one

---

[3] 1 Samuel 22:9, 17-18
[4] 1 Samuel 2:27-30; 3:11-14; 22:11-18
[5] 1 Samuel 24:3-22

incident, David came to Saul's camp and actually obtained Saul's spear and cruse of water as he and his men slept. Once again David refrained one of his soldiers from killing Saul.[6]

It would have been so easy to rid David of this brutish thorn in his side. After all, this righteous soldier was being unfairly hunted like an animal. However, David was not brutish, he was honorable. Regardless of the situation, he could not resort to an act that was contrary to the integrity of his heart. He would not lower himself to the ways of the soulish man. He had to maintain his walk of faith and obedience before his Lord.

Once again, David confronted his adversary. He first rebuked those who were to guard their king. If he had been an enemy, the king would be dead. He then asked the king why he continued to pursue after him since he was one of his loyal servants. David presented himself as a humble servant who had no intention of evil towards his king.

David also called for reconciliation. If he had truly wronged the king, then let there be a sacrifice made to right it, but if this pursuit finds its origins with men, let such men be accursed for driving him away from his inheritance in the land of Israel, possibly tempting him to serve other gods. He also rebuked the king by challenging him not to let his blood fall to the ground. After all, why would the king of Israel seek a flea as if hunting for a partridge?

This brave, honorable man once again made himself small in the scheme of things. He was not trying to stand tall in regard to Saul or Israel; he simply was trying to make his way through a trying time, brought on by a man who had resorted to becoming brutish towards him. David declared that the Lord would deliver him out of all tribulation.[7]

King Saul once again confessed that he had sinned against David. He admitted that he had played the fool and had greatly erred. There is nothing more foolish than the brutish man who wants to render evil for righteousness. Even though such a man will sin against that which is righteous, his greatest error is his failure to realize that he is simply heaping judgment upon himself. God knows how to deliver the godly out of temptation, and how to bring judgment down on the unrighteous.[8]

Saul was not the only brutish man David had to contend with in the wilderness. There was another such man by the name of Nabal. Nabal was of the house of Caleb, from the tribe of Judah. He was a rich man as far as worldly riches, but he was poor in character. He clearly served as the epitome of a brutish man who openly chose such a state. Scripture refers to him as being a churlish man. "Churlish" in this text implied he

---

[6] 1 Samuel 26:5-12
[7] 1 Samuel 26:24
[8] 1 Samuel 26:21-25; 2 Peter 2:9

was cruel, grievous, hard, impudent, rough, and stiff-necked.[9] It was said of him that he was evil in his doings.[10]

David heard that Nabal was shearing his sheep in Carmel. Nabal's shepherds had been with David and his men. This small army of David had not only ensured their well-being, but they had protected Nabal's investment. David knew of his prosperity, and inquired if he would share some of his good fortune with his men.[11]

Brutish people are void of any benevolence or compassion. They are very self-serving, always excusing away moral responsibility, mocking kindness, and quick at demeaning those who would dare try to prick their dead conscience with any type of moral obligation or kindness. Nabal was no exception when it came to responding to David's inquiry. He regarded David as a runaway slave. He gave the impression that any kindness towards David would be taking away from his servants, for he had no intention of sharing out of the abundance of his personal blessings.[12]

This is the first time we see David ready to bring vengeance on such an impertinent fool. He called his men to put on their swords. He swore that he would destroy anybody associated with this man.

God is faithful to hold back our hand in such times. David had every right to be angry, but it was not the fault of his servants that Nabal was such a fool. One of the young men of Nabal's establishment went to Nabal's wife, Abigail, to inform her of her husband's foolish words to David. The servant clearly noted that Nabal was a worthless man that could not be reasoned with. He also related how David and his soldiers were very good to them when they were with them in the fields. He also warned her that due to Nabel returning evil for good that evil was determined against him, as well as his whole household.[13]

Abigail was a woman with good understanding and who possessed a beautiful countenance. Her character epitomized the opposite of the brutish state of her husband. Unlike Saphira who went along with the wicked lie of her husband, Abigail quickly acted contrary to her husband's wickedness, and prepared provision for David and his men. She rode on an ass in order to intercept David. She met him in humility as she fell before him seeking mercy on behalf of her household. She even prophesized that the Lord would make David a sure house because he fought the battles of the Lord God, and that he would be appointed leader over Israel.

Since David was an honorable man, he was quick to repent of his determination, and extend mercy, as well as grace, to this beautiful woman and her household. David made this declaration to Abigail in 1

---

[9] Stong's Exhaustive Concordance, #7186
[10] 1 Samuel 25:2-3
[11] 1 Samuel 25:4-9
[12] 1 Samuel 25:10-11
[13] 1 Samuel 25:14-17

Samuel 25:32b-33, "Blessed be the LORD God of Israel, who sent thee this day to meet me. And blessed be thy advice, and blessed be thou, who hast kept me this day from coming to shed blood, and from avenging myself with mine own hand."

Unlike Sapphira, who experienced the same judgment as her husband, Ananias, Abigail saved the day without her husband even knowing it.[14] She understood the character of her husband, and realized he would not see the error of his ways and the wisdom of her actions. She was a godly woman who no doubt was submissive in her state as a wife before the Lord, but she did not hold to her husband's obstinate, foolish ways. She did not try to justify him before David; she simply did what was honorable in regard to him and his men. As a result, she spared the lives of those of her household, even her churlish husband, as well as kept David from shedding innocent blood. This example reveals that where one person's foolish actions may bring judgment on the innocent, the righteous actions of another may prevent it from happening.

Nabal held a feast like a king in his household, no doubt to commemorate his good fortune. After allowing her brutish husband a night to enjoy his good fortune, Abigail did tell Nabal about David the next mourning. The Scripture state that his heart died within him and became like stone. Ten days later, the Lord smote this fool and he died in his wretched state.

Nabal only enjoyed his fortune for a short season. In a way, he reminds me of the man in the parable in Luke 12:16-21. In this parable a rich man perceived that he was in control of his wealth. Since he had been greatly blessed, he decided to heap the wealth upon himself by building greater barns to contain even greater wealth so he could live in ease as he ate, drank, and was merry.

However, man is not in control of his life. He is as a cork on the ocean of life, blown to and fro by waves of circumstances that are beyond his control. Granted, man may determine the quality of his life, but he cannot determine the length of it. That determination solely rests with God, and was made evident to the rich man when God said this to him, "Thou fool, this night thy soul shall be required of thee; then whose shall those things be, which thou has provided" (Luke 12:20b)?

The reality of a fool is that he actually perceives that he is in control of his life. He lives contrary to the reality of God and eternity. He is separated from God in his independence; therefore, he has no sense that he is lacking the real essence of wisdom, righteousness, sanctification, and redemption. He sees himself as being so self-sufficient that he often lives in a state of delusion about his weakness and inept abilities as man. He is so fleshly that he perceives life from the premise that all happiness is attached to the world, and will bow down to

---

[14] Acts 5:1-11

Developing Our Christian Life

his fleshly desires. He is so indifferent to the Spirit that he mocks the unseen reality of eternity.

Solomon dealt with the fate of the fool in the book of Proverbs. It is important to point out that in our fallen condition we are all born with foolishness bound in our hearts. As a result, we are found to be a fool at different times in our lives. This is why we must possess our souls in the ways of wisdom as a means to properly address the foolishness that awaits any possible opportunity of being tripped up in our lives before God.[15]

"Being foolish" points to that which is unwise or simple in its ability to rightly perceive. It implies that a person has some raw material that must be properly developed through the ways of wisdom. According to Os Hillman's article on the different types of fools, he distinguishes four types of fools. For those who allow the wisdom of God to have its way, they are referred to as the simple fool that will make mistakes, but will quickly learn from them and make them right such as David.

The second kind of fool is the hardened fool. They are hardened by the truth for they refuse to learn from their foolish ways and humble themselves enough to receive instruction. King Saul was such a fool. It led him to a brutish state that clearly unveiled the ongoing saga of his foolishness as he digressed in his unregenerate, fallen condition.

The third type of fool mocks the things of God. Such people see anything spiritual as being irrational and nonsense. They have clearly bought the philosophies of the world, making them skeptical towards that which does not fit their worldly mindset. They are often referred to as "scoffers" or "scorners."

Then you have the fourth level of being a fool. This fool is the God-denying fool. You see this type of foolishness in Nabal. This individual is morally wicked. He ignores the disgrace he brings on his family and despises any holiness that may challenge his sick, perverted reality.

Solomon tells us that fools deal foolishly with matters. They will trust in their own hearts, and as a result, there is shame, mischief, folly, deceit, rage, false confidence, and an unteachable spirit that is associated with those who choose the ways of their personal folly. Ultimately, such fools walk according to their own darkness, and will fall into a pit of judgment.[16]

These different fools are dealt with according to their foolishness. The simple fool will meet with chastisement that will bring him or her to repentance in order to partake of God's holiness. The second type of fool will fall into his own traps. He will continue to be exposed as a fool as he heaps judgment upon himself, while tasting the bitter despair of his own folly in utter hopelessness. Judgments are prepared for the scoffer.[17]

---

[15] Proverbs 1:7; 22:15; 28:26
[16] Proverbs 3:35, 10:23, 13:16; 14:8-9, 16; 15:5; 16:22; Ecclesiastes 2:14
[17] Proverbs 1:22-32; 5:21-23; 18:12; 19:29; Hebrews 12:5-10

And, as we can see with Nabal and the rich man, God's judgment was clear and quick.

It is said that when David heard that Nabal was dead he made this statement in 1 Samuel 25:39b, "Blessed be the LORD, who hath pleaded the cause of my reproach from the hand of Nabal, and hath kept his servant from evil; for the LORD hath returned the wickedness of Nabal upon his own head." The Scripture went on to say that David sent and talked with Abigail to take her in marriage. Abigail once again presents herself in humility as David's handmaiden and servant. However, she was exalted into the position of being his wife.

At this point, Abigail would have been David's third wife. Abigail is one of the few that ranks among the wives of David that the Bible makes clear reference to in regard to her character. We know of Saul's daughter, Michal, but she was given to another man until David reclaimed her as his own wife. However, Michal was the one who mocked him when he danced before the ark of Lord. Her punishment was that she remained childless.[18]

Another one of David's wives that we read much about was Bathsheba. We know that David committed the grave sin of adultery with her, producing a child, and then had her husband, Uriah, killed because he would not innocently play into his plan to hide this sin. In spite of her association with David's sin, Bath-sheba appeared to be an honorable woman. Since she was the mother of King Solomon, she was one of five women interestingly mentioned in the lineage of David, but it was as Uriah's wife.[19]

Abigail is the one wife that never received a black mark on her character. At one point, the Amalekites took her captive, but of course, David rescued her. According to David's genealogy, she had one son by him, named Daniel. In 2 Samuel 3:3, he is also called Chileab.[20] Daniel means "judgment of God," and Chileab means "like his father."[21]

The first son of David, who was in line to the throne, Ammon, was killed by his brother, Absalom, David's third oldest son. Both Absalom, and Adonijah, David's fourth oldest son, were killed when they made unsuccessful attempts to secure the throne. We see the judgment of God in regard to these three men. Their actions revealed that they lacked integrity and were wicked. However, if Chileab, David's second oldest son, lived to be a man in the midst of such judgment, and he was like his father, he had integrity. Even though he would have the right to secure the throne, he would know whether God had ordained him as king. If he was such a man, most likely the character of his mother would have greatly influenced him; therefore, he would honorably give way to the will

---

[18] 2 Samuel 6:20-23
[19] 2 Samuel 11; Matthew 1:6
[20] 1 Samuel 30:5, 18; 1 Chronicles 3:1
[21] Smith's Bible Dictionary

of God concerning the throne of David. Like Jonathan, he would not let jealousy reign, but righteousness win out in his life.

Considering the character of Abigail, she no doubt served as a voice of reasoning in the king's court at different times. Depending on the age she lived to be, her wisdom and grace would have become a more stabilizing factor when matters appeared to be insane during David's reign. Although this is complete speculation on my part regarding her and her son, we know that one will never really step outside of his or her character no matter what circumstances may challenge him or her.

Abigail is one of my favorite examples in Scripture. She epitomized what constitutes real beauty when it came to people. Her countenance reflected the inner life of a person who knew God. She knew how to be an honorable wife in wisdom and grace even when she had to contend with a brutish husband who would never be able to honor her in a just way. She was indeed a woman who knew how to possess her soul in the midst of challenging times.

Our outer person clearly reflects our inner life. What does your countenance say about your life before God? Are you possessing your soul in challenging times, or are you becoming brutish about the matters of life in order to bring about your desired reality?

13

THE DESPERATE MAN

Following the digression of the fallen man into a brutish state is quite unnerving. There are those who choose this cruel state for it truly reflects the hardness of their wicked heart. These individuals believe that they deserve all the world offers, and mock anything that would challenge them to the contrary. However, there are those who have tasted the fruit of the unseen world. They have seen and experience this world's power, benevolence, and wisdom. These individuals know there is a just God who will bring about judgment. They may even be like Felix who trembled after the Apostle Paul reasoned with him about righteousness, temperance, and judgment to come.[1] Yet, in these people's foolish state, they will not humble themselves and give way to the truth of it.

King Saul was such a man. He had been chosen by God according to the preference of the people, anointed by the prophet, Samuel, and empowered by the Spirit, yet he became a brutish man towards righteousness. In such cases, I cannot help but think of those Scriptures that warn us of our end if we have encountered the righteous way of the next world, but are foolish enough to go back to the vomit of the old life.

The Apostle Paul challenged the foolish Galatians in their bewitched state in this way, "Are ye so foolish? Having begun in the Spirit, are ye now made perfect by the flesh" (Galatians 3:3)?

The writer of Hebrews talks about those who have been enlightened by the reality of eternity. In fact, they have tasted of the heavenly gift, the good Word of God, and the powers of the age to come, as well as being partakers of the Holy Spirit. He warns that if such an individual falls away, if it is impossible to renew him or her again unto repentance. The reason for this is that this person's attitude and actions would require the Son of God to be crucified afresh, putting Him to an open shame.[2]

The Apostle Peter has a similar warning as that in Hebrews in his second epistle. He talked about those who were in bondage to their own corruption, while deceitfully promising others liberty. The apostle presents this warning in 2 Peter 2:20-21 as follows,

> For if, after they have escaped the pollutions of the world through the knowledge of the Lord and Savior, Jesus Christ, they are again entangled in it, and overcome, the latter end is worse with them than the beginning. For it had been better

---

[1] Acts 24:24-25
[2] Hebrews 6:4-6

> for them not to have known the way of righteousness than, after they have known it, to turn from the holy commandment delivered unto them.

The apostle goes on to remind us of the proverb that warns us of a dog going back to his own vomit and the sow to the mire.

We cannot forget Jesus' warning. There are those who have managed to do great feats in His name, but who walk contrary to the will of the Father. Because of their works, they have a wrong perspective about their life before God. They see themselves being acceptable on the basis of their deeds.[3] They have failed to believe the Word where it states that God does not consider us on the basis of how we look or what we do, but according to our heart condition. As a result, the Lord of lords will reject these individuals because there is no real point of identification to His kingdom.

At this point, we could get into a big debate about whether such a person was truly saved or not. I, for one, know that I do not have the means to possess such a judgment call. We are told that we will know people by their fruit, and not whether they are truly saved. Fruits simply reveal if a person is operating in a right spirit.[4]

There are a couple of reasons we are to discern the spirit of a person. The first one is to determine if we can come into agreement with him or her for the purpose of fellowship and edification. The common ground for all true spiritual fellowship comes through the Spirit of God based on a correct perception of Jesus Christ. Keep in mind, there are many different Christ's being presented, but there is only one true Jesus that all believers can fellowship upon. The problem with some Christians is that they believe they can handle being exposed to those who have a different Jesus without being influenced by their antichrist spirit. They convince themselves that they can find other common ground upon which to fellowship without compromising their belief and understanding of the Jesus of the Bible.

However, people who do not believe in the real Jesus are enemies of God. They do not know Him and He does not know them. As my co-laborer in the Gospel, Jeannette, reminded me, in such situations Christians can become like Peter on the night Jesus was betrayed.[5] They will make the mistake of warming their hands at the enemies' fire with no real concern as to what their actions are truly saying to Jesus. These same individuals may convince themselves that they are as close as they can get to Jesus, but the reality is they are coming into a compromising place with the enemy. After all, it is the enemy's fire. Such compromise will dull these individuals' spiritual senses, causing them to be unprepared to stand for truth. And, when they are challenged about their relationship with the real Jesus, they will ultimately end up denying

---

[3] Matthew 7:21-23
[4] Matthew 7:16, 20
[5] Luke 22:54-62

that they even knew Him out of fear as to how the enemy will respond to them.

The second reason we must discern the spirit has to do with ministry. If individuals are struggling in their spiritual life, there will be a spiritual mixture of fear, confusion, and despair. We, as believers need to discern such an individual with the intent of ministering to him or her. However, God is the one who will justly judge everyone according to the inward condition of the heart. It is not within our means to put some type of formula in place by which to try to determine if people are saved. The real distinction in salvation is that the person truly has the witness of the Holy Spirit in his or her inner man. The witness of the Spirit will impress the person's conscience about matters, lead him or her into all truth about Jesus, and empower him or her to walk out the life of Christ that is being established in the person's inner man.[6]

We are clearly told to learn the lessons of the Bible and adhere to its righteous guidelines and its urgent warnings. We have such examples of people like Saul, as well as the clear warnings of Scripture about the type of lifestyle we, as believers, must be establishing. This life will identify us as one who has been delivered from the kingdom of darkness and translated into the kingdom of God's dear Son.[7]

We must admit that Saul knew the difference between the fleshly and the spiritual. He had tasted of the unseen world, but in spite of all of his experiences he never did learn how to fear God. The fear of Lord would have produced wisdom in Saul to see the foolishness of his ways, as well as develop a healthy attitude in properly confronting his unacceptable attitudes and ways in humility and repentance. In his unbelief and disobedience, he kept putting God to a foolish test with his actions. In the end, he was stripped of the kingdom of Israel and the throne, and the Lord departed from him. He not only deprived his descendants of the throne, but he became a doomed man whose very days were numbered as the king of Israel.

In spite of each judgment, Saul continued on in his godless ways. He clearly digressed to each stage of the fallen man. Once in awhile reason seemed to take hold when the contrast was made clear between him and David, but his soul had become unyielding before God. Since he had failed to possess his soul, his thoughts had become unmanageable, his emotions undisciplined, and his ways unruly.

We need to take heed of Saul's spiritual experience and digression. He is a clear example of why a man ends up becoming an utter fool in his life. Saul started out with promises, only to lose all hope of seeing those promises fulfilled. He started out as a man preferred by many, but eventually became a stench to heaven. He was given power, only to lose authority, producing weak leadership. He secured some riches and victories, but could not secure his soul. He had the potential to be great,

---

[6] John 16:7-11, 13; Acts 1:8; 1 John 5:4-13
[7] Colossians 1:13

but became a despairing, tormented despot. This is clearly the plight of man if he fails to truly possess his soul in light of eternity.

Saul had become indifferent towards the truth of his responsibilities in regard to God. Judgment had been pronounced, and now only the consequences awaited him. Although he was aware that it would be matter of time before the world he knew would come caving down around his ears, he continued to live as if he would ultimately secure what he had lost in lieu of his foolishness. Granted, he became brutish against the truth, but the reality was that he was cognizant that he would come to a defeating end. Unlike Nabal, he had not chosen the brutish state; rather, he had digressed into it because of his wrong, foolish choices that defied the living God. Since he knew the harsh consequences for the error of his ways, desperation began to take hold of his soul.

This is the final stage of the soulish man that remains bound to the ways of the world, but not living in denial or delusion about the true wretched condition of his inner soul. It is a stage of total desperation. Saul knew his ultimate end; therefore, he lived in this state. In such a condition, people live despairing over what could have been and what will never be. It is a state of vanity where all successes will be consumed by the ultimate failure to possess one's soul in light of eternity. In this despairing pit of depression folly mocks the senselessness of one's life, worldly riches leave such a person empty, and all desperate attempts to hold onto this present life bring the person closer to the brink of the abyss. This was Saul's tormenting reality concerning the ways and end of his foolishness.

He desperately sought David in order to destroy the successor to the throne, only to be brought to the reality of his own demise as king. Once again, he was about to face his dreaded enemy, the Philistines. It seemed as if this enemy had revealed the weakness of his leadership throughout his reign. Saul may have looked like a king to the people of Israel, but this enemy often revealed the quality of his leadership. Granted, he had some victories over them, but in many battles, he was often stifled, placed in a limbo position of fear and ineptness to secure the victory.

Since Saul knew that only the God of Israel could truly secure a victory for His people, he found himself in more of a desperate situation. Who could he go to, to seek counsel, encouragement, or instruction? The great prophet Samuel was dead; therefore, he could not seek him. He inquired of the Lord, but the Lord had departed from him; therefore, God remained silent.[8]

It is important to remember the vital work of the Holy Spirit. He is the one who brings conviction about sin, as well as the need for salvation to those who initially become desperate about their spiritual condition. He is the One who strips away the masks of indifference and pretence from

---

[8] 1 Samuel 28:3-6

the complacent man in order to reprove the fleshly man of his wicked ways in light of the righteousness of Christ. His purpose for such reproof is to break the natural man at the point of his arrogance with the knowledge of the judgment that awaits him. In such brokenness the soulish man will have the means to repent of his rebellion, and be born again by the life of Christ, thereby, receiving the seal of the Holy Spirit unto the day of redemption.[9]

We are warned that the Spirit will not always strive with man. He can be easily vexed or grieved by sin and indifference to the matters of God, as well as quenched by the presence of a wrong spirit or environment of deception and rebellion. Such conditions can cause Him to withdraw or depart from such an unholy atmosphere.[10] This is why when David was finally made aware of his sin of adultery and murder, he made this request as he sought forgiveness in true repentance, "Cast me not away from thy presence, and take not thy holy Spirit from me" (Psalms 51:11).

The Spirit had departed from Saul. There was no real conviction of sin that would bring him to a place of true repentance; therefore, no hope of reconciliation, just a worldly sorrow that could not be quenched.[11] There was no reproof of righteousness, just an awareness that he was about to face an irreversible judgment that would surely cost him his very life. Imagine how Saul might have felt. Desperation must have taken hold of him as never before. He had nowhere to go. He could not ignore the ensuing battle. He had to face the enemy, but he had no power, authority, or support. Heaven remained silent towards him. The reality is that the brutish man is a deluded, stiff-necked fool who is blinded to the damnation that awaits him, but the desperate man proves to be a coward because he knows and fears his inevitable end of destruction that looms before him in spite of his appeals to God.

Where would Saul turn in desperation? There was only one place in which he could appeal to the supernatural, and that was the kingdom of darkness. After all, he was a weak leader. He had valiant men such as his son, Jonathan and David, to fight many of his battles and inspire others on to victory. Even though the Lord had departed from him, people such as Samuel and David could still appeal to Jehovah God on behalf of Israel. But Samuel was dead, and out of jealousy and fear, Saul had forced David to become a fugitive.

One must wonder if Saul had a premonition about this battle. If he did, his desperation would surely escalate. He asked his servants to find him a medium even though as king, he had cut off those who had been involved with such activity in response to the Law. His servants knew of a woman who was considered a medium at Endor. No matter how one might root out such activity, there are always pockets of darkness hidden

---

[9] John 16:7-11; Ephesians 4:30
[10] Genesis 6:3; Ephesians 4:30; 1 Thessalonians 5:19
[11] 2 Corinthians 7:10

under various disguises.[12] This is true for each of our lives. We must guard our hearts at all times and test our spirit.

When the medium asked Saul who she needed to bring up, he told her that he wanted to talk to Samuel. There is a debate about whether Samuel was actually raised from his grave since the Bible clearly considers any type of spiritualism, such as witchcraft and necromancy, an abomination.[13] My opinion is that based on the woman's reaction and the words that were spoken, I do believe the Lord allowed Samuel to make an appearance. However, the sole purpose for such appearance was to pronounce final judgment on Saul.

Samuel asked Saul why he disturbed his rest. Saul admitted that the Lord had departed from him, and that he wanted him to make known what he should do in spite of the fact that he failed to obey the Lord's instructions in the past. Samuel's reply was why would Saul ask him since the Lord was not with him and he was God's enemy. Besides, He had already pronounced judgment on him because he had not obeyed God's voice in regard to the Amalekites. Therefore, the Lord had brought about that very day to execute His judgment upon the king. Not only would Saul die in defeat, the Lord would deliver Israel into the hands of the Philistines.

The people of Israel were about to taste the bitter consequences for demanding a king, and the king was about to taste judgment for his disobedient actions. Try as Saul did in his different times of desperation to change his future plight, God was going to have the final word and fulfill His judgments. Saul could not keep his life or thwart what God had established. This is the real folly of man's foolishness. He thinks that he can save his life in spite of the fact that his Creator has numbered his days. As man arrogantly strives to save his life, he actually loses the real essence of it.

Samuel's words caused Saul to fall to the ground in fear. Saul was coming to the end of his insidious existence. In such a time, the soulish man has no confidence to stand. The natural man's strength proves to be fragile as it quickly flows into a sea of hopelessness. The fleshly man becomes paralyzed in a quagmire of fear. The complacent man falls into desolation as the brutish man faces the end of his wickedness, sensing that his last bit of desperation can do nothing more than lead him into complete ruin.

This is the epitaph of the fallen man. His demise will mark the tragedy of a wasted life. Such a life is offered on the many altars of the world. These altars are marked by the different follies produced by man's independence, pride, lust, indifference, cruelty, and desperation.

The battle raged between the Philistines and Israel. It is said that the men of Israel fled, and that the Philistines followed hard after Saul and his sons. In the end, three of Saul's sons, including Jonathan, were

---

[12] Leviticus 19:31; 20:6, 27; 1 Samuel 28:7
[13] Deuteronomy 18:10-12

killed. Saul was also severely wounded, but not dead. It is not enough to wound the fallen man; he must die to ensure he will never rise from the ashes.[14]

Saul knew he was a dead man. He asked his armor bearer to finish the job to avoid dying at the hands of the uncircumcised. The truth is if Saul had allowed his heart to be circumcised from its wicked, fleshly ways, he would not be in such a dishonorable position. But who wants to kill your own king to somehow make a matter look honorable, when there is no honor to be found in any of it? The armor bearer refused to kill Saul. Therefore, out of fear, Saul fell on his own sword ending his reign, but sadly taking many men with him in his folly.[15]

The Philistines found Saul and his sons. They cut off the head of the king of Israel, along with his sons, and published their great victory.[16] It is a solemn reminder that the reign of the fleshly man will be cut off for good in righteous judgment. It will never rise again to claim any kind of glory for itself.

It is vital we understand how the fallen man digresses into utter ruin. It is not easy to follow Saul down his destructive path, but he serves as a vital example to each of us. The first book of Samuel ends with his death. We are told that valiant men came by night and took the bodies of Saul and his sons that hung from the wall of Bethshan, and brought them to Jabesh where they burned them. Then, they took their bones and buried them under a tree.[17]

The fleshly man will not survive. All that might possibly remain of a person's existence are the silent bones that show the end of all flesh, and hopefully a godly mark that identifies him or her to eternity. Let us mark the life of Saul by learning the lessons of his life. Samuel summarized the main lesson in 1 Samuel 15:22, "And Samuel said, Hath the LORD as great delight in burnt offerings and sacrifices, as in obeying the voice of the LORD? Behold, to obey is better than sacrifice, and to hearken than the fat of rams."

---

[14] 1 Samuel 31:1-3
[15] Deuteronomy 10:16; 30:6; 1 Samuel 31:4-6
[16] 1 Samuel 31:7-10
[17] 1 Samuel 31:12-13

14
THE CHALLENGE

As we follow the relationship between Saul as the earthly, fallen man, and David as the spiritual man, we can begin to see the diverse differences between the character of these two men. David often found his battle was not with the visible, uncircumcised enemies of Israel; rather, it was with the unregenerate man among his own people.

The unregenerate man is often caught in a whirlwind that causes him to spiral downward into a dark abyss of hopelessness. There is no way out of this abyss spiritually, emotionally, or mentally. The grave darkness of it will simply overpower and consume every aspect about this man's reasoning, making him into an utter fool. This is why Jesus had to experience the very depths of physical death and the grave to save us from the claims of this damnable abyss upon our very souls.

We observed how King Saul descended into this abyss. Here was a man with great potential, but he did not possess his soul; instead, he allowed the preference, activities, and desires of his soul to possess him. As we consider Saul, he failed to take accountability for his decisions, attitudes, and actions. Of course, before God he could never get away with excusing himself for his blatant disregard and unbelief towards his Creator and His ways. He could not truly blame the circumstances for his disobedience towards the simple instructions of God or the righteousness of others who would not compromise with his darkness. In the end, his death revealed the actual disgrace that the unregenerate man will experience in his folly.

The other example was David. He was a man that possessed integrity in the inner man. Integrity points to the presence of inner character that will honestly face a matter. Such honesty serves as a means to wisely give way to that which is worthy, honorable, and just. This type of integrity must come into full operation at the place where life confronts or challenges our personal reality about self and the world around us. How will we respond to reality that strips us of our fanciful notions about our personal character, strength, and life?

People vary as to where they must apply integrity. For some, they must apply integrity at the end of their conclusions. After all, they may be unmanageable in their thought process. Only by applying integrity at the end of their conclusions can they realize that God's thoughts are much higher than theirs.[1] This puts such conclusions into a proper perspective,

---
[1] Isaiah 55:8-9

causing these individuals to realize that their conclusions about their present reality are untrustworthy; therefore, they must lightly esteem them until the heavenly perspective can be established according to Spirit and truth of Jesus' wisdom.

Other people must apply integrity when their emotions are beginning to ascend upward in intensity or momentum. Such overrated, undisciplined emotions will cause these people to highly esteem what they feel as being reality. These people will judge everything according to their fickle, unpredictable, and unrealistic emotions, often charging or opposing that which is truth. When integrity is applied to the emotions at the right time, it can actually take the momentum out of their escalation, bringing proper discipline to this type of individual. Discipline at this point can bring much needed order, allowing these people to properly evaluate and discern the environment and reality around them according to Spirit and the truth of Jesus' Word.

There is another type of person that must apply integrity up front to keep his or her various images and conclusions that he or she develops about life in proper perspective. The problem with these people is that they perceive their images as being reality when they are nothing more than unrealistic concepts that will always fall short of the mark of perfection that these people are forever seeking in their worlds. Such images make these people unyielding in their attitudes of indifference, cruelty, or anger. Such ungodly attitudes reveal the weakness and ineptness of these people's standards that are constantly being adjusted behind their different façades to control their reality. As a result, they must apply integrity up front to properly recognize and discern that they cannot trust their images to connect them to the reality around them. Without an honest connection with reality, such individuals would be unable to address it according to the Spirit and truth of Jesus' example.

The last group of people must apply integrity to the facts that they develop about matters. These facts serve as cement lines that are limited because they lack dimension or the ability to be challenged, enlarged, adjusted, or discarded to ensure purity, spirit, and truth. People who operate within these lines will become unruly as they strive to rule their circumstances. As a result, these people must have the integrity to see that they are limited in their understanding. And, if they insist on their way, they will end up operating in a wrong spirit.

This brings us to the importance of having integrity. Without such integrity, the fallen man will fail to be transformed and will digress into the state of becoming an utter fool to those who have to contend with him. I cannot begin to tell you of the many situations where people digressed into a state of total insanity because they held their reality about a particular matter as the absolute truth. In the end, they destroyed relationships as they went into total delusion or denial.

The denial is always the same. People refuse to face the fact that the fallen man that is operating in them will always be at odds with the spiritual man. Sometimes, this man can show himself to be noble in

Developing Our Christian Life

some situations, but will prove to be dishonorable when challenged in regard to maintaining his particular reality and lifestyle.

This can be seen in the case of the people of Keilah.[2] Keilah was located in the lowland district of Judah. Its name means fortress.[3] However, the enemy, the Philistines, was robbing the people of Keilah of their threshing floors. David inquired of the Lord if he should deliver his poor countrymen from such oppression. The Lord told him to arise for He would deliver them. David obeyed, and the victory was secured.

When the priest, Abiathar, fled to David at Keilah after Saul murdered his family members, he warned David that Saul was coming to Keilah to besiege him and his men. You would think that after David and his men fought for Keilah, the people would be very protective of them. However, when people lack integrity, they can always justify treason in the name of self-preservation.

When David inquired of the Lord as to whether the people of Keilah would deliver him and his men into the hand of Saul, the Lord told him they would. This is the reality of the fallen man. He is treacherous, and will justify betraying that which deserves his respect and commitment. After all, in the mind of the fallen man he must live, survive, and exist no matter what part of his character or soul he must sell or compromise. This man merely thinks of sacrifice in noble terms where he will receive recognition for noteworthy acts, but not in honorable terms where he must be willing to give up his right to life, recognition, and fame to ensure real life for others.

David responded to the wisdom, instruction, and protection of his true fortress, God, by leaving behind the treachery and fickleness of the flesh (Keilah). He and his men went into the wilderness of Ziph, where he remained on a mountain. "Ziph" means battlement.[4] The battle with the unpredictable ways of the soulish man can bring us to places of struggle, harshness, betrayal, and despair, but it can also bring us higher (mountain) in our relationship with God. It is when we, as believers, are brought low by the challenges of life that we can be brought higher in Christ as a means to reach our potential in Him. In fact, the depth God is allowed to go in us will determine the height we will be brought to in our relationship with Him.

As we follow David through each challenge, we can clearly see how he overcame Saul (the flesh) by being respectable, sensitive, and obedient to the Lord. After Saul's death, the people of Judah came to David to officially anoint him as their king. For seven years, there was a struggle between the house of Saul and the house of David. Scripture tells us that the house of David grew stronger, while the house of Saul grew weaker.[5]

---

[2] 1 Samuel 23:1-14
[3] Smith's Bible Dictionary
[4] 1 Samuel 23:14-15
[5] 2 Samuel 3:1

As one gives way to God, the flesh becomes weaker in its influence in the person's life. But, we as believers must note, it might become weaker but as long as we are in these bodies, it will remain active. It will whine, occasionally try to ensnare the spiritual, and attempt to maintain its past loyalties in subtle ways, but it has no intention of conceding to that which is worthy or greater.

This clearly reminds us of the perpetual struggle between the flesh and the Spirit. At times the flesh's influence will become a whimper in the saint's life, but it is always ready to raise its ugly head out of the ashes of weakness and vanity to reclaim preeminence in each of our lives. Even though David encountered the many outside activities of the flesh in his struggles, he had to come face to face with the power it could acquire through the personal flaws of his character. These flaws proved that the spiritual man could easily be taken captive by his fleshly appetites, causing him to deviate from righteousness into iniquity.

David eventually gained the throne of Israel. He proved to be a powerful and honorable king for most of his 40-year reign. However, he also proved to be very fleshly in a couple of situations. These incidents would reveal that flaws did exist in his character, and would prove to become points of moral deviation or iniquity if he did not carefully maintain His ways before the Lord. He learned the harsh lesson that even though the flesh had become weak, it always remains ready to take charge when the opportunity arises. We see David failing in three areas, but there was only one incident that was put on his account as a blatant failure towards God.[6]

Even though David was regarded as a hero, God does not try to compromise or downplay his failures and flaws. They are clearly put forth in Scripture for our example. The first main failure is well known by everyone who has any real knowledge of this man's life. It has to do with Bathsheba.

It is important to understand how David fell into the traps of his flesh, and became soulish in his activities, giving way to the arrogant demands of the natural man, bowing down to the desires of the fleshly man, and becoming complacent towards his iniquity as he strived to hide his transgression. In fact, we will see where David actually became a brutish man, only to fall into utter desperation as he sought God's forgiveness. It was a hard lesson that would have resounding affects that not only shook his family with dire consequences, but all of Israel.

David learned that sin not only costs those who submit to it, but those who are innocent and left unprotected by the fallout it always leaves behind. In order to understand the devices that can take one captive regardless of how long he or she has served God, let us honestly follow David in his digression into the captivity and destruction that occurred due to sin in his life. Remember, the flesh is quite capable of

---

[6] 1 Kings 15:5

taking center stage in each of our lives at any time, regardless of how weak and subdued it has become by the presence of the spiritual man.

To understand how sin takes even a saint captive, we must understand that it begins with environment. One environment that seems to provide the necessary breeding ground for temptation is when there is a false sense of peace. It is easy for people to lose their spiritual edge when they fail to stir themselves up as a means to ensure their spiritual savvy. In such a state they become lackadaisical in their spiritual life. At this point, people are ready to walk or fall into the trap of temptation, because they are not prepared to recognize it.

Such an environment was present when David fell into the trap of temptation. It is stated that it was a time for kings to go forth to battle, but David remained behind. Instead of being fine tuned in battle, David found himself arising from his bed and walking upon the roof of his house.[7]

This all seemed innocent enough, but David was not sensitive enough to recognize the spiritually complacent and possibly restless state of his own soul. It was from this premise that temptation caught his eye. He saw a beautiful woman washing herself. Some believe that the woman was trying to tempt someone, but the reality is that she was doing it in the darkness of the night when even King David was supposed to be in bed. I do not believe she was trying to catch anyone's eye including the king. David was the one out of order, opting to take a walk when he should have been with his army or in his bed.

Now that David's fleshly appetites were being stirred up through his eyes, the desire of the flesh took hold as he begins to lust after her. Imagine the short timeframe this all transpired. The man who had been a spiritual giant was now becoming captive to the lusts of his flesh within seconds. Discernment was being disregarded as all reasoning went out the door. Since he was king, he could arrogantly demand that this woman be brought to him so he could taste of her forbidden fruit regardless of her status.[8]

Notice that when David inquired about her, he was fully aware that she was the wife of Uriah. Uriah was a Hittite or a descendant of Canaan. When you study Uriah's character, he was a man of integrity, fully committed to King David. Clearly, David knew and trusted him for he served as one of his bodyguards, who was mentioned as being one of "the valiant thirty" in 2 Samuel 23:39 and 1 Chronicles 11:25-41.

It was clear that David was taken captive by the fleshly man because none of the facts about Bathsheba gave him a reality check as to what he was about to do. He was bent on tasting the forbidden fruit of the wife of one of his most trusted soldiers, dishonoring himself and betraying the trust of one who was honorable. Perhaps, he was trying to convince himself that he simply wanted to talk to her, but David's intentions were

---

[7] 2 Samuel 11
[8] 2 Samuel 11:2-4

quite clear. He wanted her, and nothing was going to stop him from his fleshly pursuit.

He tasted Bathsheba's forbidden fruit, only to be faced with the harsh consequences of his lust. Bathsheba became pregnant. There was no way he could hide his sin. He could have repented and faced the shame of his wretched selfish pursuits, but his integrity and reasoning had been taken captive by the ways of the flesh. David now had to resort to scheming in such a way that his sin would not find him out. However, in his state, David did not count on Uriah being an honorable man.[9] This committed man was not driven by his lusts regardless of how beautiful his wife was. He had a responsibility to the matters of God first, as well as the reality that his comrades could not enjoy their homes; therefore, how could he? His honorable ways and practices would override the ways of his flesh.

No matter how hard David tried, he could not set up the right circumstances to hide his sin with Bathsheba. This is when he resorted to the brutish stage. He would use Uriah's honor against him by offering him up as a sacrifice in the heat of battle. In God's eyes it was murder, but in David's logic it was a matter of duty. After all, good soldiers die in battle, and Uriah was no exception.[10]

Sadly, Uriah was offered up in battle as a sacrifice so David could hide his sin. The king then turned around and married Bathsheba. It all looked so honorable to the onlooker, even though there were probably some rumors coming from the king's court. But who could rebuke the king? After all, he had the right to demand from the people of Israel whatever he desired, and they had the responsibility to give it, regardless of how improper and immoral it was.

As I consider David's actions, I wonder how a man who walked according to the integrity of his heart could stoop so low as to murder a man who was honorable, just to cover a sin of the flesh. My co-laborer, Jeannette, once remarked how people circumvent their hearts about a matter so they can justify fleshly ways, while making themselves appear as if they are honorable.

David clearly circumvented his heart. He failed to listen to its integrity because he gave audience to the flesh. His ability to reason in his mind was thrown aside as the fleshly desires were satisfied in one temporary moment of perverted ecstasy. In that moment when the flesh was partaking of the darkness of sin and death, David betrayed his heart, sacrificed his integrity, and found himself in complete opposition of God's Law. All sound boundaries had surely been cast aside for the flesh to experience that which was forbidden by the holy Law of God.

Clearly, David was in denial about his perverted conduct, and possibly was deluded about God's attitude towards it. Perhaps in David's state, he really believed that his actions were not so bad, and justified

---

[9] 2 Samuel 11:6-13
[10] 2 Samuel 11:14-21; Proverbs 28:13

Developing Our Christian Life

them because he was king. Clearly, their wicked intent along with his actions were hidden from the eyes of those in Israel. However, David looked at it, God knew, and He deemed his action of adultery as a transgression, and the murder of Uriah as an iniquity that became a blatant affront against His standard of righteousness. It is important to point out that both sins (adultery and murder) could not be covered by a sacrifice. According to God's Law, both sins required the death of the transgressor. This is why David in his prayer of forgiveness in Psalm 51:16-17, admitted that God was not requiring a sacrifice from him or would delight in a burnt offering; therefore, he could only offer the sacrifices of a broken spirit, and a broken and contrite heart. The king understood that God would never despise true repentance.

God knew David's grave transgressions and the wretched iniquity that had taken center stage in his life, and He was about to bring the king's profane ways to the forefront by the prophet, Nathan.[11] After all, this king was His servant. In spite of his hardened state brought on by sin, the light of truth could remove the blinders off of his eyes, revealing his true plight before God. Clearly, David's only hope was that he still had a heart that could be convicted by the truth.

Nathan set David up by relating a story of injustice done by one man taking unfair advantage of the kindness of another. In his righteous zeal, David became angry at such a person's lack of pity, and pronounced judgment on himself without realizing that he was the culprit. He had actually stolen an honorable man's wife, and he would end up paying restitution with four of his sons' lives.

God pronounced judgment on David. He was reminded that he was anointed king over Saul. He had been given all of the benefits of a king above all measure. But, in his time of temptation, David despised, disesteemed, disdained, or scorned God's commandments by regarding them as insignificant in the light of his fleshly desires, decisions, and actions.

Since David had killed Uriah, taken his wife to be his wife, and despised God, the sword would never depart from his house. Evil would rise up in his own house; and unlike David's actions that took place in secret, his wives would be taken by another man who would partake of their forbidden fruit in the open before all of Israel as a means to humiliate him.

King David did truly repent, and God spared his life, but his actions set in motion dire consequences that would practically rip his kingdom apart. He not only lost the son that was conceived in his adulterous affair with Bathsheba, but three sons would die by the sword as prophesied.

It is important to realize that David's action stripped him of the authority to speak into the lives of others. This was clear when his oldest son, Amnon, began to lust after his half-sister, Tamar. Eventually, Amnon deceitfully set her up in a situation where he raped her. Although

---

[11] 2 Samuel 12:1-13

his lust was great, once such perversion humiliates and strips all honor and purity from a relationship, it turns into hatred, disgust, and rejection.

Amnon, who was a dishonorable man, not only failed to see his responsibility to do right by his half-sister, but also blatantly rejected her after bringing shame upon her. In a brutish way he had stripped Tamar of her purity. Even though David knew of this wicked deed committed by his son, Amnon, he did not display the necessary authority to take the steps to rebuke and properly chastise him. He also failed to demand that his son show himself responsible and honorable towards his half-sister. Although the king was angry about it, he failed to take action against it, causing him to make the second big error in his life.[12]

Clearly, David's failure to address the blatant sin of Amnon was part of the judgment pronounced on him and his family. His lack of response to this sin became a breeding ground in which anger, bitterness, and rivalry over the throne ripped at his family, causing anguish in the king's soul while costing the lives of his first, third, and fourth oldest sons.

David's failure to address the sin of his oldest son, stirred up anger in Tamar's brother, Absalom. Absalom is the one who eventually brought swift retribution on Amnon by executing him with a sword, and fleeing to Geshur. However, by this time Absalom saw his father as a weak king. This third son of David had a natural beauty, as well as an ability to be clever and persuasive with others. He had fleshly ambitions, and clearly could see himself as an exceptional king in light of his father's weak leadership ability that had been clearly displayed among his own family. However, this arrogant young man had one problem, God did not agree with his evaluation.[13]

Through a series of deceptive moves, Absalom once again gained a foothold into his father's home and kingdom. During his clever moves, he was gaining the favor of others. Clearly, he knew how to persuade people according to his charismatic personality and his ambitions to be king.[14]

David did not know what was happening in his own family and kingdom. Whether he was blinded, in denial, or too busy with other matters of the kingdom, he was unprepared for the coup Absalom started right in his backyard. Before the king knew it, he was running for his very life.[15] The flesh will always set us up with the intent of destroying us. It was bent on destroying the spiritual man, and it would eventually bring Absalom to total destruction.

We can only guess what kind of sorrow and despair David was experiencing. His own son had betrayed him and was threatening to take away from him both the kingdom of Israel and his very life.

---

[12] 2 Samuel 13:1-22
[13] 2 Samuel 12:23-14:33
[14] 2 Samuel 15:1-12
[15] 2 Samuel 15:13-37

Developing Our Christian Life

It is at times such as these that other people's character will be tested. You have godly men such as Zadok, who will choose to guard what is of God when such insanity reigns. After all, God's presence must be maintained if order and light are ever to come back after such darkness has it way in a matter.

You have the likes of Hushai who understood that his responsibility was to obey the righteous king, even if it meant going back into the enemy's camp to thwart his plans. There are men like Ziba who saw an opportunity to take advantage in a chaotic situation to deceptively gain more of the world at the expense of others. There are those like Shimei who viewed such times as a means to curse what God had ordained, and you have people like Mephibosheth who sat at the king's table, but was taken captive due to his limitations. All he could do was wait for the king to return and reign once again.[16]

Finally, you have the plans of the soulish man. In many ways they can prove to be brilliant, but godless and already marked as being doomed. The one who best represents the darkness of such plans is Ahithophel. Ahithophel's name means "brother of foolishness." He was the grandfather of Bathsheba, and served as one of David's counselors.[17]

Although Ahithophel's wisdom was highly esteemed, he ultimately proved that the brother of foolishness is nothing more than the ways of folly. This worldly, wise man proved to be a fool when he sided with the foolish, rebellious Absalom. Clearly, this counselor thought according to the carnal ways of the world. He was the one who counseled Absalom to humiliate David by taking his concubines that were left behind, and publicly laying with them for all of Israel to see. This was not only the way to humiliate the king, but also to lay claim to his home, throne, and kingdom.

The next point of wisdom that Ahithophel gave Absalom was to prepare an army of men and go after David in his weakened state. In this manner he could be destroyed. This man's wisdom was on target. David was weak, but his God remained strong. In Psalm 2:2, we are told that the kings and rulers of the earth set themselves together to take counsel against the Lord and His words. However, Psalm 2:4 states, "He who sitteth in the heavens shall laugh; the Lord shall have them in derision."

Ahithophel's plan was about to be thwarted by Hushai who simply played on the pride of Absalom. Foolishness makes man vulnerable. When a man is soulish, it does not take much to tempt his selfishness, placate the ego of his natural man, cause the fleshly to give way to ideas of fear or ecstasy, and the complacent man to be stirred up to pursue the expectations of personal grandeur. As the complacent man reaches for

---

[16] 2 Samuel 16:1-14; 19:24-30
[17] Smith's Bible Dictionary

such grandeur, he becomes brutish in his attempts, setting him up for utter failure and destruction.[18]

When Ahithophel saw that his counsel was not followed, he saddled his donkey, went to his house, put it in order, and hung himself. The counsel of the world, regardless of how great it might be, will eventually be brought to naught by God. All that will be left is its foolishness as it hangs in utter defeat for all to see.[19]

Obviously, all the counsel of the world will be eventually brought to total failure, but what will happen to the pursuit of the fallen man's attempt to lay claim to what God has already allotted to the spiritual man? According to the example we have in Absalom, we know the unregenerate man will be set up to fall into failure and defeat. However, what is interesting about Absalom was that his vanity is what personally entangled him into the place of utter destruction. His beautiful hair that according to the *Eerdmans' Handbook to the Bible* was calculated to possibly weigh from 3½ to four pounds, got caught in the thick boughs of a great oak, leaving him to helplessly meet his fate of judgment.[20]

The ultimate fruit of the fleshly man is vanity. He is left empty, and his life serves as an example of failure, despair, and judgment. We clearly can see this in King David's rebellious son's case. He definitely wanted to be remembered. He erected a pillar and called it after his own name. However, he is not remembered as a great king, but as an utter fool. [21]

Sorrow greatly besieged David at different times of his life. Such sorrow was often the result of the consequences that followed him because of his sin with Bathsheba, as well as ignoring the same type of sin within his own family. It appears as if David learned the hard way that he could not ignore sin no matter what form it presented itself in, for it would eventually gain ground. This was brought out in the revolt of Sheba. It was quickly put down.[22]

The final incident in which King David failed was the counting of the people of Israel. God had strict guidelines in which the people of Israel were to be counted.[23] They were to be redeemed at the same time to avoid judgment. It is important to note that the account of this incident found in 1 Chronicles 21 reveals that Satan stood up against Israel, and provoked David to number the people

The word "provoke" means that David was seduced, enticed, moved, or persuaded, making him oblivious to his godly responsibility that was set forth by God in His Law.[24] Clearly, this shows us it was not within

---

[18] Proverbs 16:15-23
[19] 2 Samuel 17:23
[20] 2 Samuel 14:25-26; 18: 9-14
[21] 2 Samuel 18:17-18
[22] 2 Samuel 20:1-3, 14-22
[23] Exodus 30:11-16
[24] Strong's Exhaustive Concordance, #5496

Developing Our Christian Life

David's heart to rebel against God. Satan actually moved against him in a seductive, persuasive way. Here we see that even though David was a spiritual man with a right heart, Satan still could influence him.

Satan is a powerful foe that understands our human weaknesses. He knows how to seduce, entice, and persuade our flesh into a false reality about a matter. It is as though we lose our head for a season until God has His way in a matter. Whether we like it or not, God uses Satan to do a deeper work in His people. For example, He allowed Satan to attack Job and to sift Peter.[25]

According to the account of this incident found in 2 Samuel 24, the Lord was angry against Israel; therefore, David was incited to number the people. Clearly, the incident was not about David, but the people of Israel. There was something amiss in their environment that God would no longer tolerate. This takes us back to the reality that the people of Israel would experience the bitterness and consequences of preferring man to Jehovah God as their king.

David's actions to number the people brought retribution. He was given three choices as to the type of judgment he would submit the people of Israel and himself too. He actually chose the judgment set forth in Exodus 30:12, regarding the procedure of redeeming the people before counting them—that of a plague.

We do not know why God was displeased with Israel, but we know that in King David He had a man who knew what it meant to stand in the gap for the people. The king was willing to pay the necessary price to stay any further judgment on the people of Israel. It is true that in His holiness God will judge, but in His mercy, He will seek after one who will intercede or stand in the gap for His people.[26] The greatest example of this is when Jesus stood in the gap for each of us and paid the ultimate price for our souls. He died on the cross to redeem us. His redemption showed both the holiness of God to judge all sin, and His incredible mercy to provide a way that will silence or satisfy such judgment being wrought against His people.

David stood in the gap and stayed the judgment ready to be dispersed on Jerusalem. He started with repentance for his actions. Although he was demonically enticed, it was still his actions that brought judgment on Israel. Although God had allowed the incident to chastise Israel, David still had the means and responsibility as a godly king to offer the necessary sacrifice that would once again bring peace to the land of Israel. We must remind ourselves that this peace had nothing to do with the physical enemies of Israel; rather, it involved being at peace with the God of Israel.

Man's greatest war is with his flesh. Granted, he can fall into sin, become subject to Satan's enticement, and be plagued by circumstances and enemies beyond his control, but his biggest battle is with his own

---

[25] Job 1:6-2:13; Luke 22:31-32
[26] Ezekiel 22:29-31

flesh. It can serve as an open door for sin to take root, Satan to gain territory, and the greatest type of opposition to be waged against the holiness and sovereign ways of God.

This is why man must possess his soul. If he does not confront sin in his own life, he will fall into its traps, become enslaved to them and eventually prove weak in confronting his enemies. And, if he does not maintain his soul in the times of great testing, Satan can seduce him into a reality that will become a means of judgment.

What about you? Are you letting down the guard that must be placed upon your heart so you can properly receive, or are you failing to maintain a watch upon your thought life to ensure that your thoughts are being properly disciplined by the mind of Christ? Have you placed a bridle upon your tongue to ensure that it is properly reined in, as well as taken the blinders and false images away from your eyes so that you can see what is real? Scripture is clear that you must possess your own soul to ensure the quality of your Christian life and testimony before God and others.

15
THE PROMISE

In the last chapter we considered the challenge that man's fallen disposition personally presents to the spiritual man. As we followed David through his life, we saw that the strength of his youth was properly challenged and channeled by his relationship with Jehovah God. His character was defined in the harsh terrain and in the caves of the wilderness. His leadership was tested by temptation, sorrow, and despair. In spite of his human failures, flaws, frailties, and challenges, David did possess the promises of God through abiding confidence and fortitude.

The promises that David secured in his life before God continue to benefit God's people to this day. The promise God made to David had to do with the Messiah. God promised that He would send forth a king through David's lineage and He would establish his throne forever. This promise is also known as the Davidic covenant. We know that this pointed to Jesus Christ. David never saw his throne established in this manner, but he believed God, and knew God would, in due time, bring it forth.

The Messiah did come. He died for our sins and established a new covenant based on His redemption. This new covenant opened up the way for each believer to be part of an unseen kingdom. One day He is coming back as the King of kings and Lord of lords, and will bring to fruition the promises that were made to King David.

Clearly, King David's life serves as a valuable testimony to every believer. It is obvious that God's people must not only possess their souls, but they must do it in patience to inherit His promises. David shows us that it takes faith to walk through this world while keeping eternity in view. It takes faith to follow the ways of God when the path is not clear. It takes faith to possess His promises, and to finish the journey. Hebrews 6:12 confirms this, "That ye be not slothful, but followers of them who through faith and patience inherit the promises."

David's life shows us that the spiritual journey can prove to be difficult. There are many different types of challenges along the way. One's character is constantly being exposed, but the key for each follower of God is that during the journey he or she learns to possess his or her soul through faith, knowing that in the end he or she will possess the promises of God.

What main promise must we, as believers, make sure we possess at the end of our spiritual life? The children of Israel had to possess the

Promised Land, but Christians must possess another type of promise. Our promise has to do with possessing the life of Jesus. His life is eternal and abundant. It is a life of promise, purpose, and power.

In Deuteronomy 30:19 we read this powerful Scripture, "I call heaven and earth to record this day against you, that I have set before you life and death, blessing and cursing; therefore, choose life, that both thou and thy seed may live." It is our responsibility to determine and choose the type or quality of life we will walk out. It seems simple enough, but the reality is that most people fail to choose life; rather, they give way to the aspects of death in their life, missing the opportunity of knowing, experiencing, and tasting the life that has been ordained and freely offered to all who will but choose it.

The reason that many people fail to possess life is because since they have been given the gift of physical life, they perceive that the earthly constitutes the essence of their life; but such a life does not possess the life promised by God. The type of life we each end up possessing actually comes down to the condition of our inner being. This condition is determined by what type of life we choose, as well as how we are going to express or experience it in this present world.

There are two types of existence: one of survival in the midst of the working of death upon our life, and the other has to do with actually experiencing and living the life God has ordained for us. The type of existence we choose to express is going to be determined by what we allow to influence us, the agendas we establish, the pursuits we follow, and the lifestyle we develop. As we consider this, we must realize that in a way we will be trying to discover the essence or the real reason for our being or purpose. In such a search, hopefully we will discover what constitutes real life according to God. However, because of our fallen condition, few ever really come to terms with what constitutes true life.

Deuteronomy 30:20 actually explains the essence of life,
> That thou mayest love the Lord thy God, and that thou mayest obey His voice, and that thou mayest cleave unto him; for he is thy life, and the length of thy days; that thou mayest dwell in the land which the LORD swore unto thy fathers, to Abraham, to Issac, and to Jacob, to give them.

Although this was spoken to the children of Israel, its very principles apply to believers. It tells us what must influence us is the love of, for, and because of God. Our agenda must be to obey Him, and we must learn how to cleave to Him. This entails following Him, as we cling to His righteous ways and His everlasting Word. In this pursuit, we will learn that God is the essence of our life, and it is from this premise that our lifestyle is firmly established in godliness.

Obviously, as Christians we cannot take for granted our lives in Christ. It is not enough to develop the inward life; we must also constantly maintain it in integrity. Integrity is not just a matter of being honest, but is humble in disposition to properly receive, meek in attitude in order to accurately respond, and godly in lifestyle to ensure all matters are done in an honorable way. The Apostle Paul summarized it in this way, "For which cause we faint not; but though our outward man perish, yet the inward man is renewed day by day" (2 Corinthians 4:16).

The outward man is perishing, but for the believer, the inward man must be renewed day by day by the very life of Jesus being established in us. However, such inward renewal points to the work of the Holy Spirit. Once again, we are reminded that the difference between the fallen man and the spiritual man is the presence of the Holy Spirit. Without the identification mark of the Spirit, there would be no real distinction between the earth-bound man and the spiritual man. We know that the Spirit departed from Saul, and came upon David.[1]

As believers, it is vital to remember the importance and identification of the Holy Spirit upon our lives. People believe that religious affiliations, moral codes, positions, or certain works identify them to heaven. However, there is only one sure seal that classifies one as belonging to the heavenly kingdom until redemption is actually brought to fruition, and that is the Holy Spirit. It is the Spirit who does the work in the lives of God's people. The prophet Zechariah brought this out in his writings, "...Not by might, nor by power, but by my Spirit, saith the LORD of hosts" (Zechariah 4:6c). It is the presence of the Spirit within the inner being of a person that makes him, or her, a spiritual man. This is also clearly brought out in Scripture.[2] Without Him, there is no means in which a person can relate, interact, or know that which is spiritual, as well as properly discern that which is unseen.

In the Old Testament the Holy Spirit was the cloud by day and the fire by night. He would come down on man to empower him to fulfill His purpose, but in the New Testament, He abides in man.[3] Therefore, the presence of God is not simply in the midst of His people, it is actually in His people.

It is important to note that the cloud guided God's people by day, and the fire protected them at night. Clearly, they were to follow the cloud during the day as it moved, and they would rest in the shadow of the fire at night. These two examples pointed to the work of the Spirit. We are instructed to walk after the Spirit, be led by the Spirit, and walk in the Spirit.[4] To walk after something means to follow it, to be led by something means you are being guided in some way, and to walk in something points to walking in accordance to that which will bring protection. Such a walk will also establish one in a place or position.

The Holy Spirit is both a gift and a promise from the Father. He is a gift given upon our salvation, and a promise that must be possessed daily, to ensure a life that is empowered by the flame of heavenly inspiration and revelation. When we are walking after the Holy Spirit, we

---

[1] 1 Samuel 16:13-14; 18:12
[2] Exodus 13:21-22; 1 Corinthians 2:10-14; Ephesians 1:13-14; 4:30
[3] 1 Corinthians 6:19
[4] Romans 8:1, 14; Galatians 5:16

will be following after that which will work the essence of righteousness, godliness, faith, love, patience, and meekness in our lives. There will be no condemnation found in such a life. Walking after the Spirit allows us to acquire His inspiration and fruit, which means we must deny self so we will begin to travel in the way of life as we take on the disciplined character of our Lord and Savior, Jesus Christ. It is as we take on Jesus' disposition and mind that we will learn what it means to fight the good fight of faith so we are able to lay hold of eternal life. [5]

We must be led by the Spirit to find our identity in Christ as children of God. For example, the Holy Spirit leads us into all truth about Jesus. In turn, Jesus serves as the truth about the life that has been made available through His redemption. This life establishes us in a relationship with the Father as His children. We have been legally adopted, identifying us as heirs to an eternal inheritance. Once again, this eternal inheritance has to do with the type of life that we, as believers, will be prepared to embrace in eternity during our journey through this present world. It will be a glorious, satisfying life as we are glorified together in our precious Lord. Such a life will also make certain that through the leading of the Spirit the deeds of the body will be mortified, ensuring that we will truly live the abundant life that has been made available to us.[6]

As Christians, we must walk in the Spirit. The Apostle Paul stated that if we walk in the Spirit, we will not fulfill the lust of the flesh. In fact, we are told that since we are in Christ, we have crucified the flesh with its affections and lusts. As the old is crucified, we can put on the new life. The Apostle Paul summarized it best, "But put ye on the Lord Jesus Christ, and make not provision for the flesh, to fulfill its lusts" (Romans 13:14).

The Holy Spirit is also associated to blessed communion. As you study the work of the Spirit, it is clear that the ultimate goal for Him is to establish us in a life of sweet communion with the Father. Communion was lost in the Garden of Eden and restored by the redemption of Christ. But we must learn how to walk in the Spirit to ensure such glorious fellowship. The Spirit must bring us to a state that allows us to stand confident before the Father, as being cleansed and separate from all that is profane. He must establish the mind of Christ in us so that we can be likeminded with our Father. This is what will bring about the sweet fellowship that not only defines our life in Christ, but also enhances it in the midst of the grave darkness that is engulfing this world.[7]

The Holy Spirit also enables us to stand according to the ways of God, withstand with the truth of Jesus, and stand in the life that is being established in us according to the Word of God. We see that David learned how to walk after the ways of God, be led by the truths of God,

---

[5] Ephesians 5:18; 1 Timothy 6:11-12
[6] John 1:12; 14:6; 16:13; Romans 8:14-17; Ephesians 1:11-14
[7] 2 Corinthians 13:14

and walk in the light of communion with God. We can see it not only in the examples of his life, but in his prayers and psalms.

David also showed us that the different challenges to the spiritual man do not always come with the fiery tests, but they can also be found hidden in the drudgeries of life. These drudgeries can cause us to become comfortable and complacent in our spiritual lives.

Complacency is what sets a person up to fall into grave temptation. This is why we are instructed to possess our souls in patience. It takes a great deal of inward patience to possess the life that God has ordained for us in the different environments of the world. Whether it is the fiery ovens that test our faith, we must possess our souls in sincere confidence towards our Lord; or, in times of peace where our souls can be lured to sleep, we must snatch them from such a place to make certain that we continue to possess them, ensuring that we do not lose our spiritual edge.

Ultimately, we must possess our souls in patience no matter what the environment. If we do possess them, we can be ensured of the working of the Spirit upon them. He will have the freedom to convict us if we are becoming complacent towards His ways, renew us if we are becoming insensitive to His gentle leading, and quicken us to the lack of quality our life is taking on if we are failing to walk in agreement with Him in sweet communion.

At the end of this journey of possessing our souls, we will end up possessing the promise of life. It is hard to recognize that in our fallen state we have no real understanding of the life that Adam possessed in the Garden of Eden before his fall. It is true many are seeking after the idea or image of that life, but they do not understand that the quality of Adam's life was not based on the garden, but on his relationship with God.

Death to real life occurred when that relationship between God and Adam ceased because of his sin. This is why Jesus stated that He was the way to that relationship with the Father through reconciliation. He was also the truth about the beauty of life that comes from being reconciled back to God, and He is the essence and author of the life that is brought forth into the inner being of every believer. It is this inner life that allows each of us to discover the glorious reality of being a child of God. As God's child, we can boldly come to His throne seeking His mercy, knowing we can find grace to freely sit in His glorious presence and commune with Him.[8]

Clearly, Adam ceased to possess the life found in the garden because he failed to possess his soul when given an opportunity to do so. We as believers must possess our souls in patience to come into the place of blessed communion with our God. We must take possession of our souls daily by giving way to the working of the Spirit, the disciplines

---

[8] Hebrews 4:14-16

of God's Word, and the wisdom, righteousness, sanctification, and redemption found in the life, examples, and work of Jesus.

The Bible tells us that as believers, we have been given everything that pertains unto life and godliness. Since having escaped the corruption of this present world that entangles us through lust, we have been given great and precious promises so that we can partake of our Lord's divine nature.[9] It is clear we need to possess our souls in patience to avoid entanglements with the world so that we can through faith acquire the promises of life. Such possessions will allow us to become enlightened by the truth and light of heaven. This simply means we have indeed tasted the heavenly gift of Jesus through His Word, while partaking of the power of His Spirit.

The question is do you possess your soul? It is not an option. Scripture tells us that we must endure to the end if we are going to be saved.[10] We can only endure in patience. Such patience requires us to discipline the soul if we are going to abide, continue, and remain anchored to the Rock of Jesus in our Christian lives. Abiding is what each of us must do to finish the rest of the course that remains before us. This is the only way we can be assured that we are ready to stand in times of testing, ready to withstand in tribulation, and remain standing when darkness is consuming us.

As I consider the dark times before us, I think of King David. He faced so many obstacles and enemies. He knew the despair and sorrow of the darkness of man's heart and the world around him. But, to avoid from being driven or influenced by his circumstances, he clearly disciplined his soul as a means to possess it. He gave us insight as to this discipline in Psalm 16:8-9. Consider, meditate upon, and assimilate his words as you regard the inward condition of your soul. Perhaps his words will help you to understand how to patiently possess your soul in these precarious times, while still living in these weak, fleshly bodies. "I have set the LORD always before me; because he is at my right hand, I shall not be moved. Therefore my heart is glad, and my glory rejoiceth; my flesh also shall rest in hope."

---

[9] 2 Peter 1:3-4
[10] Matthew 24:13

Book Three

EXPERIENCING THE CHRISTIAN LIFE

By

Rayola Kelley

INTRODUCTION

Another book! Some wonder why I write books on these different spiritual subjects. There are a couple of reasons. The first one is that it is my means of not forgetting what has been revealed to me. The small glimpses I receive about these subjects are so overwhelming that I want to capture them in some way to remind myself of what I have discovered. After all, we humans are quite forgetful about such matters. In our mind we convince ourselves we will not forget such valuable insights, but because of our human limitations and struggle to maintain sanity in what often appears to be a world spinning out of control, we can easily forget the intensity, power, and lessons involving that which is eternal and heavenly.

The second reason is because it is my reasonable service to God. I have learned that what He entrusts to me, I must be prepared to give it away to others. Such a release of the things of God allows Him the means to multiply and distribute the precious manna and gems of His kingdom into other lives. I am also quite aware that these points of service may be consumed as sacrifices by the fires of sanctification, obscured by the darkness of ignorance and indifference, and possibly trampled upon by those who have no heart or vision for such matters; but nevertheless, it is my reasonable service to offer my different forms of ministry as sacrifices to God for Him to do as He pleases.

As I struggle with the compelling desire to complete what has been entrusted to me, I have to consider if there is one way to capitalize on what God has faithfully given me though the years. I recognize that what He has given me has been life. This life permeates all that He has endowed to me. In fact, each gem that makes up this precious treasure has been saturated with, as well as made distinct, by this life. This life flow contains the inspiration, motivation, and power of heaven to save, compel, sustain, and develop the inner man.

Hence enters the sacrifice of another book, which may only be seen by a few, but nevertheless, it will also serve as another reminder of the spiritual lessons that have earmarked my growth during this journey. The Christian journey is all about finding and possessing this incredible spiritual life.

Experiencing the Christian Life is a summation of the many lessons that I have alluded to or expounded on in my other books concerning Christian living. Since Christianity is about life, perhaps this book will mark the completion of this series. But it will never mark the completion of discovering the endless treasure and heavenly nuggets that have been made available to all of those who truly possess this incredible gift of God.

Ultimately, it is my hope that the reader will receive a revelation of what it means to possess, experience, and walk out, this incredible way of living as he or she embraces this heavenly life on a daily basis.

1

SEARCHING FOR LIFE

Through the different books I have written, I have discussed the matter of life. What constitutes life, and where, what, or who serves as the real source of life? This is a question we must ask ourselves even though it may appear strange, or what some people would consider as being a no-brainer. The reason we must explore this subject is because our life does not originate with us. Real life actually comes from the outside of man, which means each of us must have some type of life imparted to us, and then we must actually develop it by seeking the source of it.

We all have our different ideas about life, but the definition of it varies. When we think about life, other terms or words come into play such as the ability to function, exist, survive, and live. This brings us to the meanings of life. One meaning of life has to do with the function of breathing. Our breath points to the concept of air, wind, or spirit flowing through a person's body. The second meaning is the ability to interact with one's environment, even though in some cases, such as people in comas, such interaction can be very limited. Such interaction also points to the relationship we have with those things or people that make up our environment. The third meaning points to the concept of a person actually living the life that has been made available to him or her. How we view, approach, and walk out this life will be determined by outside influences such as culture, religion, opportunities, initiative, or circumstances.

As we consider these three meanings of life, we can conclude that without the breath of spirit flowing through and out of us there would be no life. Jesus' death on the cross confirms this. Scripture states of Him that He yielded up His spirit in order to give way to physical death.[1]

It is important to point out that the first man was made a living soul, pointing to the reality that Adam's initial breath was the Spirit of God. When Adam fell into spiritual darkness, the breath of God lifted from him and the air of the world became the breath that kept him functioning in his environment. However, instead of breathing in the fresh wind of the Spirit in sweet communion with his Creator, man begin to breathe in the air that began to erode away his physical life as he started to partake of a fallen world in which death marked the end of man's journey.

The second meaning of life involving the ability to interact points to the quality of life we develop. Life takes on its own character as to how it will respond, relate, or interact with its environment. The environment

---

[1] Matthew 27:50

that surrounds us often determines the quality of the life we are living. The one aspect of our life that sets the tone for much of our environment is the type of relationships we develop with people.

If people could discover one truth about what it means to possess quality in one's life, it comes down to this: The quality and real success of life is not what we obtain in this world, but what type of investment we leave in the lives of others. What kind of taste, impression, and attitude will we leave with those who knew us best, as well as those we encountered along the way?

There was one man whose goal was to obtain success according to the world. However, in his attempt to gain the world, his family was falling apart. Eventually, a wise counselor broke through his perception by challenging him to reconsider his idea of success. It should not be based on the world; rather, it must be considered in light of the type of relationships he had with his wife and children. This new revelation broke through the dark despair of this man. He realized that there was tremendous freedom in changing his perspective, attitude, value system, and energy from that which was lifeless to that which would bring real quality to his life. His new-found liberty not only changed his focus and attitude, but it also completely changed the despairing face of his family.

This brings us to the third meaning of life, that of actually living. When life is eluding people, they will function, exist, and survive, but they will not know what it means to live. For example, some people simply learn how to function in their physical life due to physical challenges beyond their control, while others simply develop means to exist when emotional well-being is missing. For those who operate from a premise of survival, they are learning how to play the games to avoid becoming a victim in a world that has long lost their trust.

Living life is associated with lifestyle. For example, many Americans are pursuing the lifestyle associated with the American dream. In the minds of many people to possess the American dream would make them quite happy. But who or what defines happiness for people? For those who have possessed that which has been associated with worldly happiness, many admit that such pursuits proved to be empty.

We are once again reminded that our personal lives do not originate with us. Life comes from the outside. We, therefore, must seek it from without. In fact, man looks to three sources to find and secure life. The first source he looks to is self. He thinks if he can do that which makes him happy, he will discover what it means to live.

Emphasis on self will always define life according to our selfish state. It is from this selfish disposition that we put value on what we perceive would add purpose to the aspects of our personal preferences and ways. The result is that we will approach matters according to how something will serve our purpose, make us look, or how it will make us feel. However, at the end of such selfish emphasis is nothing but a touchy reality that resents those who refuse to bow down to its need for personal exaltation. Eventually such a disposition becomes totally consumed by darkness as the person who gives way to its insatiable appetites quickly descends into the dark waters of stagnation and death. There is no semblance of life coming from such waters, for nothing can flow out of the endless abyss of self-centeredness.

Needless to say, the more people are full of self, the less they will be able to have a healthy interaction with their environment. Eventually, they will simply learn to somehow exist as they strive to maintain some semblance of self. This is why Jesus' first command to His disciples was to deny or disown self so they could truly find life. He also went on to make this statement, "For whosoever would save his life shall lose it; but whosoever will lose his life for my sake, the same shall save it" (Luke 9:24).

The second source people look to, to find life is the world. Many people perceive that if they could possess the things of the world, they would not only be successful and rich, but they would surely be happy. Solomon, one of the richest men of the world, had to admit in his writing in Ecclesiastes that after partaking of every aspect of the world that all matters attached to it proved to be empty, useless, or vain. Jesus asked what it would profit a man to gain the whole world but lose his soul.[2] He made this statement in Luke 12:15, "...Take heed, and beware of covetousness; for a man's life consisteth not in the abundance of the things which he possesseth."

As we can see, people who pursue the self-life will lose their idea of life in the end. Even though they may taste the temporary pleasures of the fruit of this existence, it will turn into disillusionment and bitterness. In the end, they will find themselves existing in a miserable state, while the essence of real life eludes them.

When it comes to the world, people eventually have to sell their souls to possess the illusive life it promises. As a result, they will become empty in their attempts to secure some lasting, satisfying happiness from the world. Ultimately, they learn to survive as they find themselves being robbed of that which could bring some purpose and meaning to their lives. In the end, they will find themselves in a despairing state of vanity and hopelessness.

The third source that people seek their life from is God. In Amos 5, God's people are instructed to seek the Lord and live. God is the source of true and lasting life. It is only by having the life He has designated for us as Christians that we will discover what it actually means to live. Jesus described this life as being eternal and abundant; therefore, living such a life takes place outside of the influences of the self-life and the illusive life the world promotes. This heavenly life identifies people who possess it as being heirs to an inheritance that is everlasting, and a type of life that will prove to be satisfying.

---

[2] Luke 9:25

Developing Our Christian Life

When we consider the life that God offers, we can begin to see what it means to live. First of all, we do not simply function in this life; rather, we are being led into this life on a continual basis by the Holy Spirit. He once again is the heavenly air that brings forth the very life of Christ in a believer. He is the very living breath that flows through each believer that inspires his or her inner man to explore the depths and heights of God. It is His wind that lifts saints above the entangling ways of the world to view all matters from a heavenly position.

It is the Holy Spirit that enables each of us as believers to interact with God on a spiritual level.[3] He is the point of agreement and fellowship with the Lord in a growing relationship. In communion, He establishes us in a relationship of oneness with our Lord to bring forth the witness that is living, powerful, and effective. To experience such a life of purpose ensures that each of us will not simply exist according to some lesser status quo, but we will fulfill our high calling as we possess the fullness of our heavenly inheritance.

It is as we walk in the Spirit that our attitude towards the world will change. We will become strangers and pilgrims in it as we realize it is not really our home. We are in fact citizens of the kingdom of heaven. Granted, as Christians we serve in the official capacity of ambassadors in this present age. As ambassadors, our main diplomatic service is reconciliation between man and God, but our ultimate destination is heaven.[4] We will never be content to remain in this world, but as we strive to fulfill our obligations according to our high calling, we will not resort to simply surviving this present age. Rather, we will occupy while becoming more desirous to finish the course that will ultimately lead us to our heavenly home in Christ.

Where are you seeking your present life? Beware of simply tacking Christ on to your self-life or adjusting Him into a worldly lifestyle. Make sure that the self-life has been completely disowned, and that your flesh has become crucified to the influences of the world. After all, the Holy Spirit will have no part in any unholy agreement or lifestyle. You must be seeking your complete life in God before you will sense His breath flowing through you, the very life of God being established in you; and that your spiritual walk through this world actually separates you to fulfill the very purpose of God in this present age.

---

[3] 1 Corinthians 2:10-14
[4] 2 Corinthians 5:19-20; Philippians 3:20; 1 Peter 2:11

2

LIVING THE LIFE

Real life comes from God, but how does this life look and express itself in us? Amazingly, the life that comes from God has a look that can be observed. It has a voice that can be heard. It has a way in which it can be tested. It has a smell to it that can be enjoyed, and a taste that can bring great satisfaction. In fact, this life can be summarized in four words: The Lord Jesus Christ.

The Apostle Paul understood that God expressed the life that He desired to give each of us in His Son, Jesus Christ. People beheld the Son and found life. They heard His voice and experienced hope. They tested His ways and found them to be righteous and eternal. They smelled the fragrance of His love and grace and discovered comfort. And, they tasted of His power and compassion and found healing and satisfaction.

As Christians, we know that the life we must possess is a life contrary to the physical life that we live in the flesh. It is a spiritual, unseen life. However, some perceive that they will experience this life in the future when they die. For others, they see this life as simply an extension of the work of God in some type of ministry or religious activities. However, Jesus explained the essence of this life in this way, "For as the Father hath life in himself, so hath he given to the Son to have life in himself" (John 5:26). In John 5:21, Jesus stated that He gives life to whomsoever He will.

We know that all that comes from God is eternal. Therefore, the life He is offering each of us is eternal. There is no end to this life. It has always existed, it is currently active, and it will always be present through the ages to come. This life can only be obtained through one avenue, and that is by receiving Jesus Christ as Lord and Savior. Jesus said of Himself that He was the life, as well as the resurrection. He also stated that everlasting life came from Him.[1] People, who received Jesus, received His life. It is not something that will become evident after physical death; it is something that is presently active in every believer.

The life that Jesus possesses and gives is also abundant.[2] In other words, it is complete; therefore, satisfying to the spiritual man. However, this life can only be realized on a spiritual level. It cannot be found in any aspect of the self-life, nor can it be obtained by pursuing the world. The abundant life can only be possessed as one seeks out the reality of God.

---

[1] John 5:39-40; 6:39-40, 47; 11:25-26
[2] John 10:10

Jesus stated in John 10:9 that He was the door to this life, and we, as His sheep must follow Him as our Shepherd through the door. This door represents His life and work, and once we enter through it, it will allow us to experience salvation, and to know the satisfaction from having life that is both eternal and satisfying.

Jesus is clearly the essence of God's life that has been made available to all those who embrace it by faith. This life is not only eternal and satisfying, but it possesses resurrection power. People must find this life through the narrow entrance of the Person, work, and words of Jesus. As a result, the Apostle Paul made this statement in Galatians 2:20, "I am crucified with Christ: nevertheless I live; yet not I, but Christ liveth in me; and the life which I now live in the flesh I live by the faith of the Son of God, who loved me and gave himself for me."

Meditate on the apostle's statement. He is declaring that his old life has been crucified with Christ. He explained in Romans 6 how this death to the old life takes place. It is through complete identification with Christ. As believers, we have been baptized into Jesus' death; therefore, we are buried with Him. Jesus' burial reminds us that our sins that were attached to the old life have been taken to the grave, and remain buried. Since we have been placed in His death, we should walk in the newness of life, knowing that we will be raised in the likeness of His resurrection.

The Apostle Paul explained the purpose for this type of identification with Jesus in regard to His death and burial in Philippians 3:10, "That I may know him, and the power of his resurrection, and the fellowship of his sufferings, being made conformable unto his death." The apostle established his attitude toward his old life before he made this statement. He declared that he counted all the things associated with his old life as dung, in order to win Christ. Winning Christ would point to the apostle knowing Him, as well as realizing the power that would be found in His resurrection. Paul understood that there was no personal righteousness found in him, and that it was through faith in Christ that true righteousness would be imputed to him.

Paul also realized there was a cost to possessing the life of Christ. He had to come to the place of fellowship with Him in His sufferings. Since Jesus' suffering caused Him to become identified to each of us in order to be made a sin offering on our behalf, the apostle only reasoned that he needed to be made conformable unto his death. It was only out of this death that the life of Jesus could be established in Paul's inner man in greater ways.

Clearly, the Apostle Paul recognized that the life that he was living was not his life; rather, it was the very life of Christ in him. The Holy Spirit could only work the life of Christ in him as he walked this life out by faith. As you follow Paul's reasoning, he concluded that since he was living the life of Christ, he must consider all that he did in light of the fact that he was dead to his old life and alive to live out the new life. This death allowed him to make the great exchange of his old life with the new as he was raised up to live out this incredible existence that is attached to the heavenly. This new life will ultimately express the glory of heaven, Jesus Christ.

This brings us to the issue of salvation. Salvation is not a matter of saying a sinner's prayer that implies all the work of salvation has been completed so that now you can go on your way, knowing you are heaven bound. Rather, the life of Christ in a person is what saves him or her. Don't get me wrong, some people have received the life of Christ by saying the sinner's prayer, but there are others who walk away with an intellectual acknowledgement that Jesus died for them, but there is no heart revelation. In summation, such individuals have not been converted to the righteous ways of God. The Word of God is clear that unless a person believes the Gospel in his or her heart, there is no assurance of salvation.[3]

The evidence of true salvation is the new life being brought forth. Obviously, there cannot be a new life, unless a person has been born again with this life. Jesus clearly stated in John 3:5 that man must be first born of water (God's Word) and the Spirit, before he can enter into the kingdom of God. Note how the water comes before the Spirit. We are told we are saved by grace through faith. However, faith comes by hearing and hearing by the Word of God. We must hear the Word for it to awaken us to our need to be saved. Once awakened to our condition, the Holy Spirit can bring conviction as to our condition of sin and the sentence of death that is upon our souls. As the conviction breaks us, we cry out to the Lord to save us. At this point the Spirit is given as a gift to take up residence in our hearts, identifying us as being born from above with Jesus' life, and sealed to receive an eternal inheritance.[4] Obviously, faith opens the door of our hearts to be born again from above. Upon believing God's Word, the eternal and abundant life of Christ is imparted into us by the presence and work of Holy Spirit.

Our born-again experience represents our infant stage as a Christian. In other words, the life of Christ must be matured in us. In his book, *Finding the Reality of God,* Paris Reidhead commented on how many Christians fail to realize how far-reaching salvation is. I would have to concur with Mr. Reidhead's evaluation. In my observation as to how people treat salvation, I noticed how some treat it as a mere doctrine, rather than a truth. Doctrine is man's responsibility towards a matter, but everything associated with the character and work of God is a truth. Salvation is a work that God has accomplished. Our responsibility towards His salvation becomes a matter of doctrine. It is choosing to have faith towards the Person of God and His work. This faith is expressed in obedience to His Word.

As we consider how salvation has been solely made a doctrine, we only have to consider "easy believism." In "easy believism" a person only has to say some sinner's prayer, and he or she is considered saved.

---

[3] Romans 10:9-10
[4] Romans 10:17; Ephesians 1:11-14; 2:8

Developing Our Christian Life

Once again, it must be pointed out that salvation is a work of God. As Mr. Reidhead pointed out in his book, it is not an experience, but it is the Person of Jesus, for, Jehovah is our salvation. He goes on to explain that the word "salvation" has four tenses. The perfect tense of salvation points to being saved from the pleasure of sin, which occurs at the point of repentance.[5]

When people truly repent, they turn away from the old life, as a means of leaving it behind or counting it as dead, in order to embrace the new life. This is the beginning of where people make the great exchange of their old life with the new life by changing direction. Without repentance, Jesus warned people in Luke 13:5 that they would perish in their sins. Sadly, some people have no idea of what they are being saved from. They think salvation is about having a better life, rather than a new life. Some people act as if they are being saved *in* their sins, rather than being saved *from* their sins. Mr. Reidhead pointed out that since most people are being told how to be saved without first understanding what they need to be saved from, many have become gospel hardened.[6]

The past tense of salvation points to being saved from the death penalty of sin, which points to the work of justification. We know we are justified by faith in what Christ did for us on the cross. It is important to point out that we are not being justified in our sins; rather, we are being justified by the reality of Christ. The Bible tells us salvation places us in Christ, as well as places Him in us. In Him, we are positionally standing justified, allowing His very life to be worked in us.

The present tense of salvation is expressed by the work of sanctification which implies one is being saved from the power of sin. At this point the life of Christ is being worked in us in greater measure to bring forth a transformation. His life is setting us distinctly apart from the old life in attitude, ways, and conduct in order to set us apart for the very work of God.

Finally, you have the future tense of salvation which points to glorification with Christ that speaks of being saved from the presence of sin. To be saved from the presence of sin points to being totally delivered from every avenue of it. It points to the complete abiding and rest that all saints will experience in the unhindered glory of God.

Glorification with Jesus also has its tenses. You have the *perfect tense* of His glory which can only be realized in our lives through suffering. You have the *past tense* of His glory which points to Christ in us, the hope of glory that is present in our lives. You have the *present tense* of His glory which should be reflecting in, through, and from our lives, and our *future tense* of glory with Him, which points to reigning with Him.[7]

---

[5] pg. 22
[6] pg. 53
[7] Romans 8:17; 2 Corinthians 3:18; Colossians 1:27; 2 Timothy 2:12

To declare we are saved in our present state is not correct. The reality of salvation is that we are being saved. Salvation must be worked in our lives, within our lives, and through our lives. This means the very life of Jesus must be formed in us. His mind (disposition or attitude) must be worked *within* our way of thinking, and His ways must be *applied* to our approach and conduct. When Jesus is formed in us, we *take on* His likeness. When His disposition is being brought forth *within* us, we will be conformed to His image. When our Lord's life is being *worked* through our lives, we will be changed from glory to glory, ultimately reflecting His glory. The Apostle Paul summarized the reality of the complete work of salvation best when he instructed believers to work out their salvation with fear and trembling.[8]

As Mr. Reidhead stated in his book, salvation is *potentially* ours at the point of repentance, it *experientially* becomes ours at the place of union with Christ, and it *effectively* will be ours through the ages to come.[9] As each of us considers these three realities of salvation, we must recognize that at repentance, salvation is occurring or becoming a possibility or likelihood, but the life of Christ must still be worked *in* our inner man for salvation to reach its ultimate *potential* or purpose in our lives.

Once the life of Christ is being worked *within* every fiber of who we are, we can begin to *experience* the reality or benefits of it. Keep in mind, the more the life of Christ is worked within us, the more we will come into union with Jesus. Such a union points to experiencing Him on a personal level. In fact, it means we will be growing up in the knowledge of Jesus.

Once that union is established with our Lord, as His life is being worked *through* us by obedience, we can begin to walk in assurance that salvation will be our *effective* reality or result in the ages to come. Clearly, when it comes to salvation it not only reaches back to the cross to bring forth repentance to provide the means for justification for past sins, and produce sanctification for the present, but it reaches forward to the unveiling of its eternal benefits.

The question that must be resolved in every person's heart is, "Am I being saved at this moment?" Salvation or deliverance may have occurred in the past from certain aspects of the old life, but if a person never allows the life of Christ to bring him or her into the present for the purpose of preparing him or her for the future, its work is not proving to be far reaching enough, nor is it being allowed to be brought to completion. Salvation that is hindered in this way will cause a person to remain in the wilderness of the barren soul, where the life of Jesus is never really realized.

What would your answer be in regard to being saved when it comes to the past, present, and future? If you can't answer this question, consider the following prayer.

---

[8] Psalm 17:15; Romans 6:5; 8:29; 13:14; Philippians 2:12
[9] pg. 22

Developing Our Christian Life

Lord Jesus,

    I now understand that I need to be saved from my sin. I am not being saved to embrace a better life, but a new life, Your life. Lord, I clearly need to be saved from the effects and working of sin upon my heart, mind, and life. The only way I can be saved is through forgiveness. I seek Your pardon so that I can receive the newness of Your life. I may not understand all of it, but I choose to believe it by faith, trusting that You will respond to my heartfelt plea. Thank You for saving me. I now give You permission to be my Lord of my life, as Your Spirit works Your life within me. Amen.

3

NOMINAL CHRISTIANITY

We now know that, as believers, the life we live is the very life of Jesus. With this in mind, we must come to terms with how this supernatural life in us can actually be reduced to normalcy. After all, this life is endued with resurrection power. It is eternal and able to bring complete satisfaction to the soul. Obviously, Jesus' life in us should prove to be a complete opposite of normalcy that is often experienced in the world. Such normalcy that is caused by the world proves to be void of any inspiration and power. Emptiness of this nature causes leanness or dissatisfaction to take place in a person's soul.

It is important to understand how Christians who have been given the means to acquire the promises of God, walk in despair or defeat. Clearly, the life of Christ is not intended to be lived on a mediocre level. His life in us is meant to enable each of us as believers to experience the depths of the challenge this spiritual life will bring in the midst of the present age, without being swallowed in the darkness of despair. Due to the power of the Spirit behind this life, we are also able to scale the heights presented by different challenges in order to develop the vantage point that inspires each of us to come higher in God regardless of the cost.

The Christian life is an incredible experience, but it must be walked out in faithful obedience to discover the inspiration, power, and purpose of it. This brings us back to why Christians fail to discover the reality of this spiritual life. There are some decisive reasons for the Christian life digressing into what appears to be a nominal existence. We are going to consider these reasons in light of Scriptural examples.

One of the greatest examples of a person being brought to the stage of normalcy in his spiritual life is Lot. Lot was Abraham's nephew. Through his journey with his uncle, he no doubt witnessed God blessing Abraham. To some extent he benefitted from the blessings that flowed down from heaven to his uncle and eventually filtered down to him. In fact, both men were so blessed that the land could not contain the fruits of their blessings, causing strife between their herdsmen. It was decided by this uncle and nephew that they needed to go their separate ways. Even though God had promised Abraham the land of Canaan, this righteous man still allowed Lot to choose the place where he wanted to reside.

Lot looked towards the east at the well watered plain of Jordan where Sodom and Gomorrah were located. His eyes were clearly attracted to the plush land, and chose to locate in what appeared to be a garden. However, he actually pitched his tent in the midst of great wickedness.[1]

The example clearly found in Lot's life is that the first step to neutralizing one's spiritual life is to choose the lush valleys of the world as a means to maintain a certain lifestyle, rather than sell all to possess the life that God has ordained. As a result of his decision, Lot actually came into the entrapments of the world. When a person tries to walk between the promised life of God and the fading, temporary attractions of the world, his or her life will take on a nominal temperature that will taste of drudgery and disillusionment. Because Lot made the choice he did for the world, he experienced three major events in his life that revealed the fruit of such an existence.

The first event that intruded into his nominal existence in this place of wickedness was bondage. Lot was basically a sitting duck in this land. As a result, he was taken captive along with his goods, by a wicked king. Abraham rescued his nephew and was able to restore back to him all of his goods. However, this example is clear. When God's people reside close to, or in the world, to benefit from it, it has a way of taking them captive and robbing them of all their goods. These individuals will eventually find themselves in tremendous bondage to it.[2] Like Lot, such Christians have to often be delivered from such bondage.

The second incident involved judgment. The stench of the land's wickedness had become a point of great grief to God. The Lord was about to bring judgment down on Sodom and Gomorrah. At this time, Lot lived in Sodom. Abraham interceded for God to stay His judgment against these two cities for the sake of ten righteous men.[3] Sadly, there were not ten righteous men to be found; therefore, the one righteous man that lived there was earmarked for deliverance. That man was Lot.

We are told that Lot's spirit was vexed over the sin that was rampant. The angels who were sent into Sodom to rescue Lot and his family, found themselves affronted in Lot's home by the grave wickedness of the men of the city.[4] Clearly, Lot tried to protect them from the men's wicked plans, but the angels had the means to supernaturally drive the men back, stopping their evil designs.

Lot was told of the impending judgment ready to be poured out on the two cities. He tried to warn his sons-in-law, but they would not listen. Eventually, the angels had to literally pull Lot and his wife, and two daughters, out of Sodom before God rained fire on the two doomed cities. We know that Lot's wife looked back on God's judgment, and was turned into a pillar of salt.

As we consider Lot, it is important to recognize that he may have been vexed over the wicked condition of Sodom, but he did not hate the

---

[1] Genesis 13:6-13
[2] Genesis 14:8-16
[3] Genesis 18:23-33
[4] Genesis 19:1-24; 2 Peter 2:6-9

sins of the city enough to flee from their influence. When we consider the incidents in Lot's life, we must conclude that in God's final judgment on Sodom, this man lost most of his possessions, including his wife.

Even though Lot was stirred in his spirit about sin, he still remained nominal in his actions towards it. What we see about Lot's attitude is that it was nonchalant towards the present age he lived in. If it were not for the angels, Lot would have been judged along with the rest of the people of Sodom. Even after being warned of the judgment to come, the angels still had to pull him out of the city.

Christians, who have a nominal attitude towards the world and sin, will also have the same type of attitude towards their Christian life. Such an attitude reveals that they have failed to choose the righteous, narrow ways of God. Since they have failed to follow the Lord into a new life, they will remain comfortable in the old way, causing defeat in their spiritual lives.

When Christians fail to separate themselves from the influence of the world and sin, they will eventually slide into some type of sin. We clearly see this in Lot's life. Obviously, his daughters had been greatly influenced by the wicked ways of Sodom. In their perverted reasoning they justified committing incest with their father as a way to propagate. Since there was some obvious deviation in Lot's character, he was easily set up to fall into their trap. Sadly, he did slide into the clenches of their entrapment, producing two offspring.[5] From the premise of this deviation, other than serving as an example to others, Lot's name faded into obscurity.

The second example of normalcy in operation among God's people was the children of Israel. The children of Israel knew all about the bondage associated with normalcy. They had been made slaves by the Egyptians. Each day found them in the same struggle to survive under the harsh tyranny of the Egyptian leaders. Eventually, it became so great, they cried out to the Lord. He sent Moses in to deliver them.

It is hard to say how the people of Israel perceived their deliverance. However, I do not think that they thought they would end up wandering in the desert. Egypt represented bondage to them, but the wilderness represented possible death, as well as a life that would possess leanness. I am sure that they had no idea that due to their unbelief towards Jehovah God, the wilderness would eventually become a graveyard to a whole generation,

As you consider the people of Israel, you realize that God did not intend for them to wander around in the wilderness for forty years. Although He provided the water and manna through those forty years, His real plan for them was to eat the fruit of the Promised Land.

Clearly, God's plan for Israel was not for them to taste the normalcy of the drudgery and leanness of the wilderness. The lot that the children of Israel experienced in the wilderness was not brought on them by God.

---

[5] Genesis 19:30-38

Developing Our Christian Life

Rather, it was brought on them by their decision to not trust God. They not only failed to trust God, but they also presumed that God would have to accept their feeble attempts to possess the Promised Land in their own flesh after they had refused to possess it by faith. The Apostle Paul summarized the essence of their attitude in Galatians 3:3, "Are ye so foolish? Having begun in the Spirit, are ye now made perfect by the flesh?"

We can clearly learn much from the children of Israel about how God's people succumb to a nominal life. God has the best in mind for His people, but because of their attitudes of idolatry and unbelief toward Him, the influence of the world, and work of sin in their lives, they will settle for less. The less in this case for the children of Israel translated into tasting the drudgery of the wilderness.

Through the years, I have found this to be true for Christians as well. God has provided everything that pertains to life and godliness. He has given His Spirit to lead and guide each of us as His people through the terrain of this world. He serves as our Rock in the storms of life, our fortress in battles, our high tower in times of adversity, and our refuge in times trouble. He is all we have need of, for He is our all in all.[6]

In spite of God being our all in all, many Christians fail to possess the complete promise of life that is found in Him. The problem rests in His people's attitude. They want the life God has promised, but they are not willing to possess it. The children of Israel wanted the benefits of the Promised Land, but they did not want to pay the necessary price to inherit it.

It is vital that we heed Israel's example. In his book, *The Saving Life of Christ,* Major W. Ian Thomas used the situation surrounding Israel in Egypt, to explain the three types of people that can be observed in the examples surrounding the children of Israel. There are those who are of the world, which are clearly represented by those of Egypt. These individuals are idolatrous and self-serving. They rely on man's strength to save them from utter destruction. These people have no intention of coming out of Egypt. They are unsaved and their doom is sealed by their attitude of rejection towards the true God of heaven.

The second group is represented by those who wander around in the wilderness. Major Thomas compared the second group of people to carnal Christians. Carnal Christians have come out of Egypt, but Egypt is not totally out of them. These individuals may hate the bondage of Egypt, but they easily forget about such bondage when challenged by the harshness of the wilderness. They keep looking back at what Egypt offered in the way of fleshly appetites, forgetting that bondage only allowed them to taste the despair of its bitter oppression, rather than the satisfying, abundant fruits of life.

Since these individuals keep looking back, they fail to look forward. For example, in front of the children of Israel was the Promised Land with

---

[6] Romans 8:14; 1 Corinthians 15:28; Colossians 3:11; 2 Peter 1:3-4

its incredible fruits. Granted, they would first have to possess this land to experience the sweetness of not only its fruit, but the liberty that allowed them to enjoy it as a people.

In chapter four of his book, *The Master's Indwelling,* Andrew Murray also pointed out the carnality of the people of Israel. God brought them out of Egypt with the desire to bring them into a new life in Canaan. However, their carnality caused them to remain in the wilderness. Murray brings out the contrast of the wilderness of carnality and the new life that could be obtained in the Promised Land. The wilderness of carnality had the children of Israel wandering backward and forward for forty years because of unbelief, while the land of Canaan offered perfect rest for them. In carnality, the people constantly find themselves going backwards by desiring and chasing after the various temptations of the world, only to discover that they must now go forward in repentance if they were going to survive the emptiness of the wilderness. It is a life of ups and downs, as well as uncertainties.

The wilderness of carnality is also a place of wants that cannot be fulfilled, and is void of any real victory over the enemies. On the other hand, Canaan represents a land of plenty, a place of victory where the enemies are conquered, and God's people enter into a place of rest because of possessing faith and assurance towards God.

When Christians keep looking back at the world because they lack the faith to possess God's promises, they will remain in the spiritual wilderness. These individuals are content with the mixture of the world's attitude about life and the beliefs and activities associated with their Christian life. In essence, these individuals basically hold on to their worldly attitude, while they adopt Christian doctrine as a means to reform or rehabilitate certain aspects of their life. However, they refuse to give up every influence of the self-life in order to go on to the ways of maturity and righteousness.

The Apostle Paul spoke about the fruits of carnal Christians.[7] Since these people perceive matters from the fleshly premise of their old life, envying, strife and divisions follow them. Due to their spiritual ineptness to properly discern matters, they must judge according to assumptions they have about others, and presumptions about God's perspective. Even though these people might get some issues right, they lack the right spirit to ensure the intent of it. As a result, they fail to be upright before God.

Righteousness represents the meat of doing God's will, not establishing an outward form of religious piousness. In carnality, Christians can maintain an outward appearance of piousness through half-hearted conduct, as they reserve the right to maintain certain ideas or philosophies of the world. This half-hearted perspective will keep them looking backward at what was, preventing them from looking forward to what can and will be.

---

[7] 1 Corinthians 3:1-3

These Christians may even come up to the promises of God, but they will never completely possess them. They do not have the heart or the desire to pay the price to possess the complete promises of God. Since these people lack the heart to pay the necessary price to possess what God has for them, they will never come to that place where they will consecrate every area of their lives to God. Consecration in this text means offering their lives as a living sacrifice so that they can discover what the good, acceptable and perfect will of God is in a matter.[8]

Jesus made this statement in Luke 9:62b, "...No man, having put his hand to the plough, and looking back, is fit for the kingdom of God." Sadly, carnal Christians give the impression they are putting their hand to the plough, but they are always looking back at the world. They display envy towards those of the world that appear to possess the type of life they desire. They cause strife in their world because they are not content with the life they can possess in Christ. Since there is a division in their heart and focus, they often experience the torment of the battle between the Spirit and their flesh.

When the Apostle Paul was contending with the Corinthians about their carnal state, he warned them that even though they would be saved, it would be through fire. If their works proved to be wood, hay, or stubble, they would be burned up in the fires of judgment.[9]

Carnal Christians will never enter into the full life of God in their present age of mediocre Christianity. They will remain in the lean state of their spiritual lives because they have never released their hold on Egypt to go forward to experience the fullness of their life in Christ. As a result, they fail to live the life of Christ as they walk in the leanness of spirit. The journey for them through this present age will prove to be an ongoing wilderness that will become drudgery and bitterness to their souls. In their dissatisfaction, they will murmur and complain, but they will not repent for their attitude towards Egypt, as they refuse to risk their fleshly life to discover the fullness of their spiritual lives.

The third type is made up of committed followers of God, who by faith enter into the promises of God as a means to possess their inheritance. These people are quick to leave the bondage of Egypt behind; and, like Joshua and Caleb will choose the way of faith. Their faith will enable them to enter into the life God has for them. These people will also have the necessary righteousness imputed to them, enabling them to maintain the quality of their inheritance.

What about you? Are you a carnal Christian that operates within the nominal levels of mediocre Christianity? If so, know that it is because you will not leave the attachments with Egypt behind in the wilderness, in order to possess a new life in Christ.

---

[8] Romans 12:1-2; Hebrews 5:11-14; 6:12
[9] 1 Corinthians 3:12-15

4

PREPARATION

We have been considering the three types of people in regard to the three spiritual levels that can be observed among those who are in Egypt. There are those who are like the Egyptians. They are spiritually dead to the reality of the one true God. These people, of course, represent the unsaved. There are those who wander in the wilderness of carnality because of unbelief. People who fall into this category are those who may be Christians, but they remain in spiritual barrenness because they will not let go of Egypt to enter into all that God has for them. Finally, you have the people who actually enter into the Promised Land to possess their inheritance from God. These people represent the saints who are embracing the life of Jesus and the promises of God by faith.

The key to understanding the Christian walk is that it is a process. The process that Christians must go through challenges different areas of their lives. For example, God must first bring the person out of Egypt, a type of the world. Deliverance from the entanglements of the world occurs so that one can truly become identified to the life that God has for him or her.

Egypt clearly revealed the world with it various poison fruits of idolatry, paganism, and humanistic philosophies. These fruits are made to look and taste good as they entangle people into the enticing web of the dark delusion of its deceptive ways, resulting in death. Because of this destructive web, the only way people will leave Egypt is when they have been brought to a state of sheer desperation. Desperation of this type is due to the world's unbearable bondage. Such bondage occurs at the point where the demands of Egypt became so great and undesirable to the person that he or she becomes desperate to find relief from the heavy blanket of despair.

It must be pointed out that relief is quite different from deliverance. Those seeking relief do not necessarily desire to be delivered out of Egypt; rather, they simply want their situation to change in order to experience relief from the bitterness brought on by their circumstances. After all, these people are quite comfortable in Egypt, but grave bondage can create an unbearable taste in these people's mouth. This discomfort can be related to the eagle stirring up the nest to expose its thorny side. The uncomfortable nest will force the eaglets out of their comfortable safety zone to begin the process of reaching their potential in the heights of the air currents.

God was allowing the comfortable nest of Egypt to be stirred up for His people so that they would spread out their immature wings in order to

Developing Our Christian Life

trek off into the wilderness to some unknown land or destination. God would be there to ensure that they would not be destroyed. The Lord brought this out in Exodus 19:4, "Ye have seen what I did unto the Egyptians, and how I bore you on eagle's wings and brought you unto myself." However, the stirring of the nest can all prove quite unnerving to a soul. It points to total deliverance from what is familiar to discover one's potential. The main problem with people who want relief rather than desiring complete deliverance is that they may come out of Egypt, but Egypt does not always come out of them.

This was true for the children of Israel. Most of them brought with them the worldly thinking of Egypt even though they had found themselves in bondage to its oppressive ways. After all, Egypt was what they were used to. Even as slaves, they knew what to expect from the powerful and tyrannical leadership. But, to travel to an unknown place is another story. As a result, these people failed to realize that they were being completely delivered from all the influences of Egypt that pointed to not only tyrannical bondage for them but the seeds of death.

Sadly, the people of Israel had accepted the influences of Egypt without realizing that these influences had established their perspective. The perspective the Jewish people had of themselves was that they were slaves. From this perspective they would never be able to realize their potential to become a great nation. They were willing to accept crumbs from the Egyptians, when God wanted them to partake of the best fruits of the Promised Land.

It was only the bitterness of the grave bondage that finally forced the children of Israel to desperately cry out to God for deliverance; and it was fear created by the death of the Egyptians' first-born that finally released them out of their place of bondage and sorrow. Needless to say, they were initially excited about their deliverance, but the way proved to be hard and challenging. The way led them right into the wilderness. It was not the fastest way to the Promised Land, but it was the way they needed to walk to ensure preparation to possess the land. After all, these slaves had to become soldiers.

The Christian walk involves a process as well. Instead of being led the easiest and fastest route to secure the promises of God, Christians are led by way of a narrow path that proves to be unattractive and hard. However, the hard way creates the necessary endurance that must be present to possess the promises of God. Hebrews 6:12 gives us this insight, "That ye be not slothful, but followers of them who through faith and patience inherit the promises."

The boundaries of this narrow way often prove to be too simple for the worldly perception, allowing people the right to sway or take detours from the path. These boundaries merely serve as guideposts that point the way, but do not hedge people into the narrow path. These two boundaries are Spirit and truth. The Spirit will gently guide, while the truth can prove to be comforting, as well as firm, sharp, and uncompromising. It will ultimately expose and separate people according to their heart condition.

It is vital that God's people understand the process of preparation that takes place. It is important to point out that as Christians, our process will make us ready to walk in the way we are being called to. It will prepare us for our destination.

We know that saints are preparing for the glory of eternity. They walk in the light of Jesus, submit to the leading of the Spirit, seek to do the Father's will, and focus on their heavenly destination. However, those who walk according to the flesh are on a broad path of destruction.[1] They are walking in darkness according to the world, they are submitting to the god of the world, being led by their fleshly appetites or feelings, and seeking to please their self-life. In such a life these people have no real focus outside of this present age. Sadly, the darkness of delusion is blinding these people to their ultimate destination of damnation.

If you ask these people if they prefer heaven, most of them would probably answer yes. However, they are not preparing themselves for the environment of heaven. They are living as children of hell, preparing to taste the complete bitterness of the judgment that awaits them.

One of the individuals that we can follow in his preparation is Moses. He was raised in the courts of Pharaoh. No doubt he was prepared by the best form of education. He was probably being groomed to be a leader in Egypt. However, Moses knew who he was. He was not an Egyptian. He was a Hebrew who rightfully deserved to taste the harsh taskmaster of slavery.

Moses also had a sense of his destiny. He knew that he was spared from being a slave, trained to be a leader, and separated for a mission. Hebrews 11:24-27 gives us special insight into this man. He refused to be called the son of Pharaoh's daughter; instead, he chose to suffer affliction with the people of God. Instead of enjoying sin for a season, he chose the reproach of Christ as being of far greater value than anything Egypt could offer him. He understood that the real reward was not of this world.

Although Moses had a sense of his destiny, he was not prepared to carry out his mission. He had zeal, but not wisdom. He had knowledge, but not experience. He had strength, but not the meekness to properly channel it. Clearly, God had to take him through a process that would reach into his very soul and spirit in order for him to be prepared to carry out the destiny set before him.

The preparation Moses would have to endure would take place in the wilderness. The wilderness has many meanings, but it pointed to barrenness, leanness, harshness, and endurance.

This brings us to the concept of barrenness. Barrenness points to a condition or environment where there is no vegetation or fruit. It points to a wasteland that has no real potential. Although Moses had a sense of

---

[1] Matthew 7:13-14

his destiny or commission, he had to first lose all awareness of it so God could actually define it according to His eternal plan. For forty years Moses traveled the barren terrain of the wilderness as a shepherd. Each year the sense of his destiny was possibly fading into the vastness of the leanness that was invading every aspect of his life.

When people lose the awareness of their destiny, they actually lose their vision. Without vision, people experience barrenness in their lives. From this vantage point, they do not perceive that they have anything of importance to offer. They are often forced to learn ways in which they are able to maintain and endure in the drudgery of it all. However, they end up with no vision past the lot that they have had to accept as their everyday lifestyle.

Obviously, Moses could not foresee that his experience of walking in the wilderness was preparing him to lead people through it. In his initial years in Egypt, he had a sense that the people of Israel had to be led out of Egypt, but he had no real direction or training past the initial deliverance. It would not be enough for Moses to lead people out of Egypt if he did not have the means to deliver them through the terrain that stood before them and into the place that represented their complete deliverance.

Can you imagine the knowledge of the wilderness Moses acquired in those forty years? His experience to survive and endure the harshness of it was vital to the leadership he would have to display. He had no foreknowledge that the children of Israel's two year stretch in the wilderness would be extended to forty years of wandering in it because of unbelief.

The other important aspect is that Moses was prepared to lead people out of Egypt and through the wilderness, but was he prepared and called to lead them into the Promised Land? We know that Moses did not lead the people of Israel into the place of promise.

There is a lot of symbolism in this example. Moses represented the Law, which could show people the ways of holiness, but could never lead them into realizing the complete promises of God. Moses was a capable leader in the wilderness, but was not a soldier that could lead people into victories in the Promised Land. He was a great shepherd, but not a great commander. As a result, Moses' leadership had to give way to the leadership of the great soldier, Joshua.

We know that Joshua represents the capable leadership of Jesus Christ. Jesus alone is the One who can lead each of us into the promises attached to the abundant and eternal life.

The example of the two different leaderships of Moses and Joshua reveal that God will prepare each of us as His people to fulfill our part in His kingdom, but we must always be aware that each type of leadership can only shine in the arena for which it was prepared. Every form of leadership which operates in its element is valuable to the furtherance of God's kingdom, but outside of its element it will prove to be limiting and stifling to those who want to go on to discover what God has for them.

The key to powerful leadership is that it recognizes when it must give way to another type of leadership that has been prepared by God to lead His people beyond the present terrain of their spiritual lives on to perfection. For every Christian leader, they can be assured of encountering their Joshua along the way. They need to be quick to relinquish their leadership of the sheep to this leader. His name is Jesus Christ.

What has God been preparing you for in regard to His kingdom? Moses was called, prepared, and then commissioned to lead the people of Israel. It took 80 years of his life for him to be prepared in different ways. Perhaps you are in your preparation stage, and are about ready to give up. Before you do, consider Moses. Give God permission to have His way in you (preparation) so that He can have His way through you based on the type or form of leadership He is establishing or has established in you.

5

TURNING ASIDE

We have been considering the man Moses. Early on in his life he had a sense of his destiny as the children of Israel's deliverer. But, at that stage of his life he had not been prepared as the shepherd they needed him to be to ensure that they were delivered out of the muddied pastures of Egypt into and through the barren wasteland of the wilderness. He had a call, but he had not received his commission or marching orders from God. He first had to be prepared.

God, in His faithfulness, will never commission His people until they have been prepared to carry out His marching orders. Moses was no exception. For forty years, he had to be put in a place where from all appearances he would lose all sense of his destiny. This meant his self-sufficiency took a back seat to the humbling reality that he was not some great leader, but a shepherd overseeing dumb sheep in a nowhere place. In such a lean, barren environment, it also meant he would most likely lose sight of the vision of his calling. Everything he had perceived in the zealous years of his youth most likely faded into drudgery. Four decades of drudgery probably seemed to have no real purpose or significance for the man who once enjoyed the abundance of Pharaoh's court.

Even though Moses was eighty years old at this point, his physical health and appearance was that of a man in the prime of his life. The difference was that he possessed the wisdom and experience of a man of his years. He was no longer zealous because of immaturity, nor was he unrealistic about the struggles that the harshness of life could bring. Obviously, he had been clearly tempered by the adversities of the wilderness. He had unknowingly been prepared to realize his calling and fulfill his commission as a deliverer.

Clearly, Moses had for all intents and purposes accepted his nominal lot in life. He would remain in the wilderness and die as a simple shepherd. This brings us to a very important aspect of preparation: that of acceptance. People who refuse to accept the reality of their humble lives will never be prepared to accept the caliber of their high calling and commission. They will never learn the lessons of life that are cleverly woven into the mosaic of the various challenges that will confront them. As a result, they will never gain a healthy perspective about their place in the scheme of eternity.

The truth is, Moses could remain as a simple (humble) shepherd in the wilderness until his death. However, he would be the shepherd of an entire nation that he would finally lead to the Promised Land, even after forty years of wandering around in the wasteland of unbelief.

The main purpose of preparation is to bring a person to a state of humility before God. All the overrated fluff and stuffing of preconceived notions, personal strength, and self-sufficiency must be knocked out, burned out, and left behind in the wilderness. Humility is the only state in which a person will be prepared to hear God's call upon his or her life.

After forty years on the backside of the desert, God was about to intrude into the normalcy of Moses' life. Most people fail to realize that if God makes an appearance into their world, it is not with pomp and circumstance, but in an unlikely way that might elude their very attention if they are not careful to stop long enough to discern what is happening in their environment.

For Moses, it was a bush that caught his attention. No doubt there were plenty of bushes in the wilderness. They all appeared the same, so why did one bush out on the desert cause Moses to stop long enough to ponder what was going on? This bush was aflame with something that was out of the extra-ordinary. It was burning with a fire, but yet not consumed by it. Moses recognized that activity taking place as being great. We know that such greatness is associated with God.[1]

Keep in mind this was an ordinary bush, yet it was on fire, but not being destroyed. We also recognize that it was not the bush that was extraordinary; it was the fire. The fire represented the presence of God. It pointed to His holiness.

As we consider this situation, we must recognize any old bush would have served the same purpose in the same situation. This bush reminds us that any person will do when it comes to God doing His bidding. Such a person could point to you or me, but we first must allow ourselves to be properly prepared.

God came to meet Moses in the wilderness. Not only had Moses finally been prepared to lead the children of Israel, but they were also prepared to follow. Everything was now in place for God to give Moses his marching orders.

For Moses to encounter the Lord in this burning bush, he had to turn aside from the normalcy of his life to consider the phenomenal happening that was taking place. There are four actions we see taking place in regard to Moses' response in Exodus 3:3: "And Moses said, I will now turn aside and see this great sight, why the bush is not burnt."

First Moses stopped from doing that which was normal. So many people will not stop from doing their normal activities to consider if God is in a matter. They are so busy running straight ahead at full speed, that they could easily miss the burning bushes in their life. People need to stop and consider if God is trying to get their attention before they run head long into nothingness.

---

[1] Exodus 3:1-3

The second type of movement Moses made was that he turned aside. Much of what God does is accomplished away from the worldly focus of daily activities. His different intrusions often manifest themselves on the sidelines of our many daily demands. Therefore, we must not only come to a stop, but we must also turn aside to encounter Him. This means we must fine-tune our spiritual peripheral vision to not only connect with the present reality around us, but to also properly discern God's intrusions or interventions.

The third thing Moses did was that he made a decision to see what was actually going on. How many people look, but never see what is really going on? When it comes to God's intervention, it is not enough to simply look His way; you must actually see Him in a matter to properly hear Him.

This brings us to Moses' final response. He stopped and turned aside to see what was going on so that he could understand. People who look without seeing have no intention of really understanding. They are not open to what is happening nor are they interested in changing their view or perspective of a situation; therefore, they fail to connect to the reality around them.

The reason Moses' response is so important is because when Moses turned aside to see, God called out to him from the burning bush. Have you ever known people who were on such a dead run that they couldn't hear you call out to them? To get a person's attention, he or she must be stopped, as well as become open and willing to tune in to their environment.

In the military they use the command "attention," to bring people to a place where they were prepared to stop their present activity and turn aside to carry out a matter. In such a state, individuals are prepared to hear and see in such a way that they are able to properly understand the command. God had to get Moses' attention, because He was going to require Moses to not only turn aside from normalcy, but to step outside of the routine of what was considered his present life.

As Christians, we must consider if God gives us a burning bush that is able to grab our attention, would we be willing to stop long enough to consider it? For Christians, this bush would not only manage to get their attention, but to set their lives aflame with a new vision and purpose. The truth is there is such a "bush" present in the midst of Christians. It is the cross of Jesus.

Granted, for Christians, it is not a burning bush, but an old rugged cross that lifted Jesus above this world. This object speaks a powerful message that has the ability to set hearts aflame with passion, purpose, and vision. Even though this fire appears as if it would consume everything it touches, it simply purges, redefines, and empowers those who encounter it. We know this fire to be the Holy Spirit.

As a Christian, I am aware that my biggest challenge in my Christian life is to keep my burning bush ever before me. It is my stake as to my heritage and the mark that points me to eternity. It serves as my reality check, as it reminds me of my humble beginnings as a child of God. It must become my daily place of identification as I choose to become identified in the death, burial, and resurrection of Jesus in regard to my decisions and daily walk. It is in such identification that I will become more like Him.

Jesus' cross is the object that reminds me that the life I now live is the life of Christ. Since it is His life, then all matters must line up to Him, His examples, and will. Each time I choose to line an attitude, decision, or response up to Him, different aspects of His life will be worked into my inner man by the Spirit of God.

The Apostle Peter talked about the barrenness that can occur in our spiritual lives.[2] This barrenness is made evident because one does not really possess the virtues of Christ. These excellent qualities include diligence, faith, excellent character, knowledge, temperance, patience, godliness, brotherly kindness, and benevolent love. The apostle goes on to explain that if these virtues do not abound in Christians, it is due to the fact that such individuals are barren or unfruitful in their knowledge of the Lord Jesus Christ.

The Christian life is brought forth as the characteristics of Christ are being unveiled in and through the lives of believers. However, as believers, we cannot take on such virtues if we do not really know Jesus. At the cross of Jesus, it ceases to be about our personal identity as the great exchange takes place. The exchange is that my right to my selfish, worldly life dies at the point of the cross. Death of this nature means to become lost in Jesus' work of redemption in order to gain a new life that will be ablaze with resurrection power. In a sense, we must be consumed by His life and in His life. If we fail to experience this total identification at the cross, we will remain ignorant in our knowledge or understanding of our Lord.

In such ignorance of Jesus, we will fail to put on His life when our attitude about matters is being challenged, thus preventing our minds from being transformed. If we do not know what pleases Him, we will not know how to ensure the integrity of His life that comes through obedience. The darkness of such ignorance will keep us from learning of His disposition. And, if we do not walk in the ways of righteousness according to His examples, we will never be conformed to His likeness. Without His likeness there will be no lasting fruits established by our lives. Clearly, to be fruitful in our lives, we must not be barren in our knowledge or understanding of who Jesus is and must be to us.

Jesus' cross also reminds us that we must begin with humility to receive this life. As the Apostle Peter pointed out, the reason people lack the excellent characteristic of the Christian life is that they have become

---

[2] 2 Peter 1:5-9

blinded to spiritual matters. Their inability to see from afar is the result of them forgetting that they have been purged from old sins.

Every Christian stands on the same level at Jesus' cross. There are none being exalted because they have great means, gifts, money, or insights. Everyone is standing level at the cross because they are in need of God's intervention. There is no self-sufficiency, notable strength, or incredible abilities taking center stage. All silently and humbly stand at the cross in need of forgiveness, reconciliation, and restoration.

Sadly, the drudgeries of life can cause believers to become spiritually dull towards God. As a result, their eyes become dim, their hearing becomes muffled, and their discernment loses its sharpness. Since they have lost their spiritual edge, they can no longer see afar into the distance. It is the ability to see into the far distance where one can occasionally gain subtle glimpses into eternity.

When Christians lose their way because the world is beginning to consume them, they need to stop. The reason for stopping is to remember the burning bush that serves as their stake, and once again become acquainted with it. They must remember their humble beginnings so that they can turn aside from all their worldly demands to see or behold their burning bush. The cross of Jesus clearly stands unique above all other spiritual places, reaching far above this present world to the very throne room of God. They also need to remind themselves that their burning bush represents a new life, a high calling, and a glorious future. They must remember their old life ceased in the world, and now they walk in the newness of life according to a heavenly perspective.

This new life is not just any life; it is the life of Jesus. And, every time we as believers turn aside to embrace this new life in faith and obedience, we are embracing the extraordinary. Every time we give way to this life in godly submission, we are allowing the extraordinary to change the ordinary terrain of our lives. Each time we gain a bit of Jesus' life, the flame of the Holy Spirit is fanned to stir us up in greater devotion and purpose.

Believers, there is nothing normal about the life of Christ that is in each of us. There is no drudgery attached to the life of Christ that is being lived out on a daily basis. If there is any drudgery present in your life, all you have to do is stop and identify it. You will find out that what is proving to be boring and exhausting in your present existence is actually attached to the world with all of its demands, temporary pleasures, and foolish ways.

Saints of the Most High God, when was the last time you stopped running the race of the world, and turned aside to locate your burning bush? If you did, was the burning bush close or far away? Could you feel the intensity of its heat, or could you barely see a small ember in the distance?

Let me suggest to you that if you have not recently taken the time to behold Jesus' cross, it is time to stop and turn aside. And, when you behold it, remember the love, sacrifice, and hope that glows within the powerful flames of the incredible message that surrounds this tree. Remember the work of redemption, the gift of life, and the Promise of the Holy Spirit. Remember that as believers, we have been given everything that pertains to life according to Him, as well as what pertains to godliness because of Jesus' redemption. Remember, when you turn aside to consider Jesus' cross, you just might feel that flame of the Holy Spirit bursting forth to purge, consume, and empower you to once again discover the incredible blessings of the gift of life that has been entrusted to you.

6

ENCOUNTERING HIS PRESENCE

Moses had been in the wilderness of drudgery and normalcy for forty years. From every indication, he had accepted his lot in life. The memories of his past life had probably become dim in light of the barren wasteland he confronted every day. Nothing had really changed in the terrain of his existence for the past forty years; that is, until he observed a burning bush.

Moses knew there was something great about the burning bush. It is not that a bush can't burn for it can; it is that when a bush burns it will naturally be consumed by the fire. However, this bush was not being destroyed. Clearly, there was something extraordinary going on. Moses not only stopped to consider what he was witnessing, he actually turned aside to see what was truly happening.

His actions produced a response. A voice called out from the bush. Talk about something extraordinary happening. It had to appear as if the bush was talking to Moses. However, we know that it was the angel of the LORD who was calling him from out of the midst of the burning bush.

Who is the angel of the LORD? "Angel" means messenger, but when the voice called out to Moses, it was identified as the voice of God. Clearly, the messenger in this incident was God. This brings us to what Person of the Godhead would actually serve as a personal messenger on behalf of the throne of God. Most people would agree that the Word, who was introduced in the Gospel of John, was serving as the messenger. If this is true, then the pre-incarnate Jesus not only had intruded into Moses' reality, but He was about to change the direction of his life.

Since God was speaking to Moses, it was obvious that he was actually encountering the presence of God. It is important to take note of what it means to <u>stand</u> <u>before</u> the presence of God. When we consider the word "presence," it points to the appearance or expression of something that can be sensed in some way. In fact, it sets up an environment that will express support, or encourage a certain response.

When it comes to God's presence, it can express itself in different ways. The environment that is established by His presence will give people a sense of how they are to stand and respond to Him. For example, Moses in this incident simply stood before Him. In other cases, people simply witness His presence, some stand as close to His presence as they can, while others sup in His presence, ascend into the midst of His presence, or are completely overcome by His presence.

Clearly as we consider the different incidents surrounding the presence of God, we will begin to discover that His manifestations are clearly an expression of His Person in some way. But His presence also sets up the environment in order to invoke the correct response from His people that He is so deserving of.

Obviously, it is important to note what kind of environment is being set up by God. In this case what does it mean for individuals to stand before the presence of God? No doubt standing before the presence of God involves a serious matter that will require one's complete attention and commitment.

God was about to give Moses His marching orders. When people receive their orders, they must stand at attention before the one who is sending them. Moses was actually standing at attention before the Holy God to properly receive his instructions. However, receiving His marching instructions was not God's first order of business.

God's order is very important to understand. We see there is separation and preparation, but what Moses needed to foremost understand at this point of time was not necessarily his marching orders, but who was actually sending him on this mission. The proper authority must first be established before the commands can be given. Moses needed to understand who was commissioning him to carry out a very extraordinary mission.

Most Christians think what they need to first understand is what their mission is according to God's will and plan. Although knowing the mission is vital, the main understanding they first must come to terms with is who God is. This is true for any situation where a person is being sent to represent someone or something. Does the one who is commissioning him or her for a mission have the authority and power to enable the one he or she is sending forth to see a matter or mission brought to fruition?

In order to establish His authority, God first established the type of attitude Moses needed to have towards Him. Consider how God set up the environment that would produce a proper attitude. His first command to Moses was, "Draw not nigh hither: put off thy shoes from off thy feet, for the place whereon thou standest is holy ground" (Exodus 3:5b).

Moses was told he could not approach the Lord until he first took off his shoes. You cannot approach a holy God without first preparing yourself through some type of separation. After all, wherever the presence of God is, people must cease from being casual, flippant, or foolish. They must quickly develop a proper fear, knowing that if they fail to correctly recognize the character of God as a means to accurately perceive what He is saying, they will bring dishonor and displeasure to Him.

We can actually observe this in the life of Jacob. On his way to his uncle's place, he stopped at Luz to rest for the night. God actually intruded into Jacob's dreams. Jacob witnessed a ladder that was set up on the earth whose top reached into heaven. He witnessed the angels of God ascending and descending upon it. Jacob saw the Lord standing at the top of it. We know the Lord that was at the top of the ladder was Jesus in His pre-incarnate state.[1] The reason we know this is because Jesus clearly stipulated to the Jews in John 5:37 that no man has seen or heard the Father. Since Jacob saw the Lord and heard Him, we must conclude that this was the Word mentioned in John 1:1 who was revealing Himself to Jacob, as well as speaking to him.

Jesus also made reference to the place of the ladder in John 1:51 when He told Nathanael that he would witness the angels of God ascending and descending upon the Son of God. The Apostle Paul made this statement about the One who would become our personal ladder to heaven in Ephesians 4:9-10, "(Now that he ascended, what is it but that he also descended first into the lower parts of the earth? He that descended is the same also that ascended up far above all heavens, that he might fill all things)." For Jacob, Jesus was standing at the top of this ladder, but for us He descended to the bottom of it. And, when the cross lifted Him up above the world, He became the actual ladder between man and heaven in order to reconcile man back to God.

When Jacob awoke from his dream, he realized he had encountered God. However, he was not jumping up and down with foolish glee; rather, he was afraid. He recognized how dreadful the place would have been if he had met the holy God in judgment, instead of God establishing and reaffirming the covenant with him He had made with his grandfather, Abraham. Jacob marked the place by renaming Luz, "Bethel," the place of God, where he had acknowledged that he witnessed the actual gate of heaven.[2]

Moses' shoes represented the contamination of the world. After all, each of us must walk through this world. We cannot help but be tainted by its various influences. The dust of its vanity often clings to our soles, the mud of its wicked compromises can become like glue as it thickens and hardens against our inner resolve to walk uprightly, its garbage causes a stench to follow us, and the decay of it tries to rob us of an effective testimony.

For this reason the Apostle Paul instructed Christians in this manner, "And your feet shod with the preparation of the gospel of peace" (Ephesians 6:15). To shod one's feet is to prepare him or her for the journey. Each of us are to walk according to the Gospel, in light of the abiding place of reconciliation and peace of our loving Savior, our risen Lord, and our soon and coming King.

It was at this time that God introduced Himself to Moses. He would identify Himself to the great patriarchs such as Abraham, Isaac, and Jacob. God would use this point of identification to confirm the covenant

---

[1] Genesis 28:10-13; John 1:1-3; 1 John 5:7
[2] Genesis 28:16-19

He had made with Abraham. This covenant was also a means for Moses and the people of Israel to establish a personal stake in God's promises as His people. It was not God's intention for them to be slaves. Through Abraham, He had promised them a land to bring them forth as a great nation. As a nation, these people were meant to be the head, not the tail among the heathen people of the land. However, they had been brought into slavery because they forgot their real purpose in this world. It was not to become part of the world, but to remain separate from it as a means to represent Jehovah God as a holy, peculiar people in the midst of grave spiritual darkness.[3] In truth, the world had taken them captive, causing them to taste the bitterness of tyrannical oppression.

Although a covenant identified the people of Israel to Jehovah God, it was God that actually identified them to the rest of the world. Out of all the people of the world, they were the only ones who knew about the real God of heaven. They were the ones who possessed the true light and the truth about man's real plight. They alone possessed the knowledge concerning life and death. Jesus made this important statement to the Samaritan woman about the knowledge that the Jews possessed because of their identification to Jehovah God, "Ye worship ye know not what. We know what we worship; for salvation is of the Jews" (John 4:22).

Abraham understood that his real portion of his inheritance was not land, rather it was God Himself. God made a covenant with Abraham to establish a people in which a redeemer could be brought forth. The birthright to salvation that has been freely offered to all through faith came through the Jews by way of their Messiah, our Lord. But, if individuals do not possess the reality of God's life, then they will have no claim to the unseen inheritance, nor will they have any part in His kingdom. For this reason, Abraham was not looking to possess the Promised Land; rather, he was looking beyond it to a city made by the hands of God. In summation, he was not looking to possess the Promised Land of Canaan, but to behold, partake of, and rest in the blessed promise of communion with his God in the future unveiling of the New Jerusalem. Granted, the Promised Land had abundance to partake of on a physical level, but the new city would have the unending glory and beauty of the King of kings to forever satisfy the real inner need and longing of man's soul.[4]

For Christians, we are also a peculiar or special people who make up an unseen kingdom, a holy nation of priests. Our inheritance is the very eternal life of Christ. His life identifies us to our future home with Him in glory.[5] Sadly, many who wear the title of "Christian" are more caught up with what the world can give them instead of the true inheritance that

---

[3] Genesis 15:1-18; 17:1-14; 26:24; 28:12-15; Deuteronomy 14:1-2; 28:13
[4] Genesis 15:1; Psalms 16:5; Hebrews 11:8-10; Revelation 21:9-27
[5] John 5:25-29; Ephesians 1:11-14; Titus 2:14; 1 Peter 2:9

identifies them to the kingdom of God. These people's identification with the world is bringing them into captivity to the claims and destruction of the world. As believers, we must always keep in mind that the Holy Spirit in us, is actually preparing us here on earth to live in the holiness and beauty of our soon coming Lord.

Moses needed to understand that the people of Israel's deliverance was not just a matter of bringing these individuals out of grave captivity, but it also was God's way of honoring His covenant with Abraham.[6] The great leader, Moses, was to lead the descendants of Abraham to the Promised Land in light of the covenant God had made with the great patriarch. This was God's way of aligning Moses' focus in the right direction. Everything he did would have to be in light of this one goal.

What about Christians? We are part of a covenant.[7] How does God introduce Himself to His people in this present age in order to establish or reestablish the covenant? It is simple. He introduces Himself through His Son. When Jesus was lifted up on the cross, it clearly established the new covenant. Every believer must come by way of the cross to truly be introduced to God. As Christians, we must remember that Jesus died on the cross to align our life to the covenant. Instead of possessing the land, we must allow Him to possess us so that we can walk according to His life in us.

As we consider Moses standing before the presence of God, we must take note of what God wanted to do. He wanted to get Moses' attention, prepare the environment, establish His authority, and introduced Himself in light of the covenant He made with Abraham. This is God's order when it comes to standing before His presence. God does not make Himself known unless He has a purpose in mind. Ultimately, that purpose will result in worshipping Him in attitude, commitment, and service. Such worship will bring glory to Him as He shows Himself mighty through His servants, on behalf of His people.

---

[6] Exodus 3:8

[7] If you would like to know more about covenants, see the author's book, *The Place of Covenant* in Volume 1 of her foundational Series.

7

THE COMMISSION

We have been following Moses in his preparation to stand before Jehovah God. All godly preparation will always bring God's people to a state of humility. Clearly, God had prepared him; now He was about to commission him. Moses needed to understand who was sending him to do the impossible. Jehovah God would go before him in preparation for the great deliverance that was about to take place for the people of Israel. What Moses needed to do was to trust and obey God by carrying out the commission.

We can only imagine what Moses was thinking and feeling when he first encountered God. Was he thinking that the whole matter was surreal? Was he feeling overwhelmed by awe? The Word does not tell us, but what we do know is that God gave Moses a clear map, "Come now therefore, and I will send thee unto Pharaoh, that thou mayest bring forth my people, the children of Israel out of Egypt" (Exodus 3:10).

Moses had been prepared to lead the children of Israel, but was he emotionally and spiritually ready to obey? His answer gives us much insight into his perception, "And Moses said unto God, Who am I, that I should go unto Pharaoh, and that I should bring forth the children of Israel out of Egypt" (Exodus 3:11).

Moses' response reveals that he had been brought to a humble state. He was asking the Lord why He would bother to consider or use him for such a task. However, God faithfully assured him that He would be with him in all matters, and that He was giving him a token. He also pointed out that when Moses brought the people out of Egypt, that he would serve Him on the mountain.

We all want to have mountaintop experiences with God, but we want to avoid the preparation that first must take place in the barren wildernesses of our lives. The reality is that as Christians, we are not meant to live in and for mountaintop experiences. Rather, we are meant to walk through the valleys of humiliation so that we can share and become identified in our Lord's glory. It is one thing to experience His glory, and another to share in His glory.

God had introduced Himself to Moses as the God of Abraham, but Moses asked the Lord what name he should give the children of Israel when they inquired about the God who sent him. It is interesting to see how God introduces or presents Himself to people. God had introduced Himself at the point of heritage and covenant to Moses, but how would He introduce Himself to the children of Israel?

The people of Israel would know that God is the I AM THAT I AM.[1] What does it mean for God to be the I AM? It first of all points to His character which is indescribable as to the eternal depth or height in which it can reach. He is simply who He is. In fact, He has always been who He is, today He continues to be who He is, and He will remain who He is in the future.

The idea of God being the I AM points to His presence as well. The reality of His presence denotes present reality. There is no past or future in Him. He knows, oversees, and influences all matters. Since He is always who He is, He is also present in the activities of the universe. In Him all matters exist, function, and operate. There is nothing that happens that He is not clearly aware of or involved in. He is all-sufficient and all-powerful to bring about matters.

The term "I AM" is also active. In other words, the great I AM is able to carry out what He has ordained. Once again, this points to His sufficiency, authority, power, and strength to bring forth a matter.

Once God was clearly established as the "I AM" to His people, then Moses could take the next step by introducing the I AM as the LORD God of their fathers, the God of Abraham, Isaac, and Jacob.[2] In fact, God begins all introductions of Himself with the words "I am."

Over twenty centuries ago, another voice was heard. The voice of Jesus rang through the corridors of time, connecting the past with the present, and the present with the future, as He introduced Himself as the "I am." In regard to the past, Jesus declared that as the "I am" He existed before Abraham. For the present, He introduced Himself as the bread of life, and the giver of Living Water to all of those who would come to Him. When it came to the future, He introduced Himself as the resurrection. However, the religious people of His day tried to silence His voice, but centuries later the introduction continues to reach the ears of those who possess a seeking, open heart towards God.

Consider the progression that took place in God's introduction of Himself to the people of Israel. He first introduced Himself in a general way to them. In other words, He is the great I AM to His creation. This term speaks of His incredible character, authority, and power. But now He presented Himself in a personal way. He is not only the great I AM of creation, but He was the "I am" to the children of Israel's patriarchs. He is the God of their heritage or lineage. He is the God of Abraham, Isaac, and Jacob. In fact, their forefathers had believed, obeyed, followed, worshipped, and served Him.

God also clearly instructed Moses to gather the elders of Israel together and tell them that the God of their fathers had personally appeared to him, acknowledging what was happening to the people of Israel in their slavery. It is interesting to note that God stated He had

---

[1] Exodus 3:14
[2] Exodus 3:15

actually visited the children of Israel to become a first-hand witness of their oppression.[3] It is not that God did not know their situation, but He was making it a personal point of identification. After hearing their cries, He visited them in their plight, saw their oppression, and was ready to deliver them out of slavery and bring them to the Promised Land. Also, the mention of the Promised Land also pointed back to the covenant that God had made with Abraham.

In this presentation to the elders there were three witnesses verifying the authority that Moses was being sent in by God. First, there was God appearing to him, then there was the connection with the people of Israel's forefathers, and finally there was the covenant. As a result, God assured Moses that the elders would receive him.

The elders were to become an important aspect of Moses' commission. These men were to initially go with Moses to present Jehovah's case to Pharaoh. Moses' first attempt to deliver one man from Egyptian oppression made him a wanted man in Egypt. Forty years later, he would come back to Egypt as a deliverer of Jehovah God's people. Not only would he have God going before him, but he would also have the elders going with him to face the Egyptian leader. They were to inform Pharaoh that The LORD God of the Hebrews had met with them, and that on His behalf they are beseeching the Pharaoh to let the people of Israel journey three days into the wilderness so they could sacrifice to their God.

God also warned Moses that Pharaoh would not agree to such a request, but He would use the leader's refusal to show Himself mighty on behalf of the people of Israel. He also promised that they would find favor in the sight of the Egyptians and that they would not leave empty-handed.[4] Obviously, in His righteousness, God would not let the children of Israel leave Egypt without being compensated for their 400 years of service as slaves.

It is important to see how fast regression can take place in man when he considers a matter of God in light of his own strength. Moses began to see the obstacles loom right in front of him. God's commission started out with the fact that He was sending him as His people's deliverer and ended with the people of Israel leaving with the riches of Egypt. God had laid out every detail of the plan, the reaction of the Pharaoh, and the end results. It was also made quite clear that Moses was not going in his own power. In his humanity Moses was not equipped to deliver these people, but in the power of God, the people of Israel would be delivered. In spite of God presenting His case in a clear manner, Moses could only see the obstacles looming in front of him.

First, Moses did not have faith in the elders. He perceived himself as standing alone in facing the Pharaoh. He had a good point. People are

---

[3] Exodus 3:16
[4] Exodus 3:19-22

naturally suspicious, but God had already stated that He would give him a token. He actually gave Moses two signs: the rod and his hand. The rod became a serpent and the hand became leprous. Rod points to authority or power, while the hand points to service. It is important to note that the hand was placed closest to the bosom to change its condition. This shows that when a matter of God comes from the heart of the person and the hand is cleansed of all worldly involvement, there will be authority present to confirm a matter. [5]

God always will give His people a token to verify His claims. As Christians, we have the hand of God upon us in the form of the Holy Spirit, and we carry the rod of the Word of God. Christ's blood was spilled on the ground so that we could be identified as part of the covenant. We walk according to the power of His Spirit, we stand according to the authority of His Word, and we are established in new life because of the covenant.

You would think the witnesses God presented would silence all of Moses' concerns. However, he had one more concern. He felt he did not have the words to deliver the message. After all, he had been with the sheep in the wilderness for forty years. The Lord reminded him that He is the One who made man's mouth. He is the one who can cause the ear to hear and the eye to see. He is Jehovah. With this presentation, God commanded Moses to go, and He would serve as his mouth, as well as teach him what to say. [6]

The Lord has given a similar promise to Christians in Mark 13:10-11,
> And the gospel must first be published among all nations. But when they shall lead you, and deliver you up, take no thought beforehand what ye shall speak, neither do ye pre-meditate: but whatsoever shall be given you in that hour, that speak ye; for it is not ye that speak, but the Holy Ghost.

We know that the Holy Spirit is the real teacher. He is the One who will lead us into all truth. [7]

Moses' digression as the simple servant of the great Jehovah God became evident at this point. Consider his request, "And he said, O my Lord, send, I pray thee, by the hand of him whom thou will send" (Exodus 4:13). We are told that the anger of the Lord was kindled against Moses. Digression takes place at the point of unbelief. Moses did not believe that God could handle what he considered to be a speech problem on his part. He did not trust Him to show Himself mighty in his weakness.

God agreed to send Moses' brother, Aaron, because he could speak well. But, beware of what you ask for. Moses did not need his brother Aaron to speak the oracles of God. Scriptures show that Moses verbally confronted Pharaoh without the help of Aaron. He must have found his

---

[5] Exodus 4:1-9
[6] Exodus 4:10-12
[7] John 16:13; 1 John 2:27

tongue somewhere along the way. The fact was that Moses' answer to prayer became a hindrance to him in many ways. Aaron was the one who constructed the golden calf when Moses was on the mountain, as well as siding with his sister Miriam to rebel against Moses' leadership. It is important to point out that it was Moses that received the call, not Aaron. Aaron was once removed from the actual call to deliver the children of Israel.

Together Moses and Aaron obeyed God. Most people know the rest of the story. Whether they have read it in Scriptures, heard the story while involved with church activities, or watched it being played out on the movie screen, there are very few in America that do not know something about the incredible feat that was accomplished thousands of years ago in regard to the children of Israel's deliverance.

However, a greater feat was accomplished only 20 centuries ago. Instead of a nation being delivered, all mankind was provided a way to be delivered. Instead of the Red Sea parting, the earth parted and shook in light of an empty tomb. Instead of the Egyptian army being defeated, death was defeated. Instead of many Passover Lambs being prepared to be sacrificed as a means to identify God's people, as well as cover them from judgment, one Lamb was completely utilized for the sake of mankind as He was offered by God on the cross. This Lamb became identified to man in order to take away the sin of all who would believe, as well as serve as the Bread of life to those spiritual pilgrims on their journey through this world. Instead of a nation rising out of the barren wilderness to possess a great land, one man arose from the grave to possess the hearts of men. We know that man's name to be Jesus Christ, the Son of the Living God.

As Christians, we have all been commissioned to share this victorious message to the Pharaoh's of the world, as well as those who reside in this present age, and with those who clearly are slaves to its tyrannical systems. The question is, how many of us have digressed away from the authority and power found in the life provided to us to carry out this commission, to a place of unbelief? Such unbelief is the result of making God too small in light of our own personal ineptness.

8

EXPERIENCING THE MOUNTAIN

Many people have unrealistic ideas about God. It is easy to get caught up with the supernatural and miraculous aspects of Him. We often conclude that if we could just see God operate on our behalf like the children of Israel, we would never have any doubt or unbelief challenging our spiritual life. However, such a perspective is untrue. The supernatural or the miraculous is not what makes us stand when challenged. It is the faith towards God that we choose to apply in regard to our own spiritual state before our Lord that enables us to withstand such challenges.

The supernatural and miraculous simply confirms a message or faith that is already active, but it will never create faith in people's hearts. In fact, the small seeds of faith are already in receptive hearts, ready to be brought forth into fruits of everlasting life through simple trust and obedience. To confirm this thought, consider Pharaoh. If these types of events could have such an impact on stiff-necked people, Pharaoh would have conceded to let the children of Israel go into the wilderness to rightfully worship their God. However, he became hardened towards God when he failed to concede in his heart that the God of Israel was the true God of heaven, thereby, he personally owed Him obedience and worship.

Faith takes root in tender hearts towards God. Moses had such a heart. Each time he confronted the arrogant, idolatrous, Pharaoh, his tongue was loosened to boldly display a greater measure of faith and authority. Each judgment that the Egyptians tasted because of their leader's stubbornness, exalted both Jehovah God and Moses in the Egyptians' eyes. Like their leader, these people may have initially been ignorant about Israel's God, but because of His judgments, they knew who He was, and they also knew who was greater in power and majesty than all other gods in spite of their leader's stiff-necked rejection of Him.

Before deliverance could take place, God had to humble Pharaoh before His people and bring down all the idols of Egypt. This was necessary to establish the preeminence of Jehovah God. In the end, Egypt would taste ten major judgments against its gods, shaking every aspect of its culture and the lifestyle of the people. Keep in mind that our various idols are determined by the type of culture that cultivates our society, and the type of lifestyles we adopt because of them.

For example, one of the great idols of America is the American dream. There is nothing wrong with dreaming about a productive life.

However, the American dream has nothing to do with establishing a productive life that is beneficial; rather, it surrounds money, material possessions, and presenting a certain appearance and lifestyle that gives the impression of success. Sadly, this concept of the American dream has produced a materialistic society that does not deal in reality. Instead of lives proving to be productive, many have become selfish and self-serving which have produced pleasure seekers who want to be entertained. The work ethic has lost its luster with each succeeding generation. Since there is no real substance behind such a self-serving lifestyle, selfishness and frustration grew as socialistic, Marxist philosophies clearly found a receptive ground in the empty lives that such a materialistic society will ultimately produce. For many young people any change will do other than the nothingness that has engulfed their meaningless lives. Since these individuals lack any real wisdom, they will not be able to see the end results of such destructive ideology. Granted, they may float, flounder, and become lost in the culture of unproductive nonsense and emptiness that is now prevalent in our society, but what they will end up embracing is a culture of death. Cultures of death lead to complete, utter ruin.

The reason there is no substance in world-centered lifestyles is because God has been thrown out of every arena as the idol of money with its false sense of power, self-sufficiency, and security has been elevated. He has been replaced with vain pursuits that even include that of man-made religion, as well as adjusted to fit any new age, cultic belief, or pagan practice that has appeased the fancy of man. As a result, man has been exalted in the place of God in many different ways.

God had to expose the foolish, idolatrous ways of the Egyptian people. He had to show how fragile they were in light of His power. Perhaps the people of Israel had been at the mercy of the Egyptian people, but now these Egyptians were at the mercy of Israel's righteous God.

We know that the final judgment was death to all the first-born of Egypt. This included their sons and livestock. What a high price these people had to pay for the foolish and idolatrous ways of their leader. However, this high cost pointed to the high cost God would pay for each of us. His Son, the first-begotten, would be offered up on the cross for all mankind. For Israel, the death of the first-born allowed them to rise out of the dust of slavery as a great nation. For believers, the death of God's only begotten Son allowed them to rise out of the ashes of sin and death as a Church, a holy nation of priests, in whom the kingdom of God would be brought forth in power and glory.

It is fascinating to study the way in which the people of Israel had to travel.[1] Although their footprints have long ago faded beneath the dust of

---

[1] If you would like to journey with the children of Israel, see the author's book, *The Victorious Journey* in this same volume.

Developing Our Christian Life

the barren wilderness, the children of Israel left an indelible impression that will never be wiped from the pages of God's Word. For the former slaves, it would prove to be a journey of discovery. These people would taste the vanity of their ways, witness the greatness of God's ways, and taste the bitterness of failure and judgment brought on by unbelief.

One of the greatest marks of these people's journey would be a simple mount in the middle of the desert. They would arrive at this destination three months after they had been delivered out of Egypt. Here, they would be encamped around this mount for almost two years.[2]

Clearly, there was much symbolism being implemented in all that was being established for these poor souls, but they could not be seen or appreciated. Like all mankind who are slaves to sin, the people of Israel had also been in a similar slavery for four hundred years. They were delivered through the Red Sea which represented baptism that pointed to separation, as well as death to their old life. They found themselves in the grave of the wilderness for three months, only to be brought to a mount that appeared to have no real significance.

The name of the wilderness and the mount was Sinai. Sinai means "thorny." No doubt this wilderness had it share of thorns, but for the children of Israel, it was where God chose to establish His name and presence in their midst. It would take almost two years to establish a witness of His character and work.

Obviously, it is one thing to be called by God and another matter to establish a testimony of Himself in the lives of His people. In the past, as a believer, I have zealously pursued my calling, while failing to have my Sinai experience. In fact, it is believed that Sinai is an antitype of the Christian's Pentecost. Without the witness and testimony of the presence of God in our midst, there will be no evidence of His life or distinction upon us. We as believers must be clearly established in our lives in Christ before we can be effective in our true calling.

The people of Israel had been physically delivered from Egypt, but they had not been separated from its influence on their inner man. In order for this separation to take place there had to be a shaking, cleansing, and a testimony of God being firmly established among them.

It is important to point out that before God shakes, cleanses, and establishes a testimony, there must be preparation. Moses went up to God in Sinai, and we see the Lord calling out of the mountain to him. The Lord was about to establish His power and commitment to the children of Israel. How does God establish His power to the people of Israel: by having them remember what He has already done on their behalf. God told Moses to remind the children of Israel what He did to the Egyptians. He then described His commitment of how He actually bore them on eagle's wings and brought them to Himself.[3]

---

[2] Exodus 19:1-9; Numbers 10:11-12
[3] Exodus 19:3-4

It is from this premise that God gives conditions that will allow Him to fulfill His desire that He possessed for His people. He told Moses that if His people will obey His voice and keep the covenant, then they will become a peculiar treasure that will be regarded above all the people of the earth. They will also become a kingdom of priests, a holy nation.[4]

After these instructions, Moses brought God's message to the elders. Obviously, God was trying to prepare the people for the type of testimony He was about to set forth in their midst. Consider the response of the people in Exodus 19:8, "And all the people answered together, and said, All that the LORD hath spoken we will do. And Moses returned the words of the people unto the LORD."

Keep in mind, Moses only heard the voice of God. God's presence was not manifesting itself to him. We can hear a person's voice without experiencing his or her presence. It would be the same as talking to someone on the phone.

When the people agreed to accept God's condition, Moses returned to the mountain to give God the verdict. This is when the Lord informed Moses in what manner He would make His presence known, as well as the purpose for His presentation, "And the LORD said unto Moses, Lo, I come unto thee in a thick cloud, that the people may hear when I speak with thee, and believe thee forever" (Exodus 19:9a). The Lord wanted to confirm Moses' leadership as well as His words. The people would not only see, but they would hear as well. The conditions were set forth in Exodus 19:11-15.

The first manner of business for the people of Israel had to do with preparation. They needed to sanctify or cleanse themselves. This required them to wash their clothes and to refrain from sexual intimacy in order to be ready on the third day for the Lord's presence. It is hard to know what the people of Israel expected on the third day, but the actions required of them should have given them some idea as to what they might encounter. Separation and cleansing clearly pointed to establishing a holy environment.

The second requirement involved setting boundaries to protect the people from possible judgment. These boundaries should have given them a stronger sense of the God of Israel. He demands holiness from His people because He is holy. Boundaries had to be set as a means of warning the people of Israel against trespassing against and touching what God had designated as being holy.

On the third day the presence of God came down on the mountain. There was smoke and fire, as well as thundering and lightning that accompanied the thick dark cloud that ascended on the mount, causing the mount to shake. According to Revelation 8:2-6, such a display of God's holiness and power also occurs in heaven. There was also the

---

[4] Exodus 19:5-6

voice of the trumpet that was so exceedingly loud that it caused the people to tremble.[5]

Moses led the people to the lower part of the mount. There they heard the voice of the trumpet being sounded. It became louder and louder. Moses spoke, and God answered him by a voice. The Lord in His presence and power came down on the mount and called Moses to come to the top of the mount to meet with Him.[6]

Keep in mind, God's presence sets up the environment. What was God's presence saying to the people of Israel, and how would they respond to it? Moses had been prepared to meet with God. In his first encounter with Him, he *stood before* His presence to receive his commission. However, in this incident, he had to *ascend into* the presence of God in order to meet with Him.

What did the Lord want to give Moses? He first instructed Moses to warn the children of Israel not to break through the boundaries because they would die. However, we also know it was at Mount Sinai that Moses received the Law and the instructions about building the tabernacle. According to Hebrews 8:5, Moses had to make the tabernacle according to the pattern that God revealed to him in the mount. The Law and tabernacle were to serve as a testimony of God in the midst of Israel. The Law would declare His holiness and the tabernacle was the place in which His name would be established and His presence would reside in their midst in some form. For example, His presence served as a cloud during the day and a pillar of fire at night. The cloud pointed to His gentle leading and the fire to His protection.

This brings us to the people's reactions towards the presence of God. We already know that they trembled at His presence. Exodus 20:18-21 gives us insight into their reaction. It tells us that they actually moved as far away from the mount as they could get. Once again, there are people who do not mind the presence of God in their midst, but who likewise do not want to let Him intrude into their way of thinking or living. It was clear that these people were shaken, but they would not humble themselves enough to find out what God was trying to cleanse them from. It was brought out in Exodus 20:22-23 that God was showing that He was the true God who was living, and who wanted to actually commune with His people. Because He was the one true God, they must not resort to the ways of Egypt by making lifeless gods of silver and gold.

God was trying to shake lose their association with idols. Obviously, these Jewish people dreaded Him, but they had not come to the place where they truly regarded and honored Him as God. As a result, they stood far away from His presence to avoid personally hearing Him. These people asked Moses to speak to God on their behalf and to speak

---

[5] Exodus 19:16
[6] Exodus 19:17-20

to them on behalf of God. In a sense they removed themselves from any personal communion with Him, as they insisted that another stand between Him and them. They did not want to personally deal with their God.

God's presence in Mount Sinai was trying to prepare His people to understand the seriousness of the testimony of the Law and tabernacle that He was entrusting to them. The Law revealed how far away man is from God, but the tabernacle revealed that a way can be provided to those who desire to come into a real place of communion with Him. Moses is such an example. After all, he allowed the dark cloud to shut him in with God. It was as though he had been consumed by it. However, the harsh reality of idols is that they keep people from desiring the place of communion with God, and will allow them to erect something else, an image or man between God and them.

The Law clearly declares that all men stand as sinners, doomed to taste the consequence of death. However, God established another type of tabernacle or temple among men that possessed His name and presence 20 centuries ago. Instead of the temple being a place, it was actually a person. In John 2:19-22, Jesus spoke of His body being the temple. It was through His death on the cross that God would provide a way for every person to come into His very presence, in sweet communion and without fearing judgment.

Christians cannot live the Christian life without the living testimony and presence of God in their midst. It is true that Israel had their Mount Sinai, but we as believers have our Pentecost. The Law and tabernacle would identify the people of Israel to Jehovah God, but the presence of the Holy Spirit would serve as a seal to identify believers to their spiritual inheritance until they realize the fullness of their redemption.[7]

The Law would be kept before the children of Israel, while the Law would be written upon our hearts by the Spirit. The tabernacle had to be moved according to the presence of God, but as temples of God, the Spirit of God goes everywhere we go. The children of Israel witnessed God's presence, but as believers, we experience it. The children of Israel often removed themselves or departed from the presence of God that was in their midst, while believers should learn what it means to be moved by His presence, rather than left behind.

There is a clear difference between the two covenants established by God. People could outwardly conform to the first one, while those of the second covenant must be transformed from within. Although the first covenant was holy and perfect, the second covenant proved to be better or excellent because it was able to bring people to a state of holiness and perfection before the Lord.

The question is simple. How close are you to experiencing the unhindered presence of God? Have you ascended towards gaining a

---

[7] Ephesians 1:11-14

Developing Our Christian Life

greater life in Christ? Have you been shut in with the Father in communion by the presence of His Spirit? Or, have you stood far off from the secret places of God because of fear and uncertainty? As we will see, being afar off from the presence of God is simply too far away from possessing the life God has ordained for you.

9

SUPPING IN THE PRESENCE OF GOD

As we follow the children of Israel through their journey, it is important to note that they did not go anywhere without God's presence in their midst. God's presence in the midst of His people was both His promise and heart desire. He stated that He wanted to walk in the midst of His people. This was necessary to identify them to Him, and to establish a relationship with them that would be forever binding in their hearts and minds.

However, when they encountered the presence of God in His holiness, they witnessed the dreadful reality of His righteousness. Moses had encountered God in a burning bush. He was made to understand that wherever God's presence was, it was to be treated as holy ground. However, the mountain experience revealed God in His holiness. For Moses, he stood before the presence of the Lord in the environment of holiness, but for the children of Israel they were standing before holiness. Such a presentation of God caused them to want to stand afar off from Him, rather than be close to Him.

Obviously, God's presence expresses itself in different ways. Remember, the presence of God is to create a certain sense of who He is according to the environment in which He is manifesting Himself. The environment is meant to determine attitude and approach towards Him. For Moses, he was instructed to approach God in a certain way by taking off his shoes. However, for the children of Israel, they could witness his holiness, but they could not touch it or ascend up into it without paying the price of their life. It was clear that for people to withstand the judgment of God's holiness, they must be first prepared and called.

As we consider the event that was about to take place, we can begin to understand why God presented Himself in such a manner. He was about to give them the Law that proved that all men were incapable of coming to Him without some type of sacrifice, covering (atonement), or intervention due to the disastrous affects of sin.

God would also give the pattern for the tabernacle in which His glory would reside. The Law would reveal man's hopeless, doomed condition in light of God's holiness, while the tabernacle would have to be established as a holy environment to ensure God's glory would reside in the midst of His people. The giving of the Law and the pattern of the tabernacle proved to be serious business. In both cases the Hebrew people could not be flippant or casual about their attitude or approach to them.

We also see God's presence manifesting itself in other ways in regard to the Jewish people. It could be seen as a cloud that identified the tabernacle and guided the children of Israel through the wilderness. It also manifested itself as a fire at night that brought distinction, as well as comfort and protection to them. In a way, the presence of God among the children of Israel served as a constant witness to them about the reality of God abiding in their midst. Such a witness would also assure them that His promises would be brought forth on their behalf.

Even though the presence of God was dreadful to the children of Israel at Mount Sinai, He wanted them to understand His real heart towards them. They were not separated from Him because He was holy, but because they were sinners. He had not caused this separation; rather, man in his independence, rebellion, and idolatry was the one that created such a separation.

God had clearly shown His intention towards them when He delivered them out of bondage from Egypt. He did not deliver them so they could remain separated from Him; instead, He delivered them so they could have a relationship with Him. He wanted them to understand that because of His holiness, He first had to provide the way that would enable them to approach Him. The Law would show why they were separated, but the sacrifices would reveal the way in which man could stand, walk before, and honor God in his life. The tabernacle would not only reveal the inward condition man must have to approach God, but the reality that it is up to each individual to personally establish a right relationship with God.

As Christians, we realize that God provided the way in which all men can now approach Him without fear of judgment, rejection, and death. Jesus said of Himself, I am the way to the Father. We know that He fulfilled the Law, became a sacrifice that took away our sins, and revealed that the real temple of God would become man. Instead of just the presence of God being in the midst of man, it would now reside in him.[1]

Like the Hebrews in the wilderness, the presence of God also ensures every aspect of Christian living. In fact, believers are, in a sense, consumed by the presence of God if they are truly abiding in the life that has been ordained by the Lord. Christians do possess His presence in them through the indwelling of the Holy Spirit. They have been positionally placed in the presence of God since they have been seated in high places in Christ Jesus.[2]

---

[1] Matthew 5:17-18; John 14:6; Romans 10:4; 1 Corinthians 3:16-17; Hebrews 10:3-18

[2] 1 Corinthians 6:19; Ephesians 2:6

As a result, believers are to stand before the presence of God in faith, ready to obey. They are to pursue after God's presence as they follow after the Holy Spirit in obedience to Christ to secure their life in Him in righteousness, godliness, faith, love, patience, and meekness. They are to be led by the Spirit into an intimate relationship with God as His children. The Apostle Paul confirmed this when he stated that those who are led by the Spirit, are known as the children of God. If Christians are following after the presence of God and being led by His presence, they will learn what it means to walk in the Spirit. If they learn to walk in the Spirit, they will not fulfill the lust of the flesh, nor will they be under the yoke of the Law. Rather, they will be walking according to a more excellent law, the law that is of the Spirit of life that is found in Christ Jesus.[3]

Another aspect of God's presence in the life of the Christian is the presence that comes from the throne. God's presence descended upon Mount Sinai, and God called Moses up to the mountain for instructions. Likewise, the Holy Spirit descends on God's people through the manifestations of gifts. Through these gifts believers are edified with wisdom, revelation, and prophecy through means such as instructions, encouragement, exhortation, and warnings. God's presence within assures a right state and His presence around us ensures the right walk, but the presence from above ensures agreement and power. It connects us to the throne of God as we line up to His will about a matter, and walk it out in the power of the Spirit and in obedience to His Word.

As we consider Moses at Mount Sinai, we have to somewhat conclude that Moses ascended up into the presence of God at different times to receive certain aspects of the Law. Moses would share these ordinances with the people, who in turn agreed to keep them.[4]

This brings us to another aspect of God's presence. When God is present, man must worship Him. The Lord told Moses to bring Aaron and his sons, along with seventy elders to worship Him from afar, for only Moses could come near to Him.[5]

Before the leaders of Israel came near to God to worship Him from a distance, Moses read the covenant to the people and sprinkled the blood of the burnt and peace offerings upon the children of Israel.[6] The burnt offerings represented consecration, while the peace offering pointed to some type of reconciliation.

Aaron, along with his sons and the elders followed Moses to the place where they were to worship God from afar. However, at this place of worship, they actually saw the God of Israel. We know that the person of the Godhead that they beheld was the Word, or the Son of God in His

---

[3] Romans 8:1-2, 14; Galatians 5:16-18; 1 Timothy 6:11
[4] Exodus 24:2-4
[5] Exodus 24:1
[6] Exodus 24:5-8

pre-incarnate state. The reason we know this is because Jesus clearly stated that no one has heard the Father's voice or seen His shape. We are told that even though these men saw God, He did not lay a hand of judgment on them.[7]

It is interesting to note that these men went with Moses to worship God, but ended up supping together in His presence.[8] They could not draw near to Him but He drew near to them. This incident shows us two aspects about God's presence: 1) Man may not come or be able to always come close to God without possible consequences, but God can sovereignly choose to come close to man without him having to fear destruction; and 2) acceptable worship allows God to draw near to us. It also serves as a door into communion or agreement with God. It is in such communion that one can begin to partake of His very life.

There are two types of communion. One is where man sits to receive matters of God. I have learned that when people sit down to eat, they are the most receptive to hear, share, and receive. Some of the greatest types of ministering has taken place at such moments. After all, sharing serves as a point of communion.

The second type of communion is where one comes into a place of total agreement. For believers, this points to them actually coming into the Most Holy Place where they simply sit in the presence of God to enjoy His company. In a sense it would be like sitting on the Father's lap, and simply enjoying the type of relationship that has been clearly allotted to each of us by Christ's redemptive work on the cross.

We see this in the case of the Jewish leaders sitting in the presence of God, partaking together. Clearly, they were receptive to receive. For Christians, Jesus gave this invitation to them in Revelation 3:20, "Behold, I stand at the door, and knock; if any man hear my voice, and open the door, I will come in to him, and will sup with him, and he with me." It is easy to get caught up with the many different substitutes that can replace our life in Christ, but there is only one place that will ensure the integrity and passion of this life and that is in communion or agreement with God.

It is our Lord that often must make the necessary advancements to bring us back to center in our relationship with Him. In my life I have become deceived by good works, dulled down by compromise, and exalted by spiritual knowledge to such a point, I did not realize His presence had lifted off of my life. My connection with heaven had been broken, but in my ignorance, I continued on in the same foolish manner. However, I had a sense that something was missing. The joy of my salvation was gone, the passion I once had for Christ had been replaced with fleshly sentimentality towards what seemed to be good causes, while my spiritual knowledge about the matters of God lacked life and power. The state that it produced in me was emptiness that mocked me.

---

[7] Exodus 24:9-11; John 1:1; 5:37
[8] Exodus 24:1-11

At the end of this state of nothingness was the harsh awareness that Jesus was missing. Granted, I had heard a slight knocking, but I was too busy or caught up with my activities to investigate. I knew there was much lack in my life, but I was consoling myself because of my personal overrated evaluation of the so-called "good deeds" that I had done in the name of religion. Even though I was aware that God's balances did not rate my good deeds in the same way I did, it was my way of throwing a bone to Him to ease my conscience until I got my personal act together.

The more I tried to get my act together, the deeper I spiraled down into my pit. One day I finally hit the bottom of my pit as I finally came to a place of repentance. I felt myself becoming broken, which left the essence of my Christian life laying in many pieces and fragments. I found myself desperately seeking God's mercy and forgiveness for the mess I had made of my life. At that time, I did not realize that my brokenness had brought me to a state of humility. Such a state serves as a form of worship that God will not despise. In fact, He will draw near to such an individual.

At that time, the most incredible thing happened; the Lord brought me into the inner chamber of communion. It was at this time I realized that I had strayed away from the center of my life, Jesus. In order to come back to the center, I needed to accept His invitation to come to His table of communion and partake of His life as it was broken and imparted to and in me by the free-flowing Living Water of His Spirit. It was almost like sitting at His feet, simply learning of Him.

Supping in the presence of the Lord allows us to get our bearings. It allows us to enjoy Him and Him to enjoy us. We can partake of His divine nature, and know the pleasure of being part of His kingdom, realize His promises, discover His plan, and become part of His purpose in the present age we live in. The Apostle Peter made this statement, "By which are given unto us exceedingly great and precious promises, that by these ye might be partakers of the divine nature, having escaped the corruption that is in the world through lust" (2 Peter 1:4).

The Jewish people had been delivered from the corruption of Egypt. The leaders now sat and supped in the presence of God. Surely, they realized that God wanted a relationship with them that would prove to be excellent in every way. They could trust Him, as well as follow Him into His promises.

It was at this time of supping with the elders in the presence of God, that He once again called Moses to come up into the mount. God wanted to give Him the Law written on tables of stone so that he could teach it to the people of Israel. As he rose up, Moses gave the elders instructions. He told them to tarry or wait for him until he came again.[9]

This reminds me of the people in the upper room on the day of Pentecost. They had been told to tarry until they were endued with power

---

[9] Exodus 24:12-15

from on high. It is said of these people that they all continued with one accord in prayer and supplication. In other words, these people would wait in expectation for the power.[10] But, would the people of Israel wait in expectation for Moses' return?

Supping in the presence of God is a prelude to a possible time of preparation or waiting in expectancy for God to bring something forth. The Jewish people were waiting for the Law to be etched in stone, while the people in the upper room were waiting for the promise and gift of God.

It is important at this time to point out that Moses' servant Joshua came with him, but he could only go so far. Moses' example shows us that we can only come higher alone. It is our life in Christ, and we must possess it for ourselves. In the case of Joshua, he shows us that we may not be able to experience the presence of God through others or for others, but we need to get as close as we can to where God is, waiting in preparation, readiness, and expectation for the time we can have our own experience with Him.

Have you supped in the presence of the Lord? Is Jesus knocking on the door of your heart right now because He has been left out or left behind in all of your religious activities? If He is, take this time to open the door and discover what it means to sup in His presence as you partake of His divine nature and His Living Water.

---

[10] Luke 24:49; Acts 2:14

10

WAITING BEFORE GOD

Aaron and the elders were told to wait for Moses and Joshua until they came back off the mountain. God was calling Moses up into the mountain to meet with Him. When Moses went up into the mount, a cloud covered it. It is said that the glory of the Lord abode upon Mount Sinai for six days, and upon the seventh day God called Moses out of the midst of the cloud. In this example, we see Moses <u>waiting in</u> the presence of God.[1]

Moses had to wait for six days on the mount. How many of us would wait in complete silence? Most likely Moses was praying, meditating, and silently waiting for God to intrude into the silence. Such a time would be a test to his faith. Genuine faith allows God's people to wait in patience until a matter or promise is brought forth by God. Hebrews 6:11-12 confirms this, "And we desire that every one of you do show the same diligence to the full assurance of hope unto the end; That ye be not slothful, but followers of them who through faith and patience inherit the promises."

People who have faith wait in hope and expectancy. Faith believes that a matter will happen, while the attitude of expectancy keeps people aware of what is going on, thereby, keeping them open before the Lord to receive from Him. Moses believed that God was going to give him the tablets that contained His commandments. Therefore, the issue was not whether God was going to do what He said; rather, it was a matter of timing as to when He would fulfill the expected end that He promised.

It is vital that Christians learn to wait or tarry before God until a matter is brought to fruition. Waiting prepares God's people to receive His promise. In the state of waiting, they are alert and expecting the Lord to bring a matter to completeness. Their attention is being disciplined and their emotions are being funneled according to the hope or expectation, producing a humble state before the Lord. In this state the inward man is being prepared to receive, as well as respond to what the Lord wants to entrust to the person. The famous Scripture in Isaiah makes this declaration, "But they that wait upon the LORD shall renew their strength; they shall mount up with wings as eagles; they shall run, and not be weary; and they shall walk, and not faint" (Isaiah 40:31).

---

[1] Exodus 24:15-16

Believers, who wait in faith, are literally waiting upon the Lord. In a sense, they are resting in confidence upon Him as their abiding Rock. They are not moved by doubt, pushed by the winds of uncertainty, or buffeted to utter despair by the coldness of silence. They are simply believing, abiding, and resting on the Rock.

The believers in the upper room were also told to tarry. When you realize that the countdown for the fifty days of Pentecost started when Jesus was offered up as the meal offering, and then put into the ground as the seed for the first-fruits, you can calculate that He spent three days in the depths of the earth, plus the 40 days He was seen by others until His ascension. At this point 43 days are accounted for. This leaves seven days remaining from the Passover until the Feast of Pentecost. Such calculations imply that the believers who tarried in the upper room before the promise of the Spirit came upon them waited the same amount of time as Moses did on Mount Sinai before the Lord finally spoke to him.[2]

Notice what the children of Israel witnessed from their position. God's glory was like a devouring fire. From all appearances, God's holiness not only appeared to swallow Moses, but it also looked as if it was consuming him. Consider in what way the Holy Spirit manifested Himself on the day of Pentecost to those in the upper room. The new believers heard a sound from heaven that sounded like a rushing mighty wind that filled the place. Then, cloven tongues as of fire sat upon each of them.[3]

It is clear to see why Mount Sinai is considered a type of Pentecost. The difference is that Moses was engulfed by the holy presence of God, while the Spirit of God filled up the new believers' lives as a means to distinguish and empower their lives and tongues. For Moses, his experience on Mount Sinai was to receive the Law in order to establish the spiritual conduct for His people, as well as to receive the instructions for building the tabernacle, a place that would be distinguished as God's dwelling place. For the New Testament believers, they were being established as the temples of God, but their tongues were set apart by the fire to fulfill their commission of preaching the Gospel, as well as teaching others to observe the commandments of the Lord.

Waiting for God is a form of godly discipline. It first of all disciplines the inner man to come to a place of quiet confidence before the Lord in light of hope or expectation. It also disciplines the walk. Waiting ensures that we as believers are ready to follow, while we inwardly remain still before the Lord. Such discipline ensures that we will not lag behind our Lord, but we will not get ahead of Him either. We will learn to be ready to follow when His presence lifts. We will choose to follow after His presence as it moves, and we also will allow it to lead us as it guides. As

---

[2] Acts 1:2-9
[3] Exodus 24:17; Acts 2:1-4

the Spirit guides us, we ultimately will discover what it means to walk in accordance to God's presence as we come into step with our Lord's yoke.

Moses gave Aaron and the elders the strict instruction to wait or tarry for him. Keep in mind, these men's faith would be tested as well. Did they possess the faith to believe and the expectancy to prepare themselves for what God would be entrusting to them as a people or nation?

The children of Israel had experienced great miracles on their behalf. They had stood before the dreadful presence of God's holiness. They had witnessed the fire of His glory. These people had asked Moses to be the intercessor between them and Jehovah God, allowing them to stand afar off, while witnessing the intensity of His holiness. They had agreed to obey the covenant and the Law that had been established for them that would distinguish them as a peculiar or special people.

Moses had entered into the fiery presence of God to receive not only the commandments written in stone, but the instructions for the tabernacle. There was no time limit to how long this would take. As a result, Moses had told Aaron, his sons, and the elders to tarry.

Most of you probably know the story concerning the children of Israel waiting for Moses. He was on that mountain longer than they anticipated. It would take faith on the part of the children of Israel to simply wait for Moses to come down, since they would not know the status of his condition. In summation, they would have to mix faith with what they had previously experienced, witnessed, and agreed to in order to stand firmly on what they could not see until the expectation was realized. After all, there was no timeframe given as to how long Moses would be on that mount.[4]

This is why God's people must walk by faith and not by sight.[5] God does not work according to timetables. As His people, we must always choose to trust Him regardless of the waiting period that is involved. Sadly, the opposite is true in most cases. The prophet Isaiah gives a vivid summation of this state, "For thus saith the Lord GOD, the Holy One of Israel: In returning and rest shall ye be saved; in quietness and in confidence shall be your strength: and ye would not" (Isaiah 30:15).

The people of Israel assumed that something must have happened to Moses and would not wait for his return. Since Moses appeared to be out of the picture, so was Jehovah God. And, since the mediator was absent, they apparently concluded that they could also disregard their agreement with God to recognize and worship Him as their only true God.

These people went to Aaron, the man who should have insisted that the people wait for the promised expectation of Moses' return. They

---

[4] Hebrews 4:2
[5] 2 Corinthians 5:7

asked the leader to make them a god that they could worship. As a leader, Aaron should have maintained the example of tarrying, while trying to reason with the people about their idolatrous decision to seek another god. He should have exhorted them to believe in the one true God, even if they could not see anything on the horizon. Sadly, the man who should have been waiting ended up heeding the people's request.[6]

Aaron commanded them to bring gold objects, in which he designed a golden calf, an object that was greatly worshipped by various pagan cultures at that time. Sadly, the people became excited about this object. They had worshipped God after being delivered through the Red Sea. They had benefitted from His leadership and provision, but at this point it is as though He no longer existed as a lifeless golden calf took center stage of their focus, affections, and worship.

Their enthusiasm for the golden calf caused Aaron to take one more step. He built an altar and made a proclamation, "...Tomorrow is a feast to the LORD" (Exodus 32:5). Think about Aaron's example. Aaron made an altar to an idol and declared a day to worship and feast before this altar in the name of the Lord. There are some modern congregations doing the same thing. They have devised various activities that find their inspiration from the imaginations and doings of man. Their enthusiasm around the worldly altars that have been constructed as a place of worship, prove to be contagious to those who are weak in their faith. Then, these people try to cover up their idolatry by dedicating it all to Jesus. They are simply tacking Him on to receive some type of approval or credibility for their worldly, idolatrous practices and heretical teachings. Since Jesus has been tacked on, they can now worship and feast before these ungodly altars. Such feasts produce pagan practices that end up defying any reason or common sense.

The events surrounding the intrusion of God into the midst of mankind are always marked by times of waiting for the promise. How many years did Noah wait as he prepared the ark before the flood came? How many years did Abraham and Sarah have to wait for Isaac? How many years did the children of Israel taste the bitterness of slavery and wander as sojourners before they were brought forth into the Promised Land? How many years did the Jewish people spend in captivity in Babylon before they returned to their land? How many years did many of the Jewish people like Simeon and Anna in Luke 2, wait for the Messiah to come? In fact, some are still unnecessarily waiting for His first advent.

These are just a few examples of the waiting God's people had to endure before a promise was fulfilled. However, there is a great waiting period taking place right now. Like the Jews, we as believers, are waiting for the coming of our Lord Jesus Christ for His Body, the Church. In fact, the Body of Christ has been in waiting for over 2,000 years. Jesus' instructions to His Church are as clear and decisive as Moses was to

---

[6] Exodus 32:1-2

Aaron and the elders. He instructed those of His Church to possess their souls in patience by watching, being ready, as well as always being in prayer so they will not be caught off guard. This diligence would assure them that in the end they will not be found to be worthless servants at His coming.[7]

During each waiting period the hearts of God's people are tested. Instead of mixing faith with what they know is true, many are giving way to unbelief and falling into the snares of idolatry. As a result, these individuals end up putting their Lord to a foolish test. After all, they do not know when He is coming, or when they will have to stand before Him and give an account for their deviant ways and practices. They assume that they will be ready for His coming. Meanwhile, they are going to partake of the world as much as they can before the master returns home and finds them to be the unfaithful servants they are.

Imagine how Moses felt when God ceased in His instructions, and commanded him to turn aside from the eternal to contend with the ways of that which was fleshly and temporary--mainly idolatry. It is clear that the children of Israel were out from under Egypt's tyrannical rule, but Egypt's idolatrous influences remained intact in the Jewish people. The Lord said of them that they were stiff-necked, and He was about to cause His wrath to burn against them. He wanted to cause Moses' descendants to become a great nation.

Moses was a servant of God and a mediator on behalf of the people of Israel. In addition, in his humble state, he had no desire for his descendants to become a great nation. As a result, he stood as a mediator on behalf of the Jews, as he reasoned with the Lord about these people's foolishness. He reminded the Lord of His promises and covenant to Abraham.

God repented of the evil He was about to bring on the children of Israel, leaving it up to Moses to deal with them. Moses came down from the mountain bearing the stone tablets to only hear and witness the idolatrous practices of the Hebrews. His anger began to burn. Moses cast the tablets down, breaking them at the base of the mount. His gesture signified that the children of Israel had certainly broken the Law of God.

Moses broke down their idol, reduced it in the fire to liquid, then ground it to powder and made the idolatrous children of Israel drink it to partake of its bitterness. He separated those who were zealous for the Lord from those who were shamefully exposed by their idolatrous preference and ways. The Levites were the one who zealously stood with Moses as they were told to take the sword and execute judgment on those who stood on the side of the idol.[8]

---

[7] Matthew 24:42-46; Mark 13:32-37; Luke 21:19, 34-36
[8] Exodus 32:21-29

What has the Church been doing for two thousand years? As you study the history of the Church, there has been like separation and judgment occurring in the Body. There have been times when those who were considered part of the Church married the world in some way and embraced its idols and philosophies. However, a firebrand would come forth with truth, creating a wave of reformation to sweep through the land. The sword of persecution would often answer such reformation, causing those who were caught in the crossfire to choose who they were going to believe and serve. Through the centuries the real members of the living Church always found themselves being separated from the religious system that demanded worship and obedience. They sometimes stood alone, only to find that there were others willing to set aside the temporary age they lived in, and become identified as a living sacrifice ready to be offered up for the sake of the Christ and His Gospel.

The reason that Christians fall into the traps of idolatry is because they have not learned to wait in expectation. They have never allowed their small measure of faith to be refined while waiting upon the Lord to move. They do not want to be tested, proved, and exposed. They are hoping to skip the valleys of humiliation and the silent plateaus of waiting until God speaks or moves. As a result, they never establish depth to their faith, character in their walk, and witness any fruition of God's promises.

What about you? Are you the one on the mountain waiting upon God, or are you the one in the valley waiting for someone to give you some spiritual direction? The difference between the mountain experience and the valley is expectation. Genuine faith stands, waits, and moves according to the expectation of possessing the life that God has promised. As a result, such expectation will ultimately lead people to embrace and partake of God's promises.

11

THE TENT OF MEETING

The children of Israel failed to wait for Moses. They had no real expectation towards God. In summation, they had no real faith towards God. When people are waiting for God, they do so because of faith in His Person and faith towards His faithful, perfect ways. They choose to believe that He means what He says, will do what He promised, and will bring about a matter according to His perfect will, His good purpose, and for His glory.

The problem with the children of Israel is that they had a mixture.[1] They had experiences with God, but they maintained their idolatrous mindsets and ways. If God performed according to their mindset or operated according to their understanding, they would acknowledge Him. But, if matters started to become unpredictable, then they had other options to fall back on. In fact, they could create their own god that would best suit their purposes.

This brings us to the harsh reality that people without sincere faith towards God will possess other options in regard to what they will put their faith in. For example, if God fails to perform according to personal standards, then people have other idols waiting in the background to take center stage in their lives. In such cases, the true God becomes optional, while the idols become the source of their reliance and solution.

I learned early in my faith walk that as long as I had options as far as my faith, I did not have to learn what it meant for me to live or walk in light of heavenly expectations. As long as I secretly maintained my worldly options, I could avoid the fiery ovens that would refine and enlarge my faith to embrace the expectation of eventually experiencing the faithfulness and fullness of God in a situation.

Since the Hebrews did not live in expectation of God, they resorted to a substitute that had no life or power. This is what can happen to those who call themselves Christians. The Apostle Paul warned that in the last part of the end days there would be a falling away from the truth. Those who do not love the truth will find themselves being swept up by a great wave of delusion that will plunge them into judgment.[2]

It is important to understand that there is a difference between how truth will affect people and how deception works on them. People must be led to the truth by the Spirit. Such truth will always have a sobering

---

[1] Hebrews 3:15-4:2
[2] 2 Thessalonians 2:3, 10-12

connection to the reality that is happening around these individuals. However, deception is a wave that finds its height in sentiment as it creates a different reality. In other words, people sense, feel, perceive, or think a matter is right because of how it affects their notions, imagination, perception, or ideas. It actually stirs up their sentiment towards their personal conclusions, seducing them into a false reality. As they get more caught up with how this false reality is affecting them, the wave of deception gains height and momentum as it begins to rush towards the shores of judgment.

Sadly, I have watched various waves of delusion flowing in and out of Christendom, taking with it those who do not love the truth. As the wave enfolds these individuals, they become harder to reach and warn in regard to the judgment that is awaiting them. After all, in their minds they know they are right, and those who do not agree with them are wrong.

The wave of idolatry clearly rolled in and through the camp of Israel. As people became caught up with its momentum, they were unaware that the shores of truth and judgment proved to be closer than they had thought. Not only did they have to taste the bitterness of their decisions and actions, but many paid with their lives.

We, as believers, need to take heed to the children of Israel's idolatrous example. We need to not only let our idols fall to the ground in judgment, but we must get rid of secret idols of the heart and mind that become our option when God fails to be the solution that is acceptable to our notion about a matter. By getting rid of such idols, it will allow us to mix faith in what we know about God in light of the experiences we have had with Him and the instructions we have been entrusted with. Faith that is mixed with these factors will create the expectation of seeing a matter brought forth according to God's perfect ways, promises, and plan.

It is also important to recognize what happened to the testimony of God that was serving as a temporary place of worship until the tabernacle of God was established according to the heavenly pattern. This testimony was known as the tent of meeting. This temporary meeting place represented God's presence in the midst of His people, and that He indeed dwelt among them, as well as walked among them. However, the camp had been defiled by idolatry. God's testimony or presence would not remain in such an unholy environment.

Moses moved the tabernacle outside of the camp.[3] If people wanted to resolve the issue with God, they would have to come outside of the defiled place to seek Him.

Being taken outside of the camp is also what happened in Jesus' case when He was taken to the cross. The cross represents the believer's altar. Jesus was led outside the camp of man's perverted religion and the unholy activities of the world to be offered up on the altar

---

[3] Exodus 33:7

of the cross.[4] Likewise, we as believers must individually seek the Lord outside of the different camps that represent man's religion and the world's influences to find Him. In essence, we must find what is eternal.

Moving outside of the camp is a very important principle to remember or consider for our own lives. God will have no part in that which is unholy. He cannot honor, come down, or move in such an environment. As a result, we see this type of environment being advocated in the New Testament. Keep in mind, God wanted His name and presence to be upon His tabernacle or temple. He wanted to dwell in the midst of His people.

As Christians, we serve as the temple of the Holy Spirit.[5] Sacrifices are to be offered from the altar of our hearts, service is to be rendered before God in humility and meekness, and ministry that is pure must be offered to others.

The Apostle Paul lays out the type of inward environment that must be present for God to live and walk in our midst. He made this statement in 1 Corinthians 3:17, "If any man defile the temple of God, him shall God destroy; for the temple of God is holy, which temple ye are." In 1 Corinthians 6:19-20, he reminds people that as God's temple, we do not belong to ourselves. Since we belong to God, we should be glorifying Him. However, if we give way to the flesh, we will defile the temple and bring judgment upon ourselves. If we let self reign instead of Jesus, we will defile the temple, while walking under condemnation. If we come into agreement with the world, we will be committing spiritual harlotry or fornication, bringing the wrath of God upon us.

The children of Israel had erected an idol in the camp, and had defiled the whole camp. As a result, some had tasted the wrath of God. Since they had defiled the whole camp, the tent of the meeting was moved outside of the defiled camp; therefore, the people had to seek God for themselves. They had to make the necessary effort to come outside of the camp to properly worship Him.

It is amazing that the children of Israel did not worship God at the foot of Mount Sinai, yet when His presence came down on the tent, they worshipped Him. Some worshipped Him from the doors of their tents. Others worshipped Him outside of the very tent of meeting. Then there was Joshua who was in the tent with Moses and remained there to experience all he could, and finally you have Moses who spoke face to face with God.

The percentages of people who come into the place of intimacy with God are few. Most people prefer to worship God from the safe distance of their religious comfort zones. Some people venture outside of the religious camps to seek and worship God, while a few will come as close

---

[4] Hebrews 13:10-14
[5] 1 Corinthians 3:16; 6:19

Developing Our Christian Life

as they can to experience His presence and worship Him. However, those who enter into that place of intimacy with God are even fewer.

This brings us to the different relationships people have with God. So many Christians stand outside of what constitutes true fellowship with God. These individuals are content to be associated with Christianity, while observing those who are pursuing a closer relationship. There are those individuals who want more of God, but many times they find themselves striving in their own strength, while watching others enter into a greater relationship with the Lord. Then, there are those who dare to pay the price to know God, and are ever brought so close to Him; and, finally you have those very few committed individuals who have left all behind to enter into the place of intimacy with God.

Moses entered the tabernacle as various people stood at the door of their tents, while others were waiting outside of the camp at the place of the tent. When Moses entered the tent, the cloudy pillar descended and stood at the tent door. We have already considered how Moses <u>stood before</u> the presence of God, <u>ascended into</u> His presence, <u>supped</u> in it, and <u>waited in</u> His presence. We know that in the first situation, Moses was going to receive His marching orders. When he ascended into His presence, he was going to receive the Law and pattern for the tabernacle. When he supped in His presence, there was fellowship and instruction, and when he waited in His presence, he did so in expectation of seeing a matter come to fruition.

We are told that the presence of God was standing at the door of the tabernacle. It was not burning, nor did it display darkness. It was like a cloudy pillar. There are a couple of things we must note about God's particular presentation of Himself in this matter. He descended as a pillar, a column, or platform.[6] We know this is the type of presence the children of Israel followed in the wilderness. This pillar descended while still pointing upward in the form of a cloud or covering. We know that this cloud or covering is most likely the Holy Ghost because of what the prophet, Isaiah, said in Isaiah 30:1, "Woe to the rebellious children, saith the LORD, who take counsel, but not of me; and who cover with a covering, but not of my Spirit, that they may add sin to sin."

This brings us to the purpose for the presence of the Lord to stand at the door of the tent. The Lord wanted to speak to Moses face to face, as a man speaks to his friend. Jesus gives us insight into why God wanted to have this type of encounter with His servants in John 15:15, "Henceforth I call you not servants; for the servant knoweth not what his lord doeth: but I have called you friends; for all things that I have heard of my Father I have made known unto you." In the fiery bush, God gave Moses his marching orders. In the dark, consuming presence of His holiness, God entrusted the Law and the pattern of the tabernacle to Moses. However, in the case of His presence coming down, it was for

---

[6] Exodus 33:9-10

the purpose of supping, speaking, or walking among His people. What an incredible contrast the Word gives us, concerning how God's presence sets up certain environments in order to invoke His people in a proper way.

It is interesting to note what took place between the Lord and Moses. Moses understood that he had found grace in His sight. He requested that the Lord show him the way, as well as give him a compelling desire to know Him. However, Moses had a reason for presenting his particular case to the Lord. The Lord informed him that He would honor his request. This is when Moses made this request, "I beseech thee, show me thy glory" (Exodus 33:18b).

Moses had an incredible relationship with the Lord. He had been in His presence in various ways. He had been the one who was not only sent by God, but was used by God to do great feats on behalf of the children of Israel. He had a friendship with God that brought intimacy to their relationship. Yet, we see where Moses wanted to know Him more. He was not content to simply accept his present position, even though it far outweighed the distant relationship that the rest of the people of Israel had with God. Moses wanted to behold His glory.

Presence establishes environment, but glory establishes the reality of God in light of His unending majesty. Moses wanted to experience the reality of God's splendor. In fact, the Lord described His glory as His "goodness." In this text God's goodness pointed to the unveiling of His indescribable beauty, which creates well-being in His people that often finds its origins in His grace and mercy.[7] It was here that God admitted to Moses that he could not see the fullness of His glory head on without dying. However, He would allow him to see the back part of His glory. For God to allow Moses to even witness the back of His glory, He would first have to place him on a rock by placing him in the cleft of it, and then He would cover him with His hand while He passed by. He told Moses that when He took His hand away, he could see the back part of His majesty.[8]

To me this is one of the most incredible pictures of the Christian life. We have been placed on the foundation of our Rock, Jesus, but we have also been put in the cleft of this eternal Rock. After all, God has placed us in Christ who serves as our wisdom, righteousness, sanctification, and redemption. Our very person is actually hid in the life of Christ who also serves as our ark. It is in Christ that we see the different aspects of God's majesty being unveiled to us and in us.[9] For example, His pure wisdom is imparted into our lives to discover His perfect order, while the eternal ways of His righteousness are constantly being established before us to walk in, His incredible sanctification is worked in us as we

---

[7] Strong's Strong Concordance; #2898
[8] Exodus 33:20-23
[9] 1 Corinthians 1:30; 3:11; Colossians 3:3

take more of His likeness on, and His glorious redemption is continually being realized in our lives. As a result, we can look fully in the face of the Son of glory as a means to receive this incredible life, knowing that we will see God without being afraid of judgment.

This brings us to the realization that we not only have been placed in a position and environment of holiness, but we are to walk after the ways of holiness, and be led into holiness. Clearly, we must walk according to a state of holiness in accordance to the presence of holiness that is evident in our lives through the indwelling presence of the Spirit. This state and presence of holiness ensures that ultimately we will possess the source of holiness, the life of Jesus.

Jesus' life in us represents the holiness that is being worked in us and through us. Once again, as Christians, we are reminded that we are not only placed in God's presence, surrounded by His presence, and connected by His presence, but we also have His presence in us. We have the life of Jesus in us through the abiding presence of the Spirit of God. We must walk in this presence to ensure a holy life. As Christians, we are not to walk according to the old life, but according to the new, holy life of Christ in us.

The Apostle Peter gave these instructions in 1 Peter 1:13-16,
> Wherefore, gird up the loins of your mind, be sober, and hope to the end for the grace that is to be brought unto you at the revelation of Jesus Christ, As obedient children, not fashioning yourselves according to the former lusts in your ignorance But, as he who hath called you is holy, so be ye holy in all manner of conversation, Because it is written, Be ye holy; for I am holy.

Christians do not have any other option when it comes to being holy. As believers, our minds must be disciplined by that which is holy. Our dispositions must be in line with the revelation of Christ that has been outlined in Scripture and revealed by the Spirit. Our attitudes must be transformed by the Spirit, rather than conformed to the ways and lusts of the present world. Obviously, as Christians, we are being called to be holy, which entails the inner man being established in holiness, the outward environment of our homes and churches becoming holy to ensure fellowship with God and each other, and our way of living must be holy to ensure a powerful testimony that can clearly be read by the world.

What about your life? Are you content in your present life in Christ, or are you desirous to know more about him? Have you committed your whole life to God because you truly possess the life of Christ, or do you maintain a right to live your life, because you still lay claim to it? Do you understand that holiness is necessary to ensure that you properly worship Him? Remember, as Christians, everything about our lives must set us apart from the world and must identify us to our holy God. Does your life set you apart from the world and identify you to the Christian life?

12

THE PURPOSE OF GOD'S GLORY

Moses' request was to behold the glory of God. However, he could not witness the fullness of God's glory and live to tell about it. In Christ dwells the fullness of the Godhead bodily. In other words, man looked upon the very glory of God 20 centuries ago without dying. However, God's glory was also veiled in humanity.

As Christians, the only way we can experience and walk out the Christian life is according to the presence of God. However, the purpose of the presence of God is to establish the glory of God in our lives. Without the right presence, God's glory will be missing.

Once again, we must remember that presence points to the person of someone actually being present as a means to interact, influence, or lead, while glory points to the light, beauty, or honor that actually distinguishes someone as to the person he or she is. As Christians, we must walk according to the presence of God in order to reflect our Lord's glory.

In chapter two, I made reference to the different tenses of this glory as it is worked in our lives as believers. For review purposes we need to consider these tenses again. Remember, it is the Holy Spirit's responsibility to work the life, light, or glory of Christ in us. There is the *perfect* tense of this glory which involves suffering. The Apostle Paul stated in Romans 8:17 that we must suffer with Him so that we may be glorified together.

The *past* tense of His glory being worked in us points to the expectation that we possess, due to being born again. Colossians 1:27b talks about the expectation we have been given, "Christ in you, the hope of glory."

We have the *present* work of His glory taking place, which is being made evident in us when we actually begin to reflect His life to those around us. 2 Corinthians 3:18 tells us that we, as believers, should be as open glasses (mirrors) in which Jesus' image is being constantly brought forth in and through our lives. As His likeness is being worked in us, it will also be unveiled through our lives to others in greater ways.

The more we live in and according to the Spirit, the more our inner man will be changed to reflect Jesus' glory. As believers, we are continually being changed to conform to His likeness. We need to realize that such change is preparing us for our *future* glory, where the fullness of Christ's life and power will be completely realized in us. It is in our future glory in Christ that we will live in His unhindered majesty, knowing our fellowship with Him will be forever and unbroken, and that we will also rule with Him.

It is vital that we understand how the glory of God works. It is ongoing in our lives. Moses' experience in this area reveals this work. After encountering God's glory, Moses was instructed to hew out two tables of stone like the first ones that were broken, and to be ready to go up into the mountain again. We know that Moses witnessed the backside of God's glory, but what was the purpose of such an encounter?

Remember that Moses wanted to know God in a greater measure. He sensed that he needed to witness His glory for such a desire to be satisfied. How did this encounter with God's glory cause Moses to know Him in greater ways? If you follow Moses into his next meeting with God, you can begin to understand how the glory of God affected Moses' life. As we are about to see, it enlarged him to receive a greater revelation of God.

It is important at this time to consider the different places that Moses encountered God. He encountered Him in the wilderness. This points to how God intrudes into our normalcy to present Himself to us. We see that Moses was called up into the mountain to meet with God. This symbolizes the reality that God is always calling us higher in our life with Him. God met Moses at the door of the tent of the meeting to talk face to face with him as He would a friend. Such a meeting points to sweet fellowship. As we follow Moses in each of his encounters with God, we can see how his relationship with his Creator changed.

Moses' first meeting with God served as an introduction as God revealed His identity and Moses' commission. The introduction took place from a burning bush. In his second real meeting with God, he ascended up a mount into the fire. In his third meeting, God descended in a pillar of cloud to talk face to face with him as a friend. Clearly, the relationship that had been established between God and Moses culminated with Moses requesting God to show him His glory or majesty.

Now we come to the significance of God's glory. It actually prepared Moses to see Him in greater ways. How can we, as believers, see something until we have been given a greater light in which to see it? This is why the Apostle Paul made this declaration, "But we all, with open face beholding as in a glass the glory of the Lord, are changed into the same image from glory to glory, even as by the Spirit of the Lord" (2 Corinthians 3:18). (Emphasis added.)

The truth is, as believers, we are constantly walking by a limited light of understanding. Our understanding of our Lord must be continually enlarged so that we can see glimpses of His infinite character. Each glimpse allows His life to be established in us in greater measures, causing us to take on His likeness. This is why Christians are given this command in Matthew 5:16, "Let your light so shine before men, that they may see your good works, and glorify your Father, who is in heaven."

Keep in mind, Moses had lost his initial vision, but now he is prepared to receive his real vision. And, what would that vision consist of? Would it mean he would have a greater ministry or see greater miracles? Is this not what most Christians think of when it comes to receiving a vision from God?

Most Christians know about Proverbs 29:18 that states, "Where there is no vision, the people perish; but he that keepeth the law, happy is he." In my initial years as a Christian, I used to think vision was all wrapped up with calling, ministry, or spiritual accomplishments. However, I discovered that calling, ministry, or spiritual accomplishments had nothing to do with vision. My calling gave me a sense as to how ministry would be carried out, while true ministry is clearly described in Scripture as one of reconciliation. However, I had to admit in my first years of ministry, I did everything in my own strength, according to my own concepts. I tried to bring about spiritual accomplishment according to my perception, but I constantly hit one wall after another wall of hindrances, defeats, and frustration.

This was Moses' problem in his initial years of zeal. He had tried to deliver one Hebrew man from oppression, and ended up becoming a fugitive in the wilderness. He learned what many servants of God learn after all their energy has been spent on vain attempts to bring about desired results for the sake of God. The prophet Zechariah summarizes this lesson, "...Not by might, nor by power, but by my Spirit, saith the LORD of hosts" (Zechariah 4:6c)

God is the one who does the work of His kingdom in and through His servants. It is the Spirit of God that must inspire work, as well as empowering the vessel to carry out such work to ensure that God receives glory. This reality was made quite obvious to Moses when it was the Lord who delivered the people of Israel, and not His servant.

If calling, ministry, or spiritual accomplishments do not entail vision, then what type of vision must God's servants have to finish their course? Moses' encounter with God gives us valuable insight into this answer in Exodus 34:5-7,

> And the LORD descended in the cloud, and stood with him there, and proclaimed the name of the LORD. And the LORD passed by before him, and proclaimed, The LORD, The LORD God, merciful and gracious, long-suffering, and abundant in goodness and truth. Keeping mercy for thousands, forgiving iniquity and transgression and sin, and who will by no means clear the guilty, visiting the iniquity of the fathers upon the children, and upon the children's children, unto the third and to the fourth generation.

The new vision every servant must receive to finish the course is a greater revelation of their Lord. It was the Lord who passed before Moses, not some vision of ministry or accomplishments. It was the Lord who proclaimed His name or character in relationship to His people. He is the One who is merciful towards us in our depravity, gracious towards us in our search for Him, long-suffering towards us in relationship to repentance, quick to bestow His goodness upon us, and is the essence of truth. He is the One who offers mercy, pardon, and judgment to each generation according to their darkness and sin that is often passed down through influence, example, and conditioning.

Keep in mind, vision has to do with our focus, emphasis, and goal. To finish the course, our focus must be on God. To ensure the integrity of our agendas, our emphasis must be to possess the life that God has ordained for us. Our goal should be to take on His likeness so that we truly reflect and represent Him in this dark world. As you can see, vision should be and must be about God. He is our portion or inheritance. He is our source of life and hope. He is the only way we will find liberty and truth in the midst of the insane darkness that clearly reigns in this present age.

It is interesting how Moses responded to God's introduction. Granted, Moses probably intellectually understood that God possessed these traits, but now they were being revealed to his spirit as truth, which brought life to his spirit and substance to his soul. The reason I know that these truths were becoming revelation to Moses, is because he made haste to bow his head towards the earth, and worship God.[1]

To me it has always been interesting to observe in Scripture how people approached or responded to God. When Moses first encountered God, he simply took off his shoes, but there was no sign of real worship. We see him ascending up the mountain into the cloud to meet God, supping before Him, waiting before Him, and talking face to face with Him, but this is the first time we see such awe overcome him that he bowed his head in humility and worshipped God.

No doubt Moses had worshipped God throughout his life, but this new revelation of God caused him to automatically worship his Creator. This is the intent of all new revelation. It must bring us to a higher caliber of worship in devotion, adoration, and service.

It is from the premise of worship that Moses once again interceded for the stiff-necked Hebrews. He did it from the grounds of finding grace before God, which allowed him to stand in the gap for the people of Israel. He asked the Lord to go with them and lead them to their earthly inheritance. After all, Jehovah God was their spiritual inheritance, and regardless of their status as former slaves of Egypt, and their present status as strangers heading for the new land, they were already the richest people on earth. Sadly, many of these individuals failed to possess their true inheritance in the end. Such a harsh reality should serve as a sober warning to Christians as well.

Once the vision is established, then the commission will be renewed. Keep in mind that personal calling simply determines how we will carry out our commission in God's kingdom. The problem that many well-

---

[1] Exodus 34:8

meaning servants of God run into is they put emphasis on calling, rather than commission, because they lack the correct focus as to their real purpose as servants of the Most High.

It is important at this time to understand how the Lord renewed Moses' commission. As Christians, we all have the same commission as far as preaching the Gospel and making disciples of Jesus. The Jewish people also had a like commission as well. It was God's heart that His people possess the fullness of their inheritance. For Israel, their inheritance was both spiritual and earthly, but for Christians, their inheritance is spiritual. Granted, they may receive earthly blessings along the way, but their real inheritance is the eternal, abundant life of Jesus.

The Lord will renew commission by establishing a covenant. We see this in the case of Moses in Exodus 34:10,

> And he said, Behold, I make a covenant: Before all thy people I will do marvels, such as have not been done in all the earth, nor in any nation: and all the people among whom thou art shall see the work of the LORD; for it is an terrible thing that I will do with thee.

A covenant does two things, it will show what God will do to bring about a matter, but it will also establish the responsibility of the other party to ensure that the integrity of God's part is properly honored, received, and maintained. For example, God's part of the covenant He established with Moses was that He would drive the pagan people out of the Promised Land, but the Hebrews' part was that they would destroy all the pagan and idolatrous idols and altars of these people. This was the way to ensure that His people would be established in complete loyalty, devotion, and worship of Jehovah God.[2]

Let us now consider the covenant that has been established with every blood-bought saint. The covenant that God made with us as believers is one of redemption. We have been redeemed by the blood of His Son. What does this covenant tell us about our responsibility to the Lord? Let me summarize this in light of our commission.

We have been purchased: As Christians, we do not belong to ourselves. The Apostle Paul informed us that we belong to God. Therefore, we are here to serve Him, not ourselves. Our service to our awesome God must be done in the spirit of joyfulness, something that was not only lacking in the attitude of the children of Israel, but also caused judgment to come down upon them. We should be bondservants who live to please our Lord, not servants to sin with its deadly claims and tentacles of death that will work on our lives.[3] We are here to carry out our Lord, Owner, and God's bidding.

We are no longer under the curse of the Law: God's Law could only condemn us in our sin. It had no way to justify us as long as we were

---

[2] Exodus 34:11-17
[3] Deuteronomy 28:47-48; Matthew 20:28; Romans 6:0-22; 1 Corinthians 6:19-20; 7:21-23

serving sin. Therefore, we were under the very curse of it, as it held us in subjection to it. Through Jesus' redemption, we have been delivered from the tyranny of sin and made subject to a more excellent law, which is the law of the Spirit of life in Christ Jesus.[4] We are commissioned to tell people about this great deliverance through the preaching of the Gospel.

We have been reconciled back to God through Jesus' redemption. Man was clearly separated from God due to sin. However, Jesus became sin for us so we could be made in the righteousness of God. Jesus' substitution on the cross points to the great exchange that was made as a means to bring us back into fellowship with our Creator. Since Jesus' act on the cross resulted in reconciliation, we have been told, as believers, that we have also been entrusted with a ministry of reconciliation.[5]

We have been given a seal that will ensure our complete redemption. As Christians, we have been redeemed from the past masters of sin and Satan, but we must continually be redeemed from the powerful influences of self and the world. In the future we will fully realize redemption when we are taken out of this world to receive the complete inheritance of the promise of eternal life. The presence of the Holy Spirit in us serves as the seal that will identify us to this inheritance. Since we have been given the spirit of wisdom and revelation, we must walk in the light of it as living epistles that clearly share the hope of this inheritance with others.[6]

Have you ever encountered God's glory? What revelation did you receive? Have you walked in the light of the revelation according to obedience to the vision you were entrusted with, or has the light turned into darkness because of unbelief? Perhaps you have never experienced His glory because you are content to say in the door of your tent or witness His glory from outside of the real meeting place of fellowship.

It is up to each person to establish his or her own relationship with the Lord. The extent of our relationship for each of us with the Lord has not been determined by Him, but by us. If we have failed to experience the presence of God in greater ways, it is because we have settled for what we have become accustomed to in our religious life. Such contentment is not godly, but fleshly, self-serving, and will eventually digress into a state of unbelief.[7]

---

[4] Romans 8:2; Galatians 3:13; 4:5
[5] 2 Corinthians 5:18-21; Ephesians 2:13-18; Colossians 1:20-21
[6] 2 Corinthians 3:2-3; Ephesians 1:7-14, 17-18
[7] 1 Timothy 6:6-12

13

REFLECTING THE GLORY OF GOD

People walk according to the vision they possess about God and the essence of what they think life should be. Vision points to revelation. Therefore, as believers, we will walk according to the revelation we have of our Lord. The level or type of revelation we possess will be based on our spiritual maturity, calling, or responsibility. It is important to understand this principle because too many Christians arrogantly or unfairly consider themselves or others in light of their personal revelation. Such an attitude will produce elitism, resulting in these individuals becoming very judgmental. Obviously, the fruit that is produced from such comparison is contrary to the fruit of the Spirit.

Moses was walking according to his revelation of God. Each revelation varied according to the relationship he had with God and the responsibilities that were being entrusted to him. A good example of how revelation varies with God's people is Joshua. Joshua served Moses. He was with him on the mountain and remained in the tent of meeting when God's presence came down. Joshua was as close as he could get in Moses' personal encounters with God. In the end, Joshua would become the great military leader who would lead Israel into the Promised Land. In Joshua 5:13-15, we read the revelation of God that was given to this great soldier. The Lord introduced Himself to Joshua as the captain of the hosts of the LORD. Although Joshua would lead the people into battle, it would be the divine captain of heaven who would go before him and his army, and actually secure victory on their behalf.

Have you had a revelation of Jesus? Are you walking according to this vision or has it been dulled down by a false light that has become more attractive or persuasive to you? It is important for each of us to realize that we have some type of light in us. If it is not the light of Christ, then the light that a person could be walking in is nothing more than darkness. For example, when people walk according to self, they walk in a state of denial about truth as they harbor anger towards the one true God who will not bow down to their selfish whims. When individuals walk according to the world, they walk in ignorance about reality because they harbor humanistic philosophies. Such philosophies cause them to become disillusioned and mocking towards truth. When people walk according to man's dead religion, they walk in delusion about God. Such delusion is due to the fact that they have come under the powerful influence of the substitute light of the antichrist spirit, while becoming self-righteous towards truth.

Life also points to the type of light or understanding people walk in. Jesus said in Matthew 6:22-23 that the light man possesses will be reflected through the outlet of his soul, which is the eye. If the light of man is really darkness, he will not only walk according to this darkness, but his soul will be full of it. For those who walk according to selfish preferences, life will be consumed by a tormenting darkness that experiences an occasional relief brought about by sentimental or temperamental happiness. When such darkness comes to those who walk according to the encroaching dark philosophies of the world, there is only temporary relief that comes from fleeting happiness as life proves to be illusive and frustrating. For the self-righteous, their formidable darkness proves to become too rigid and unbearable, as they harbor a fanciful notion about experiencing a future full of reward and recognition. This is why Jesus warned to take heed how we actually hear or perceive a matter based on our particular understanding.[1]

The type of life or light we walk in or according to will be greatly affected by that which influences us. Keep in mind we all start out with a clean slate as to our attitudes and ideas concerning life. People write on those slates, establishing our particular light or understanding of something.

The Word of God confirms that it is God's desire to influence our understanding to ensure we are walking in and according to His light. Consider how Moses had been instructed to hew two tables of stone. He was then called up to the mountain so that God could engrave His Law on those stones. Once something has been engraved, it is set forever. As Christians, it is the Holy Spirit who desires to write God's laws upon the fleshly tablet of our hearts. Hence, James exhorts us, as believers, to put away all filthiness and wickedness so that we can receive with meekness the engrafted Word, thereby, saving our souls.[2]

This brings us to a very important point. People's slates must go through cleansing to rid them of the darkness that has influenced their attitude towards life and God before the Holy Spirit can engrave God's Word upon them. Such individuals must first learn how to humble themselves before God so that He can write on the slate of their pure hearts His life-changing, liberating truths. Keep in mind that if the slate is not first cleansed then there will be confusion when God tries to engrave His Word upon it.

Through the years I have watched Christians struggle with confusion. The darkness of the old life makes people stiff-necked towards God's truths and ways. God wants to write upon the slate of each person's

---

[1] Luke 8:18
[2] Exodus 34:1; Hebrews 10:16; James 1:21

heart His truths that will make him or her free, but human nature has a tendency to cling to the former slate of the old man. As the Lord presents these truths with the desire to engrave them upon His people's hearts, many of these individuals can hit the gray area of confusion because God's truths prove contrary to their understanding. Such people must first repent of the unbelief associated with their stiff-necked ways in order to be cleansed from the idolatry that reigns within the confines of the stony tablets of their hearts.

Minds that have been cleansed become transformed minds that no longer think according to this present world.[3] Believers who have transformed minds walk according to a heavenly beat that is contrary to the requiem chant of the present age we live in.

Obviously, Moses' encounter with the presence of God was transforming him. No doubt part of Moses' preparation entailed cleansing his mind of former influences. When God finally appeared to Moses, he was a humbled man who had no real sense of any personal worth. Once he obeyed the Lord, we see a man who became bolder in the courts of Pharaoh. In the power of God, the Red Sea parted at his command. He alone ascended up into God's presence to receive the Law and pattern for the tabernacle.

It is vital that we follow Moses' personal progression. His progression reveals how God's influence changes the inner person, determining who that person will ultimately become. Such an identity will influence how we, as believers, express the life that is being established in us. For Moses, he was brought down to the abominable status of a shepherd. He was humbled by and in the wilderness, but when he encountered God, his status was changed from a mere shepherd of sheep to that of a deliverer and leader of God's sheep. He became a servant to God and a mediator to the people. In the end, he had established such a relationship with the Lord that he spoke to him face to face as a friend.

Due to his relationship with God, Moses found favor with his Creator. The grace that God extended towards His servant gave Moses boldness to request that He show him His glory. To be exposed to God's glory prepares a person to come to a place where God's glory will shine forth through him or her.

It is one thing to be exposed to God's glory and another matter to reflect it. Moses had been exposed to God's glory, but it was not yet reflecting in His life. How does one become a mirror of God's glory? It comes back to being brought to an enlarged inner state where you are able to receive all that God has for you in that particular situation. Once a person comes to such a receptive state, then he or she must sit and wait in His presence.

Moses was once again upon the mountain for forty day and forty nights. In that time, he was in the presence of God receiving the

---

[3] Romans 12:2

engraved tablets of the Law. When he came down from the mountain, his face reflected the glory of God.[4]

Sadly, the people of Israel were afraid of this powerful reflection being in their midst.[5] They could witness God's presence from a distance, but they had no real desire to enter into it. They could wait for Moses to bring God's instruction, but they had no intention of simply waiting for God to speak to them. They did not mind dancing before the altar of an idol, but they feared becoming a reflection of God's glory in this dark world. Just as God's glory was veiled by the consuming cloud of His holiness, Moses' face was veiled to hide the reflection of God's glory from the people.

We are reminded once again that the Bible declares that all have sinned and fallen short of the glory of God. Man was designed to reflect his Creator's glory, but because of sin, God's glory has been marred or hidden from man behind the veil of darkness that now covers his heart and mind. As long as a person continues in sin, he or she will fall short of experiencing and being identified by God's glory. It is this glory that comes from the life of God being established and erected in the lives of His people. As saints of the most high, this glory serves as the light of our soul and the reflection that can be seen in our eyes and on our countenance.

The Apostle Paul talked about Moses' veil in 2 Corinthians 3:6-18 in relationship to the glory that even exceeds the glory that was evident on Moses' face. The glory that exceeds that of Moses is the Holy Spirit. In God's presence Moses received the manifestation of His glory through the receiving of the Law, but for you and me as Christians, we actually possess this glory through the abiding presence of the Holy Spirit. The only way this glory will manifest itself to others is as the life of Christ is being established more and more in the believer.

Christ and His life are the essence of glory to every believer. James referred to Jesus as the Lord of glory. The writer of Hebrews states that Jesus' person served as the brightness of His own glory. Finally, the Apostle Paul made reference to the riches of the glory of Jesus' inheritance in the saints, as well as stipulated that it is Christ in us that serves as our hope of glory.[6]

The veil Moses had to put on to cover the visible manifestation of God's glory in light of the Law, symbolized the veil that is upon the minds and hearts of those who are still lost in the darkness of sin and death. The Law revealed the harsh reality of sin in light of God's glory. When the children of Israel looked upon the glory that manifested itself on Moses' face, they became afraid to even come near to him. Perhaps

---

[4] Exodus 34:28
[5] Exodus 34:29-30
[6] Ephesians 1:17-18; Colossians 1:27; Hebrews 1:3; James 2:1

they feared that the light of the glory would indeed reveal the devastation that sin had upon their lives and which continued to work in them.[7]

Moses would put the veil on when he spoke the words of God to the people of Israel, but he would remove it when he entered the presence of God. The Apostle Paul made reference to the custom of the Jewish men wearing their prayer shawl over their head. This practice symbolized how these men would not enter into prayer time without first covering their shame brought on by sin.[8]

The Apostle Paul explained how the veil remains to this day on the hearts of people, even when Moses is being read, but that it has been taken away from believers by Jesus Christ. Since the veil of shame has been taken away from the minds and hearts of the Lord's people, the Holy Spirit now has the liberty to restore them as living epistles—mirrors that surely reflect the life that is being brought forth through them. Unlike Moses who hid the glory of God behind a veil, believers must let the glory of Jesus' life shine forth through their open faces, regardless of the actions and attitudes of others.[9]

Christ is the only one that can remove the veil from people's hearts and minds. He does this so that individuals can once again discover their potential of reflecting His very glory in this dark world. Obviously, as Christians, we are not here to reflect the darkness of self, the world, or man's religion. We are to serve as the crowning glory of God in the midst of this lost, despairing world.

Has Jesus taken away the veil of shame from your mind and heart? Are you now reflecting His glory? Keep in mind, the light you are walking according to will reveal what kind of attitude you have towards life and God.

---

[7] Exodus 34:30; 2 Corinthians 3:12-15
[8] 1 Corinthians 11:4-7
[9] Exodus 34:32-35; 2 Corinthians 3:2-3, 14-18

14

MINISTRATION OF RIGHTEOUSNESS

We have been considering what it means to live the Christian life. Most people think that the Christian life is something we must seek out, find, or devise as we travel though this world as strangers and pilgrims. However, it is not the Christian life we must seek, but the One who is the source of this life. We are unable to find this life unless we possess the intent to discover how to live it as we come to terms with the One who has given it as a gift.

Obviously, the Christian life is not to be devised through trial and error or adjusted according to the present age. In other words, as the Lord's servants, we do not purport how others are to live this life out, while we muddle through the changes and challenges of this present world. The truth is we already have a blueprint of it in the Word of God that is applicable no matter the age or times we live in. We do not plan this life out before we attempt to live it, because a pattern has already been clearly established for us to follow through the examples and teachings we have been given by Jesus. As commanded, we must follow the pattern.

The Christian life is walked out according to the light of Jesus in obedience to the instruction of the Word, and in the power and presence of the Holy Spirit. After all, this life is Jesus' very life that is eternal and abundant. This is why it is called the Christian life or the Christian walk instead of being referred to as the Christian belief, religion, or system.

Jesus' life must penetrate every arena of who we are, who we are to become, and who we actually allow ourselves to become. Who we are is determined by our makeup and attitudes, who we become will be established by the type of decisions we make in regard to who or what we serve, and who we allow ourselves to become will be determined by who or what we come into agreement with. Obviously, we are who we are, but whether we reach our potential depends on what master we serve and what spirit we give way to. The master we serve will determine or change our attitude, while the spirit will influence what kind of light is being reflected in, through, and from our lives.

This brings us to the one main distinction that must be evident in God's people; that is, the reality of His presence. As we have considered the concept of presence through this book, we have seen that it is God's desire and promise that He would be present in the midst of His people. He wanted His presence to flow down, in, and through His people, as He actually led His people with it.

For the Christian, we have the presence of God in us as a point of fellowship and identification, but He also wants His presence to flow from above, in us, and through us, as it fills us up to empower us in our walk and testimonies. And, since our life is also hid in Christ, His presence abounds around us as a means to protect, lead, and guide us in our spiritual journey.

When people think of God's presence, they usually think of an experience that made them feel good or left them with some type of emotional sensation. As we have already discovered, the real truth is that God's presence is meant to set up the environment that will prepare us to meet with God in a right attitude. The right attitude ensures that we will approach God in the manner in which we will properly receive from Him. Let us now consider how the different aspects of God's presence prepared Moses.

Response to God's Presence	Preparation	Power
Stood	Commissioned	Deliverance
Ascended	Received the Law	Ministration of glory
Supped	Communion	Beheld God's glory
Waited	Vision	Reflected His glory

The presence of God will lead us to the glory of God. Moses represented the glory of the first ministration. Ministration points to the way a matter is attended or type of service. Moses was given the Law to minister to the people of Israel. The glory of the Law was that it was holy and perfect in every way. There was no deviance, prejudice, or darkness to its ways. However, the glory of the Law exposed the darkness of fallen man. It was to reveal that man in his present state was and is a transgressor of God's holy Law and deserves death. This is why it was hard for the rest of the people of Israel to look upon the glory of Moses' face. According to the sources of my information, pure whiteness is the expression of God's glory, bringing an obvious contrast between His light and people's darkness.

The people of Israel also experienced the presence of God, but in different ways than Moses. They did not have a relationship with God like Moses had. Due to their inner state, they simply witnessed the presence of God from a distance. They were fearful of the darkness of His presence. Yet, the darkness was necessary for it veiled His holiness, while in a sense reflecting their inner state of sin, idolatry, and paganism. They remained removed from God by one mediator, Moses, who struggled under the great burden of it. Let us now consider how the glory of the ministration of the Law affected these people in their deliverance and journey.

Presence	Fruits	Results
Introduction to the great I AM	Greater oppression from the world.	Deliverance
Leads them out of Egypt	Testing	Wilderness
Dreadful at Sinai	Mediator Requested	Idolatry
Lifts from the camp	Judgment	Worship

The glory of the Law came from outside of man, to shine upon his hopeless plight. Since the eternal Law of God could not justify man in his lost state, its very light was to not only cause man to see his hopeless plight of condemnation, but to cause him to look beyond his state to see where the light of the Law was pointing to.

The Apostle Paul stated that the Law was a schoolmaster that pointed to the solution God provided to address man's plight. He explained who could be found at the end of the Law in Romans 10:4, "For Christ is the end of the law for righteousness to every that believeth." We know that Jesus fulfilled every aspect of the Law to satisfy its demands for righteousness and judgment.[1]

When we consider the Christian walk, it is not unusual to see Christians fall through the cracks when it comes to experiencing the life God intends for each of them. They fall through the cracks, not because

---

[1] Matthew 5:17-18; Galatians 3:24

they have a distinct commission as Moses was given, but like the children of Israel, they remain distant from real fellowship with God.

As Christians, we need to personally encounter the presence of God to walk out the Christian life. We need to learn to fellowship in His presence so we can take on our Lord's very glory.[2] However, like Moses in his forty years in the wilderness, many of us have been bogged down in the nominal demands of every day life. As a result, we sort of bounce from one activity to another as we consider much of what we do to be a normal way of life. We have no idea that a large amount of what we encounter in this present life serves as points of testing as to how we are handling the life of Christ, as well as a time for preparation to walk out the lessons or revelations established by such testing in greater measure. Preparation is the means of separating us unto the commission and calling that is attached to this incredible life.

Let us now consider the type of environment we need as believers in the following table on the next page, to ensure God's presence, as well as how His presence and glory should be translating in our lives.

---

[2] Psalm 17:15; Romans 6:5; 8:29; 2 Corinthians 3:18

Environment	Presence	Jesus' life	Results
Born Again	Dwells in you	Endowed with His eternal and abundant lives	Sealed to an eternal inheritance
Deny Self	Follow after in obedience.	Developing His life in us.	Realizing the hope of glory in us.
Become crucified	Led in the ways of righteousness.	Become completely identified with His life.	Experiencing His glory through suffering.
Being filled up with the Spirit	Descends upon you.	Walk according to His life	Connected to His heavenly glory.
Fellowship	Supping in it.	Enjoying His life.	Partaking of His glory
Intimacy	Abiding In it.	Walking out His life.	Reflecting His glory.

The Law ministered condemnation; therefore, its glory needed to be covered up by a veil. However, Jesus ministers the glory of righteousness that was unveiled in His humanity as our example. It is important to understand how these two different glories were reflected. The glory of the first ministration was God's holiness. It simply reflected how far away man was from God. The second type of glory was reflected through the humanity of Jesus. Holiness and righteousness are interchanged when it comes to God. However, in Jesus' humanity righteousness was reflected in light of what it means for man to have right standing before God, in God, and because of God. This righteousness was established by the work of redemption. Unlike the holiness of God that clearly distinguished how far away man was from Him, the righteousness that can be unveiled in humanity serves as a mirror that brings contrast between those who are dead in their sins, from those who are walking according to the life of Christ in them. In the first reflection, man stood doomed, but in the second reflection, man not only could see where he is under God's wrath, but he could also see beyond judgment to what has been provided for him. The provision of God would allow him to have right standing before Him on the basis of what Jesus accomplished on the cross.

As a result, the Apostle Paul pointed out that the glory of righteousness exceeds the Law in glory. The second glory was much more excellent because it offered man a way in which he could be counted as righteous in God's sight. In fact, through faith believers have been placed in a position of righteousness in Christ. They have been clothed in the white linen robe of His righteousness through the covenant established by His blood. As a result, they are commanded to follow after righteousness in spirit and truth. In other words, believers are to follow Jesus in the paths of righteousness through the powerful conviction and leading of the Spirit.[3]

The Christian life gives us a very distinct picture of how believers are to walk. They are to follow after the Holy Spirit in the ways of righteousness and obedience, be led by Him in subjection as a child of God, and walk in Him in submission and meekness according to the life they are called to live as a visible testimony to others. In summation, believers must follow after the essence of God's presence, be led by His presence, and walk in His presence. They must also sup and abide in it to ensure victory in this present world and to finish the course that leads them into the next world.

It is the presence of God's Spirit that ensures the environment is right for the Lord to intrude into our nominal lives and call us into the service of the extraordinary. His holy presence must be present to ensure that we are prepared to listen and properly respond in obedience. His abiding presence will determine the vision that we must have of Him in order to be prepared to receive and carry out our commission. Ultimately, His presence will lead us into His very glory, where our vision of Him will be enlarged and refined by a greater revelation of the depth and life we are being called to.

The secret to the Christian life is that since, we as believers, possess the life of Christ, we have the means to possess the focus or vision of Christ in His glory. As we maintain the integrity of this vision, we will allow the life of Christ to be worked in us resulting in revelation. Such revelation can only come forth out of obedience to God's Word.

---

[3] Psalm 23:3; John 10:25-27; Romans 4:1-9, 1 Corinthians 1:30; 1 John 1:7; Revelation 19:7-8

Developing Our Christian Life

It is as believers obediently walk according to the revelation they have received, that they will find their lives being consumed by the ongoing reality of Jesus in His glory. His glory will cause the old life and way in each of us to cease to be as we become more like our Lord in attitude and disposition. As the light of His glorious life consumes each of us, we will discover that His life is indeed pulsating through our very beings. As self-sufficiency ebbs out of us, and we are filled up by the very glory of heaven, we will realize that the power we walk in truly belongs to the Holy Spirit who is leading each of us in the way we must go. As the Spirit leads, He will also work Christ's disposition in us, while occasionally overshadowing us with the wisdom and revelation of heaven.

Following Moses into the life that caused him to encounter God's presence in different ways gives us a picture of what we will encounter as Christians. Ultimately, we should be led into a place where we can experience God's glory, revealing to us why our present ministration of glory is more excellent than the ministration of the Law. Instead of simply revealing the devastation of sin working in us, we will see how Jesus became sin for us so that we could be made into the righteousness of God.[4]

As believers, we take so much for granted. The presence of God was in the children of Israel's midst, but His glory was concealed in the Most Holy Place of the tabernacle. There was only one man who was invited to come and commune with God in this most holy place, at the mercy seat, between the cherubim, and that was Moses.[5]

Consider what Moses had to experience in his journey before he first encountered the presence of God. Think about what the children of Israel witnessed about God's presence on Mount Sinai. Some of the leaders of Israel supped in the presence of God, but ended up participating in idolatry. When God's presence came down outside of the camp, some of the people of Israel stood in the door of their tents to worship God, others went outside of the camp to worship Him, and Joshua was inside the tent worshipping, while Moses was talking to God face to face as a friend.

The difference between Moses and the children of Israel came down to the type of relationship that Moses had with God. When it comes to the New Testament Church, God came down in the flesh to tabernacle among His people, as well as give them His Holy Spirit so that the way could be opened for nominal man to experience the extraordinary life that is clearly developed in God's presence.

As Christians, the way has been clearly opened to us to have an intimate relationship as children with God. We have an open invitation to come and commune with our Lord. We have the means to worship God from the altar of our hearts, as we honor Him in the right spirit in light of

---

[4] 2 Corinthians 5:21
[5] Exodus 25:22

His truth. We have the glory of our Lord residing in our midst, as we are endowed with and surrounded by His presence.

As a result, there is no excuse as to why we as Christians fail to reflect the glory of our precious Lord. It is His glory that makes His people stand distinct. Sadly, there are those who have not really ascended spiritually into the mountain to establish a relationship in the presence of God. These people are easy to recognize because they become uncomfortable with the evidence of this presence in other people's lives.

The presence of God will continue to challenge, expose, and reveal the spiritual state of His people. What His presence often reveals are the attitudes, responses, and emphasis that His people have in regard to the world. The reason it reveals the relationship each of us has to the world is because many of God's people are not necessarily concerned about whether God is truly in their midst. They are not interested in meeting with Him and receiving from Him. After all, they have their associations with Him, religious identifications, noble causes, spiritual experiences, and personal forms of piety. They perceive themselves rich, even though they often lack spirit, life, and passion towards the matters of God.

Consider the day we live in. If the presence of God is missing, the light that is actually being reflected will reveal such a state. Without God's presence in the midst of His people, there is no true light in which people can properly walk. There is no real guidance or protection. Such a state will desensitize people in such a way that they will become like Samson, incapable of even discerning that the presence of the Lord has departed from their midst, leaving a spiritual vacuum that must somehow be filled.[6] Sadly, it will be filled with substitutes that are associated with fleshly desires and worldly philosophies and practices. The image that will be reflected will not be the life of Jesus, but various forms of darkness that present themselves as false, deceptive lights of religion and piousness.

As His people, we would assume that nothing would be tolerated or accepted unless God's presence has confirmed a matter and His glory has sanctified it. However, God's people react four ways to His presence. We have the example of Moses. He wanted more of God, and would not be content until he encountered Him in a greater way. However, you have people like Adam who hid from the presence of God because of sin. You have people like Cain who departed from the presence of God to become vagabonds, fugitives from God because they do not want to repent and come into submission to the righteous ways of God. Finally, you have people like King Saul. The presence of the Lord departs from them because of their independent spirit and rebellious ways.[7]

---

[6] Judges 16:20
[7] Genesis 3:8-10; 4:12-16; 1 Samuel 18:12

Developing Our Christian Life

People who hide or depart from the presence of God stand afar off from Him, and never learn how to worship Him in Spirit and truth. We also can see differences in people's relationship with God. There are those who step outside of their comfort zones to begin their journey to discover His presence, but they often must overcome the fear of the unknown to embark into the inner chambers of fellowship. Then, there are those who get as close as they can as a means to prepare themselves to enter into all that God has for them. In fact, these people's desire is to be a Moses who will end up standing in the presence of God and talking face to face with Him as a friend.

If people do not have the presence of God to gauge their spiritual condition, they will stray from that which marks the center focus of their lives. Each age has found those who consider themselves God's people actually drifting away from the center of what is true, right, and acceptable to God. The farther people get away from the center, the more indifferent, deluded, extreme, and insane they become in their religious beliefs and practices.

As believers, the test is simple. If the God of the Bible is not the center of our focus, understanding, hope, and purpose, then Jesus is not the foundation, the Gospel is not the power of God unto salvation, the Holy Spirit is not the One who is working in us, the Word will not be our final authority, and we will end up establishing our own form of truth or reality.

It is obvious that there is only one true Christian life. It is distinguished by the abiding presence of God within, the powerful presence of God from above, and the incredible presence of God that abounds. Clearly, His presence hides His saints in Jesus' life.

If the presence of God is missing from our life, we can be assured we are not born-again. If the presence of God is not obvious in the outer sanctuary of our lives, we can be assured that there is no real connection of fellowship to heaven. If the presence of God is absent from our churches, we need to close their doors because it is all a religious game. If it is missing from our activities, we can be certain that there will be no power or godly love present, and that such works will be considered reprobate by God.

We need God's presence to experience and walk out the life of Christ, but there must be total abandonment to our Lord. This requires inward consecration from any attachments of the world, as well as an outward dedication to the ways of righteousness. Like Peter, this often means Satan is allowed to sift us to ensure true conversion.

Perpetual conversion to the ways of God will establish a right attitude that allows us to learn what it means to take the faithful steps of Abraham towards God's promises, as well as develop a disposition to come to a true place of repentance like King David. Such repentance will end in contrition of spirit and brokenness of one's heart over sin. In summation, those who are far from God's presence need to repent for the darkness created by their unbelief.

Consider the following table in order to come to terms with God's presence. Meditate on the conditions that will ensure God's presence or cause it to lift. Prayerfully consider where you are on the following chart. Be open and quick to respond in a proper way to ensure the purity, integrity, and validity of your Christian life.

Example	Reaction to God's Presence	Type of glory that was reflected
Moses	Desired more of God.	God's holiness
Adam	Hid from it.	Independence
Cain	Departed from it	Hatred towards Righteousness
Samson	Unaware that it had lifted from him.	Perversion of the flesh.
Children of Israel	Stood afar from it.	Idolatry
King Saul	It departed from him	Rebellion
King David	Asked the Lord to not cast him from it.	Forgiveness and restoration of fellowship

We have tremendous examples to consider about God's presence. But how many believers understand the importance of experiencing and living the Christian life in light of His abiding presence? King David understood the importance of God's presence. He stated that it was in His presence that the fullness of joy would be realized. He went on to say his desire was to behold God's face in righteousness, for his soul would be satisfied, and he would be assured of awaking in His likeness.[8]

As Christians it is our responsibility to make sure that we come to the place where we walk in the presence of God, ensuring that we have fellowship and intimacy with Him. As promised by 1 John 2:6 and 3:2, by learning how to desire, seek, find, follow after, and abide in His

---

[8] Psalms 16:11; 17:15

presence, we will take on our Lord's likeness and reflect His wisdom, righteousness, sanctification, and redemption to the rest of the world.

As a Christian, what light are you walking according to? Are you actually taking on the likeness of Christ as you discover what it means to walk and abide in His presence?

***

We have taken quite a journey to discover the Christian life. I do hope in this spiritual odyssey that you have discovered what constitutes this extraordinary life that we know as the "Christian walk". It is not a religion or belief system. It is actually the abiding life of Christ in each of us that identifies us to this incredible walk. It is the presence of God that serves as a witness to its validity, as well as ensures that this incredible life is properly being developed and brought forth in us. It is the glory of Jesus shining forth through us that reflects the quality of this life to others.

As a Christian, I have had to endure many rough terrains in my spiritual life to discover and experience the real essence of my life in Christ. The terrain of my fleshly ways caused me to war against the Spirit. The terrain of my selfish disposition caused the truth to become shrouded in darkness, while the terrain of man's religion caused tremendous confusion in me. But, in the end God's faithfulness to reveal the source and essence of this life ultimately delivered me from unseen bondages and brought me through the drudgery and normalcy of the different terrains that had comprised the great barren wilderness of my soul. The journey also led me to the different mountains of His glory to be transformed into Jesus' very likeness in different ways.

Although this life has proved to be overwhelming, I have learned in such times that the old me is truly being consumed by the new man that is being established in me by the Spirit of God. At times, I have been weary with coming to places where my character revealed a great gulf that was separating me from that which is Spirit and life. Then, I had to choose righteousness and fling myself on the great Rock in faith. As a result, I have occasionally experienced brokenness over my sin, while at other times I have encountered His great strength to overcome. In some cases I have even found the place of rest, as He delivered me to the other side of my despair to discover the power and righteousness of His eternal character and His victorious life.

My spiritual pilgrimage has made me realize that my different encounters with God's presence are actually preparing me to live in His presence for eternity. The sanctifying work of the Holy Spirit to make me into Jesus' likeness as a means to reflect His glory is in preparation for that day when I will be no more for I will be consumed by His glory. In His glory I will enter into the place of unhindered rest, fellowship, service, and worship before His holy throne.

The closing challenge is simple. As a Christian, are you living the life of Christ in the presence of His Spirit in daily preparation to embrace the fullness of your inheritance in the next world? The Apostle Paul summarized it best in Ephesians 3:16-21,

> That he would grant you according to the riches of his glory, to be strengthened with might by his Spirit in the inner man; That Christ may dwell in your hearts by faith; that ye, being rooted and grounded in love, May be able to comprehend, with all saints, what is the breadeth, and length, and depth, and height, And to know the love of Christ, which passeth knowledge, that ye might be filled with all the fullness of God. Now unto him who is able to do exceedingly abundantly above all that we ask or think, according to the power that worketh in us, Unto him be glory in the church by Christ Jesus throughout all ages, world without end. Amen.

Book Four

THE POWER OF OUR TESTIMONIES

By
Rayola Kelley
Copyright © 2008

INTRODUCTION

One of the aspects of my Christian life that I have taken for granted for the past 30 years has been my testimony. Understanding the concept of testimony early in my Christian faith helped me to establish my Christian walk. This encouraged me to develop a greater testimony as I experienced the different points of spiritual growth.

Over the years I have asked Christians for their testimonies. The reactions have varied. One individual became furious with me, and rudely told me that since I was in her home, she was the one to ask the questions. Of course, she never asked me to give my testimony. On the other hand, other people would share about their different religious influences, affiliations, and experiences. But few have ever given me a testimony, and even fewer have ever bothered to ask me if I had one.

Recently, I have become aware that the Christianity that is being expounded today does not stress, teach, or explain the necessity of having a personal testimony. As a result, the edification that testimonies brought to God's people in the past is becoming extinct. Contrast, encouragement, or challenge is missing from much of the Church.

In our discipleship program, we required the disciples of Christ to give their testimonies. This has been one of the ways in which we are able to discern whether a person truly understands redemption, as well as exposes the level of a person's spiritual maturity.

Due to many misunderstandings about this issue, an in-depth teaching on testimonies was presented to those who were sitting under the auspice of Gentle Shepherd Ministries. This book is the product of the teaching and the testimonies that were presented.

It is our desire that Christians begin to understand the importance of their testimonies, and become more established in them. It is also our hope that the testimonies in this book will edify the reader in his or her spiritual journey.

1

WHAT IS A TESTIMONY?

As pointed out, one of my frustrations with the Church is that many Christians have no concept of testimony. When asked about their Christian testimony, I hear about their church affiliation, doctrine, pastor, and church programs. Such emphasis sounds religious, but is nothing more than sounding brass and tinkling cymbals. There is absolutely no substance behind any of it. The reason for this is because the church, doctrine, pastor, or programs cannot establish a testimony that will stand when tested, tried, and judged.

Consider what a testimony is. When you think about testifying in a court of law, you are actually verifying a matter. Your words become a matter of record that can be proven and confirmed in some way. Therefore, you are serving as an eyewitness who is bringing affirmation to something that is being established or has already been established based on evidence. This evidence results in personal conviction as to what is true. Therefore, when people give a testimony, they are actually testifying of something that they know without a doubt to be true because of the evidence already presented and what they have witnessed in their personal lives.

The next aspect of our testimony, as Christians, is what we are testifying about, as well as what record we are establishing as being true. This is where the confusion begins to cloud the real issue about testimonies. Are we testifying that a particular church, denomination, school of thought, philosophy, theology, or doctrine is true? Therefore, what are we declaring for the record to those around us?

The Apostle Paul gives us this insight in 1 Corinthians 2:2, "For I determined not to know any thing among you, save Jesus Christ, and him crucified." Clearly, the testimony we are to share as believers is not about churches, denominations, influential religious leaders, or beliefs. Our testimony should be about the Person of Jesus Christ.

Obviously, if we are testifying about matters surrounding a person, we must come from the premise of some type of evidence. According to the Apostle Paul, there are various evidences, including eyewitnesses, to verify the truth about Jesus. First, he was a personal eyewitness to the reality and revelation of Jesus. You have the inner core of those who were Jesus' followers, as well as others who were His disciples. These individuals witnessed His teachings and miracles. In fact, the Apostle

John stated that Jesus did so many miracles that the world could not contain all of the books that could have been written about them. Some watched Him die, while others prepared His body and placed Him in an empty tomb. Historical records written by such individuals as Josephus have verified all of this. And, we cannot forget that there were also over 500 eyewitnesses that testified of one aspect of His life—that He had actually risen from the grave. In fact, the main criterion of being an apostle of the New Church was that the person had to be an eyewitness of the life, ministry, death, burial, and resurrection of Jesus Christ. There were the disciples who also watched Him ascend to heaven with the promise that He would return one day.[1]

This brings us to the next part of a testimony. What should we be declaring about Jesus? Obviously, we must be affirming the record about Him that has already been established in the Word of God. It must be a living reality to our hearts. However, most professing Christians fail to properly answer this question about their testimony. Sadly, in my encounters many do not appear to have any consensus as to what they need to be declaring. The closest declaration is that Jesus "is my Savior."

If you have this premise to start from, count yourself fortunate. However, even this premise can lack understanding. It seems that more and more people do not have any real concept as to why Jesus is a Savior. In other words, what is He saving them from? Granted, they have some terminology down, but how many of these individuals possess any real meaning behind their statements or words? Obviously, they can talk the talk, but they still appear ignorant about the real matters surrounding Jesus Christ and His death on the cross.

As Christians, we can only declare what has already been established as truth. Obviously, our declaration is not based on blind faith but on something that has already been established, reinforced, and confirmed on a consistent basis for the past two thousand years. What every Christian should be testifying about is that the Gospel is indeed true.

What is the Gospel? The Apostle Paul declared that the Gospel is the power of God unto salvation.[2] I remember asking a person who belonged to a well-known cult how she knew that her cult was right about the matters of life and death. Her testimony was that she had this "burning in her bosom." Obviously, this woman was not beginning from any premise that had already been verified. She was beginning at the point of some emotional experience. In her mind, the experience confirmed her present conclusion.

When I asked this lady about what gospel her cult was advocating, she could not answer the question. She continued to declare that she

---

[1] John 21:23-25; Acts 1:2-11; 15-26; 9:1-19; 1 Corinthians 15:3-9
[2] Romans 1:16

knew her particular church was true in its claims because of the "burning in her bosom." However, her "burning" meant nothing to me. I was not looking for some type of experience, for even Satan can come as an angel of light and penetrate our innermost being with a destructive lie that will seem more real than the actual reality around us. Such lies will falsely confirm one's heretical belief or experience as he or she continue to remain blind to the destructive path that he or she is on. [3]

The Gospel I understand is not based on experience, but on actual evidence. I do not believe it blindly, nor do I follow it in some delusion based on wishful thinking. I do not hope it is true; rather, I believe that it is true because of the evidence that has confirmed and identified the source of my experiences. The source of my evidence is God.

Sadly, Christians are not much better at answering the question of what is the Gospel than the lady in the cult. After all, we as believers are commissioned to preach the Gospel. Recently, our missionary work was opened wide to the Hispanic people of our community. When posed with this question, some of these Hispanic people explained that to them preaching the Gospel meant taking the Word of God with them.

The Gospel is not the Word of God, but a message that has been firmly verified as being true by God's Words. As Christians, we are commissioned to preach a message that is found and confirmed in the Word of God. This message is the "good news" that has been extended to everyone who will believe it. We know this message is about the Person of Jesus Christ. In fact, He is the light in the Gospel that is often veiled by Satan to those who will not choose the way of faith towards God.[4]

We have already mentioned much of the Gospel. It is that Jesus died, was buried, and rose again. This is the consistent message of all those who truly have believed the Gospel of Jesus Christ.[5] You see the Apostle Peter proclaiming it in Acts 2:22-36. The Apostle Paul declared the same good news at different times. He also explained how Jesus was put to death, but how God raised Him up in three days. It was this same Jesus that he had met on the road to Damascus who forever changed his direction and life.[6]

This glorious message possesses the power of God unto salvation. Is it enough to quote the Gospel or must it be a reality? According to the Apostle Paul, it must become a reality by believing it in the heart. To believe something has the same intensity as saying, "Amen." "Amen" means "so be it." In other words, the matter is true, but it must be

---

[3] 2 Corinthians 4:3-5; 11:14
[4] Mark 16:15; 1 Corinthians 15:1-4; 2 Corinthians 4:3-6
[5] If you would like to understand the Gospel of Jesus Christ in a better way, see the author's, entitled, *The Presentation of the Gospel* that can be found in Volume 5 of her foundational series.
[6] Acts 13:16-39; 22:1-23; 26:1-23

realized and fulfilled in one's life to become a personal reality that changes and guides a person. And, once it is believed in the heart, a person will be born-again from above of water and Spirit.[7]

Once the person believes the Gospel in his or her heart and confesses that Jesus is Lord, that person will experience the new birth. This means that the Holy Spirit imparts the very life of Jesus into a person's inner being. As the new life is worked into a person, he or she begins to be transformed by the very disposition of Jesus in his or her perception, will, intellect, and emotions. It is the new life in a believer that begins to make him or her into a new creation. This new disposition also leads to developing a relationship with God through Jesus Christ. As Jesus stated, He is the way, the truth, and the life. This life comes through reconciliation with the Father. Reconciliation points to access into a relationship with God.[8]

The simple message of the Gospel is capable of saving a person. Consider the following testimony of *Marietta McCollough*. Notice how her desire to possess a greater revelation of Jesus Christ takes center stage in her life.

***

My parents divorced when I was four. I had always been raised in a Christian home, but never really knew who God was. In church we always sat in the pews that were a few rows from the front, and if we decided we were going to go to sleep, we would think twice, because Mom would thump us.

I always remembered from the time I was four that my mother, along with my siblings and me, kneeling down beside our beds and praying. When we were finished, we would then say the Lord's Prayer (Matthew 6:9-13). I knew in my heart it was a beautiful prayer. However, I never knew until years later what the prayer meant. I continued to go to church with my family. But I noticed that the kids in my church were not any different than the kids I hung around with at school. As a result, I could never really see any true salvation.

I remember as I was growing up, the saying my mother would always quote to me. It was Genesis 6:3a, "And the Lord said, My spirit will not always strive with man." I never really thought much about that verse until years later. My mom worked two jobs to support us. She was very strict with us as far as going to movies, bowling, playing, and so forth. Mainly, she did not want us to get caught up with worldly things. Now I can look back and see why, but at the time I was always angry because all my friends appeared to be having fun while I had to stay home.

Years went by, and I remember as a senior in high school I always wanted to become popular like the other girls. God honored my dream. I

---

[7] John 3:3, 5; Romans 10:9-10
[8] John 3:3, 5; 14:6; 2 Corinthians 5:17; Ephesians 2:13-17

Developing Our Christian Life

was elected Home Coming Queen during that year. But, even with all the excitement, I knew that there was still something else missing in my life.

Months later, on a Saturday afternoon, I was sitting on my front step crying, and seeking God for forgiveness. I asked Him into my heart. This encounter was brought about by an incident. The night before, after playing a basketball game, my girlfriend and I went out to have fun. We had a little too much fun, and I woke up driving down the middle of a bar pit about 20 feet away from hitting a telephone pole head on. God was gracious and merciful to spare my life.

After high school I went on to college. That summer I had an opportunity to get a good job, so I quit college and went to work full-time for an accountant. Just when I thought my life was under control, I felt there was something amiss in it. Sometimes I would go to church and see people jumping up and down. I was not used to this type of display, but I thought that this must be the way to get real with God. This is what I thought Christianity was at the time, even though it seemed weird to me. However, I was still empty inside.

At that time, I could see all my family and friends getting married and divorced, so I told myself that I was not going to get married until I was 27. A day before I turned 27, I married my husband, Don. Because Don knew God and went to church, I thought at the time that this was the right move to make. I never bothered asking God, because in my mind I was doing the right thing.

I decided since Don was a godly man, I would go with him to church. When we did manage to go, we were just in time for their religious hype and the sermon. In spite of all the religious activity, I would still come away empty. However, I knew I still needed to go because it was the right thing to do.

A few years went by and I met Krista Dinatale where I was working. I later learned that she was part of Gentle Shepherd Ministries. One Saturday, we decided to come in [to work] and bring projects up to date. While we were there, she started talking to me about Jesus. She asked me what my testimony was. I told her that I went to church. She stated, "No that is not your testimony." I just knew I had a blank stare on my face because no one had ever asked me for my testimony before. I didn't really know what one was, but I do remember when I was younger, people stood up and gave praises for the good things that had happened to them. Then, that is when she asked me if I was saved. I told her yes, and then she told me that is your testimony.

A few Sundays after the incident with Krista, I was attending church and they gave an altar call. I went forward with a heavy heart, because I just knew something was wrong with me. I was not happy like all the other Christians. They prayed for me, but I did not feel any movement of the Holy Spirit. Later I realized that He was missing from the many activities of this church.

About six months to a year later I started going to the meetings conducted by Gentle Shepherd Ministries. At the time, we had Bible studies on Thursday and Saturday evenings in a private home. I started to see the difference between religion and the real Jesus. I could see truth and sincerity being preached and taught. I knew I wanted what the others had. I asked God to help me find what they had through prayer and reading the Scriptures.

God has helped me grow one step at a time. Sure, I know I will go through some tough times, but I am willing to do what it takes to have all of Him. I look back now and know that God has really met every need of my life. Without knowing Him I would still be empty and out in the world trying to find out who I am. The Scripture that sticks in my mind is Jeremiah 29:13, And ye shall seek me, and find me, when you shall search for me with all your heart."

2

THE PURPOSE OF SALVATION

Up to this point we have been talking about the Gospel. Jesus died, was buried, and rose again on the third day. However, there is one part of the Gospel that has not been clearly presented. It is why Jesus died for us.

It is not unusual to observe how people can become quite sentimental towards Jesus dying for each of us. However, the reason He died for us will quickly replace any sentimental notion with sobriety. Jesus did not die for us because He was some noble man, nor are we worthy of such a sacrifice. As you truly consider His ordeal on the way to Calvary, there was no reason for Him to die. Other than saving a criminal named Barabbas, His death seemed useless, senseless, and unfair. From all appearances, He was not noble for dying on a cross. Rather, He was a fool to allow people to crucify Him.

The Word of God declares that Jesus was not some noble man, but that He was the sacrificial Lamb of God. When you study the concept of the sacrificial lamb, you will realize it has to do with atonement and death. The first lamb we usually remember in the Bible is in relationship to the first Passover. An innocent lamb had to be sacrificed; its blood marked the doorposts of each Hebrew home to spare the Jewish family from the judgment of death upon every firstborn. Without the identification of the blood, the firstborn sons, as well as the firstborn of the flocks would die that night.[1]

As the Law was set up, it explained the necessity of animal sacrifices. The blood of these animals was used to make atonement for sin. Atonement was used as the means to cover a person's sin. Therefore, when God looked down after a sacrifice was made for sin, the sin was covered, sparing the person from tasting the consequences of judgment pronounced by the Law upon such actions. These sacrifices were ongoing, but even they could not cover certain sins such as blatant idolatry, adultery, witchcraft, and murder. The penalty for such sins was death.[2]

The purpose of the Law was to show man that he was a transgressor against the holy Law of God, doomed to taste the judgment pronounced upon all sin—that of death or separation from God. This brings us back to God's sacrifice. The Word tells us that Jesus Christ was the Lamb of

---

[1] Exodus 12:1-30
[2] Leviticus 16; 20:10; 24:17; Hebrews 9:6-7, 11-22; 10:4, 10-22

God who took away the sin of the world. As a result, the Gospel begins with the reality that Jesus died for our sin. It was God who provided the only sacrifice that would take away all sins and serve as the means of reconciliation between God and man.[3]

Jesus dying for our sins is the main theme of the Gospel. It is about God redeeming us from the influences, workings, and activities of sin upon our soul. This is a revelation that needs to reach into our very being. The reason is because some Christians have no idea that they are sinners. They think Jesus died to spare them from certain unpleasant aspects of life. However, Christ did not die so we could have a perfect life; He died so that we could obtain life through Him.

Sin is a robber, murderer, and is out to destroy everyone who gives way to its dictates. It robs of truth, kills hope, and destroys any aspect of life. Consider the following testimony of *Javier Animas*. Born in Mexico, he has been in the United States for over 20 years. It was in America that he discovered and met Jesus Christ as his Lord and Savior. He and his family have been part of the Gentle Shepherd Ministries' family since 2006. They are very evangelistic in their community.

As you will see, in his former life, Javier struggled with various issues throughout his life due to his home environment and the influences of the culture and the world around him. He finally came face-to-face with the real issue of his inner struggles, that of sin.

***

This is my testimony, but first I want to give thanks to God because He allows me to give him glory and honor. He has given me an opportunity to testify of His greatness. I think that He has chosen me since before I was born. But I chose to follow a wrong path. I willfully started down the broad path by making bad decisions.

This path started when I was a young child. I would behave badly; but, about five years ago Jesus Christ's mercy became real to me. Before I received Him, I had tried everything that was called sin. I was a very sinful man, but I repented. Do not think that after I received Christ all the problems went away. But I didn't sin anymore and I separated myself from it. There was a huge difference in me.

Let me give you some examples. In the past when a problem would come up, I would try solving it my own way based on what would work for me. It didn't matter if I had to lie or sin in some other way. If a rumor would come up, or if someone rebuked me, I would not stay quiet. I would rebel against everything and everyone. I used to like to steal, lie, fornicate, and do all other sorts of things. Now I clearly handle matters

---

[3] John 1:29; Romans 2:12; 3:20; 6:23; 7:7, 12-13; 1 Corinthians 15:3-4; 2 Corinthians 5:18-19; Galatians 3:24; Ephesians 2:14-18; 1 Timothy 1:9

differently. With the wisdom that my Lord gives me I can say, "no" to all such temptations and sin.

Now I am able to tell you that if you put Him before all else in your life, He will deliver you from all wrong. I lie not to you about such a matter. God is good and His mercies are everlasting. By now you can see that I used to be a very bad person. I would like to tell you in detail just how much of a sinner I was, but that would take too long. Sin was my path and my way of life.

Long story short, I was a big sinner, but God forgave me, and now here I am testifying about His forgiveness and salvation. I am not ashamed of the Gospel of Christ. I want to serve Him all the days of my life, for one day I shall see Him.

I hope this testimony edifies you in some way. I know that some of these other testimonies have edified me, and still continue to do so. I love to see how many other people have repented of their sins, and are saved through the mercy and grace of our Lord. Now they are testifying about it, and telling others where God has brought them in their lives. This shows me that God is the same yesterday, today, and will be forever. Amen.

***

Christians often find themselves in various struggles in their new life in Christ. The problem is that many consider Christ's salvation in light of being saved from their present life situation, but not from their way of thinking, being, and living. Jesus does not save us from life itself with it challenges, losses, hardships, and toil. He saves us from how sin is influencing and working in our lives. It is the influence of sin on our fallen condition that justifies selfishness, personal rights, and wrong conclusions. It is the workings of sin upon our deceptive heart that makes us bitter, judgmental, and unforgiving. It is the activities and ways of sin that makes us prefer darkness, along with its ways of unbelief and death, to the life and liberty we could find in Jesus. This is the reality of sin in operation.

As you consider the aspects of the influences of sin, you will realize that Jesus saves us from the dictates, claims, and the destructive ways of sin. However, He must also save us from the workings of sin. This means we must be saved from how sin is now affecting our lives through the ungodly influences that have conditioned us in our perception, mindsets, conclusions, and lifestyles. He must also save us from the activities of sin that operate through temptations, fleshly lusts, and the attractions of the world.

The misconception for most people is that Jesus saves us from hell. In reality, Jesus saves us from the consequences of sin that is in operation. The consequence of sin is death or separation from God. Such salvation will spare us from God's judgment of death upon sin.

Therefore, we are spared from experiencing the eternal damnation of the lake of fire. The reason we are being spared in this manner is because we deserved such punishment.

I used to think that Jesus came to save me from hell. As I began to understand that salvation is deliverance, I realize that salvation is for now.[4] In other words, I do not need to be saved from hell in my present state; I needed to be saved from the ways of spiritual death that will ultimately lead me to the place of utter separation from God.

However, once a person is in hell, it is too late for him or her to be delivered. It is appointed for man to die once, then judgment.[5] Hell is simply a temporary holding place of judgment for those who refuse to receive deliverance in this present world from the consequences of sin. Since the consequence of sin is a permanent death or separation from God, hell will eventually be cast into the lake of fire that will burn forever. Both environments will compliment those who wanted no part of God. Both are void of God's life, presence, and intervention. God will simply be honoring the person's desire to be free from any aspect of His life, character, ways, and intervention.

Meanwhile, people need to be saved from the sin that reigns, perverts, and entangles them into the ways of death. God's mercy has to reach through the reign, perversion, and entanglements of sin to bring hope of deliverance. Those who have been saved had to be drawn to the hope of life by the Father. The Holy Spirit had to convict them of their sin, as well as their need for righteousness to avoid the judgment to come.[6] It is only as the Father draws and the Spirit convicts, that the sin laden-sinner begins to hear the invitation of Jesus, "If any man thirst, let him come unto me, and drink" (John 7:37b).

Jesus explained the importance of His invitation in John 4:14 to the Samaritan woman who was given a verbal invitation to partake of this Living Water, "But whosoever drinketh of the water that I shall give him shall never thirst, but the water that I shall give him shall be in him a well of water springing up into everlasting life." This water is what produces everlasting life.

Surprisingly, over the years, I have heard many Christians talk about Jesus' deliverance in terms of circumstances, but some of these individuals have failed to realize Jesus' true deliverance is not of a physical nature, but of a spiritual one. God's love did not reach through circumstances to save people from unpleasant conditions. Rather, He reached through the darkness of men's souls with His light to save them from the ways of death. This light is the very life of Jesus.[7]

---

[4] 2 Corinthians 6:2
[5] Hebrews 9:27; Revelation 20:14-15
[6] John 6:44; 16:7-11
[7] John 1:4-5, 3:14-21

Clearly, Jesus' salvation is not associated with deliverance from bad circumstances but from spiritual darkness. The Apostle Paul made this statement in regards to this matter, "But God commendeth his love toward us in that, while we were yet sinners, Christ died for us. Much more then, being now justified by his blood, we shall be saved from wrath through him" (Romans 5:8-9).

Understanding what God is saving us from is of the utmost importance because it is going to determine the type of attitude that will be developed towards God and His redemption. If people think God is delivering them out of an unpleasant life, they will see Him as "a daddy" who is at their beck and call to spoil them with the things of the world, ensuring a wonderful life. Or, perhaps they will think of Him as a "Santa Claus" who will fulfill their list of desires.

However, if a person realizes he or she has been saved from the consequence of sin, he or she will develop an attitude of appreciation and gratitude for God's mercy and grace. His mercy reminds such people that He has refrained from bringing deserved judgment upon them. His grace will reveal that He is showing favor to them, not because of who they are, but because of who He is. Such people will realize that God did not save them *from* their despairing life; rather, He saved them *unto* His everlasting life.

People who see God as saving them from what is unpleasant never change their attitude about God or life. People who see God as providing the means of inheriting eternal life through the redemption of Jesus approach matters from a state of humility. Clearly, the premise in which people start their spiritual journey will determine not only their attitude, but whether they will finish the course.

The other aspect of salvation is that Jesus did not save us to change our circumstances; rather, He saved us to make us into new creations. The real work of salvation involves changing the inner man, not the outward circumstances.[8] This means that the inward disposition is being changed so that sin can no longer influence it in the ways of darkness, work the ways of death into its perception, and use its activities to lead a person into the traps of destruction.

It is only as believers grow in the knowledge of the depth of their sin and in the revelation of God's love and redemption will their state of humility enlarge. Such enlargement will cause them to grow in gratitude. The Apostle John stated the type of affect God's benevolent action would have on one who had an understanding of it, "We love him, because he first loved us" (1 John 4:19).

The Apostle Paul's attitude towards Jesus' life being realized in him was one of total abandonment. He counted all matters loss or dung so

---

[8] 2 Corinthians 4:16; 5:17; Ephesians 4:22-24

that he could win Christ.[9] He gave this testimony in relationship to his conversion,

> This is a faithful saying, and worthy of all acceptance, that Christ Jesus came into the world to save sinners, of whom I am chief. Nevertheless, for this cause I obtained mercy, that in me first Jesus Christ might show forth all long-suffering, for a pattern to them who should hereafter believe on him to life everlasting. Now unto the King eternal, immortal, invisible, the only wise God, be honor and glory forever and ever. Amen (1 Timothy 1:15-17).

The question is what have you asked Jesus to save you from? Perhaps it is some circumstance. Maybe you are experiencing a great loss. However, the real reason Jesus died for you and me was to save us from the workings and consequences of sin. If you have not made peace with Jesus at this point, you must consider whether you have been born again of the Spirit and of His Word.

Consider the following testimony of *Rich Ralston*. He has been with Gentle Shepherd Ministries since 2005. He has also been involved with the local rescue mission, as well as helped form an international ministry. His testimony reveals his search for something that would address his inner struggles.

***

When I was a boy, my parents told me there was a God. This declaration was due to the fact that when I was a baby, I almost died from a defect with my mitral heart valve. After radiation treatments on my heart, a lady doctor told my mother the only hope I had was for them to pray. My mother reminded me once in awhile about God sparing my life, but we never attended church. I can only remember going to church three times as a boy.

As a teenager, my attitude about God changed from thinking that God cared about me, to a doubtful and rebellious attitude. My mother, having a nervous breakdown and spending three years in a mental hospital, brought on such thinking. I could not understand how God would allow my mother to suffer in such a way.

When I started attending college, I became involved in Buddhism and Karate. I was trying to find purpose in life, and peace within myself, but I could never find any peace. It was during my college years that I was influenced by philosophies that caused me to become an agnostic in my worldview. I wanted somebody to prove to me that God was real before I would believe.

After I graduated from college and got married, I worked with a Christian and a Jehovah's Witness. Between these two men asking me questions and trying to share their faith with me, they sparked within me a new interest to find out more about God. All this time, I still had an

---

[9] Philippians 3:7-8

empty feeling inside about my real purpose for living, as well as lacking peace from within.

I began praying to God to show me who He really was. I did this for months. In 1978 I decided that maybe I needed to clean up my life before God would be interested in me. My wife and I decided to buy a juicer, and to start eating healthier. I met a lady name Louise who sold juicers.

Louise began to ask me questions about what I thought about God. I told her I had no use for religion. She agreed with me and told me what really was important was a personal relationship with God through His Son, Jesus Christ. She told me that God made a way for me to have peace with Him by what His Son, Jesus Christ, did when He died on the cross for my sins. She told me that, "The wages of sin is death, but the gift of God is eternal life through Jesus Christ, our Lord" (Romans 6:23).

She reinforced my hopeless condition when she told me that, "All have sinned and come short of the glory of God" (Romans 3:23). She pointed out that I needed a Savior to forgive me of my sins. She went on to explain that salvation was a gift of God, not something that I had to work for or earn.

Louise was making it clear that I could never be good enough in my own efforts to achieve eternal life. "For by grace you are saved by faith, and it is not of yourselves, it is the gift of God: not of works, least anyone should boast" (Ephesians 2:8-9).

She went on to explain that Jesus Christ was the only way to salvation. Therefore, I needed to receive Him into my heart as my Lord and Savior, as well as ask Him to forgive me of my sins. "For as many as received him, to them he gave power to become the sons of God, to those who believe on His name" (John 1:12).

I prayed with her and received Jesus Christ as my Lord and Savior. I felt like a heavy weight had been lifted off my shoulders. For the first time in my life I knew I had real peace with God. I then realized that I now had real purpose for my life, and that was to get to know this God who forgave my sins and gave me eternal life.1 John 5:13 states, "I write these things to you who believe in the name of the Son of God so that you may know that you have eternal life."

I felt like I was a new person inside because all the guilt from the past was gone, and I had a new sense of purpose and peace within me. The Bible says, "If any man be in Christ he is a new creature: old thing are passed away; behold all things are become new" (2 Corinthians 5:17). This is how I came to know the Lord Jesus Christ.

***

Give it a Try

As Christians, each of us should have a record or testimony of our salvation. If you do not possess such a record, you better settle the issue of your eternal destination right now. Humble yourself before the Lord.

Acknowledge your sin and your inability to save yourself. Ask Him to come into your heart and save you from the consequences of your wretched condition of death and destruction. By faith, receive Jesus into your heart as your powerful Savior and risen Lord.

However, if you truly have received the Lord, but have never really given your personal testimony, it is time you give it a try. It should be a natural extension of the life you are establishing in Christ. If you are still unsure about what an effective testimony entails, Rich Ralston has prepared a simple outline that you can easily follow in preparing the record of your salvation. All you have to do is choose and insert the right answer.

If you don't mind, I would like to briefly share with you what Jesus means to me. Before I received Jesus Christ as my Lord and Savior, my understanding about Him was very limited/somewhat limited/well understood/ confusing to me.

I grew up in a family that knew/didn't know/pretended to know the Lord. Our family regularly attended/seldom attended/never attended church. Principles about God were taught to me/ seldom taught/never taught by parent/parents. My life before I came to know Jesus lacked direction/lacked real purpose/was without meaning/ was filled with emptiness/ filled with anger or bitterness or resentment/ filled with fear/ filled with uncertainty/ was without love/etc.

I was told about Jesus by my mother/father/relative/friend/pastor/co-worker/while attending church service/listening to a radio/television program/etc. He/she/they shared Bible Scriptures such as Isaiah 64:6; Romans 3:10, 23; 6:23; etc. that explained to me that I was a sinner and needed a Savior. He/she/they also told me that I must confess and repent of my sins, and receive Jesus Christ as my Lord and Savior in order to have eternal life. He/she/they also told me that Romans 10:9, 10 says in simple terms "That if you confess with your mouth, Jesus is Lord, and believe in your heart that God raised him from the dead, you will be saved. For it is with your heart that you believe and are justified, and it is with your mouth that you confess and are saved." I asked Jesus into my heart and life on date (if you know it).

Since I have confessed and repented of my sins, and have received Jesus as my Lord and Savior, my life has changed for the better. I know that I truly have eternal life. I now have purpose, direction, and hope for today as well as the future. Even though I may have problems in my life, Jesus said in the Book of Hebrews 13:5, "I will never leave you nor forsake you." I know He is with me forever.

3

OVERCOMING HINDRANCES

One might wonder why it is important to have an established testimony. The Apostle John gives us insight into the necessity for having a powerful testimony, "And they overcame him by the blood of the Lamb, and by the <u>word</u> <u>of their</u> <u>testimony</u>; and they loved not their lives unto the death" (Revelation 12:11). (Emphasis added.)

We will overcome with our testimony. Needless to say, our testimony is established upon the everlasting covenant that was verified and sealed by the blood of the Lamb. Our testimony, in a sense, serves as an initial stake in which we can consider the matters of life. If a matter does not line up to, compliment, agree with, or reinforce our testimony, we have the simple means of discerning it. In the case of lies, fears, and heresy, we will be able to recognize and flee from their influences in our lives.

This is why testimonies must grow. I have been born again for over 30 years. If there were no indications of growing, changing, and becoming mature in my Christian life, I would have to examine myself to see if I am really in the faith. I realize there are different levels of maturity among believers for various reasons, but there should be some indication that a person has truly come to an understanding of salvation. Even the Apostle John makes reference to the fact that there is a witness, or knowing, in one's spirit concerning his or her spiritual condition. Of course, one must not be under the darkness of delusion to ensure he or she is able to honestly examine his or her fruits.[1]

There was a story about a man who participated in a church program that had to do with spiritual growth. One of the requirements in the program was that everyone needed to write out their testimony. When it came to his written testimony, all he had was a date written down. When questioned about the date, he stated that he was saved on that day. Before that day nothing really happened, and after that date, nothing of significance had happened. Not long after this incident, this man ended his life.

Our testimony is not based on some date, but on the reality that Jesus Christ came into our lives to save us. This man's stake had no substance. It could not change his life, bring meaning to his existence, or serve as a place of hope. It was simply a date where he said a prayer or made some kind of confession, but it never went any further. Granted, he

---

[1] 2 Corinthians 13:5; 1 John 5:5-13

may have changed some aspects about his lifestyle, but the inner man never was enlarged to embrace the impossible, the incredible, and the magnificent.

Christianity is a life. It is the life of Christ in us, and His life is eternal. Therefore, the one aspect of His life is that it is ongoing. It is meant to change, enlarge, and bring purpose to every believer. Life that remains stagnant in a believer becomes unbearable. Life that lacks challenge becomes aimless. Life that is never enlarged by learning lessons of life becomes spiritually small and dull. Life that is not disciplined becomes useless. Clearly, the life of Christ must be experienced and lived out in every arena of our lives. It is meant to make us into new creations that become living expressions of our Lord and Savior.

Years ago there was a pastor who challenged the group I was part of to consider whether we had grown in our testimonies. As I considered my testimony, I realized I had become more arrogant in what I knew about the Bible, but was going backwards as far as my character and lifestyle. I also realized I could not be honest about my present testimony. As a result, I hid my hypocrisy behind a spirit of self-righteousness, while trying to give the outward impression that my spiritual life was on target. However, this man's challenge did not escape my conscience.

Yearly, I try to challenge those who are under my care to consider whether they have grown spiritually. There are reasons why people's testimonies are not growing. Let us now consider these reasons.

1) The first reason a testimony is not growing is because a person is not born again. Many people claim salvation based on some religious association. As stated, no one but Jesus can save a person. Therefore, if an individual has not made peace with God through the redemption of Jesus Christ, he or she is still miserably lost in his or her sins. If you are such a person, you need to go back to the Gospel message, ask forgiveness, and receive the complete work of Jesus' redemption in your heart.

2) The second reason a testimony is not growing is because a person is walking in some type of sin. The Apostle John is clear that if you are truly born again, you will not be able to walk in sin. In other words, the new disposition (heart and spirit) in you will not be comfortable with sin.[2] Even though you may be giving in to some type of sin, the conviction and war taking place in the spirit will be strong and unbearable. Eventually, you will give way to the convicting power of the Spirit because you cannot stand the void sin is causing in your life.

3) Another reason that believers' testimonies do not grow is because they are not developing a healthy attitude towards God

---

[2] Ezekiel 36:26-27; 1 John 3:8-10

and life. This is due to religious and worldly influences and preferences. Man's religion creates a cult mentality where people are indoctrinated by man's interpretation of Scripture. As a result, they are not open to the Spirit of God to challenge, change, and bring proper instruction. The influences of the world will cause spiritual dullness in a believer. He or she will lose his or her edge to properly discern that the life of Christ is either being drowned out by the demands of the world, or it is being sucked out of the person due to unholy agreement with the spirit of the world.
4) The fourth reason that a testimony fails to develop is because the person has not decided to follow Jesus. It is a matter of consecration. Such an individual is simply playing the religious game to get by while he or she is living life according to personal preferences.
5) In other cases where testimonies are becoming stagnant, Christians are actually angry with God. God has failed to bow down to these people's way of thinking. In reality, these people are fleshly and immature. Their reason for being Christians is not because they realize they need salvation, but because they see it as a means to benefit their self-serving ways.
6) The final reason Christians' testimonies do not grow is because they have made bad decisions due to ingratitude and selfishness. As a result, they are not obeying God, but walking in unbelief.

It is important to point out that if a Christian is a new convert, he or she should at least possess a testimony of being born again into the kingdom of God. Such a person may not understand the implications of his or her new birth, but he or she should understand that Jesus saved him or her from sin.

On the other hand, people who have been Christians for at least five years should have a good foundation as to what they believe. Those who have been part of the kingdom of God for ten years should be able to share about experiencing God in personal ways. Christians who have tasted of the Spirit and Word for 15 years should be expressing maturity in attitudes and actions. They should be displaying godly wisdom.

As you can see, there should be evidence of some type of spiritual growth in a Christian. This growth is not based on what a person is doing for God. Rather, it is based on what the person is allowing God to do in and through him or her. Salvation clearly is His work and bidding.

If you consider your testimony and it has not grown, then examine the above reasons as to why it is stagnant. Once you identify the reason, then you will be able to match the problem with the intent to right the wrong attitude. In fact, you will be able to see a correlation between what is preventing you from growing in your testimony with the following attitudes or practices that could be present in your life.

We have already stipulated that in the first scenario a person needs to be born again. Today there are many making a confession of Jesus, but how many of these individuals have truly been born again? Perhaps, they have failed to recognize their hopeless plight due to the influence, workings, and activities of sin? Maybe it was an emotional whim or wishful thinking for them to go forward and go through confession and prayer. However, if it did not eventually go beyond the mental and emotional arenas into the heart where it became truth, one cannot be assured of being saved. A person must truly be born again in the spirit if he or she is going to inherit eternal life.[3]

When people are walking in sin, there is also a tendency to ignore, deny, or justify it away. Therefore, all tendencies toward sin are to simply delude each individual about his or her particular spiritual condition. Each believer must demand personal integrity up front towards the Word of God.

The Word of God is sharp and meant to rip away any false cloak or justification to expose the sin that is reigning. At this point, a person must repent by agreeing with God's evaluation about a matter, and turning from any independence, self-sufficiency, or right to have life on his or her terms. This is best summarized as denying self through godly repentance and total abandonment from the ways of the world, the flesh, and self-fulfillment. It is total abandonment that allows a person to abide in Jesus. If a person is abiding in Christ, he or she will not give in to the reign of sin.

Wrong preferences point to idolatry. People, who are idolatrous, prefer and love the world more than God. Their heart possesses the wrong treasures and their minds are being conformed to this present world. Idolatry always finds it source in the focus of the affections of one's heart.[4]

Jesus' instruction to His disciples to deny self, pick up their cross, and follow Him was and continues to be simple. However, to execute it can prove to be challenging. Who wants to deny self the right to life in order to learn the discipline of obedience through faith towards God? Who wants to taste death to the self-life in order to be prepared to follow Christ? And, who wants to follow Christ into uncertain territory to simply gain His life? However, this is the consecrated life. In spite of the justification for avoiding such a life, it is not an option, but a natural response of those who are truly disciples of Jesus. It will bring His followers into agreement with God about all matters regarding Him and the life He has made available to each of us.

---

[3] John 3:3, 5
[4] Matthew 16:24-26; John 15:22; Colossians 3:2; Hebrews 3:12-15; 4:12

Developing Our Christian Life

The reason most people become angry with God is because they have a very high opinion of themselves. In other words, they feel they deserve the best. In reality, they deserve hell, but their arrogance has blinded them to the spirit of pride that is freely operating in their lives. Such people give the impression that Jesus did not really die for their sin; rather, He died because they were worthy of such sacrifice. As a result, they are totally missing the spirit or intent as to why Jesus had to redeem each of us on the cross. Since they do not understand the basis of the Gospel, they are failing to come to terms with His mercy. Mercy, not pride, produces humility and gratitude that allows one the freedom to embrace His grace in an appropriate way. However, these people are operating within jealousies, insecurities, anger, bitterness, resentment, unforgiveness, and hatred.[5]

People, who walk in unbelief towards the Lord, have no fear of the Lord. As a result, they walk in the foolishness of rebellion and delusion. They will continue to make the wrong decisions because they will not recognize God's authority in their life. As a result, God will not be able to bless them, as they continue to make the wrong decisions because there are no boundaries or discipline in place.

Each believer must remember that he or she will face God and give an account to the Lord of all, as to why he or she did not establish a powerful testimony. There will be no excuse on judgment day for spiritual immaturity. God has given us the necessary tools to be established upon the Rock of ages.

Consider *Carrie Seaney's* following testimony. Carrie has been part of this ministry for over 20 years. She has a powerful way of sharing her testimony through song and has made six CDs. She is an elementary teacher, acknowledging the grave importance of this mission field. She is ever striving to enlarge her abilities to reach her potential. Her initial foundation in regard to her Christian faith was founded on her religion. Consider her struggles to wade through the different obstacles of sin, idolatry, deception, and pride in order to come to terms with Jesus.

***

My life is a gift of grace. God has been faithful to bring me to the place of great need. I need Jesus and His Gospel. On the other hand, Jesus brought me to the place of decision. By His mercy, grace, love, and faithfulness, I decided to love the truth. The truth proclaims Jesus is the Son of God, God Incarnate, the Messiah, and my personal Savior. Within my heart, He has put the need to serve Him and proclaim the Good News of His death, burial, and resurrection. He has brought me from darkness into the light.

My journey from the darkness to the Light began with a bad decision. As a very young child, I opened myself up to the demonic realm. Instead

---

[5] Matthew 6:15; Romans 12:3; Hebrews 12:15; James 3:13-17; 1 John 2:9-11

of turning to Jesus to be my friend when faced with loneliness and despair, I embraced fantasy and imaginary friends. These imaginary friends, Leanna and Tommy, were demons with powerful rights in my life. They filled me with lies and worked treachery within my heart. The treachery and lies eventually led to wanting my father to die, even praying he would die. This produced tremendous condemnation and unbearable darkness within me.

Unfortunately, my journey from the darkness to the Light has its starting point in religion. As far back as I can remember my family attended church every time the doors were open. We could have been fighting on the way to church, but the moment our red Mercury, with the sticker boldly declaring, "I love Sunday School", pulled into the parking lot, we put our game faces on. Our family became the model of the pious Christian family.

In Sunday school, I knew all the right answers to the questions, but I did not know Jesus. He was a concept, not my Lord. I believed I sincerely received Jesus into my heart when I was young, but I did not live a victorious life in Christ. In seventh grade, I watched a video series about the End Times. The series impacted me greatly. I remember praying to God that I would choose Him, rather than give in under the pressure of death.

My teenage years were spent seeking recognition in sports, academics, and religion. At eighteen, while traveling alone from Oregon to Idaho, I rolled and totaled the bronco I was driving. I remember thinking to myself in the midst of the accident that I could have died. I know without the shadow of a doubt that God intervened on my behalf. After all, I should have been killed. The driver's side was totally smashed. Others confirmed the possible ramifications of it after they saw the vehicle and witnessed the fact that I was not injured or dead.

Still sober from the near-death experience, while at a "Christian" retreat, I asked God to really know Him like the people in the Bible. From this point, the darkness from my sin began to become an incredible burden. I could no longer keep my sins hidden behind closed doors and religious cloaks. My skepticism became apparent. My immaturity became glaringly obvious. My anger and hatred raised their ugly heads. My selfishness and arrogance became a noose around my neck. I began to withdraw and isolate myself. I hated life as well as myself.

From this point, my journey from darkness to the Light started to show signs of hope. I was sitting outside the college dorm of one of my friends, working up the courage to be sociable. For some weeks, I had been thinking about suicide. For no merit of my own, Jesus simply met me. I don't know why I spoke to Him, but He was there with me. Pathetically, I told Him that He could have me if He wanted me. I was washed with such light and hope. I felt so clean. I went in and told my friends. They looked at me like I was nuts. I had never had so much

Developing Our Christian Life

hope. As a result, I did not care what they thought. I remember saying over and over, "Jesus is real. He is real!"

I would love to say that everything was perfect from that point on, but it wasn't. I went on a few detours. Life was not turning out the way that I had dreamed it would. I was not married. I believed that I was not supposed to be anything but a wife and mother. Yet, I was sent to be a part of the new yearlong student teaching program. I was terrified.

At this point in my life, I truly believed that I was stupid, and I was pretty sure a requirement for teaching was intelligence. My game plan was to hide as much as possible; however, the program was not set up for sliding by unnoticed. I was not prepared or disciplined enough to succeed. In the eighth month of the nine-month program, I had a nervous breakdown. I had passed enough credits to earn a degree in Applied Studies with an emphasis in education.

With this failure to burden me, I took a job working with children who had severe behaviors. I took the job because I felt incompetent to do anything else, and it was a way of punishing myself for my failure. It was horrible. I quit after eight months. I went from job to job, but always ended up back in a classroom. I was miserable, so once again I called out to God for help.

I moved in with a roommate and began to attend her church. There was a handsome man who met my standards and we became friends. I was driving to my parents' house, when God spoke to me. I had a decision to make. Did I want this man or God? Without much thought, I said aloud, "I choose You, Jesus." Within three weeks, there was no man and I walked through the door into Rayola, Jeannette, and Krista's front room.

I was a sad case. I had gone to church my entire life, and I knew nothing of the Word of God. I didn't even know what "God Incarnate" meant. But I did know that the truth was being presented to me. I had a wall of skepticism up, but inside I was crying out, "Jesus, Jesus!" I knew that this was my chance to know Jesus. I went home and called for another appointment. Again, I cried out to God. Please God, please have Rayola ask me to the fellowship.

Unsure as to whether she was stepping over some line since I was already attending a church, Rayola cautiously invited me to attend their fellowship. I attended and drank in the Word of God. The first thing to go was my fantasy life that had been a part of my life since I was real young. Then, with encouragement from Rayola, I enrolled to go back to college to get my teaching degree. Without her support, I would have quit again.

About three months into my internship, I moved in with Krista. When I moved in with her, I left a lot of my old life behind. I began to hold the line with family and friends, even allowing God's sword to come down in relationships so that I could know Jesus. Krista's testimony that she lived every moment of every day exposed my sin and became a means of contending for my soul.

Clearly, I was not an easy person to deal with. I still had unresolved issues plaguing me, as well as refusing to give up my rights to protect myself from being vulnerable before others. When I asked Krista why she put up with me, she told me God told her to. After a year, God brought a separation between Krista and me. I needed to grow up and discover my own identity in Christ. I had always hidden behind family, religious cloaks, and even friends.

I was sitting on the fence, refusing to make a decision to take responsibility for my own life in Christ. I was now all alone, just my demons and I. Feeling rejected and angry, I stormed at God. I was doubting my salvation, and in my rebellion, I was beginning to set my path on destruction. Then, He met me. Using Krista, He said, "Just take one step at a time." I made my decision. I chose to love the Truth one step at a time. So, I take my journey from the darkness to the Light one step at a time.

The Light is Jesus. He is my Savior, my friend, my hope, my husband, my help, my God, my King, my Lord, my place of peace, my future, my Teacher, my Shepherd, the Giver of my life, my Creator, and my Master.

4

LEARNING OF JESUS

Obviously, our testimony will grow. Granted, the actual record will not change, but our understanding of God and the salvation He has provided will be constantly marked by the revelation and intervention of eternity. God's character is beyond comprehension, and our salvation possesses the eternal life of Jesus. Since we are in a finite state in our flesh, we have yet to discover and experience the eternal perspective that awaits those in glory who possess the life of Christ.

The reality of our life in Christ is that since it is eternal, it will enlarge us to embrace greater depths and heights in regard to the character and work of God. After all, in our finite state, we must be enlarged to embrace the infinite. This enlargement is not always pleasant, but necessary if we are going to grow in our testimony.

As we have already pointed out, our testimony is not based on religious experiences, affiliations, leaders, or activities. It is strictly based on Jesus Christ. Jesus is not only our religious foundation that must be clearly established beneath us, but He is also our cornerstone that all activities, lifestyles, and practices must line up to in Spirit and truth.[1]

Sadly, few people build their lives in line with and within, Christ. They may have a religious foundation, but it is made up of the "sands" of man's influence and Satan's deception. People may be lining up to some religious pillar, but it is like Lot's wife. It stands silently in remembrance of something that has already been judged for its worldly, idolatrous, and pagan agreement.[2]

Jesus is the only foundation and cornerstone that will ensure life. To establish Jesus as our foundation, we must apply faith. This is the problem with many Christians; they have failed to apply faith to the Word of God. They pick and choose what they will believe or apply to their life. The areas of the Word that do not serve their worldly philosophies or self-serving agendas and pursuits are discarded or redefined. As a result, they have a mixture in their foundation that will crumble into sand when challenged by the storms of life.[3]

The writer of Hebrews brings this matter into perspective, "For unto us was the gospel preached, as well as unto them; but the word

---

[1] 1 Corinthians 3:11; 1 Peter 2:6-8
[2] Genesis 19:26; Luke 17:32
[3] Matthew 7:24-27; 21:42-44

preached did not profit them, not being mixed with faith in them that heard it" (Hebrews 4:2). What is not properly mixed with faith is rendered useless. It will fail to profit the person in the way that is beneficial and lasting.

When it comes to the cornerstone, people mix various aspects of their lifestyle to the words, teachings, and examples of Jesus. They can mix elements of their culture, religious influences, or practices to the cornerstone, stripping Jesus of His power and authority in their lives. The reality of the cornerstone is that all other stones, or in the case of Christians, all aspects of their life must be shaped according to the cornerstone. For the foundation, it ensures that we will *stand in* the storms of life, but for the cornerstone it will enable us to *withstand* the storms of life.

As you can see in some cases, faith is not being properly mixed in regard to the foundation or the cornerstone.[4] As a result, where faith is missing, sin is reigning in ignorance, rebellion, and darkness.[5] The problem is that in ignorance, people will erect their own god. They will fall in love with this god and be fiercely devoted to it, but it is an image or a concept that represents the best of their imagination.

When it comes to rebellion, people will insist that God see it their way in order for them to show faith towards Him and obedience to His Word. However, God will not bow down to people's way of thinking. As a result, rebellion turns into anger towards God. It will judge Him as being a fake or unfair because He did not come into agreement with their best attempts to get it right or to adjust life to their particular religious standards.

Finally, man will walk in darkness according to his own reality and delusion about God and his spiritual condition. He will not only live in ignorance about God, but he will live in denial about his sin and fruits before God. He will convince himself that he is planted on the true foundation when in reality the real Jesus is missing. He will delude himself about lining up to the cornerstone, when in fact his false reality is serving as his real cornerstone, blinding him to the fact that he is standing near the abyss of destruction.

Receiving Jesus as Savior and Lord is the beginning of establishing a relationship with God. After all, Christianity is all about having a relationship with our Creator. In this relationship, we discover who God really is.[6] You cannot discover the reality of God through other means such as church, pastor, spouse, parents, or friends. Each person is responsible to establish this relationship with God through Jesus Christ on his or her own. As believers, we not only find our life in this

---

[4] If you would like to understand more about genuine faith, see the author's book *In Search of Real Faith* in Volume 2 of her foundational series.
[5] Romans 14:23
[6] Hebrews 11:6

relationship, but we also come to terms with our purpose on earth. Clearly, our testimony grows only as our relationship with God develops.

It is in a relationship with God that our perception of God enlarges. Such enlargement comes by revelation. It is as our perception enlarges by the reality of God, that the Holy Spirit is able to bring greater revelations to truths concerning God. Since the Spirit is unveiling the deeper revelation of God to our spirit, God's Word becomes living. The very life of Jesus will begin to flow or pulsate through our minds into our hearts. It will instruct, exhort, comfort, and impact our way of thinking and being. In summation, it will transform our mind.[7]

In many cases, people have made God too small. If God is small, how can people apply faith to His Word? After all, He is not big enough to bring it about. Therefore, people will automatically put faith in personal strength, abilities, or knowledge to bring about a matter. In the areas where faith is missing, unbelief will reign, causing the heart to become hardened towards those truths about God that would challenge the darkness of their unbelief.

Jesus' command is simple, "...learn of me... (Matthew 11:29b).[8] Most believers start out with zeal for Christ, but lack true knowledge of Him. This often surprises people. They have some concept of Jesus, but this concept is abstract or lacks dimension. Either way, a person's perception of God is confusing, unrealistic, or it lacks life.

It is not enough to know *of* God or know *about* God, one must *know* God for him or herself. The knowledge that lacks revelation and life in regard to God will prove ignorant of His character and ways. He is holy in His character, which brings clarity to who He is and how He expresses Himself. He is perfect and righteous in His ways, which will define the ways He will meet us individually to reveal Himself to us. However, to experience revelation and life, we must apply faith to the Word of God. His Word must become truth, as well as practiced to encourage an environment in which God can freely reveal Himself in a relationship. Such faith is actually counted as righteousness to us.[9]

We must learn who God is. He must become real and living to us. His ways must become light, His words food, and His examples instruction. We learn of God by learning of Jesus. Jesus clearly stated that when His disciples beheld Him, they were seeing the Father. Therefore, what we discover about Jesus, we are also discovering about the Father. As John stated, those who learn of the Father will

---

[7] Romans 12:2

[8] If you would like to come to a greater understanding of the Person, life, and work of Jesus, see the author's book titled *He Actually Thought It Not Robbery* in Volume 2 of her foundational series.

[9] Psalms 18:30; 23:3; Romans 4:3, 9; 10:2-3; Hebrews 12:14; 1 Peter 1:15-16

automatically come to Jesus.[10] Each discovery of Jesus will make the reality of God more vivid and alive to us.

As a result, Jesus is commanding us to learn of Him. Notice, He is not instructing us to learn about Him, in other words, gain knowledge about Him. Rather, He is telling us to learn of Him. The word "of" indicates a point of reckoning as to the origin or reason of a matter.[11] In this case, we must learn that Jesus is our source, as well as our place of reason in the scheme of things.

The more we learn of Jesus, the more we will discover about the Father. For example, we must learn of Jesus' disposition—that of humility. Jesus reveals that we must come to the Father from a state of lowliness or humility. We must approach the Father in such a state in order to experience His mercy, grace, and promises.

Jesus also had an attitude of meekness. Such meekness reveals a willingness to yield to the will of the Father. Such yielding will bring us into line with the Father's purpose for our lives and others. However, that purpose cannot be revealed until one is meek.

As we learn of Christ, the more we will unlearn the ways of the world. We have been conditioned or conformed to the world in our thinking, attitudes, and conduct. To strip away the influence of the world, we must have the proper contrast. In this case, the proper contrast is Jesus. In fact, the Holy Spirit will use the truth and examples of Jesus to convict us of what is righteous, as well as our need to line up to such righteousness in the right spirit and in truth. As we come into agreement with the righteous ways of God, we begin to unlearn the ways of the world. This means our mind is being transformed by the revelation of God's ways.[12] The more we learn the ways of the God, the more we will be brought to an understanding of God. Notice, we will come to a greater understanding of God's infallible character and ways, but we will never fully understand God in His majesty until we are no longer hindered by the flesh.

The Apostle Paul's goal was to come to a greater knowledge of Jesus. He was ready to count all matters of his life and the present world as useless dung to possess a greater insight into his Lord and Savior. He wanted to apprehend this knowledge as well as be possessed by it.[13] As you study Paul's attitude, you will realize that he valued Jesus Christ above all other matters of life. His example clearly reminds us that we must learn to value our Lord above all other attractions and desires. Such a process involves counting the things that now hold our affection as being useless in light of possessing Jesus in greater measure.

---

[10] John 6:45; 14:7-11
[11] Matthew 11:29
[12] John 16:7-13; Romans 12:2
[13] Philippians 3:7-8, 12

Developing Our Christian Life

The Apostle Peter talked about being barren in the knowledge of Jesus in 2 Peter 1:8. As you follow his thinking in 2 Peter 1:3-9, you begin to realize that there is a process in gaining and maintaining this knowledge of Jesus. It begins from the premise of godliness. We have been given all things that pertain unto life and godliness through the knowledge of Christ. Once again, our source is Jesus, and all tools that are needed to walk in life and godliness towards Him are obtained through knowing Him.

However, to walk in His life and in godliness, there must be diligence present in our character. In other words, it is an earnest matter that requires personal care and eagerness. In our diligence, the first element we must add is faith. As we choose to respond in faith, we must add virtue. Virtue points to adding excellence to our faith to ensure its purity.

Once excellence is added to a matter, then knowledge can follow suit. After all, faith is in place to keep knowledge in perspective, and excellence is present to challenge such knowledge to graduate to wisdom. Wisdom is knowledge in action. Knowledge is disciplined through temperance. Temperance is maintained with patience. Patience points to experience.[14] The trials of experience will express itself in godliness. Godliness will always manifest itself in kindness towards others. Kindness that has its origins in godliness will serve as a form of love.

Love is the end of the process. It is this process that makes a person abound in the knowledge of Christ. It will produce lasting fruit that will be pleasing to God and others. However, many do not abound in this type of fruitful life. The reason for this is because they are barren in the knowledge of the One they must grow to love, Jesus Christ. These individuals have forgotten that they were purged from their old sins. As a result, they have become blind to their spiritual condition, as well as to their real source of hope.

The Apostle Peter's constant desire was to bring believers to the remembrance of the source of their Christian faith and life. Likewise, we must never forget what Jesus did for us. He died for us so that we might abound in His life, not remain stagnant and unproductive in our former life. He died for us so we could grow in a relationship with God, not so we could continue on with our relationship with the world. He died so we could enjoy sweet communion with God, not so we could continue on in unholy agreements. Believers are missing it because they easily forget in the midst of the worldly attractions and challenges that their hope, life, and all they have need of is found in a growing, thriving relationship with the Lord Jesus Christ.

Prayerfully consider if your testimony has grown. As you do so, think about your conclusion in light of my testimony which follows. This part of my testimony represents a turning point in my Christian life. It also marks

---

[14] Romans 5:2-5

a tremendous time of spiritual growth. Perhaps you will be able to relate to my struggles and my discovery.

***

My greatest testimony of God is that He is faithful. He was faithful to save me from a cult that had indoctrinated me in the ways of death. He first began to draw me away from this cult to His Son when I was experiencing despair over my personal failures. My cult had taught me that I could become acceptable through works, but I was aware that sin was very much present in my life. Sin caused such hopelessness in me. I had nowhere to go. After all, I knew about God, but I did not know how He was the answer to my sin problem. After all, my idea of God was vague, making Him indifferent and cold to my plight.

However, through a series of events, God reached through my hopelessness, and showed me that He had provided a solution to my sin problem through Jesus Christ. Amazingly, it was liberating to know that I was indeed a sinner, and that my sins had actually been dealt with at the cross through the death, burial, and resurrection of Jesus. However, I still had foolishness bound in my heart. I did not understand death to the self-life. Therefore, I brought foolishness and immaturity into my new life with Christ.

As I look back, I realize this foolishness put God to many foolish tests in my life as I took one detour after another. I took the detour of religion and found myself in idolatry. I took the detour of self-righteousness and found myself in hypocrisy and compromise. I took the detour of being zealous for God, only to realize that I was missing something. After seven years of detours, I came to the end of myself. The fruit I tasted from my despairing life had no joy. I had lost the joy of my salvation.

One day as I sat in complete misery due to my unhappy state, the faithfulness and tenderness of God began to penetrate my soul. Suddenly, I found myself on the floor crying out for mercy. It was as if all the flood dams of my wretched soul begin to burst forth in repentance. I felt myself being broken as the floodwaters begin to cleanse me. I was on that floor for over two hours, crying, repenting, and confessing my sins and failures.

But something glorious happened. My Lord picked me up and gently took me into the Most Holy Place. The reason I know this is because all of a sudden, I realized I was in His presence. I knew I was forgiven, being restored, and for some surprising reason, I knew He was still going to use me in spite of myself. It was so glorious. After all, I had never been in His presence. I had felt His presence, but I had never been in His presence. The joy of my salvation once again flooded my soul as it had when I was first saved.

It was such sweet communion. It was so wonderful. When I came out, I was ready to consecrate my whole life to tell the world about that place, the secret place, the Most Holy place of communion. But I felt a hand on my shoulder. It was my Lord's hand. I did not understand why He was restraining me. I remember stating, "Lord, I want to tell everyone that this place with You really exists." His voice broke through, "Rayola, what have you done for me?" The list of good deeds, even witnessing, went through my mind, but all I could do was stand with my head down in shame because they were insignificant in light of all my failures and in comparison to what He did for me on the cross.

Then, He asked another question. "Rayola, what have you done with Me? Have you walked with Me, supped with Me? What have you done with Me? It suddenly occurred to me what had been missing all along in my detours of religion, self-righteous attempts, and religious zeal. Jesus was missing. His words to me at that time did not involve a commission to go forth, but rather an invitation to sit at His table and learn of Him.

This is the problem with most religion with all of its activities. Even in its best form, Jesus is often missing. Is Jesus missing in your religious activities?

It was only when Jesus took His rightful place in my life that I began to see the error of my ways, learn the lessons of righteousness, understand consecration, and begin to grow in a relationship with God. Clearly, I had so much to learn because I wasted years of being foolish, religious, and ridiculous.

I had to learn the lessons of God's heart. One of the lessons has to do with our commission. He wants His people to be discipled. To disciple someone means that the character and ways of God are lifted up as the standard with the intent and hope of applying such revelations to attitudes and lifestyle. It is the reality of Christ that changes hearts, minds, and lives, not religion, movements, activities, or doctrines, but the actual reality of our sweet Jesus. I have been a witness of this many times.

I had to learn about His way of doing. You see, the matters of heaven and of men's souls are His business. I once witnessed an actual revival. God did not use the churches or any great tent meeting. God came from the outside of religion and man's best attempts, and begin to draw and convict young people of their wayward lifestyles. These young people, who were in drugs, alcohol, and perverted lifestyles, were encountering miraculous interventions of God, while freely drinking from the wells of salvation. I was aware of this revival because for some reason God allowed me to be right in the middle of it and witness it.

These young people were coming to me, seeking something that was real. I would simply share with them about Jesus and His truths, and God would touch, draw, convict, and save them. Space does not permit me to share the miracles that surrounded this revival, but what I can tell you is that it was God's doing. It was not my doing, some church's doing, or any pastor's doing, it was God's doing. There were those who wanted to jump on the bandwagon and take credit for God's doing. In some cases, it became a matter of competition or a platform to some pastors. And sadly, in such cases where man gets involved in the doings of God, he will always pervert and touch God's glory. However, every bit of it was God's doing.

I realize that if God does not do it, it will not last. Eventually, some of these young people went to the wayside and some continue to serve Him. But such details are not my concern, because it is God's affair. What I do know is that God wants a relationship with each of us, and that in my case He was faithful to bring me forth into a living union with Him.

I am not trying to con you. The Christian life is challenging, especially when you sell out to Him. There are many times I just wanted to forget it all and walk away. However, when I peered back to my old life, all that remained had either been destroyed by the devastation of sin or purged by the sanctifying fires of God. Every time I came to this point, I came to the same conclusion that Peter did in John 6 when Jesus asked him if he would also go away like many of the other disciples who had been offended by some His teachings. Peter's answer best explains my conclusion, "Lord, to whom shall we go? Thou hast the words of eternal life. And we believe and are sure that thou art that Christ, the Son of the living God" (John 6:68b-69).

5

CONSECRATION

One of the major turning points in the Christian life usually begins with some type of consecration. Consecration is an act of holiness. It means separating oneself from that which is unholy in order to be separated unto that which is holy. In other words, it cuts ties with unholy agreements or alliances in order to come into agreement with God.

Holiness for the Christian is especially brought out in the concept of serving as priests. The priests of the Old Testament had to go through a process to be made acceptable to God. After all, they were to minister to and before God and to man. They were to do service in the tabernacle as they ensured an environment in which the light and presence of God could reside in the midst of man. They ministered continually before God's altars, His table, and the candlestick on behalf of others.[1]

The temple and priests of the Old Testament served as a shadow of things to come. The shadow was fulfilled in the redemptive work of Christ.[2] Christians now serve as both the holy sanctuary or temple and the priest. Ministering must be ongoing to ensure the flame and presence of God. As New Testament priests, Christians are to minister to God in sweet fellowship with Him, they minister before God with their sacrifices of praise, and they minister to men as they offer the life of Christ through such means as being living examples and good deeds.[3]

However, many Christians fail to fill their position as priests. They may serve a church, a ministry, or some type of leader, but they fail to serve God with acceptable sacrifices, as well as serve others in a way in which God is glorified. Such individuals often end up tacking Christ on to a worldly Christianity. Their sanctuaries fall into disarray, and they lose their way as their life becomes empty from useless activities that are devoid of real, eternal significance.

While consecration is an *act* of holiness on man's part, sanctification is the *work* of holiness, and is done by the Spirit. As stated, consecration involves some type of act of separating from the unholy. This consecration begins when a person presents his or her body as a living sacrifice. Sacrifice points to some type of death. As believers, we must decide to die to our present life to live in light of the power that has been

---

[1] Hebrews 9:1-7; 10:1-4-14; 13:15-16; 1 Peter 2:5, 9
[2] If you would like to understand the different shadows in the Bible, see the author's book, *Follow the Pattern* in Volume 2 of her foundational series.
[3] 1 Peter 2:5, 9; Hebrews 13:15-16

imparted to the believer in his or her new life. In fact, each of us as believers must decide to continually embrace death to the self-life until we gain Christ.

Consecrated sacrifices can be compared to the burnt offering in the Old Testament. Such an offering was in light of a person consecrating something totally to God. The fire was applied to this offering until the fire consumed it. The smoke from the altar served as a sweet savor to God.[4]

There is much that must be burned up by the sanctifying fire of God. The Holy Spirit represents the fire on the altar of the heart. Sanctification is therefore the work of the Holy Spirit to separate a person to God for service. Once the sanctification process is in full swing, a believer must once again consecrate self to walk the godly life out in practical ways. Consecration of this nature becomes separation unto the ways of God.

Consecration on the part of the believer usually marks spiritual growth. As you consider some of the testimonies in this book, you can see where some of these individuals consecrated themselves to God. They made a commitment of separation in order to experience God in a greater way.

Believers usually are brought to the place of consecration by way of decisions. The reality of God is always bringing people to the valley of decisions. There are Christians who appear to want to do a balancing act between the world and Christianity. As they try to walk the fence of indecision, the fence becomes narrower and harder to balance upon, and it begins to wobble with insecurity. Eventually, the wind of truth comes along and knocks these people off of the fence, forcing them to make a decision about which master they are going to serve.

It is all about service. We all serve something. Some serve the flesh, self, and the world. This simply means they are serving the god of this world, Satan. There are others who pick how they are going to serve God. These people will have a mixture because they are not applying faith towards God to every decision or aspect of their Christian life. This mixture will cause them to be unprofitable in their Christian life, as well as in the present world.[5]

Consecration involves a commitment to pay the price to gain Christ. Gaining Christ involves knowing God. The price has to do with the world, the flesh, or self. It is at this point we must decide to die to the unholy influences around us in order to live unto God. This decision must be daily as we decide to live unto death for the purpose of living totally for Him. In such a time, different points of reliance are exposed and priorities and values are redefined.

Consecration will happen many times in a Christian's life. In consecration, God is calling His servant higher for the purpose of greater service. To accomplish this, God has to periodically strip away layers of

---

[4] Leviticus 1; Romans 12:1; 1 Peter 1:2
[5] Hebrews 4:2

self, the influence of the world, or the enticements of the flesh to expose idols, wrong priorities, selfish agendas, and self-serving rights. As each layer is stripped away, God puts His finger on other aspects of our personal life that are hindering us from abandoning all to serve Him in a way that He is worthy of.

The initial separation of consecration can occur in two ways. It can come with the brokenness brought on by sin. In my testimony, my brokenness brought me to a separation from the dictates of my flesh. The reality came from the depth of my soul that I needed to be set free from my state, or die in my misery because I could no longer go on in my wretched condition. My brokenness over my sin invoked the mercy of God, and Jesus brought me into the Most Holy Place to discover complete forgiveness, as well as receive the promise of restoration. Such an experience causes one to fling all upon God in love, devotion, and total abandonment to know and serve Him.

However, consecration comes also from sensing leanness in the soul. It is at this point that the separation of consecration must take place. However, we have a tendency to hold on to certain aspects of our lives. This is when the battle between the Spirit and the flesh occurs.

Each battle reveals that we do not want to trust God with that particular aspect of our life. We want to hold on to it for some reason. As we struggle over our right to maintain some aspect of our life, we become restless and discontent. We are walking in and out of the shadows of unbelief and rebellion. Our attitude proves to be foul, our soul heavy, our heart restless, and our spirit uneasy. This is where a person is restless in his or her present life. He or she knows that there is more to his or her spiritual life. Such restlessness causes the person to see that his or her present state is not acceptable. At this time, such a person will cry out to God to possess more of Him. As a result, consecration may mark a time of great struggle and adversity. It is during this time that faith is often tested by fire as a means to refine and establish it in greater measure.[6]

The prayers of consecration have always been answered, but not in a pleasant manner. For most people, it costs the life they presently know. Everything is thrown up in the air. This is necessary for God to turn a matter around for the sake of righteousness. When I have ministered to believers who find themselves in the turbulent waters of separation, they are in a tremendous struggle over their faith in God. They cannot understand why such adverse challenges are happening to them. As I have questioned them, I am able to pinpoint a time in which they cried out to God to be separated from their present life so that they could come into a greater place of communion and service. Upon the identification of their prayer, they are able to understand why they are

---

[6] 1 Peter 1:6-9

now in the midst of a raging storm. God is answering their prayer to come higher in their lives in Him.

I came face-to-face with this very reality in my personal life. I was living a life that many desire in America. Boats, snowmobiles, bikes, ATVs, RV's, and stuff for camping and other activities surrounded me. As I considered all of this stuff, I realized how empty it was in light of eternity. It was at this time I came face-to-face with the vanity of the world.

So many people put stock in the things of the world. Sadly, people spend all their life trying to accumulate these articles in the name of fun, security, and life. In the end, some are wise enough to realize that these things cannot add meaning or purpose to life. In a way, these things may represent the best the world has to offer, but when it comes to eternity, they often prove to be idolatrous and frivolous. Ultimately, they not only become a source of vanity, but they become a burden that leaves one empty.

As I considered this harsh reality, I recognized that I did not want to settle for such a vain, insignificant substitution for the abundant life that can only be secured in Christ. I needed to discover and experience the life that Jesus had for me no matter the cost. I cried out to God, "Lord if I cannot serve You, take me home right now because life does not make sense." Within a year my world was turned upside down.

My experience was far from pleasant. But I learned that the world entangles us into its false glory with things. These ties can quickly lose their luster, causing us to chase after other things to fill our empty lives with stuff. In the end, we discover that we have not become rich because of things, but lean in spirit. James gives us this perspective, "Hearken, my beloved brethren, Hath not God chosen the poor of this world to be rich in faith and heirs of the kingdom which he hath promised to them that love Him" (James 2:5)?

Those who are rich in this world can prove to be self-sufficient. However, they do not realize that their reliance is on the world and not in God. As they become more reliant on the world, they become poor in their life before God. Sadly, the false glory that is attached to the world will blind them to their spiritual poverty. Like those of the Laodicean Church, they will think they are rich, when in reality they stand wretched before God.[7] They will not realize how fragile their world is until the vanity of it is exposed in light of their spiritual condition.

Consecration will cause different types of poverty in each separation to bring a person into his or her rich life in God. The cost or the losses will vary. How tightly one is holding on to a matter will determine the extent of the sorrow that he or she will experience when the time comes for him or her to let go of it. Jesus reminds us of the attitude that ensures

---

[7] Revelation 3:14-19

Developing Our Christian Life

that one gains the heavenly treasure of God in Matthew 5:3, "Blessed are the poor in spirit; for theirs is the kingdom of heaven."

We must recognize that the things of this earth leave us wretched, while the things of heaven will cause us to be rich in spiritual treasures and blessings. However, we cannot hold on to the things of this present life and gain the blessings of the next. We must let go of the present age, to gain the hope of the next world.

Consider the following testimony of *Krista (Dinatale) Storlie*. She was involved with Gentle Shepherd Ministries as a team member for two decades. She married in 2019 and is now involved with her new family and church. She understood that it was not enough to be a Christian in name or association only. She had to live the life that was set forth by her Creator.

***

My initial years of growing up were spent in what society would call a normal family life. My dad worked, my mom was a housewife, and there was my dog Pup-Pup and my sister. My childhood allowed me to be a normal kid building forts, climbing trees, coloring, crafts, riding my bike, and swimming.

Occasionally, when visiting my relatives, I would question my life when I realized there was a difference between my aunt's family and mine. They went to church and sang songs about Jesus. They appeared to be complete and at peace, a life that seemed unobtainable and unrealistic to me.

My grandmother in Little Rock, Arkansas, mimicked the same life. My memories of our visit with her were of her talking about Jesus, her prayer groups, and church affiliation. Once in awhile, I would even venture to church with my relatives, but I would come away questioning its significance. It all appeared as if it was just a religious preference. After all, my life with family and friends was satisfying enough.

However, my so-called "controlled world" came crashing down at age nine. My parents divorced. There had been fighting between my parents, and I reasoned that perhaps there would be peace in our home. Since we were given a choice as to who we would live with, my sister and I chose our mother thinking she was the more nurturing parent. Contrary to my conclusions, my sister and I were met with total devastation when we realized that, in a sense, we lost both of our parents in one day. Overnight my mother jumped into the party scene. Her moral conduct went out the door as she began to drink heavily, bring men home with her, and she even exposed us to the drug scene. By the time I was in high school my mother was on her fourth marriage.

My life became consumed by loneliness, fear, and pain. I concluded that going to church, as suggested by my relatives, might fill the emptiness of my soul. However, my mother would have nothing to do with God. As a result, at age 13, I began to go the same route as my mother. Although I was excelling in sports at school, and maintaining good grades as a means to receive affirmation, I was sneaking out at night, drinking, smoking, carousing, and dabbling in drugs to somehow fill that big black void in my life.

However, I discovered that the enticements of the world were insatiable. As my vanity grew in its demands and desires, I felt myself sinking deeper into a black hole. I had a sense of my sin, and knew that it was leading me straight to hell. I could see that all my plans and aspirations were becoming illusive. I could feel the vise grips of my reality tightening even more around me as the man I thought I would marry left, while my mother was depending on me for emotional support. I could not keep up in my college education. My life was spinning out of control, and no one seemed to care. Nothing seemed to suffice. The heavy burden of sin was becoming too great for me to carry. I had nowhere else to look but up.

The only place I sensed I might find peace was at the church where my relatives attended. I do not remember the sermon, but I can remember the precious words to one of the songs that broke through the darkness of my despair to bring hope, "washed in the blood." After the song had penetrated my heart, I was prepared to receive the simple invitation of the pastor when he stated that no sin was too great. If someone needed his or her burden of sin lifted through forgiveness, Jesus' death on the cross served as a place of pardon. In fact, sins were not only remitted from the slate, they were buried in the deepest part of the sea to be remembered no more. On that day in May of 1987, nothing could have stopped me as I ran to the altar and knelt before God and man, raised my arms and wept. I cried out for mercy, and asked Jesus to forgive me and to come into my heart as my personal Savior.

I was excited about my conversion, but my zeal gave way to the nominal ways of religion. I went to church when the doors opened, sang in the choir, and even got married to someone in the church six months later. It all looked so perfect except something was missing. Although I had a conversion experience, nothing had changed much in my lifestyle. I watched questionable movies, made decisions without any regard to God's plan, and did my religious duties such as reading the Bible and praying when it fit within my time schedule. Obviously, I was talking the talk, but not walking the walk.

It was clear that in all my religious activity I was not being encouraged in a consecrated life. Such a life would ensure that Jesus was not just a name that I hid behind, but also a Person who must be "all in all" and Lord. Instead of salvation being an awakening that happened at my conversion, it would become a reality that I worked out in my life daily through submission to the Spirit and obedience to the Word.

Obviously, I was standing on the outskirts of Christianity, while walking in condemnation due to my lifestyle. As a result, desperation was

Developing Our Christian Life

invading my soul. I needed to know Jesus in a more intimate way, but how? One day while stopped at a stop sign, the desperation flooded my soul. From the depths of my spirit, I gave God permission to bring me to a place of knowing Him in greater ways no matter what it cost me.

The cost for my consecration would be realized in a matter of days. Before I knew what hit me, my marriage fell apart. I was left heartbroken and completely devastated. I felt betrayed by God and everyone in my life. Once again, I was being forced to look up and cry out to God.

God heard me, and stepped on the scene. This is when He put Rayola and Jeannette into my life. They gently guided me through the despair of my life, as they challenged me to get into the Word and discover God for myself. That is when I began to learn that my life in Christ could only be realized outside of the nominal ways of religion. For six years I had tacked Christ on to a worldly "Christian" lifestyle while I hid behind the cloaks of religion. Like the parable of the sower and the seed that fell among the thorns, I was caught up with the cares of this world. God allowed me to give way to, as well as experience and taste, the bitter dregs of my flesh, selfishness, and weakness. I was like the Shalumite girl in the book of the Song of Solomon who loved the shepherd, but was lured into the world and tempted by her elusive desires. And, like her, I realized that the insatiable lusts of the world just left me hungrier and thirstier for my Lord.

The Lord had clearly brought me to a decision. Would I choose Him or my flesh? I chose the lover of my soul. I realized nothing outside of Jesus makes sense. God called me to leave family, friends, and the security of the world to follow Him in ministry with Rayola and Jeannette. This ministry with them started in the backside of the wilderness where He honored my prayer by having me sit at His feet to know Him in greater ways and learn His Word. He has given me a contrast of what true ministry is. Ministry is not trying to be someone of significance, but true ministry is becoming a servant of all.

It's been a long and narrow road, but through it all I am discovering greater revelations of Him in the form of His abiding faithfulness. I have taken more detours, but He has been faithful to refine my faith. At times, He has brought me face-to-face with my pride and selfishness, proving there is no good thing in my flesh.

He continues to go deeper as He brings me to crossroads of decisions. Like Peter, my heart is to trust Him with everything, and be willing to lay down my life at any price to follow Him. The scriptures in John 6:65-67 summarizes the vivid reality about those who walk in unbelief. Jesus' heartfelt words continue to challenge me, "Will you also go away?"

My continued focus and desired reality is like Paul to,

> ...count all things but loss for the excellency of the knowledge of Christ Jesus, my Lord; for whom I have suffered the loss of all things, and do count them but dung, that I may win Christ...That I

may know him, and the power of his resurrection, and the fellowship of his sufferings, being made conformable unto His death (Philippians 3:8 & 10).

6

DETOURS

One of the matters of life that greatly affects our testimony is the detours we take in our Christian walk. As you read these testimonies, note the detours that were taken along the way by these different individuals.

It is important to understand the difference between a "path" that one is on and the "detours" one may take. The Bible speaks of two distinct paths in Matthew 7:13-14, "Enter in at the strait gate; for wide is the gate, and broad is the way, that leadeth to destruction, and many there be which go in thereat; Because strait is the gate and narrow is the way, which leadeth unto life, and few there be that find it."

The word "path" means a course one is actually traveling. Course points to going from one point to the next. In other words, it is mapped out. One's initial course in this world begins with the premise of selfishness. It is a broad path because it allows for every activity that the world offers, the flesh desires, and self pursues. Therefore, people have much leeway to explore the different aspects of the type of life the world offers. The problem with this path is that it is the way of death.

Granted, this path of death looks correct in the eyes of those who are justifying every fleshly, wicked way, but it leads to death and destruction. Death means there is no life in the activities of the world. Perhaps, there are moments of ecstasy, but this is not real life. Ultimately, one will simply taste of the forbidden fruits that contain the seeds of eternal death because such fruit appeals to the different aspects of his or her flesh, but its euphoria is temporary, empty, and deadly. Each time a person partakes of such a fruit, death robs the person of any real semblance of life. The mind becomes darkened, and the conscience more desensitized to its darkness. Despair begins to take root as the broad path enlarges with empty promises that leave a person in depression. It all proves to be miserable.

As many Christians have discovered in the past, detours that veer off from the narrow path will also take them on many different pursuits that will be void of lasting satisfaction. For example, some people feel that worldly relationships or a family would fill their emptiness, but these things can prove to be heart wrenching. Obviously, even as Christians, we can take what some would consider to be good, but it will not allow us to find the essence of our life in Christ. Even the good and acceptable things in life can prove to be detours. After all, they cannot bring any real peace, meaning, or satisfaction.

As you consider the path to destruction, there are no real detours. There is no need for them. Such a path embraces everything that a person could desire or pursue. It offers everything that can be imagined, that is, except real life. It allows for any practice, philosophy, or pursuit. In fact, it will accompany the traveler merrily on his or her way with ample justification. It deludes, pacifies, and makes promises, but all of it is to blind the person as to the course he or she is on. It is a path that explores the emptiness of vanity, the fruit of death, and the ways of destruction. Ultimately, it leads to the abyss of hell. The writer of Proverbs gives this insight as to why so many walk this path of ruin, "There is a way which seemeth right unto a man, but the end thereof are the ways of death" (14:12).

The other path is the strait, narrow path. It is important to realize everyone is walking on the same road of life. However, some are walking in the opposite direction. The terrains and the end of the journey are quite different on each path. The part of the road that is broad and attractive leads to hell. The opposite direction of the road narrows and becomes rough and unattractive. In fact, it is strait, meaning very narrow. It is hard to travel for it has many different obstacles and temptations along the way. These obstacles and temptations along the way are what cause people to take the detours.[1]

The detours will be discussed after we understand the makeup of the strait path. The path is narrow because it begins with one Person, the Lord Jesus Christ. It is a hard course because it is disciplined by the way of the cross which entails self-denial and death to the fleshly ways of the old life.

The natural consideration for some people who become disillusioned with the broad path is how do they change their course or the direction that they are walking in? After all, no one really wants to walk in the ways of death, but many fail to recognize that the course they are on may embrace many options and ways, but it remains the same path that leads to spiritual ruin. Sadly, most people on this path refuse to heed any warning as to the emptiness or disillusion of the path that they are on.

To change one's direction, a person must repent. Repentance means the person is actually turning away from the direction or course he or she is walking by turning around to face God. True repentance is not just a turn around in direction, but in attitude and approach. A person will have a change of attitude about a matter. In other words, he or she will actually come into agreement with God's evaluation about an activity or practice. Once the attitude is changed, then a person's approach towards a situation or subject will change as well.

---

[1] For further consideration of how hindrances and detours affect our lives see the author book titled, *From Prisons and Dots to Christianity* in Volume 7 of her foundational series.

Developing Our Christian Life

Consider the following excerpt from the testimony of *Jose Lopez*. Born in Mexico in the midst of poverty, as a young man he began to walk the broad path of death and destruction trying to find some type of meaning and semblance to his life. Trying circumstances eventually brought him to America where he discovered Jesus. He eventually had to face the vanity of some of his pursuits including those that were religious.

Jose has a tender heart towards God. In a testimony he shared with the men at the local mission, he admitted that his family considered him a "good son", but he realized that one's best is filthy rags before God. His vision is to go back to Mexico to share the Gospel with those in bondage to lifeless religion, oppressive cultural influences, and the entanglements of sin.

***

When I was younger, my parents used to make me go to church, even though they didn't attend. I did not like to go to church. The only reason I would attend services was because there was a little restaurant next to it. I would go straight into the restaurant after church and eat fried chicken. Since my church worshipped idols, I basically grew up praying to an idol known as the Guadalupe. Nobody ever showed me or stressed that the Bible was the Word of God, and that such idolatry was considered an abomination to God.

When I was much older, I got a job at a factory and met my wife, Marisol. We fell in love and had our first child, Jose. When Jose was born, he was all purple. The doctor said that because he did not breathe when he first came out, some of his brain cells had died. They told us that he might not live, and that if he did, he might be a "vegetable." In our ignorance we thought God was punishing us because we were not yet married. I prayed to the Guadalupe to save my son, and if she did, we would name him after her. So, we named our son Jose Guadalupe Lopez. Now we know who really saved our little Jose's life, the Almighty God.

After this I came to the United Sates in hopes of finding a better life for my family, and treatment for my son. I came with this plan, but God had other plans. After a year, I sent for Marisol and Jose to come live with me.

Our neighbors were Christians and would invite us to come to their church, but we would tell them that we were Catholics. However, we did tell them that we would go with them some day. When we finally did attend their church, we thought it was very different from the few times we had attended the Catholic Church because there were no images and idols to pay homage to. We ended up going a second time. This is when we both gave our lives to Jesus. After that our lives were not the same. I thank God for all of his blessings and for my family.

I would also like to share an incident that happened last year that once again reminds me of God's faithfulness. I was driving to work and there was black ice on the road. I tried passing a car and slid on the ice. I saw that I was going to crash into a light pole. I cried out to God. The light pole broke, but the car had turned in such a way that all the windows, except the windshield and the window on the driver's side broke. The car was totaled, but thank God, He kept me safe from injury and death. I thank God for His mercies and His grace. I thank Him for keeping me safe.

***

Jose certainly changed direction in his life. Obviously, such a change points to repentance. Repentance causes us to face the light of the world—Jesus Christ. This light is glorious, and it is the light that shines forth through the glorious Gospel message.[2] Obviously, Jesus is the light of hope, for He offers redemption to all who will believe on Him.

However, behind the glorious light of Christ looms the cross. This is where the path becomes hard. It requires identification with Christ in His death, burial, and resurrection. There is death to the self-life, and the old way of living is buried, ensuring that the new life of Jesus comes forth in resurrection power.[3]

Sadly, many people stand in the light, but fail to become identified to Jesus. Scriptures are clear; we are not called to stand in the light, but to walk in the light.[4] Those who stand in the light will eventually become disillusioned with their life in Christ. The reason they become disillusioned is because the light does not stay in one place. The Bible instructs us to follow Jesus, not stand around and simply consider Him. When the light moves and we fail to follow Him, darkness can begin to invade our focus as we lose sight of Jesus. At this point, the fire that was burning in our souls becomes dimmer as we fail to seek out our life in Christ.

This brings us down to detours that Christians find themselves walking in. Clearly, when Jesus saves a person, he or she is being saved from the path he or she is presently on.

Once people are on the path of life, they must become identified with death to discipline their walk. In other words, there is a dying out process that takes place on this hard and narrow path. Most new believers start out with zeal that lacks knowledge.[5] This zeal can prove to be nothing more than a "flash in the pan." It is there one minute and gone the next. However, the light is not a matter of personal zeal, but the life of Jesus that must be kept in proper perspective as His life is worked in us,

---

[2] 2 Corinthians 4:3-6
[3] Romans 6:1-14
[4] Ephesians 5:8-15
[5] Romans 10:2-3

Developing Our Christian Life

through us, and out of us. This takes commitment. As believers walk the way of the cross, it will discipline them to endure the hardness of the way.

In fact, the children of Israel began to complain because the way to the Promised Land was proving to be hard. Although they were provided with all of their needs, they became weary with the hard way, and started to complain. The consequence of their ungrateful attitude was swift. God sent fiery serpents among them. They bit the people, and many died. The people quickly repented. Amazingly, God did not remove the serpents; rather, He provided a means in which people could be delivered from the deadly bite of the serpents. However, the people had to look to what was ordained by God to be saved from death.[6] Jesus spoke of this incident in John 3:14-16 in relationship to His being lifted up on the cross to take the sting out of the bite of death.

Obstacles that are meant to test people along the way can actually tempt them to take a detour away from the narrow, hard path of Christianity. A detour is a deviation from the direct path. Deviations can divert a person from finishing the course.

There are the usual temptations of the self-life, the flesh, and the world along this narrow path. However, the test of each of these temptations comes from the same sources: Satan and truth. Both will test the heart of people to expose their place of dependency.

Temptations are part of the path. Although we are given a way out of temptations, few recognize how such temptation serves as a means to drive them from the course of life. These diversions can hinder and bring people to spiritual ruin. The main door for most temptation is pride.[7]

Pride maintains the right to pursue certain aspects of life. It serves as the platform for the flesh to be enticed into the entanglements of the world. The Apostle Paul identified the attitude that would not become entangled with the world—that of a soldier.[8]

As soldiers, we have our marching orders. It is to preach the Gospel, and make followers of Christ. There is nothing earthly or fleshly in these marching orders. In fact, we have been given the full armor, along with the necessary footwear in order to bring the Gospel of peace to others.[9] As Isaiah 52:7 declares, "How beautiful upon the mountains are the feet of him that bringeth good tidings, that publisheth peace; that bringeth good tidings of good, that publisheth salvation; that saith unto Zion, Thy God reigneth."

Soldiers must keep their focus on the mission to finish the course. Anything that diverts the soldier is not only a detour, but also often points to treachery towards one's mission, and betrayal of his or her position.

---

[6] Numbers 21:4-9
[7] 1 Corinthians 10:12-14
[8] 2 Timothy 2:3; James 1:13-15
[9] Matthew 28:18-20; Mark 16:15; Ephesians 6:10-17

As stated, when traveling the broad path, there are no real detours. We can find people searching for God on this path because of disillusionment towards their present life. Of course, they are looking in the wrong places. They need deliverance from their despairing life, but are at a loss as to what it will take to find hope in the midst of their plight. They do not realize that what they need to be delivered from is not their miserable circumstances and way of life, but the particular path they are on. There is no life in the way they are walking. The torment of an empty life is not due to the circumstances of life, but to the affects of sin upon the heart and mind.

The narrow path is designed to not only bring deliverance from the dictates and consequences of sin, but to bring healing where the sin of others has left its ugly bruising upon the spirit and soul of a person. Such deliverance shows Jesus as the Victor, and His redemption as the source of all victory over the bondage, wounding, and consequences of sin.

This brings us back to detours. The types of detours we as Christians often take expose the weaknesses in our character. In fact, this is where we have to face the idols that have been cleverly disguised. In this case it is not a matter of victory over sin, but one of confronting the source of our detour, and overcoming it.

Detours are meant to teach us valuable lessons about the character of God, the real meaning of life and the wretchedness of self. It is in light of our weaknesses that we discover the faithfulness and grace of God. He alone becomes sufficient in the testing and trials of life. He is the One who never forsakes us on our detours, and begins to call us back to the path of life and righteousness. The struggle often becomes greater as each detour leads to emptiness, while the Spirit gently seeks to persuade us to come back to the place of satisfaction and rest in our Lord.

As I look back on my many detours, I realize how God made them count in my life. The lessons about life I learned on those foolish detours have established wisdom and sobriety in me. Their unveiling of the different weaknesses in my character allowed me to give way to the work of the Spirit to establish integrity and compassion in those areas. However, the real value in my detours resulted from me discovering the depths of God. He was always there to comfort me when I came face-to-face with the depths of my wretchedness. He gave me encouragement when I wanted to give up in the midst of the failures and trails of my detours. When I came face-to-face with the emptiness and foolishness of each detour, He reminded me of the satisfaction and joy that can only be found in Him. He proved to be faithful when I was being unfaithful to Him and my calling, as well as merciful and full of grace when I repented.

Today, I contend with Christians who are about to take detours. My advice is to avoid them. However, most people have to learn the hard way, just as I did. Our arrogance convinces us that we are an exception to the rule, and those who would try to stop us are ignorant and foolish.

My prayer for these individuals is that they will not be so stiff-necked that they prolong the process, or that they would not be foolish enough to get themselves into situations where the consequences and affects on their lives are irreversible.

Since God is able to take the worst of a matter and turn it around for good, I do not feel that my detours were a waste. As a result, the bitterness and shame of them never turned into unresolved matters that haunt me; rather, they turned into stepping-stones that have allowed integrity to be established in my many flaws. These stepping-stones have made me an overcomer in certain areas where my self-life, the flesh, and the world, once freely reigned.

As you consider how detours affect your life, you will realize that they can prove to be a powerful tool in your testimony. However, the power does not rest in the details of one's detours, but in the character and intervention of God to bring one back from the deviations to the path of life. In fact, those who have overcome in the different areas of their life via a detour prove to have authority. This authority gives them credibility in what they say. They can encourage those who, due to personal detours, feel like failures to consider the faithfulness of God to restore them. They can speak from experience to those who now taste the shame, defeat, and emptiness of their detours, telling them about the restoration that awaits them at the Father's house.

Consider the following testimony of *Maria Salgada Animas*. Maria grew up in Mexico. She was part of a family of 18 children. Her father was abusive. But, as you can see in her testimony, there is no detour too great for God to reach the prodigal child who is beginning to realize the disgrace of being in and partaking of the different pigpens of this perverse world.

***

When I was five years old there was a pastor whose last name was Rivera. I remember that he was the first man who introduced my family and me to Jesus. Jesus received me in His arms and I received Him in my heart. Sadly, I saw much hypocrisy in my father when the pastor visited us. The joy of his presence was short lived once he and his companion left our house; but Jesus had me in His arms so that I could look to Him and not my father.

I was 13 years old the last time I heard the preaching of the good news of salvation in my hometown. From then on all hell broke out within me. When I was 16 years old, I found an opportunity to escape from my family by getting married. I met my future husband at a wedding, and knew him for five months. We decided to get married. He was a total stranger to everyone, including me. But it was me who had the reins of my life. We migrated to the United States to California. Sadly, we had to face that we didn't love each other. Our relationship only lasted a short time.

I moved to Illinois with my sister, and discovered I was pregnant. My brother-in-law told me to abort the child. He said I was too young (at 17) and beautiful to have such a big responsibility. Immediately, in my heart there was something that told me not to give in to his temptation. Even though I was doing what was right, I felt rejected because I refused to sacrifice my child.

I moved in with my other sister who belonged to an apostolic church. To make her happy I received Christ in my heart again, and was baptized with the denomination. But, once more, the Christianity that was being displayed seemed hypocritical, making me question whether I wanted to even be a Christian.

Once again, I turned from God. All that time, I knew that His mercy and love was over me, but I didn't realize how far He would have to go to keep me from the many dangers that could easily trap one who was disappointed and unsure.

I thought that I was so intelligent, but in reality, I was a puppet in the hands of the enemy, full of selfishness and pride, giving way to sin and transgression. I perceived myself as being better than anyone else. I just knew I had the whole world to myself.

My immature attitude brought me to the point where if I wanted something, and didn't have it, I would do anything I could to possess it, even steal. I acquired $500 dresses, as well as shoes to match them. The friends I chose to hang around with had to be rich, even though I was always portraying a false impression of my financial status.

When I was 19 years old, I moved back to California. There I got involved with a man who was possessive and violent. In spite of my foolish decision, I continued on the same bad path, ignoring the calling of the voice of the One who loves my soul, the One who left everything behind in order to be dressed in humanity to pay for my soul on a cross.

At the age of 24, after being mistreated and physically abused by my violent partner, I finally decided that it all had to end. Sadly, this decision did not come until Oscar, my young son, stood between me and the gun that was being pointed at me. Oscar yelled, "Look out, look out, Mom, he is gonna kill you!" My eyes were opened to the reality of this terrible, abusive relationship.

We went to a refuge where my family of four was helped in locating a house. It was a new beginning for my three children and me. However, I still had the reins of my life, doing all kinds of worldly activities.

One day while taking off my makeup, I saw a great emptiness in my life that friends, expensive-brand clothes, and relationships could not fill. Everything was gray without flavor or purpose. I fell to my knees and cried like never before. I said, "God if you are real, make Yourself real to my life. Save me from my sins, clean me from all of my iniquities, forgive me of my sins and transgressions, and come into my heart. Take the reins of my life. Be my Lord, my Savior, my King, and my Redeemer. I need you."

A verse came to my mind that I had learned as a young child: "Come now, and let us reason together, saith the LORD: though your sins be as scarlet, they shall be as white as snow; though they be red like crimson, they shall be as wool" (Isaiah 1:18). I don't know how long I was there on my knees, but I fell asleep. When I woke up it was a new day, and there was no more darkness in my soul. The sun was bright, and the birds were in the trees singing. I appreciated life again. I felt that the Lord truly forgave me. I felt like a new creature. Jesus had filled the void in my soul. I am so thankful that even though I was in sin, He extended his holy hand and saved me from the consequences of it.

I went into the house and prayed to God, asking Him to let me become His servant, and to teach me so I could learn to walk in His ways. He reminded me of the Scripture in Psalms 119:105: "Thy word is a lamp unto my feet, and a light unto my path."

I was looking for a place to fellowship, but the churches all looked alike. Something was missing. They appeared to be doing their own thing. My Christian neighbor invited us to her church. We began to attend it. To me it was the soundest doctrine I had ever heard, but the women looked at me with suspicion because I was young and attractive, posing some unseen threat to their husbands. Obviously, they did not care to see the intentions of my heart. I prayed to God that he would give me a husband so that I would not be a threat to anyone.

I met Javier at a fitness center. Sadly, I didn't wait for God to answer my prayer according to His timing. I decided that since he was attractive, that God must be giving him to me. I loved him from the beginning. He did move into my house, but because of some threats that he was receiving, we moved to Idaho.

The Spirit of the Lord was convicting me of what I was doing. I knew it was wrong. The idea of giving him up was more than I could bear. I would cry before the Lord, telling Him that I loved this man, and that He was asking too much of me. Eventually, I found myself at the crossroads. A decision had to be made.

By this time we had a one-year-old daughter. I was watching TV when I heard the song, "Change my heart O' Lord." I fell on my knees and asked the Lord to forgive me. I could not go on with this life of sin. I told Him that if I was going to serve Him, it would be on His terms and not on my terms. Peace came into my heart once again.

I had in hand $1500. I rented a U-Haul and put all of our belongings in it, and headed for Florida. I was very sure that what I was doing was correct because the desire of my heart was to please my Lord and God. The U-Haul rental was $900. I was left with $600 for the expenses of hotel rooms, food, and gas. Before we hit the road I told the Lord that He knew how much money was in my purse, and that I would trust Him to work out the details, for He would never leave me nor forsake me. When we arrived at our destination in Florida, there was $20 left in my purse.

Three weeks later Javier was there looking for us. He recognized that he was doing wrong. We decided to come back to Idaho with the promise of marriage, which was eventually fulfilled.

When we got back to Idaho, we rented an apartment. We started to attend church. Javier even started attending church with us. He received Christ, and from that point on our lives were different.

We still have challenges, but the Lord continues to teach, and He brings forth greater revelations of Himself. I even became aware that there was more to my life in Christ than religion and emotional hype. I even told Him there had to be more than lifeless religious activities. I gave Him permission to bring us to the fountain of life. He answered my heartfelt request by bringing us here to this ministry [Gentle Shepherd Ministries].

The Lord continues to transform our hearts and minds. There is not enough paper to tell you all the beautiful things, as well as all the miracles that He has done for me. I have indeed witnessed His mercy and grace.

7

EXPERIENCES

One of the many aspects of Christianity is the experience that comes out of the journey. Keep in mind, Christianity is a walk. On this incredible journey to discover the real meaning of life, you cannot help but see different terrain and encounter different experiences along the way.

Experiences in the Christian walk are another important feature in powerful testimonies. Detours can result in authority being established, but experience produces wisdom, and will often expose, develop, or validate our level of maturity in the kingdom of God.

Experience points to experiencing the different aspects of life. As individuals encounter and partake of life, they become more aware of the challenges of it. These experiences often help people to have an understanding about what other people may be experiencing or will experience. It actually gives them the power to speak into people's lives.

The Apostle Paul talks about where experiences fit into our Christianity in Romans 5:3-4, "And not only so, but we glory in tribulations also, knowing that tribulation worketh patience, and patience, experience; and experience, hope."

As you consider this scenario, you begin to realize that experiences come out of tribulation. The life in Christ is full and satisfying. It is full because it is an existence that experiences life's different aspects in order to discover God in the midst. It is satisfying due to the contrast that it brings to one's life.

This contrast comes out of experiencing the vanity of the world and experiencing the abundance of Christ. This contrast becomes more evident in light of the world. You can have much of the world and still know the bitterness of vanity. You can be poor in the world, but discover the riches in Christ.[1] Being rich towards God ensures satisfaction.

It is in tribulation that patience is developed. Patience points to character. We must have character to stand and endure. Endurance is necessary if we are going to learn the lessons of life that will produce wisdom from above. We also will discover the treasures of God that are found in Christ Jesus.

---

[1] James 2:5

Sadly, most people resent tribulation and shy away from developing patience. The result is that they never develop the character to endure. Endurance brings about depth, not only in character, but also in knowing the person of God and understanding His ways. Remember, testimony establishes or confirms a record already given about God. He is constant in all matters in accordance with His character. Patience allows one to discover God's unwavering consistency as he or she walks by faith in the ways of His life. It is in patience that God is able to unveil certain aspects of His character in greater measure. Each revelation establishes a person more in his or her testimony. In a sense, it establishes the foundation or Rock of Jesus under the individual.

The other aspect of experience is that it actually connects biblical theology with reality. When experience connects Christian theology with reality, Christianity ceases to be a mental concept or belief, and becomes living and transforming. So many Christians have a hard time accepting present reality. They are often adjusting, ignoring, or trying to change reality to fit their fanciful notions about life. In such situations Jesus is often tacked on as a point of credibility or for the sake of conscience, but is never sought out as the only solution to the different challenges of life.

In order for God to have His way, believers must honestly face life. However, without the reality of Jesus, life becomes unbearable to face. Therefore, experience takes what a person correctly believes about God and confirms it as being true in practical application and living. As a result, the truths about God become a reality that can be applied to the challenges and circumstances of life.

It's the application of the truth of God's Word to everyday reality that proves the Bible is as applicable today as when it was first inspired. It does address every problem and situation that can confront a person along the way. It brings in wisdom to convey viable instructions, as well as warns and contends with a person's way of doing. It prepares a person to face life head on, instead of avoiding it. It produces hope and instills integrity.

Sadly, Christians do not always get beyond the mental concept of Christ to the living reality of Him. This is why godly experiences are important. They establish a person in his or her life in Christ. Such experiences not only give believers needed wisdom about the matters of life, but they can produce compassion. Compassion is necessary in true ministry.

The Apostle Paul put adverse experiences in this way in 2 Corinthians 1:4-7,

> Who comforteth us in all our tribulation, that we may be able to comfort them which are in any trouble, by the comfort wherewith we ourselves are comforted of God. For as the sufferings of Christ abound in us, so our consolation also aboundeth by Christ. And whether we be afflicted, it is for your consolation and salvation,

which is effectual in the enduring of the same sufferings which we also suffer; or whether we be comforted, it is for your consolation and salvation. And our hope of you is steadfast, knowing that, as ye are partakers of the sufferings, so shall ye be also of the consolation.

Experiences are not only necessary in being effective ministers, but in having a powerful testimony. This brings us to what we will be experiencing. We will actually be experiencing God. The real reality of the Christian life is that we are to come into a full relationship with God. It is in this relationship that we will hear, see, taste, touch, and smell the sweetness of God. In summation, we will partake of the divine nature of God. Partaking of the divine nature points to an assimilation of the life of Christ into our very life.[2]

The Apostle John actually speaks of his personal experience with Jesus in his first epistle in 1 John 1:1-2,

That which was from the beginning, which we have heard, which we have seen with our eyes, which we have looked upon, and our hands have handled, of the Word of life (For the life was manifested, and we have seen it, and bear witness, and show unto you that eternal life, which was with the Father, and was manifested unto us).

Consider how John's personal experience with Jesus became a point of personal validation and confirmation as to his testimony. He declared that he had actually heard, seen, and touched Him. As a result, he could bear witness or testify of the eternal life that is available to each of us through Him.

The Apostle Peter testified of his experiences with Jesus in his second epistle.

For we have not followed cunningly devised fables when we made known unto you the power and coming of our Lord Jesus Christ, but were eyewitnesses of his majesty. For he received from God, the Father, honor and glory, when there came such a voice to him from the excellent glory, This is my beloved Son, in whom I am well pleased. And this voice which came from heaven we heard, when we were with him in the holy mount (2 Peter 1:16-18).

In these testimonies, we can see where people actually heard the voice of the Father. This voice confirmed Jesus' identity. We read where physical eyes beheld Jesus' glory as God. The Apostle Paul not only saw the light of Jesus on the road to Damascus, but he also heard His voice. In Paul's second epistle to the Corinthians, He talked about how the life of Jesus serves as a fragrance not only to God, but also to Christians and the unsaved. In other testimonies Samuel heard the voice of the Lord, while King David spoke of tasting of His goodness.[3]

---

[2] 2 Peter 1:3-4
[3] 1 Samuel 3:4-10; Psalm 34:8; John 1:14; Acts 9:4-6; 2 Corinthians 2:15-16

These experiences are not based on theology, but on the character and move of God. Through the years I have had many experiences with God during various challenges of my life. For example, in adverse times, He became my Rock. In the valleys of humiliation, He revealed Himself as a loving, sacrificial, caring Shepherd. In the pits of despair, He proved to be an understanding friend that never left me nor forsook me. In desperate times, He proved to my powerful Deliverer and God. Each experience with God confirmed what the Bible has already established as a living testimony of His character. In each experience, He has constantly proven to be a loving, faithful God in all that He does.

However, it is important to discern experience. There are many people who assume their spiritual experiences constitute reality, rather than testing the spirit behind the experience in light of the Word of God. Experiences that are of God will simply confirm His Word and become a point of revelation, wisdom, and growth in our spiritual lives.

Experiences that do not originate with God will always refuse to become subject to the Word of God. These experiences create a separate reality that Satan can use to seduce and delude a person into delusion. Such a reality will make these individuals' experience seem more real than the truth of God's Word. In fact, these individuals prefer their reality to the truth of the Word.

Such deluded people can be easily discerned if you look beyond all of their religious rhetoric and claims. The biggest indicator is that these people become unrealistic about spiritual matters. They are so proud of what they know, or of who they think they are that they are arrogant and unteachable. In fact, they make everything subject to their way of thinking and being. After all, their bigger than life experience has enlightened them. Since this experience was so real to them, they perceive that there is no way that it can be a counterfeit of the truth.

This is how many cults begin. I cannot tell you how many people had an experience or revelation that supposedly "enlightened" them to the truth. The one common denominator in these times of enlightenment is the claim that Jesus is not God. Such a lie is the first affront against God's Word, His character, and His authority. It comes back to the same lie of Genesis 3:1: ...Hath God said?" In summation, "Did God really mean what He said?" "Surely, God did not mean it in that way." Experiences in this type of situation become a false light that will blind these individuals to the destructive path they are on.[4]

As we have seen, experiences are a big part of the saint's testimony. It not only validates the faith of these individuals in God as to what they have declared, but it becomes a valuable means of ministering to others.

Think about how you have experienced God, and how it validated your faith towards Him and established you more in your testimony.

---

[4] 2 Corinthians 11:1-4, 13-15

Developing Our Christian Life

Consider the following testimony of *Kitty Miller*. Kitty has been involved with Gentle Shepherd Ministries since 1999. She reveals that her experiences from her past have influenced and shaped her life in Christ. Like most of us, Kitty still struggles with different aspects of her Christian life, but her experiences with God's love and faithfulness continues to draw her back to center. She also reveals that she not only had to be saved from sin that affected her lifestyle, but also sin that perverted her mindsets, attitudes, and perceptions about God and life.

***

Even when I was very young, I knew that there was a God. Please note, I didn't say I knew Him because I did not really know Him until much later in my life. But, looking back at my life, God's love was always there. He was and is faithful and loving to the point that He brought about circumstances and events to get my attention in order to save me from sin and self.

My mother and father divorced when I was an infant. My mother took me with her to Oregon. We lived in a small sawmill town where my mother pulled lumber off of the green chain. One day she got all dressed up in an emerald green satin dress, and went to town. From that point, my life changed and moving became a constant companion in my life. Sometimes I lived with my mother, experiencing emotional and physical neglect. When I lived with other families, I was left prey to abuse as well.

But God did place a very nice lady in my life in one of the families that I lived with. She cared about me and introduced me to Jesus. It was at this time that I received Jesus into my life. Unfortunately, this introduction was short-lived as I was always moving. I do remember many of the old hymns and one of my favorites was, "At the cross, at the cross where I first saw the light and the burden of my heart rolled away." However, it would be many years later that God would actually take away my burdens.

Finally, around age 10, I was placed in a detention center in Oregon due to my mother's obvious neglect and abandonment. Eventually, the court placed me in a foster family. By this time in my young life, I had developed many wrong mindsets, attitudes, and perceptions about life. I learned how to convince people to enter in with me as a means to receive acceptance. I was a success at conforming due to my deep need to belong and to be loved. As a result, I was eager and willing to conform to get such acceptance by the world's standards.

I spent a great deal of my life, even into my adulthood, trying to get people to accept and love me. I created different realities in my mind that I could run into for safety, especially since I didn't think at the time that God really loved me. Abandonment, and the scars that surrounded my past, had engulfed me for years. I reasoned that since my own mother and father didn't love me, why would God? As I was to learn much later, I had become angry with God because of my past; therefore, the years that followed proved to be one detour after another.

My new foster family consisted of a single lady. She was a believer, but I only found religion in the church she attended. I didn't find Jesus Christ, so I left and went where my friends were. I was exposed to church camps and fun things, but there was no real contrast to be seen between the world and religion. I saw no real commitment to Jesus Christ. Unchallenged, my life basically remained empty, as I wandered around like a lost sheep.

With my past baggage intact, I entered into marriage, which resulted in three children and a divorce. I failed to discipline my children, failing both my children and God. This great failure caused me to walk away from what little I knew of God.

I remember the incident very clearly. I believed that I had rights to a better life since my childhood was a disaster. I had been nothing but a victim of the sins of others. Therefore, I wanted God on my terms. My perception of God was that He owed me a better life. I learned later that I had developed a victim mentality. This mentality engulfed my whole attitude. This attitude revealed my disposition. The state of my inner man determined my perception of God. Yes, I believed there was a God, but I gave way to self-pity. The realities I had created centered around personal survival. Needless to say, it all proved to be idolatrous, as I ran into my mind rather than to God.

I moved from Oregon to Idaho after being single for six years. It was at this time that I took another giant detour—I re-married. All the while I was still searching for God in all the wrong places. For a short time, I became involved in a church that turned out to be a cult. After leaving the cult, I went to another church that proved to be spiritually dead.

Details are not necessary as I also had issues from my past that I had not properly dealt with. These issues created some of the problems, but the bottom line is that the man I married the second time did not honor, love, or respect me. The marriage ended in divorce.

Over the years God in His love and faithfulness had placed in my heart an on-going desire for more of Him. While I was still in my second marriage and living here in Nampa, I came across the book, *Hidden Manna* by Rayola Kelley and Jeannette Haley. This book began to change my life. The night that I started reading the book, I saw God's faithfulness, and in His love, He met me in a caring and tender way that I had never known before. God really did know who I was, and that He really loved me. I needed and wanted to know this in a desperate and personal way.

God actually started with what I most desperately needed, love, His love. I spent that night laughing, crying, confessing my sins, and asking God to forgive me of my sins. I also asked for more of Him. All I knew was I wanted more of whatever these two authors had that wrote the book. It was obvious they knew God.

Developing Our Christian Life

    I spent considerable time trying to locate Rayola and Jeannette. To my surprise, they were living not far from me. Contact was made, and that is when Rayola, Jeannette, and Krista of Gentle Shepherd Ministries entered my life. God used the book and these ladies to show me that there were people out there who really knew God.

    The process has been long, and they have been very patient with me along the way. They cared and loved me in a way that I didn't know people loved other people. They hung around even when I was stupid and ignorant about what I thought I was supposed to do because I did not know how to be me. I knew all about conforming, performing, and whatever else I had learned early in life to get my desired acceptance from the world, but I did not know how to really interact with people in a healthy relationship.

    God used these three ladies to help me identify the cycles that I ran around in and often would get lost in. Eventually I would get stuck in the ruts that I created with my thinking and useless activities to try to keep my world together. God also had to identify my different forms of reality that I operated in. It seemed like an impossible feat, but He was faithful to reveal each one to me. Needless to say, I had to ask for His forgiveness.

    Obviously, I did not really possess God's perception. My thinking resulted in ungodly behavior that did not bring glory to God. Upon this revelation, I made a decision that I wanted to run to Him for His perspective. I wanted His reality and truth.

    God has been very patient, long-suffering and faithful with me. One would think by the time you get in your sixties that you are supposed to know something. I have come to find out I truly know very little unless I see God's perspective. I continually marvel at how He continues to reveal Himself to me in personal ways. I have learned to ask for His perspective and not to rely on what I personally think is real and true. I know that the Word of God is real, it is the truth, and I am continually seeking this truth for my life. I am His child, He is my Father, my husband, my Savior, and my Redeemer. He continues to call me higher in Him so that my life will glorify Him.

8

EMPHASIS

Every testimony has an emphasis. Emphasis has to do with the impression or importance that is being stressed about a certain matter. The benefit of a testimony of Jesus is that it enlarges with each new revelation of Him.

Keep in mind that Christ is infinite in His character and ways. Therefore, our testimony will always be ongoing, as well as expand to include other areas of our lives which help to enable us to relate to others in a personal way.

Before I go on to explain the emphasis of a person's testimony, we must first remind ourselves of the purpose of our testimony. We are testifying of the character and work of Jesus Christ.

This brings us back to the Gospel of Jesus Christ. There are two main ways the Gospel of Jesus Christ is proclaimed. These ways are through preaching and the sharing of our testimony. When we preach the Gospel, we are proclaiming Christ's redemption, which was secured through His death, burial, and resurrection. We can emphasize certain aspects of this message, such as how He died for our sin, or perhaps His burial, or maybe His resurrection. But it will always be in conjunction with the devastation of sin, the mercy and love of God towards us in our doomed plight, and the resurrection power to bring forth new life in us.

However, when it comes to our testimony, it will not be a matter of proclaiming the Gospel, but sharing our experiences about the impact this incredible message had in our lives. Of course, the Gospel message will be present in our testimony, but we will be sharing it as to how the very life of Jesus has impacted our lives. Sharing our personal experiences in regard to Jesus is a way to verify that the Gospel has been confirmed as being true and living. For either the Gospel or our testimony to have any affect, Christ must indeed be real to our hearts, as well as serve as our ultimate reality.

The longer a person has been a Christian, the more experiences there should be to draw from. Once again, we are reminded of our need to grow in our knowledge or testimony of Christ. For example, I have been a Christian for over 30 years. My experiences with God and His Word vary and should be evident by a greater testimony. The beauty about a greater testimony is that I am not limited to my salvation experience. I have much more to share; therefore, my testimony can embrace a variety of areas and challenges, allowing me to relate on a personal basis to others so that I can actually minister Christ at the point of their need. Don't get me wrong, my salvation experience stands at the core of my testimony. I have indeed been forgiven of my sins and saved from the consequences of it by what Jesus did on the cross. Granted, everyone needs to be saved, but ministers of the Gospel need to be able to relate to others in practical ways.

The reality of Christ is that He can meet us at any need, challenge, and problem, as well as comfort and encourage us in our losses. However, Christian servants will not understand this unless they have allowed Christ to meet them at their own personal points of need. As all true servants of God know, they cannot lead people in their spiritual lives where they have never been themselves.

We, as believers, must tread those places that represent challenge of character, loss of rights to self, the idolatrous influences of the temporary world, and the despairing failures of the flesh. We must face the essence of our pursuits for life in order to face the vanity of our self-serving dreams, the emptiness of the world, the perversion of the flesh, and the fruitlessness of all personal attempts and self-sufficiency.

We must face these aspects of life so we can endure the pain of emotional loss, the challenges of suffering and persecution in times of testing, and the refining of our faith in the fiery ovens. It is often easy to compromise in these areas, but we must remember what the essence of the Christian life is. It is best described by the Apostle Paul in Colossians 1:27, "To whom God would make known what is the riches of the glory of this mystery among the Gentiles, which is Christ in you, the hope of glory." Our hope to realize the fullness of God's glory in our lives is solely found in Christ.

Emphasis in our testimony helps remind us of what God has done. It helps us focus on what needs to be brought out for the edification of others. For example, after 40 years of experiences, I have to consider what will best suit those I am sharing with. I inquire of the Lord as to what I should emphasize about my testimony.

One such gathering comes to mind. As I inquired of the Lord, He reminded me of His faithfulness in different areas of my walk. As a result, I shared about His faithfulness to this particular group. Those who were present walked away edified in their lives and were also encouraged in their faith in God.

We see the Apostle Paul doing the same thing in Acts. Depending on whom he was speaking to would determine his emphasis and the approach of his presentation. For example, in Acts 22:1-22, his testimony was directed at the Jews. He was presenting it from the premise of his Jewish roots. In Acts 26:1-23, he gave his testimony in light of the fact that he was speaking to Gentiles. He made a reference to his Jewish heritage, but his emphasis was in regard to the worldly influences of those days. The Apostle Paul made this statement, "For though I am free from all men, yet have I made myself servant unto all, that I might gain the more" (1 Corinthians 9:19).

The Apostle Paul also made this statement about his testimony in 1 Timothy 1:14-16,

> And the grace of our Lord was exceedingly abundant with faith and love which is in Christ Jesus. This is a faithful saying, and worthy of all acceptation, that Christ Jesus came into the world to save sinners; of whom I am chief. Howbeit for this cause I obtained mercy, that in me first Jesus Christ might shew forth all long-suffering, for a pattern to them which should hereafter believe on him to life everlasting.

This is what you would refer to as a mini testimony. The apostle tells us that his testimony can serve as a pattern to show the long-suffering of God towards us in regard to our salvation. Paul had an incredible experience with Jesus. It was an experience that not only impacted his life, but those who heard it.

Consider the following testimony of *Oscar Careno*. At the time of writing this testimony Oscar was 21 years old. He has a disability. He was diagnosed as having a form of autism. He displays a keen intelligence, as well as a tremendous musical ability. In fact, he occasionally conducts the band at a local high school. In Oscar's testimony you will see that what profoundly impressed him about his salvation was the need to worship God through singing. Although Oscar understands the Godhead and knows what Jesus did for him on the cross, his main concern is to express this revelation through the gift of music. He also realizes that out of salvation comes sincere worship. Not only consider his desire to express his salvation through music, but also note his heart to honor God with the gift he has been entrusted with.

***

A long time ago, before Iziquia and Steven [his siblings] were born, before I met Javier who is my dad [step-father], I was living in California with my family. We were living in a small apartment. I was only a child at the time. I didn't know who Jesus Christ was, that He was truly God Almighty in the flesh. I also didn't know there were God the Father and the Holy Spirit. My mom took my brother, sister, and me to church every Wednesday night and every Sunday morning and evening. When she took me to Sunday school, I was very nervous. All the children would stand in front of the congregation to sing and praise God, but I would not sing. I was afraid to sing, because if someone heard me singing, he or she would say, "His singing voice is weird."

My life was starting to change with Jesus as time went by, but I would still refuse to sing to Him. I struggled with others making fun of me. When my family moved to Idaho with my dad, Javier, we lived in a new home in Boise. We went to a new church, but I still didn't want to sing, even in front of my mom and dad. I didn't want to sing when I was in elementary, junior high, and in high school. It was still rough on me when some students made fun of me. No matter where I went as a Christian, even when my family went to a different church, I would still feel lost at singing to God.

When my family and I moved to Nampa, we started to attend the fellowship of Gentle Shepherd Ministries. As the days went by, I was starting to sing to the Lord. I felt great joy in my heart that the Lord is always watching over me, similar to Jehoshaphat, the king of Judah along with the people when they were singing and praising God in a difficult time. The Lord protected them from their enemies. I will never forget that when I sing and praise to Jesus, I am singing, praising, and honoring the Father as well.

***

The other aspect in regard to emphasis of a person's testimony is that of calling. Many times, our testimony reveals how God has prepared us to accept our calling. Consider the Apostle Paul. He was Jewish, but in his encounter with the real Jesus, he was called to evangelize the Gentile world. Paul never forgot his Jewish roots and always started at the synagogue. But, in his encounters with the Jews, he experienced rejection of the message, as well as persecution. Therefore, Paul went to the Gentiles and preached the Gospel.

In my personal situation, I wanted to know the Word of God so I would never be deceived again. This desire was based on being saved out of a cult. It was my pursuit to know the Word of God that brought me to the revelation of how powerful it is. When I finally encountered a personal revelation of Jesus Christ, I realized the need to teach the Word with power and authority in order to prepare the right environment to encourage revelation. The ultimate emphasis of both my desire to know the Word and prepare others, came out of the deep realization that people need to not only grow in the knowledge of Jesus, but also grow in a relationship with the Living God.

Consider the different emphasis of your testimony. Follow it in light of calling. How much of the emphasis of your testimony has also led you to understand and fulfill your calling?

In the following testimony, you will see the emphasis of the Christian life being impressed upon this person's life at a young age. *Jeannette Haley* has been involved in various aspects of ministry for years. In 1989, together we founded Gentle Shepherd Ministries. For years she taught various Bible Studies, as well as conducted seminars and retreats along with me. As a professional artist, she taught painting. In 1996, her life drastically changed when she lost the use of most of her voice due to Spasmodic Dysphonia. What does a person do when he or she loses their means to communicate, especially when the person is a minister and teacher?

Jeannette had to fight to overcome despair. She had to be open to be redirected in her life before God. As a means to express herself, she began to write Christian novels. When she recognized the need for Bible Studies and quality Christian stories for young people and children, her emphasis and talents were once again redirected back to her roots—that being the need to influence and impress upon the hearts and minds of children and young people the need to love Jesus and follow Him.

Jeannette has overseen the Sunday school in our past fellowships, as well as writes and provides materials from studies to stories as a means to establish the young people in their lives with God. In fact, her children's books have led young people to Christ as well, as inspired them in their faith. With this in mind, enjoy the roots and inspiration of her testimony and how it has affected her calling.

***

Before I even became enrolled in kindergarten, I recall my great-grandmother talking about Jesus. Her entire life was consumed with the reality of Christ, making quilts and other things to send to missionaries, and personal evangelism. One of my fondest memories of her (when I was still a child, but older) was her going to her door and calling to all the neighborhood children to come in and sit down in her tiny living room. There she taught them songs about Jesus as she played her old-fashioned pump organ.

My journey with the Lord began with what I call a "drawing" in my heart to learn all I could about Him. As I look back, I know that the Father was calling me right from the start. In my formative years, I did attend Sunday school and church. In Sunday school I had dedicated teachers who taught the way of salvation and insisted on Bible memorization along with the great hymn, "Holy, Holy, Holy." Hymns are as much a part of learning sound biblical truths as is the Bible.

In those days, children sat on hard, wood pews with their family during the entire church service. There was no talking, movement, or running around. After all, we were in God's house, hearing God's Word (even if children couldn't understand it all), singing songs about God, and praying prayers to God. Impressed upon my heart was an incredible awe or reverence for the Lord, and the desire to please Him.

Sometime before, or when, I attended Jr. High School, my parents gave up church because of a hireling shepherd who came in and took over the church. After that, I lugged the big, black family KJV Bible that some friends had given my dad under my arm, and walked several blocks alone to a local community church in order to attend Sunday school.

Fortunately, I have always loved to read. Great-grandma provided me with a Moody Bible Institute Bible Correspondence Course, which I loved to do. She also made sure that I received good Christian books, such as the Danny Orlis series, and literature. I listened to the Back to the Bible children's program every Saturday morning on the radio. I mention all this to emphasize how important it is to get the Word into children while they are young.

By the time I was thirteen, I had a keen sense of God's holiness, man's sinful condition, the great price that Jesus paid on the cross for our sins, and the reality of eternal life that would be spent in one of two places—heaven or hell. There was no frivolity or silliness attached to these sober realities. I believed I was a sinner, I asked Jesus to save me and come into my heart, and I shared the Gospel with others.

At sixteen, as I lay awake meditating on the Lord one night, He called me to follow Him. It was a very distinct call. I responded with a poem (long lost to time) and committed myself to Him, to go wherever He called, and do whatever He asked me to do. By this time, my mother was becoming upset with my decision to be a missionary. She said, "You'll die in some jungle in Africa." Pleasing my mother had always been a strong influence in my life. Her idea of living was not committing one's life to God. She claimed to be a believer, but not to the point of ever talking about Jesus, reading His Word, or putting Him first. Her influence was overpowering.

Even though I knew the plan of salvation, I had been taught that all you had to do was "accept" Jesus into your heart and you were eternally saved, regardless of how you lived. For many years I took a lot of detours, even though I went to church. No one told me that Jesus must be more than my Savior, but that He must be Lord of my life as well. Although my heart never turned away from Jesus, my footsteps did through a series of wrong decisions based on personal needs and unrealistic standards.

Finally, in the 1980's, through a series of God-ordained events, as well as being part of a Spirit-filled church that discipled me for five years, and much seeking to *really know Him, through genuine repentance,* I committed my entire life to God regardless of the cost. In the end, it cost me everything, including husband, home, friends, family, inheritances, reputation, financial stability, and material possessions. It even cost me the church I attended, and eventually my health. But, I had gained the reality of Christ outside of any man-centered religious system. It may have been the "end" of my life as I knew it then, but it was the beginning of a life with God that continues to this day as I continue to serve Him, and grow in the knowledge of our Lord Jesus Christ.

9

CULTURAL INFLUENCE

How does culture affect our testimony? In order to answer this question, we would have to understand what constitutes culture. Culture actually determines what type of lifestyle a person will adopt. It influences taste, preference, approach, and conduct. It will determine emphasis. In other words, in some cultures, families are everything. In other cultures, education takes the forefront as to what is important. As you can guess, people of diverse cultures also develop differently in their emotional and intellectual arenas as to agendas.

This brings us to customs. Cultures give people a sense of identity. Through customs and practices people gain a sense of belonging. They feel that they have an anchor to go back to, to get their perspective. Ultimately, each culture will also determine moral values, as well as social accountability. It is often from the vantage point of culture that people judge a matter.

When you study the concept of culture, you realize that it comes out of the idea of cultivation. Anything that has the potential to grow in any area must be cultivated in some way. It is the cultures of the world that actually cultivate people. As you ponder this, it gives valuable insight into the type of influence cultures have on the people.

When it comes to the Gospel, you realize that it must not only meet a person in his or her culture, but it must address and challenge the capacity of each culture to bring identity and purpose to a person. Granted, cultures may determine social conduct and reform, as well as religious emphasis, but none of them can save people from the dictates of sin and its consequence of death. If Jesus does not take center stage in a person's life, then Christianity will be adjusted according to the attitudes and values established by the culture. Such a mixture will defile Christianity, while Christianity will cause an identity crisis for such people as they try to combine the worldly and heavenly together.

The Gospel of Jesus Christ will ultimately challenge any cultural influence. The reason it will is because at the basis of culture is idolatry and paganism. Granted, idols may be hidden under different disguises such as family obligations and education, while paganism may be covered up by social reforms that promote the idea of a better life, but nevertheless, idolatry and paganism are the basis for all worldly cultures. The idols may vary with each culture and the expression of paganism may look different to the so-called "civilized" practices of other cultures, but it all has the same faulty foundation. Such a foundation reveals a mixture of everything from wisdom to religion and moral responsibility. However, its wisdom will prove to be sensual, its religion superstitious, and its moral practices hypocritical and perverted.

As an American, I thought according to my culture. When God began to deal with me at the point of my cultural influences, I realized that I was one spoiled person. I resented any challenge to my comfort zones. I fought against coming to any type of poverty in my life that would force me to become totally dependent upon God. I avoided being brought face-to-face with my weak character, and raged against any change in my American mentality.

God was long-suffering with me in my struggles. One day I realized that I may be an American, but as a Christian, I must not think like one. My citizenship was tied into the kingdom of God; therefore, I must have the mind of Christ. I must truly become separated from the ways and practices of this present age. And, since my culture found its premise in the philosophies and systems of the world, I had to deny its importance to my way of thinking, and become crucified to its philosophical systematic influences on my life and attitude. After all, these philosophies and systems are under the influence of the god of this world, Satan.[1]

Clearly, I had to develop the mind of Christ, instead of being a good flag-waving American. This required me to make Jesus the center of my life in order to respond according to a heavenly calling and purpose.

The Gospel of Jesus can meet a person in any culture, but our Christian life and testimony must transcend our culture. The reason for this is because the greatest point of bondage for most people can be traced to their cultural influence. They often adjust the things of God to their culture, rather than line up their way of thinking to the high calling they have in Christ Jesus.

The main reason we must have the mind of Christ and adjust our way of thinking to the Word is to change our attitude.[2] Since our culture initially serves as our vantage point, it produces our attitudes towards life.

To have the mind of Christ means to have the attitude of Christ towards the matters of life. Attitudes determine behavior patterns. To exhibit the life of Jesus, we must take on His attitude. His attitude will enable us to properly discern personal attitudes that are contrary to the way things must be. As we line our attitudes up to Christ, we will begin living according to the attitudes that are being established.

Since culture determines the way we conduct ourselves in all matters regarding life, we must wade through our attitudes about these matters.

---

[1] 2 Corinthians 4:3-4; 6:14-18; Philippians 2:5; 3:20; Galatians 6:14
[2] If you would like to consider the way a Christian must think to express the attitude of Christ, see the author's book titled, *Think On These Things* in Volume 2 of her foundational series.

After all, people's conduct can clearly reveal the strengths and weaknesses of their culture. It is important to note at this point that where there are strengths in a culture, you will also find prejudices attached to such strengths. In other words, the strengths of my culture will make me feel superior to someone who is of a different culture.

As far as weaknesses in each culture, you can discover the means in which to capitalize on, control, or abuse the people of that particular culture. Obviously, our cultures will set us up to be destroyed in some way. In fact, the only culture that has survived through the breakdown, reforming, and destruction of different societies and cultures over the centuries has been the Jewish culture. Granted, modern-day Israel is plagued by unbelief towards Jehovah God, and is liberal and immoral in some of its practices. But, at the core of these people stands a belief that was clearly established upon the true God of the Bible. Through much persecution, these people have been preserved due to the watchful eye of Jehovah God. They actually stand as a visible memorial and witness of the fact that there is only one true God who has made Himself known through the centuries through the existence and living testimony of the Jewish people.

In our ministry, we have had the blessing of working with a couple of different cultures. They have brought insight to us about the powerful influence of culture upon people's lives. Regardless of the culture, it puts people in bondage in some way. You can find beneficial traits or practices in each culture, but even that which is beneficial is often taken into extremes. Ultimately, even the beneficial traits that could be commendable become defiled.

For example, America esteems liberty. This is good, but because of the sinful, immoral, and religious mentality of some Americans, this liberty has been used to mock and abuse the freedom of others. The harsh reality is that there is no balance that can be found in man outside of God. God is the only one who can bring balance to that which is beneficial and grace to that which is weak. Otherwise, the strengths of each culture will set people up for defeat, and their weaknesses will cause their strengths to eventually cave in around them.

In another example, we have worked with a culture that is very laid back in its attitude towards life. The people of this culture enjoy getting together and celebrating whenever there is an opportunity to do so. This practice has reminded me that I must take time to enjoy the life God has given me. However, the flip side of this attitude is that it lacks the balance of sobriety. Without sobriety, people can prove to be irresponsible in different areas of their life, thereby, revealing that behind the laid back attitude is fierce independence that often refuses to be responsible.

This is why throughout history cultures seem to redefine themselves. Each great culture gives in to that which is less, causing a digression. Consider the Egyptian, Maya, and Aztec civilizations, (to name a few) and what they eventually gave way to because of their idolatry and pagan practices.

In a way, it is almost as if the only thing remaining from each great culture is their paganism. Even their gods are redefined and repackaged along the way. What was once considered true in that particular past age is now looked upon as a myth. These myths are studied simply to get insight into the former glories of each culture. For example, consider the mythical gods of the Greeks. To the people of this culture centuries ago these gods were real. They even built great temples to some of these gods, but now these very same temples either stand as a shadow of what once was, or they have been completely destroyed.

However, there is one God that stands true among all other gods. He is the God of Abraham, Isaac, and Jacob. He is the God that gave the Law which still stands as the model to all other laws. Twenty centuries ago, this God actually became flesh to walk among man. He stepped into time and humanity. He not only came to change the influence of the world upon man, but He also changed the direction man walked and how he regarded life.

Jesus had to deliver man from the idolatrous and pagan influences of the worldly culture upon his mind and heart. He had to give him an eternal perspective before his focus allowed him to consider anything outside of what was and is considered normal and acceptable. This deliverance must be complete, or it will defile a person in his or her understanding of God.

My testimony of Jesus is about a Savior who delivered me from the worldly, the nominal, and the insane reality of culture, man-made religions, selfishness, and paganism. This deliverance has not been an easy one, but a prized one that I thank Him for. I no longer want to think like an American. Rather, I desire to have the mind of Christ so I can think in terms of His kingdom.

Below are a couple of testimonies from believers who grew up in the Hispanic culture. Sadly, some families have been torn apart in their home country as parents or relatives have sought means in America to provide a better life for those who have been left behind. Sadly, some of the very things that have oppressed these people in their culture have been brought by them into this country.

Keep in mind cultures not only influence lifestyles, but mindsets. We all take a certain amount of pride in how our particular culture has civilized us, such as in the areas of music, art, and literature. Needless to say, this perception can blind us to that which truly oppresses us. Conflict arises when two different cultures collide. It is not unusual to see the older generation try to maintain the old ways of their culture, while the younger generation begins to adopt the different ways of the culture they now live in.

For the believers who come to America looking for a better life, they still must realize that their real hope in life can only be found Jesus

Christ. Their desire to experience a better life must not solely be to pursue a financial base. Rather, they need to seek Christ, desire forgiveness for any sins, and they must seek ways to be delivered from mindsets that rob them from possessing the life that God has ordained for them.

Consider the following testimony of *Marisol Lopez*. Marisol grew up in Mexico, had a Catholic background, was abandoned by her father at two, lived with grandparents, had to contend with a rude stepfather, lost her mother when she was 16, and tried to support her siblings. Like most people in any culture, she struck out against the confusion, emptiness, and loneliness of her life by taking the path of rebellion. She joined a gang to find someone or something that could give her a sense of belonging and purpose. Here are some excerpts from her testimony. Consider how her way of life robbed her of any real purpose or satisfaction, leaving her empty and lost.

***

I remember when I was a little girl I was taught that there was a God, but I was never taught where to look for Him; rather, I was taught to pray to the saints. To me it was normal to pray to dead people, but I still had a feeling of emptiness in my heart. However, I ignored it.

As the years passed, many issues in my life were left unresolved [such as her mother's death and (Marisol's) relationship with her]. I kept working so that some of my family members wouldn't have need of anything. Years passed and I continued in my rebellion. I loved to go to parties and dances. I thought and felt like I was doing the right thing. As a result, I spent many years going down this wrong path.

At age 19 I met a man, Jose. When I think back, I feel that God put him in my path. He was a noble man, and with him I felt he actually understood and loved me.

At age 20, I had my first child. I felt for the first time that I would have a real family. When Jose was born, I fell in love with God and life once again. However, Jose was born with a disability. I prayed fervently to the Virgin Mary, but she never answered my prayers. We immigrated to the United States to find treatment for our son. After a year of separation from Jose, and due to financial challenges, we ended up settling down in California.

We had some neighbors that would talk to us about Christ, but I would tell them that I was Catholic. We even baptized our daughter, Laura when she was born. But the neighbors never gave up telling us about Jesus. One day they invited us to go to church with them. The first time I went with them I was so scared. I would tell myself that it was a satanic church because the people cried, yelled, jumped, and even fell to the ground.

Days passed and I felt a great necessity to go back to that church. In fact, I told my husband that we needed to go back. He questioned me to see if I was sincere. I assured him that the necessary assurance was there. From that day on, I felt something in my heart. The emptiness was being filled. Along with Jose, we received the Lord Jesus Christ into our lives. The people rejoiced with my husband and me in our newfound faith and hope. I felt they really cared for us. They taught us the ways of the Word of God.

We never missed a day of church or Bible Study. Then I understood what it was that I was missing. When Christ came into my life, everything changed. I never really had understood how important I was to Jesus Christ.

I am learning to be a true servant of God. Now that my eyes are being opened by His truth, I completely feel that God has filled that feeling of emptiness that was within me. I no longer feel anger towards my mother or my sisters. Now all I have to do is teach my children the ways of our Lord and of truth. I see and know that there is a mighty God, creator of the universe and of my life.

***

Marisol still struggles with living in the midst of two diverse cultures. Her Hispanic culture is embedded in how she perceives life. However, she is now living in a culture that is totally different, but possesses certain attractions that she cannot ignore.

As I watch this balancing act of two cultures going on in people's lives, I can see how some take the different practices of America and simply adjust them to their culturally influenced perception. It is interesting to see the type of combinations that can come out of such a mixture.

In *Karina Lopez's* following testimony, you can also see how age and culture influences testimonies. Karina is Marisol's sister-in-law. She is going on 17 (at the time of this writing) and is becoming what we would call Americanized in her way of thinking. Even though her Hispanic roots weigh heavily upon her, she has admitted that the American culture is more attractive because it offers her opportunities that would not be readily available in Mexico. In her testimony, she shows us that all people are basically the same, yet clearly distinguished by the cultures that influence their perceptions.

***

I lived with both of my parents until I was about seven years old. I have always lived around my mom's family. My dad would drink every weekend. During those times he used to get aggressive with my mom.

My dad was also overly protective of me. I remember once he hit my mom just because I was crying. He had actually thought she had hit me. That is the way life was. My dad and mother always ended up fighting every time he got drunk.

Eventually my mom met a man, and we moved in with him. He was nice, but I would do everything possible to keep my mom's attention on me. The truth was I was jealous of him. However, this is the place where I first heard of Jesus.

My mom met a lady named Roma and her brother Mauricio. They told her about Christ, and we started to attend their Bible Studies, as well as church every Sunday. I knew about God, but I had never received His Son as my Savior. It was one night at a Bible Study for young people when we were praying, that I finally received Christ Jesus into my heart.

From that point on life changed a lot. Our family rejected my mom and me because of our newfound faith, but I found my real family in Christ. We didn't talk to our family for about three years. We moved out from that man's house and went to live alone. Although it was just my mom and me, the Lord was faithful to provide. We never lacked any needs such as food.

We would go to the Bible Studies every Tuesday and Thursday and to church on Sunday. I remember once on a Tuesday night that I didn't want to go to the Bible Study because I didn't want to miss my favorite cartoon, Pokemon. Later I learned that this cartoon was a trap of Satan to keep children away from God. It actually perverts the minds of children. At first it was hard to stop watching the cartoon. It seemed to be harmless, but I realized that it would not benefit my life in any way.

After three years, our family started to look for us to restore communications. We started to talk to them about Christ. They would listen, but never received Christ as their Savior. After some time, we once again moved to the town where my grandma lived. We lived in a house that was located in front of hers.

About a year-and-half later my mom and I moved from Mexico to California. My dad had moved to the U.S. when I was eight. I was now 14 and had not really missed him. My mom had raised me alone in his absence. She was very strict with me, bringing some much-needed discipline and security to my life.

Admittedly, I didn't really have a reason to come to the U.S. but now I have realized that it was the Lord who brought me here. In the time I have been here, I have been through a lot of different experiences. I have learned from them, and most importantly, I know that Jesus, my Lord, is the one who has helped me. He has given me favor and strength to go through the different challenges. I also know that He loves me, and He is faithful to never leave me alone. This has allowed me to understand that I need to do His will, as well as let Him guide my life.

10

ESTABLISHING YOUR CHILD'S TESTIMONY

One of the things I stress to parents is the need for them to help their children establish their own personal testimony. As you can see, for my co-laborer, Jeannette, her testimony started at the tender young age of four. We often think that there is a certain age in which children all of a sudden become smart enough to understand the simple message of the Gospel. However, Scripture refutes such an attitude.

We are told that a child will lead. The greatest way children lead is by their simple approach to life. They have not yet been made mocking, sneering skeptics by the education of this present age. Their values have not been conditioned or perverted by pride and prejudice. They are still inquisitive about the simple matters of life. They have not quite come to the place where they are demanding their independence. Granted, they may be trying to get their way, but they are not demanding independence from the authority and protection of their parents. As a result, Jesus used children more than once as valuable examples to the adults. In summation, He was establishing that as adults we must regress so that we can take on the trusting disposition of a child to truly be converted.[1]

The testimonies from children you will be reading in this chapter was given back in 2006 when this book was first published. Many of them are now married and have their own children. Our prayer is that they have held tight to their faith and are raising their children to love Jesus.

Consider the following testimony of *Iziquia Animas*. At the time of this writing, she was nine, but her testimony started when she was five. We have watched her grow in her understanding of what salvation is about. Enjoy her simplicity and sincerity.

***

I remember that when I was five years old I lived in a little house and my mom introduced me to God through Jesus. She read me Bible stories even though there were no pictures. The first and second churches we went to were pretty religious. Then Poncho [her brother] invited us to another church (Gentle Shepherd Ministries' Fellowship). Since then I

---

[1] Matthew 18:1-6; 19:13-15

have been learning about Jesus. I am sure that I will go to heaven because I am saved. I know God has a calling for me somewhere in Mexico or in the United States. In the Bible it says to preach the Gospel to every creature on earth, and that is just what I am going to do. And, someday I know that I will go to heaven.

***

Iziquia had a real sense of God early in her life. The truth is that parents must begin to set up an environment in which a child can discover the reality of Jesus from the moment they are born. The environment points to the spirit that is in operation in the home. The spirit in the home will encourage division, conflict, or agreement. It will give a sense of peace or uncertainty. Sadly, it is hard for adults to realize that these little people do indeed sense the unseen influences that are inspiring, motivating, or driving those around them.

The one thing that I have constantly witnessed in families is that the children are insecure about their place in the family. They have no sense of belonging or protection. Needless to say, children do not know how to explain this insecurity so they act up and act out to somehow silence or resolve the fact that their environment is disjointed. They are hoping that those in their small world will somehow respond in such a way that they will be made to feel secure in their environment.

There are simple reasons why children lack security in their environment. It means that two important elements are missing: order and agreement. More and more homes are out of order. In fact, I spent a couple of months teaching our adult Sunday school about order. It all started when some new families came into our fellowship. Although somewhat self-conscious about their children's behavior, I could actually see their struggle over the issue. It is not that they did not desire for their children to know how to properly conduct themselves; it is that they lacked the understanding or tools to bring about such a task. It was clear that order was missing in their families, but it was also obvious that much of what they understood about childrearing came from the examples in their own childhood.[2]

The Bible is clear that our God is a God of order.[3] If there is no order, there is no means of bringing security or proper instruction to our children. Children's behavior is the product of their environment. A home where a child is wearing the so-called "pants of authority" will be out of order. Such a child will become unmanageable, demanding, and unlikable to those who have to contend with him or her outside of the

---

[2] If you would like to understand more about healthy families and childrearing, see the author's book, *Bring Down the Sacred Cows* in Volume 4 of her foundational series.

[3] 1 Corinthians 14:33

home environment. A home where children will not recognize the authority of their parents will become a battleground, rather than a sanctuary. Such miserable children will later fall prey to the destructive elements of society that will offer some type of discipline and acceptance such as gangs and satanic covens.

It is hard to convince parents, who view their "tolerance" towards unacceptable behavior from their children as a sign of love, that it is really communicating the opposite. In fact, the Bible tells us that such a reaction is one of hate. Love will properly bring the necessary boundaries to a child.[4] It is within these boundaries that children will find security.

Even children do not interpret indifference as love. They translate such tolerance as a means of placating or pacifying them because they are a matter of inconvenience. In fact, such tolerance is viewed by children as the parents' selfish means of getting them off their back so they can do their thing.

When you tell parents that they can influence their children's behavior beginning from the crib, they look at you as if you are insane. However, it is true. We can actually train our children in the way they should walk beginning from the time they are babies.[5] The key rests in our responses to their behavior.

For example, children cry to get our attention. Such crying will become the avenue in which they will initially develop their behavior. Granted, new parents must learn the different cries of their babies. For example, there will be a different cry when a baby is hungry, tired, sick, or just wants his or her way. Parents need to communicate support and protection, but they must let the baby know that they will not respond to the cry that demands its way. Babies quickly learn that their needs will be met, but not their demands.

If babies do not learn this important discipline, then as they grow older their cries become one of frustration and anger. I cannot tell you how many times we have had to listen to one and two-year old children scream uncontrollably in our fellowship because it was their means of getting their way.

I remember taking one little girl out of the fellowship. She would work herself up into an uncontrollable rage. Various people contended with her in the gentlest way, but she was angry. She had no form of discipline or security. She had been allowed to run without any restraint or instruction. She was lacking much-needed boundaries that would give her a sense of security.

As I stood watching this little girl cry uncontrollably, I asked God for wisdom. Immediately, the answer came to me. I took the little girl by the shoulders, looked into her face and with a firm but loud voice so she could hear me through her anger, rebellion, and insecurity, told her that

---

[4] Proverbs 13:24; 19:18; 29:16-17; 1 Corinthians 13:5-6; Hebrews 12:5-11
[5] Proverbs 22:6

she was *WRONG!* I made the statement twice. After the second time, she stopped crying. The truth of God actually set this child free. I remember she came up to me to be consoled, but instead I reached down and gave her couple of light swats on her padded bottom because it was her little game. She needed to do what was right, and walk back into the fellowship on her own volition. I never thought a simple statement that was reinforced by light swats would cause her to realize that her behavior was totally unacceptable and would no longer be tolerated. She has been a different child ever since.

In another situation a little two-year-old boy also cried to get his way. His parents were also struggling with his aggression towards his other siblings. Once again, I could see a child that was angry because the burden of being in charge of his life was too great for his small shoulders. He did not have the means, wisdom, or strength to call the shots in his life or in his home. As the Bible tells us, foolishness is what is bound up in the hearts of children.[6]

I asked the parents' permission to contend with the child. This time I simply picked him up when he was crying for his way and held him. For close to 45 minutes the child angrily and aggressively struggled against me. His parents supported me by turning their back on him when he cried for them to deliver him from my hold. Eventually, the child realized he was not in control. He reluctantly submitted and was released. He rarely cries for attention in our fellowship, and when he does, it is softly as he automatically marches towards the door with his dad behind him until it is resolved. His parents have even commented on how his behavior has changed.

Disciplining children never has to be extreme, but it must be consistent. They must know you are serious about bringing constructive order to their lives. They must learn how to conduct themselves according to environment. For example, they will conduct themselves differently in church, school, or at someone's home than if they were home or in a park playing. Those in authority must set constructive boundaries to establish what acceptable behavior is. Constructive boundaries will cause the children to feel secure.

This brings us to the next aspect of behavior, and that is attitude. Behavior is going to determine attitude, and attitude is going to reinforce behavior. Children who are not in order will develop terrible attitudes towards any authority. As you study the progression of training a child, you will realize that by disciplining behavior, you will be able to persuade the mind in the right way. For example, a disciplined child will be able to receive instruction and will eventually discern what behavior is appropriate according to the environment.

Once the mind is swayed in a right way, you can influence the heart. Attitude is the manifestation of the condition or disposition of the heart. If

---

[6] Proverbs 22:15

a child has not learned to respect authority through proper discipline, then he or she will develop an indifferent attitude towards it. When authority challenges such a person, he or she will end up rebelling, raging against, or mocking it. Hence, enters a rebellious, hateful attitude. Such an attitude will reveal itself in children starting usually from the age of seven or eight. When young people have developed this attitude, it means bad habits and patterns will be present in their behavior.

Most parents believe their children will grow out of bad behavior, but this is not true in most cases. Bad behavior will be firmly established if it is not properly challenged, and will express itself differently depending on the child's age. Sadly, the destructive results of this can be seen in the younger generations who appear to become more and more indifferent to authority and responsibility.

The second element that is a must in order to establish secure environments for our children is agreement. As Christians, our agreement must begin with God. We must agree with Him about what it means to invest in our children. They are His heritage, and one day parents will present these precious gifts back to Him. Since God is our Creator, He knows that discipline is needed to train children in the way that they should walk.[7]

Training does not mean conditioning a child to think or act a certain way. Training points to showing a child what is acceptable in regard to behavior and attitude. Children must realize that there are consequences for bad behavior and attitudes, and benefits for acceptable behavior and attitudes. It is from these two boundaries that a child will learn how to overcome foolishness by making the right decisions in regard to how he or she will conduct him or herself. It is in this environment that children are taught to own their own life by taking responsibility for their actions and attitudes.

When I was growing up, I was referred to as a "good kid." However, I was keenly aware of consequences due to bad behavior because of the discipline I encountered. My healthy fear resulted in me making decisions based on the possible consequences I might receive. In such times I figured that the foolishness I was about to embark upon in order to experience some temporary pleasure or unrealistic expectation was not worth the possible consequence that might follow. Therefore, the vanity of my foolishness was denied and I maintained some right standing with those around me.

It is vital that Christian parents first come into agreement with God's take on childrearing, and then they can come into agreement with each other about how to properly train a child. The problem in many Christian homes is that this agreement is clearly missing between the parents. One parent believes in discipline, the other is lenient, or we should say "tolerant." The parent that believes in discipline may be excessive or

---

[7] Psalm 127:3; Proverbs 22:6

unwise in handling a matter, which will cause him or her to lose important credibility in the eyes of the spouse and the children. Children are very aware of this lack of agreement between their parents and will often play one parent against the other as a means to get their way. This creates a chaotic and confusing environment that lacks security. As Jesus stated, a house divided against itself will fall.[8]

I have also witnessed homes where one parent is constructive in discipline and the other one is tolerant. I use the word "tolerant" instead of lenient because tolerance is a way of ignoring bad behavior, while being lenient can be a way of showing mercy. God will not tolerate bad behavior or wrong attitudes from His people. However, He can show lenience towards those who are struggling with a matter. Parents who refuse to confront bad behavior and attitudes are being tolerant, which is sending a very bad message to their children. It is saying that it is all right for them to act like undisciplined little heathens who have never been taught what is proper. It is sending a message that it does not matter what kind of person he or she becomes.

It is interesting to observe children's attitude towards a tolerant parent. They are insecure, frustrated, angry, and disrespectful. They doubt this parent's level of love and commitment to them. It appears that they are wrestling to get their way, but in reality, they are testing the parent to see if mom or dad will ever clue in, step up to the plate, and stop them from spiraling downward towards utter despair and rebellion.

Children need to see agreement between their parents. Parents do need to back each other up when it comes to holding the line of proper discipline. Even though children will initially challenge such lines, it will bring order and security to their lives. They will also discover their place in the family.

It is from the premise of order and agreement that a right environment can be established in which children can be established on the immovable Rock of Jesus. The main key is that the environment that is established must be conducive to ensure the right spirit and to uphold truth.

Parents need to realize that spiritual investment must be made in children if they are going to love God and develop a strong testimony. In Deuteronomy 6:6-7 we read these words,

> And these words, which I command thee this day, shall be in thine heart; And thou shalt teach them diligently unto thy children, and shalt talk of them when thou sittest in thine house, and when thou walkest by the way, and when thou liest down, and when thou risest up.

Obviously, parents must keep the reality of God ever before their children. It is important to point out that there is a balance to the Christian life. Christianity does not mean we should be stoic around our

---

[8] Matthew 12:25

Developing Our Christian Life

children to give an impression that the religious life is a burden. We do not serve a dead Savior, but a risen Lord. I believe children should know that Christianity encourages people to celebrate life in a constructive way. The children in our fellowship have participated in constructive activities outside of the fellowship. Some of these activities involved evangelizing, while enjoying certain pleasures of life. Our children must realize it is not a life of dos and don'ts; rather, it is the means in which to discover a satisfying lifestyle that is balanced and productive.

There are three ways in which a testimony can be established early in the child's life. The first tools that can prove to be very effective are stories. Parents need to tell or read stories from the Bible. This will help make God an important part of the child's life. It will set up a healthy attitude towards God.

In our group of young people there is a four-year-old named Esteban (Stevie) Animas. Every morning, he wants his mother to start out with a story. His mother uses this desire as a means to relate Bible stories to him. His favorite story is David and Goliath.

The people in our fellowship have taken a great interest in the progression of our children in regards to what they understand. Stevie has made some interesting steps. When he was three he was given an opportunity to share with the Sunday school class about Jesus. This is what he said: "I trust God. I am thankful for Jesus. I want to be the donkey God uses." (He had heard about Balaam's donkey.)

Recently, Stevie was sitting at the table with some other children. He made a simple statement that allowed us to see into his simple understanding of Jesus. He stated that only Jesus could heal your heart.

In other testimonies of our children by the names of Laura, Pamela, and Brenda, they made similar statements such as: "I'm thankful for having God in my heart and having wonderful parents. I love Jesus." And, "I am thankful for being saved. I love Jesus." It is true that children will lead us in so many enjoyable ways if we will properly invest in them, and learn to listen to the simple revelation the Spirit will bring to their hearts about spiritual examples and truths.

When you consider most of the testimonies of our young people, Bible stories have served as a valuable foundation for what they initially do understand about God. It is from this foundation that basic truths can be reinforced. Consider how the stories of the Bible affected *Jared McCollough's* testimony. Jared was an eighth grader when he shared his testimony in front of the rest of the fellowship.

***

When I was a little kid, I went to a church in Caldwell. I knew there was a God, but I did not know him very well. When I went to church, I went there to get prizes and to sing songs, but God was not very important to me. Then one Wednesday the pastor of the church was talking about

God. He was saying people that weren't saved needed to come and give their hearts to God, as well as to get the burdens off of their chest. I really wanted that, so I went up to the front and asked Jesus into my heart. I felt really good, but then a year or two later I stopped going to that church.

My mom started these Bible lessons on all the heroes of the Bible like David and Samson. They were really informative. They told a lot about each person. Then a few years later my mom started going to Gentle Shepherd Ministries. She wanted my dad and me to come. After a while we did, but we only went to the Sunday services, but stayed home on Wednesday. I realized that I needed to go Wednesday so I could learn even more about Jesus. After learning about God, I am still amazed at what he can do. I now have an understanding of God. I know He has a lot of power, and can do anything. And, He is the only one that can save us from going to hell.

***

The second tool is very important for establishing credibility in regard to the Christian life for young people, and that tool is examples. Children are trying to find their identity. Therefore, they imitate the ones who influence them. Parents need to beware that their children are watching them. They are hearing what they are saying and they are watching how they handle the matters of life to see if their words and attitudes agree with their actions. Christian parents must discipline their personal lives in order to ensure there is credibility to their claims about Christ. If children fail to see agreement between words and lifestyles, they will eventually become skeptical and rebellious towards what they hear.

For example, in children's minds, they assume that if you say something, it must be true. However, truth can only be confirmed if it is backed up with responsible actions. This is why many parents lose respect and credibility with their children. They do not mean what they say, or say what they mean. Such inconsistency will cause insecurity for children as they struggle with what they can trust in their limited worlds.

Once again, we are reminded of how important the environment is which happens to be the third element in ensuring that your children will develop their personal testimony of Jesus. They must be constantly exposed to God, His truth, and His ways. They must see Christianity in action. It is not enough for children to see their parents read the Bible; they must see them living it.

In working with young people, I have seen how their home environment influences their attitude and responses towards God. Children who have genuine spiritual investment taking place in their lives seem more tuned in to life in general. They have more inclination towards God and His truths. I know when the life of Christ is missing at home, children are not ready to meet Him on Sunday. There is often a great struggle to get them to a place where they are ready to receive the nuggets of truth.

Thanks to dedicated Sunday school teachers and the people in the fellowship, our children are exposed to prayer, the Word, ministry, and fellowship. They are considered an important part of the Body. Each one has his or her place in our spiritual family. As this is being written, our four-year-olds are learning the books of the Bible and the Romans' Road, as well as memorizing short verses of the Bible weekly. Our youth are also memorizing Scriptures, as well as doing Bible Studies at home, and are expected to pay attention on Wednesday night and during Sunday services. At different times they are even asked what they have learned.

The problem today is not that we expect too much out of our children, it is that we expect too little out of them. They are never challenged to reach a higher bar to discover their position, abilities, talents, or potential. They are left to their own devices as they give way to the various vanities of life that dull them down towards God.

Our children also need to become acquainted with the Holy Spirit so they will be able to properly discern their environment. They must learn how to partake of the Word of God so they will be able to know how to possess His life. As they embrace the reality of God, they will be able to make the right decisions, consider their calling, and even count the cost in light of following Him. Righteousness will become their natural preference as the Word becomes life and truth to their souls.

Children, regardless of their tender age, need to be properly challenged to replace the foolishness bound in their hearts with sobriety. As they mature, they need to be aware that there are dire consequences if they fail to possess the salvation of Jesus. Consider *Katie McCollough's* testimony. I met her when she was five years old. She gave this testimony before the fellowship when she was in the fifth grade. However, I heard the first part of her testimony as her and her mother tearfully related it to me when she was only six years old.

***

My mom and I were sitting on the couch watching this movie, and people were being thrown into a fire. I turned to my mom and said, "Mom, I don't want to go to hell." She then said, "You are not going to hell, Katie. All you have to do is say, "Dear Jesus, please come into my heart and forgive my sins. Amen."

After that my whole life changed. I had to make some right decisions, and I am still trying to make them with God's help and by getting into the Word. I know by doing what is right it will help me to know God better and grow stronger in Him.

I also know God has put a calling on my life to go somewhere in the world and minister to people that don't know Jesus.

***

Our children need a spiritual legacy that will prepare them to embrace their heavenly inheritance. Today, I hear about the desires of parents to give their children everything that they did not have when they were growing up. Sadly, over the years each generation has lost a sense as to what is important. As a result, each generation has tried to fill the emptiness of their lives with stuff, drugs, sexual immorality, and endless activities that have no real eternal significance whatsoever.

These same parents strive to protect their children from the reality of life. However, life will touch their children at different times with its harsh realities of challenges, suffering, and death. Our children must learn to stand according to the character and word of God, and not according to the empty vacuum of the world.

Consider the testimony of little *Jose Lopez*. At eleven, he is small for his age, sits in a wheelchair, and has a hard time communicating. Little Jose is a miracle. The doctor told his parents at his birth that he would literally be a vegetable, and not to expect him to live long. It was through this trying situation that his parents began to see God's hand upon his life. They watched him struggle through various physical challenges such as surgeries to horrendous seizures due to his cranium being too small. At times, these seizures would rob him of his very breath. As a result, surgery was planned to correct the situation. But, once again God interceded on his behalf, and the surgery never happened. Even the doctors were shocked because they could not figure out how this serious, life-threatening situation was corrected.

Jose is very sensitive towards the Lord. He sometimes tries to sing during worship service. He understands more than most people give him credit for. For example, he knows and understands two languages. He is also very aware of other people's struggles. Jose's mother, Marisol, translates his simple testimony.

***

From all appearances I was normal, but was born with a disability. I do not know why. (At this point he shrugged his shoulders as he threw his arms up in the air.) Since the treatment was expensive, my dad came to America as a means to get the necessary help for me. I came to California at age three. I was immediately put into therapy. At that time, I could not even roll over.

The doctors in Mexico told my parents I would be a vegetable, but they did not know God. We eventually encountered people who knew God. Life began to change because of prayer. We then knew God could change my situation. As time went by I could sit up, move my legs, eat by myself, chew, and swallow food.

When I was six years old, I went to a Christian Church where I gave my life to Jesus. From that time on God began to show Himself mighty on my behalf.

***

As you can see, the quality of little Jose's life has proven to be challenging. However, God has used it to reveal Himself to those who encounter this young boy. What would the world be like if it was not for the likes of little Jose, as well as the many other children who love Jesus?

Once again, we are reminded that our real hope will not be found in this present world. Perhaps little Jose will never know what a "so-called" normal life is like. However, because of his simple testimony, he lives in light of hope. Therefore, what is being denied him in this present life, he will be able to realize to the fullest in the next world because of what Jesus Christ accomplished on the cross for each of us.

11

COMMITMENT

When we talk about the power of our testimony, we are also talking about the level of our commitment that we have towards our Lord. There is no real testimony without a genuine commitment to the One whom believers are testifying about. This commitment is necessary to ensure that one will maintain his or her testimony when challenged.

Jesus talked about one of the things that we must understand about our testimony. In Luke 21:13-15, He gives us this insight, "And it shall turn to you for a testimony. Settle it, therefore, in your hearts, not to meditate before what ye shall answer; For I will give you a mouth and wisdom, which all your adversaries shall not be able to gainsay nor resist." Clearly, we must settle in our hearts what we are going to believe. We will not have to think about our response, because it will be a natural response that will be inspired by wisdom from above.

Consider the following testimony of *Yolanda Robledo*, written when she was 17 years old. She has displayed an evangelistic heart, and is gifted in many ways, but due to various challenges in her life, she has struggled with many issues.[1] One of those issues was the matter of her salvation. She had to settle it in her heart in order to overcome the confusion caused by some unwise ministers.

***

When I was younger, we lived in California and attended church there. I was really little so I didn't understand very well, but they would always tell us that Jesus loved us.

When I was about five years old, we moved to this [Nampa] area. We attended a church in Caldwell, but our Sunday school never really taught us about salvation. When I started the third grade, we started to attend a different church. There, they taught us a little bit about salvation, and a whole lot of religion.

At home, my mom would always tell my brothers and me about salvation, and would ask us if we wanted Jesus to come into our hearts.

---

[1] If you would like to understand the core of the matters of life that continually affect us, see the author's book, *"The Issues of Life"* in Volume 5 of her foundational series.

Developing Our Christian Life

One day, I accepted the invitation by going into my room and asking Jesus to come into my heart and save me. I had realized that we were all sinners; therefore, Jesus needed to save us.

At our church preachers would come and go. I remember one in particular asked me, along with two other girls, to come to the front. Before this, we had already asked Jesus to come into our hearts and save us. But this preacher said that we were not saved, and that we needed to be. We all looked at each other with surprised looks on our faces, and then we looked at him like he was crazy. However, we went through the motions again, and asked Jesus into our hearts, just to make him quit bugging us. After that, I really started to question my salvation. A couple more preachers did the same thing, and then I really started to question my salvation. I was totally confused.

The Lord brought my family and me here to this fellowship. Now I am very sure that I am saved by the mercy of God. I have also learned so much in the short time we have been here.

***

Obviously, our testimony must be a matter of the heart. Jesus talked about those who draw near with their mouths, but their hearts were far from Him.[2] It is clear that if one is going to stand for something, he or she must believe it in the heart. Those who do not believe the matters of God in the heart will simply make Christianity into a religion, rather than a matter of discovering real life. This is the problem with some Christians. They say the right things, but it is a point of theology rather than a matter of living, being, and experiencing the life that is being established in them. Our testimony as Christians must be established in our minds as being viable, and settled in our hearts as truth in order for it to become a natural extension of what we say and how we live.

As we consider the concept of commitment, we will realize that lasting commitments are motivated by the love of God. God so loved the people of the world, He made a commitment to give His only begotten Son. Jesus so loved mankind that He made a commitment to allow Himself to be offered up as a sacrifice.

Godly love is a commitment to be upright before God and to do right by others. Clearly, our testimony will develop depth because of growing in the knowledge and love of Jesus. Such a commitment also points to being steadfast, abiding, and enduring.

When we think of being steadfast, we are reminded of a hope that cannot be moved and of an unfeigned faith that will withstand when challenged in the fires of affliction.[3] The key about being steadfast is the focus. We must keep our focus on the One we are called to follow and

---

[2] Matthew 15:8
[3] Hebrews 3:14; 6:19; 1 Peter 5:7-11

serve. Our focus will line our affections up to the One who we are placing our loyalty in service to, and our faithfulness in regard to our devotion.

Such steadfastness will actually allow us to abide in confidence. The established testimony of Christians possesses an abiding anchor that is clearly established on the immovable Rock of Jesus. Abiding in such a confidence serves as our strength. We can stand in confidence of what we know, for it has already been established as truth.

It is the strength that comes out of the abiding confidence that enables us to endure adversity that would challenge us in our testimony. Such strength serves as the steadfastness in our focus and resolve not to compromise what we know is true.

Once we have settled a matter in our heart, we can commit our ways to the Lord. Testimonies often declare the ways of God. His ways not only prove to be faithful, but they enable us to experience His power, intervention, and faithfulness. As we commit our ways to God in order to line our life up to Him, we will discover the ways of God.[4]

It is not enough to know the ways of God, we must walk in them to experience the presence, promises, and will of God. Out of this commitment, true reconciliation will come.

We are told as believers that the Lord has committed to us the work of reconciliation. The word of reconciliation points to the actual core of our testimony. Through our declarations about His character and work, God has the means to reconcile man back into a relationship with Himself. How can people know about a matter unless they are told? Our testimony will bring to light the need for people to repent, so they can be saved. In salvation, they will experience healing, hope, and restoration. They will know what it means to be at peace with God.[5]

There is another important aspect of commitment that leads to reconciliation. It will bring us to a place of agreement. When people have a testimony of something, it points to them coming into agreement with others who maintain a similar experience. Agreement is a point of strength and confirmation.

For Christians to possess a testimony of Jesus means that they came into agreement with the Word of God in relationship to sin and salvation. Those who have already discovered Jesus' salvation will also confirm this agreement.

Such initial agreement identifies believers to a new King, Lord, and kingdom. However, this agreement must be established in greater ways to ensure a steadfast commitment. This commitment is established at the point of agreeing with God's Word, which possesses the true testimony or record as to who Jesus is.

It is important to realize that our initial agreement with God comes at the point of Jesus' work of redemption. However, to come into

---

[4] Psalm 37:5
[5] Romans 10:14; 2 Corinthians 5:18-19; Ephesians 2:13-18; Colossians 1:20-21

agreement with the heart of God and with other believers, we must come into agreement at the point of the character and person of Jesus. We must become likeminded. The way we become likeminded is to partake of Jesus. Jesus is the Bread from heaven.[6] It is from this premise that believers come into agreement to partake of Him in sweet fellowship or communion.

Today there is much debate about who Jesus is. As a result, there is very little fellowship. If there is agreement at the point of Jesus, it sometimes turns out to be an intellectual agreement, but not one that is established in Spirit and truth. In other words, the intellectual perception of Jesus simply makes Him a concept. The perception that comes out of the revelation of the Spirit, who uncovers deep truths about Him, makes Him a living person who is totally God and totally man.

The more a person partakes of Jesus, the more precious the fellowship becomes between those who have agreement. Over the years I have met many Christians. It is easy to recognize the ones who have encountered Jesus in the secret places of communion. These are the people I find agreement with. This agreement is unspoken, but you immediately know there is an agreement. You are actually able to share some of the deep encounters you have had with the Lord. These people not only understand, but they will edify you through confirmation of truth, encouragement, and sharing.

Consider the following testimony of *Jane Rodriguez*. After years of sitting in a church pew, she realized there was so much more to the Christian life than religion. In her pursuit to experience a fuller life in Christ, she discovered this agreement. Today, she has a powerful testimony and life in the Lord. No doubt some of you will relate to her struggle to find a life of agreement and fellowship in Christ.

***

I grew up in a church that my family had been members of for generations. I am thankful that my parents took me to church and gave me a spiritual foundation. They made sure I knew the doctrines of our denomination. I always believed in God and prayed. But, I didn't have a <u>personal</u> relationship with Him.

I knew the verse in James 4:8a, "Draw nigh to God, and he will draw nigh to you." But, I didn't realize that if you keep on drawing near to Him, He will keep on drawing nearer to you. I didn't really understand what it meant to walk out my belief or faith in God.

A few years ago, I recommitted and rededicated myself to Him. He knows when you are serious about knowing Him, and wanting to walk in obedience. I learned to focus on Him, and imagined Him surrounding me and residing in me. He began to give me an understanding I didn't have

---

[6] John 6:32-35, 48-58; Philippians 2:2

before. I learned that reading the Word was not the same as studying it. Reading is good! But, really studying it made me see so much more in it (like eternal life). This is what keeps a close relationship with Him. This is the way to have peace and joy.

I still struggle with the things of the world pulling me away from the center of my life and hope. I learned that what I feed myself is very important. I am more selective about movies and what I will watch on TV, regardless of what may be going on in my surroundings.

Keeping my family close is important to me. I even work at helping family members stay close. Satan loves to pull families apart. I've been through some things I don't want to go through again. But, even commitment to family can take away from time at the feet of Jesus. One of my favorite lessons is picturing Jesus at the head of the triangle in my marriage. It gave me some peace to know if I look to Jesus first, He will take care of the rest. It helped me give up my right to having my way. When I let the world pull me away, I feel agitated. I am thankful that the focus of this fellowship is finding the truth about who the Jesus of the Bible is, and what God wants us to know.

In my old church I read verses about examining myself, but until I studied what it meant, I didn't really know how to. I liked learning practical steps about how to examine myself. Like checking my motives. Do I just want to come out on top, or do I really want to be part of the solution? I used that one a lot.

There are many side stories to my testimony. But, the main theme of my testimony is that if we draw near to Him, and truly seek Him, He will draw near to us and reveal Himself to us.

The church I was raised in teaches that the Holy Spirit comes into us when we are baptized. They sprinkle baptize at two weeks old or so. They say, "Do you renounce the devil and his wicked ways?" Needless to say, the sponsors are the ones who speak for the baby and say, "I do." They say the child's name and say, "I baptize you in the name of the Father, the Son, and the Holy Ghost.

As I grew up, I saw Scriptures about water baptism, but never noticed the Bible talks about water baptism and being baptized with the Spirit. It was all the same to me. I worked with a lady who the Spirit sort of bubbled out of. I wanted to be more like her.

Years passed and I took many detours. A friend invited me to her Bible Study, and I began learning things I had never heard. I had never studied the Word like this before. I began attending Sunday service as well. One day our minister said, "I sense there are those who wish to go higher in our Lord." I thought, "It is me! I want to go higher."

We were praying and I said, "Lord, I want to know you for myself." I felt myself going higher. I was praying fervently, and I knew a change was taking place.

After I left the fellowship that day, I sinned. I don't know why I did such a stupid thing. I had certain temptations in my life that I struggled with, but this was not one of the temptations that would lure me to fall. Of course, Satan was right there helping me to justify it, "It is such a small thing. It won't really matter."

I asked for forgiveness that very night. I couldn't forget it, and I asked for forgiveness again a few days later just to make sure. When I asked for forgiveness the third time, I felt that the Lord was saying, "Let us move on." I said, "Lord, test me again, I won't fail. Test me."

In 2004, I went though a yearlong test involving finances. My husband didn't have a job for eight months. I determined to trust God, and it was amazing how many times and in how many ways He provided for me and met my needs. I learned that He was trustworthy. I knew it was so, because it says so in the Bible, but I found out in very personal ways. I talked to Him more that year than I ever had before, and He was right beside me all the way.

I was given missionary books. Since we could not afford to go places, I read several of these books about these committed servants. I couldn't believe how missionaries go for days with nothing. I'm so glad they tell their personal stories. I began to see how much I had. I thought only people with much more money than I would ever have were the ones who were heaping upon themselves. I actually found I could do with much less. I went shopping in my closet, and found things I had forgotten were there. I learned the difference between needs and wants.

I had heard many times that God would provide for our needs. When we looked up what God considered our needs are, the verse defined them as food, water, and clothing. I was shocked that shelter wasn't on His list, let alone all the things that adorn our shelves.

Near the end of the year, I knew the lesson (or test) was almost over. We were always praying that my husband would get a job, and he did. Well, he got two jobs. He worked at one three months, and then went to a second job where he still works.

I was wondering why, if the Lord wanted me to learn all that I learned that year, why my husband was the one who lost his job and I still had mine. And, then I understood that God wanted me to be a good steward with the money I earned. I had always heard that God blesses us so that we can help His people, but I found out He wanted me to help with His work.

The day the lesson ended, (and I knew this lesson was finished that day) I cried and felt joy and felt cleansed. I was amazed that our Lord would devote so much time to stretch me in my faith and commitment. The next day He gave me a bonus. He knew it was coming, but I didn't. I received a $2 an hour raise. So, I also learned that His timing is perfect. I had always heard that it was, but He showed me that day.

In this glorious time of growth, the Word of God has come alive for me. In the church I grew up in, we would sing, "Lord, to whom shall we go? You have the words of eternal life." Now these very words have taken on a new and very special meaning.

There are many special people, and indeed my entire extended family, who still attend the church I was member in for over 50 years. I love these people and care about them. I try to share what I can in a quiet way so that I won't offend anyone.

One time I made a remark to my sister and cousin about what I was learning without thinking about how they would take it. I was thinking only in terms of sharing with those who were the dearest and closest to me. I wanted them to know what was happening in my spiritual life. I didn't stop to think about them still being in the church of our family. Later, it dawned on me that they might have been offended.

God's Word tells us to share with love and with the intent of helping others to come to know Him in a personal way. It is true my family and I grew up with a good foundation due to our church, but I was missing the awakening and the knowledge of the Holy Spirit. I wanted them to know there is so much more to this glorious life in Christ. I want them to join me in growing and expanding in a personal relationship with God that will indeed bring them higher.

12

WE WILL OVERCOME

God's Word is very clear in Revelation 12:11 that we will overcome the advances of the enemy with our testimony. It is hard to believe that having an inner confidence in a record that is 20 centuries old will enable us to overcome. However, the record became a recorded event that cannot be denied. It actually was a fulfillment of a series of promises that were given to God's people at the beginning of the human race. The first promise can be found in Genesis 3:15.

These promises pointed to the coming of the Messiah, the Christ, the one who would redeem us from sin and death. Jesus said of Abraham that the great patriarch saw the day when He, the Promised One of God would come, and rejoiced in it.[1] The books of the various prophets are laced with prophecies concerning Jesus' advents. However, the promise and record of Jesus must become a personal, living testimony that we will not only stand upon, but we will live according to.

As Christians, we are commissioned to preach the Gospel and to make disciples of Jesus' followers. We carry the living reality of the Gospel, as well as been given the means by which we can disciple others.[2] But, we also possess something that is able to confirm the Gospel and become a point of authenticity to disciple others. We possess a personal testimony.

Clearly, there are three ways in which God reaches out to people. These ways have different purposes behind them as to what they are designed to reach, or impact, in a person's life. However, the Holy Spirit must be the One who is anointing, inspiring, and empowering the believer in his or her claims to ensure that his or her outreach will have the necessary impact on the recipient's life.

Let us now consider these three avenues that God uses to reach out to people. Keep in mind, each avenue is meant to reach different aspects of man. Each aspect must have the touch of heaven on it to ensure that God will have His way in the lives of others.

As previously stated, we are *commissioned* to *preach* the Gospel. However, the Holy Spirit must anoint us. Preaching is meant to break the yoke of bondage by stirring up the *inner man* to consider the truth. This is necessary so the person can begin to _hear_ the truth about his or her

---

[1] John 8:56
[2] Matthew 28:18-20; Mark 16:15

spiritual plight. Anointed preaching can bring conviction to the soul in regard to sin, righteousness, and judgment. It appeals to the spiritual state of man in light of his spirit being dead, asleep, or spiritually dull towards the things of God.[3]

Discipling others involves *teaching*. This is why we are *commanded* to teach others to observe the teachings of Christ. However, such teaching must be *inspired* by the Holy Spirit, and *established* according to the Word of God. Inspired teaching will challenge people to receive the truth so they can *see* the reality of God. It will bring the necessary contrast between righteousness and that which is unacceptable, profane, and considered vain to God. Such teachings will address spiritual growth in light of one's potential in the kingdom of God. It often appeals to *the mind* with the intention of transforming how it perceives the issues of life. The reason we are commanded to teach is because there are various ways we bring wisdom and instruction to others, such as through example, obedience, attitudes, and words. We need to remember we are walking epistles that are constantly being read by others. Our lives do speak loudly, and as Christians, our conduct must be honorable. To be honorable, we must be benevolent in our actions, meek in our attitude, and steadfast in our words.[4]

Finally, we have our testimony. It clearly adds *credibility* to our Christian life. When sharing it, we must be *empowered* by the Holy Spirit. It is meant to appeal to the *heart* in order to stir up the desire for the truth. In this case, a person can *know* that it is a truth that has been confirmed and personally experienced, and that he or she can possess it. In a way, it serves as a *touch* from heaven. It does address the spiritual environment of a person in light of salvation. It also can serve as a means to encourage people in their faith. Testimonies should never be about how bad we were or how far we have managed to come in all of our religious attempts, but how powerful and faithful God was to reach us in our plight, in order to deliver us from the ways of death, give us hope, and bring us to the place of victory.

As you can see, the Gospel serves as the foundation of our testimony, while teaching serves as the cornerstone to our testimony. The Gospel speaks of identification to the life of Christ in us, while discipleship points to experiencing the life of Christ as it is being worked in us and through us by obedience. However, when the opportunity arises, rather than preaching the Gospel, I can stand on the power of its message when I share my testimony. When I share my testimony with others, it can become a means to stir up their lifeless soul, teach valuable truths, or disciple them in the ways of God.

---

[3] Isaiah 10:27; Mark 16:15; John 16:7-11; 1 John 2:20
[4] Matthew 5:17-19; 28:19-20; Romans 12:1-2; 2 Corinthians 3:1-3; Philippians 2:5

Developing Our Christian Life

For this reason, our testimony is considered a powerful tool.[5] In all honesty, it must be a natural extension of our life. We are not only to share it, but we must be living out the reality of the claims of our testimony before others. To preach, teach, or share in light of God's kingdom, we must be humble in spirit, meek in attitude, pure in heart, unfeigned in our faith, and single in agenda, priority, and purpose.

The common denominator of the Gospel, righteous teachings, and sure testimonies is Jesus Christ. He is the truth that serves as the <u>light</u> in the Gospel. He is the <u>absolute</u> truth that brings authority to the teachings. And, He is the <u>unchangeable</u> truth that brings credibility to our testimonies. As a result, we must recognize that we are clay vessels that have been designed to carry this message and living witness of Christ wherever we go.[6]

As believers, we must be willing vessels that are ready to be used at all times. We possess something that is a matter of life and death to those who are lost. To withhold such information not only reveals a lack of love, but a disregard for the heart of God towards His creation. Since we possess this insight, we are responsible to preach, teach, and share it with whosoever will listen and believe.

When we come down to the bottom line of this matter, we must recognize that as believers we possess the truth. Truth serves as the sharp sword that will expose, test, and challenge. It is capable of making a person free, as well as bringing a person to a point of decision and separation or judgment.[7] It is absolute and will not be changed regardless of the conclusions of others. Ultimately, when all is said and done, truth will remain standing.

At the crossroads of truth, people will either receive it or reject it. As a result, we, as vessels of God, must speak the truth for three reasons: 1) To take away all further accusations from God's character. In the end, no man will be able to accuse God or His servants for not caring. 2) To bring a person to a decision about God, His Gospel, and the ways of His truths. We cannot save people, but we can offer the truth of salvation, grace, and godliness to them. It will bring individuals to a decisive decision about God. 3) To bring a righteous, clear contrast so that others can clearly see their destructive path, unrighteous ways, and ungodly attitudes.[8]

It is the uncompromised truth of God that gives authority and power in preaching, teaching, and sharing one's testimony. It allows one to stand for truth in preaching, to withstand affronts made against truth in teaching, and enables one to stand on it when sharing his or her testimony. After all, a testimony is like a foundation; the life that comes

---

[5] Revelation 12:11
[6] John 14:6; 2 Corinthians 4:4-7; Hebrews 13:8
[7] Matthew 10:34-35; John 8:32; 17:17; Hebrews 4:12
[8] Isaiah 55:11; Ezekiel 3:17-20; Joel 3:14

from teaching establishes the outward structure; and, the preaching and reality of the Gospel is the glue that confirms our faith and holds the different aspects of our Christian life together.

When you realize that the truth of Jesus stands at the core of the Gospel, the teachings of the Bible, and the powerful testimonies of those who believe Him and in Him, you will understand that it will cause a reaction. If preaching truth manages to stir up people out of their spiritual dullness, they can either receive it or become angry and hard towards it. If truth becomes the sharp sword in teaching, it can edify people in their faith or insult them in their unbelief.

This brings us to the power of our testimonies. As Christians, we know our testimonies have been established by an everlasting covenant that was brought forth by the blood of Jesus. According to the great cloud of witnesses in Hebrews 11, many were willing to give up their lives to experience a greater resurrection. Clearly, they did not love their lives unto the death.

As we consider preaching, teaching, and sharing, we begin to see how powerful our testimony can prove to be. People can reject the Gospel and debate godly teaching, but they cannot rob a person of their personal testimony. It is important to once again note that Paul's testimony varied with the crowds. Our testimony is versatile, and can prove to be a powerful tool in any situation. We can make it personal to reach the hearts of others to minister life and hope. Since testimonies are based on personal experience, they prove to be simple, pure, and devoid of rhetoric. If a person is sincere and passionate in his or her testimony, it can be presented in a clear and concise way that will penetrate a broken or hard heart.

Since this book is about the power of our testimonies, it is vital as believers that we come to terms with being a living witness of Jesus Christ. If you have never written your testimony, or perhaps it has been a couple of years since you have updated your testimony, now would be a good time to consider the claims and quality of your witness.

Below is a simple outline for establishing a message, teaching, or testimony. It is merely a suggestion because most Christians eventually develop their own way of presenting the truths of God to lost or hungry sheep. However, if you are new to such presentations, this outline will help give you some valuable insight.

A. Start out with one main theme.
B. Once a theme is established, you must consider how you will approach it.
C. Your approach will be based on your emphasis, or what you want to bring out or highlight about the theme.
D. This approach and emphasis should be in line with personal experiences with God, and not head knowledge or what you have heard from others.

Developing Our Christian Life

E. You should have three main points to back up your emphasis. For example, if you are emphasizing personal relationship or communion, you would share why it is valuable, the lessons you have learned, and how it has brought growth to your life.
F. If you are preaching or teaching, you must back your points up with at least two scriptures. If sharing, you must have Scripture ready to back up your claims. This means you must personally study the Word, as well as ask the Holy Spirit for personal revelation that will penetrate the mind and heart of others. Remember, you cannot lead people any further than you are in your life before God. Be willing to be transparent about personal struggles and challenges.
G. You must bring your listeners to a clear, concise conclusion in regard to your theme. Make sure you connect your emphasis with your theme so you can bring people a clear understanding.
H. Do not bore people by trying to bluff your way through a matter. They will know whether you have the goods. Stick to what you personally know is true. It is okay to admit when you do not know something.

The real goal of this book is to challenge every reader to make sure they have a testimony of Jesus Christ. This testimony is not based on some experience or feeling, but what has been clearly established by the Word and is being brought forth by the Spirit of God. As we have seen throughout this book, such a testimony will serve as a witness of every believer's salvation.

Jesus' salvation is the main thread that connects every theme and Scripture in the Bible. It is the proclamation, declaration, and claim of every blood-bought saint. It is what each believer has chosen to believe, and what he or she chooses to walk according to in this present world. In fact, every believer finds agreement at the point of his or her testimony concerning the redemption of Jesus Christ. It is because of the believer's testimony that he or she is able to identify and fellowship with others concerning the Bread from heaven in sweet communion.

In his epistle, the Apostle John summarized the power behind the witness of Jesus' salvation in 1 John 5:9-12.

> If we receive the witness of men, the witness of God is greater; for this is the witness of God which he hath testified of his Son. He that believeth on the Son of God hath the witness in himself; he that believeth not God hath made him liar, because he believeth not the record that God gave of his Son. And this is the record, that God hath given to us eternal life, and this life is in his Son. He that hath the Son hath life; and he that hath not the Son of God hath not life.

The final question is simple. Do you have such a witness in your life? If so, you will possess an overcoming testimony that has the power of life and heaven behind it. Such power will enable you to be an overcomer in this present age.

Book Five

THE VICTORIOUS JOURNEY

By
Rayola Kelley

Copyright © 2006

INTRODUCTION

Christianity is an incredible journey of a lifetime, but it was not until I realized this truth that I developed the right perspective about my life in this present world. Even though I found myself suffering from inner conflict and confusion, I never realized that these mental and spiritual disturbances were a result of an improper attitude about my life in God.

I found there were various factors that blurred this reality. One was the influence of the world. I never realized the hold the world had on me until I came face to face with the many detours that had taken me down dead-end streets of vanity.

Another influence was the idea of life. Life pretty much revolved around me, myself, and I. The great influence of "I" in my life kept me from seeing the different paths I veered on. I was harboring a false sense of security that was based on how something made me feel. Later, I learned that feelings are temporary, but the end results of the foolishness caused by the "I" factor can prove to be irreversible.

There were many other factors that influenced my understanding. However, it was only when God put the revelation of the Christian walk into the terms of being a journey that my perspective changed to embrace the infinite and powerful reality of this incredible life. It changed my way of thinking about a life that revolves around me, into the reality that the essence of real life hinges on my relationship with God through Jesus Christ. This relationship can only be realized if I learn to regress and become as a child before God, a humble bondservant to Jesus, and part of a glorious bride that will experience eternity with the true lover of my soul.

Since I have come to terms with the Christian life being a journey, I have been able to face the obstacles and challenges in a more realistic way. I realize that the journey here is a time of preparation for eternity. This has caused me to become excited, knowing that I will discover rewards that will last forever.

I do hope each reader will enjoy this incredible journey that will lead him or her through various spiritual terrains that are found in this present world, and hopefully will ultimately bring each sojourner home in order to experience the hope of the abundant and eternal life.

1

HUMBLE BEGINNINGS

How does the spiritual journey officially begin for the Christian? The answer is simple: It begins when one is truly born from above. Jesus said, "...Verily, verily I say unto thee, Except a man be born of water and of the Spirit, he cannot enter into the kingdom of God" (John 3:5).

I experienced the born-again experience in the midst of "easy believism." Coming forward and simply repeating the "sinner's prayer" often marks this "easy believism." During that time period, the concept of being "born again" had also become a popular fad or craze. Sadly, the exaltation of this experience as a fad blurred the necessity of being truly born again if a person is to enter the kingdom of God. When the hoopla died down, the concept of being born again was put on the shelf and treated as an outdated, overrated spiritual theme.

Spiritual birth is not a fad, theme, or concept, but a truth that must be experienced. It is supernatural in nature and represents a miracle that comes from the outside of man, his environment, and the dictates of the world. It is a birth of a new life that is totally wrought by God, and given to man by the simple response of faith.

This brings us to the importance of the experience of the new birth. Regardless of how many times a person says a "sinner's prayer," unless he or she has been born of the water of the Word and the Spirit, he or she cannot enter the kingdom of God. Just like a natural birth, the conception of this new life by faith takes place in the inner being of man at the point of the spirit, and will manifest itself in and through the soul of man.

This spiritual birth occurs when a person comes to the end of self, only to find failure, disillusionment, and hopelessness. For me, I had to come to the end of my religious piousness to discover that I was a hypocrite at best and totally spiritually depraved at worse.

This harsh reality caused me to spiral downward into an abyss of fear and hopelessness. I felt fear because if I could not work my way to God, I was forever doomed, even though I had no concept of what spiritual doom and ruin meant. I felt hopelessness because I could not work my way to heaven. The dilemma grew as I struggled with what appeared to be an impossibility of me ever meeting the real God of heaven.

The spiritual gulf between God and me escalated as I became more aware of my spiritual poverty.[1] I wanted to be good, but my motives mocked me, my attitudes declared my goodness to be a façade, and my good deeds were hollow as they echoed the emptiness of my own spirit and soul. I felt myself getting further away from a God who seemed impersonal, uncaring, and harsh. After all, could He not see that I was trying to be good and give me a break? In many ways, it appeared that He had turned a deaf ear to my struggles.

Through a series of events, I started to hear and read about Jesus. I knew of Jesus because my religion had taught me that He came by way of a manger, and that He died for the sins of the world. However, in my mind, Jesus always remained a sweet babe in a manger who became a noble man in life.

In many ways, this noble man, Jesus, had a name, but remained faceless. He did kind deeds, but it was because He was good. He was the Son of God, which was nothing more than a title that held no meaning.

Like most people, I knew of Christ, but I did not personally know Him. I had a vague understanding of Him, but it was so vague that He had no identity, no real purpose, and no point of personal identification with my plight. He was just out there, and was only brought down to a limited reality at Christmas time.

Eventually, the light of Jesus began to penetrate my heart through the Gospel. It began to dawn on me that I was a sinner, unable to save myself. Out of love, God sent His only begotten Son to die on the cross for my sins. He bridged the gap that I had become overwhelmingly aware of. All I had to do was believe in my heart this truth and God would save me from spiritual ruin.[2]

For the first time in my religious life, I was introduced to the work of grace. Jesus had closed that gap between God and me, which was an act of grace. Granted, I did not deserve it, but, by faith, I received the incredible gift of eternal life that was freely being offered to me.[3]

I cannot tell you the relief that the reality of Jesus' death on the cross brought to my heart. It explained to me my desperate plight and provided the means by which I could be delivered. This reality penetrated my sick soul, as my darkened mind conceived it as truth. As a result, I received Christ into my heart as Lord and Savior.

As I considered the struggles I had been through, I realized I had been broken by the reality of my depravity. However, as the hope of Jesus penetrated my tormented mind and broken heart, comfort began to flood my soul as a healing balm, bringing joy to my spirit.[4] I would

---

[1] Matthew 5:3
[2] John 3:16-18; Romans 3:23; 6:23; 10:9-10; 2 Corinthians 4:3-4
[3] Ephesians 2:8-10
[4] Matthew 5:4

learn that being spiritually broken was a necessary part of spiritual growth. I would find myself being broken at different stages of my walk, making me more pliable in the Lord's hands.

Jesus, who had been a vague concept, now became alive as He came into my heart through the Holy Spirit to abide in and with me. His very presence stipulated that I had been born again with a new life that was from above. I had a new spirit and heart within me.[5]

It was a glorious time. Things quickly changed for me as my life took on new meaning. Even though the Bible was still foreign to me, I could look back and see that God was making me into a new creation, where old things pass away and all things become new.[6] Now, I was saved, home free, and on my way to heaven; therefore, I figured I had nothing more to worry about. All I needed to do was go to church, read the Bible, and pray, and I would fulfill all of my religious duties.

As I look back on my attitude, I not only see the immaturity of a babe in Christ, but I realize that I had adopted that attitude that comes out of "easy believism." Such an attitude declares, "I'm saved, all is well, for now I am on my way to heaven." Even though there was evidence of salvation in my life, I did not understand that the Christian life brought a price with it. I was told that all I needed to do was believe and life would be much better. I was too fresh to this new life to know it was a walk that involved personal restraint, a cross that implicated death to everything associated with my old life, and a journey into unknown territories.

Even though I did not totally grasp my new life in Christ, I enjoyed my position as a child of God. I had a sense that there was a power that held me, but I did not realize that the position and power was allotted to me, giving me the right and power to live the Christian life.

Sadly, I began to define Christianity according to my religious concepts, comfort zones, and strong influences that dictated my spiritual environment. It would take various detours before I would learn that salvation is a life that begins with the humble beginnings of a spiritual birth. This birth simply marks the beginning of a new, spiritual life that must be discovered, embraced, and walked out.

Like all new life, there must be progression beyond the infant stage to come to a place of maturity. This maturity can only occur as salvation is worked in, through, and out in a person's life.[7] In order for this life to be worked in, through, and out, it must be walked out every day in obedience to the ways of God.

The problem with trying to walk out this life is that a person will take many detours before he or she discovers the true path. As I look back, I can distinguish four major detours that I would like to share with you. These detours are planted firmly in my mind because I eventually

---

[5] Ezekiel 36:26
[6] 2 Corinthians 5:17
[7] Philippians 2:12

learned the lessons of each of them after becoming weary with going down the same road or around the same mountain. Each of these detours will be discussed in greater lengths in future chapters.

The first detour I had to contend with was the world. It is hard to believe how much the world influences our philosophies. However, I discovered on my many detours that it was a strong thread that penetrated every area of my life.

The world is designed to subtly rob believers of their life in God. For example, in the midst of all the worldly attractions and activities, it is easy to forget the sacrifice of the Lamb of God. It is comfortable to become self-sufficient when all is well. It is convenient to con and delude oneself about personal character, as long as adversity is not testing and challenging it. Sadly, exaltation of self creates a fantasy or delusion that is reinforced by the philosophies of the world. This delusion remains intact until reality slams against it.

I recognized that each time I went down a path that was designed by the world, I encountered nothing more than vanity. Eventually, I was able to see how the influences of the world undermined true faith, causing unbelief and skepticism, which always hindered me from walking the walk.[8]

Another detour I quickly found myself taking was that of religion. According to James 1:27, "Pure religion and undefiled before God and the Father is this, To visit the fatherless and widows in their affliction, and to keep himself unspotted from the world." Real religion is not made up of rituals and practices, but of righteousness that is clearly reflected in attitude and actions.

I had been saved out of a man-made religion, but I began to allow man to define my perception of Christianity. Any time you allow man to define your personal life and walk, no matter how righteous it might be, you will end up with a religion that is nothing but a personal cult. Cults operate within the dead-letter of the Word.

In fact, almost all cults are humanistic because they often lead back to man's influence. Whenever man's concepts and ways serve as the substitute, it means an antichrist spirit is in operation, exalting another Jesus. This leads us back to the source of all deception and counterfeits: Satan. If the source goes directly back to Satan, it means it has occult influences. Regardless of the counterfeit, the right spirit will be missing, as well as the true light and work of God.

When religion goes back to man, it will mean nothing to the follower because his or her beliefs belong to another. When it comes to personal attitudes in regard to God and life, they are based on the attitudes of those who are influencing the individual the most. Personal actions will always be in line with those who have the person's loyalty. Eventually, if the person has an open heart and loves the truth, he or she begins to

---

[8] Matthew 13:22 refer to Romans 10:17

Developing Our Christian Life

realize that Jesus has been replaced in his or her life as the source and conscience of his or her walk.

The problem is that man-made religion offers benefits that entice the flesh and feed egos. For example, it can advance your knowledge, but it cannot give life or authority. It can make you appear righteous, but it cannot cleanse you of your depravity and filth. It can give you a sense of possessing special secrets and truths, but it will cause you to miss the real treasure of heaven.

Sadly, man-made religion always drowns out the Christian life as it becomes a replacement for a relationship with God through Jesus Christ. And, without a vital relationship with God, there will be no life or growth.

The next detour was that of intellectual pursuit. I had been deceived, and my goal was to know the Word of God in such a way that I would never be deceived again. It was a noble gesture with the wrong motive and emphasis. My motive was conceit and my emphasis was knowledge, instead of truth. In the end, I knew the Bible well and could argue any point of it. However, the Word had no authority and power in my life to bring about personal change. Its lack of authority was due to the fact that I had rendered this powerful sword into controllable pieces. It did not have the power to penetrate my religious façade, let alone reveal my heart to expose my real spiritual condition.[9]

I hid behind my religious knowledge, while deluding myself about my attitudes and actions. I convinced myself that I had good intentions and that I would overcome bad practices. But in reality, I was not an overcomer. Only those who overcome will truly reap the benefits of heaven, according to the messages to the seven different churches in Revelation 2-3.

As a result of my motive and emphasis, I became judgmental, instead of discerning. I developed a board in my eye that supposedly allowed me to see other people's discrepancies, but actually blinded me to my own spiritual conditions. In the end, I even judged God as I replaced truth with knowledge.

Another detour I took was that of religious causes. I avoided facing my spiritual condition by promoting what I call noble causes in the name of Jesus. I managed to cover up my personal struggles by doing religious deeds. These causes and deeds replaced my lack of devotion, as well as hid the fact that I was failing to carry out the great commission of preaching the Gospel and making followers of Jesus.

Each detour brought me to the end of myself. I began to realize that I had put my confidence in the world, religion, man, self, and deeds, but not in God. As I was brought face to face with the vanity of the world, the fake light of religion, the cursed arm of the flesh (man), the lust of self, and the emptiness of deeds, the Lord revealed that it was all idolatry.

---

[9] Hebrews 4:12

Idolatry always seems to cause at least 98 percent of the spiritual detours in our lives. Each detour shows the priority that we are harboring, the right to self that we are claiming, and the selfish motive that is behind our pursuits. Its presence in our lives reveals a divided heart, lukewarm devotion, self-exalting pride, and a stiff neck.

Idolatry makes one consistent claim: that the individual does not love God with all of his or her heart, soul, mind, and strength. When the love of God and a love for God are missing, one will find treachery lurking at the door of his or her heart.[10]

Treachery often clothes itself in the false light of self-righteousness and in fake nobility. The false light of self-righteousness makes a person righteous in his or her own eyes, while fake nobility will occasionally admit that it is wrong in a vague way, but will never confess or repent. In other words, it appears as an honorable cloak that hides blatant rebellion. Individuals who operate in fake nobility are either deceived about self or liars, because they know they have no intention of coming clean of their rebellion.

As I have studied the lives of many servants of God, I realize that the greatest temptation often comes at the point of great victories or when the person is nearing the end of his or her spiritual journey. We can see these two scenarios in the lives of the Prophet Elijah and King Solomon. Sadly, when a person gives in to the temptation, the individual will begin to experience valleys of defeat, fear, and depression.

I have been traveling the Christian Road for years, but in the back of my mind, I am aware that I could fall into the trap of victory and blow it right before I cross over the finish line. I am aware that I could become too secure or smug in my life and fail to see the traps of the enemy. I could become lifted up in my heart and would have to be brought down in judgment.

I keep thinking about the Apostle Paul's words in 2 Timothy 4:7, "I have fought a good fight, I have finished my course, I have kept the faith." Paul declared that he had finished the course set before Him. Notice, he said "my course." God has a course specifically designed for each of His followers.

This reminds me of the prophet in 1 Kings 13. God gave him specific instructions when He sent him to pronounce judgment on the idolatrous king Jeroboam. Temptation caught up with him as he rested under a tree. He had not completed God's instruction. The actual temptation would appear to be insignificant and certainly not unreasonable, but it caused him to take a detour from the course that God had clearly set before him. As he was sitting in direct disobedience to God, judgment was proclaimed. As a result, the man never finished the course.

The one thing I had to take note of was the fact that this prophet's name is conspicuously missing. I am not trying to spiritualize this, but it

---

[10] Hosea 6:7; Mark 12:29-31

is a fact that names were important in the Old Testament. They actually said something about the person, the time in which the individual lived, or sometimes made reference to the person's mission. The fact that his name was not mentioned caused me to speculate if God was trying to reinforce a principle.

Revelation 2:17 states,
> He that hath an ear, let him hear what the Spirit saith unto the churches; To him that overcometh will I give to eat of the hidden manna, and will give him a white stone, and in the stone a new name written, which no man knoweth save he that receiveth it.

It stuck me that if a person was going to receive a new name, then he or she must finish the course set before him or her.

One might be wondering how a person could keep on course. The Apostle Paul gives us a clue in his statement in 2 Timothy 4:7. It comes down to the three F's of Christianity: Fight the fight, be faithful to finish the course, and maintain the faith.

The fight implies that it is not an easy road to travel, and the greatest challenge is to endure. Satan loves to wear down the patience of the saints; and, in the fast pace of our culture, many Christians offer all their time, resources, and energy upon the different altars of the world. This leaves them with very little strength to even stir themselves up to seek God's strength to fight the battle. Like Hitler in his attempt to conquer the world, Satan is initially taking over much territory with very little resistance from those of the religious world.

Faithfulness to God is what keeps a person on the right course. It actually gently steers an individual down the right path without him or her even being aware of the leading that is taking place. Christians who are faithful will take each step of faith according to the responsibility or task that lies before them. The power of faithfulness is that it always deals in the present, instead of looking ahead for greater things. Steps of faithfulness will always bring a person to greater service and victories.

To keep the faith implies having to maintain or hold on to the faith that was first delivered to the saints. This means holding on to the character and person of God. The Apostle Paul clung to his life in Christ. He was always moving forward to apprehend more of Jesus or to be apprehended by Him. There is no indication that Paul ever simply waited for this life to come to him. He relentlessly sought this life, based on his faith in the Son of God.[11]

It is important for each person to determine if he or she is on the right course. If you have never been born again, you have not even started. If you have officially started this journey, but you are on a detour, it is time to recognize the futility of your pursuit and repent. Genuine repentance will cause you to turn around and begin your journey back towards God. The final consideration is, are you on the course God designed for you?

---

[11] Jude 3; Philippians 3:12; Galatians 2:20

If you are not, you will find yourself becoming very dissatisfied with all aspects of your life, even your Christian life.

Even though the spiritual journey may be hard, the Apostle Paul summarized the blessing of it in this way, "Henceforth there is laid up for me a crown of righteousness, which the Lord, the righteous judge, shall give me at that day: and not to me only, but unto all them also that love his appearing" (2 Timothy 4:8).

2

THE PURPOSE

Why is the Christian faith a journey instead of a religious exercise or practice? The answer is easy because the goal of this spiritual journey is to discover what constitutes true life. Many people perceive their lives to be made up of the things of the world, as well as the right to live their life in any manner they choose, and the pursuit of success according to what they value. Some summarize life in one concept: the pursuit of personal happiness. These ideas of life are illusive and idolatrous. These desires are so deep in many that they have become gods that they relentlessly pursue. The reason they fervently pursue these different idols is because they believe that at the end of their pursuit everything will be as they have imagined and desired.

In order to possess their concept of happiness, people have to become the god of their worlds as they manipulate their reality to acquire the desires of their heart. It all seems harmless until reality brings them to the end of themselves where they realize that even if they could accomplish such a feat, any type of fruition of it will always fall short of their expectations. Many become disillusioned as these pursuits elude them, causing anger and depression.

Sadly, there are many people who want to be gods of their particular world or "little kingdom" as a means to manipulate their environment to comply with their idea of reality. They cannot imagine how their concept of life is far from reality and will bring them into opposition with the one true God who only operates in truth. This truth can only be realized as reality is being addressed in a forthright manner.

Jesus said in John 10:10 that He gives abundant life. This life is satisfying and complete. Many Christians fail to obtain this life because they hold on to their concepts of experiencing life on their terms. To define life on personal terms means a person will define life according to the world and the lust of the flesh. Jesus put this pursuit into perspective, "For what is a man profited, if he shall gain the whole world, and lose his own soul? or what shall a man give in exchange for his soul" (Matthew 16:26)? As you can see, such a pursuit will cause a person to lose his or her own soul.

We know that the Christian walk is to be a journey. As stated, the goal of this journey is to discover what constitutes real life and to possess it. Life is defined as having the ability to respond or interact with the environment. For example, man was made a living soul, so that he could interact with God. Without this interaction with God, the essence of life will be missed, causing man to walk in death and darkness.

The born-again experience is the means to give man the ability to once again interact with his God in a relationship. It is in this relationship that a person can discover the real aspects and benefits of this incredible life.

Sadly, until people begin to walk out the Christian life, they have a perverted definition of it. Often people's unrealistic concept of life will cause the real source of life (God and His righteousness) to look pale in comparison. Such a comparison in light of their fantasy will cause them to reject the real essence of the satisfying life God desires to give them.

People's idea of life is often tied into that which is temporary, but real life is meant to not only be abundant, but eternal. The abundant life is for now, while the eternal aspect of the complete life in Christ will not be realized until one embraces the reality of eternity. In fact, man was created to operate in the eternal. This is why physical death is a harsh reality. Even though physical death is only death to life as people presently know it, it is a shock to their very beings because they cannot perceive their present life coming to an end, especially since the breath of God "marked" mankind with the seal of eternity.

The concept of life for most people is based on how a person's present life is, and anything outside of his or her comprehension seems unrealistic. Therefore, when the temporary aspects of the world are considered in light of eternity, it causes confusion and fear, proving that no one can understand the real basis of life when it is based on that which is temporary.

People also look to the temporary to bring substance to their life. Since many depend on the world, they look to it to sustain their life only to realize that like the world, such temporary substance fades away. The life that the world offers is illusive and lacking any real quality of life. Jesus made this clear when He said, "...Take heed, and beware of covetousness: for a man's life consisteth not in the abundance of the things which he possesses" (Luke 12:15).

Quality of life does not consist of what a person possesses, but what possesses him or her. The Apostle Paul talked about being apprehended by a greater reality that caused him to forget those things that were behind, and reach forth unto those things which were before him.[1]

The apostle's attitude showed how he abandoned the temporary to embrace the eternal. He realized that everything outside of Jesus was useless. Therefore, his attitude towards the temporary allowed him to focus on the eternal. He knew his life was not behind him, and that it was not based on his earthly identity, religious accomplishments, and worldly recognition. He counted such things as being dung. He knew that real life

---

[1] Philippians 3:5-14

came from outside of all of these elements, and his goal was to not only know this life, but to possess it and be possessed by it.[2]

The spiritual passageway to this incredible life has been designed to prepare each person to finish the course. If people fail to walk the course set before them by God, they will not be properly prepared to endure the hardship of the obstacles they will encounter on this journey. They will be unable to overcome the world, subdue the enticement of the flesh, and cause Satan to flee.

This journey is meant to establish godly character, which lies at the heart of real Christianity. It is a way for a person to exercise unto godliness as he or she walks this incredible life out in practical ways.[3] By exercising unto godliness, there will be a separation from that which is unholy, while meekness is worked into the person as he or she submits to the Holy Spirit. Such meekness will be displayed through temperance that reveals itself in upright conduct.

To properly understand this journey, we must grasp what it is not. We already know that it officially starts when we are born of water and Spirit.[4] We also know that even though many take detours on this journey, it is a passage or course that has already been personally designed by God for each individual. Since God has designed this course, it reveals this spiritual journey has a destination.

The perspective that there is a spiritual destination makes this spiritual journey of great importance. Most people take detours because they do not have any particular destination in mind. They end up going with the flow or pursuing accomplishments that have no eternal significance or meaning. They look inward to self or outward to the world to discover life. However, few look upward to Jesus to find this life. In the spiritual realm, people either ignore the spiritual, bringing it down to a worldly nature, or, they chase after the supernatural to gain spiritual insights, ending up with dangerous substitutes. Both attitudes keep people from seeking to know God in an intimate way. This has opened many up to be carried away by every wind of doctrine.[5]

Jesus gave up the glories of heaven and set His face towards Calvary.[6] Nothing could deter Him from His goal to obtain life, for whosoever would believe upon His name, character, or work would receive this life. Like Jesus, we need to set our focus on the destination. This would serve as a powerful deterrent from taking unnecessary and foolish detours.

What kind of destination are you preparing for, heaven or hell? Where is your focus, inward, outward, or upward? Keep in mind what

---

[2] Ibid
[3] 1 Timothy 4:7
[4] John 3:5
[5] Ephesians 4:14
[6] Luke 9:53; Philippians 2:6-8

Hebrews 9:27 says, "And as it is appointed unto men once to die, but after this the judgment."

The next aspect of this spiritual journey we must consider is that it should not be treated as a vacation. We Americans live for our vacations. We imagine, plan, and prepare for them, sometimes a year in advance. When vacation time arrives, many end up disappointed because it did not live up to their expectations. In fact, most people need another vacation after their vacation.

Many people treat Christianity as if it were a vacation from reality, where they will experience bliss, fun, and pleasure. Make no mistake; Christianity will not spare anyone from the trials of this present world. It is not a means to escape reality, but the way by which a person is provided the means in which he or she can face reality in order to come to truth.

It is in truth that a person can find freedom from the disheartening reality of the world. After all, Jesus is the truth and a person's only source of rest and lasting pleasure. His reality should penetrate every aspect of each of our lives. He is not some insignificant part of reality—He is reality. To tack Jesus on or compartmentalize Him is to do away with the real place of rest and protection.[7] Therefore, the strength found in Christianity comes with the ability to face reality, in order to embrace the truth of Jesus, thereby, experiencing both rest and pleasure in this world.

Jesus left the beauty of heaven to travel through this world. In other words, He gave up all that heaven possesses to embrace the worst the world could throw His way. His journey was not a vacation. The persecution He suffered was not fun and the cross He bore was not pleasurable. He never took a vacation away from the Father. Everything Jesus did was in consideration of His Father's heart and will, and He found His truest form of joy in His intimate union with Him.

Jesus is our example. Are you willing to give up the vainglories of this world to embrace the beauty and light of heaven—Jesus Christ? Are you looking to Christianity to fulfill a fantasy of a blessed life of fun and pleasure? Perhaps you even want to take a vacation from God because you are still clinging to the vanity of the world to fulfill your needs and give you pleasure.

The spiritual journey does not point to some future moving trip either. Many Christians consider this spiritual journey in consideration of the future and not in light of the present. They see the Christian life in terms of first experiencing the life the world has to offer, while doing a few good things to keep God off their backs. They hold onto the things of the past, such as unforgiveness and wounds, in order to claim the right to live outside of the Word. Or, they excuse themselves from taking present responsibility due to a lack of devotion. They store up things for the future, for the time when they will feel financially secure. In their minds

---

[7] Matthew 11:28-29; John 8:32-36; 14:6

when they are financially secured according to the world, they will be able to sell out or abandon all to serve God.

Sadly, if they fail to sell out when they are called, they never will. There will always be excuses, and time will pass them by. Ultimately, such individuals will see their service to God as always being in the future. I have seen this sad scenario many times. Such people never get around to selling out and truly serving God.

Meanwhile, many Christians continue to live for self as they think of the spiritual journey in the future tense. They put roots down in this world and store up worldly treasures in case God fails them along the way. All of their treasures lead back to the lusts of the world, and not to God.

Christianity is a journey that needs to be prevalent in our life on a daily basis. To effectively take this journey, a person must travel lightly. Hebrews 12:1 states, "...let us lay aside every weight, and the sin which doth so easily beset us, and let us run with patience the race that is set before us."

This verse shows us that the journey is much like a race that will test our patience. We must lay aside those things which will keep us from effectively running this race, such as our associations with the world, the dictates of the flesh, and the influences of sin.

Are you one of those who are weighed down, or are you ready to walk the walk? 1 John 2:6 states, "He that saith he abideth in him ought himself also so to walk, even as he walked." The key to walking this walk is found in abiding in Jesus. He is the One who gives individuals the ability to travel this spiritual passageway.

The Christian walk is not a sightseeing excursion. Many Christians embrace the idea of Christianity to "see the sights," which can include anything from blessings, miracles, and religious entertainment, to signs and wonders. These sights may excite the fleshly appetites and responses, but they do not constitute real life.

These sightseeing Christians watch others as well. Such people are unrealistic about what constitutes real Christianity, and become judgmental towards those who do not live up to their expectations. They remind me of armchair quarterbacks. They expertly play the game from the comfort of their armchairs, but the truth is, they are on the sidelines and not in the game. When you are in the middle of the real battle, you have a different and often limited perspective as to what is going on.

Sightseeing is for the spectator, not the participant, and there is no exception in the kingdom of God. The Christian walk is a walk of faith, not a walk according to sight. Granted, there are many treasures to discover, mysteries to uncover, and riches to be possessed. However, these blessings are all spiritual in nature, and can only be discovered as one walks out the Christian life.[8]

---

[8] 2 Corinthians 5:7; Ephesians 1:3

For example, the greatest treasure we must discover is the unspeakable gift from heaven, Jesus Christ. The greatest mystery we must uncover is Christ in us, the hope of glory. The riches that are to be obtained can only be found in the eternal inheritance that belongs to all the children of God.[9]

Are you just along for the ride and the show? If you are, it means you are a spectator, not a participant of the Christian journey.

When you combine those who consider Christianity in light of a vacation, a future moving trip, or a sightseeing experience, you have people who simply think, talk, dream, or plan to take the spiritual journey, but never do it. As a result, they fail to make their life in Christ and their calling a reality. They are hearers of the Word, but not doers of it.[10]

The ones who *think* about the journey may work it out in their mind, but never act it out in practicality. In fact, they waste much of their energy in thinking about what they are going to do, rather than simply doing it. Proverbs 3:5-7 puts this intellectual exercise into this perspective, "Trust in the LORD with all thine heart; and lean not unto thine own understanding. In all thy ways acknowledge him, and he shall direct thy paths. Be not wise in thine own eyes: fear the LORD, and depart from evil."

These Scripture verses in Proverbs show that these people do not trust the Lord, but have put their confidence in their own understanding. As a result, they have failed to seek Him in all their ways so He could direct their steps. They see themselves as being wise, yet they do not fear the Lord, and will not recognize that they are operating in evil or idolatry.

Those who *talk* about the Christian life, but who fail to reach great heights are simply manifesting an exercise in emotions. These people get on an emotional high by talking about spiritual truths or plans, but they never carry them out because of fear. They actually fear reality, because it rarely rises up to meet their expectations. Therefore, they avoid it by bluffing their way through with talk.

Talk is cheap and these people are not willing to be tested on any other terms but their own. If they do not get the emotional sensation they desire, they will give way to frustration, give in to anger, and become skeptical. They falter in their spiritual life, because they have not set their affections on things above.[11]

The people who only *dream* great dreams rather than be faithful with what is in front of them, make up what I refer to as the dreamers. They have grandiose dreams that they can present in such a way that you actually think it is reality. Sadly, these people believe the fantasy to be reality. In their mind, it is already accomplished, even though they have

---

[9] 2 Corinthians 9:15; Ephesians 1:3-14; 2:7; Colossians 1:27; 2:2-3
[10] James 1:22-25
[11] Colossians 3:1-2

done absolutely nothing. Eventually, they begin to operate in delusion that identifies them as fools.

The dreamers like to see themselves in greatness, but they are not willing to pay the price of a servant. They want it handed to them without any toil, because, in their minds, they actually deserve it. Jesus made this statement in Luke 14:28, "For which of you, intending to build a tower, sitteth not down first, and counteth the cost, whether he have sufficient to finish it?" If a person is not willing to pay the price, then let it be known that such dreams are nothing but vain imaginations, that will eventually rise up and judge God unfairly.

Finally, those who have great *plans* for Christ's kingdom are often motivated by self-exaltation. When such people pursue their plans, their underlying motivation is to build earthly kingdoms, rather than further the kingdom of God. Their vision is inward towards personal abilities and outward as far as drawing certain procedures from the world to accomplish this feat. The possible bigness of these religious kingdoms replaces true anointing, the vision for lost souls, the preaching of the real Gospel, and the heart for the mission field. The reality of God, His truth, message, and ways being established in us, are replaced with worldly financial security, prestige, and success.

These types of individuals are not co-laborers with God. Rather, they are just laboring to ensure that their plan is brought to fruition, regardless of God's will and plan. Of course, it is all in the name of Jesus, and considered righteous. However, Psalm 127:1 states, "Except the LORD build the house, they labour in vain that build it: except the LORD keep the city, the watchman waketh but in vain." Man's labors apart from God are all done in vain no matter how religious they may appear.

We are not just to think, talk, dream, or plan, we must do that which is right before God. We must walk this life out or it will have no meaning to it.

This reminds me of the incident when King David was instructing Solomon to build the temple. King David had it in his heart to build it, but because he was a man of war, God gave the responsibility to Solomon who was a man of peace. This did not stop King David from taking an active role in it. He laid out the pattern, drew up the plans, and put aside the means by which to acquire the material. As a result, the king said this to Solomon in 1 Chronicles 28:10, "Take heed now; for the LORD hath chosen thee to build an house for the sanctuary: be strong, and <u>do it</u>". (Emphasis added.)

God has given every Christian the pattern of Jesus Christ and the detailed plan of the Christian life or journey in His Word. He has given every believer the means to accomplish this feat through the power and anointing of the Holy Spirit. Therefore, all the Christian has to do is <u>do it</u>!

Steps of obedience, which include following the pattern, adhering to the plans, and surrendering to the Holy Ghost, will enable the wayfarer to discover the life God has for him or her. This life is eternal and can only be found in Jesus Christ.

Jesus said, "I am the way." In other words, He is the pattern that serves as our example that we must follow to complete the journey.[12]

In the same verse, He went on to say, "I am...the truth." He is the reality that prepares the person to walk in spirit and truth. Since He never changes, reality remains the same. This reality has the potential to make a person free.[13]

He ended the thought with this statement, "I am...the life." He is the life that we must possess. He is not only the essence of eternal life, but He is the source of the abundant life that contains the riches of heaven. He is the life that God is trying to work within each believer.

This life leads to an intimate relationship with the Father. Jesus confirmed this, "I am the way, the truth, and the life: and no man cometh unto the Father, but by me" (John 14:6). The spiritual journey is meant to lead a person into a relationship with the Father where there is healing, restoration, and peace.

Have you discovered this life (or relationship), or are you treating Christianity as a vacation, a future move, a sightseeing tour, or a fantasy that tantalizes the mind and emotions, but is never walked out? If you are not sure, ask God to show you, because if you do not walk the walk, you will never discover the depth and power of a relationship with God; therefore, you will never possess the life He has for you.

---

[12] John 14:6
[13] John 8:32

3

THE DISPOSITION

In order to take this spiritual pilgrimage, a person must have the right disposition to become a spiritual wayfarer in this world. The Apostle Peter confirmed this in 1 Peter 2:11, "Dearly beloved, I beseech you as strangers and pilgrims, abstain from fleshly lusts, which war against the soul." Peter is referring to the saints as strangers and pilgrims in this world. He is beseeching or exhorting them to maintain the integrity of this status by abstaining from fleshly lusts.

James 1:14-15 gives this insight into the destruction of fleshly lusts, "But every man is tempted, when he is drawn away of his own lust, and enticed. Then when lust hath conceived, it bringeth forth sin: and sin, when it is finished, bringeth forth death." Fleshly lust has to do with the world. The Apostle Peter talked about having to escape the corruption that is in the world through lust. Obviously, fleshly lust opens us up to the world. John tells us in his first epistle that the world is made up of the lust of the flesh, the pride of life, and the lust of the eyes. In other words, it is designed to attract us through lust into the entanglements of the world, bringing us to spiritual ruin.[1]

The enticements of the world are all fleshly in nature, which explains their alluring abilities. However, they are vanity and can only serve as a temporary utopia or fix. This temporary fix enhances the fleshly taste buds to pursue more fulfillments. Each pursuit enlarges the appetites, creating a spiritual vacuum that will eventually cause leanness to the soul.

The Apostle Peter warns the saints in 1 Peter 2:11 to maintain the life they have in Christ, by abstaining from fleshly lusts that result in death. Sadly, many Christians are not heeding Peter's warning. They are actually partaking of the things of the world which clearly opposes Scripture.

The world is our enemy, but it serves as a present constant reality to each of us. We have to live and operate within its boundaries. We struggle with it because much of the world is neither good nor bad. Therefore, how can we be separate from it and still function? This once again brings us back to the enticements of the world—the emphasis that

---

[1] 2 Peter 1:4; 1 John 2:16

we put on the things of the world. The answer rests with where a person's heart or affections are being directed.[2]

As Christians, we should be directing our affections towards God. This means partaking of the things of God due to the fact that all believers have escaped the corruption that is in the world. However, the reality is that if we as Christians have escaped, some appear to have run back into it. There is no real distinction between many who call themselves "Christians" and the world. This unhealthy relationship with the world has caused them to have an ungodly mixture in their lives before God. The result is spiritual dullness, which prevents believers from properly discerning the holy from the unholy.

James 4:4 makes this statement about any type of close association with the world, "Ye adulterers and adulteresses, know ye not that the friendship of the world is enmity with God? Whosoever therefore will be a friend of the world is the enemy of God." It is spiritual adultery for the Christian to have friendship or a close association with the world, because it results in an ungodly mixture that causes inconsistency, hinders spiritual growth, and strips the believer of his or her authority and power to overcome. This inability to overcome will ultimately produce a weak Church that will easily fall prey to Satan.

Spiritual adultery manifests itself when Christians lack love, passion, and commitment towards God, and towards the Person of Jesus. Such manifestation reveals that the heart is far away from God, regardless of what is being said or done.[3]

1 John 5:4-5 goes one step further to make this declaration, "For whatsoever is born of God overcometh the world: and this is the victory that overcometh the world, even our faith. Who is he that overcometh the world, but he that believeth that Jesus is the Son of God?" The Word of God is decisive. If a person is born from above, he or she will be overcoming the world. The reason for this victory is because such an individual truly believes that Jesus is who He says He is.

In John 16:33, Jesus gave us this insight into why a person who believes in Him will overcome the world, in spite of the challenges and tribulations it presents, "These things I have spoken unto you, that in me ye might have peace. In the world ye shall have tribulation: but be of good cheer; I have overcome the world."

When you read John 13-16, you realize that Jesus is telling His followers what to expect from this world. The world will hate them because it hated Him. He explains that the reason for this animosity is because the Christian is not of the world, because He has chosen him or her out of it. This clear distinction will create enmity between these two distinct kingdoms, because the Christian will serve as both the salt that

---

[2] Matthew 6:23; Colossians 3:2
[3] Matthew 15:8-9

will cause a reaction from those who belong to the world, and the light that will expose the heart attitudes inspired by the world.[4]

Sadly, so much of the world has been allowed into the Church in attitudes, practices, and philosophy, that, even now many sincere believers are unable to see how full of the world they are. The influence of the world seems harmless enough, but in reality, it has the ability to lull the Church to sleep, as it devises means to lead innocent and well-meaning believers to the slaughter. Today these two entities often come into an unholy agreement to promote the same emphasis in the name of peace, political correctness, and unity.

Jesus guaranteed His followers that they would not have an easy time in this world, but that through Him they could overcome and be able to find true peace. As He stated in John 14:27, "Peace I leave with you, my peace I give unto you: not as the world giveth, give I unto you. Let not your heart be troubled, neither let it be afraid."

Today, many Christians are in the midst of conflict, because there is no real distinction in their attitudes, speech, and practices from the unbeliever. They have one foot in the world and one in Christianity in an attempt to bring both worlds together, so that they can have the best of this present world, and still experience heaven. In most cases, they can remain comfortable in these two worlds, because much of the Church does not call for separation from the present age. These individuals can juggle both worlds without being challenged or confronted; that is, until someone begins to bring the contrast between these two entities. Then, the conflict between the Spirit and the flesh begins as the Holy Ghost starts to bring conviction.[5]

This inner struggle not only takes place in their personal lives, but it affects their other relationships. People become miserable as they continue to attempt to hold on to both worlds. This misery will eventually cause resentment towards the One who demands that they make a choice between these two entities. Jesus spoke about this resentment in Matthew 6:24, "No man can serve two masters: for either he will hate the one, and love the other; or else he will hold to the one, and despise the other. Ye cannot serve God and mammon." The influence of the present age not only chokes out the power and purity of the Word and work of God in people's lives, but they will not have the authority to overcome. Their testimony will be rendered ineffective.

Most Christians do not realize that Christianity and the world denote not only two opposing worlds, but also different spirits. In fact, the spirit behind true Christianity and the spirit of world will not mix when brought together. And, when there is such an unholy mixture in the believer, it signals some serious spiritual problems.

---

[4] John 15:18-19
[5] John 16:8-11; Galatians 5:16-18

The Christian, who is overcoming through Christ, is under the power of the Holy Spirit, but the Christian, who is subject to the world, comes under the domain of Satan. Ephesians 2:2-3 gives this insight,

> Wherein in times past ye walked according to the course of this world, according to the prince of the power of the air, the spirit that now worketh in the children of disobedience: Among whom also we all had our conversation in times past in the lusts of our flesh, fulfilling the desires of the flesh and of the mind; and were by nature the children of wrath even as others.

The spirit of the world works within disobedience and will result in judgment. Therefore, Christians who are greatly influenced by the world will often find themselves at odds with God. They will actually come under the spirit of the world and thus begin to feel rebellion rising up within them as they begin to claim rights. The more the world has inroads, the greater the disobedience and the carnality of the Christian.

A carnal Christian works on a fleshly, intellectual level, making him or her subject to the attitudes of the world. The world's influence in a Christian's life will translate into rebellion, complacency, insatiable, worldly appetites (paganism), or depression. These influences will cause such individuals to become lukewarm in their life towards God as the world chokes out their life in God.[6] They will also become agitated when they are challenged to choose between the world and the cross.

The cross for the Christian represents death to all the powerful influences of the world. The Apostle Paul described this death in this way in Galatians 6:14, "But God forbid that I should glory, save in the cross of our Lord Jesus Christ, by whom the world is crucified unto me, and I unto the world."

Carnal Christians, who want to maintain their right to experience the world, avoid becoming crucified to its influences. After all, these influences need to be killed outright. Why do believers want the right to hold on to the world? It comes down to their disposition or attitude towards it.

Disposition is based on the person's perception of something. This perception determines what a person values and pursues. Therefore, the real attraction to the world that many Christians possess and maintain comes down to their perception of it.

Worldly perception is very self-serving, because it is based on the notion of how the world can benefit the person's personal goals and desires. As long as a person sees the world as offering something of value, he or she will cling to it. Since worldly goals and desires are inspired by self-centeredness, it will open a person up to the world's deception.

A person's attraction to the world cannot cease until his or her disposition is transformed by the renewing of the mind by the Spirit of

---

[6] Matthew 13:22

God. The Apostle Paul makes reference to this in Romans 12:2, "And be not conformed to this world: but be ye transformed by the renewing of your mind, that ye may prove what is that good, and acceptable, and perfect, will of God."

In order for the mind to be transformed to redefine a person's perception of the world, he or she must come into agreement with God's perspective or definition of it. This disposition does not take place until the world's importance or values are actually redefined by the individual, and he or she begins to adhere to the scriptural instructions concerning it.

It takes the Holy Ghost to change a person's ungodly disposition towards the world, but it takes the Christian to show the proper attitude or response towards the issues of life to ensure that he or she does not become entangled in the world again. The Apostle Paul gives insight into the first response a person must have in regards to the world in 2 Corinthians 6:14-18. Let me highlight some of these instructions.

> Be ye not unequally yoked...what agreement hath the temple of God with idols...Wherefore come out from among them, and be ye separate, saith the Lord, and touch not the unclean thing; and I will receive you, And will be a Father unto you, and ye shall be my sons and daughters...

The person must become separate in attitude, affections, speech, and practices from the world. This separation includes such things as not coming into agreement or fellowshipping with that which belongs to the world, which is the way a person touches the world. An individual must not touch the things of the world, because they will defile the person, making him or her spiritually dull.

After a person separates from the influence of the world, he or she must flee the attractions of the world when he or she encounters them. The word "flee" means to run away, to shun, or to escape from.[7] The world has tentacles; therefore, it has the ability to once again entangle a person into its web, even after he or she has been separated from it.[8] Therefore, it is vital that Christians guard themselves against these tentacles by fleeing the world's attractions.

There are three main avenues by which the world can once again entangle a person. These avenues are in compliance with the three means by which a person is attracted to the world: the lust of the flesh, the pride of life, and the lust of the eyes. The first avenue is found in 1 Corinthians 6:18, "Flee fornication. Every sin that a man doeth is without the body; but he that committeth fornication sinneth against his own body."

"Fornication" in this text means unlawful lust that includes all illicit sex and spiritual harlotry. This sin points to sinful acts carried on in the

---

[7] Strong's Exhaustive Concordance of the Bible, #5343
[8] 2 Timothy 2:3-4

flesh that are thought to bring satisfaction. Such activities bring a person into spiritual agreement with the practices of the world.

We see this agreement even in the Church as it seeks the world's methods and practices to promote or attract more people to its many denominations. Although the leadership justifies these worldly practices in the name of Christ, it is often no more than adopting the world's ways to compete for more money and prestige. In most cases, it has nothing to do with lost souls, but with money and power that comes with numbers.

The Apostle Paul tells us that the love of money is the root of all evil. The root of this evil has to do with the fact that money is associated with such pursuits as power, prestige, and success. Such a pursuit gives people the means to justify and compromise character and honesty in their practices, while in the Christian world, it justifies merchandising men's souls.[9]

The agreement between the world and the Church has caused many churches to become organizations that are clothed in an appearance of righteousness, but are void of power and life. The Church's attraction is no longer Jesus being lifted up, but a promise of a religious cloak that will hide the world's influence behind a façade of righteousness. Such a façade maintains a religious appearance, but in attitude and practice there is no real separation from the world. As a result, much of the visible Church has lost its savor to make a difference in the world.[10]

The other part of fornication is spiritual harlotry. Spiritual harlotry points to a Christian who is prostituting him or herself with the world. This prostitution points to a person selling him or herself in the area of perversion and destruction. The examples of this spiritual harlotry can be found in addictions, pornography, pleasure, and lusts. The world's goal is to make people dependent on its various systems. This dependency becomes spiritual harlotry as the world begins to serve as the person's source of life and salvation.

The second avenue of the world that entangles many into its deadly tentacles is idolatry. The world is full of idols, and 1 Corinthians 10:14 commands, "Wherefore, my dearly beloved, flee from idolatry." This instruction was in relationship to Israel in the wilderness. They were prone to idolatry, for they had lived within the environment of idolatry in Egypt for four centuries. (Egypt is a type of the world.)

God brought the children of Israel out from Egypt, but the idols of Egypt remained erected in their hearts and minds. Whenever life became difficult in the wilderness, the Israelites looked back to Egypt, and murmured against the one true God. This brought judgment upon them more than once.

---

[9] 2 Peter 2:1-3
[10] Luke 14:34-35; 2 Timothy 3:5

Developing Our Christian Life

In 1 Corinthians 10:13, we read, "There hath no temptation taken you but such is common to man: but God is faithful, who will not suffer you to be tempted above that ye are able; but will with the temptation also make a way to escape, that ye may be able to bear it." Many Christians quote this scripture, but they fail to recognize the context of it. This verse is preceded by this instruction, "Wherefore let him that thinketh he standeth take heed lest he fall."

We see 1 Corinthians 10:12 making reference to the sin of pride. In fact, the greatest idol of man is pride. Christians fail to recognize that they are vulnerable to the traps of the world due to pride. Pride either inspires or gives way to all idolatry. It sets people up to fall into their own traps, as they become deceived about their ability to flirt, toy, or play games with the world without consequences. How wrong they are!

Whenever pride reigns, man will look towards the world for perspective and purpose. For example, many people stumble over Jesus, because He does not fit their religious notions, or He is considered foolish because of the world's presentations. In each of these scenarios, it all comes back to man's pride, which is arrogant and unteachable. This is why there are so many cults, and why many are attracted to the occult.

God has given every believer a way to escape the destruction of the temptation of sin, but many people fail to take the way out, because it requires humbling self and fleeing all idols. All idolatry serves as an open door for temptation to entice and defeat. Therefore, all Christians must recognize the idols of the world and flee from them, as soon as they encounter them.

Believers cannot successfully flee idolatry until they neglect the claims and rights of pride. As long as one gives way to pride, the world will serve as its platform of exaltation and the flesh as the attractive bridge to the world. As long as pride reigns in unhindered vainglory, idolatry has both free reign and an open door.

The third avenue can be found in 2 Timothy 2:22, "Flee also youthful lusts." When you consider this type of lust, you realize that it involves the lust of the eyes. The youth especially get caught up with this form of lust because it serves as a point of identity for them.

For example, many young people believe that they must fit into the world, so they must present themselves a certain way, by wearing certain clothes, adhering to popular fads, and advocating a particular morality, while walking and talking a certain way. Sadly, many lose a sense of self, as they succumb to the psychology of the world and peer pressure. They become lost in a bigger identity that lacks stability, because it is an image that hinges on temporary fads without regard to individual personality.

Needless to say, when people look to the world for satisfaction, importance, and identity, they are showing dependency on the world. This is why people are told to flee worldly enticement. Such a response will change their focus, thereby, changing their emphasis. Once a person flees these worldly enticements, Scripture stipulates what he or she must pursue. 1 Timothy 6:11 says, "But thou, O man of God, flee these things; and follow after righteousness, godliness, faith, love, patience, meekness."

2 Timothy 2:22 states, "Flee also youthful lusts: but follow righteousness, faith, charity, peace, with them that call on the Lord out of a pure heart." Christians are commanded to flee enticements of the world, but they must fill up their vacant lives by following and pressing after that which is righteous (upright), godly (lining up to God's character), of faith (in our walk), inspired by godly love (motivation), maintained through longsuffering (character), and under the control of the Holy Spirit.

If a person follows after these godly virtues, it will put him or her on the right path, allowing for the Spirit of God to transform his or her disposition towards the world. The world will become less and less important, as Jesus becomes more and more consuming.

It is important that, as Christians, we examine our disposition. Are we conforming to the world, or are we being transformed, so we can effectively take this spiritual pilgrimage? And, if we are being transformed, what kind of attitude will manifest itself to clearly reveal to others that we have been set apart from the world in every aspect of our lives?

Before you can examine the correct attitude towards the world, you must determine what your disposition or attitude towards it is. Are you a friend of it or are you an enemy of it who is aware that it will rob you of your life in Christ, kill your testimony, and destroy your faith?

4

BECOMING A SOJOURNER

As you have learned from the last chapter, our attitude towards the world will determine what kind of emphasis we will put on it. This attitude will also establish what kind of relationship we will have with the world. There are four types of dispositions towards the world that will establish the type of relationship we will have with God through Jesus Christ.

The first type of disposition is that of the *victim*. Many people become victims of the world as they fall prey to Satan's various snares or traps of lies and temptations. These traps include such things as addiction, abuses, and perversion. These people find themselves being forced to sell their souls to maintain a semblance of existence, while drowning in despair, loneliness, and hopelessness. Such victims are in total bondage to Satan's devices and cannot see any way out of the prison they find themselves in.

The second disposition belongs to the *associates* of the world. These are the people who play on the plight of the victims. They often use the victims as well as seek out the innocent, foolish, and lonely to further their wicked pursuits. They operate under the guise of success, as they promote the work of darkness and wreak havoc in people's lives.

These people have willingly sold their souls to the power of darkness in the hope of gaining wealth, prestige, and power. They are cruel in disposition and are only interested in climbing the ladder of success and power, regardless of who they hurt or use on their way up.

The third group is those who *prostitute* themselves with the world in order to enjoy its many pleasures. These pleasure seekers do not care what they sell along the way, as long as the pleasure keeps coming. These individuals are self-centered and rarely deal in reality. They become more flippant about possible consequences as their appetites enlarge with each taste of the world's pleasures.

The fourth group is comprised of those who are *sojourners*. They are simply passing through this world. They do not plan to stay long enough to become a victim of Satan's various devices. They are repulsed at its wicked ways, and are not impressed with its pleasures because they see it all as vanity.

Obviously, when we study these four different dispositions, the only correct one would be the sojourner. But, how many Christians have remained victims to the world because of entanglements that are still clinging to them? These Christians struggle with guilt, condemnation, and defeat.

Other Christians are associates with the world. They see themselves as simply using the world for their own purposes, but are blinded to its traps that will set them up for a destructive fall. Once this type of Christian falls into the trap, he or she can end up becoming skeptical of truth and become a mocker of God.

Then there are the Christians who are seeking certain pleasures from the world. These pleasures are not necessarily good or bad, but they can constitute an unhealthy desire that will cause believers to come into an unholy agreement with the world. This type of prostitution will end in complacency, lust, and misery.

If Christians are sojourners in this world, they will serve as strangers and pilgrims that Peter made reference to in 1 Peter 2:11. Hebrews 11:13 gives us this insight about the spiritual strangers and pilgrims traveling through this world, "These all died in faith, not having received the promises, but having seen them afar off, and were persuaded of them, and embraced them, and confessed that they were strangers and pilgrims on the earth."

The real strangers and pilgrims of the world walked in faith in their God and embraced His promises, even though they never witnessed them coming to fruition. They confessed by their lives and mouths that they were not of this world, and that they belonged elsewhere. In fact, Hebrews 11:38 stated this about them, "(Of whom the world was not worthy)."

When you study the scriptural concept of a stranger and the historical perspective of a pilgrim, you get a powerful picture of what these two terms mean for the Christian. A stranger is a foreigner whose stay in a place is temporary. In the scheme of things, this foreigner is simply a visitor, heading to a permanent or final destination.

As strangers, all of the surroundings are foreign to them such as customs, language, and culture. They are not acquainted with the idiosyncrasies of their environment, nor do they care to be for their affection and focus are elsewhere. Therefore, their temporary abode has no real attraction.

Philippians 3:20 states, "For our conversation is in heaven; from whence also we look for the Saviour, the Lord Jesus Christ." This verse tells us that our focus is heavenward. The more intent our focus becomes towards heaven, the stranger the world will become to us.

We can see this attitude in the lives of many saints. For example, Abraham was given many impressive promises, but in Genesis 15:1, his greatest possession is defined, "After these things the word of the LORD came unto Abram in a vision, saying, Fear not, Abram: I am thy shield, and thy exceeding great reward."

First of all, we see that Abraham was given a vision. Proverbs 29:18 tells us that where there is no vision, people perish. Today, Christians lack spiritual vision and are falling into the various traps of Satan. This is why Jesus instructed Christians in the end days to watch in order to be aware of their spiritual lives and the times they live in.[1] Such a condition points to spiritual blindness.

Spiritual blindness means that one is spiritually dull and unable to properly discern what is around him or her. Discernment is necessary in walking out this spiritual pilgrimage, because without it, one is unable to properly judge what is happening.

As you study the life of Abraham, you can see that he left his old way of life behind him and became a stranger in this world. It must have been an overwhelming experience as he faced a world that was foreign to him. God assured him that he needed not to be afraid of his status as a stranger, for He would be with Him.

Some Christians fear becoming strangers in this world. They hold on to the old life or old ways, instead of abandoning all to know Jesus. Yet, being a stranger in this world allows a person to discover Jesus in a more personal way.

In Numbers 35, God provided six refuge cities throughout Israel for the manslayer, stranger, and sojourner. These cities offered protection and were to remind Israel that they were strangers in Egypt until God brought them forth as sojourners in the world. They wandered around in the wilderness until God led them to the place that He had given Abraham: the Promised Land.

The number "six" reminds man of his imperfection that causes him to be vulnerable to defeat, but the city symbolizes how God is man's real refuge.[2] In fact, the refuge cities are a type of Christ. Christ serves as a means of escape and protection to every heavy-laden sinner who is seeking rest from guilt, as well as a place of hope to hide in. Colossians 3:3 confirms this refuge, "For ye are dead, and your life is hid with Christ in God."

To enjoy the protection of the refuge city, one must be within its gates. This was brought out in an interesting incident that took place in 2 Samuel 3. There had been war between the house of David and the house of Saul after Saul had been killed and David was crowned king. Within the courts of King Ishbosheth, Saul's son, was a man named Abner. Abner was over the army, but became strong in the kingdom, due to Ishbosheth's weak leadership.

Ishbosheth accused Abner of defiling one of Saul's concubines. This made Abner furious with the king and he contacted David to make peace with him. While Abner was on his way home from making peace with David, Joab, one of the leaders in David's army, heard about the peace agreement. Joab had cause against Abner because he had killed his brother in one of the skirmishes. Joab devised a plan to bring Abner back

---

[1] Matthew 24:42-43; Mark 13:32-37; Luke 21:36
[2] Joshua 20:7

to Hebron where Joab met him outside of the gate. There, Joab killed him.

The reason this incident caught my attention is that Hebron was a refuge city.[3] If only Abner had made it through the gate into the city, he would have been protected from Joab's vengeance. If Joab had killed Abner within the city, he would be considered a murderer and prosecuted, but because Abner was outside of the gate, he was not protected, making him open prey to man's vengeance.

Jesus is not only the Christian's refuge city, but He is also the door or gate. One must enter into Him to be delivered from the wrath to come.[4] As you can see from the example, it matters little how close you are to the gate, you must enter into the safety of Jesus to be assured of protection. Are you one of those who still remains outside of the gate and protection of Jesus?

Jesus welcomes and protects all strangers of every age who seek His auspice. The gate is not closed, but thrown wide open. However, a person must enter through the gate, seeking refuge from the uncertainty and strangeness of the world. Once inside of the gate, there is nothing to fear from the foreign environment.

Abraham was also told that the Lord was his reward. This man of faith realized that the quality of his life was not based on future promises, but on the present reality of his God. Because Abraham's focus was on a heavenly mark, it set the course he would walk. Hebrews 11:8-10 summarizes this man's journey through a strange land, but it also decisively states his secret for his success, "For he looked for a city which hath foundations, whose builder and maker is God."

If only Jesus' sheep had Abraham's vision, they would not become entangled with this world. They would consider themselves strangers in it, as they pursued their heavenly destination, the unhindered glory of the lover of their souls.

Pilgrims are different from strangers. Strangers are on their way to a destination, while pilgrims are in search of a place that allows them the freedom they so long for. These people are restless in their spirits. They not only desire to worship God, but they always sense there is more, and they seek to find it. As they seek to know God and understand their place in Him, they become more determined to secure this place. In the case of pilgrims, the freedom they seek is that of being able to worship God according to their religious convictions and teachings.

American history is greatly marked by the humble beginnings of the pilgrims. These people resented the religious oppression they suffered in Europe. They stood distinct from the European ways and culture, as they reckoned the government wicked and the culture worldly and unholy.

---

[3] Ibid
[4] John 10:7-9; 1 Thessalonians 5:9

Developing Our Christian Life

Due to their strict adherence to separation from both, they tasted the bitterness of persecution.

It is not enough to be a stranger in attitude; you must be a pilgrim in disposition. The pilgrims' desire was to freely worship God. When given the opportunity to pursue this freedom of worship, they abandoned the life they knew, and willingly faced unknown hardships and possible death. To these people, hardship and death were a reasonable price to pay to be able to properly love, serve, and worship their God.

The hardships were indescribable for the pilgrims who came to America, and many died before they saw the fruition of their commitment. However, their abandonment to possess the uncompromised, holy life serves as an example to every saint of God. Obviously, these individuals viewed the world as an enemy. They saw the world's government as a wicked, tyrannical taskmaster that stood in their way of properly worshipping their God. They not only rejected the world, but they cared little about their own welfare. They knew that without the reality of God in their midst, life meant nothing.

If only the followers of Jesus had such a disposition towards the world and an undying devotion to God. They could be assured of standing distinct in the present darkness. Not only would they have power in their prayer closets, but they would also have the unhindered ability to worship God.

God formed man to worship Him. It is within every living being to become an avenue or vessel of praise unto God. Today, the importance of worship is either downplayed or commercialized. It is either a term without meaning or a form of idolatry, as people exalt their particular form of worship.

God deserves worship, and it is a very important part of the saint's life, but many do not know how to worship. This was brought out in the incident with the Samaritan woman in John 4. This woman's main concern was to know how to properly worship God. We actually see Jesus taking time to meet with her and answer her question. He made this valuable statement to her, "But the hour cometh, and now is, when the true worshippers shall worship the Father in spirit and in truth: for the Father seeketh such to worship him. God is a Spirit: and they that worship him must worship him in spirit and in truth" (John 4:23-24). If only Jesus' bride had the same concern about knowing how to properly adore her bridegroom, her families and fellowships would greatly change.

The truth is much of the Church lacks power because many are not searching for a life or a place that would be pleasing to God. This lack of spiritual adventure exists because many are not dissatisfied with this present world; therefore, they see no need to abandon it to seek out a greater life in Christ.

Sadly, many Christians are not sojourners due to the place the world holds in their lives. They have put roots down in this world and they intend to stay. As a result, they are missing the life that God wants to bestow upon them.

This brings us to another important aspect of this spiritual journey: that of identification. When you study the lives of those who have successfully made this spiritual pilgrimage, you will see that it was about identification.

This is clearly brought out in the life of Jesus. Jesus was a stranger in the world He created. He was a pilgrim, as He rejected the ways of man's religion and the world. His ultimate goal was to bring the liberty to worship God to those who would come seeking Him.

In order to accomplish this feat, He became identified with mankind. He took on the disposition of a servant, and allowed Himself to be fashioned in the form of man. He was tempted in all areas, but without sin. On the cross, He became a sin offering. As the Lamb of God, He actually became an exchange or substitute for each of us.[5]

The path Jesus traveled on earth serves as our pattern. He became identified with each of us on His journey; therefore, we must become identified with Him in our walk.[6]

As a stranger, we must separate from this world. Our vision must be heavenward and daily we must seek Jesus out as our refuge. We must avoid becoming too familiar or comfortable with the world. The only way we can do this is to deny self and abstain from the many attractions of the world. This denial can only effectively be done in light of our heavenly destination.

As pilgrims, we should be restless in our hearts until we find our place of worship and rest in Jesus. We must be repulsed enough by the activities of the world, that we seek ways to recklessly abandon ourselves to discover a greater life. This abandonment is not only a form of consecration, but it points to the application of the cross. The application of the cross points to death to what we know, in order to embrace what our hearts should be desperately seeking—the means to worship God in spirit and truth.

This spiritual journey is the way of self-denial and the cross. It will lead one into total identification with Jesus. In the end, this can be our glorious claim, "I am crucified with Christ: nevertheless I live; yet not I, but Christ liveth in me: and the life which I now live in the flesh I live by the faith of the Son of God, who loved me, and gave himself for me" (Galatians 2:20).

How about you? If you have roots in this world, you will never become a stranger. If your affections are directed towards it, you will never be a pilgrim. If you have agreement with the world in some way, are you a victim, associate, or one who prostitutes yourself with it? Are you truly a stranger in attitude and a pilgrim in heart, or are you losing

---

[5] 2 Corinthians 5:21; Hebrews 4:15
[6] 1 John 2:6

Developing Our Christian Life

your spiritual status by becoming more entangled with the devices of this world?

5

THE PATH

A pilgrimage means that one must follow a route or travel a certain path. Matthew 7:13-14 states that there are only two spiritual paths that people will travel, "Enter ye in at the strait gate: for wide is the gate, and broad is the way, that leadeth to destruction, and many there be which go in thereat: Because strait is the gate, and narrow is the way, which leadeth unto life, and few there be that find it."

The way every spiritual stranger and pilgrim must travel begins with a strait gate, but one must enter through it to discover life. Luke 13:24 gives us this sobering scenario about this gate, "Strive to enter in at the strait gate: for many, I say unto you, will seek to enter in, and shall not be able."

Every time I read the scriptures in Matthew and Luke about the gate, they serve as a "neon warning sign" to me. The idea that many will try to enter into this gate, but few will find it brings a sober reality to me. This picture causes me to not only want to come to terms with this gate, but examine my own life before God. Am I one of those who are seeking to enter into it, but actually missing it? Am I so arrogant as to assume that I am okay, or am I so religious that I think I have a corner on what is right and acceptable to God, thereby, passing by the gate?

This has caused me to do an intensive study on the gate in order to come to terms with it. These three scriptures give a thorough description of it. First, there is only one such gate, and we must conclude that it appears as unattractive because it is strait and narrow. Since this gate is straight and hard, it means that there is difficulty attached to it that implies personal cost. You must also find this gate, which means you must search for it.

The idea that you must find this entrance implies three possible scenarios: 1) it can be easily overlooked, 2) there are many other gates that are similar to it, which will cause confusion, or (3) it is hidden.

As I studied the characteristics of this gate, I realized that it clearly described one entrance. Jesus revealed the identity of this gate in John 10:9, "I am the door: by me if any man enter in, he shall be saved, and shall go in and out, and find pasture." This verse clearly shows that the entrance to the spiritual life is not a religion, denomination, belief, or philosophy, but a person, Jesus Christ.

When I meditated on the fact that the gate is the Person of Jesus, I could see that in the midst of religion, intellectual pursuits, and religious activities that He would be easily overlooked. This is why it is not unusual to look to many different things, other than Jesus, or get caught up with the many different religious side attractions that cause one to leave Him behind.

I also realized that there are many different Christ's being presented today, but there is only one true Jesus who is able to save. For example, there is the "holiday" Jesus who remains a baby in the manger who is considered only at Christmas time, or the Jesus that never comes off of the cross at Easter. There is the "historical" Jesus who is a matter of history but who is not living today. Then, there is the "religious" Jesus who is one of the way-showers, a representation of God, a great prophet, an incredible teacher, the spiritual brother of Lucifer, or Michael the archangel. There is also the "nice guy" Jesus who just wants to adhere to all of our needs and wants. All of these Christ's have similar qualities, but are clearly not the Jesus of the Bible.

Every time I come to the realization that there are so many different Christ's, I remember what Jesus said to Peter in Matthew 16:13, "...Whom do men say that I the Son of man am?" Everyone starts out with others defining Jesus for them. Sadly, many remain in the shadow of others' presentation of Jesus, rather than seeking to know Him on a personal basis.

It matters little as to what others say about Jesus. The question remains the same, "...But whom say ye that I am? (Matthew 16:15)." It is upon this one question that rests a person's eternal destination. A person can believe there is a Jesus, but if he or she does not know the real Jesus, he or she remains lost. A person can know about Jesus, but unless Jesus is a personal revelation, there will be no indication of salvation, authority, and power.

This brings us down to the final point of why many fail to enter into the gate of life. Jesus, the Son of God, is hidden from those who are in darkness. Since He is hidden, one must seek to find Him. Is it any wonder that scriptures such as Amos 5:6 instruct, "Seek the LORD, and ye shall live..."?

Jeremiah 29:13 instructs us to seek God with all of our heart. God can honor a seeking heart by taking away the veil that prevents a person from seeing Jesus for whom He is. God must reveal Jesus before He is able to save a person to the uttermost.[1] Jesus confirmed this after Peter declared His identity, "Blessed art thou, Simon Barjona; for flesh and blood hath not revealed it unto thee, but my Father, who is in heaven."

People can walk around with knowledge of Jesus, but it takes a revelation from God for a person to truly embrace the Jesus of the Bible and experience His life. Have you such a revelation or are you walking around content with some type of impersonal or dead knowledge of Jesus Christ?

---

[1] 2 Corinthians 3:16; 4:4-5; Hebrews 7:25

Jesus is not only the gate, but He is the way in which a person must walk. He said of Himself in John 14:6, "...I am the way..."

Isaiah 30:21 gives us this insight into the way, "And thine ears shall hear a word behind thee, saying, This is the way, walk ye in it, when ye turn to the right hand, and when ye turn to the left." Two thousand years ago, God's voice declared the way—the way of Jesus; therefore, every believer must walk in it. Jesus confirmed this when He instructed His disciples, "...Follow me, and I will make you fishers of men" (Matthew 4:19).

As the way, Jesus became the example to man. He visibly revealed two distinct patterns that man must follow in order to walk in the way. The first example is found in John 13:14-16—that of a servant. Jesus showed His followers three parts to the pattern of servitude in disposition, attitude, and action. First, His disposition was that of lowliness and His attitude was that of meekness. You cannot be a faithful servant if there is any self-importance reigning.

The second part of this pattern is that He gave way to something worthy and greater than His humanity—the Father, "...not my will, but thine, be done."[2] Jesus never did anything outside of His Father's will. He stressed this importance to His disciples, "I can of mine own self do nothing: as I hear, I judge: and my judgment is just; because I seek not mine own will, but the will of the Father who hath sent me" (John 5:30).

As you study this scripture, you begin to realize that as a servant of God, His followers must not do anything outside of their Master to ensure effectiveness. If a life of servitude is maintained within the boundaries of the Master, all will be done in the atmosphere of what is considered righteous and acceptable. Therefore, it is up to each servant to seek the will of the Master and not pursue his or her own will.

The third part of the pattern of servitude is that of obedience. Obedience to the Master is motivated by love, and will bring credibility and clout. Jesus came into subjection to the Father's will in order to obey Him. As a result, He was given a name above all names. And, in the foreseeable future, there will be a time when every knee will bow and every tongue will confess that He is Lord, to the glory of the Father.[3]

Godly obedience comes out of suffering. This brings us to the second example that Christ left us, found in 1 Peter 2:21, "For even hereunto were ye called: because Christ also suffered for us, leaving us an example, that ye should follow his steps." There are three parts to the pattern found in suffering. They are 1) self-denial, 2) focus, and 3) sacrifice. Each point of this pattern points to godly character and perfection that is being worked in the person, allowing the individual to

---

[2] Luke 22:42b
[3] Philippians 2:5-11

Developing Our Christian Life

overcome. If a person fails to walk this second pattern out in his or her life, he or she will never be an overcomer.[4]

Jesus' example shows a man who *denied Himself* of being entangled in the enticements of the world. This type of self-denial always ends in physical or mental suffering, as it gives way to godly discipline. Jesus' denial came out of love. As a result, He overcame the world.

We see the culmination of Jesus' love on the cross, but we witness Him overcoming the world in His temptation in the wilderness. Satan tempted His flesh, pride, and the lust of the eyes, but He refused to give way to the temptations by believing the Word, upholding the nature of God, and looking beyond the kingdoms of this world.[5] As a result, He was able to make this statement in John 16:33, "These things I have spoken unto you, that in me ye might have peace. In the world ye shall have tribulation: but be of good cheer; I have overcome the world."

Jesus set His face towards the cross. When a person sets his or her focus on something, it implies that a matter will be accomplished regardless of the price that it might require. Jesus mentioned this price in Luke 14:28, "For which of you, intending to build a tower, sitteth not down first, and counteth the cost, whether he has sufficient to finish it?"

This intense *focus* brought Jesus to the Garden of Gethsemane where He denied His flesh of its right to life, and submitted to the will of the Father. Because of this denial, He overcame the flesh and was brought to perfection as man. Hebrews 5:8-9 confirms this, "Though he were a Son, yet learned he obedience by the things which he suffered; And being made perfect, he became the author of eternal salvation unto all them that obey him." (Emphasis added.)

On the cross, we see Jesus' *sacrifice*. He gave way to a greater and eternal purpose, and not only redeemed man, but also overcame Satan. Hebrews 2:14 confirmed this, "Forasmuch then as the children are partakers of flesh and blood, he also himself likewise took part of the same; that through death he might destroy him that had the power of death, that is, the devil."

Acceptable sacrifice cannot happen without the love of God. True love replaces the essence of self. Therefore, a life without the motivation of God's love will fall short, as the focus will be missing, and the sacrifice will be thwarted or considered unacceptable by God. Today, many Christians act similar to the heathen, as they display love that is fleshly and a worldly focus that produces double-mindedness. Rather than becoming a living sacrifice to prove what is the acceptable will of God, many act as martyrs. As martyrs they justify glorying in their own religious deeds.[6]

---

[4] Hebrews 5:8-9
[5] Matthew 4:1-11
[6] Romans 12:1; 1 Corinthians 1:31

The work of the cross in the lives of God's people is about a dead sacrifice that is ultimately being made alive unto God for His use and glory. This brings us down to the straight and narrow path of the Christian.

The characteristics of the narrow gate are not solely pointing to the person of Jesus, but to the cross that served as His altar. The cross is the only object that fits the description of being straight and narrow. Straight means standing close, or narrow.[7] The boundaries of the cross are quite narrow. They are meant to rid people of any excess spiritual baggage that would beset them in their spiritual walk. This type of separation points to consecration or total abandonment.

"Narrow" means afflict, suffer, tribulation, and trouble. This implies the work of the cross. Luke 13:24 tells us that we must strive to enter into this gate. "Strive" means to struggle, contend, endeavor, fight, or labor to accomplish something.[8] Both of these words imply travailing. Acts 14:22 makes this interesting statement, "Confirming the souls of the disciples, and exhorting them to continue in the faith, and that we must through much tribulation enter into the kingdom of God."

Christianity is often presented as a nice walk in the park. But, as one can see from these Scriptures, it has a narrow gate that is unrelenting and unbending. The construction of this gate has been established to deal with the old man, so that the believer can embrace a new life. This brings us to the struggle that occurs at this gate.

Many people try to enter this life through other avenues, instead of through the narrow gate. This is their way of avoiding death to the self-life. They try everything from good works, to majoring in religion as a means to avoid the hardness of this entrance. They often erect another Jesus who would not require them to enter this narrow gate of suffering and death. Yet, Jesus' words about this gate still echo in the Scriptures as He refers to those who try to enter in elsewhere, as thieves.[9]

I can remember my encounter with this gate. I fought hard against embracing the cross. I recall talking about Jesus' death in sentimental terms for years, but I never became identified with Him in His death. I still shake my head at my foolishness because I later learned that there was nothing sentimental about Jesus and the cross He had to bear. It was a tragic unveiling of the depravity of man, as well as the glorious revelation of the intervention of a loving, merciful, and holy God.

I never realized that the cross would reveal my depravity. What we must recognize is that there is nothing sentimental or glorious about such a revelation. In fact, it was humbling and so abrasive against my pride that I literally felt I would not survive the whole ordeal.

---

[7] Strong's Exhaustive Concordance of the Bible, Greek, #4728
[8] Ibid, #2346 and #75
[9] John 10:10

Developing Our Christian Life

    The narrow entrance stripped away any fantasy or romantic notions I had about the Christian walk. The narrow gate cut into every fiber of self-importance, and exposed the harsh reality that I had nothing to offer in and of myself. I was a worthless vessel that needed to be broken down and put through the process of molding and refining again. And, if any value were to be found in my life, it would come from that which was heavenly.[10]

    This is when I felt the hands of Jesus. I knew that I had encountered the base of the cross. However, in my humbled state, Jesus was able to reach down and lift me up above the devastation of the cross. It was at that time that I realized that the cross is all about identity. Identity points to relationship, and relationship is all about abiding. 1 John 2:6 states, "He that saith he abideth in him ought himself also so to walk, even as he walked." This scripture tells us that we cannot walk as Jesus walked, unless we abide in Him.

    Jesus called His disciples to follow Him, but He also stated that He was the Vine, in John 15. Life comes from Jesus, but one must be abiding in Him. Such "abiding" points to a living relationship with God. In this relationship all dependency will be totally on Jesus. As the Vine moves, so does the branch.

    Jesus, who is the Vine, must also lead as a Shepherd. The sheep that belong to Him will follow as they hear His voice.[11] He is the Master as well, and His servants will do as He did. He teaches with examples and powerful words, and His students will respond to His examples as well as respond in obedience to what He teaches.

    Every part of the believer's life should be abiding in Christ. Every attitude must be an expression of Him, every aspect of the Christian life must be touched by His will, and every action must be according to His influence and purpose.

    The Christian life is about Jesus, and anything outside of Him will be in vain. Everything that is not done in light of Him will display darkness and defeat. And, anything that fails to manifest Him will rob a person of all power and authority.

    The journey is about preparation, but we must enter through the gate. The gate is about death to the self-life to live life unto God. This gate opens to the way. The way is about learning how to walk as Jesus walked. His walk led Him to a cross of death, but later, it gave way to resurrection power. His walk brought Him by way of humility, suffering, and death, but through it all, He overcame the world, the flesh, and Satan.

    Jesus' secret for this victorious life was the fact that He abided in the presence of the Father. He did not walk unless instructed, and He only walked according to the Father's design. His life was about the Father

---

[10] 2 Corinthians 4:7
[11] John 10:4-5

and doing the Father's business. This is how Jesus walked, and this is how His followers must walk.

A Christian's life hinges on abiding in the precious Vine. It should be about Jesus and doing His bidding. It is about giving way to something worthy and greater, to embrace the glorious reality of heaven, the precious Son of God.

Have you entered the gate of life? If you have, are you walking according to the way of heaven or are you struggling against the work of the cross that is found in light of Jesus' glorious redemption? Are you trying to get a grasp of the Christian life as you try to figure out how to accomplish it in your own strength, or are you surrendering all to the work of God being done in and through you by His Spirit?

6

THE BROAD PATH

We observed from the last chapter that a gate that consists of a person rather than religious beliefs and philosophies is what actually marks the entrance into the spiritual life. The actual gate is unattractive because it forms a cross that requires self-denial and death to the self-life. Since it is not obvious to the naked eye, we are told that we must find this gate. Once we find it, we must then strive to enter in for there are many worldly entanglements and excess baggage of self that cause people to fail to enter in.

The harsh reality of this gate is that few will find it, even though they may seek for it. Due to the various excuses of man and the narrow and unattractiveness of the entrance, many miss the actual gate, putting them on the broad path.

The broad path is popular because it can be adjusted to fit one's beliefs and philosophies. It is the path of least resistance, and considered wise and acceptable to the world. It is honored for its tolerance to embrace all, and promoted for its ability to fit into any philosophy. Although many hail these various attractions, they are the very characteristics that have made this popular path not only attractive, but also broad and destructive.

In the Word of God, the examples of those who chose the broad path are many. Their reasons for choosing this broad road and the impending consequences vary, but they clearly serve as warnings and examples for us to heed.

Each of these examples served as counterfeits to what is real and acceptable to God. By studying the counterfeit along with the righteous example, we can get a clear picture of the individual who will choose the path of least resistance.

The first one to choose this broad path was *Adam*. Adam had it all in the Garden of Eden, but in his heart, he desired independence from God's reign. Independence means the self-life wants to be God, bringing the individual into opposition to God's authority. This desire caused Adam to toy with transgression in his heart.[1]

When the opportunity presented itself through the serpent beguiling Eve, the desire took action in the form of blatant disobedience. When confronted, the self-life refused to humble itself and take accountability

---

[1] Job 31:33

for its transgression. The results were devastating, Adam and Eve were banned from Paradise, while the consequences of death, toil, and sweat would plague the man and all of his descendents.[2]

Jesus Christ is considered the second Adam. The right response can be seen in Jesus as He submits Himself to the will of the Father, and allows the self-life to be poured out in the Garden of Gethsemane. From this point He chooses the narrow route of Calvary.[3]

Adam's oldest son, *Cain*, is the next person who chose the path of least resistance. His downfall came at the point of allowing his emotions to reign. The problem with emotions reigning is that they encourage so-called "rights," and will create an unrealistic reality.

Cain gave in to his jealousy in regard to God accepting Abel's sacrifice, while rejecting his. His jealousy gave him the right to be angry, as well as justified him giving in to his base desire to deal with the situation according to his emotional momentum. This resulted in Cain committing murder.

When a person walks according to base, undisciplined emotions, he or she not only proves to be touchy in his or her responses, but fickle in his or her commitment. This emotional condition causes a person to be unrealistic, impulsive, and untrustworthy.

The consequences that Cain paid were that he left the presence of the Lord and became a spiritual vagabond. He built the first city with man-made government. City life removes man not only from the earth from which he was formed, but also from his need for God to rule his life.[4]

Cain's brother Abel proved to be the opposite example of Cain. Cain brought God his best, but in his mind, his sacrifice was about who he was and what he had accomplished. Abel realized that his sacrifice had nothing to do with him, but with the character of God, and he chose the narrow path of righteousness. In fact, his sacrifice pointed to the sacrifice of Jesus Christ.[5]

When man operates on the emotional level, it will always come down to himself rather than God. As a result, he will miss the whole point of what it means to have a life in God.

The next person who took the broad road was *Ishmael*, the son of Abraham. In the life and attitude of Ishmael, you can see how arrogance operates. All arrogance begins when man takes matters into his own hands. We see this scenario when Sarah took her barrenness and desire to provide Abraham with a son as an excuse to give Abraham her handmaid, Hagar.[6]

---

[2] Genesis 3
[3] 1 Corinthians 15:45
[4] Genesis 4
[5] Hebrews 11:4
[6] Genesis 16

Developing Our Christian Life

    Ishmael was the product of that union. You can see how arrogance manifested itself in Ishmael towards the blessings and promises of God. He was fierce, and actually mocked the things of God when he mocked Isaac. In the end, his seed became fierce competitors with everyone, including those chosen by God.[7]

    It is important to point out that arrogance makes a person a bondman. Hagar and her son were put in this category in Genesis 21:10 and Galatians 4:22-31. They were kept from partaking of the promises of God. These are the consequences for those who allow arrogance to rule in them.

    Isaac was the one who partook of God's promises. He was God's fulfillment to a promise He made to Abraham. His conception was a miracle, and his life testified to God's faithfulness and ability to do the impossible. As you study the people who partake of God's promises, you will see that they walk the narrow path in fear and trembling.[8]

    The next person who took the broad path was *Esau*. From all outward appearances, Esau looked all right, and he was what most would consider a real man. He hunted and lived off the earth, and appeared to be self-sufficient. However, God said of him in Hebrews 12:16 that he was a fornicator and a profane person.

    The reason God considered Esau in this light was because he was a man who lived by the flesh. The old man freely reigned through the dictates of his flesh, and as a result he sold his birthright.[9] The old man is indifferent to the things of God, and will ultimately only value that which serves the person in the immediate situation.

    The consequences Esau paid were too great even for him. Not only did he sell his birthright, but he also lost his blessing as the eldest son. Rightfully, he did not deserve the blessing, and was rejected from receiving it. When he sought the blessing with tears, he found no place of repentance where he could change the outcome.[10]

    The opposite scenario of Esau was his brother Jacob. Jacob was not like the self-sufficient Esau. Although, Jacob was considered to be a thief, he knew what he wanted. His emphasis was not on this earth, but on the future. For example, unlike his self-serving brother, he wanted the birthright, and showed both shrewdness and wisdom in securing it. Since he secured the birthright, it was only right that he received the blessings. With his mother's instruction and help, he recognize the opportunity to receive the blessing as well. Even though Jacob appeared shrewd, his emphasis showed that he valued something of greater significance and substance. It showed that his vision was beyond the present moment, and actually embraced something that had eternal

---

[7] Genesis 16:10-12; 21
[8] Philippians 2:12; Hebrews 11:11
[9] Genesis 25:29-34
[10] Hebrews 12:17

significance in God's plan. Interestingly, the word "plain" that was used to describe Jacob in Genesis 25:27, means complete, gentle, perfect, undefiled, and upright.[11] This is why God said he hated Esau and loved Jacob.[12]

As a result of his inner resolve and desire, Jacob received both the birthright and the blessing. After a long process, he came home as Israel, the prince, who prevails with God. Before he died, he even blessed the Pharaoh of Egypt.[13]

As you study those who value the things of God, you will see people who are watchful and aware of significant opportunities around them, as they walk the narrow path.[14] Keep in mind, the narrowness of the path is what keeps a person sharp or discerning.

The next example happens to be a group of people known as the Israelites. The *Israelites* missed the narrow opportunity to enter into the Promised Land because of something called presumption. Presumption finds its origin in pride, and is displayed in being stiff-necked. The Israelites presumed that since they were God's chosen people, He had to put up with their many complaints and rebellion. In other words, God had to honor them in spite of their attitudes and actions. At first, you see God's long-suffering towards them, but at the right time He began to chastise them. Eventually, His chastisement turns into judgment as people escalate in their presumptions.

You can see this presumption in operation in Numbers 14. Ten out of twelve spies brought back an evil report to the children of Israel about the Promised Land, causing the people to murmur against Moses, Aaron, and God. It was at this point that God decided to destroy these stiff-necked people and make Moses into a great nation. Moses interceded on behalf of Israel, and God repented or withdrew from destroying them, but pronounced judgment on them: The present generation would not enter the Promised Land.

The next morning, some of the Israelites rose up to enter the Promised Land. They had repented and presumed that God would overlook their rebellion and allow them to enter in. Once again, we see that presumption puts the emphasis on the person's good intentions, while disregarding the character or judgments of God. It is like children who presume that if they plead long enough, they can convince their parents to let them have their way. Moses warned them that their presumption would lead to death. They ignored his warnings and many fell by the sword.

We see this presumption in operation in the days of Jesus. The Israelites took pride in being descendants of Abraham, rather than

---

[11] Strong's Exhaustive Concordance, #8535
[12] Malachi 1:3; Romans 9:13
[13] Genesis 31:24-32; 47:7-10
[14] Matthew 24:43-44; Luke 21:34-36

cherish their spiritual life before God. John the Baptist made this declaration in Matthew 3:9, "And think not to say within yourselves, We have Abraham to our father: for I say unto you that God is able of these stones to raise up children unto Abraham."

Presumption is a major problem in the Church. Many presume they are Christians because they said a "sinner's prayer," attend church, read the Bible, live a decent life, or are attracted to spiritual things. However, such things could be based on the person's high opinion of self, and not on the knowledge or character of Jesus. The Christian life is produced through a relationship with the Living God in the growing knowledge of Christ, and will produce visible fruits as people walk this life out daily in practical ways.

The consequence for the Israelites was that they died in the wilderness of unbelief. Presumption always puts faith in the person's assumption or position and not in God. This misdirected faith produces a hard heart and unbelief towards God.[15]

Caleb's example is the opposite of the example left to us by the Israelites of his day. He was a man who walked the narrow path by faith. His faith was a product of his heart and life: he wholly followed God. Because of Caleb's tremendous faith in his God, God honored him when he entered the Promised Land. This faith allowed him to conquer and possess a land of giants and walled cities.[16]

The next person who took the broad path of popularity was *Orpah*, the daughter-in-law of Naomi. Orpah was a Moabite, and she represents those who stand at a crossroad between the God of Israel and their old life of idolatry and paganism. Sadly, this Moabite chose to walk the broad path of her old life, as she went back into idolatry and paganism.[17]

As you study those who take the broad path back to their old life or old ways, you realize it is the most convenient way. You begin to recognize that many reject the narrow way because it is unknown and frightening to them; therefore, they choose to go with what they are used to.

As you study the few verses about Orpah, you can see where she cried and wept about the prospect of losing the companionship of her mother-in-law, but she still went back to the old way. The Orpahs of the world are full of good intentions, but they have no inclination to pay the price. They comfort and justify themselves that they felt the tug on their heart to choose the narrow way, but looked at the circumstances and deemed it too hard. The Orpahs will always turn back at the crossroads.

The opposite contrast is Ruth. Orpah wept about her mother-in-law leaving, but Ruth clung to her. As Orpah was on her way back to the old life, Ruth was making this declaration,

---

[15] Hebrews 3
[16] Numbers 13:6, 30; 14:6-9, 37-38; Joshua 14:10-14; 15:14
[17] Ruth 1:4-15

...Intreat me not to leave thee, or to return from following after thee: for whither thou goest, I will go; and where thou lodgest, I will lodge: thy people shall be my people, and thy God my God: Where thou diest, will I die, and there will I be buried: the LORD do so to me, and more also, if ought but death part thee and me (Ruth 1:16-17).

The consequences for going back to the old way are that a person will disappear and be remembered no more. When you consider that people's names will be blotted out of the book of life, you can begin to see how one's existence would disappear from all memory.[18]

For Ruth, who walked the narrow path of total devotion, she became the great-grandmother of King David. Since she is named in the lineage of Jesus in Matthew, she will always be remembered.[19]

The next person who walked this broad path was *Samson*. God had given Samson strength and honor. However, Samson had a weakness. He gave in to his lust for women, and came under the captivity and rule of the Philistines who represent the world.[20]

Samson truly shows what happens to a person who allows his or her lust to draw him or her into the enticements of the world, bringing him or her under the spirit of the world.[21] Samson unwisely thought he could handle the temptation of Delilah. He failed to realize that outside of the protection of God, a person will be overcome by the world, and will become its victim. Samson ended up betraying his heart and his God (the source of his strength), and selling his strength and honor for the sake of lust.

The consequence of Samson's action is that the Lord departed from him without his even discerning it. When the Lord departed, his strength went with Him, causing Samson to become vulnerable to his enemies. His enemies subdued him. The Philistines put out his eyes. He was then taken into captivity to be used and humiliated.[22] It is important to point out that the world will spiritually blind a person to his or her enemies, causing vulnerability and destruction.

The opposite contrast to Samson is Joseph, the son of Jacob. Joseph was enticed with the lust of the world and fled from it. Although he was resented and unfairly imprisoned for choosing the narrow path of purity and holiness, God eventually exalted him as a leader, second to Pharaoh in Egypt. As a result, he was used to save his family from famine and death.[23]

---

[18] Exodus 32:32; Psalm 69:28; Revelation 3:5
[19] Ruth 4:17-22; Matthew 1:5
[20] Judges 13-16
[21] Ephesians 2:2
[22] Judges 16:17-21
[23] Genesis 39:7-20; 41:38-44; 50:17-20

Developing Our Christian Life

The next person who traveled the broad path of destruction was *Eli*, the priest. Eli traveled the broad road of complacency. Complacency means that a person has no passion or initiative to go contrary to that which is comfortable, self-serving, or convenient.

Eli's sons were wicked and serving as priests in the temple. He confronted his sons about their sin, but failed to take any action against them since he was benefiting from their wicked ways.[24] In my observation, the more people ignore or compromise with wickedness, the more they become passive towards actually dealing with it in their own personal lives or in their homes. We see the extent of this passivity in Eli when God pronounced judgment on his household. When he heard the judgment, his attitude was, "So be it."

David Wilkerson, in his August 19, 2002 publication, voiced his concern over how a passive attitude seems to be engulfing the men and young people in the Christian realm. The dreadful conclusion to this situation is that it matters little how you may warn or contend with these people. Their attitude will remain as Eli's, "So be it," Sadly, these people's hearts are neither cold nor hot towards God. They are unreceptive. It is as if they are deaf or incapable of responding to the things of God.

I have struggled with understanding this same attitude in people. At one time, I thought the complacent attitude invading the hearts and minds of many Christians was like that of the Laodicean Church in Revelation 3. Yet, this attitude seems even more indifferent than those of Laodicea. At least the people of Laodicea had an opinion as to their Christian status because they thought they were spiritually on the right path.

I began to realize that the complacency I have encountered today is more dangerous. At least the people in Laodicea were deluded, but the complacency people exhibit today is not from delusion, but is a product of total indifference. They really couldn't care less if they are on the right or wrong path. Like Eli, whatever happens, happens.

The problem with complacency is that it will keep a person in a state of indifference until it is too late to respond. Eli was casual about the impending judgment; but, when it occurred, his response was not one of indifference. He actually fell backwards when he heard the news and broke his neck.[25]

Eli did not realize that the judgment that would fall on his house would affect all of Israel. The consequence was that the glory of the Lord departed from Israel. Eli had displayed fake nobility when he was willing to accept the judgment of God, but in his complacency he failed to see that his lack of response would cost all of Israel.

---

[24] 1 Samuel 1:12-17, 22-25
[25] 1 Samuel 4:17-18

The glory of God has departed from many homes and churches; and how many remain indifferent to that reality? As the Church, do we care that Satan is winning, and that many souls are on the broad path of destruction? As followers of Christ, do we care about whether or not we are just talking the talk, while hypocritically not walking the walk? Are we content in holding others to spiritual accountability, while failing to hold ourselves accountable for personal attitudes and actions? Such hypocrisy does not declare our righteousness before God or others, but our foolishness. Eli was a fool, and he died a foolish death.

The opposite of Eli was Samuel. Samuel responded to God and walked the narrow path of obedience. He contended with Israel's rejection of God as their king, confronted the sin of King Saul, and lived a life that was beyond reproach.[26]

This brings us to contending with complacency in our own lives. If a person is complacent, he or she is not striving to enter into the narrow gate. This person will just be getting by as he or she sits as close to the gate as possible, secretly hoping that all of his or her religious activities will satisfy God when the time comes. Sadly, complacency puts the person on the path of least resistance that will end in destruction. Even though a person's spiritual condition may not matter now, it will down the line. And, as Eli along with the five foolish virgins in Matthew 25 discovered, it will be too late to change the course.

The key is turning from the broad path of complacency, and repenting of indifference. Eli tried to confront the sin of his sons, but failed to ask God to deal with his own complacency. It was Eli's unwillingness to deal with the sin of his own life that allowed his sons to freely practice wickedness.

The problem with complacency is that people either do not care about their deficiency of spiritual fervor because they lack any inclination to repent, or they do not see any real need to change their indifferent attitude. It is true that one may not feel like repenting right now, but it is important to repent of any complacency. A person needs to ask God to revive and put a fire in his or her spirit that will inspire him or her to pursue and possess all that God has for him or her. The victory over complacency is to decide to do what is right, regardless of feelings. Obedience to what is right is a form of discipline, and is the only measure that will properly confront and deal with any spiritual indifference in a person's life.

The final example we will be considering is *King Saul*. King Saul was a man who gave in to rebellion, which causes man to be exalted over God. All rebellion puts a person on the broad path of destruction because it allows for independence, emotional dictates, arrogance, fleshly preferences, presumptions, idolatry, lustful pursuits, and

---

[26] 1 Samuel 3; 8; 12:3, 13, 15

complacency. As you study Saul's life, you can see these different attitudes and sins.

The consequences for Saul were far reaching. In his first rebellious act, God took the kingdom from his heirs. In his second act of defiance, God personally rejected him from being king of Israel, and showed him that he would rip the kingdom from him. We see that after God rejected him as king, the Spirit of God departed from him, and an evil spirit tormented him. In his final demise, we see that he was so desperate to hear from God that he resorted to consulting a witch in regards to his last battle.[27]

King Saul's example should create some sobriety in each of us. He shows us that rebellion will set a person up for a fall, resulting in, everything of value being ripped from that person's grasp. Saul not only walked in judgment and condemnation, but his soul was tormented. We see him operating in fear, driven by insecurities, subject to jealousies, opposing the real servants of God, and ultimately, being exposed as an utter fool.

The opposite of King Saul was King David. David's secret was that he was a man after God's own heart. He walked the narrow path of integrity before God, and, as a result, he was said to be perfect in his walk. When you study David's life, you will see where it was noted that he behaved himself wisely in all of his ways. In other words, he walked before man in uprightness and before God in faith and obedience.[28]

As you study the broad path, you will realize that it is easy to be on it. There are so many entrances to this path that are enticing to the flesh, appealing to pride, and attractive to the eye. Up front, it is comfortable, convenient, and offers no resistance. However, in the end, it will mock, torment, and destroy your soul.

Consider the following table on the next page, and see what path you presently are on. Be honest with yourself as to whether you are striving to enter in the narrow way, or whether you are on the broad path of destruction.

---

[27] 1 Samuel 13:14; 15:22-28; 16:14-15; 28:7-25
[28] 1 Samuel 13:14; 18:14; I Kings 9:4

Person	Type of Walk	Response To God	Worldly Remorse	Contrast	Type of Walk
Adam	Independence	Tolerance	Excuse Self	Jesus	Submission
Cain	Emotional dictates	Offended	Rights	Abel	Righteousness
Ishmael	Arrogance	Mocked the things of God.	Refused to Repent	Isaac	Partook of the promises.
Esau	Old Man	Despised the things of God.	Self-pity	Jacob	Strived for the things of God.
Israel	Presumptions	Blinded to the things of God.	Repented outwardly	Caleb	Faith
Orpah	Old Life	Good intentions	Felt Bad	Ruth	Clung to the things of God.
Samson	Lust	Desensitized towards God.	Bound Up	Joseph	Purity
Eli	Complacency	Indifference	No need to repent	Samuel	Obedience
King Saul	Rebellion	Flippant	Outward emotions	King David	Integrity

7

THE ANATOMY OF DEFEAT

We cannot talk about the broad way without revealing the source behind people's preference to walk the ways of destruction. Many Christians have misconceptions about Christianity. They think it is just a matter of saving a soul, when in reality the whole essence of Christianity comes down to possessing the life God has for a person. This requires a person to not only walk out this life, but also fight a good fight along the way.

By studying the children of Israel's journey to and in the Promised Land, one can see the anatomy behind defeat and destruction. It would serve Christians well to not only come to terms with the Hebrews' journey, but to consider the mistakes they made when they entered the Promised Land. Keep in mind, the Promised Land is symbolic of the promised life that is available to every believer.

Many Christians think the place of defeat is in the wilderness. The wilderness is not a place of defeat, but one of testing.[1] The Israelites were not in a struggle for their existence because it was beyond their ability to maintain any real life in this harsh atmosphere. They had to solely depend on God to provide for all of their needs. The real issue in the wilderness came down to whether the children of Israel would ever come to the point of total reliance on Jehovah God.

Such reliance was necessary for Israel to develop the faith they needed to possess the Promised Land. This was brought out when the twelve spies came back to report on the environment and terrain of this land.[2]

The Israelites were close to entering into all that God had promised Abraham. However, they chose to listen to the bad reports about giants, rather than trust in God who had provided for their needs every step of the way. It was at this point that they showed that they still operated in unbelief. Because of their unbelief, a whole generation of Hebrews never entered into the Promised Land.[3]

This brings us to the real battle that occurs for every sojourner in the kingdom of God. As previously discussed, it is not a matter of just coming up to the gate that leads to the promised life, one must enter into

---

[1] Deuteronomy 8:2
[2] Numbers 14
[3] Numbers 13:27-33; 14:1-10; Hebrews 3

it. The other important aspect of this life in God is that one must personally possess it.

The Israelites never entered the Promised Land because they refused to possess it. They considered obstacles such as giants, horses, and iron chariots, rather than the abiding reality of their all-powerful God. In their minds, they were already defeated; therefore, there was no need to enter in.

There are Christians who are like the Israelites. They walk up to the narrow gate leading to their spiritual lives, but because of obstacles they never enter in. They view themselves as already overcome by the obstacles that appear too great to subdue.

Forty years later, a new generation came to the Promised Land. Unlike their fathers who died in the wilderness, they were ready to enter in. As you study their feats, you can see them as a gigantic army that entered in and swept the land as God went before them.[4]

Joshua 21:44 tells us that God gave Israel rest in this land and delivered their enemies into their hands. Judges 1:2 also talked about God delivering the land into Joshua's hand. It must have been an incredible victory that created much zeal and enthusiasm, but it was not enough for God to deliver the land to Israel. Every tribe had to possess their own inheritance. In other words, God had won the war by delivering the land to the children Israel, but there had to be personal battles fought in order to possess it.

To understand the battle, one must understand the mandate God gave the children of Israel. They had to rid the land of the Canaanites to prevent unholy alliances and pagan practices.

For the Christian, Jesus wrought a mighty victory on the cross. He won the war over the enemies of the soul, but Christians have a responsibility to fight a good fight in order to possess the life God has for them. The Apostle Paul talks about this battle in his many epistles.

In Romans 8:37, he speaks of being more than a conqueror through Jesus, while in 1 Corinthians 9:26, he talks of fighting the fight, and bringing his body into subjection so he would not be a castaway. In Philippians 3:12, we see that Paul is trying to apprehend this life, while in Philippians 3:14, he is pressing towards the prize. In Ephesians 6:10-18, he describes the armor, and in 2 Timothy 2:3, he talks about enduring as a good soldier.

Some people would accuse me of advocating the need to earn salvation. It is very clear that God delivered the Promised Land to the Israelites, but they had to possess it. This possession was not a matter of earning or securing the land, for it was already theirs for the taking; rather, it was about overcoming personal enemies that would prevent them from inhabiting it, and ensuring God's blessing on their inheritance.

---

[4] Joshua 12

Developing Our Christian Life

This is true for the Christian. Salvation is a free gift, but the life of Christ must be experienced in a personal way. However, there are various obstacles or enemies that would prevent embracing this life. There are three such obstacles or enemies that will keep a person from entering in. We have already made reference to these enemies, but let us consider them in light of Israel and the Promised Land.

God gave the Israelites these instructions in Exodus 23:31-33,

> ...for I will deliver the inhabitants of the land into your hand; and thou shalt drive them out before thee. Thou shalt make no covenant with them, nor with their gods. They shall not dwell in thy land, lest they make thee sin against me: for if thou serve their gods, it will surely be a snare unto thee.

In Deuteronomy 7:16-18, they are given similar instructions,

> And thou shalt consume all the people which the LORD thy God shall deliver thee; thine eye shall have no pity upon them: neither shalt thou serve their gods; for that will be a snare unto thee. If thou shalt say in thine heart, These nations are more than I; how can I dispossess them? Thou shalt not be afraid of them: but shalt well remember what the LORD thy God did unto Pharaoh and unto all of Egypt.

The first truth one must keep in mind is that Jesus has already won the victory on the cross. It is a matter of driving the defeated foe out of the territory. The word "drive" implies action. One of the enemies that comfortably resides among God's people is passivity when active faith is called for.

We see this passivity within the tribes of Israel. After the land had been subdued and some of the tribes were already making moves to drive the enemy out of their inheritance, seven tribes remained content in being in the Promised Land, but not taking any action to secure a personal inheritance. Joshua rebuked these tribes in Joshua 18. He knew the value and quality of the land, so he told the tribes to send men out to walk the remaining land and decide what they wanted to possess. After they made a decision, they were to return, and then they would cast lots for their inheritance.

The reason Christians are passive or complacent is because they have no concept about the eternal inheritance that awaits them. Ephesians 1 talks about this inheritance, but many have never walked this life out to discover how real it is. As a result, many remain content to settle with the idea of an eternal and abundant inheritance, even though they are failing to possess it for themselves.

The next instruction God gave His people was not to make any covenants with these enemies or their gods. To ensure that the Israelites would not come into agreement or unholy alliances with the heathen of the land and their cultures, God commanded them to consume the people and show no pity towards their plight.

God wanted to wipe out the memory and practices of these people because He knew if they remained in the land, the children of Israel would be ensnared or trapped by the destructive tentacles of idolatry and paganism, causing them to sin against Him. The problem that the people of Israel had is true for today. Complacency causes a show of tolerance towards enemies. This tolerance is often based on indifference that comes from a lack of fear of God.

People who lack the fear God are arrogant in attitude and mocking towards their so-called "enemies". They often fail to see enemies for the threat that they are. We see this in Adam's life. Satan was in the Garden of Eden, but Adam ignored him and never took his presence seriously. As a result, Adam gave way to rebellion and brought death upon all creation.

Do you tolerate the enemies of your soul by convincing yourself that you can handle them? And, what enemies fall into this category? The world with all of its lust easily falls into this class of enemies. This would include anything that may entice you to come into agreement with its spirit. The spirit of the world is capable of robbing you of purity, discernment, and your testimony of Jesus.

Sadly, the children of Israel did not drive all of these enemies out of the land. As you read the account of each tribe in the book of Joshua, many of them failed to conquer certain enemies. In some cases, they overcame them, but instead of driving them out, they made them slaves. As a result, an angel of the LORD pronounced this judgment on them in Judges 2:2-3,

> And ye shall make no league with the inhabitants of this land; ye shall throw down their altars: but ye have not obeyed my voice: why have ye done this? Wherefore I also said, I will not drive them out from before you; but they shall be as thorns in your sides, and their gods shall be a snare unto you.

The Word of God is clear about what God's people need to do with their enemies, but few obey. His people show tolerance to such things as the world, the flesh, and Satan. They are indifferent to the instructions of God, and often mock His warnings and instructions concerning the enemies of their souls.

One wonders when God's people are going to fear Him enough to heed His instructions. The answer could be, when it is too late to change the course of the situation.

This brings us to the actual snare that each of the enemies uses to ensnare man's soul into Satan's spider web. The last part of Judges 2:3 answers the question, "...and their gods shall be a snare unto you."

Every enemy of the soul represents some form of idolatry. Let us consider the modern-day idols of America. For example, the flesh exalts lust to serve as an idol, while pride places self on the throne, and the eyes exalt the things of the world in the place of God.

Developing Our Christian Life

Idolatry causes various spiritual problems by determining attitudes and focus, while establishing or reinforcing a wrong heart condition. The greatest point of defeat in idolatry will come at the point of focus. People will naturally walk according to their focus. If a person is walking contrary to God, there is no way for his or her attitude to be challenged or his or her heart to be exposed. In a way, a person who has a wrong spiritual focus will prove to be spiritually blinded.

There are five obstacles that catch people's attention and lead them into idolatry. The first culprit is *pride*. Pride either gives man a high, unrealistic opinion about his spiritual condition or it makes him a suffering victim and martyr when he encounters the consequences of judgment for his actions. Sadly, many Christians are motivated by personal pride in regards to Christian service. Such service is not about God, but about bringing adoration, acceptance, and recognition to self. These people will sacrifice their lives to serve God, but will fail to obey in spirit and truth to ensure that God is glorified.

The solution to pride is humility, but pride refuses to humble self, and when humility is absent, there will be no repentance. Repentance means a person is turning from walking according to self and coming into submission to God. Therefore, believers must ask God to work Christ's humility in them, to change both their attitude and focus.

The next major focus among people is *fear*. Fear is when individuals put their focus on their abilities to solve problems, whether it is with their minds, strength, or talents. Needless to say, people are limited or miserably fail to solve the problem, causing them to focus more on the obstacles. As they focus on the problem, the problem escalates, ending with people fainting in their mind.

Hebrews 12:3 gives insight into the solution for such a focus, "For consider him that endured such contradiction of sinners against himself, lest ye be wearied and faint in your minds." God's people must never look to self or consider the obstacles, but look to Jesus.

Another focus is *temptation*. Temptation comes by way of the enticement of the world. If a person focuses on the point of temptation, he or she will automatically give way to it. How do people allow temptation to have its way? Here are some of the reasons that temptation subdues a person: The person 1) thinks it cannot touch or affect him or her, 2) toys with the idea of how the temptation will satisfy lust, feed the ego, and add to his or her life, 3) denies or mocks the power and consequences of the sin behind it, or 4) allows it to delude him or her about its nature.

The solution to temptation is to flee from it. Do not delude yourself about the tentacles that are attached with every temptation to entice, deceive, and draw a person into its deadly trap.

The next focus that can cause people to fall into destruction is *circumstances*. God uses circumstances to shake people's foundations. It is usually the last resort, but in desperation to be free from the inconvenience or uncomfortable situation, man will often look to God to change the circumstances, so that he can merrily go on his way.

I must make an important statement at this point. We may want God to change the situation when He is trying to use circumstances to change us. My co-laborer and I have had a lot of circumstances throughout our ministry that have changed the way we think, look, respond, or act in different situations.

The solution to circumstances is faith in the character of God. Allow God to be God, by trusting that He is in control and working in His people's lives with eternity in mind.

The final source of focus can be Satan. Satan was allowed to "boil" Job, "sift" Peter, and "tempt" Jesus in an attempt to destroy His mission.[6] People often operate in extremes with Satan. They either give him too much attention, or they try to ignore him altogether. Both attitudes towards Satan can be destructive. We must always remind ourselves that Satan is not more powerful than God, but he is more powerful than man.

To give too much credit to Satan will take away from the majesty of God, but to not recognize when he is working will give him free reign to do his bidding without any hindrance. God uses Satan for His own purposes. He uses him by setting boundaries on him to test His people in order to bring them higher in their life with Him. He has given believers authority in Christ, an armor that will protect, and a weapon that will put Satan on the run. The solution to overcoming Satan is to submit oneself to God and respond in repentance and walk in humility. This will cause Satan to flee.[7]

This brings us to the source behind those who walk the broad path. As you study the lives of those on the broad path, you realize that they do not love God with all of their heart, soul, mind, and might. Their loyalties are divided, while their focus is more on their idol than on God.

The children of Israel became divided between the idols of Canaan and Jehovah God. These idols set them up to become slaves to wicked leaders as shown in the book of *Judges,* as well as caused them to walk between two opinions.[8] Like Solomon, the Hebrews did not set out to become idolatrous, but they subtly fell into its trap because the snares were firmly in place. 1 Kings 11:4 gives us this insight into the trap that so cleverly ensnares, "For it came to pass, when Solomon was old, that his wives turned away his heart after other gods: and his heart was not perfect with the LORD his God, as was the heart of David."

Ezekiel 36:26 tells us that God will give His people a new heart. In 1 Samuel 10:9, God gave Saul a changed heart, while in 1 Kings 1:29, He gave Solomon largeness of heart.

---

[6] Job 1:6-12; 23:10; Luke 22:31
[7] James 4:6-11
[8] 1 Kings 18:21

Developing Our Christian Life

    The heart that God gives His people has the desire and capacity to respond and obey Him.[9] Sadly, even with a new heart, many fail to respond in uprightness towards the things of God. As they respond to the world, the flesh, and Satan in an idolatrous manner, their heart becomes hard and complacent towards the things of God.

    You can actually see the cycle of an idolatrous heart. Like Solomon, it becomes divided in loyalties. This division will produce a heart like Solomon's son, Rehoboam, who did evil because his heart was not prepared to seek the Lord.[10]

    The heart that is unprepared to seek God will eventually walk in the sins of idolatry. We see where Rehoboam did evil, but repented when God sorely chastised him. However, in the case of his son Abijam, he walked in the sins of idolatry and reigned for only three years.[11]

    When you study the progression of the idolatrous heart, you will see that it starts out as worldly, and eventually becomes stony. If this heart is not changed through real repentance, it will digress into a hard heart.[12]

    King David had a perfect heart. When you study his heart, the first thing you will see is that it was fixed upon God. This means that his focus was solely on God, and there were no other loyalties or masters.[13]

    The second quality about David's heart was that he walked before God in integrity.[14] Integrity in this text points to completeness and uprightness.[15] As you study David's life, you will see that this integrity translated into receiving reproof, repenting of sin, and walking humbly before God and men.

    To gain a better picture of a perfect heart, one must study the lives of those who were considered to be righteous before God. The one consistent ingredient that you will find in these people's lives is that they chose to do that which was right before God. For example, Asa took down the altars of the strange gods and Jehoshaphat sought the Lord and walked in his commandments. King Jotham prepared his ways before the Lord and Hezekiah opened the doors of the temple after they were closed by his wicked father.[16]

    King Hezekiah showed the intensity of his commitment towards God as he called for the temple to be sanctified, as well as made a covenant with the Lord. He proclaimed a Passover and destroyed all of the altars

---

[9] See Ezekiel 36:26-27
[10] 2 Chronicles 12:14
[11] 1 Kings 15:1-4; 2 Chronicles 12
[12] See Matthew 13:1-23.
[13] Psalm 57:7-11
[14] 1 Kings 9:4
[15] Strong's Exhaustive Concordance; #8537
[16] 2 Chronicles 14:3; 17:4; 27:6; 29:3

of idols. He sought God in crisis and interceded on behalf of his people.[17] In the end, he brought much needed spiritual reformation to Israel.

King Josiah was another man who stands out because of his righteous response to God. He had a tender heart and quickly responded to the reading of the Law. He made a covenant with the Lord to walk after Him and to obey His commandments with all of his heart. He went throughout Israel and destroyed all idolatrous altars. This king's commitment stayed God's judgment from Israel until after his death.[18]

The contrast between those who give in to the broad path of destruction and those who choose the narrow way of righteousness reveals that it all comes down to a choice of the heart. Those on the broad path choose to give way to already established cycles of rebellion and idolatry, thereby, hardening their hearts. Those on the narrow path choose the ways of righteousness, causing their heart to become tender towards God.

What does your heart say about your life before God? Is it becoming hardened towards the things of God or is it becoming tender towards God, as righteousness becomes "meat" and "life" to your spirit and soul?

---

[17] 2 Chronicles 29:4-11; 30:2, 14, 17-19; 32
[18] 2 Chronicles 34:21-33

8

TRAVELING THE WAY

The Christian journey is a strenuous walk, but the rewards it carries with it are incredible. The Apostle Paul understood this and declared in Philippians 3:14, "I press toward the mark for the prize of the high calling of God in Christ Jesus."

In 2 Timothy 4:8, Paul made this statement, "Henceforth there is laid up for me a crown of righteousness, which the Lord, the righteous judge, shall give me at that day: and not to me only, but unto all them also that love his appearing."

In the last couple of chapters, we considered the two distinct paths that people will travel. There is the broad path that is popular, easy, and attractive to travel. Many walk this broad path as they adjust their lives to whatever is natural, convenient, or preferred. As they give way to worldly, fleshly dictates, they blindly head for the abyss of ruin and destruction. Revelations 21:8 confirms the judgment awaiting those on the broad path, "But the fearful, and unbelieving, and the abominable, and murderers, and whoremongers, and sorcerers, and idolaters, and all liars, shall have their part in the lake which burneth with fire and brimstone: which is the second death."

The other path is the narrow gate that one must strive to enter into, in order to begin to travel in the way of eternal and abundant life. Sadly, few will find this gate; therefore, they will end up on the broad road that leads to destruction. This brings us to the need to understand some important facts about traveling the way of the cross, the way of Jesus.

First, it is a walk that prepares a person for eternity. People are actually determining their eternal destination and rewards by how they are presently walking. They are either preparing for heaven where the presence of God resides, or they are preparing for hell where the essence of life is missing. They will be given rewards on that fateful Day of Judgment, or all of the so-called "works" of a person will be burned up by the purifying fires of judgment.

Secondly, God will direct a person's steps. Psalm 37:23-24 states, "The steps of a good man are ordered by the LORD: and he delighteth in his way. Though he fall, he shall not be utterly cast down: for the LORD upholdeth him with his hand." These verses state that the Lord orders the steps of a good man. God's people often miss the reality that it is God's good pleasure to order the steps of His people, but they must be in the way. To walk in the way means there is protection because the person is being obedient to God. In fact, the writer in Psalm 119:133 made this request, "Order my steps in thy word: and let not any iniquity have dominion over me."

Proverbs 16:9 tells us, "A man's heart deviseth his way: but the LORD directeth his steps." Interestingly, God can direct the steps of His people in spite of their heart. We see this in the children of Israel's case as God actually established their steps on their way to the Promised Land. These people took personal detours of idolatry and sin, but God was faithful to lead and direct them.

The Lord sovereignly directs His people's steps through circumstances, but the secret of victory is determined by how they respond to His leading. For example, the children of Israel walked in the way God led, but failed to respond in faith and obedience when it came to entering into the Promised Land.

The final aspect of this journey is that everything we do is being recorded. Proverbs 15:3 tells us, "The eyes of the LORD are in every place, beholding the evil and the good." People often think God does not have time to consider all of their ways. They believe that darkness covers them, and that their thoughts are too many or too insignificant for God to notice. How foolish people are to consider God in light of their limited and perverted understanding and ways.

We clearly see this foolish attitude in Ezekiel 8. The priests thought they could hide their idolatry in the secret chambers of the temple. However, the Lord was aware of their conduct. It provoked Him to anger, and He made this declaration, "Therefore will I also deal in fury: mine eye shall not spare, neither will I have pity: and though they cry in mine ears with a loud voice, yet will I not hear them" (Ezekiel 8:18).

Ecclesiastes 12:14 says, "For God shall bring every work into judgment, with every secret thing, whether it be good, or whether it be evil."

Matthew 12:36-37 states, "But I say unto you, That every idle word that men shall speak, they shall give account thereof in the day of judgment. For by thy words thou shalt be justified, and by thy words thou shalt be condemned."

Proverbs 16:2-3 give us this insight, "All the ways of a man are clean in his own eyes; but the LORD weigheth the spirits."

As we can see, the Israelites were walking in the way, but their words and motives tripped them up. They took detours because their hearts were hard due to unbelief, their necks stiff from arrogance, and their steps inconsistent because of disobedience.[1]

This is one of the problems with some Christians today. They appear to be on the way, but they are just going through the motions. They display either passiveness or fanaticism, but few have a passion for God where they walk daily according to His ways and will.

---

[1] Numbers 14; Hebrews 3

Developing Our Christian Life

Sadly, like the Israelites, many who think or refer to themselves as being Christian will not finish the course. They will trip over some idol, give way to some sin, and ultimately walk in unbelief as they perish in the devastation of their spiritual wilderness.

God's people must keep in mind that they will be judged for what they do, say, and think. Their motives will be unveiled, and all points of arrogance will be exposed for the sinister culprits that they are. The Apostle Paul put it this way in 2 Corinthians 5:10, "For we must all appear before the judgment seat of Christ; that every one may receive the things done in his body, according to that he hath done, whether it be good or bad." It is vital that Christians do not lightly test their spirit, ignore those things that are undisciplined, fail to examine their motives, or fail to judge their ways.

With this in mind, let us now consider the children of Israel's steps and learn valuable lessons from their journey that is recorded in Numbers 33. The initial part of their journey started with the death of the firstborn of the Egyptians.[2] The death of the firstborn is what freed the Israelites from slavery, and ushered them into a new life with God.

The death of the firstborn in Egypt reminds the Christian of the death of Jesus Christ, the only begotten Son of God. His death on the cross would serve as the key that would unlock the prison doors to all those who are tired of the captivity brought on by sin. Embracing Christ's redemption wrought on the cross ushers an individual into a new life with God.

The first place of importance is Ethan.[3] Ethan stood on the edge of the wilderness. This may simply mean the place that marked the end of cultivated lands and the beginning of the wilderness. However, in many ways, it served as a place of distinction and choice. It was from this place that one could view the contrast between the abundance of the world that was represented by Egypt and the harsh barren wilderness that is often experienced when one truly sets out to seek and find God.

For the Christian, Ethan serves as the harsh entrance into a new life in God. It is where separation occurs from everything that represents the old life. It represents self-denial, abandonment, consecration, and abasement. Even though this place stands at the edge of what many consider to be the difference between life and death, each one must choose what is generally considered to be the way of death, to embrace real life.

The next place the Israelites came to was the Red Sea.[4] Although many consider the Red Sea in light of the parting of the water, 1 Corinthians 10:1-2 gives us the spiritual significance of this place. "Moreover, brethren, I would not that ye should be ignorant, how that all

---

[2] Numbers 33:4
[3] Numbers 33:6
[4] Numbers 33:8

our fathers were under the cloud, and all passed through the sea; And were all baptized unto Moses in the cloud and in the sea."

Ethan points to separation, but the Red Sea represents total immersion into this new life. Clearly, after the Red Sea, there is no turning back. Baptism for the Christian is symbolic of him or her separating from the old way to become totally identified with Jesus in His death, burial, and resurrection.[5]

As you consider the whole picture of this journey, there are three types of terrain that the Israelites had to enter and pass through. These different terrains point to the Gospel. The Red Sea represents the entrance to death and cleansing, while the wilderness is symbolic of the grave where all residues of the past are left, and the Promised Land points to the new or resurrected life. What a powerful representation of the journey one must travel to embrace the full life of Christ.

Three days into the wilderness, they came to Marah. It was at Marah that they encountered bitter waters that they could not drink.[6] A tree cast into the waters made it sweet. For the Christian, Marah represents the bitter-sweet reality of the spiritual walk. It cost God His Son, as He offered Him upon the altar of the tree, the cross. This altar was placed in the midst of wretched humanity. In spite of the many struggles that Christians have in this world, they can always find sweetness at the foot of the cross of Jesus, as they embrace His forgiveness and His glorious life.

After the bitter water, the Israelites came to Elim. Elim had 12 fountains of water with 70 palm trees. It was an oasis in the desert. What a contrast this place was from the bitter springs of Marah. To the Christian, these fountains not only point to the wells of salvation but the Living Waters. Isaiah 12:3 states, "Therefore with joy shall ye draw water out of the wells of salvation."

John 7:37-38 assures, "...If any man thirst, let him come unto me, and drink. He that believeth on me, as the scripture hath said, out of his belly shall flow rivers of living water."

The fountains symbolize Jesus, while the waters point to the Holy Spirit. Jesus is the only one who can uncap the Living Waters in a person's spirit and soul. It is up to Christians to learn to draw from the fountain of the life of Jesus in order to partake of the Holy Spirit.

There were 12 such fountains at Elim, which pointed to governmental perfection. As Isaiah 9:6-7 states, "...and the government shall be upon his shoulder...Of the increase of his government and peace there shall be no end, upon his kingdom, to order it, and to establish it with judgment and with justice..."

There were 70 palm trees. The number 70 points to perfect spiritual order, carried out in spiritual power and significance. Only the Holy Spirit

---

[5] Romans 6:3-5
[6] Exodus 15:23-26; Numbers 33:8

can bring perfect order, power, and significance into Christians' restless and uncertain lives.[7]

Next, we see Israel camping by the Red Sea, which brought the Israelites to their first major wilderness. The harsh wilderness that Moses made reference to in Deuteronomy 1:19 was comprised of five wildernesses. These wildernesses represent different aspects of Christian growth.

Ethan marked the first wilderness. According to *Smith's Bible Dictionary*, Ethan was in the wilderness of Shur. We know this represented a place of choice and separation, but their journey through this wilderness was not a long process.

The second wilderness was the wilderness of Sin. This is where Israel was tested to show that they were still rebellious in attitude and idolatrous in heart.[8] Everything must be tested in order to reveal the character and heart attitude of a person. Deuteronomy 8:2 confirms this, "And thou shalt remember all the way which the LORD thy God led thee these forty years in the wilderness, to humble thee, and to prove thee, to know what was in thine heart, whether thou wouldest keep his commandment."

A significant place in the wilderness of Sin was Rhephidim, which means "rest" or "stay."[9] Rhephidim was a place of rest, but the Israelites could not remain there long because it was a place of drought as well.

All wilderness experiences will reveal personal spiritual drought. The key to satisfying the soul comes down to finding a place of rest, even in the midst of challenges and harshness.

Today, many Christians are restless in their spirits because they have not found rest in the only place they can, Jesus Christ.[10] This restlessness causes them to take detours in their life in the attempt to satisfy their thirst, only to find greater spiritual desire to partake of more.

The third wilderness was Sinai, and this is where Israel received the Law to show them how far removed from God they were in their hearts. It was here that the children of Israel had to learn the lessons of waiting on God, and abiding in His presence in the midst of the extremes of life.

One of the lessons a person must learn is that, in order to abide in Christ, a believer must learn to rest in Him no matter what is pressing against him or her. The reason that God's followers must learn the lesson of abiding in the challenging times is because they never learn it in the good times. It takes adversity of life for one to learn how to abide in the midst of extreme elements.

---

[7] The representation of numbers can be found in E. W. Bullinger book, Number in Scripture.
[8] Numbers 33:11
[9] Number 33:14
[10] Matthew 11:28-30

The fourth wilderness is not mentioned by name, but described by the different places that Israel stayed. For example, the places named in Numbers 33:17-36, from Hazeroth to Kadesh made up this wilderness. This wilderness was called the wilderness of Paran or "wilderness of wandering."[11] It was where Israel wandered for forty years, making this region a graveyard for the rebellious generation that refused to enter into the Promised Land.

The final wilderness was Zin.[12] This wilderness was just before the Promised Land. It actually led the Israelites to Mount Hor where Aaron died. The wilderness of Zin represents putting off what remained of the old, in order to put on the new. It was a place of preparation to not only enter into the Promised Land, but to possess it.

The harsh places of life operate in extremes. For example, silence or loneliness can drive people mad, the wind of adversity can cause isolation, the restless heart of challenges can cause weakness, and the lack of satisfaction, resentment.

Trying to keep up with every place the Israelites camped or traveled through could boggle the mind. The reality is that every place was significant to reach their destination. These places may just be names, but the Israelites had to face the terrain and challenge of each area. They could not see the end of their journey nor always understand the route they were taking. However, they realized that they did not have to concern themselves with such details, because God was leading the way.

It may seem to those who study the children of Israel's steps that much of their spiritual journey was unimportant, but God had an eternal perspective in view as each place and step had been ordained by Him. These places not only represented steps towards a complete new life, but important lessons that were meant to prepare them for the Promised Land.

Throughout the years of traveling the way of Christ, I have learned the lessons of when to rest, when to fight, how to be abased, and how to properly receive. These are all vital lessons I learned in the wildernesses of my life, but I realize the difficulties were designed to bring me into a place of total dependency on God.

It is dependency on God that allows one to experience His character. As one experiences different aspects of His character, he or she is collecting treasures that will add value to his or her testimony.

The most consistent testimony of those who have learned to depend on God is that He is faithful. Psalm 89:1 declares, "I will sing of the mercies of the LORD for ever: with my mouth will I make known thy faithfulness to all generations." This testimony will be passed down from generation to generation.

---

[11] Smith's Bible Dictionary
[12] Numbers 33:36

Developing Our Christian Life

It is in the spiritual wilderness that a person's life is established in God through a relationship with Him. It is the harshness of the wilderness that instills the character that is so necessary in order to enter into all that God has for each individual.

Have you entered through the narrow gate into the wilderness? If you have, take courage and know that this part of the journey is important for spiritual maturity. Embrace the wilderness by giving God permission to have His way in your life.

9

THE CALL

As stated, the spiritual journey begins with the new birth experience. This is when a person turns from an old life to embrace a new life in Christ. However, this walk cannot go forward until the call of God reaches a person's heart. Until this particular call comes, a person will have to wait at the gate for the Shepherd.

Jesus said in John 10:16, "And other sheep I have, which are not of this fold: them also I must bring, and they shall hear my voice; and there shall be one fold, and one shepherd." My understanding of this scripture is based on other people's explanation of how the shepherds of Jesus' day would keep their sheep in a centralized, enclosed area overnight. In the morning, they would call for their sheep, and upon hearing the voice of their shepherd, the sheep would separate from the other sheep and follow him. Obviously, Jesus' call goes out among humanity to gather those who belong to Him. In fact, He talks about going after that one lost sheep in Luke 15.

Matthew 20:16 makes this statement, "So the last shall be first, and the first last: for many be called, but few chosen." Throughout scripture, one can see God calling people, but few respond. Those who do will be chosen to carry out His plan and will.

One of the first people God called was Adam. Adam had just eaten of the forbidden fruit. His spiritual nakedness was unveiled; therefore, he made a cloak of fig leaves. Genesis 3:8-9 gives us this account,

> And they heard the voice of the LORD God walking in the garden in the cool of the day: and Adam and his wife hid themselves from the presence of the LORD God amongst the trees of the garden. And the LORD God called unto Adam and said unto him, Where art thou?

Of course, God knew where Adam and Eve were, but they needed to recognize that they were hiding from God because sin had made them spiritually naked, causing shame. In a way they had become lost to God, and God had become lost to them. They stood exposed for their rebellious deed, and knew that they could not confidently stand before God. Therefore, they tried to hide their spiritual condition behind fig leaves and their physical presence in the midst of trees.

Today, many people try to hide from God behind various cloaks of personal righteousness and deeds in the midst of spiritual ignorance, delusion, and darkness. Like Adam and Eve, He knows each person's location and is calling him or her unto Himself. Sadly, most individuals never realize how far away from life they are because of their spiritual darkness and delusion. Spiritual delusion allows them to justify walking away from God down a path of death and destruction.

God begins early in man's life to call him to Himself in the garden of life. Sadly, many ignore His call, while others have become desensitized to it. Over the years, the world has been successful in drowning out His voice with fleshly attractions and rebellion.

In spite of the fact that God is calling, man continues to hide from Him behind flimsy cloaks. However, God's call goes forth for the sake of each individual.[1] He is calling so that a person will take note of whether he or she is personally hiding from Him. It is God's desire to give individuals a reality check that would cause them to allow His light to reveal truth, resulting in liberty, reconciliation, and restoration.

How about you? Have you heard God's simple call, "Adam (man) where are you?" Have you allowed His light to reveal your sin, His love to enfold you in forgiveness, and His commitment and devotion to you to bring wholeness to your soul?

The second incident where God contended with man is found in Genesis 4. This time God is not calling for man to recognize where he is spiritually, but to examine himself and take responsibility for a wrong disposition. Most of us know about Abel and Cain. God accepted Abel's offering and rejected Cain's. In Genesis 4:6, we see God contending with Cain about his attitude towards the situation. Cain's countenance was reflecting his disposition. He had been offended by God's rejection of his sacrifice, but rather than face his attitude, he justified it and transferred his anger towards Abel.

Cain refused to heed God's voice and killed Abel. The call that goes out from God is in regard to Abel in Genesis 4:9, "Where is Abel, thy brother?" The pattern is being made clear between these two incidents. The first question to Adam had to do with where he was located in regards to his relationship with God, while the second question to Cain had to do with the location of his brother. The second call went forth to reveal Cain's heart attitude towards Abel. A person's disposition and fruit will be based on a person's relationship with God and his or her disposition towards others.

People's attitudes towards others, reflect their true heart before God. This is why all commandments can be summarized in the two commandments to love God with all your heart and to love others as yourself.[2]

Instead of confessing to God his wicked deed, Cain tried to get around his murderous actions. However, God already knew what he had done. He was giving Cain an opportunity to humble himself, repent, and

---

[1] John 15:22
[2] Mark 12:29-31

confess, but Cain felt he had a right to be angry, choosing the broad path of self-pity. His unwillingness to repent forced him to go out from the presence of the Lord.[3]

The disposition of many Christians can be seen by their countenance. They walk in unbelief because of idolatry, and are angry because when truth is presented, it offends them. They are disillusioned because of heresy and dissatisfied because they are stiff-necked. They are cruel due to arrogance and unforgiving because they feel life has treated them unfairly.

Like Cain, you can see that sin lies at the door of their hearts, but if you confront them, they become angry. And, if their sin is exposed, they become full of self-pity. In the end, those who hold to such a disposition fail to ever repent.

Jesus' initial call to everyone is to repent. He declares in Luke 13:5, "I tell you, Nay: but, except ye repent, ye shall all likewise perish." It is simple to repent, but the arrogant heart refuses to humble itself, the stiff-necked will not bow in submission, and the flesh will not surrender its rights.

As we study Adam, we can see where God is calling man to expose himself to His presence and be restored. With Cain, God is calling upon man to be forthright about his disposition and action to prevent him from sin, thereby, avoiding the need to leave His presence. This shows us that God's initial call to man is to give him a reality check about his spiritual condition. Notice that Adam hid from God, while Cain refused to heed His warning and had to leave His presence.

If man hears the initial call for repentance, it is because truth has penetrated a receptive heart. Such a penetration will give such an individual a sense of the depravity of his or her own soul. Once man responds to the initial call to face his condition, he will be prepared to hear and respond to the next call.

This is evident in the life of Isaiah. In Isaiah 6, the prophet saw the Lord, and his first awareness was how holy God is and how unclean he was. Upon his confession of his uncleanness, a live coal from the altar cleansed him. It was after the cleansing that he heard the voice of the Lord saying, "...Whom shall I send, and who will go for us" (Isaiah 6:8)?

Isaiah responded to the call, "Here am I; send me" (Isaiah 6:8).

Sadly, many people never hear this call. Like Adam, they hide from the truth, and when truth rips away their flimsy cloaks, they respond in anger and resentment. Like Cain, they prefer the darkness of their wicked actions, rather than the presence of the Lord.[4]

The one element about God's call is that it goes out to individuals rather than to the masses. For example, God did not call Israel. Rather, He called Moses and sent him to deliver the children of Israel. This

---

[3] Genesis 4:16
[4] John 3:19-20; 15:22

Developing Our Christian Life

confirms that a person's life and walk are personal, and will come down to the type of relationship he or she has with God.

This truth is brought out in Abraham's life. Genesis 12:1 tells us, "Now the LORD had said unto Abram, Get thee out of thy country, and from thy kindred, and from thy father's house, unto a land that I will shew thee." As one studies God's initial call to Abraham, he or she can see where God was calling him to come out and be separate. In fact, there are three areas in his life that God was calling for separation in Abraham's life. These areas of abandonment result in three types of separation.

The first separation is that of consecration. This is where the person separates from those things that would hinder him or her from wholly following God. Therefore, God's initial call to Abraham was that of consecration.

The second separation points to preparation and anointing. This is where the person is being separated for something. In the case of Abraham, he and his descendants were being separated from the rest of the nations to bring forth the Messiah.

The third type of separation is sanctification. This is where a person is being separated unto God. As you follow the life of Abraham, you will see that he was separated unto God in a personal way, and as a result, he became known as a friend of God.[5]

You can also see these three forms of separation in the life of Jesus. He was separated from heaven and His glory for the purpose of becoming the Lamb of God who would take away the sin of the world. In His humanity He was separated to do the will of the Father, which resulted in His third separation as an anointed vessel to carry out His mission as the Lamb and His ministry as the Messiah. The ultimate separation for Jesus in His humanity occurred on the cross where He had to die on the cross, taste the judgment for sin, and embrace death. However, His resurrection proved that He was victorious over the grave and death.[6]

Man is responsible to consecrate himself, but as far as the other two separations, they are the work of God. God will prepare, anoint, and sanctify His people to do His work. The purpose for this separation is so God's people will come deeper in a relationship with Him.

The first form of consecration that was required of Abraham entailed him leaving his country or source of worldly citizenship behind. His country represented the world, along with cultural influences and practices. God first must call His people to come out and be separate from these influences, because the world will drown out the Word of

---

[5] James 2:23
[6] Philippians 2:6-8; John 1:29; 1 Corinthians 15:51-57

God.[7] Therefore, for people to truly hear the deep things of God, they must come out from all the activities of the world.

We see this in Jesus' life. Crowds followed Him, but many times, He separated Himself from the crowds and His disciples to seek a quiet place where He could effectively commune with the Father.[8]

The next separation Abraham had to adhere was from his kindred. "Kindred" points to relatives such as parents, grandparents, uncles, aunts, and cousins. Today, family has been greatly exalted. The push for strong families often overrides the call of God in a person's life. The truth is, family can be the greatest deterrent to wholly serving God.

Earthly family represents identity, but a person's life in Christ is going to be separated from any earthly associations. In fact, a person must display the likeness of Christ, and not that of an earthly family. This is why Jesus' response to the man in Luke 9:62 who wanted to go bid farewell to his family was clear, "...No man, having put his hand to the plough, and looking back, is fit for the kingdom of God."

It is important for followers of Christ to realize that they will leave their earthly family or old life behind when they adhere to Christ's calling. The calling of God is strictly designed for the individual and not the whole family. It is an individual pursuit that will often leave all worldly associations behind in pursuit for that which is priceless.

To leave families who are on the broad path to destruction or in pigpens of pagan and idolatrous cultures is hard for some Christians, but they must leave the souls of family members in the hands of God. Each follower of Christ must let the old go, to single-heartedly follow Christ into a life marked by eternity.

As believers pursue this life, they must remember that their life is not behind them but before them. To look back because of devotion to relatives shows divided loyalties, to remain in limbo concerning earthly matters reveals unbelief, and to take detours because of earthly associations exposes wrong priorities. Each Christian must choose to reach out and embrace the life that is before him or her, because to do otherwise will mean the individual is not fit for the kingdom of God.

The final separation in God's initial call to Abraham came concerning separation from his father's household. This separation points to parents and siblings. We know that Abraham's father was an idolater and that he died in Haran.[9]

Much of the separation that takes place has to do not only with pagan cultures, but also with the idolatry they advocate. Joshua reminded the children of Israel in Joshua 24:2 that their fathers, who

---

[7] 2 Corinthians 6:14-18; Matthew 13:22
[8] Matthew 14:23; Mark 6:31; Luke 5:16; 22:41
[9] Genesis 11:32; Joshua 24:2

Developing Our Christian Life

dwelt on the other side of the flood up to the time of Abraham's father Terah, served other gods.

How many Christians' parents serve other gods? God will call His people away from the influence of other gods. In fact, if believers cling to these gods by clinging to family, His sword will come down, causing a necessary severance between any unholy alliances. Keep in mind, God is a jealous God and will not share worship with any idol.

Jesus talked about this sword that will divide families in Matthew 10:34-36,

> Think not that I am come to send peace on earth: I came not to send peace, but a sword. For I am come to set a man at variance against his father, and the daughter her mother, and the daughter-in-law against her mother-in-law. And a man's foes shall be they of his own household.

I know that in my own case, this sword has come down between my family and myself. They probably think my devotion to God is fanatical, misdirected, or cultist. They reel in hurt and rejection, but the real issue does not lie with my love for them, but my devotion to God.

As I have followed Jesus over the years, so much of this world has lost its meaning, importance, and glitter. Where family previously and unsuccessfully filled certain aspects of my life, I now experience a complete satisfaction through Christ. Due to this satisfaction, I do not care to look back at what once was as far as worldly relationships. This has caused those of my family to speculate about the person I am now. Like Jesus in John 7:5, my view of life has come into question, but it matters little, because I have heard His voice and I understand the necessity for separation.

This separation continued throughout Abraham's life. We see a division coming between Lot and Abraham in Genesis 13:7-13. In a way, this separation determined Abraham's inheritance.

As I have studied the Christian life, I realize that I cannot share my spiritual inheritance with others any more than the five wise virgins could share their oil with the five foolish ones in Matthew 25. Many times, a person's decisions about his or her life in Christ will determine the quality of his or her inheritance. I have learned that the more I choose Jesus and His righteousness, the more value is added to my spiritual inheritance.

One of the most sorrowful separations that happened in Abraham's life was the one that took place between him and his oldest son, Ishmael.[10] This separation took place so that the purity and integrity of the inheritance remained intact. Sarah insisted that Ishmael was not to share in Isaac's inheritance, and God confirmed it.

This example shows me that it is about inheritance, and it is up to me to maintain the purity and integrity of the inheritance I have through

---

[10] Genesis 21

Jesus. Like Isaac, it will be an inheritance that cannot be shared with those who do not have the same spirit or heart.

Separation is also necessary to receive what God has for a person. This is brought out in the case of Moses. Moses was separated from his family at a very early age. In spite of this separation, he was aware that God called him to deliver the Israelites from the oppressive bondage of Egypt. However, he first had to go through a separation from country and kindred before he could become the deliverer. Moses was forced to leave country and kindred behind after he asserted himself to be a deliverer by killing an Egyptian in defense of a Hebrew.

When a person is being separated for a work of God, he or she must first go by way of the valley of humiliation. Every real servant of God is brought to this place. These stout-hearted saints will suffer various losses, such as the initial vision (or calling), material wealth, prestige, and reputation.

This valley of humiliation may vary for different people. For Isaiah in the courts of heaven, it lasted only a couple of minutes, but for Abraham, there were thirteen years of silence. Moses spent 40 years in the wilderness, David spent at least ten years running from King Saul, and Joseph spent years as a slave and prisoner in Egypt. However, as you consider the results and examples of those who were prepared by God through the adversity of separation and humiliation for His work, you can see that it brought maturity and leadership.

Humility is a quality that can only be worked in a person as he or she senses his or her depravity in light of God's holiness. The greatest awareness that is realized in the valley of humiliation is just how incapable an individual is to control his or her world and please God.

The *Encyclopedia of Sermon Illustrations* gives some wonderful illustrations of how humility works. One of the illustrations had to do with thinking in terms of God's gifts being placed upon shelves, one above the other. As the Christian grows in character, the easier it is for the different shelves to be reached. However, the concept of humility would change such a picture. God's gifts that are on shelves are located one beneath the other. Therefore, it is not a matter of growing taller, but of stooping lower to locate His best gifts.

My first valley of humiliation lasted four years. To this day, I thank God for that tough experience for a couple of reasons—the first one being that it was an answer to one of my prayers. I had asked God to never let me take credit for His work in and through me. I greatly feared touching His glory, because I had a sense of my incredible pride and a desire to be a "somebody" in His kingdom, as well as in the sight of others.

Secondly, I realized that until the pride issue was honestly confronted and dealt with at the appropriate time, I would be a useless vessel. I knew as long as pride reigned, I could not trust my motive and perception because matters would always be about me and not Jesus Christ.

As I look back, I initially resented going through the process God had to take me through before He could really entrust me with the treasures of heaven, but I value it today. I realize that it was in this process that some of the greater points of character were worked into my life.

Forty years of being in the wilderness made Moses a meek man. We know that God once again established Moses' call from a burning bush. He not only became a great deliverer, but the one who received the Law and spoke face to face with God.[11] As you study Moses' life, you can see that he was being fine-tuned to not only hear and receive the deep things of God, but to impart them to others.

God also addresses people according to their potential. This can be observed in the life of Gideon. In Judges 6:12, the angel of the Lord appeared to him as he was secretly threshing wheat, and said, "…The LORD is with thee, thou mighty man of valor."

Gideon did not appear to be a man of valor as you consider how he protested his plight in secret. However, one needs to remember that God sees the future potential of a person. Therefore, all a person has to do is respond to the present call of God for Him to bring the individual to his or her potential. God looks for people who know their weaknesses, but have an obedient heart. As the heart responds, God is able to show His might and strength, which he did through Gideon. As a result, this man did prove to be a mighty man of valor.[12]

As separation occurs and the believer begins to respond to God, his or her life will be fine-tuned to hear the still small voice of God.[13] The still small voice implies a whisper that can only be heard in the secret chambers of intimacy. Such intimacy points to relationship.

The initial call of Jesus after repentance is of a personal nature. He invites people to come unto Him and partake of the various wells of salvation that can bring salvation, healing, reconciliation, and restoration.[14]

His second call is to deny self, pick up the cross, and follow Him. The first two parts of this call points to total consecration or abandonment, but the last part of the call to follow Him implies preparation, discovery, and service. Jesus not only leads his sheep from something, but He leads them into a new life that will entail service and worship.

The final call is found in the Song of Solomon, which is, "Come away with me."[15] The call of consecration will make you a stranger in the world. The second form of separation will make you a pilgrim, who will not be

---

[11] Exodus 3-4; 19-20; 33:11
[12] Judges 6-7
[13] 1 Kings 19:11-13
[14] Matthew 11:28-30; John 6:35; 7:37-39
[15] Song of Solomon 2:10, 13

content until your potential is fulfilled. However, the third type of call is to bring you apart, to the inner chambers of fellowship. It is a time of walking in the garden of communion and enjoying the sweetness of the Lover of your soul. It is also during this time that a person speaks face to face with the Son of God, taking on a reflection of His glory and coming forth as a friend of God.

I have shared this story many times, but there was a time in my life that my greatest goal was to be known as a faithful servant of God. One day, a godly woman looked into my eyes and told me that the Lord desired to call me "friend." I suddenly realized that the Lord was not looking for servants among His people. Rather, He was looking for those He could truly call friend. "Henceforth I call you not servants; for the servant knoweth not what his lord doeth: but I have called you friends; for all things that I have heard of my Father I have made known unto you" (John 15:15). It is in intimacy that the greatest sanctification takes place in our lives.

Today, Christians are content with hearing His call, but how many are consecrating themselves for the purposes of God? How many are graduating from the status of servant and become a friend of God?

The Christian journey is all about discovering the reality of God in a personal, intimate way. If you come to the end of your journey, but you never discover the beauty, majesty, and friendship of the Lord, you have missed the whole purpose of this Christian journey. You will be like the children of Israel in the wilderness. They were susceptible to idols, always looking back to Egypt, shrinking in front of obstacles, and wandering in the wilderness of unbelief.

The secret of all spiritual giants is that their main goal and focus is to possess eternity. This eternity is summarized in the consuming reality of God Incarnate, who made these declarations to the Apostle John, "...I am Alpha and Omega...Fear not; I am the first and the last...I am he that liveth, and was dead; and, behold, I am alive for evermore, Amen; and have the keys of hell and of death" (Revelation 1:11, 17c, 18).

10

LET MY PEOPLE GO

Have you ever watched a horse race? It appears as if the horses are anxious and biting at the bit as they wait for the gates to open. While lined up and waiting for the starting gates to open, I often wonder if the time of waiting for both the horses and their riders seems like an eternity.

For the last nine chapters, we have been preparing to take a journey. We have managed to identify the right gate, map out the route, and understand the purpose of our journey. The next step has to be the journey, right? Wrong! There is always an intense time of preparation for the spiritual traveler before he or she can be on his or her way. God's people must go through much preparation before the gates are opened. This truth can be seen in Jesus' life. He spent 30 years in obscurity being prepared for ministry that lasted a little over three years.

Moses spent 40 years in the backside of the desert, and then experienced a short time in Egypt before the parting of the Red Sea, two years at Sinai, and at least eighty days on the mountain shut in with God. After that, he spent another 40 years in the wilderness with the children of Israel. The miracles and victories in his life were minor compared to the trials, tribulations, and testing. In the end, Moses was never allowed to enter into the Promised Land with Israel.

The spiritual journey is more about preparation than service. It is plagued with drudgery, while only dotted with occasional victories. The valleys of humiliation greatly outnumber the mountaintop experiences.

Many Christians have a hard time accepting the reality of true Christianity because it has been presented as a life of blessings, and not one of hardships and drudgeries that eventually produce lasting rewards. As a result, many Christians give up at the starting gate or in the midst of testing, and go home. Jesus witnessed this in His own ministry.

In John 6, Jesus presented some hard sayings that could not be intellectually grasped or accepted by many of His disciples. John 6:66-67 tells us the response of the majority of His followers, "From that time many of his disciples went back, and walked no more with him. Then said Jesus unto the twelve, Will ye also go away?"

Much of Christianity is made up of waiting for the gate to open, so that a person can move forward into service. And, such times consist of what many call drudgeries. In fact, establishing the Christian life in the midst of what is often considered drudgery is one of the biggest challenges. This means applying Christian practices and teachings to everyday life in what appears to be insignificant.

For example, when you are working, whether in or out of the home, you must not be, "...slothful in business; (but) fervent in spirit; serving the Lord;...Not with eyeservice, as menpleasers; but as the servants of Christ, doing the will of God from the heart" (Romans 12:11; Ephesians 6:6). (Parenthesis added.)

At home with family, you should, "Be kindly affectioned one to another with brotherly love; in honour preferring one another" (Romans 12:10).

In your relationship with other Christians, you should, "Bear ye one another's burdens, and so fulfill the law of Christ" (Galatians 6:2).

When it comes to spare time, a Christian needs to be "Redeeming the time, because the days are evil" (Ephesians 5:16).

The real test in drudgery comes down to faithfulness. If you begin to do that which is pleasing and right to God in these insignificant times, it will produce a disposition of thankfulness and the virtue of faithfulness. This allows God to honor you in the drudgeries of your life, making such times a blessing rather than a burden that results in depression and self-pity.

In the years that Jeannette and I have been in ministry together, we have felt like we have been waiting at the gate most of the time. Occasionally, the gate has opened, but we have found other gates or obstacles down the road that have stopped us. At first, I became depressed because the gate never seemed to open for us. However, when it did open, I really did not enjoy the race because it proved to be a time of testing that carried tremendous demands.

Once again, we are waiting for the gate to open, but we are not anxious for it to open as in the past. We now wonder if we are ready for the race. We have learned that drudgery may seem endless, but when you are in the race, you can be left behind if you are not prepared to run it.

Through the years, I have learned that drudgery makes you wonder if God is going to use you. However, once you are in the race, you wonder if you are going to complete it. Therefore, drudgery tests your faith, while the actual race will expose your motives and character.

The children of Israel are a good example of the waiting and preparation before deliverance occurred. They had experienced drudgery through slavery. It is important to keep in mind that the children of Israel had been in Egypt for over 400 years. God had blessed them in various ways. As a result, it caused the leaders of Egypt to not only notice them, but to fear their numbers and seize the opportunity to make them slaves.[1]

---

[1] Genesis 15:13; Exodus 1:7-11

Developing Our Christian Life

This slavery brought a reality check to the Israelites. The main reality check was that they were indeed strangers in Egypt. Their lineage went back to another man, their beliefs were rooted in another God, and their homeland was located in a distant land.

Saints are strangers in this world. Their lineage goes back to the Son of God, their beliefs are rooted in the reality of His character, and their citizenship is located in a far distant kingdom.[2]

This harsh reality check made the Israelites turn back to Jehovah God and cry out to Him in total desperation. Their cries reached their merciful God, and He began to set in motion their deliverance.[3]

Sadly, many people will not cry out for deliverance until their bondage becomes so unbearable that they can no longer tolerate the oppression. The key word here is "tolerate." People have a tendency to tolerate anything as long as their lives remain in a semi-comfortable mode. When life is tolerable, individuals can be conditioned to accept greater bondage without becoming desperate. After all, Egypt was a rich nation, and the Israelites benefited from the crumbs of this great society.

After years of bondage, however, their taskmasters had become cruel in their demands. These drastic conditions caused the Israelites to be stirred up out of their comfort zones and spiritual lethargy to reconsider their roots and Jehovah God. Therefore, intense bondage served as the leverage that would allow God to reclaim a nation, keep His covenant with Abraham, and show Himself mighty.

The harsh reality is that everyone is in bondage to sin.[4] Many live comfortably in sin until they realize that their life has no substance or meaning. In fact, life does not make sense if God is not the source of it. Such reality throws many people into an identity crisis. This identity crisis is what will often cause people to seek the one true God.

God called Moses out of the wilderness to lead the children of Israel out from bondage. Can you imagine what the Israelites possibly thought when Moses stepped on the scene? "Praise God, we are out of here!" They probably had high hopes that after Moses' meeting with the Pharaoh that the oppression would lift and they would be on their way.

Most of us know the story about Moses' encounter with Pharaoh. He went to Pharaoh and delivered God's message. However, Pharaoh did not tremble at the message of Jehovah God. After all, he was considered a god in His own land, and had his own gods. He had no knowledge or need for the God of Israel.[5]

In fact, Egypt had many gods, and according to their mathematical equation, if one god failed, there were others who could humble this strange God of Israel. Instead of bringing deliverance to the children of

---

[2] Philippians 3:20
[3] Exodus 3:4-10
[4] Romans 6:17-18
[5] Exodus 5:2

Israel, Moses' request brought greater bondage upon them. The bondage was so oppressive that the Israelites cried out against Moses.[6]

This brings us to another reality, people who do not know the true God have no respect or regard for Him. They will often mock and challenge Him to prove Himself. I even see this attitude among Christians who are devoted to an idea, concept, or belief about God, but are ignorant of the God of the Bible. *Daniel 11:32* addresses the necessity to know the true God, "...but the people that do know their God shall be strong, and do exploits."

God warned Moses that Pharaoh would harden his heart, but through the time of testing, He would prove that He was the one true God. As you study the ten plagues of Egypt in light of Egypt's idols, you will realize that God was humbling all the gods of Egypt in front of both the Egyptians and the Israelites.

God's miraculous and awesome judgment upon the Egyptians caused His name to be known throughout the pagan nations. In fact, His reputation preceded Him in such a way that Rahab, the harlot of Jericho, recounted to the two Israelite spies the events that had taken place 40 years earlier.[7] She said that the God of Israel struck terror in the hearts of the people.

As I thought about the fear that the pagan nations displayed towards God during that time in history, I realized how Israel had actually lacked that fear for Jehovah God. As you travel with them, you can see it was only after they had been greatly chastised that they showed any healthy fear or recognition that the God of Israel was holy and deserved awe, obedience, and worship.

Sadly, this also appears to be the case for much of the visible Church in America. The Communists show more awareness towards the power of God's Word than Christians where freedom of religion has been the rule. Many believers are taking the Word for granted, along with God's love and grace. As a result, much of the visible Church appears to be weak and vulnerable.

The truth is no nation or people can stand before the God of Israel. He alone is God. Isaiah 42:8 declares, "I am the LORD: that is my name: and my glory will I not give to another, neither my praise to graven images."

Isaiah 45:21-22 tells us, "...and there is no God else beside me; a just God and a Saviour; there is none beside me. Look unto me, and be ye saved, all the ends of the earth: for I am God, and there is none else."

God's main goal was to become Israel's God. Israel had been in the midst of paganism and idolatry for over 400 years. They had a spiritual mixture that would prove to be their downfall in the wilderness.

---

[6] Exodus 5:6-23
[7] Joshua 2:9-11

Developing Our Christian Life

Many Christians have a mixture because of the powerful influence of the world. Today, I am watching God humble the gods of America, but few in the Church are recognizing what He is doing. Much of the body of Christ actually believes that the humbling of these American idols is the work of the devil, and the Church is simply failing to take the appropriate measures. Instead of calling for repentance and brokenness about the idols that have been erected in the hearts and minds of professing Christians to stay the hand of God's judgment, the Church is calling for prayer and fasting to push back the devil.

It is important to stress, God must become your God. He is the only sure rock and foundation by which a person will be able to stand in the midst of tribulation, and withstand the attacks of the enemy. He will humble every idol out of mercy, and allow the necessary bondage to cause each of us to reconsider our roots, lineage, and hope.

The process of humbling the gods of Egypt took time, but through it all, God made one consistent demand on Pharaoh, "Let my people go."[8] It is important to note that the God of heaven laid claim to the children of Israel. He made it clear to Pharaoh that they did not belong to him; therefore, he had no legal claims upon them. He must let them go!

The Word tells us that saints have been bought with a price; therefore, the world or its god, Satan, has no legal claims on them.[9] However, like Pharaoh, Satan does not want to let go of those who once freely served him, which causes an intense battle before deliverance takes place.

The battle that transpired between Pharaoh and God reveals the arrogance of man and the sovereignty of God. Mankind and the powers of darkness can try to outwit, outlast, and remain immovable before God, but He will reign in the end. This was evident as the most important god of Egypt, Pharaoh, was humbled by the death of his firstborn son, which resulted in the ushering in of the deliverance of the Israelites.

By God humbling the idols of Egypt, He broke the stiff necks of the Egyptians. They began to fear the God of Israel, and when God brought their final god down before Him, the Egyptians not only insisted that the children of Israel leave, but they provided them with supplies and riches. The riches of Egypt served as a payment for the Israelites' service for hundreds of years of slavery.[10]

There is a progression in the requests and struggles to secure the freedom of Israel. The first request can be found in Exodus 5:1, "…Let my people go, that they may hold a feast unto me in the wilderness." The first request was for the Israelites to be set free to celebrate life. All the feasts that God established required not only celebration of the life that

---

[8] Exodus 5:2; 6:11; 7:14; 8:1; 9:1; 10:3
[9] 1 Corinthians 6:20; 7:23
[10] Exodus 3:22; 6:1; 11:2;

God provided, but also sacrifices to pay homage to the One who gave them life.

As long as people are in bondage, they cannot celebrate the essence or source of their life, which is God. God is calling His people apart from the atmosphere of Egypt to discover real life.[11] Real life is first found in recognizing and worshipping the true God of the universe.

This is true for Christians. As previously written, this spiritual journey is about discovering the life that God has for each of us. Therefore, the Lord calls believers apart from the world, so they can discover, embrace, and celebrate the life He has given them.

Another important part of this deliverance had to do with the children of Israel taking a three-day journey into the wilderness to sacrifice, to stay any judgment.[12] As you will see, the wilderness is symbolic of the grave. The three days represents the sacrifice of God, Jesus Christ, being in the grave for three days to silence judgment on sin, and to secure victory over death for all who believe upon Him. Later, we are told where the three-day journey in the wilderness led Israel—to Marah, the place of the bitter springs.[13]

In Exodus 7:6, the request goes one step further, "…Let my people go, that they may serve me in the wilderness." It is this request that is constantly put before Pharaoh from this point on.[14] For years, Israel had served Egypt. Now, God is laying claim to their service. People can only serve one master at a time. The children of Israel did not belong to Pharaoh. They had simply been taken captive because of circumstances beyond their control. God was taking the reigns back of His people and calling them forth to serve Him.

Christians are servants of God. They owe God total allegiance. However, because of the influences of the world, they can prove to still be divided in their loyalty to Him. This division serves as a breach in the wall in their spiritual life, and allows the world and Satan to penetrate their lives with temptation.

Service in this text also points to worship.[15] God understood the importance of the Israelites establishing their religious life as soon as they were out in the wilderness. At the core of active and godly religion is worship. Godly worship has various characteristics. It has praise, which serves as a celebration of God. Within genuine praise is thankfulness. This virtue is the means by which people celebrate the spiritual bounty and beauty of what God has brought to their lives. We see that all celebration hinges on who God is and what He does for us.

---

[11] 2 Corinthians 6:14-18
[12] Exodus 5:3; 8:27
[13] Exodus 33:8
[14] Exodus 8:1, 20; 9:1, 13; 10:3
[15] Strong's Exhaustive Concordance of the Bible, # 5647

Developing Our Christian Life

Jesus said that we are to worship God in spirit and truth.[16] A spirit of meekness breeds humility. Humility allows us to receive truth in a righteous manner. Therefore, true worship and humility walk hand in hand. In fact, thankfulness sets up an environment that produces humility before God. As one considers the blessings of God in the right attitude, he or she will be in awe of the faithfulness of God. This awe will automatically humble the heart, bow the neck, and bend the knees before the God of power and majesty.

Humility is the key that unlocks the door of communion. The ultimate goal of real worship is to lead the worshipper into the very presence of God. Quietness of spirit, and not exaltation, marks this communion as one sits humbly in the overwhelming presence of God Almighty.

There were times that Pharaoh agreed to let the children of Israel go, but then, he would put conditions on their journey. In Exodus 8:28, he told them that they could not go far away. Obviously, he wanted them close enough to control them.

The problem with a close association with Egypt is that it would cause God's people to operate on the outside fringes of their real life in God. Egypt represented the world. God had to totally separate His people. This separation would change their dependency from Egypt to Him. This is true for Christians as well. Believers who combine the world with Christianity prove to be carnal. They remain on the outside fringes of their life with God, always looking in at the possibilities of this incredible life, but never entering in. Therefore, God had no intention of allowing Israel to stay in the reach of Pharaoh. Israel belonged to Him, and the Promised Land was her destination.

Satan would keep every one of God's people in his claws, but heaven is the destination of every believer. And, God knows how to loosen the grip of any tyrant who would prevent His people from finishing the course and embracing His promises.

Exodus 10:8 says, "And Moses and Aaron were brought again unto Pharaoh: and he said unto them, Go, serve the LORD your God: but who are they that shall go?"

Moses' answer in Genesis 10:9 is, "...We will go with our young and with our old, and with our sons and daughters with our flocks and with our herds will we go; for we must hold a feast unto the LORD."

Pharaoh became upset at the prospect of the little ones going on this journey. He made this statement in Exodus 10:11, "Not so: go now ye that are men, and serve the LORD; for that ye did desire." The little ones represented affections. Pharaoh knew if he kept the little ones, the children of Israel would look back towards Egypt and eventually come back to those they left behind.

Exodus 10:24 gives us Pharaoh's next chess play, "...Go ye, serve the LORD; only let your flocks and your herds be stayed: let your little

---

[16] John 4:24

ones also go with you." The flocks represent provision. If the children of Israel did not have their needs met or any way to sacrifice to God, it would defeat their purpose and they would have to return to the tyranny of Egypt. Moses was not about to leave anyone or any necessary possession behind.

These examples show Christians that everything about their lives must be committed to God. If affections are left behind, they will look back to the world. If they are sent out in the wilderness without proper provision, they will go back to the world. God had to bring a complete separation, by bringing all of Israel out with the proper provisions. Proper provisions would alleviate any reason for any of His people to go back to their old ways of life.

Through the ordeal, Pharaoh refused to humble himself, serving as an obstacle to God's people.[17] In the final showdown, Pharaoh made this statement to Moses, "...Get thee from me, take heed to thyself, see my face no more; for in that day thou seest my face thou shalt die" (Exodus 10:28).

Moses' reply was: "...Thou hast spoken well, I will see thy face again no more" (Exodus 10:29).

This brought about the final judgment upon Egypt: The death of the firstborn. The death of an innocent lamb ensured that death would pass over Israel, and it was the death of the firstborn of Egypt that opened the prison doors of bondage for the children of Israel.[18]

Both the lamb and the firstborn point to the sacrifice of Jesus who secured the means of redemption for all who would believe upon His name. As in the days of Israel, the Passover Lamb, God's only begotten Son, opens all of the prison doors, so that believers can be translated from the kingdom of darkness into the kingdom of light.[19]

Everyone needs to be delivered from the tyranny of Pharaoh (Satan and sin) and the influences of Egypt (world). However, one must consider whether or not he or she is desperate enough to pursue God, or if he or she is tolerating bondage. Perhaps you are at the gate anxiously waiting for deliverance, but are you ready?

Bondage is a terrible weight, but freedom can become a great test. If God delivers you, will you go into the wilderness to establish your life in him, or will you desire freedom without God and resent godly disciplines? Keep in mind the reason why God delivers His people from the bondage of the world and Satan. He delivers them so that they can serve and worship Him.

Everyone who claims to be a Christian has been delivered for the purpose of service and worship. But how many are abusing this spiritual

---

[17] Exodus 10:3
[18] Exodus 11-12
[19] John 1:29; Romans 8:29; Acts 4:12; Colossians 1:13

freedom by coming once again under the bondage of sin, the world, and Satan? Heed the warnings of the Apostle Peter,

> For if after they have escaped the pollutions of the world through the knowledge of the Lord and Savior Jesus Christ, they are again entangled therein, and overcome, the latter end is worse with them than the beginning. For it had been better for them not to have known the way of righteousness, than, after they have known it, to turn from the holy commandment, delivered unto them. But it is happened unto them according to the true proverb, The dog is turned to his own vomit again; and the sow that was washed to her wallowing in the mire (2 Peter 2:20-22).

11

THE WILDERNESS OF SHUR

How sweet is spiritual liberty? Israel was about to find out. After the death of the firstborn in Egypt, God opened the gate of bondage, and Israel came out from harsh slavery into the care of His glorious leadership. Exodus 13:17-18 states,

> And it came to pass, when Pharaoh had let the people go, that God led them not through the land of the Philistines, although that was near; God said, Lest peradventure the people repent when they see war, and they return to Egypt: But God led the people about, through the way of the wilderness of the Red Sea: and the children of Israel went up harnessed out of the land of Egypt.

In this verse, we see God recognizing the vulnerability of Israel. The vulnerability of someone or a people will determine the route God will take them. As you follow His care and concern towards Israel, you will see He was a doting Father, a protective husband, a considerate Master, and a loving God. He summarized His care towards Israel to Moses in this way in Exodus 19:4, "Ye have seen what I did unto the Egyptians, and how I bare you on eagle's wings, and brought you unto myself." What an incredible picture of how detailed God is about leading His people through the maze of the present world.

God's desire was to bring Israel to Himself. This desire has not changed in regards to the Church. Jesus' invitation is to come to Him. He longs to sup with us in an intimate and personal way.[1]

Moses said this about God's commitment to Israel in Deuteronomy 32:10-11,

> He found him in a desert land, and in the waste howling wilderness; he led him about, he instructed him, he kept him as the apple of his eye. As an eagle stirreth up her nest, fluttereth over her young, spreadeth abroad her wings, taketh them, beareth them on wings."

This Scripture verse shows us that God highly values and keeps His people ever before Him. He stirs them up and out of their comfort zones to bring them higher, and then bears them up in power. It is a beautiful picture indeed. However, many of His people fail to see His care, commitment, love, and protection.

---

[1] Matthew 11:28-30; John 6:35; 7:37; Revelation 3:20

Exodus 13:21-22 tells us how God guided Israel,

> And the LORD went before them by day in a pillar of a cloud, to lead them the way; and by night in a pillar of fire, to give them light; to go by day and night: He took not away the pillar of the cloud by day, nor the pillar of fire by night, from before the people.

Although not as visible, the Church has a similar guidance in the presence and leadership of the Holy Spirit.

The children of Israel had been set free to know and serve this caring God who would bear them up in His power and lead them in His ways. However, would they take the opportunity to know Him? You would also think that such a caring God would bring Israel into a blissful place. Instead, God brought the children of Israel to the Wilderness of Shur.

Shur means "a wall" and most likely received its name from a fortified Arabian town that was located east of the ancient head of the Red Sea and on the eastern border of Egypt.[2] The concept of wall points to protection or adversity. The direction "east" often symbolizes judgment or separation. As you put together the idea of a wall and judgment from the east, you have a picture of separation, adversity, hindrance, or being buffeted.

The wilderness is a type of grave, and Shur represents the work of the grave: that of separation. Separation is marked by adversity, and as we are about to discover, on this part of the journey, Israel would not be exempt from the adversity caused by separation.

The wilderness of Shur is also known as the wilderness of Etham. As stated previously, Etham marked the end of the cultivated lands and the beginning of the wilderness. This place was near the Seven Wells, which were located about three miles from the western side of the ancient head of the gulf. Etham means "bounded by the sea."[3]

This sets up another descriptive picture as we begin to realize that the Red Sea represented the initial wall of adversity or buffeting to the children of Israel. The number "seven" also implies that some type of perfection will take place. The concept of "well" often points to the work of God on behalf of man.

The Lord warned Moses of the upcoming adversity that would face Israel in Exodus 14:3-4, "For Pharaoh will say of the children of Israel, They are entangled in the land, the wilderness hath shut them in. And I will harden Pharaoh's heart, that he shall follow them." As you study this scenario, you will realize that Pharaoh failed to humble himself enough to recognize and acknowledge that it was Jehovah God who secured Israel's deliverance. He still considered his opposition as being against mere man, in spite of all the miracles and judgment.

---

[2] Smith's Bible Dictionary
[3] Ibid

One would think that Pharaoh would have the sobriety or understanding that all that befell him was not due to a man named Moses, but to the God of Moses. His attitude towards God reminds me of the foolish words of the infidel Voltaire, "Even if a miracle should be wrought in the open marketplace before a thousand sober witnesses, I would rather mistrust my senses than admit a miracle."[4]

Although Pharaoh witnessed one miracle after another, he still refused to fear Jehovah God, acknowledge Him, and humble himself before Him. This attitude caused him to reconsider Israel's departure, resulting in anger.

Obviously, Israel's separation from Egypt was not complete. They had gone out with a high hand, meaning the Israelites left in an exalted position, instead of in destitution.[4] However, the leader of Egypt was not ready to let Egypt's slaves go. This set up the scene for one final miracle that would clearly separate Israel from Egypt, once and for all.

In order to perform this incredible separation, God brought Israel to the Red Sea. The Red Sea served as a wall of possible destruction to Israel, while the Egyptians were hedging them in like vise grips from the opposite direction.

It is interesting to note that there were three distinct separations that took place in this incident. The first separation is found in Exodus 14:19-20,

> And the angel of God, which went before the camp of Israel, removed and went behind them; and the pillar of the cloud went from before their face, and stood behind them: And it came between the camp of the Egyptians and the camp of Israel; and it was a cloud and darkness to them, but it gave light by night to these: so that the one came not near the other all the night.

There was a decisive distinction made between Israel and Egypt. Israel was in the light of God, while Egypt was in total darkness. We see that, in this case, Egypt encountered the wall of adversity, while Israel was secure in the fortress of its protection.

As a person follows the light, the darkness will become more defined. The reason there is a greater distinction is because light points to cleansing from sin and agreement in God. 1 John 1:6-7 states, "If we say that we have fellowship with him, and walk in darkness, we lie, and do not the truth: But if we walk in the light, as he is the light, we have fellowship one with another, and the blood of Jesus Christ his Son cleanseth us from all sin."

The next separation after cleansing is becoming identified with God. Identification occurs in baptism and implies that one's life is now hidden in God. Exodus 14:21 gives us a description of this baptism,

---

[4] Encyclopedia Of Sermon Illustrations; ©1988 by Concordia Publishing House, #433

[4] Exodus 14:8

Developing Our Christian Life

> And Moses stretched out his hand over the sea; and the LORD caused the sea to go back by a strong east wind all that night, and made the sea dry land, and the waters were divided. And the children of Israel went into the midst of the sea upon the dry ground: and the waters were a wall unto them on their right hand, and on their left.

Here we see that an east wind pushed back the water and dried up the land for the Israelites.

1 Corinthians 10:1-2 tells us that the Israelites were under the cloud, passed through the sea, and were all baptized into Moses in the cloud and sea. Like the Israelites, each member of the Church is baptized by the Spirit into one Body. And, the head of this Body is Jesus.[5]

The third separation is death. For the Israelites, the waters of the Red Sea served as a wall of protection, but to the Egyptians it became the means of judgment and death.

> And the LORD said unto Moses, Stretch out thine hand over the sea, that the waters may come again upon the Egyptians, upon their chariots, and their horsemen... the LORD overthrew the Egyptians in the midst of the sea... there remained not so much as one of them (Exodus 14:26, 27c, 28c).

God had humbled the idols of Egypt, but at the Red Sea, He humbled the strength of Pharaoh. Like the modern missiles of today, chariots and horses often determined the strength of a nation. Pharaoh sent the strength of Egypt to bring Israel back to the land. As we can see, Egypt's strength crumbled before Jehovah God.

People have four main layers that must be dealt with before they can learn reliance upon God. As you will see, each wilderness separately unveils and addresses each of these layers. The first layer represents the strength of man.

It is not unusual for man to rely upon personal strength, but the truth is, man does not have any real strength in and of himself. Granted, personal strength is developed, but without food, water, and the proper means of maintaining it, man would be unable to survive. This is why Jeremiah 17:5 states, "Thus saith the LORD; Cursed be the man that trusteth in man, and maketh flesh his arm, and whose heart departeth from the LORD."

Strength comes from three sources, the land, the world, and God. When God brought Israel to the wilderness, the first source of strength (that of the land) was quickly alleviated. Such land is unproductive and not able to sustain life.

The horses and chariots represented the world's source of strength. This is the source that man often looks to in establishing authority and displaying power. God made this statement in Deuteronomy 17:14c and 16,

---

[5] 1 Corinthians 12:13; Ephesians 5:23

> ... and shalt say, I will set a king over me, like as all the nations that are about me.... But he shall not multiply horses to himself, nor cause the people to return to Egypt, to the end that he should multiply horses: forasmuch as the LORD hath said unto you, Ye shall henceforth return no more that way.

God ultimately revealed the vanity of the strength of the world as He overthrew the Egyptians in the midst of the sea.

This brings us to the final source of strength—God. God is the source of lasting and sustaining strength. Zechariah 4:6 declares, "...Not by might, nor by power, but by my Spirit, saith the LORD of hosts." Therefore, it matters little how much power a people or country may display if God is against it. He can bring any nation or people down with one act.

Psalm 144:15 says, "Happy is that people, that is in such a case: yea, happy is that people, whose God is the LORD." The nation who fails to recognize the leadership, authority, and power of God will lack character. Without character, the people of that nation will lack the fortitude to stand in crisis and withstand the onslaught of the enemy.

The example of Egypt proves that the strength of the world is outward, and lacks the proper foundation to stand. Even in the Church, there are people who are Pharaohs, depending on the world for strength. They trust their own strength to survive, endure, and overcome. They try to intimidate people with an outward show of might in order to cover up their inward emptiness. They try to stand their ground with indifference and control, or bully people with empty threats. However, such sufficiency represents vanity. 2 Corinthians 3:5 puts it in this perspective, "Not that we are sufficient of ourselves to think any thing as of ourselves; but our sufficiency is of God."

If you are a Pharaoh, you need to know one important fact. You are coming down. God will humble you at the point of your strength to show you how much pride and fear is behind your hot air, and that before God it will be abased. Luke 18:14b confirms this, "... for everyone that exalteth himself shall be abased; and he that humbleth himself shall be exalted."

Israel made it to the other side of the Red Sea, while there was not one Egyptian who survived the ordeal. God delivered Israel and brought Egypt down into the depths of the sea. If God is going to be God in your life, there must not be one shred of personal strength left to rely on. It is now up to God to provide in the wilderness. After all, you are officially dead to the life that is maintained by personal strength or the world.

This miraculous event caused the Israelites to rejoice for they had stood still and watched the salvation of the Lord. It was a glorious time.[6] However, people are fickle. At one point, the Israelites were rejoicing

---

[6] Exodus 14:13, 28; 15

over God's miraculous victory over Pharaoh's army. Then, the next time you read about them they were grumbling.

The Israelites were taken three days into the wilderness after their encounter at the Red Sea, only to find no water. It is important to note that initially it was requested that Israel be allowed to travel three days into the wilderness to have a feast and sacrifice to God. This was actually instructed to stay judgment.[7] However, instead of celebrating their deliverance, new life, and sacrificing to God, they ended up murmuring.

Exodus 15:23-24 says, "And when they came to Marah, they could not drink the waters of Marah, for they were bitter: therefore the name of it was called Marah. And the people murmured against Moses, saying, What shall we drink?" Here at Marah the people encountered the harsh reality about their journey. Some of it would prove to be a mixed bag that included adverse challenges that would bring bitterness to their souls.

Moses cried unto God and He showed him a tree that he cast into the waters. This tree made the waters sweet, so the Israelites could freely drink of it. How many of you have cried out to God, and He showed you a tree? This is a beautiful representation of the work of the cross. The bitter springs represent people's spiritual condition. They have been poisoned with sin, defiled with the stagnation of rebellion, and rendered useless by endless compromise with the world. However, in the midst of this bitterness, God placed a tree, the cross, and allowed His Son to drink every drop of the bitter cup of judgment for us on that tree. Jesus Christ drank of this bitter cup, so that people could partake of the sweet Rivers of Living Water.[8]

The wilderness of Shur is a powerful picture of the power and deliverance that is wrought by the Gospel to those with a searching heart. The Red Sea introduces us to Jesus' death, while the wilderness represents the grave. The bitter waters point to the harsh reality of sin, while the tree points to redemption and healing.

It was at this place that God spoke these words in Exodus 15:26,

...If thou wilt diligently hearken to the voice of the LORD thy God, and wilt do that which is right in his sight, and wilt give ear to his commandments, and keep all his statutes, I will put none of these diseases upon thee, which I have brought upon the Egyptians: for I am the LORD that healeth thee.

Is not Jesus' work on the cross about healing? "But he was wounded for our transgressions, he was bruised for our iniquities: the chastisement of our peace was upon him; and with his stripes we are healed" (Isaiah 53:5).

---

[7] Exodus 5:1, 3; 8:27
[8] John 7:37-39

If God's people would learn to not only rejoice in the victorious times, but also to joyfully embrace the bitterness of this life, sweetness will come out of it. This sweetness is not about service or greatness. It is about the Person of Jesus being manifested in a person's life.

By embracing the bitterness of this life, it will bring you to the refreshing waters of Elim. The Red Sea points to identification through death, the wilderness to the grave, the tree to the cross, but Elim points to Pentecost. It had twelve fountains or wells and 70 palm trees.

The wells or fountains pointed to Jesus Christ and His work of redemption, while the water represented the Holy Spirit. It was Jesus who baptized those waiting in the upper room with the Holy Ghost. Jesus has much to offer any weary traveler, lost wayfarer, and wounded soul. He is the Great Physician who came to meet man right where he lives. He is the great I AM, always operating in the present in a gentle, incredible way. As a Shepherd, He oversees the needs and cares of those who belong to Him. He serves as the door to communion, as well as the Anointed One, the Christ, the Son of the Living God. Like the serpent in the wilderness, He was lifted up on the pole, or cross, above man's hopeless plight to bring salvation. He also serves as the light of the world that cleanses. He is the life of man that lasts forever and the way to peace. Jesus is the truth about God, the Bread of life that sustains, and the Giver of the Living Water that refreshes. He is the Vine that gives nourishment.[9]

Elim means "strong trees."[10] As one partakes of Jesus' qualities, he or she will become as Psalm 1:3 declares, "And he shall be like a tree planted by the rivers of water, that bringeth forth his fruit in his season; his leaf also shall not wither; and whatsoever he doeth shall prosper".

In the Wilderness of Shur, we see the Gospel, as well as experience Pentecost. We taste the bitterness of the cross, as well as the sweetness it will ultimately bring forth through identification with Jesus Christ.

Separation in Shur is distinct and complete for the spiritual wayfarer. The Israelites no longer belonged to Egypt for they became hidden in the cloud. Are you hidden in Christ?[11]

There are many valuable lessons to draw from in the wilderness of separation. The greatest theme of Shur, besides separation, is ridding man of personal strength, so that he can give way to God. Have you allowed yourself to be separated in the Wilderness of Shur? Is your personal strength intact? These are issues that people must confront before going further. Resolve any of these matters, and let God be God in your life.

---

[9] Acts 1:5; John 6:35; 10:1-10; 14:6; 15:1-8
[10] Smith's Bible Dictionary
[11] Colossians 3:1-3

12

THE WILDERNESS OF SIN

The next stage of the journey brought Israel to the Wilderness of Sin. This wilderness implies a time of testing. It points to the concept and working of sin, revealing man's need to come face to face with this terminal disease of the soul. This disease is manifested in the lust of the flesh. That which is done in the flesh results in death.

James 1:14-15 says, "But every man is tempted, when he is drawn away of his own lust, and enticed. Then when lust hath conceived, it bringeth forth sin: and sin, when it is finished, bringeth forth death." A statement was made in the *Encyclopedia of Sermon Illustrations* in reference to Judas' betrayal leading to the crucifixion of Christ. It related Judas' betrayal to the flesh. If uncontrolled, the flesh will also lead to a person's eternal death.[1] True to its name, the Wilderness of Sin became a place of great testing and enticement to the children of Israel.

Exodus 16:1 gives us some insight into this wilderness. "And they took their journey from Elim, and all the congregation of the children of Israel came unto the wilderness of Sin, which is between Elim and Sinai on the fifteenth day of the second month after their departing out of the land of Egypt." The Wilderness of Sin was a tract of land that was between Elim and Sinai. Notice how they arrived in this wilderness in the second month. The number "two" represents differences that bring contrast.[2] This contrast is obvious, as this wilderness is between Elim, which means "strong trees," and Sinai, which means "thorny."[3]

They arrived on the 15th day. The number "15" (3 x 5) is comprised of completion or divine perfection and grace.[4] The children of Israel had been completely separated from their former life. This separation was so complete there was no way for them to turn back. Such a separation was an act of grace on God's part, as a way to protect them. If one turned back, he or she would not be worthy or fit for God's kingdom.[5]

I have experienced His grace in this manner. Through a series of events, I left my hometown in disgrace after a divorce. My life was in

---

[1] # 617, pg. 135
[2] Number In Scripture, E.W. Bullinger, pgs. 92, 96
[3] Smith's Bible Dictionary
[4] Number In Scripture, pg. 257
[5] Luke 9:62

such disarray that I knew I would never be back nor did I have any desire to look back. The Lord had brought a complete separation to protect me from any romantic or unrealistic emotions about my former life. This not only proved His grace to me, but it gave me the liberty to pursue my new life in Him.

This brings us to grace. When we think of sin in light of salvation, grace follows closely behind. The Wilderness of Shur points to deliverance. If true to form, we will see God's amazing grace follow closely behind in the Wilderness of Sin.

There is a spiritual progression with each wilderness. The Wilderness of Shur was a place of complete separation. The children of Israel were totally separated from Egypt (the world) through the miraculous intervention of God. It was also here that God dealt with the first layer of dependency within man—his strength.

Each wilderness represents a different aspect of the grave. For Shur, it represented the work of the grave—that of separation. However, the Wilderness of Sin represents the product of the grave, that of death. As we are about to see, death deals with the second layer of dependency that man looks to—the flesh.

The Israelites had come from the bitter springs of Marah to the fresh waters of Elim. There, they had partaken of the 12 wells as they rested under and around the 70 palm trees. This was a time of preparation for the Wilderness of Sin.

For the Christian, this is representative of coming by way of the cross, in order to experience the power of Pentecost. It is important to recognize this path, in order to understand the preparation necessary to face the Wilderness of Sin.

Jesus gives us a glimpse of the challenge this wilderness represents when He went from the waters of Jordan into the wilderness to be tested by Satan. The testing lasted forty days and proved to be intense.

Jesus' disciples picked up this path of testing after His ascension. They were told to tarry until they were endued with power from above.[6] This waiting was a preparation for the next phase of their Christian journey. Acts 1:8 gives insight into the next part of the journey, "But ye shall receive power, after that the Holy Ghost is come upon you: and ye shall be witnesses unto me both in Jerusalem, and in all of Judea, and in Samaria, and unto the uttermost part of the earth."

The key word in this verse is "witness." This word in this text implies martyr.[7] A martyr is one who suffers death. As we are about to see, the flesh must die daily in order for God to reign. The problem is that the flesh puts up a fierce fight to live, which causes various challenges and will result in defeat.

---

[6] Luke 24:49
[7] Strong's Exhaustive Concordance and Dictionary, #3144

This brings us to the importance of grace in light of the flesh. Confronting personal strength, as one must, in the Wilderness of Shur is a harsh reality. Such a reality is due to the fact that a person's greatest point of strength marks the most vulnerable place of weakness. Once a person comes face to face with this reality, he or she can resolve to accept the vanity of personal strength and go on to the next stage of personal growth without too much contention.

The flesh is a different battle. It is alive and well, and it is harder to confront and deal with because it hides. This enemy will only raise its head when it is being tested. We see this in the case of the children of Israel in the Wilderness of Sin. It was not long after entering this wilderness that the people of Israel began murmuring against Moses and Aaron.[8] They were hungry, and they quickly realized that there were no resources. They considered the environment they were in and concluded that it was a death sentence.

In a way, they accused Moses and Aaron of playing a cruel trick on them. Instead of delivering them from bondage, the people concluded that these two men were actually leading them into the clutches of death. The Israelites were right in a sense. Although the dying out process for the flesh is a lifelong process, the wilderness provided the front row seat to participate in this process. This part of the journey would allow the Israelites to see the depravity of the flesh. The wilderness was a means to execute a deadly blow to the flesh. However, before a blow could be executed against the flesh, it had to raise its head in protest.

It was here in the Wilderness of Sin that the flesh would expose itself at different times as the Israelites faced challenges, uncertainties, and inconveniences. The visible manifestation of the flesh was the insidious murmuring that came out in the times of testing.

Murmuring involves an obstinate attitude that expresses itself in the form of complaining. This action is the opposite of faith because it refuses to get past what it feels and sees to simply trust God. It begrudges because it is spoiled, and does not want to endure any inconveniences. It lacks patience due to the fact that the appetites of the flesh become more intense. Ultimately, it manifests resentment because the flesh refuses to be disciplined.

Since this incident was early in their journey, God showed them grace. Grace gives God's people the opportunity to spiritually mature. This can only occur as a person walks by faith. As you will see later, this grace can turn into chastisement or judgment if people fail to grow in it. Failure to mature in God's grace causes people to abuse it, resulting in chastisement.

In Exodus 16:12, God said this to Moses, "I have heard the murmurings of the children of Israel: speak unto them, saying, At even ye shall eat flesh, and in the morning ye shall be filled with bread; and ye

---

[8] Exodus 16:2

shall know that I am the LORD your God." God is Jehovah Jireh, the provider. As our provider, God gives His saints what they have need of. Sometimes, He gives in abundance, while at other times there is only enough provision to satisfy the immediate need.

The Apostle Paul gave this insight into this subject in Philippians 4:11-13,
> Not that I speak in respect of want: for I have learned, in whatsoever state I am, therewith to be content. I know both how to be abased, and I know how to abound: every where and in all things I am instructed both to be full and to be hungry, both to abound and to suffer need. I can do all things through Christ which strengtheneth me.

Paul knew where his strength came from, and was content and confident.

God's provision is a way to remind believers that He is the One who provides for all of their needs and bounties. His faithfulness in this area reveals His character and intentions. Jeremiah 29:11 says, "For I know the thoughts that I think toward you, saith the LORD, thoughts of peace, and not evil, to give you an expected end." God wants to provide His people with all of their daily needs. Learning to rely upon Him for all needs is a way for God's people to learn the dynamics of faith.

Notice in this situation, Israel failed to look to God. Instead, they were looking to Moses and Aaron as they murmured. The focus of the Israelites was on man to solve a problem that required a supernatural intervention.

The flesh looks in every direction to satisfy its needs except upward. Since the flesh is carnal and lacks discipline, it prefers to complain rather than pray. After all, it is easier to complain than to exercise faith that requires the personal discipline to deny the flesh any audience.

God provided quail that night. They covered the ground until Israel had her fill. And, the next morning, the Israelites caught their first glimpse of the bread from heaven. Exodus 16:4 says, "Then said the LORD unto Moses, Behold, I will rain bread from heaven for you; and the people shall go out and gather a certain rate everyday, that I may prove them, whether they will walk in my law, or no."

Obviously, God was going to use a daily provision to test the Israelites. This test would not come by way of this provision being withheld from them in some way, but by how they handled it. This is true in regards to all things that come from God. They serve as points of testing our motive and tendency. For example, they were only to gather enough bread for their daily needs, except on the sixth day. On the sixth day, they were to gather enough to last through the Sabbath.

The procedure of gathering this bread daily was instilling the lesson that it is God who provides according to our daily needs. However, man must be faithful to receive and partake of it in a proper manner. Such a principle was reinforced when some of the Israelites foolishly gathered

Developing Our Christian Life

more than they needed. The next morning, the bread had worms and let off a stench. True to His word, on the sixth day, they could gather enough for two days, and its freshness remained intact. In regards to God's provision and their needs, this bread provided a visible lesson for the Israelites to grasp.

It is a fleshly habit to try to collect, hold on to, and save excess stuff as a means to store it up for the future in order to secure one's survival. This is contrary to one of God's principles found in Matthew 10:39, "He that findeth his life shall lose it and he that loseth his life for my sake shall find it." It is not up to us to try to hold on to or preserve our life. Obviously, to find true life, we must be willing to lose the life we now know. This does not, however, mean that we shouldn't be wise and prudent when we see troubled times heading our way.

The lessons surrounding the bread from heaven hold the same lessons that the believers need to learn. God is our provider. We need not murmur. Rather, we need to learn to pray for our daily needs. Jesus confirmed this in Matthew 6:11, "Give us this day our daily bread."

Today, many Christians in America are murmuring against God. These murmurings are not a result of being deprived of personal needs. Rather, they are the result of the fleshy appetites not being fed on a consistent basis.

There is a difference between needs and wants. The Wilderness of Sin has the ability to teach us the difference if we will only learn. Jesus defined our needs in Matthew 6:31-32, "Therefore take no thought, saying, What shall we eat? or, What shall we drink? or, Wherewithal shall we be clothed? (For after all these things do the Gentiles seek:) for your heavenly Father knoweth that ye have need of all these things." We see that all humanity has the three needs, which are food, drink, and clothing.

Wants are luxuries that people desire to heap upon themselves. These wants are nothing more than fleshly appetites. They will cause one's focus to be fleshly, and his or her pursuits to be vain and useless. This will cause the individual to be ineffective, even in his or her prayer life. James 4:1-3 summarizes the results of these lusts,

> From whence come wars and fightings among you? come they not hence, even of your lusts that war in your members? Ye lust, and have not: ye kill, and desire to have, and cannot obtain: ye fight and war, yet ye have not, because ye ask not. Ye ask, and receive not, because ye ask amiss, that ye may consume it upon your lusts.

Needs can be satisfied on a temporary basis, while wants enlarge the appetites, and bring dissatisfaction and discontentment.

It is a crucial lesson for Christians to learn the difference between needs and wants. Most people regard faith in light of pursuing wants when they pray. They overlook the fact that God provides for all of our needs.

We have the contrast between needs and wants in the Wilderness of Sin. The quail addressed the wants of the Israelites, and proved to be a luxury they could live without. The bread filled their need to sustain life. This bread was known as "manna." It was small, but it came down in abundance. It had a taste that was sweet to the taste buds. However, it would eventually melt in the heat.[9]

We know that this bread from heaven was symbolic of Jesus. Jesus said in John 6:32-33, "...Verily, verily, I say unto you, Moses gave you not that bread from heaven; but my Father giveth you the true bread from heaven. For the bread of God is he which cometh down from heaven, and giveth life unto the world."

It was in the Wilderness of Sin that the Israelites were commanded to rest. "...To morrow is the rest of the holy Sabbath unto the LORD" (Exodus 16:23). The rest that God was referring to was to cease from regular activities and take time to enjoy the essence of life. This would have been strange to the Israelites because they had served as slaves for over 400 years.

Sadly, many Christians do not understand rest, even in the midst of abundance. The demands and entanglements of their various wants stress many individuals. They equate fun with rest, when in reality it often leaves people empty. Jesus Christ fulfilled the Sabbath by becoming the believer's rest. "Come unto me, all ye that labour and are heaven laden, and I will give you rest" (Matthew 11:28). Rest means to step outside of daily activities and worries and rest in Christ. It is a way to refresh the soul and gain Jesus' perspective.

Have you separated your needs from your wants? Have you learned to rest? If you have not learned these two lessons, you will be discontented and stressed out on your spiritual journey.

---

[9] Exodus 15:15, 21, 31

13

THE VALLEY OF REPHIDIM

The next place the Lord led Israel was to Rephidim. It means a place of rest or stay.[1] This was a valley that was located between the Wilderness of Sin and the Wilderness of Sinai. The problem with Rephidim is that it had no water.

Valleys represent places of humiliation. This humiliation usually comes by way of an old test. In other words, it is in the valleys that a person finds out if he or she has learned the lessons encountered in the wilderness.

God had proved His endearing faithfulness to the Israelites. He had delivered them out of Egypt and parted the Red Sea. He made the bitter waters of Marah sweet, as well as provided quail and manna for food. He had heard their murmurings and showed grace.

Once again, Israel is brought to a place of testing. This test is not a new test, but an old test. Exodus 17:3 shows us that Israel clearly failed this test, as they gave way to the flesh. "And the people thirsted there for water; and the people murmured against Moses…"

God had proven in the past that He could provide water. Apparently, Israel forgot about His past acts of faithfully quenching their physical thirst. Instead of looking confidently to God to solve the water shortage, the children of Israel once again looked to Moses.

In times past, Moses immediately went to God. However, in this situation Moses gave the Israelites a stern warning, "Why chide ye with me? wherefore do ye tempt the LORD…" (Exodus 17:2)? Israel was putting God to a foolish test. Although God showed grace in this situation, one can begin to sense that the next test Israel failed would most likely result in judgment.

Moses cried out to God. He instructed Moses and the elders to go up to the rock in Horeb, which was located in Sinai.[2] 1 Corinthians 10:4 gives us this insight about the rock, "And did all drink the same spiritual drink: for they drank of that spiritual Rock that followed them: and that rock was Christ."

In the first place, Israel lacked water, and God showed Moses a tree. This tree pointed to the cross. In the second incident, God instructed Moses to go to a rock. Moses was told to strike the rock once. This

---

[1] Exodus 17:1
[2] Exodus 17:6

action pointed to Jesus being smitten for the sake of man's eternal well-being. Isaiah 53:4 says, "Surely he hath borne our griefs, and carried our sorrows: yet we did esteem him stricken, smitten of God, and afflicted."

Exodus 16:6 stated that God would stand before Moses. When I pondered this scenario, I could see God actually standing between Moses and the rock. If this picture is true, it clearly points to Jesus as God Incarnate.

Divinity was standing before Moses, and as he was striking the rock, he was, in a sense, striking God. This is an awesome picture of Jesus Christ not only standing in the gap for each of us, but also becoming a substitute for us on the cross.

Water came out of the rock. This points to the reality that believers are born of water, "...Verily, verily, I say unto thee, Except a man be born of water and of the Spirit, he cannot enter into the kingdom of God" (John 3:5).

Water is refreshing to those who are thirsty. However, the Living Water from Jesus has a far-reaching significance. Jesus brought this out in John 4:14, "But whosoever drinketh of the water that I shall give him shall never thirst; but the water that I shall give him shall be in him a well of water springing up into everlasting life."

Obviously, the water that came out of the rock had to be taken to the Israelites who were still at Rephidim. If God's people could only rest in His caring and committed character, they could always be assured that the Living Water would be brought to them.

We see Jesus going out of His way to meet the Samaritan woman at the well in John 4. He wants to bring the water to those who are thirsty and weak. Are you like the woman at the well, willing to receive it? Are you desperate enough to partake of this water or are you maintaining what little life you possess in your own power?

Between these two water incidents, we have the complete picture of Jesus dying on the cross. God provided both the altar (the cross) and the sacrifice (Jesus). We can also see how the Son of God becomes a point of testing to everyone. The Apostle Paul made this statement, "But we preach Christ crucified, unto the Jews a stumbling block, and unto the Greeks foolishness" (1 Corinthians 1:23).

The first place where the Israelites murmured about the water was called Marah, which means bitterness. This shows the bitterness caused by the bondage of sin. The second place was given two different names--Massah and Meribah.[3] Messah means temptation, while Meribah means strife and contention. The flesh is not only tempted by the world, but it tempts. In this case, it tempted God with its insidious murmuring. It also caused strife and contention between the people of Israel and Moses.

---

[3] Exodus 17:7

We see this in the case of Isaac. He encountered strife and contention over two wells his father, Abraham, had initially dug.[4] Instead of battling over the wells, he went on until he dug two other wells that ended with his establishing a relationship with the Living God.

Isaac's example shows us there will be a war between the flesh and the Spirit. And, as long as the flesh reigns, there will be conflict. As long as there is conflict or contention, man will not have the liberty to enter into a relationship with God or enjoy Him.

The flesh always causes conflict and war. People are forever giving way to its temptation of pettiness, vanity, lust, and worldliness. Therefore, it is not surprising that Israel fought their first battle at Rephidim with the Amalekites.[5]

Amalek is symbolic of the flesh. We are given important insights into the conflict that exists with the flesh. The first insight is found in Exodus 17:14, "And the LORD said unto Moses, Write this for a memorial in a book, and rehearse it in the ears of Joshua: for I will utterly put out the remembrance of Amalek from under heaven." God reveals that the flesh will one day be completely put down. For you and me, this will not happen until our corruptible flesh is put off and we reach our heavenly home. The flesh will always raise its head when least expected, and every time it does, there will be a battle between it and the Spirit.[6]

The second reality about the flesh is found in Exodus 19:16, "For he said, Because the LORD hath sworn that the LORD will have war with Amalek from generation to generation" (Exodus 17:16). This verse shows us that the Lord is at war with the flesh, but He will be victorious.

How will the flesh be subdued? The battle with Amalek clearly outlines the battle plan. Moses commanded Joshua to take men to fight the Amalekites. Obviously, we must fight the battle with the flesh. This shows us that we cannot ignore the flesh, allow it to rule unchallenged, or avoid the conflict with it. We must confront it for the enemy that it is.

Joshua and his army did not fight this battle in their own strength. Moses had to stand on top of the hill and lift up the rod. As long as the rod was lifted up, the Amalekites lost ground, but as soon as Moses' wearied and let the rod down, the Amalekites prevailed.

The rod represents the Word of God. There is authority in the Word as long as it is obeyed. Obedience to the Word is a powerful way to overcome the flesh. However, we must constantly partake of it to ensure that we will be victorious.

Eventually, a stone was placed under Moses to uphold him during the battle. The stone is symbolic of Jesus Christ. As long as the Word is founded on Jesus, there will be power to not only prevail over the enemy, but to drive him back.

---

[4] Genesis 26
[5] Exodus 17:8-16
[6] Galatians 5:17-21

There is another important aspect about this battle. Exodus 17:15 says, "And Moses built an altar, and called the name of it, Jehovah-Nissi." Jehovah-Nissi means "God is our banner." A banner was lifted up to bring identification to the army. Moses clearly recognized that God was serving as Israel's banner.

Jesus is the Christian's banner. As long as He is lifted up as a person's only source, focus, life, and armor, he or she will be victorious over the flesh. Romans 13:14 says "But put ye on the Lord Jesus Christ, and make not provision for the flesh, to fulfill its lusts thereof."

Is Jesus being lifted up? What kind of water are you partaking of? Are you putting on the Lord Jesus and walking by the Spirit to ensure that the flesh is being subdued? Or, are you complaining about your life because you are drinking of the bitter waters of consequences, strife, and contention? You need to know that Jesus will bring the waters to you, if you will repent and cry out in faith.

14

THE WILDERNESS OF SINAI

Israel came to the Wilderness of Sinai in the third month of her journey from Egypt to the Promised Land. Exodus 19:2-3 sets up the next part of this journey, "... and had pitched in the wilderness; and there Israel camped before the mount. And Moses went up unto God..."

As previously stated, the wilderness represents the grave. There are different aspects of the grave. Each wilderness reveals these aspects. For example, the Wilderness of Shur represents the work of the grave—that of separation. Man is being separated from his old life and old way to embrace the new.

The wilderness of Sin is symbolic of the product of the grave—that of death. Saints must count themselves dead to the old life. They must leave romantic and unrealistic notions about their old life in the wilderness. These notions will only lose their power in the midst of the adverse elements of life and the faithfulness of God.

The Wilderness of Sinai pointed to the purpose of the grave—that of preparation. Pitching their tents was the first indication that Israel was at the stage of this preparation. Preparation would never occur for the Israelites as long as they were on the move. They first had to come to a place of abiding.

Learning to abide is a hard lesson to apply to life. Man's natural tendency is to try to change what is unpleasant, rather than learn quiet confidence towards God. Such confidence entails trusting, waiting, and obeying. Sinai would bring this lesson to the forefront, serving as a special abiding place for Israel.

This brings us to the purpose of spiritual preparation. The main goal of this type of preparation is to establish a person in his or her life in God. This establishment represents new life being embraced and coming forth. We see this in the case of Jesus.

Jesus was in the grave for three days and nights. He took all of our sins with Him. After three days in the depths of the earth, He came forth with a glorified body. The Apostle Paul talked about this glorified body in 1 Corinthians 15:40-53.

The grave also reveals the vanity and futility of man. This harsh reality is summarized by where man puts his confidence. The different wildernesses expose misdirected confidence. For the Wilderness of Shur, personal strength was exposed for its vanity. In the Wilderness of Sin, the flesh raised its head to show how foolish it was to trust it at any level. When it comes to Sinai, it revealed the folly of idolatry. These different areas of confidence intertwine with each other. For example, the flesh causes people to put false reliance in personal strength. And, whenever the flesh is reigning, idolatry will be discovered.

Israel came to Sinai in the third month. The number "three" implies completion. This period of time pointed to Israel's spiritual life being completed. The number three is also seen in Exodus 19:11, "And be ready against the third day: for the third day the LORD will come down in the sight of the people upon Mount Sinai." The Israelites were given three days to prepare themselves to meet with God. This preparation involved sanctification or holiness.[1]

"Holiness" means to set apart. There are two separate works of holiness. First, there is consecration. This occurs when man makes the necessary commitment and determination to separate himself from that which is unholy. It is the *act* of holiness.

The second type of holiness is sanctification. This represents the *work* of holiness that is done by the Holy Spirit. For the Israelites, it meant washing their clothes as an outward work of cleansing.[2] However, real sanctification has to do with the Holy Spirit cleansing the inward person, and separating him or her unto God for His use and purpose.

God required this preparation to set Israel apart from pagan nations. Exodus 19:5 gives us insight as to how God would set His people apart, "Now therefore, if ye will obey my voice indeed, and keep my covenant, then ye shall be a peculiar treasure unto me above all people: for all the earth is mine."

God was about to establish a covenant with the nation of Israel. This is God's usual procedure when He is about to set a person, group, or nation apart for His purpose. We see this with Christians. Our covenant with God is based on the blood of Jesus.[3]

The integrity and intention of the covenant with Israel would be revealed in the Law. This Law provided the insight into the very character of Jehovah God. The sights and sounds that engulfed Mount Sinai would confirm this revelation, causing great fear among the Israelites.

Exodus 20:18-19 gives us a clear description of the sights and sounds that caused Israel to react in a fearful way.

> And all the people saw the thunderings, and the lightnings, and the noise of the trumpet, and the mountain smoking: and when the people saw it, they removed, and stood afar off. And they said unto Moses, Speak thou with us, and we will hear: but let not God speak with us, lest we die.

According to *Smith's Bible Dictionary*, this particular area is a natural amphitheater. Sounds from this area have been heard as far away as

---

[1] Exodus 19:10-11
[2] Romans 15:16; Exodus 19:10
[3] Hebrews 8:6-9:7

100 miles. There is no doubt that the sounds were amplified enough to make an impression on the children of Israel, no matter how far away they were from the mountain.

The children of Israel received a glimpse of God's holiness and immediately withdrew from His presence. They realized they could not stand in His presence without someone standing in the gap. This awareness caused the children of Israel to ask Moses to be their mediator.

Sinai's first lesson is that no person can stand before God on the basis of his or her personal righteousness. Man cannot meet and stand before God because of His holiness, and God cannot accept man because of his depravity.

Christians look for mediators, but not because they sense God's holiness or their personal depravity. They are usually looking to leaders to serve as mouthpieces to relate God's heart to them. Sadly, few Christians realize they already have a mediator. He is a man, and the Apostle Paul identifies Him in 1 Timothy 2:5, "For there is one God, and one mediator between God and men, the man Christ Jesus."

Jesus Christ is an effective mediator. His main goal is to lead people into an intimate relationship with the Father. He revealed this goal in John 14:6, "...I am the way, the truth, and the life: no man cometh to the Father but by me". When believers look to any man other than Jesus to serve as their mediator, they become one step removed in their relationship with God. This distance is often replaced with man-made religion.

Israel could have it all, but failed to embrace the opportunity to know God. These people stood afar off from Him, putting their total trust in mere man to convey God's very thoughts and heart to them. In such a setting a mediator could prove to be beneficial.

For example, the Israelites could remain indifferent to God, thereby avoiding personal accountability and responsibility. And, when they disagreed with Moses' instruction, they could excuse their disobedience. After all, Moses was simply a mere man who could be disregarded when something was inconvenient or too demanding.

This is one of the major reasons Christians seek out mere men to stand in the gap, rather than Jesus Christ. They can see, touch, and communicate with a living person. They can hide behind this person's leadership, while claiming ignorance for unacceptable conduct. This perverted reliance on man is nothing more than idolatry. Such people may declare that they want to hear God, while silently doubting His intention and concern for them.

Sadly, many human mediators are put on a pedestal. Over the years, I have been put on such a pedestal, knowing that I would eventually be brought down. The usual method for bringing a mediator down is to crucify him or her with the tongue. The mediator's crime in most cases is that they prove to be quite human, instead of being God Almighty.

This is one of the harsh realities of ministry. The greatest challenge for a minister of the Gospel is to remain vulnerable before God, while avoiding becoming too transparent to those who carry rocks around with them. In fact, rock-carrying Christians are always quick to pick up the nearest rock when they become disillusioned or hurt. This judgmental practice reveals carnality and immaturity. In the end, these people often cause much damage to the real servants of God and the work that is being done for the sake of Christ.

God wanted to establish a relationship with the people of Israel, but they excused themselves. Moses became their intercessor and experienced the intimacy that every Israelite had been given an opportunity to encounter. This brings us to an important example, that God's kingdom is established *within* one person at a time. Luke 17:21 states, "Neither shall they say, Lo here! or, Lo there! for, behold, the kingdom of God is within you."

John 3:16 declares, "For God so loved the world, that he gave his only begotten Son, that whosoever believeth in him should not perish, but have everlasting life." Like the world, God offered Israel the right to enter into this intimate place of communion with Him. However, only a few like Moses will separate themselves from the masses to experience this incredible wonderment.

Moses' spiritual journey enables Christians to understand the path of intimacy. This patriarch first encountered God in the wilderness. He was a lowly shepherd left on the backside of this harsh place. It appeared as if he would live his life out in solitude, until one day he came face to face with a burning bush. God used an ordinary bush to gain Moses' attention and speak to him. He called him out of isolation into leadership.[4]

God empowered Moses with a rod, and backed him up with one miracle after another. The Egyptians thought of him as great, while Israel experienced and benefitted greatly from the authority of his leadership.[5] Through it all, God had guided Moses every step. He had met him in every challenge and crisis.

Moses was well acquainted with God's voice. However, Sinai represented Moses coming higher in his relationship with God. We see a representation of this in Exodus 19:3, "And Moses went up unto God, and the LORD called unto Him out of the mountain." In Moses' first meeting with God, God met with him in the burning bush. In Moses' second encounter with God, he went up into the fiery mountain to meet God.

Moses spent forty days and forty nights in the presence of God in two different incidents. It must have been a glorious time because after his second time of separation on the mountain, Moses' face reflected

---

[4] Exodus 3
[5] Exodus 4; 11:3

God's glory. He had such a relationship with God that he talked to Him face to face.[6]

God's invitation to Moses was to commune with Him at the mercy seat. This desire for communion graduated from supping and waiting in His presence to Moses making that one incredible request, "I beseech thee, shew me thy glory."[7] Moses could not remain satisfied with just hearing God's voice, he had to experience Him. Although he experienced His presence, Moses had to see God's glory.

This should be the heart of every Christian. Christians must avoid being content to occasionally hear His voice. They must harbor a desire to go higher in order to experience Him in greater ways. This height should inspire them to see His glory.

John 1:14 describes God's glory in this manner: "And the Word was made flesh, and dwelt among us, (and we beheld his glory, the glory as of the only begotten of the Father,) full of grace and truth." God's glory is found in His only begotten Son, Jesus Christ.

Basking in the glory of Jesus would help all believers fulfill their highest calling—to reflect Him to a hopeless world. 2 Corinthians 3:18 says, "But we all, with open face beholding as in a glass the glory of the Lord, are changed into the same image from glory to glory, even as by the Spirit of the Lord." Are you reflecting the glory of the Son of God?

Moses went up the mountain to God and came down with the Law. The Law was to reveal the holiness of God and the depravity of man. It proved that men were spiritually standing afar off from God because of sin. The distance that existed between man and God revealed that men were incapable of pleasing Him in their own strength or on their own merit. This reality was to establish the children of Israel on the immovable Rock of salvation. The Rock of salvation pointed to Jesus Christ.

Galatians 3:24 tells us that the Law served as a schoolmaster who would lead a person to Jesus Christ, seeking justification. This search brings a person to the end of any self-righteousness to the One who is the fulfillment of the Law.[8]

God initially introduced the Law to Israel through the Ten Commandments. The first three commandments addressed the core of the separation between God and man—that of idolatry. Idolatry lies at the heart of rebellion, divided loyalties, compromise with the world, and indifferent devotion.

The first three commandments confirm that a person's life must begin with The One True God and end with a life committed to Him. He must be exalted, worshipped, and served. He must become the place of strength, rest, communion, and refreshing.

---

[6] Exodus 33:11; 34:29
[7] Exodus 33:18
[8] Romans 10:4

The fourth commandment was for the benefit of man. It reminded man that he must set a day apart to come into a place of spiritual rest where such worship and communion would be encouraged, observed, and maintained. In 1 Peter 3:15 Christians are called to sanctify the Lord in their heart, to ever keep Him before them as a means to be ready to give an answer of the hope in them.

God's presence must be evident to ensure rest, worship, and communion. On Mount Sinai, God gave a pattern for the tabernacle.[9] This tabernacle would serve as the place where His presence would reside in the midst of Israel. It would become a place of sacrifice, celebration, and worship.

The presence of God is a must for people's spiritual life to be established. Without His presence, their worship is vain, their religion empty, and their testimony powerless.

The Israelites had to have their spiritual lives established in their Jehovah God, in order to stand against and withstand the idolatrous practices of the pagan nations as a means to remain standing on the Rock. When the proper spiritual foundation is missing, people will be vulnerable in the midst of idolatry. This was confirmed when Moses delayed his return from the mountain in his first separation unto God. The children of Israel began to speculate about his absence. This speculation caused them to fill the void by erecting a golden calf.[10]

Israel's idolatry gives insight into this blatant sin. Obviously, the people were still looking to Moses for their spiritual well-being. This hidden idolatry of dependency on man led to the physical practice of worshipping the golden calf.

The fact that the children of Israel could quickly erect another idol implies that they did not love Jehovah God. Exaltation of any god is a heart matter. The Israelites had been quick in accepting Moses as their intercessor, instead of desiring to know God in a personal way. As a result, God never became a priority in their lives. He simply remained an option, instead of a way of life and One who was worthy of worship. When Moses failed to return, Jehovah God also failed to exist in their minds.

It is in times of uncertainty, fear, and doubts that a person's true god is unveiled or resurrected from hidden places. Most idols in America are hidden in the hearts and minds of people. These people may go around claiming they believe in the God of heaven, but as soon as they are tested, their real idols rise out of the ashes of disillusionment.

These hidden idols find their origins in the vain imaginations or speculations of man's mind. They are nothing more than superstitious in nature. Superstition points to spiritual ignorance, and it reveals that people do not know the real God. Without the knowledge and the

---

[9] Hebrews 8:5
[10] Exodus 32:1-6

presence of the real God, there is emptiness in the soul. This emptiness becomes the breeding ground for idolatry, as idols are quickly erected to fill it.

The reality of idols is that they are nothing more than man's design and construction. The prophet Isaiah talks about the folly of man creating his own gods. He gives this description of the foolishness of idolatry in Isaiah 44:17-18,

> And the residue of it he maketh a god, even his graven image: he falleth down unto it, and worshipeth it, and prayeth unto it, and saith, Deliver me; for thou art my god. They have not known nor understood: for he hath shut their eyes that they cannot see; and their hearts, that they cannot understand.[11]

Although idols are lifeless, man endows them with power by giving them identity. Such identity gives them authority and purpose in a person's life, allowing this pseudo-god to serve as a sick substitute for the real God. This sick substitute will dull the spiritual eyes of the worshipper.

If your personal wilderness exposes your idols, do not look to them, but repent. Recognize that you are the one who has given your idol rights in your life. Acknowledge that it is a personal affront against the one true God. Ask God to bring the idol down, as He did Dagon in 1 Samuel 5.

Once the idol is down, submit your life to God, so He can establish His life in you. Establishing your life in God takes time. It will require you to exercise faith. Such exercise means you must choose to abide, trust, wait, and obey.

The wilderness of Sinai shows us that the spiritual life is a series of choices. The children of Israel usually made choices to follow the path of least resistance. This means they gave in to the flesh, looked to man, and declared that the God of heaven had failed by erecting their own idol.

God wanted to rid the people of Israel of their idols in order for them to establish a complete life in Him. This actual process can be observed in Sinai. He gave the children of Israel the Law to establish righteous boundaries. It was in this wilderness that the tabernacle was constructed, the priesthood established, and sacrifices offered.

As we consider this process in light of the Christian life, we can see similarities. For example, the Word of God establishes righteous boundaries. Believers serve as the temple of the Holy Spirit. It is the Spirit's presence in the Christian that ensures life, and His gentle guidance that leads to all truth and reveals God's will.[12]

Christians make up a lively priesthood. They are to minister to God in communion and to man in servitude. They also serve as living sacrifices

---

[11] Also see Psalm 115:4-8; Isaiah 40:19-22; 41
[12] John 16:13; 1 Corinthians 3:16

in which the life and fragrance of Jesus will bring glory to God, as they prove what the acceptable will of God is.[13]

How does one secure this life in God? The idols must be judged. When Moses came down into the camp, he rebuked the children of Israel for their idolatry. He then asked who was on the Lord's side. The Levites came forward. Moses commanded them to execute judgment. Exodus 32:28 tells us the final results, "And the children of Levi did according to the word of Moses: and there fell of the people that day about three thousand men."

Exodus 33:7 tells us that Moses took God's temporary dwelling place and pitched it outside of the camp. Once again, we can see a beautiful representation of Jesus. He was taken outside the camp to die for us. This means He was taken outside of the religious activities of the people of Israel and their traditions to secure man's salvation.[14]

The camp had been defiled by Israel's idolatry. God could not dwell in the midst of the children of Israel until consecration and atonement had been made. When the tabernacle was taken outside of the camp, the presence of God came down on the tabernacle. The children of Israel responded in four ways. This response shows the four types of worship that comes out of purging.

Exodus 33:10 gives us insight into the first response, "And all the people saw the cloudy pillar stand at the tabernacle door: and all the people rose up and worshipped, every man in his tent door." This group of people typifies those who worship afar off. They are content to stand at the doors of religion and approach God through ritualistic methods.

The second type of worshipper can be found in Exodus 33:7, "…And it came to pass, that every one which sought the LORD went out unto the tabernacle of the congregation, which was without the camp." Those who are seeking God represent this next group. They must step outside of the comfort zones of accepted religious practices and personally pursue God. These people represent the remnant that consecrates themselves in order to know and encounter God in greater ways.

Joshua represents the third group. Exodus 33:11 tells us, "…but his servant Joshua, the son of Nun, a young man, departed not out of the tabernacle." Since Joshua was not a priest, he could not go all the way into the inner place of God. However, that did not stop him from being as close as he could be to the presence of God. Obviously, Joshua was not content to be in any other position. As a result, he was the one chosen to lead the children of Israel into the Promised Land.

Moses points to the final group of worshippers. He went all the way into the tabernacle, into the Most Holy Place, and communed with God between the Cherubim on the mercy seat. Exodus 33:11 gives us this insight about Moses: "And the LORD spake unto Moses face to face, as

---

[13] 1 Peter 2:5, 9; Romans 12:1-2
[14] Hebrews 13:10-13

a man speaketh unto his friend." Moses was the type of person who would not settle to worship God except at His feet. We see the reality of Moses' worship as he reflected God in his countenance, showed His authority in his leadership, and withstood his enemies in power, confidence, and obedience.

Consider these four examples of worshippers. Which group do you fit in? If you are part of the first group, you are missing the real essence of the Christian life. You will never know the satisfying reality of God. Are you part of the remnant that is making its way to experience the presence of God? Or, are you a Joshua who is as close to the reality of God as you can be? As a result, you could easily become a Moses, as God's Spirit faithfully leads you into the Most Holy Place of communion.

15

JUDGMENT

Numbers 33 specifically identified four wildernesses that Israel traveled through to get to the Promised Land. Journeys always involve the unknown. For example, detours will cause travelers to depart from the main road, and unexpected obstacles have been known to force wayfarers to veer off in the wrong direction. Construction zones take the sojourner on uncertain twists and turns.

This can be clearly seen in the case of Israel. There were only four different wildernesses standing between Egypt and the Promised Land. However, due to detours of rebellion, obstacles of temptations, twists of betrayals, and turns due to consequences, the journey was prolonged. What would have been a journey through four wildernesses was extended to embrace a fifth wilderness. What would have taken a little over two years to accomplish was stretched out over a 40-year period.

This next leg of the journey proved the most revealing to the children of Israel. Were they prepared to enter into the Promised Land? After all, they had established their spiritual life in Sinai, and had actually remained there until every detail of their religious life was completed and brought to fruition.

They looked like a fine-tuned group or machine as they marched towards the Promised Land. Each tribe had its position along with banners to identify their particular group. From all appearances, they seemed ready to enter into all that God had promised.

According to the record that we have, after judgment had fallen on the children of Israel for idolatry, they lived a quiet, peaceful existence in Sinai. God provided for them every day, giving them manna from heaven and water from the rock.

Obviously, they had a complete life in God. Their tabernacle was established, their priests set apart, and their God faithful. However, God did not intend for His people to stay in Sinai. He brought them to this place to enable them to establish a life in Him so they could possess the Promised Land.

After two years in the different wildernesses, the children of Israel were on their final part of the journey. They only had one more wilderness to journey through, and then, they would arrive at their destination. They had come a long way. I am sure they had an expectancy that they were close to being in the land God had promised, thereby, establishing their own nation.

Developing Our Christian Life

Numbers 10:11-12 tells us that in the second month of the second year, the cloud was taken up from off the tabernacle of the testimony. This cloud came to rest in the wilderness of Paran. The wilderness of Paran was not identified in Numbers 33. According to *Smith's Bible Dictionary*, Paran was not mentioned because it encompassed a wide region. However, the many stations from Hazeroth and Kadeash that were located in this region were clearly noted in Numbers 33:17-36.

Paran is also clearly marked by incidents that reveal the children of Israel's spiritual state. They had experienced God's grace and faithfulness. This wilderness was about to reveal whether the children of Israel learned the lessons of the past wildernesses, and if they had properly applied them to their lives.

Numbers 10:33 tells us the order in which the children of Israel traveled to Paran, "And they departed from the mount of the LORD three days journey: and the ark of the covenant of the LORD went before them in the three days journey, to search out a resting place for them."

The Ark of the Covenant went before Israel. This ark represented the presence of God preparing the way. This altar was made up of the mercy seat and Cherubim. It held the Law, a jar of manna, and later the budding rod of Aaron in its belly or compartment. Notice how it would lead Israel to a place of rest.

To the Christian, the Ark of the Covenant represents Jesus. He is the point of mercy, the end of the Law, true manna from heaven, and the budding rod of life. Jesus also prepared the way for every Christian through teachings and examples. He came out of obscurity, was baptized in the Jordan, and tempted in the wilderness. He walked in humility and obedience before the Father. In the end, He went to the cross, gave up His spirit, was buried, and rose again. He ascended into heaven and now prepares a place for all believers. Therefore, all a Christian has to do is walk in the way of Christ.[1]

Moses' prayer for their journey was simple. "...Rise up, LORD, and let thine enemies be scattered; and let them that hate thee flee before thee. And when it rested, he said, Return O LORD, unto the many thousands of Israel" (Numbers 10:35-36). The prayer of Moses acknowledged that God must fight the battle; therefore, let His enemies be scattered. Today, many claim this motto in song in regards to personal enemies. A Christian's main concern should be towards those who thwart the work of God. Their request should be as Moses' was, "...scatter your enemies O' God so that your will may be accomplished."

When Israel initially started this journey, God showed amazing grace. As the children of Israel got further along in their journey, God's grace turned into warnings and finally judgment. In Rephidim, we see the first warning directed at the children of Israel for their rebellious attitude. They were told that they were proving or testing God. After all, they had

---

[1] Matthew 3; 4; John 14:1-3; 1 Corinthians 15:3-4; Philippians 2:6-8

witnessed miracles and experienced God's faithfulness through manna from heaven. There was no excuse for their rebellion of unbelief.

The wilderness of Sinai was the first indication that God was not going to wink at or tolerate Israel's rebellion any longer. When the children of Israel erected the golden calf, judgment did fall upon them. Exodus 32:27-28 sets up the scene,

> ...Thus saith the LORD God of Israel, Put every man his sword by his side, and go in and out from gate to gate throughout the camp, and slay every man his brother, and every man his companion, and every man his neighbour. And the children of Levi did according to the word of Moses: and there fell of the people that day about three thousand men.

This brings us to how the wilderness of Paran exemplifies the grave. The wilderness of Shur represents the work of the grave—that of separation. The wilderness of Sin is symbolic of the product of the grave—that of death. Sinai points to the purpose of the grave—that of preparation, while the wilderness of Paran represents the reality of the grave—that of judgment.

In the wilderness of Paran, we see nothing but judgment. When Jesus took our sins to the grave, it served as the last means of judgment upon sin. This judgment would silence the consequences of sin once and for all for those who by faith hid in the reality of God's abiding faithfulness, everlasting promises, and majestic power.

This brings us to the final layer of man that must be exposed and properly dealt with in the wilderness. Each of these layers represents some type of dependency that is not only temporary and foolish, but destructive. The wilderness of Shur exposed the vanity of personal strength, while the wilderness of Sin revealed the foolishness of the flesh. The wilderness of Sinai unveiled the folly of idolatry, while the wilderness of Paran ripped away the façade of man's best to expose the ultimate idol of humanity—pride.

Personal strength finds its origins in the flesh, while the flesh finds its inspiration in idolatry. Underneath idolatry is pride. The wilderness of Paran revealed the attitude and manifestation of this idol. For example, one of the outward manifestations of pride is complaining. Numbers 11:1 reveals God's response towards this outward manifestation, "And when the people complained, it displeased the LORD: and the LORD heard it; and his anger was kindled; and the fire of the LORD burnt among them, and it consumed them that were in the uttermost parts of the camp."

At the core of pride are rights. These rights will declare that all fleshly inconveniences are unfair. This shows the flesh in full operation. God's response to this manifestation of pride is to consume it.

God resists and hates pride.[2] He has no tolerance for this idol. It serves as an affront against everything He is and stands for. Sadly, this

---

[2] Proverbs 6:16-19; James 4:6

is the one sin that freely reigns in homes and churches. It can easily be observed in others, but will blind the individual of its presence and reign in his or her life. This idol must be consumed by the constant, abiding reality of God. Every time pride raises its head, the reality of God is able to quickly quench it.

In spite of the judgment, God still shows grace. Numbers 11:2 states, "And the people cried unto Moses: and when Moses prayed unto the LORD, the fire was quenched." God responds to the desperate cries of His people and the humble intervention of His servants since grace can only be shown at the point of need and humility.

The next judgment occurred because the people were lusting after the things of Egypt. They began to remember the fish, cucumbers, melons, leeks, onions, and garlic. Although the manna was sufficient to meet their needs, their pride was demanding that the flesh be fed. As the flesh loomed in front of the children of Israel, they began to resent God's provision. This is another fruit of pride—ingratitude.

People who look back operate from selective memories. The children of Israel were choosing to remember the variety of food available in Egypt, but conveniently forgot that they were slaves. This makes me wonder just how much of this food did the people of Israel really enjoy in the midst of their slavery. God had delivered them because the oppression was so great that their cries had reached Him.

Sadly, people only remember what they want to recall in the context that best serves their personal desires. Such memories are selective and unrealistic, but they allow people to justify their right to complain and rebel.

In the process of pride calling "foul" about what they lacked in the area of food, the children of Israel revealed their attitude towards God's provision. They actually resented it. They failed to recognize that they did not deserve anything from the hand of God, and that all they possessed was an act of grace. Ingratitude always shows contempt towards God.

God gave the children of Israel what they desired, but it turned into judgment.[3] This is an important example for Christians to keep in mind when they insist on having it their way. When God gives in to such self-serving demands, it will not prove to be a blessing, but a form of judgment. Numbers 11:33-34 bears out this harsh reality,

> And while the flesh was yet between their teeth, ere it was chewed, the wrath of the LORD was kindled against the people, and the LORD smote the people with a very great plague. And he called the name of that place Kibroth-hattaavah: because there they buried the people that lusted.

Apparently, the children of Israel had not learned their lesson. They failed to leave much of their fleshly appetites back in the wilderness of Sin.

---

[3] Numbers 11:18-20, 33

Pride will always rebel against leadership and claim supremacy. The Apostle Paul gives us insight into this supremacy in Romans 12:3 and Galatians 6:3, "...not to think of himself more highly than he ought to think;...For if a man think himself to be something, when he is nothing, he deceiveth himself."

This supremacy can be especially seen in leadership. Miriam and Aaron were considered leaders, but they could not accept being second to Moses.[4] They wanted to be exalted. Pride refuses to accept a humble position; therefore, it is always in competition with those in higher positions.

At the heart of pride is treachery. Treachery looks for discrepancies in the lives of those that it is ready to betray. Needless to say, it never has to look far to find the means to judge the person in question, as well as justify treacherous acts. Since Moses was upright, Miriam and Aaron found what they considered to be a discrepancy in Moses' marriage. He had married an Ethiopian woman who was considered an outsider. Miriam and Aaron may have thought they found the means to bring proper accusation against Moses, but all they revealed was their own prejudices. Prejudice is also another mark of pride.

God's evaluation of the man Moses can be found in Numbers 12:3, "(Now the man Moses was very meek, above all the men which were upon the face of the earth.)" God did not have a problem with Moses. He knew what He was doing when He chose him to lead Israel. Miriam and Aaron were simply making a bid for Moses' position without God's approval.

God's response to their blatant disrespect towards His chosen leader can be found in Numbers 12:9-10, "And the anger of the LORD was kindled against them; and he departed. And the cloud departed from off the tabernacle; and behold, Miriam became leprous." Miriam only had to suffer this leprous condition for seven days. Obviously, it was a lesson that both Miriam and Aaron never forgot because they never again opposed Moses' leadership.

This brings us to the Promised Land. The children of Israel expected to go in and claim their promise from God. But, once again, pride raised its head. Twelve spies had been sent into the Promised Land to scout it out. They had discovered that God's description of the land was correct, but they did not expect to encounter the obstacle of giants. Ten of the spies brought back an evil report. The children of Israel began to murmur. It was as though they forgot the miracles of their previous deliverances and provisions. They failed to recognize that God had helped them overcome Amalek in Rephidim. Their forgetfulness opened the door to the next fruit of pride—unbelief.

In the kingdom of God, the door of opportunity may only remain open for a short time before it closes. This time allots the necessary

---

[4] Micah 6:4

Developing Our Christian Life

opportunity as to the type of decision that a person makes towards God's will, promises, and ways. Such was the case as far as Israel entering the Promised Land. It was not a matter of debate as to whether the children of Israel would enter the Promised Land, but a matter as to when this event would occur.

God would definitely fulfill His promises to Abraham, but the children of Israel would determine the timing. This would hinge on faith. If they chose to give way to unbelief, the door of opportunity would close, but if they chose to believe God, they would enter into the Promised Land.

When Israel refused to trust God and focused on the obstacles, the door of opportunity was shut. Judgment was pronounced. The ten spies immediately died in their unbelief, while the rest of Israel would wander in the Wilderness of Paran until the older generation died out. The amount of time they wandered was determined by how many days the spies were in the Promised Land. They had been in the land for forty days; therefore, the people would wander around the wilderness for forty years.[5]

Pride would not allow some of the Israelites to face the consequences for their unbelief. They decided all they had to do was say they were sorry and God would change His mind. After all, they were from the seed of Abraham and God had shown leniency in the past.

This conclusion came out of presumption. Deuteronomy 1:43 confirms this, "So I spake unto you; and ye would not hear, but rebelled against the commandment of the LORD, and went presumptuously up into the hill."

God's judgment stood as these individuals discovered when they were attacked and driven back to the wilderness. The children of Israel would reap the consequences for their rebellious pride and their disposition of unbelief because they refused to enter into all that God had promised.

The wilderness of Paran became marked by judgment. A Sabbath-breaker was stoned. Two hundred-and-fifty men from Korah challenged the leadership of Moses and Aaron, only to be swallowed by the earth. The judgment of the men of Korah caused the children of Israel to murmur against Moses and Aaron. Fourteen thousand people died by a plague before Aaron could stay the judgment.[6]

Judgment being satisfied is one of the outstanding characteristics of the grave. This judgment is necessary to ensure new life. We see this in the case of the budding rod. The Lord was becoming impatient with the children of Israel challenging His choice of leadership. He instructed the leaders of the different tribes to bring a rod representing each tribe. The Lord gave this instruction in Numbers 17:5, "And it shall come to pass, that the man's rod, whom I shall choose, shall blossom: and I will make

---

[5] Numbers 14:32-35
[6] Numbers 15:32-36; 16

to cease from me the murmurings of the children of Israel, whereby they murmur against you."

The next day, the results were in, "...The rod of Aaron for the house of Levi was budded, and brought forth buds, and bloomed blossoms and yielded almonds" (Numbers 17:8).

The Lord told Moses to put the rod in the Ark of the Covenant for a token against the rebels. This was God's way of taking away the murmuring to stay future judgment. It was also an act of grace that showed that God did not take pleasure in judging rebellion. His heart was and is to show grace and bring forth life and blessings.

The budding rod is a beautiful picture of Jesus' death, burial, and resurrection. Like the rod, His body was lifeless. After being put in the belly of the earth for three days, He came forth in resurrection power and newness of life. This proves that when God touches something that is dead, the grave loses its claim over it. Hence comes this victorious cry, "O, death, where is thy sting? O grave, where is thy victory" (1 Corinthians 15:55)?

The wilderness of Paran showed the harsh reality of the grave. As long as personal strength, the flesh, idolatry, or pride is reigning, God cannot show His grace. If grace is not present, then judgment will be operating.

It is easy to abuse God's grace by putting Him to a foolish test. This often means missing the door of opportunities. The end of such acts constitutes the greatest tragedy for humanity—people failing to enter into the complete life found in God.

How about you? Are you tasting the reality of the grave because you are failing to enter into the life God has prepared for you? Do not miss the opportunity to discover God and the life He has for you.

16

WILDERNESS OF ZIN

The children of Israel finally came into the wilderness of Zin. They had been wandering around in the wilderness of Paran for around 38 years, while the older generation died off to give way to a new generation that would possess the land. Did the wilderness of Paran make an indelible impression on this new generation? Had they learned the lessons about God and the rebellion that kept the older generation of Israel from entering into the Promised Land the first time around? We are about to find out the answers to these questions.

To understand the significance of the wilderness of Zin, we must consider how we are introduced to this wilderness. "Then came the children of Israel, even the whole congregation, into the desert of Zin the first month: and the people abode in Kadesh; and Miriam died there, and was buried there" (Numbers 20:1).

Miriam was one of the leaders of Israel. Micah 6:4 says this about Miriam, "For I brought thee up out of the land of Egypt, and redeemed thee out of the house of servants; and I sent before thee Moses, Aaron, and Miriam." Miriam was mentioned with Moses and Aaron. Exodus 15:20 refers to her as a prophetess.

When you study her life, you see her as a young girl who proved to be mentally alert when it came to her baby brother Moses in the river Nile. As a woman, she led Israel in praising God for His deliverance in Exodus 15:20-27. Her death at Kadesh in the wilderness of Zin is the first indication that God was about to change leadership. "Kadesh" means holy. There was a separation taking place so that God's purpose can be fulfilled. Obviously, this change was necessary for the children of Israel to possess the Promised Land.

Miriam's death introduces us to the significance of the wilderness of Zin in the spiritual journey. We are once again reminded that each wilderness represented different sources that man puts his confidence in. The wilderness of Shur points to the vanity of personal strength, the wilderness of Sin symbolized the foolishness of the flesh, Sinai exposed the folly of idolatry, and Paran pointed to the ultimate idol of mankind—pride. Now that each of these layers has been exposed and stripped away, what is left? The wilderness of Zin represented the source behind all of these layers—the disposition of sin.

Adam's rebellion in the Garden of Eden resulted in this disposition, which has been passed down to each generation. It plagues every person who is born into the human race. We see the representation of this disposition in Miriam.

Miriam and Aaron rebelled against Moses in Numbers 12. Since her name was mentioned first, she was probably the instigator behind the rebellion and discontentment. God's judgment upon her rebellion was leprosy. Leprosy represents the work and destruction wrought by the disposition of sin.

This disposition can be hidden behind religious piousness and activities, but it will always instigate rebellion against the authority of God. Rebellion expresses itself in the vanity of personal strength and the foolishness of the flesh. It will harbor the folly of idolatry, and lord itself in the exaltation of pride.

Miriam's death signaled the changing of the guards in the wilderness of Zin. Man starts out being a slave to sin as it lords over him with destructive enticements and temporary attractions. This leadership must cease as the old is put off in order to put on the new.

Putting off the old in order to put on the new is clearly described in the New Testament. The Apostle Paul brought this out in Ephesians and Colossians, "That ye put off concerning the former conversation the old man...and that ye put on the new man...put off the old man with his deeds; And have put on the new man ..." (Ephesians 4:22, 24: Colossians 3:9-10).

The wilderness of Zin represented the door to the new life. This new life cannot come forth until the disposition of sin is confronted and properly dealt with. It must be put down in order to put on the new. This means that when the old raises its head, a person must not give in to its enticements and attractions. Each time this disposition is disciplined through self-denial, it loses its power and influence over a person.

Zin is the fifth and final wilderness before the Promised Land. This is a beautiful picture of grace. In spite of the disposition of sin, grace can and will prevail where there is submission, humility, and death to the entanglements of the old life. This incredible attribute of God can reach into the greatest depths of this disposition to deliver a person from its entanglements and claims, to bring forth victory. The Apostle Paul said this about grace in Romans 5:20-21, "Moreover the law entered, that the offense might abound. But where sin abounded, grace did much more abound:...That as sin hath reigned unto death, even so might grace reign through righteousness unto eternal life by Jesus Christ our Lord."

The fact that Israel had survived the forty years of wandering around in the wilderness proved God's grace. His grace is often expressed in His faithfulness to preserve His people in the midst of great challenges and circumstances. Deuteronomy 8:4 confirms this, "Thy raiment waxed not old upon thee, neither did thy foot swell, these forty years."

This brings us to the final aspect of the grave. The grave is a vital ingredient of the Christian's life. One can never understand the walk unless he or she comes to terms with the grave. It is part of the Gospel that is the power of God unto salvation.[1] Therefore, the grave must not be ignored or overlooked. Rather, it must be embraced.

This is why the wilderness was an important aspect of the Israelites' journey. Let us now consider the different characteristics and works of the grave as depicted by these five wildernesses in the following table.

Wilderness	Type of Confidence	The Purpose Of Wilderness (Symbolic as the grave.)	The End Result of the Wilderness
Shur	Personal Strength (Vanity)	The work of the grave.	Separation from the old life.
Sin	Flesh (Foolishness)	The product of the grave.	Death to the flesh.
Sinai	Idolatry (Folly)	The purpose of the grave	Preparation for the life of God
Paran	Ultimate idol of mankind (Pride)	The reality of the grave.	Judgment on rebellion and pride
Zin	Disposition of sin	Victory of the grave.	New life coming forth

The wilderness of Zin represents new life coming forth in resurrection power. For God's people, the grave is not the end, but the door leading to a new beginning. This new beginning will be provided by God's grace and wrought by His sacrifice and power. Therefore, the grave must never be shunned or ignored, but embraced.

For the saint, the door of the grave is an entrance into a greater life in Christ. In order to embrace this new life, the work of the grave must be complete. There must be a separation from the world and death to carnal affections. All idols must be put under the feet of Jesus, while judgment on pride and rebellion must be satisfied. Every last ounce of self must be exposed, and what is left must be proven to ensure a new life without a divided heart, double-mindedness, undisciplined appetites, and worldly affections.

---

[1] Romans 1:16

The first residue of self the children of Israel encountered in Zin was linked to the flesh. The flesh raised its ugly head to complain about a lack of water in the wilderness of Zin. Numbers 20:2-3 says, "And there was no water for the congregation: and they gathered themselves together against Moses, and against Aaron. And the people chode with Moses..."

Keep in mind that this was a new generation. Over forty years had passed between the parting of the Red Sea and the different miracles of providing water in the wilderness of Shur and Sinai. Many of these people were young or not even yet born. As Lamentations 3:22-23 reminds us, "It is of the LORD'S mercies that we are not consumed, because his compassions fail not. They are new every morning: great is thy faithfulness."

This generation of people had witnessed God's caring intervention every day, as He gave them manna from heaven. Familiarities of this type cause people to overlook the touch of the supernatural as they begin to take even the miraculous for granted. These people were about to be a recipient of God's mercy and grace in a miraculous way. The incident would almost be a repeat of what happened over 40 years before at Mount Horeb. Moses turned to God for the solution, and God gave Him instruction about obtaining water from a rock.

The instructions were different than the previous ones. In the first incident, the elders were the only ones to witness the miracle. In the second situation, the whole congregation was to witness the miracle. "Take the rod, and gather thou the assembly together, thou, and Aaron thy brother, and speak ye unto the rock before their eyes; and it shall give forth his water, and thou shalt bring forth to them water out of the rock: so thou shalt give the congregation and their beasts drink" (Numbers 20:8).

This brings us to the second residue of self, that of self-sufficiency that manifests itself through personal strength and pride. Sadly, this self-sufficiency was exposed in the leadership and not in the congregation.

God wanted to sanctify Himself in the eyes of the children of Israel.[2] "Sanctifying" in this text means to pronounce, dedicate, hallow, and prepare.[3] God wanted to pronounce His identity through this miracle, rededicate the children of Israel for His purpose, and prepare them to enter in to receive what He had for them.

Moses was told to take the rod, but only speak to the rock.[4] This was different from the first incident when Moses was told to smite the rock once with the rod. "Smiting the rock" pointed to Jesus dying on the cross, while speaking to it would represent Jesus as being alive and serving as High Priest.

---

[2] Numbers 20:12
[3] Strong's Exhaustive Concordance, #6942
[4] Number 20:8-11

The two incidents with the rock are a beautiful representation of the complete ministry of Jesus as man on our behalf. As man, He was sacrificed as the Lamb of God in order to redeem us. However, three days later, He rose from the grave and now serves as our High Priest in the courts of heaven. All we must do is speak to Him in prayer and faith, according to His will, and He will answer us.[5]

Moses failed to speak to the Rock. Instead, he struck it twice. Moses did not understand the implication or representation of his actions, but Christians should recognize the seriousness and tragedy of his disobedient actions. Moses' actions were like declaring that Christ's work on the cross the first time was not enough. He had to be smitten and crucified afresh. Hebrews 10:26 and 29 gives this sober warning,

> For if we sin willfully after that we have received the knowledge of the truth, there remaineth no more sacrifice for sins...Of how much sorer punishment, suppose ye, shall he be thought worthy, who hath trodden under foot the Son of God, and hath counted the blood of the covenant, wherewith he was sanctified, an unholy thing, and hath done despite unto the Spirit of grace?

Moses had failed to obey God. This rebellion had not simply started with outward disobedience, but with taking credit for God's work. Numbers 20:10 states, "...Hear now, ye rebels; must <u>we</u> fetch you water out of the rock?" (Emphasis added.) Moses' claim came from self-sufficiency. When self takes credit for God's work, it is the same as touching His glory. Any time man touches God's glory, it will defile God's work. In the end, Moses and Aaron were sanctified in the eyes of Israel, instead of God.

It is easy to take credit as a leader for the things of God. Often undue glory is accredited to leaders because they are the visible figurehead. In my own life, I have to guard against taking credit for the invisible work of God in my life. It would be easy for me to take honor for His wisdom, love, and commitment that abound in my heart. I could fall into this arrogant trap and begin to think these incredible gifts God has entrusted to me are a result of personal abilities and value, instead of His grace.

God pronounced judgment on both Moses and Aaron in Number 20:12, "...Because ye believed me not, to sanctify me in the eyes of the children of Israel, therefore ye shall not bring this congregation into the land which I have given them." Moses and Aaron, who represented the initial leadership of Israel, would not be allowed to enter into the Promised Land. It was as if God was doing away with everything that represented the old way, including the leaders.

From all appearances, God was harsh in His pronouncement of judgment on Moses and Aaron. However, God's ways are higher than

---

[5] Matthew 7:7-8; Hebrews 7:25-26; 1 John 5:13-15

man's, and once an individual gets past what appears unfair, he or she can begin to see there is an eternal perspective.[6]

In fact, for the Christian, there is incredible representation in the areas of Moses and Aaron. For example, Moses represented the old covenant of the Law. For the Christian, the old (Law) gave way to the new, Joshua. "Joshua" in Greek means "Jesus." Jesus is the manifestation of truth and grace. It is clear that the new points to the work of grace or favor being extended to man.

The representation of the old giving way to the new again was clearly fulfilled on the Mount of Transfiguration in Matthew 17. Three disciples witnessed Jesus speaking to Moses and Elijah. No doubt these two men were considered heroes to the disciples, which were confirmed by their reactions towards them. Moses represented the Law, while Elijah represented the prophets.

The disciples' excitement turned into fear as they heard the voice of the Father, introducing Jesus as His beloved Son. Matthew 17:7-8 tells us the rest of the story, "And Jesus came and touched them, and said, Arise, and be not afraid. And when they had lifted up their eyes, they saw no man, save Jesus only." (Emphasis added.) Both the Law and the prophets gave way to Jesus. He alone was standing. He was recognized, acknowledged, and exalted by the Father.

Aaron represented the old priesthood. It had to be put off to give way to the new. The priests of this old priesthood had to continually stand before God, as they performed their duties in the tabernacle. They offered up sacrifices, filled the lamp with oil, put fresh bread on the table of Shewbread, and offered up incense. The ongoing ministry of these priests revealed that their work before God was never finished or completed. The sacrifices could never satisfy the judgment on sin, the oil would run out, the bread would become stagnant, and the burning incense of intercession would cease.

For the Christian, this old priesthood had to give way to a new priest. This new priest was of the order of the Melchizedek priesthood. His name is Jesus, and He would offer the one sacrifice that would satisfy judgment on sin once and for all. He offers the oil (Holy Spirit) that is in abundance, serves as the fresh bread from heaven, and ever makes intercession for His people. Hebrews 10:12 states, "But this man, after he had offered one sacrifice for sins for ever, sat down on the right hand of God." (Emphasis added.)

Jesus, the High Priest, would finish the work on the cross and sit down on the right hand of God. Today, He faithfully intercedes for believers, "Wherefore he is able also to save them to the uttermost that come unto God by him, seeing he ever liveth to make intercession for them" (Hebrews 7:25).

---

[6] Isaiah 55:8-9

Aaron died on Mount Hor, but Jesus was transfigured on the Mount of Transfiguration. The glory of the old must give way to the glory of the new. The Apostle Paul makes reference to this in 1 Corinthians 15:53-55,

> For this corruptible must put on incorruption, and this mortal must put on immortality. So when this corruptible shall have put on incorruptible, and this mortal shall have put on immortality, then shall be brought to pass the saying that is written, Death is swallowed up in victory. O death, where is thy sting? O grave, where is thy victory?

When the old gives way to the new, death is overcome and the grave silenced. This is a beautiful picture of the flesh of man giving way to the eternal life of Christ. As the Apostle Paul declared in 2 Corinthians 4:16, "For which cause we faint not; but though the outward man perish, yet the inward man is renewed day by day." This renewing can only happen as the old gives way to the new.

The more self is put off, the more battles will be won. This is the secret of overcoming. We see where Israel overcame the Canaanites in Numbers 21:1-3. However, even in the midst of victories, self can cause discouragement.

Numbers 21:4 tells us that the children of Israel became discouraged because of the way. The way of God is long and tough, but it is all about preparation. As Israel later discovered, wandering around in the wilderness is not the same as conquering the Promised Land. The wilderness was mild compared to the challenges of the Promised Land. In fact, the real work begins in the Promised Land. The difference between wandering in the wilderness and subduing the Promised Land is that you can see yourself making headway in the Promised Land.

Much of the Christian life is comprised of wilderness. It appears as if the person is not getting anywhere in life. However, to God, it is not the distance one travels, as much as the preparation one gives way to in order to be victorious. The biggest battle in the Christian life is not with enemies such as Satan. Rather, it is with self. More people actually lose on the personal home front than they do on the battlefields. Self resents going through the process, and grumbles and complains. It refuses to be denied, or allow itself to be crucified along the way. It wants convenience now, comfort at all times, and all matters resolved immediately. It wants to live and exert itself in every area. Ultimately, it will bring judgment on a person.

We see judgment in God's response to Israel in Numbers 21:6, "And the LORD sent fiery serpents among the people, and they bit the people; and much people of Israel died." Grace abused will turn into judgment. The fallen disposition came out with a vengeance, and God responded with the fiery serpents. God's response drew a quick reaction from Israel. The children of Israel quickly repented and asked Moses to request that God take away the serpents. God did not take away the serpents. Rather, He provided a solution.

The serpents represented sin, Satan, and death. For example, sin brought the serpents, Satan used them to destroy lives, and their bite was that of death. This example reveals that sin must be put down, Satan overcome, and death conquered.

God's means of confronting these three elements was not to take them away, but to lift up a solution and place it right in the middle of the devastation. This would cause the Israelites to confront their sin in light of the solution. They would begin to understand how faith in God would enable them to overcome the serpent, while taking the sting out of death.

Jesus explained this solution in John 3:14-15, "And as Moses lifted up the serpent in the wilderness, even so must the Son of man be lifted up: That whosoever believeth in him should not perish, but have eternal life." Regardless of sin, Satan, and death, God has provided a solution in Jesus' death on the cross. The serpent that was lifted up on the pole was brass or bronze. Brass represented judgment on sin. By lifting Jesus up on the cross, sin, Satan, and death were judged and their power subdued.

Today, Jesus stands in the midst of destruction, lifted up by an old rugged cross. All man has to do is look to Him by faith, acknowledge and receive Him as Lord and Savior. As a person embraces Him as God's only solution, he or she is cleansed by the blood of Jesus of all unrighteousness caused by sin. The empty cross reminds us that Satan is being put under the feet of Jesus. The empty grave declares that as the Resurrected Lord He took the sting out of death.[7]

We see enemies rising up against Israel to curse them, but God prevented their advancements by blessing Israel. This is what happened in the case of Balaam. Balak was a leader of Moab. He wanted to hire the prophet Balaam to curse the children of Israel. Balaam consulted God, and He instructed him to not curse them because He had blessed them.[8] Balaam wisely turned down Balak's request, but was tempted a second time by financial gain. Money blinded Balaam, and he put God to a foolish test by consulting Him again about the same matter. God never changes His mind about such matters, but He turned Balaam over to his lust, and gave him permission to give way to Balak.

An angel waited in the way to bring judgment upon Balaam. This is where a famous jackass not only protected a fool, but was able to talk to him. Balaam's faithful beast spared his life three times, only to be beaten each time. After the third injustice, God gave the jackass a voice, allowing Balaam to see his foolishness, as well as the angel that had been sent to bring judgment upon him. It was only by the intervention of an insignificant jackass that Balaam avoided God's judgment at that

---

[7] 1 John 1:7
[8] Numbers 22-23

moment. In the end, Balaam could only bless Israel for God had chosen to bless the people.

Christians are the most blessed of people. This blessing does not mean that Christians have it easy. Rather, it points to the fact that God will preserve the blessings designated for them.

When one is putting off the old, it is not unusual to encounter idols along the way. Numbers 25:1 tells us "And Israel abode in Shittim, and the people began to commit whoredom with the daughters of Moab." Israel joined itself to Baalpeor, one of the gods of Moab. This immediately brought swift judgment down on Israel.

This idolatry brings us back to Balak and Balaam. Balak was a leader of Moab. He had offered Balaam money, but Balaam was not allowed to curse Israel. However, this did not stop him from sharing other means that could bring down Israel. Apparently, Balaam knew human nature, and realized that the vulnerable area of mankind is idolatry. Numbers 31:16 states, "Behold, these caused the children of Israel, through the counsel of Balaam, to commit trespass against the LORD in the matter of Peor, and there was a plague among the congregation of the LORD." Apparently, he shared this knowledge with Balak who used it to tempt Israel into spiritual harlotry.

Balaam's end was that of the sword. Numbers 31:8 says, "... Balaam also the son of Beor they slew with the sword." People are susceptible to idolatry. One must remember that idolatry will bring quick retribution. Those of Israel who were involved in the idolatrous escapade with Moab were slain, and their heads hung up before the Lord. These actions served as a fierce lesson and reminder that God will not tolerate this sin among His people.[9]

Christians must flee all idolatry.[10] They must guard their hearts against any divided loyalties. They must choose the way of victory, so that the new life will come forth. Therefore, they must not hold on to personal strength, give way to the flesh, bow down to idols, and exalt pride. Believers must put off the old by humbling themselves before God and submitting to His will and way. Such action will allow them to experience the many blessings of God, as well as possess their spiritual inheritance.

The children of Israel were coming to the end of their journey, but were they ready to enter into the Promised Land? No. There were four additional events that had to take place. Foremost, the Law needed to be read.

"Deuteronomy" means "repetition of Law." Israel needed to understand the terms by which they could ensure God's blessings. The reading of the Law was a way of reminding them of their God. There are

---

[9] Numbers 25:3-5
[10] 1 Corinthians 10:14

admonitions throughout Deuteronomy for the children of Israel, making sure they did not forget their God or His Law.

The Bible serves in the same capacity for the Christian. It reminds and upholds the character of God, and instructs each believer in righteousness. There are also reminders of humble beginnings at the cross, upright responses of love, and Jesus returning for His bride.

Another noticeable event for Israel that had to take place was establishing and dividing the inheritance between the tribes of Israel, as well as designating refuge cities.[11] This pointed Israel forward, as well as established their identity in God.

For saints, their inheritance reminds them that they are sealed by the Holy Spirit, possess rights as children of God, and that their lives are hid in Christ.[12] This inheritance not only shows believers who they are, but gives them valuable insight into the future.

The next event was turning the leadership over to Joshua. The old had to give way to the new. Moses laid his hands upon Joshua, consecrating him as the new leader over Israel. This was the means of setting him apart and imparting authority and anointing of the Spirit of God.[13]

As Christians, we must turn over all reins and control of our lives to the King of kings and the Lord of lords, Jesus Christ. He has been anointed to deliver, lead, heal, and restore us into a living relationship with God.

Finally, Moses had to die. It is interesting to note where each of these leaders died. Miriam died at Kadesh in the wilderness of Zin. This shows that the disposition of sin must initially be dealt with before the person can embrace what God has for him or her.

Aaron died on Mount Hor. This mount actually rose up out of the wilderness of Zin. It is located at the edge of the land of Edom, while the mysterious city of Petra is located on its eastern side. Zin means "flat" and Hor means "mountain."[14] This wilderness and mountain stand as a contrast between the nominal (Miriam-sin disposition) and that which stipulates glory (Aaron-priesthood). Since Aaron was a High Priest, he had the opportunity of experiencing God's glory. He was taken on the mountain, which points to the concept of glory. However, Aaron represented a priesthood that caught only small glimpses of the real glory of heaven within the many shadows of symbolism, but could never be fully grasped. The reason for this is because Aaron pointed to the priesthood that was earthly in nature and religious in practice.

---

[11] Numbers 34-36
[12] Ephesians 1:11-14; John 1:12; Colossians 3:3
[13] Deuteronomy 34:9
[14] Smith's Bible Dictionary

Moses died on Mount Nebo. "Nebo" means prophet.[15] The particular range that housed Nebo bordered the Dead Sea, but it was from here that Moses could peer into the Promised Land. He was the only one out of the three leaders who would be given the opportunity to see the promise of God from a distance. But, when you think about it, this is how all of the great men of God of the Old Testament viewed their future Promise, Jesus Christ.[16] Such a view points to the incredible, far-reaching eyes of unfeigned faith.

Moses was the prophet and the lawgiver. Both the names of the mountain and the Law pointed to Moses' impact on the children of Israel. The Dead Sea pointed to death, while the Promised Land pointed to life. The mountain represented his glorious leadership and the Law, as well as his inability to complete the task. Like the Law, Moses stood in-between life and death as he led Israel. Like the Law, which could only point people to Christ, Moses could only stand at a distance and point the children of Israel to the Promised Land. Like the Law, Moses could never lead people into the complete life God had for them. Ultimately, he could only subject himself to the inevitable—death to the old to ensure victory of the new.

There is another important representation in Moses. He never entered the Promised Land in his earthly lifetime, but he did enter in. He was one of those on the Mount of Transfiguration. Obviously, Moses could enter in because Jesus was the fulfillment of the Law; therefore, the Law (Moses) could give way to Jesus, and be established in its rightful place as the new comes forth in power, authority, and anointing.

What about you? Are you putting off the old to put on the new, so you can enter in and possess your inheritance?

---

[15] Ibid
[16] John 8:56; Hebrews 11:39-40

17

CROSSING THE JORDAN

Moses' death brought Joshua and the children of Israel to the Jordan River. This river bordered the Promised Land; therefore, it served as an obstacle to the children of Israel. They had to cross over Jordan to inherit the promises of God.

The river Jordan seems like an insignificant river in the scheme of things. The word "Jordan" means "descended." According to *Smith's Bible Dictionary*, this river's course is a little more than 200 miles. It varies in width from 45 feet to 180 feet. It starts from the foothills of Mount Hermon and runs through the Sea of Galilee down to the Dead Sea. It is known for its rapid descent.[1]

The Jordan River not only served as a border marking the Promised Land, but it played an important part in the history of mankind. John the Baptist introduced the Man, Jesus Christ, the Promised Messiah, publicly at the river Jordan.

Jesus was represented by the ladder of Jacob in Genesis 28:12 where prayers ascended and promises descended. It was at the river Jordan that Jesus connected with man. He would serve as an embodiment of answered prayers and the fulfillment of God's promises.

For Joshua and the children of Israel, Jordan was where promises were made and reclaimed. Joshua 1:6, 7 and 9 capitalize on these promises,

> Be strong and of good courage; for unto this people shalt thou divide for an inheritance the land, which I swear unto their fathers to give them... observe to do according to all the law... that thou mayest prosper... Be strong and of a good courage; be not afraid, neither be thou dismayed: for the LORD thy God is with thee whithersoever thou goest.

Jordan also served as a place of preparation. Joshua 1:11 states, "...Prepare you victuals; for within three days ye shall pass over this Jordan, to go in to possess the land." Once again, we see the number "three" which points to the Gospel. The message of the Gospel is Jesus' death, burial, and resurrection.[2]

---

[1] Some information taken from New Open Bible, © by Thomas Nelson, Inc.; pg. 119 in New Testament.

[2] 1 Corinthians 15:3-4

Developing Our Christian Life

The children of Israel would go down into the Jordan and come forth in their new life. Likewise, Jesus would go down into the grave by way of death and be raised in newness of life.

The river Jordan would be a place of remembrance of keeping vows and promises. The tribes of Reuben, Gad, and the half a tribe of Manasseh had wanted to claim their inheritance on this side of the Jordan because of its plush land. This was agreed to as long as they helped the rest of Israel secure the Promised Land on the other side of the river. They were reminded of this agreement in Joshua 1:13, "Remember the word which Moses the servant of the LORD commanded you..."

For believers, this river was where the first unveiling of the Living Word took place. Jesus was declared the Word in John 1:1. Christ was the visible reality that God never forgets His promises. In Jesus, promises were fulfilled, salvation offered, and everlasting life realized.

In Joshua 3:5, Joshua told the people to, "...Sanctify yourselves: for to morrow the LORD will do wonders among you." "Wonders" point to miracles or acts too marvelous to imagine.

Marvelous wonders were witnessed in the life of Jesus. His teachings astonished people and His miracles caused many to rejoice. The real wonderment surrounding Jesus was not His acts, but who He was. The prophet declared that one of His names would be "Wonderful".[3]

The Ark of the Covenant would pass before the people and descend into Jordan. This ark represented the presence of God to Israel, but to the Christian, the ark points to Jesus Christ. "Then cometh Jesus from Galilee to Jordan unto John, to be baptized of him" (Matthew 3:13).

The Red Sea represented man becoming identified with God's life, cause, and purpose. It was a type of baptism for the Israelites that separated them from the world (Egypt) and totally identified them to God. For the Christian, Jordan represents a different identification and baptism. It is where God Incarnate, Jesus Christ, became identified with man in water baptism.

Jordan may seem insignificant to much of the world in light of other rivers, but its history is alive. God in the flesh stepped out of obscurity right into the pages of history at this river. As a result, man would never be the same.

The Jordan River represents the very essence of man. Like the Jordan, man's life seems insignificant, especially when compared to eternity. James 4:14 says this about man, "...For what is your life? It is even a vapour, that appeareth for a little time, and then vanisheth away." Like the Jordan, man's life can count for something. If man's life is marked by the salvation of Jesus, it has a history that goes back to an old rugged cross and a future that is secured. This type of life can make a difference, for it will find its source and power in Jesus.

---

[3] Isaiah 9:6

Jordan was very shallow in parts. Its depths could range from three feet to 45 feet. People without Christ are shallow. Those who do not allow Christ to have His way will lack character. People who fail to pay the price to know God will remain immature. The shallow parts of people's lives will cause them to be carried away by their flesh and erroneous doctrines.

Today, many, including Christians, are running to and fro to find purpose. They often find themselves being carried away by winds of doctrine, tickled by feel-good philosophies, and influenced by the latest fads of society.[4] Eventually, reality mocks their attempts to find such hope outside of a relationship with God, and they become skeptical or disillusioned.

Each empty pursuit either deceives or produces discontentment. Fear, arrogance, and anger become by-products as people fail to consider that there is no life or purpose outside of identification with Jesus Christ.

The Jordan River is also dirty and yellow in color. This was one of the complaints of the Gentile officer, Naaman. He was seeking healing from the prophet Elisha.[5] Elisha told him to go and wash in the Jordan seven times and he would be healed of his leprosy. Naaman was insulted with the idea of going to the Jordan. He knew of cleaner and better rivers. One of his aides reasoned with him and he obeyed. He was miraculously healed.

The color of the Jordan River is symbolic of people's spiritual condition. Weighed down by the filth of defilement and the stain of sin, they become less and less attractive. They continue to fall short of God's glory, as their best is revealed as filthy rages. Their hearts are tested and found to be wicked and deceitful.[6]

The Jordan River descends 1200 feet above sea level down to 1286 feet below sea level. It descends at a rate of 25 feet per mile. There are 27 rapids between the Sea of Galilee and the Dead Sea. The Dead Sea represents the lowest point on earth.[7]

Like Jordan, sin always leads man downward into stagnation, ruin, devastation, and hopelessness. It will bring a person to the lowest point in his or her life before he or she is swallowed up by utter despair.

This point was brought out in a story (or legend) about the painting of the *Last Supper* by Leonardo DaVinci. DaVinci searched for the right people to pose for Jesus and each disciple. He found an innocent young man, 19 years of age, to pose for the sinless Jesus. Over the years, he located the different disciples until he only had one left, Judas Iscariot. He wanted to find someone who looked like he would betray his own

---

[4] Ephesians 4:14; Colossians 2:8; 2 Timothy 4:3-4
[5] 2 Kings 5
[6] Isaiah 64:6; Jeremiah 17:9-10; Romans 3:23
[7] Smith's Bible Dictionary & Open Bible, pg. 119 in New Testament

mother. He visited various prisons, looking for just the right man to fill the bill. Finally, he located a man in prison who was paying for a life of crime. For six months, he painstakingly painted him to create the desired look and atmosphere.

When DaVinci was finished, he told the guard to take the prisoner away. As the guard was leading the man away, he suddenly broke loose and came to DaVinci. "DaVinci, do you not recognize me?" the man cried.

DaVinci studied him for a second and admitted he did not know him. The man then declared, "Oh God, have I come down so low, you painted me five years ago as Jesus."

Although I do not know if this story is true or just a legend, it does reveal the destructive power of sin. It made Jesus unrecognizable on the cross.[8] I have watched it make people old before their time. I have seen soft looks turn into hard looks, caring eyes turn into eyes that radiate anger, and beautiful countenances become disillusioned by skepticism and bitterness.

Sin not only destroys, but it leads to the greatest point of judgment—spiritual death and hell. Romans 6:23 states, "For the wages of sin is death, but the gift of God is eternal life through Jesus Christ our Lord."

Matthew 10:28 makes this declaration, "And fear not them which kill the body, but are not able to kill the soul: but rather fear him which is able to destroy both soul and body in hell."

Jesus made the greatest descent of all, from heaven to earth. He came from the Sea of Galilee to the shallow, yellow waters of Jordan to become identified with you and me. He came from the Mount of Transfiguration to valleys of demon-possessed people to secure our salvation on the cross. As believers, we must ascend from the depths of our depravity and embrace Him on the cross, to become identified with His righteousness. Proverbs 13:15 summarizes the harsh reality of walking in the ways of sin, "Good understanding giveth favour but the way of transgressors is hard."

In spite of Jordan representing the harsh reality of man, it also serves as a place of hope. After all, Jesus came to Jordan. The Ark of the Covenant came to Jordan to lead the Israelites over to the other side. It passed before the people. Joshua 3:7 says, "And the LORD said unto Joshua, This day will I begin to magnify thee in the sight of all Israel, that they may know that, as I was with Moses, so I will be with thee."

Joshua would be exalted as a leader at Jordan, and Jesus would be introduced as the Son of God at this river. God magnified Joshua with a miracle, while Jesus was honored with the Spirit of God. Joshua was also magnified in the eyes of Israel, while Jesus would be exalted in the hearts of those who would believe.[9]

---

[8] Isaiah 52:14
[9] Matthew 3:16-17; John 1:31-34

The priests brought the Ark of the Covenant down to the Jordan out of obedience, while Jesus was led down to Jordan because of righteousness. Obedience to God results in acts of righteousness. And, when the priests came to the river and stepped in, the waters parted. When Jesus stepped into Jordan and was baptized, the heavens parted.[10]

This brings us to an important principle in the kingdom of God. The priests had to step into the water before it would part. People usually want God's intervention to inspire them before they obey. This example shows us that obedience must come before God will intervene. His Word should be enough of an inspiration for a person to respond in faith. Such faith allows God to do the miraculous and make a way through any obstacle.

The priests obeyed and the waters of Jordan parted. This allowed the Israelites to cross over to the Promised Land.

Out of obedience, Jesus came down into the shallow, dirty waters of Jordan. He also came down into the midst of humanity's filth and depravity to become identified with man in every way. He did this to bring healing, salvation, and restoration. And, like Naaman at the River Jordan, if we come to Jesus in faith, we will be healed, restored, and made whole, regardless of the depth or length of our filth.

Like Naaman, many people are looking for something elaborate and glamorous that will bring healing and salvation. This is why they have a hard time believing that an unattractive object like a cross and an unrecognizable man on the cross hold the key to their healing.

The insignificant and the unattractive are the reality of the Christian life. So much of what we do in our daily lives may seem meaningless in light of eternity, but one incident can change the terrain of our lives. The reason the Christian life seems nominal is because it is not on a descent, but on a slow ascent. Like Israel, believers must cross over from the insignificant to experience the blessings of following Jesus.

You may be on a descent right now in your life due to sin and rebellion. You might think it is fun and exciting to ride the rapids of Jordan. You will gain speed and momentum that will cause you to lose control, and your fun will turn into fear. It will not take long for you to learn the vanity and foolishness of your fast descent into utter ruin. The end is always the same—the Dead Sea. Therefore, heed my warning, you need to cease from any downward plunge in your life.

What will it take for a person to stop the descent? John the Baptist tells us how to stop this descent "...Repent ye: for the kingdom of heaven is at hand" (Matthew 3:2). Repentance stops the descent of destruction and allows a person to cross over into a new life.

The Ark of the Covenant led while the people followed. Jesus came to the Jordan to lead people by example. When John the Baptist refused

---

[10] Matthew 3:16

Jesus' request to be baptized by him, Jesus said, "...Suffer it to be so now: for thus it becometh us to fulfill all righteousness" (Matthew 3:15).

Jesus became identified with man in the Jordan to become an example of righteousness. Therefore, followers of Jesus must do those things which will fulfill all righteousness in their lives, as well as in God's kingdom.

The children of Israel were commanded to carry 12 stones over with them to serve as a memorial of the parting of the Jordan. The Christian's memorial is the cross and it stands on the other side of the Jordan. It reminds us that Jesus' body was symbolic of the veil in the temple that stood between man and God. Like Jesus' body, this veil was torn, allowing the saints to enter into the promises of God.[11]

These promises are realized in prayer and intimacy with God. Intimacy points to a relationship that leads the Christian into the new life. At such a point, believers can cross over their Jordan and boldly approach the throne of grace.[12]

Jesus was always descending for the sake of humanity. However, it is important for saints to realize that if they follow Him, they will always be ascending upward in the ways of excellence. Even identification with the cross brings them upward. Following Jesus into the grave will bring them upward in resurrection power and new life.

Jesus came from the Sea of Galilee to Jordan and will lead Christians through their own "Jordan" to discover a fruitful life. He will ask each of us to cast our nets into what seems to be barren waters, only to find fish. He will lead us through unpredictable storms. He will walk on the water during contrary winds, and cause them to be still during the dark night of the soul. But, as He calms the storms, you will realize that you were in His hands all the time.[13]

This is important for Christians to remember. Much of the work in the Christian field can seem barren. Unpredictable storms will arise, threatening to destroy everything the Christian has accomplished. Giants will threaten the way, religion made up of man's traditions will buffet the truth, and Satan will lay traps along the way. But, remember, Jesus spoke to the storms, God destroyed the enemies, truth won over man's religion, and the cross declares that Satan was defeated.

Have you crossed over to possess your inheritance or are you still on the other side of Jordan? Remember, Lot's spirit was vexed on the wrong side of the Jordan.[14] If you remain on the wrong side of the Jordan, you will taste the reality of Jordan, the judgment of the wilderness, and the destruction of Sodom and Gomorrah.

---

[11] Hebrews 10:19-22.
[12] Hebrews 4:16
[13] Matthew 14:23-33; Mark 4:36-41; John 21:6
[14] 2 Peter 2:6-8

Keep in mind that your inheritance is on the other side of the Jordan. Jesus has gone before you and is waiting. Quit settling for less and cease from being obstinate. Stop the descent of your spiritual life by repenting and crossing over. Make the commitment to follow Jesus, your personal Ark of the Covenant.

18

ROLLING OFF THE OLD

Gilgal is a picture of what it means to enter into a new life. For the children of Israel, it served as a time of preparation, remembrance, rededication, and embracing a heavenly vision. It was a place where the old reproach of Egypt, rebellion, and idolatry were rolled off, so that Israel could partake of the new.

The children of Israel had crossed the Jordan River. The miraculous events of parting the Jordan River quickly spread among the Canaanites and their leaders. The hearts of these pagan people began to melt.[1] In spite of their military might, they already sensed that they were doomed. They had to admit that Israel was not just another nation, for these people believed in the God of heaven. Under His auspice, as mere slaves, the children of Israel were delivered from one of the most powerful nations, Egypt. Jehovah God had parted the Red Sea, and provided for the children of Israel as they wandered around in the wilderness. How could these uncircumcised, unholy people stand before such a great God and His people?

Fear is an effective tool to defeat enemies. The children of Israel probably had no concept of how their former escapades with Egypt and their journey through the wilderness were causing great distress to their enemies. Even though the harlot Rahab from Jericho informed the spies of the fear that her people had in regards to Jehovah God and His people, they could not have imagined how far-reaching it was.[2] As the people of Israel rejoiced, the pagan nations trembled. Life was about to change for everyone who now resided in the Promised Land.

Christians fail to remember that all of their enemies were defeated at the cross of Jesus. Satan was put under Jesus' feet, flesh was counted as dead, pride was stripped of its false authority, personal strength exchanged for His strength, and all idols brought down.[3] Since Christians fail to realize the authority and victory of the cross, they live in fear and bondage to their enemies. Satan enslaves them with lies, the flesh entices with lust, pride reigns in delusion, personal strength exalts itself only to be brought low, and all idols undermine faith, while such idolatry is being maintained in spiritual ignorance.

---

[1] Joshua 5:1
[2] Joshua 2:9-11
[3] Romans 16:20; Hebrews 2:8-15

This brings us to the purpose of Gilgal. This place may seem insignificant, but without it the children of Israel would not have been spiritually prepared to enter into the Promised Land. It was here that the old would be rolled off in order to embrace the new. In fact, "Gilgal" means rolling.

It is not unusual for Christians to bypass Gilgal. They do not realize how important this point of preparation is for spiritual well-being and endurance in possessing the life God has for them. Gilgal represents a new beginning, but it is also a reminder that there is an extensive battle ahead.

Gilgal shows the procedure of becoming spiritually prepared. The first instruction God gave Joshua was to make sharp knives and circumcise those who were uncircumcised. Joshua 5:7 states, "And their children, whom he raised up in their stead, them Joshua circumcised: for they were uncircumcised, because they had not circumcised them by the way." This shows the irresponsibility of the children of Israel. This was a serious matter. Moses failed to circumcise his sons, and he almost lost his life.[4] Surprisingly, God did not judge the children of Israel for failing to keep the covenant of circumcision.

God established circumcision as a covenant with Abraham in Genesis 17:10, "This is my covenant, which he shall keep, between me and you and thy seed after thee; Every man child among you shall be circumcised. And ye shall circumcise the flesh of your foreskin; and it shall be a token of the covenant betwixt me and you." Cutting the foreskin represented cutting away that which defiles a person. All male children at eight days old were to be circumcised. The number "eight" represents new beginnings. It was to serve as a visible mark on all the males of Israel that they have been set apart by God.

Ruth Specter Lascelle in her book, *Jewish Faith and the New Covenant,* shows how circumcision was the appropriate way of marking a covenant. Covenant comes from an Arabic root word that contains the idea of cutting. Therefore, some form of cutting served as a physical mark that established a covenant between parties. For the children of Israel, it not only set them apart as peculiar among pagan nations, but it identified them to Jehovah God. It reminded them that they had a unique purpose and mission in the world.

This visible sign was to serve as a binding contract that not only was a symbol of being separated, but an identification mark. It signified that Israel indeed belonged to Jehovah God and that they were set apart to represent Him.

The children of Israel, in their wanderings, had failed to ensure that every male had this distinguishing mark. However, God would not allow the children of Israel to possess His promises until the covenant was

---

[4] Exodus 4:25-26

Developing Our Christian Life

clearly reestablished. They needed to have the identifying mark that associated them with Him.

The physical circumcision pointed to a greater meaning or significance—spiritual circumcision. Some Jewish people pride themselves on being Jews. They are religious in practices, such as circumcision, keeping the Sabbath, and Passover. However, as one follows the real intent of circumcision, he or she begins to see that the most important identification is not outward, but inward.

John the Baptist addressed the arrogance some Jews maintained because of their physical lineage to Abraham. "And think not to say within yourselves, We have Abraham to our father: for I say unto you, that God is able of these stones to raise up children unto Abraham" (Matthew 3:9).

This distinct mark of circumcision did not make the children of Israel special. Rather, it was to remind them that they belonged to the one true God. Identification and obedience to Jehovah God are what would make them distinct as a peculiar people among the pagan nations.

The Apostle Paul explained the circumcision that must occur that will associate a person to Abraham, "But he is a Jew, which is one inwardly; and circumcision is that of the heart, in the spirit, and not in the letter; (of the Law) whose praise is not of man but of God" (Romans 2:29). (Parenthesis added.)

Spiritual Jews are those whose hearts have been circumcised. God made reference to this in Deuteronomy 10:16, "Circumcise therefore the foreskin of your heart and be not stiffnecked." This shows us that those things that are defiled in our lives must be cut off, to ensure purity and righteousness.

For the children of Israel, a sharp knife was used, but for Christians, it is the sharp sword of the Word of God that will be used to circumcise the heart. "For the word of God is quick, and powerful, and sharper than any twoedged sword, piercing even to the dividing asunder of soul and spirit, and of the joints and marrow, and is a discerner of the thoughts and intents of the heart" (Hebrews 4:12).

The penetrating truths of the Word of God are able to cut through worldly philosophies and godless excuses, and silence insidious foolishness, as it rips away religious nonsense. This surgery will expose the motivation and intentions of the heart. As the sword cuts away the hard foreskin of stony and indifferent hearts, the old source of identification will give way to a heart of flesh that will be able to respond to God.

Ezekiel 36:25-26 makes reference to this heart surgery,

> Then will I sprinkle clean water upon you, and ye shall be clean: from all filthiness, and from all your idols, will I cleanse you. A new heart also will I give you, and a new spirit will I put within you: and I will take away the stony heart out of your flesh...

There is also a reference made to water in the Scripture in Ezekiel 36. Cleansing in this text is spiritual and also pointed to the Word of God. Ephesians 5:26 states, "That he might sanctify and cleanse it (the Church) with the washing of water by the word." (Parenthesis added.)

Circumcision at Gilgal was God's way to roll away the reproach of Egypt.[5] Remember, Egypt represented the world and the old life. In some cases, the reproach can be such a part of a person's life that he or she must have it cut away before it can be rolled off. This is why spiritual circumcision is vital to Christian growth and maturity.

Associations with both the world and the old life will bring shame, rebuke, and disgrace to saints. God's heart is to separate His people from it, and then roll off its reproach so that His people can walk in newness of life. Hebrews 10:20-22 gives us this perspective,

> By a new and living way, which he hath consecrated for us, through the veil, that is to say, his flesh; And having an high priest over the house of God; Let us draw near with a true heart in full assurance of faith, having our hearts sprinkled from an evil conscience, and our bodies washed with pure water.

An uncircumcised heart makes a person a stranger to God. Ezekiel 44:7 states, "In that ye have brought into my sanctuary strangers; uncircumcised in heart, and uncircumcised in flesh, to be in my sanctuary, to pollute it." If your heart remains uncircumcised, you are polluting your life in God, and He will not be able to claim you as His.

For the children of Israel, circumcision was a form of rededication to God. This shows us that Gilgal is a place of rededication where people come back to God, allowing Him to lead them into all that He has for them.

The children of Israel abode at Gilgal until they were whole.[6] God does not call His people to activities when they are being set apart. When one is going through circumcision, whether physical or spiritual, he or she must be healed from the deep cuts. Both the separation and the healing must be made before going into battle to be an effective soldier.

Wounded Christians who have gone into battle before being healed and restored are bigger targets and more susceptible to defeat. Christians need to learn the lesson of waiting that must take place at Gilgal. God must be allowed to prepare, heal, and restore His people before they go forth. This lesson can come back to haunt those Christians who go into battle, but who are on the mend, and not whole mentally, physically, or spiritually.

At the appointed time, they kept the Passover.[7] The Passover had been the last festival they prepared and celebrated before being

---

[5] Joshua 5:9
[6] Joshua 5:8
[7] Joshua 5:10

delivered from Egypt. Now, it would be the first feast they celebrated in the Promised Land.

The first Passover was about death passing over God's people, ensuring deliverance and life.[8] The Israelites had passed through the Jordan into this new life. The first Passover celebrated freedom from harsh slavery, but this Passover would be celebrating new life as they considered the old life being rolled off.

For the Christian, the Passover points to Jesus' cross. Each believer comes to the foot of the cross, seeking mercy, grace, and forgiveness. At the cross, sins, cares, burdens, and personal righteousness are rolled off so that life can be received in abundance.

Like Israel's deliverance from Egypt, the Christian's journey begins with partaking of the sacrifice of the Lamb of God. Deliverance from any bondage always points to humble beginnings. Like the children of Israel, believers must not forget the sacrifice and intervention of God to bring them to a new life. This is why Christians observe Communion.

The manna ceased to fall from heaven, and the children of Israel began to eat of the old grain of the land. God had fed Israel for over forty years in the wilderness, but now He was providing the land that would allow His people to partake of its many fruits.

Many people expect God to hand them a perfect life. They are disappointed when He only provides what they need. They expect blessings to rain upon them even though many refuse to partake of what has already been provided. Many fail to realize that circumstances determine and change the means of provision. This may be why people either complain about God's provision or they ignore it. Ultimately, many end up taking His blessing and gifts for granted.

To partake of the fruit of the Promised Land, the Israelites had to possess the Promised Land. In order to possess the blessings of the Promised Land, they had to overcome their enemies. Israel benefited from God's provision, but now they were about to partake of His promise. This example proves that God provides according to the need. In the wilderness, God rained manna down upon them, but in the Promised Land, they had to possess the land to partake of what He provided.

God's two types of provision also point to two types of tests. The manna tested the hearts of the children of Israel. The land would test their character and faith.[9]

This example can clearly be observed in Christianity. God provided Jesus as the manna from heaven. This bread was freely given, but it is up to the Christian to pursue and partake of Jesus by faith.[10]

The manna ceased, and Israel's deliverance from the old was complete. For the Christian, it points to Jesus' finished work on the cross.

---

[8] Exodus 12
[9] Exodus 16:4; Deuteronomy 8:1-7; Joshua 1:7-9
[10] John 6:32-35; Matthew 10:8; Ephesians 2:8-9

Like the manna, He had finished His particular work, and now, it is time to go on to possess the fruits of this promise.

The people of Israel were told to eat of the old corn of the land. This corn is not the same as our corn in America. They believe it to be some type of wheat, but the significance of this corn is that it pointed to the fruit of the land and seeds that will reproduce.

The land was already fruitful and provided abundantly for the needs of the children of Israel. Christians who partake of the life of Christ will have a fruitful life. Philippians 4:19 states, "But my God shall supply all your need according to his riches in glory by Christ Jesus."

This fruitful life comes from the seed of the Gospel, which consists of the death, burial, and resurrection of Jesus Christ.[11] Therefore, the seed is the very life of Jesus. He confirmed this in John 12:24, "Verily, verily, I say unto you, Except a corn of wheat fall into the ground and die, it abideth alone: but if it dies it bringeth forth much fruit."

The wilderness represented the grave. Israel had been in the grave for over 40 years. They had encountered every level, characteristic, and work of the grave. It had been a dying out process, but now it was time for the seed (national Israel) to come forth and produce fruit for God's glory.

Christianity is marked by death that is meant to produce an abundant, fruitful life. It is a life that finds its only source in Jesus. John 10:10 and 15:5 confirm this, "I am come that they might have life, and that they might have it more abundantly...I am the vine, you are the branches. He that abideth in me, and I in him, the same brings forth much fruit: for without me you can do nothing."

Finally, Joshua encountered the Joshua of the New Testament: Jesus Christ. In Joshua 5:13-15, Joshua encountered a man who had his sword drawn. Immediately, Joshua challenged this man's intentions, "...Art thou for us, or for our adversaries?" The Man introduces Himself as the captain of the hosts of the LORD. "Captain" in this text means chief, general, lord, master, prince, and ruler.[12] There is only one Person who would hold this position in the courts of heaven, Jesus Christ.

Apparently, Joshua recognized the significance of this title, and fell down and worshipped Him. If this being were simply an angel or messenger of God, he would not allow such worship. Only God deserves homage.

The Ark of the Covenant was a shadow of Jesus. However, Jesus must never remain a shadow to those who claim to know Him. They must desire to know, love, and see Him. He will personally meet with His people and reveal Himself in a real and mighty way.

---

[11] 1 Corinthians 15:1-4
[12] Strong's Exhaustive Concordance, *#8269*

Joshua represented the man of the hour for Israel, but Jesus represents the Man of the age.[13] Joshua was the leader of Israel, but Jesus is the leader of the hosts of heaven and will one day reign as King of kings and Lord of lords.

Joshua was strong, alert and respected, but his greatest strength was his humility. Humility always recognizes and gives way to those who are worthy. This humility was evident in Joshua's life. He was closest to Moses. He was at the door of the tabernacle when others remained at the door of their tents. He was one of the spies who stood against unbelief and encouraged Israel to possess the Promised Land the first time around. He spent forty years wandering in the wilderness because of other people's unbelief. Amazingly, he was not bitter, hateful, or upset. He was a godly man who not only graciously accepted the judgment, but also became the leader who would lead Israel into the Promised Land. He was able and willing to enter in and do battle.

Joshua's character was founded on humility and formed in righteousness before God. As a result, he recognized the One who was truly worthy, and responded accordingly. The man who was a leader of Israel fell on his face and worshipped the One who would be known as the Son of Man.

Learning to worship is an important lesson. All major moves in the kingdom of God must begin and end with worship. In worship, you can gain a heavenly perspective and a sense of direction.

The man who was magnified in the sight of Israel now took his shoes off before One greater than him. The shoes represented the defilement of the world. A shoe is the one object that touches the rudiments of the world and becomes engulfed in filth. This is why Jesus washed only Peter's feet in John 13. When Peter requested that He wash his whole body, Jesus said, "...He that is washed needeth not save to wash his feet, but is clean every whit..." (John 13:10).

Joshua's example of taking off his shoes shows us that we must not only roll off that which is hindering and defiling us, but we must separate from the unholy. Keep in mind, Joshua was on his face worshipping the captain of the LORD'S host, but now, he was removing his shoes before this man in order to stand upright on holy ground. This upright position allowed Joshua to stand in the gap, and receive orders and encouragement.

Jesus was Joshua's last vision before he was to lead Israel into battle. This not only served as a heavenly vision, but it showed who would determine the victory for Israel. Jesus must be our first, present, and foremost vision. As John declared in Revelation 1:1, "The revelation of Jesus Christ, which God gave unto him, to show unto his servants things which must shortly come to pass..."

---

[13] Matthew 28:20

The captain of the LORD'S host had His sword drawn. He was the one going before Joshua to secure the Promised Land. He is the victorious leader. And, if His people are going to be victorious, Jesus must be the leader who goes before, as well as the victor who is exalted and worshipped.

The vision of Jesus in the Promised Land revealed that possessing the life God has for His people does not rest with personal attempts, but with the intervention of God. Joshua's example shows us that mere man must give way to the Victor to ensure victory.

Are you at Gilgal? If so, are you rolling off the old through spiritual circumcision and separating yourself from that which is unholy by separation? Are you rededicating your life for the purpose of following God and possessing your life in Christ? Have you eaten of the old corn (grave and death), in order for the fruit (resurrection of new life) to come forth? Are you abiding in Him? Have you recently met Him so that you can give way to His leadership, worship Him, and stand before Him in awe and uprightness?

19

POSSESSING THE LAND

The children of Israel were now in the Promised Land. They had rolled off the reproach of the old, and were ready to possess the new. Possessing the new is a long-drawn-out process. There are various obstacles and giants to overcome. It would be easy if God had simply done away with enemies, and let the Israelites possess the land without the battle.

God does not work that way. Possessing the land was as much of a preparation for maintaining it as it was to serve as a blessing. It would test the children of Israel's character and faith. Would they endure the battle, while clinging to the reality that their enemies had already been defeated? Would they give up before they finished the course, and fail to possess all that God had for them?

This is true for the Christian life. Many Christians make a mistake when they think that once they receive Jesus into their lives, they have arrived. The Christian life is simply there for the blessings and the good life. They need to realize that, like the Israelites in the Promised Land, receiving Christ is just the beginning. It is the door to embark on the new life. This door represents the beginning of this incredible journey. In fact, it will take time to experience the different aspects of this new life and possess it in its abundance.

The Apostle Paul said this in Philippians 2:12, "Wherefore, my beloved, as ye have always obeyed, not as in my presence only, but much more in my absence, work out your own salvation with fear and trembling." Christians must work their salvation in and out of their lives by faith in God and obedience to His instructions.

This brings Christians to the important lesson of the Promised Land. The lesson is that the Christian life is a journey, and is not about what we as believers do, but who we are before God.

The wilderness revealed the depth of depravity. It exposed the vanity of personal strength, the foolishness of the flesh, the folly of idolatry, and the exaltation and delusion of pride. These layers simply covered over the culprit of humanity—the fallen condition of man. As a person encounters each layer of the fallen depravity of man, he or she must conclude with Paul's discovery about his wretched self—there is no good or beneficial thing in the flesh.[1]

---

[1] Romans 7:18

People have a tendency to avoid this harsh reality. They put sins into categories. By avoiding the more blatant sins, they delude themselves into thinking that they are good. In reality, such a concept is more of a blatant affront against God and His word. This form of delusion is indifferent to God and blinded by personal wretchedness.

The wilderness was a means to expose the depravity of man through the unveiling of an ungodly disposition and the manifestation of visible sins. It was a way of separating and judging these sins in order to prepare the Israelites to be a holy nation. As a holy nation, these people would stand distinct in the midst of idolatry and paganism.

The Promised Land would address the fallen disposition in light of God's holiness and eternal plan. His holiness would not only reveal how depraved and wicked man was and is in his way of thinking, doing, and being, but his tendency to compromise with the unholy.

I have witnessed many Christians who have exposed themselves to the unholy. The harsh reality is that it does not even vex their spirit. It is as if they are spiritually dull, unable to properly discern. Sadly, what people allow themselves to be exposed to speak volumes about their spiritual commitment and life before God. Callousness to the unholy just proves that a person has become fleshly or carnal, making him or her incapable of discerning spiritual matters.[2]

Romans 3:23 tells us that all men have sinned and fallen short of God's glory. Few Christians understand the implication of this harsh reality. Man does not fall short because of what he does, but by what he fails to be in light of God's plan and purpose.

God formed Adam to be a reflection of His glory in creation. When Adam disobeyed, he fell into a state of darkness from his original state of having the ability to reflect God's glory. This darkness snuffed out Adam's potential to reflect the light and the glory of God.

This darkness has caused man to prefer and operate in darkness. It represents anything from delusion, superstition, and wickedness to self-righteousness. These works and coverings of darkness give a person a false sense about what is acceptable and holy. Delusion of this nature is capitalized upon as people clothe this wretchedness with religious garb that allows for compromise with the unholy. Such false clothing helps them to believe that they are okay without humbling themselves and paying the price to know and please God.

People begin to evaluate righteousness according to their own personal whiteness. According to Isaiah 64:6, this whiteness is nothing more than filthy rags before God. These filthy rages are compared to the menstrual rags of a woman. This visual picture not only gives a person a sense of how unholy this personal whiteness is to God, but it also shows what a stench it is to Him.

---

[2] 1 Corinthians 2:14

Developing Our Christian Life

    Personal whiteness can be summarized in a simple way. Anything a man does that is good through his own means and strength is as filthy rags to God.[3] The only goodness that is acceptable to God is the righteousness that belongs to Him. This righteousness is wrought in our lives by faith as we come into obedient submission to the Holy Spirit.

    As long as we judge spiritual matters by our own spiritual whiteness, we will never understand God's holiness. In fact, personal whiteness causes one to be blind towards God, dull towards His voice, and unable to discern the holy from the unholy. Such individuals unknowingly can call good evil and evil good because the things of God will offend them in their rebellion and unbelief.[4]

    Out of love, God will bring these people to a crisis. Recently, I experienced a healing crisis. This crisis occurs when you start cleansing your body. Your body will dump all the toxins into your system to be eliminated. Your system becomes a toxic dump waste that your body is not able to deal with fast enough, making you sick.

    In this healing crisis, your body becomes sensitive to the things that would counteract its work. It will become repulsed to certain foods and smells. It can show allergic reactions to foods that undermine its work. For the first time, a person becomes keenly aware of what is good and acceptable to his or her own well-being.

    God brings a similar crisis to a person. This spiritual crisis gives him or her acute awareness of how far away from the mark of God he or she is. It is like being unmasked or uncovered to reveal what you look like, in light of God's holiness

    This uncovering will break a person, causing deep sorrow and mourning. In a way, this is the heavy hand of God upon a soul that needs to come to terms with his or her depravity before there can be healing, restoration, and victory. Praise God for the crisis and His heavy hand. He so loves us that He will contend with us.

    The Promised Land will bring about such crises, as we are about to see. Personal strength will rise up, the flesh will try to dictate, idols will entice believers along the way, and pride will occasionally reign with a vengeance. However, the Promised Land will uncover their source, and demand that the deviation within character of God's people be confronted and properly dealt with to ensure victory.

    The Promised Land was about Israel possessing the land to fulfill God's promises to Abraham. For Christians, it is different. It is about God possessing our hearts and lives in order to fulfill His eternal plan through His people. This means that the Christian's life serves as the territory that must be conquered and set apart for God's glory.

    Three things must occur for God to possess a person's life:

---

[3] Isaiah 64:6
[4] Isaiah 5:20-23

1) Hearts need to be penetrated and changed by the sword or Word of God. [5]
2) The Spirit must transform the mind so that a person will develop the mind of Christ.[6]
3) Finally, the person must walk as Jesus walked, in total submission to the will of the Father.[7] This submission means that a person is giving way to the work of the Holy Spirit. As one gives way to the Holy Spirit, that area of his or her life becomes the domain of God.

The Promised Land shows believers how to make their lives in God personal and all-consuming. It reveals how each of us can make Christianity a personal heart revelation, rather than an indifferent religion that never gets past rituals and intellectual arrogance in order to make a heart change.

Before Christianity can be all-consuming and victorious, Christians must recognize and contend with the obstacles or giants in their path. In order to properly contend with giants, each person must personally learn the lessons of character and victory so that God can begin to take possession of their lives.

The first obstacle was Jericho. Jericho was a walled city.[8] It was shut up, not letting anything in or out of it. Jericho represents pockets of self. These pockets of self are walled in by such things as fear, control, protection, and personal rights. These walls often protect and hide vulnerabilities, hurts, wounds, or personal identity. Regardless of the reason or purpose for these walls, they keep God out. Anytime God is kept at bay, it points to rebellion and unbelief. Therefore, God clearly states that these walls must come down.

The tendency for most people is to try to ignore these walls, pretend they are not there, or just go around them. After all, Jericho is only one city. The logical conclusion is to just leave it alone, and eventually everyone will be forced out through starvation or thirst.

God's orders are clear, the walls must come down and the city utterly destroyed and burned. Where self is walled, there is filthiness and wretchedness behind it. There are also unholy alliances and compromise. It matters little as to how big or how small this walled city is—it is still part of the inheritance that rightfully belongs to Israel.

Jericho was allotted to Benjamin. "Benjamin" means son of my right hand. The reference to position points to the Son of God sitting on the right hand of God. He has paid a price for all believers.[9] Therefore, He owns each one of the saints and has the right to lay claim to every

---

[5] Hebrews 4:12
[6] Philippians 2:5; Romans 12:1-2
[7] Philippians 2:5-9
[8] Joshua 6-7
[9] 1 Corinthians 6:20; 7:23

aspect of their lives. This means He has the right to lay claim to the heart, mind, and soul of all believers.

Dealing with pockets of self is necessary. When the walls of Jericho come down, the filth and wretchedness must be destroyed and purged by the blood of Jesus and the Word of God.[10] This purging and cleansing are necessary to ensure victory.

There is a good side to this destruction. Out of it will come genuine faith. Rahab represents this faith.[11] She was in Jericho, but thanks to the scarlet cord hanging from her window, she, along with her household were saved. This scarlet cord pointed to the work of Jesus' blood on Calvary. Rahab's abiding confidence or faith came out of the ruin and destruction of Jericho. This example reminds me of Peter's words in 1 Peter 1:7, "That the trial of your faith, being much more precious than of gold that perisheth, though it be tried with fire, might be found unto praise and honor and glory at the appearing of Jesus Christ."

"Jericho" means fragrance. Christians are to serve as the fragrance of Christ.[12] To God, this fragrance is acceptable and for the Christian it will prove to be edifying. However, to the unbeliever, it will be harsh and challenging. If there are any pockets of self, this fragrance will be defiled. It will be covered up by the stench of ruin and chaos.

In Joshua 6:26, Joshua cursed Jericho. He declared that the person who rebuilt Jericho would lose his eldest son when the foundation was laid and his youngest son when the gate was erected.[13] This curse shows the seriousness of reestablishing pockets of self. It points to a cursed life that will cost deeply. It will be a life of sorrow and defeat.

The next obstacle was Ai.[14] Ai represented the ruin caused by pride. In fact, "Ai" means heaps of ruin. The children of Israel had a different approach to Ai. They had just come from victory over Jericho. Instead of recognizing that it was God who secured their victory, they had developed an unfounded personal confidence that set them up for defeat. This confidence was nothing more than pride.

Pride is not able to discern spiritual matters. There was sin in the camp, and the children of Israel were not sensitive to the fact that something was amiss among them. Because of this sin, they were not ready to confront Ai, and due to their pride, they failed to see it. Pride also assumes God is in all of the attempts that have to do with pursuing the life He has called His servants to. For example, Christians often think if they are doing something good, that God will automatically bless them.

---

[10] Ephesians 5:26; 1 John 1:7
[11] Hebrews 11:31; James 2:25
[12] 2 Corinthians 2:15-16
[13] This was fulfilled in 1 Kings 16:34.
[14] Joshua 7-8

This is a wrong perception because God weighs the spirit (or motive) we are doing something in, over the actual activity.[15]

The heart of God is not that His people be victorious; rather, it is about Him being victorious in and through them. It is the hearts and minds of the saints that serve as the real territories that must be conquered. Therefore, it matters little to God about His people's feats. He wants His character, love, mercy, grace, and will to be honored and glorified in His followers' lives.

Pride also walks by sight. The Israelites considered Ai, and concluded that they had an easy victory. They only had to send a few men in to secure Ai's defeat, rather than the whole army. This shows that Israel forgot who conquered Jericho. They had become self-confident and self-sufficient.

Self-sufficiency caused the children of Israel to make presumptions about their ability and God's expected blessing on the whole matter. In this whole ordeal, God is conspicuously missing from their considerations and plans. And, when God is missing, victory will elude people.

Scripture clearly states that God resists pride because it is treacherous, unteachable, and hypocritical. He hates the haughty look, and guarantees that the sin of pride is nothing more than a prelude to falling into shame and destruction.[16] Ultimately, pride causes a person to trip over the insignificant.

For Israel, the insignificant was Ai. When you consider the spelling of Ai, the letter "a" is so big it is hard to see the "i", yet the letter 'i' is prevalent in the name of this city. It is always the 'I' as in me, myself, and I that will trip a person up, causing him or her to fall. If there is no repentance, the fall can be right into the lake of fire.

For the children of Israel, they suffered defeat. Their pride caused them to fall as far as the ground, in fear and humility. We see Joshua on the ground, his nose in the dirt, wrestling before God. The exchange between God and Joshua is revealing. Joshua addressed God in light of the enemy and the reputation of Israel. God remained silent. When Joshua made reference to God's reputation, He then spoke. "...Get thee up; wherefore liest thou thus upon thy face" (Joshua 7:10)?

One of the major mistakes Christians make in prayer is that they make the situation about how they will look before others or how they feel about what appears to be an unfair situation. God will remain silent for it is not about the person or situation, but about His will. If an individual makes God a priority in all matters, he or she will discover how quick God is to give His perspective. This shows how we need to first honor God before He can honor us and bring about victory.

---

[15] Proverbs 16:2
[16] Proverbs 6:16-17; 8:13; 11:2; 16:18; James 4:6

There was hidden or concealed sin in the camp. A man by the name of Achan had coveted accursed things of Jericho. Achan's name means "troubler." Sadly, he was living down to his name. He had brought grave trouble to Israel, and would also bring judgment upon his family.

The tribes of Israel were assembled together to discover the person who had transgressed God's covenant in regards to Jericho. The lot fell to, and finally exposed Achan. It was at this point that Achan confessed his covetousness and transgression.

His confession did not stay judgment. It is one thing to confess sin before God actually reveals it. Once God reveals hidden sin, it means judgment. This judgment was far-reaching. Achan's possessions, livestock, and children were all taken to the valley of Achor. There, the children of Israel stoned and burned them.

One might wonder why Achan's children were stoned. My conclusion is that they knew about his sin and said nothing. Ephesians 5:11 states, "And have no fellowship with the unfruitful works of darkness, but rather reprove them." If a person knows about hidden sin, it is his or her responsibility to bring it to the light.[17] If the individual fails to do so, he or she becomes a partaker of both the sin and the judgment.

This brings us to the valley of Achor. The meaning of the name of this valley is the "valley of trouble." Valleys represent humiliation. God's judgment of Achan's hidden sin would have caused much sobriety and humiliation. After all, the Israelites had to stone him, his family, and livestock, and then burn them. They had to hear their cries as the people and animals were dying.

Humiliation is always wrought by a crisis that brings a reality check. The result of the crisis causes people to begin to seek the Lord. Even though Achor was a valley of trouble, it could easily become a place of rest. Humiliation is meant to serve as a place of calm because the person is now ready to do business with God. This readiness allows God to step on the scene and bring peace, regardless of the situation. Isaiah 65:10 states, "And Sharon shall be a fold of flocks, and the valley of Achor a place for herds to lie down in, for my people that have sought me."

Humiliation also serves as a door of hope though which to discover God's promises; however, to walk through this door means leaving sin behind and choosing the route of submission, faith, and obedience. Hosea 2:15 confirms this, "And I will give her vineyards from thence, and the valley of Achor for a door of hope: and she will sing there, as in the days of her youth, and as in the day when she came up out of the land of Egypt."

Sin brings trouble and judgment. But, praise God! He has supplied a door or gate of forgiveness, hope, and promise through Jesus Christ.

---

[17] Ephesians 5:13

After sin is taken care of, Ai now can be faced and conquered. Sin and pride walk hand in hand, but the sins of the heart must be dealt with before pride can be brought down to ruin.

The first time they confronted Ai, the children of Israel were on their own, but this time, God was with them. They showed wisdom instead of foolishness. As a result, the town was destroyed and the king hung.

The king represents the reality and much needed demise of pride. It is nothing more than a stinky, wretched carcass before God. It needs to be hung out to dry. However, the carcass of pride must not be left out too long. Leaving pride out too long can cause some people to feel sorry for its demise. They will remember how it served their purposes and begin to see it as a martyr, rather than a dead, stinky carcass that must be buried. People need to understand their pride, but avoid examining it too much. This will glorify it and give it too much power, allowing it to rise up and reign.

After the pockets of self, pride, and sin are taken care of, it is time to take stock. Joshua built an altar unto the Lord.[18] This altar pointed to worship of God and remembering what He had done. After the altar, came the reading of the Law. This was a form of cleansing and reviving. The people once again heard the means by which they could ensure God's blessings and promises in their lives.

For the Christian, our altar is the cross of Christ. After great victories or defeats, we must take time to cling to it to get God's perspective. Then, we must read the Word to cleanse and fill up the empty, vacant areas left by the pockets of self, hidden sin, and pride. Christians fail to fill these areas up and instead, live in defeat because they have not allowed the Word to establish them in a deeper life in God. The application of the Word will root them in the immovable Rock, giving much needed strength to endure, authority to overcome, and power to conquer.

There is another area that will make a person vulnerable. We see it in Joshua 9. This area represents the folly of trusting our logic. The Gibeonites knew that they were already doomed people. They devised a plan to deceive Israel. Sadly, it worked. The children of Israel fell for their deception and made a pact with their enemies. Joshua 9:14 gives us insight into their failure. They, "…asked not counsel at the mouth of the LORD."

The children of Israel were relying on their logic, instead of upon God. Their logic told them that these people were being truthful. The Gibeonites became Israel's slaves, but because of them, Israel had to fight for them. During King David's reign, this pact with them resulted in a famine because King Saul had violated this agreement, and had zealously attacked them. To satisfy the judgment upon Israel for Saul's

---

[18] Joshua 8:30-35

Developing Our Christian Life

transgression against the Gibeonites, seven of Saul's descendents were hanged.[19]

The words that God's people speak must mean truth and law. Jesus clearly instructed us not to make vows. If we do, we must keep them regardless of what it costs us personally.[20] If we fail to keep them, we will commit the sin of omission. In other words, we will fail to do right by our words, making us liars. Keep in mind; if the intent of sobriety is not present to keep our word, we are committing fraud and will prove to be liars because we have no intention of backing them up with action.

Joshua 12 tells us that Israel conquered 31 kings, but Joshua 13:1 tells us that not all the Promised Land was possessed. Joshua clearly brings out the reason for Israel failing to possess the Promised Land in Joshua 18:3, "And Joshua said unto the children of Israel, How long are ye slack to go to possess the land, which the LORD God of your fathers hath given you?" "Slackness" means abate, cease, faint, wax feeble, forsake, idle, leave, slothful, and weak.[21] It points to compromise, an attitude Jesus would not tolerate with those of the Church of Laodicea.[22]

Wherever there is compromise, Christians cease to finish the course. They faint because of fear, and they wax feeble due to a lack of authority. They will forsake their calling and become idle in their life. They will leave their first love and become slothful in their Christian responsibility. This will cause them to become weak and vulnerable to enemies.

Compromise is a passive attitude that manifests itself in flippancy and indifference. As you examine the reason for spiritual slackness, you will discover that there is no love of God abounding. Without God's love, a person will lack heart, purpose, and vision.

Joshua's solution to this is found in Joshua 18:8, "...Joshua charged them that went to describe the land, saying Go and walk through the land, and describe it, and come again to me." Like the Israelites, Christians need to walk out their inheritance. They do this by obeying the Word. As they obey the Word, they will begin to discover the treasure of heaven and get glimpses of their eternal inheritance. They will see the value of the Christian life and desire to possess more of it. They will be stirred up in their heart to embrace their possession, and become determined to finish the course to ensure the fullness and completeness in their lives.

There are Christians who are slack because they have never realized their inheritance. They have not found the Pearl of Great Price, and they have not partaken of His divine nature.[23] As a result, they have

---

[19] 2 Samuel 21:1-6
[20] Matthew 5:33-37
[21] Strong's Concordance, #7503
[22] Revelation 3:14-19
[23] Matthew 13:46; 2 Peter 1:4

no desire or care to get past the concept of salvation to allow themselves to be possessed by Jesus, so they can possess Him. To be without the Gem of heaven is a great tragedy. It is being offered to everyone, but many prefer to live in their own poverty and wretchedness.

What obstacles in your life are keeping you from being possessed by Jesus? Are there pockets of self, pride, sin, logic, or slothfulness? Are you content with just being in the Promised Land, or are you doing everything you can to truly possess it, and know and embrace your everlasting inheritance?

20

THE JOURNEY CONTINUES

This journey with Israel is a very revealing reality, as well as serves as an indelible example when it comes to the Christian life. It is easy to stand indifferent to the plight and struggles of the children of Israel, as long as we remain blind towards our own depravity. It is natural to show self-righteousness and criticism towards them, until personal examination and experience reveal there is no difference between them and the struggles and failures that can easily affront our lives.

Traveling with the Israelites can intensify for the Christians who are truly seeking truth from the ageless example of these people, especially as the human disposition is uncovered. They begin to realize that they have been greatly influenced by the world. They see the vanity of their personal strength, the foolishness of their flesh, the folly of idolatry, and the harsh reality of their pride.

The beauty about Israel's journey is that it can clarify much for Christians. They can begin to see that they are sojourners in this world. This reality becomes real as they confront each leg of the journey and become more homesick for their final destination.

The final destination is heaven. And, when Christians think of heaven, many think of gold streets and pearly gates. However, the real beauty of heaven does not rest with its physical wonders, but with its glory. John 1:14 reveals the glory of heaven, "And the Word was made flesh, and dwelt among us, (and we beheld his glory, the glory as of the only begotten of the Father, full of grace and truth."

Jesus is the glory of heaven. Revelation 21:22-23 confirms this, "And I saw no temple therein: for the Lord God Almighty and the Lamb are the temple of it. And the city had no need of the sun, neither the moon, to shine in it: for the glory of God did lighten it, and the Lamb thereof."

Many people desire heaven because this world is full of trials and struggles. However, those who understand the real glory of heaven desire to see, embrace, love, and serve the source of all glory that permeates heaven. The more a believer falls in love with God, the more he or she will become homesick for a person rather than a place. His or her focus, heart, and affections will be set upon Jesus. The world will grow strangely dim and become less and less attractive.

The Apostle Paul admitted in 2 Corinthians 5:6-9 and Philippians 1:21-24 that his preference was to be with the Lord, but he remained in this present world for the benefit of others. After many years of ministry, I understand Paul's perspective.

Like most servants of God, I started out enthusiastic about serving God. I never realized it at the time, but I was more caught up with service than with Jesus. After many different experiences and challenges, I am now caught up with Jesus. I couldn't care less about my present life or this world. I realize that I am here to serve God by touching other lives with His reality, but when this work is done, I will be ushered into His glory. This is when my real hope and joy will be realized. I will finally be home. This home will not be based on the place of heaven, but on the Person of Jesus Christ.

As I watch events escalate in this world, I become more thankful for my hope and life in Christ. I become more of a sojourner in attitude and a pilgrim in heart. I look forward to my eternal destination as I experience homesickness for Jesus. I thank God that my hope is in Jesus, and not in the temporary vanity of the world. I get excited as each day brings me closer to my destination. I rejoice as each project or scriptural responsibility is completed, because I am closer to my work and mission being completed here on earth.

Jesus Christ is my inheritance. My life is the territory that He must conquer so that I may possess my heavenly inheritance. Therefore, my prayer is that I am so consumed by His reality that nothing else matters. When I stand before Him, there will be no crack in my spiritual life caused by the erosion of the world, concealed sin, or idolatry.

When I arrive at my destination, I will rejoice on my knees as my heart cries out in humble exhilaration. I will take what crowns I have and cast them at His feet, for they will be the result of His work in my life. I will cry out of excitement, for I am before His throne and feet. Now, I can worship the One who is worthy of all recognition without hindrance, and I can thank Him for His provision of salvation and righteousness. I can bask in the fulfillment of my hope and the majesty of His unending glory.

There is another reality I will embrace at the throne of God—my new life does not mark an end, but a glorious beginning. The Apostle Paul put it in this way in Ephesians 2:7, "That in the ages to come he might show the exceeding riches of his grace in his kindness towards us through Christ Jesus." Every encounter with Jesus marks a point of new life. Every revelation points to growth, and every point of experience opens a door of new beginnings as one grows in the knowledge of the Rock of Ages, explores the depth and breadth of His character, and soars to new heights in His infinite grace.

The Christian journey is about discovering the glorious reality of heaven. For the saints, it means a new phase or a new level in their Christian growth. However, each discovery of Jesus proves that the journey does not end, but will continue into the ages to come.

Are you striving to enter in? Are you seeking the reality of heaven? If you are, you are most likely becoming more homesick, as heaven becomes more of a consuming reality than a concept. With Jesus as your focus, you will be able to enjoy and discover valuable treasures during your earthly journey that, one day you will cast at His feet in honor of His faithfulness and grace.

Biblography

Strong's Exhaustive Concordance of the Bible; James Strong, © 1986 assigned to World Bible Publishers, Inc

Webster's New Collegiate Dictionary; © 1976 by G. & C. Merriam Co.

Lectures on the Book of Acts; H. A. Ironside; Eighteenth Printing, August 1982; Published by Loizeaux Brothers, Inc

Vine's Expository Dictionary of Biblical Words; © 1985 by Thomas Nelson, Inc., Publishers

31 Kings or Victory over Self; A. B. Simpson; © 1992 by Christian Publications

Smith's Bible Dictionary, Thomas Nelson Publishers

Os Hillman, article, February 11, 2006

Eerdmans' Handbook to the Bible

The Saving Life of Christ, Major W. Ian Thomas

Finding the Reality of God, Paris Reidhead, © 1989

Number in Scripture; E. W. Bullinger; Kregel Publications

Encyclopedia of Sermon Illustrations; ©1988 by Concordia Publishing House

Jewish Faith and the New Covenant; Ruth Specter Lascelle, © 1980

The Master's Indwelling; Andrew Murray; © 1983 by Whitaker House

About the Authors

Rayola Kelley and Jeannette Haley are ordained ministers of the Gospel. Rayola was born-again and saved out of a cult in 1976 while serving in the U.S. Navy. Her spiritual journey continued through extensive discipleship, before following the Lord's call upon her life into full-time ministry 30 years ago, when, with Jeannette Haley, she founded Gentle Shepherd Ministries in 1989.

Jeannette was born in Seattle, and is a gifted artist and teacher that has used her various talents to faithfully, and at times, boldly share her faith. She has written Bible studies, Christian fiction and books for children that contain a strong Gospel message. .

Through the years, both ladies' gift of teaching the Word has opened many doors for them to teach adult Sunday school, oversee a fellowship for many years, hold evangelistic meetings in churches, conduct seminars, and speak at retreats. They have served in jail ministry, and are well known for gifts of spiritual insight, encouragement, and counseling. Upon being called to be missionaries in America, Rayola and Jeannette established different fellowships where intense Bible Studies and discipleship training were conducted to equip believers for the ministry. These different mission fields in America entailed working in various churches as well as working with other cultures such as the Korean and Hispanic nationalities.

Rayola and Jeannette began sending out a monthly newsletter containing articles for the Body of Christ in 1997 which continues to grow. Ms. Kelley has authored over 55 books, and numerous Bible Studies including an advanced Discipleship Course (available in both English and Spanish) that is being used in countries such as Africa, Bulgaria, Israel, Ireland, India, Cuba, and Pakistan. Among her many books is *"Hidden Manna"* which deals with destructive cycles in people and relationships, and *"Battle for the Soul"* which presents a clear picture of the battle that rages in the soul. She has written seven in-depth devotional books, including both the Old Testament and New Testament devotional study which takes the reader through the entire Bible in one year. All of her books are hard-hitting, bottom-line spiritual food for the hungry and thirsty soul to "chew" upon in order to *"grow strong in the Lord, and in the power of His might."*

Both Rayola and Jeannette currently reside in Northern Idaho where they continue to fulfill Christ's commission to make disciples through teaching, spiritual counseling, and through the internet and publications..

Please visit Gentle Shepherd Ministries Web Site at: www.gentleshepherd.com for further information, and to access Rayola's challenging and informative audio sermons.

Other Books By Rayola Kelley

Hidden Manna
Battle for the Soul
Stories of the Heart
Transforming Love & Beyond
The Great Debate
Post to Post: (1) Establishing the Way
Post to Post: (2) Walking in the Way
Post to Post: (3) Meditations Along the Way

Volume One: Establishing Our Life in Christ
My Words are Spirit and Life
The Anatomy of Sin
The Principles of the Abundant Life
The Place of Covenant
Unmasking the Cult Mentality

Volume Two: Putting on the Life of Christ
He Actually Thought it Not Robbery
Revelation of the Cross
In Search of Real Faith
Think on These Things
Follow the Pattern

Volume Three: Developing a Godly Environment
Godly Discipline
Prayer and Worship
Don't Touch That Dial
Face of Thankfulness
ABC's of Christianity

Volume Four: Issues of the Heart
Hidden Manna (Revised)
Bring Down the Sacred Cows
The Manual for the Single Christian Life
Parents are People Too

Volume Five: Challenging the Christian Life
The Issues of Life
Presentation of the Gospel
For the Purpose of Edification
Whatever Happened to the Church?
Women's Place in the Kingdom of God

Volume Seven: Discovering True Ministry
From Prisons and Dots to Christianity
So You Want To Be In Ministry?

Devotions
Devotions of the Heart: Books One and Two
Daily Food for the Soul: Books One and Two

Gentle Shepherd Ministries Devotion Series:
Being a Child of God
Disciplining the Strength of our Youth
Coming to Full Age

Gentle Shepherd Ministries Series:
The Christian Life Series
What Matter Is This?
The Challenge of It
The Reality of It

The Leadership Series
Overcoming
A Matter of Authority and Power
The Dynamics of True Leadership

Nugget Books:
Nuggets From Heaven
More Nuggets From Heaven
Heavenly Gems
More Heavenly Gems
Heavenly Treasures

Books By
Jeannette Haley
Books co-authored with Rayola Kelley:
Hidden Manna (original)
The Many Faces of Christianity (Volume 6)
Post to Post 3: Meditations Along the Way

Other Books:
Rose of Light, Thorn of Darkness (Volume 7)
Interview in Hell (Volume 7)
Interview on Earth (Volume 7)
The Pig and I
Reflections of Wonder (Devotional)

Children Books:
Little Stories for Little People
Traveler's Tales
The Adventures of Zack and Mira
The Adventures of Paul and Dana
(A House on the Beach)
The Monster of Mystery Valley

www.ingramcontent.com/pod-product-compliance
Lightning Source LLC
Chambersburg PA
CBHW021953160426
43197CB00007B/117